BOOK
of
CHILD
CARE

By the same author

Sexual Precocity

Diseases of Children

Paul in Hospital (with Camilla Jessel)

Common Sense about Babies and Children

More Common Sense about Babies and Children

BOOK of CHILD CARE

Hugh Jolly
MA, MD, FRCP, DCH

HARCOURT BRACE JOVANOVICH, PUBLISHERS

San Diego   New York   London

Requests for permission to make copies of any part of the work should be mailed to:
Permissions, Harcourt Brace Jovanovich, Publishers,
Orlando, Florida 32887

Library of Congress Cataloging in Publication Data
Jolly, Hugh.
Book of child care.
1. Infants—Care and hygiene.   2. Children—
Care and hygiene.   3. Children—Diseases.
4. Child development.   I. Title.
RJ101.J64   1984   649'.1   84–10756
ISBN 0–15–113460–X

Designed by Karen Savary

Illustrations by Laura Hartman

Printed in the United States of America
First American edition
A   B   C   D   E

Contents

Illustrations

Preface

To an author the preface is sometimes the most important section of his book. In it he aims to convey the atmosphere of the book and, in a new edition, to outline changes and explain the reasons for them.

Some books on child care are described as "bibles" by their publishers or by reviewers. I should like to dissociate myself from any notion that this is a bible of child care. There never could be such a work. This book is a distillation of my own beliefs about caring for children culled from my work with healthy and ill children and, most important, from listening to children and their parents.

A bible suggests a definitive treatise, whereas this edition of my *Book of Child Care* differs in several respects from the first, not only because it reflects a further six years of experience, but also because many suggestions from parents have been incorporated. One reviewer commented that I addressed myself to mothers more than to fathers. I have aimed to redress this balance but I think the comment could still be made because, much as I hope fathers will increasingly be involved in pregnancy, labor and the care of their children, mothers still spend more time with their children in the early years.

I have written a new section on birth, because so many new ideas are under discussion. Alternative birth methods are now being used rather than just being talked about. The relationship between mother and obstetrician is moving away from the antagonism of the induction controversy, and mothers are now being encouraged to be more in control of labor, provided the obstetrician can assume complete command if the situation demands. Some obstetricians are offering fathers the opportunity to take over the last moment of delivery so that they are the first to hold the baby and can hand him to his mother. Some are also giving fathers the opportunity to cut the cord; a symbolic step for a father in taking on the care of his baby. Young children are even being allowed to attend.

An example of the help given to me by parents is the plea that they should be left the excitement of finding out the baby's sex. Parents want to know if their baby is normal—they can discover the rest for themselves. If they desperately want a child of one sex and the doctor or midwife shouts out the other, their first reaction to the newborn baby is one of disappointment—an unnecessarily discouraging start.

The recent severe epidemic of whooping cough following the

decline of immunization has put the pros and cons in perspective. I hope parents will find the discussion of the problem helps them to make up their minds about immunization, since this must always remain a personal decision taken in the light of accurate facts. The new immunization schedules are also described. Doctors are concerned by how few girls are at present being immunized against German measles. Parents are still not always aware of the high risk to the unprotected fetus from German measles and in comparison how harmless is the vaccine, so I have stressed this point more vigorously. Alcohol too must now be counted among the items than can put the fetus at risk.

The enormous swing to breast feeding has increased the need for detailed explanation of how to achieve success. For no medical subject is so much conflicting advice given, and yet the advice is simple— throw away the clock and let the baby take charge. The preface to the second edition of this book stressed the major changes made in the composition of cow's milk preparations. The hazards of excess sodium in the milk and the importance of modified cow's milk preparations are still more strongly urged in this edition.

Further research has emphasized the protection against asthma and eczema that breast feeding gives those babies at risk. Other research has shown why breast-fed babies do not get rickets despite what once seemed to be a low content of vitamin D in breast milk. There *is* sufficient vitamin D, but the wrong part of the milk was being tested! The practical aspect of this work is that breast-fed babies no longer need to be given vitamin D supplements.

A major revolution has taken place in baby equipment, with the rise in popularity of the cloth pouch-type baby carrier and drop in the use of the baby carriage. No longer would I recommend a couple to buy a baby carriage before the baby is born, since they may find that a combination of cloth-pouch-type baby carrier and stroller suits them best.

Talking to mothers makes one realize how frequently the baby develops hiccups in the uterus. Most mothers can distinguish these from arm and leg movements because they are so rhythmical; but some are disturbed by this unfamiliar occurrence, so the subject has been added. Another new section is on security blankets.

Postnatal depression is so common and so much can be done to counter or prevent it that I have added considerably to this section, particularly emphasizing where the system (usually insensitive handling in hospitals) is an important factor in creating depression. Unsympathetic handling is sometimes also the reason for differing feelings toward two children: the one, usually the first, seems less cuddly and lovable than the second, with whom everything went well because the mother was experienced and could cope with the system. I refer to this unhappy child as "the ugly duckling," and I have become increasingly aware of the number affected as well as the amount they and their families can be helped once the reasons for the problem have been worked out.

Another common group of children discussed in this edition are "bathroom children." Some of these are ugly ducklings too. They are usually toddlers and their characteristic is that they must accompany their mothers everywhere, including the bathroom—a strong indication of the degree of insecurity felt by the child.

The section on discipline and punishment is enlarged, as is that on growth, where a chart has been introduced to help in understanding the differing rates of growth of various body systems. I have also enlarged the chapter on play, since I am now aware that many parents are worried because their toddlers or older children won't play without them. I have explained why this behavior is normal.

Preventive dentistry has advanced enormously and is far more easily accessible for all children. No parent should be satisfied with a dentist who merely deals with fillings. Every baby should enter the preventive program described, so that he can emerge at sixteen years with a perfectly shaped mouth and no fillings.

The work of the music therapist with handicapped children has become so important that her role is described in detail, along with that of the other therapists whom parents of handicapped children are likely to meet.

Bereavement featured in the previous editions, but the need for a greater understanding of the subject in a family setting has led to enlargement of this section. Children are still kept from funerals of loved ones, often with disastrous effects. The reasons why children need to mourn and to attend funerals are emphasized in order that their feelings should be better understood.

I have enlarged the section on "when to call your doctor" and in the sections on sick children have introduced a number of new subjects, including limping, inhalation of foreign bodies, Mongolian blue spot, and Toxocara—a roundworm that infests cats and dogs and is causing concern because so many children are now being infected by their pets, with serious results.

These and other medical advances have been incorporated throughout the book. Also, metric measurements have now been added.

Hugh Jolly

Acknowledgment

Any doctor caring for children is as interested in parents as in their children. This book is the result of years spent working with all kinds of parents, learning from them all the time. It could not have been written without the close help of one well-qualified person, herself a mother, who worked with me on the book. For this reason I owe a great debt to Mrs. Anderson, who has ensured that the views of mothers were incorporated from the start. We have worked together, talking through hundreds of tape recordings and discussing every subject before the seemingly endless process of drafting, criticism, and rewriting.

To Gillian Anderson I express my deepest thanks.

I would also like to thank Linda Ross, R.N., for her help in suggesting necessary changes for this American edition.

Introduction

I am often asked whether I think it is a good idea for parents to read books on child care and for there to be radio and television programs on the subject. As the author of this book I have obviously answered in the affirmative—but why?

Before answering the question it is relevant first to ask why it comes to be asked. We accept that training and advice are required for every job a man or woman undertakes. The job of bringing up our children, the most important we undertake, is no exception.

Fortunately, most of us bring to this task the in-built expertise given by our parents in the way they handled us as children. If we were "mothered" well by our parents we have at least a head start on those whose intellect is the same but whose childhood experiences were less happy. The early years of life are the most vital in laying down an individual's future pattern, as regards both whether he achieves his full intellectual potential and whether he is sufficiently secure and well rounded as a personality. Since these early years are so vital is there any reason to argue the need for child upbringing to be a subject of study, in books and other media, for all parents?

The modern mother takes for granted that she will have the advice of experts and will not have to rely on the advice of her mother. The previous generation of mothers may not necessarily be the best advisers of the present generation. This is not to belittle the enormous support grandmothers can give—it is, indeed, unfortunate that this support is less easily obtained because today's married daughters are less likely to live near their parents. But the modern mother is less convinced than her predecessors that her mother knows best. At the same time the "experts" should not be regarded as infallible; it is up to you to be selective about other people's advice, whether relatives or experts, and to decide how it applies to your own individual baby.

Today's parents are probably better at bringing up their children than any previous generation. They are more aware of the importance of the early years and, knowing this, they are more concerned not to make mistakes. A big advance is that fathers are taking a much more active interest in the development of their children. I believe this to have resulted from the acceptance that fathers have a right to be present during labor; in my hospital about 95 percent of fathers choose to be with their wives. Fathers feel pregnant as well as their expectant wives; it is natural, therefore, that having made the baby

1

together, they should share the experience of the birth. The amount of help a husband can give his wife in labor is incalculable and his resultant close involvement with their baby, from the start, can make all the difference to the family.

This book is addressed to both mothers and fathers and I am thinking of both when I use the term "you." Similarly, although I refer to your baby as "he" and "him," I am of course dealing throughout the book with boys and girls equally. Inevitably, many of you reading it will be the parents of first children but I hope that those of you who already have children will also find it of interest. More space is given to the care of babies and young children than to older children, since this is the period when information is most needed.

The first half of the book is about healthy children—their normal growth, development, and behavior, with advice on how to bring them up. The second half deals with children's illnesses and the care of the sick child. This part is more of a reference book, and I do not suggest you read it straight through, since it could be unnecessarily alarming to read about all the illnesses children can get.

The major aim of the book is to help you to enjoy your children more and have fewer anxieties about their health. If you enjoy them, you are helping them to enjoy life too. I hope that you will keep a Baby Book, but, after reading this book, I hope you will spend much more time describing the various stages of his development than in recording his weight!

I hope you will try to understand his behavior in terms of his developing personality and skills, and get away from mechanical explanations for his behavior, whether it be "gas" or "teething" on the one hand or "laziness" or "tiredness" on the other. This kind of understanding will enable you, for example, to see the absurdity of ascribing much of a baby's behavior in the first six months to gas. If you can get gas in perspective by the end of the first six months, then when the first tooth emerges at about that age you will not suddenly ascribe to teething those aspects of his behavior that were previously ascribed to gas.

I do not think there is such a thing as a "lazy" child but I accept that the behavior of some children would in an adult be called "laziness." Children have such a strong built-in dynamo of energy that if they stop being energetic, they are either physically or emotionally ill. Emotional disturbances can suppress a child's drive just as much as physical illness.

The baby who cries because he is "tired" will be all smiles once the reason for his crying is worked out, and tiredness is very unlikely to have been the cause. The normal baby when tired has the advantage over the adult that he can drop off to sleep without a moment's notice, wherever he may be.

Don't make the mistake of thinking of your baby as somebody almost generically different from a child or an adult. Parents often feel and sometimes even refer to their child as being "almost human," as though they really think of him as a different sort of being. The way you handle your child when he is a baby should basically be no different from the way you handle him when he is older. "Baby talk," in the sense of a special language for communicating with babies, is outdated because it is harmful to the normal development of language. For the same reason, this is a book about children, including babies, and not a "baby" book.

After reading the book, I hope that you will feel better able to make decisions from your own instincts on such questions as when it is safe for a sick child to get up, and that you will be less influenced by the rigid rules laid down for the upbringing of previous generations of children.

Understanding your child's behavior is helped by thinking back to your own childhood, so that you look at his needs through his eyes.

Another aim of this book is to make you better able to help your doctor care for your child when he is sick. It is right that you should know something about the meaning and importance of a child's symptoms, so that you can be in a better position to talk to your doctor on the telephone and to know when to call him for help. Today's doctors no longer sit on a pedestal doling out orders to their patients. They must have your partnership as parents if they are to get your child well as quickly as possible, and then help you to keep him well.

This Introduction and Chapter 27, on children, parents and their doctors, present my basic convictions in relation to child upbringing. Discipline, which is always regarded as a fundamental chapter in any book on child care, appears as a separate chapter but, more important, it is a continuing theme throughout the book, because it is totally bound up with a knowledge of normal child development. You have to understand the stage of development reached by your child before you punish him for his "bad" deed. No normal mother would punish her ten-month-old baby for knocking over his cup of milk—he is not being "naughty" when he does such a "wicked" thing.

I suspect that the more children you have, provided you enjoy them, the less you punish them. If this is true, it is because you understand more about child development. Although the youngest is sometimes described as being able to get away with murder and you are often thought of as being too lenient with him, I believe this relationship between you results from your greater understanding of how a child grows up.

Parents, today, expect to enjoy their children. I hope that reading this book will help you to enjoy them still more.

1

The Healthy Child

Pregnancy and Birth

Pregnancy

This is not a month-by-month, blow-by-blow account of pregnancy, but it will cover some of your possible worries as an expectant mother. These are likely to center on the way you feel you might affect your unborn baby's growth and well-being, for example, through what you eat or drink, through taking any drugs prescribed, even through your thoughts and emotions during pregnancy.

In fact, it is both natural and necessary for a woman to feel partially responsible for her baby's development rather than to wait passively while "nature takes its course." It is natural because it prepares you for your total responsibility for your baby once he is born. Concern for him long before his conventional birthday helps you to make the transition from wife to mother, and gives you practice in mothering. The Chinese recognize this by calling the day of birth the first birthday; this means that the Chinese give their age as one year older than people in the rest of the world. Concern is also necessary because it encourages you to seek and accept regular prenatal care —the most constructive single thing you can do for your unborn child. It is a good idea to keep a Birth Book, in which you record both your own and your husband's ideas, feelings, and changing emotions throughout pregnancy and labor. Remember—he is pregnant too and later will experience labor. Apart from its interest to both of you, it will make fascinating reading for your children later, when they are learning more about themselves.

Before Pregnancy

Time of Conception and Family Planning

Is there anything you should do even earlier? For example, is there an optimum time for conceiving a child? So far as the individual baby is concerned the optimum time for conception is when he is wanted by healthy and welcoming parents.

Family planning enables couples to delay or to space the birth of their children as they wish, which should increase the baby's chance of a good start. But that is not to say that every planned baby is luckier than a baby born in superficially unpromising circumstances or surroundings. Mothering, which involves feelings, is not the same as mothercraft, a technical skill, and it is not always available to order; too much waiting for everything to be just right for a baby (it never is!) may mean a first child is delayed until the mother is past her mid-thirties. On balance, the chances of having a healthy baby are best when a woman is neither at the very beginning nor at the very end of her childbearing years—so "have your babies (reasonably) young" is still good advice.

The Risk of Handicap

A few parents have to ask themselves whether they should have a child at all. If they have one handicapped baby they have a right and a responsibility to obtain advice on the odds of this happening again. Their doctor, or the pediatrician or geneticist to whom he refers them, can usually give some idea of the order of risk to parents who already have one affected child. For a childless couple who think there is a risk that they may produce a handicapped baby, it is usually only possible to advise on the general risk for the population as a whole, taking into account the age of the mother (see genetic counseling, pp. 417–18).

Prenatal Care

Why Routine Checks Are Essential

During pregnancy, the relationship between your body and the developing baby is always changing. The changes must be watched by a doctor so that anything significant or unusual is detected promptly. An expectant mother is not the best person to judge that everything is normal, because how she herself feels does not necessarily reflect her baby's state. A woman with a Rhesus (Rh) baby feels well, although her baby is being harmed by antibodies from her blood crossing the placenta (see p. 440). You might feel perfectly healthy with raised blood pressure, but if the rise went unnoticed and untreated, it could have serious results for your baby by reducing his blood supply through the placenta. Alternatively, a serious illness in pregnancy does not necessarily affect the baby, although naturally it would make you anxious about his safety.

Whether you sail through pregnancy feeling exceptionally healthy, or spend weeks being sick and feeling miserable, does not in itself appear to make any difference to the baby's health and growth. On the other hand, mothers who are distressed by being pregnant or made anxious by it may remain under stress after the baby is born;

this can influence the baby through his mother's handling of him.

It really is important that you go for routine checks throughout pregnancy, so that your doctor can make sure all is well. These checks are never a waste of time, even if you have an irritatingly long wait to see the doctor and then everything proves to be normal. At least this is reassuring and you should have had an opportunity to ask questions about anything that is bothering you. Don't be afraid to ask about even minor worries. Additionally, I hope your husband will be made to feel welcome and that he will be asked to come into the doctor's room with you.

If anything abnormal or potentially dangerous is noticed, something can be done to help if this is discovered promptly. Sometimes the doctor may decide to deliver the baby early; at other times he may be able to avert the threat of premature labor. Either of these decisions can give the baby a better start and may save his life, but they can only be taken if you see your doctor regularly, so that he can take them in time.

Your doctor will ask you to report to him between regular checks if you notice certain symptoms that could signal danger. He will also tell you how to care for your breasts during pregnancy and answer your questions about breast or artificial feeding (see Breast Feeding, Chapter 5).

X-rays

Since it is not a routine part of prenatal care for a baby to be X-rayed while in the womb, you may be worried if your doctor decides it is necessary. This may be in order to discover the position of the baby, to diagnose whether you are going to have twins, or to obtain some other piece of information that can be found out only in this way. Your worry probably springs from publicity about the harmful effects of irradiation and about the possibility of blood diseases in childhood originating from X-rays during pregnancy (see leukemia, p. 520).

Doctors are well aware of the possible risk of indiscriminate X-raying. Therefore the actual techniques used, the timing of X-rays, and the number performed are carefully controlled. The routine chest X-ray of a mother is delayed until after the third month of pregnancy so as not to risk any possible harm to the baby before all his organs are fully developed. The risk to a baby from an abdominal X-ray on his mother is remote; compared to the risk of the doctor remaining in ignorance it is negligible. In fact, your baby would be exposed to far more danger if his delivery were complicated by unsuspected difficulties which could have been revealed by a controlled X-ray before his birth. The invention of ultrasound to study many aspects of the baby before birth has reduced the need for X-rays.

Diabetes

This disorder must be strictly controlled by insulin during pregnancy. Therefore a diabetic mother will need to see her doctor more frequently than others. If you are diabetic, prenatal care is especially vital. With this special care, your baby has every chance of being unaffected, but he will possibly be delivered earlier than normal.

Effect of Drugs and Infection on the Developing Baby

You should see your doctor as soon as you suspect you are pregnant, because in the early weeks of pregnancy the baby is at the most critical stage of development and so is most vulnerable to damage from outside factors. Should your doctor have to prescribe drugs for you, it is wise, if you are hoping to conceive, to let him know that you may be pregnant.

German Measles

Paradoxically, the time when you most need to be careful is while you may still be unaware that you are pregnant. German measles is the best known of the outside influences that may seriously harm the baby during the first four months of pregnancy, but is usually harmless later. It is a mild illness for the mother but it may cause abnormalities in her baby. German measles vaccine is now available. This means that malformed babies resulting from German measles in pregnancy should become a thing of the past. If a woman has missed being immunized in childhood, she can be given the vaccine at any time. However, she will be warned not to become pregnant during the following three months, lest the vaccine damage the fetus.

Avoiding Risks

It is possible that some other infections and some supposedly harmless medicines may affect a fetus in the first twelve weeks. Yet thousands of mothers do become ill and do take various medicines without their babies being in any way affected. While the situation remains uncertain, your safest course, once you suspect pregnancy, is to avoid taking drugs without asking your doctor first. This is a safety-first measure, advisable because it has so far been impossible to clear every drug of suspicion of causing any damage to any fetus.

In the same way, it is wise to avoid infections if you can, both because it is obviously better to be well than ill while pregnant and because it has not yet been proved whether certain infections can harm a fetus. There are probably combinations of circumstances that could cause trouble in some pregnancies and not in others.

Keeping a Sense of Proportion

It is absolutely natural for you to be very concerned about the health of the baby inside you. This is all part of normal maternal feelings. But try to avoid becoming too obsessed and worried about possible dangers to your child, because many of these have no basis in reality. Of course, you should avoid unnecessary infections (by not visiting a neighbor with influenza, for instance), but don't refuse a visit to the movies because you might catch one there. If you are ill or have a symptom for which your doctor prescribes drugs, accept his decision. Remember that he must balance the unknown potential harm to the baby that may be caused by your untreated illness against any unknown potential effect of the drug he prescribes. He will choose the best one for you, bearing in mind that the well-being of the unborn child is a major consideration when treating any pregnant woman. For instance, the antibiotic tetracycline can make a baby's first teeth yellow and more liable to decay and may affect the growth of his bones. Therefore, if an antibiotic is necessary, the doctor will avoid tetracycline and choose one without known risk of adverse effects on the baby.

A small compensation for the disastrous effect on babies of the drug thalidomide is that all new drugs are screened more thoroughly than before from the point of view of pregnancy; but it remains impossible to prove that any drug is completely harmless, because it is so difficult to pinpoint the cause of many congenital abnormalities (see pp. 416f.). Even if a common drug or illness does turn out to carry some risk, it is important to remember that the great majority of pregnant women and their babies remain unaffected by the myriad of potential hazards they meet in pregnancy.

Injuring the Baby in the Uterus

You may worry about damaging the baby in your uterus should you fall or bump yourself. It is not recommended that you jump from treetops for fun while pregnant, but if you fall down the kitchen steps, it is very unlikely to harm your baby, who is well protected by the water he lies in and by the walls of the uterus and abdomen. A baby can survive the impact of a car crash that kills his mother. Occasionally, a fall can trigger a miscarriage during early pregnancy if a woman is particularly liable to miscarry at this time. A fall would almost certainly produce an "all or nothing" effect, either ending the pregnancy or leaving the fetus unharmed.

However, for your own comfort, it is worth learning the best way to bend, stretch, and carry things while pregnant. This is sometimes taught in preparation classes (see pp. 14–15), but ask for your doctor's advice early in pregnancy if there are no classes available or if these do not begin until the last weeks, particularly if you have a history of miscarriage. Sitting, standing, and even lying properly also make later pregnancy a less uncomfortable time.

Diet and Smoking

What about diet? Does what you eat affect the baby's size or health? In countries where the general level of nutrition is high and most mothers are therefore healthy, the majority of babies probably reach their full birth weight. Their mothers need only follow a normal diet to make sure of this.

The Effect of Smoking

On the other hand, smoking during pregnancy can seriously affect the health and size of the baby. Babies of women who smoke more than about twenty cigarettes a day weigh, on average, 6 ounces (170 g) less than nonsmokers' babies. The difference cannot be explained away on the grounds that smokers and nonsmokers belong to different income groups, eat different quantities, or have different temperaments; it is due to the harmful effects of nicotine, which reduces the amount of blood, and therefore of food substances necessary for growth, reaching the baby.

Does it matter if your baby is 6 ounces (170 grams) lighter than your nonsmoking neighbor's? Of course a larger baby is not automatically healthier or better than a smaller one. What is to his disadvantage is being born 6 ounces (170 grams) lighter than he should be; in other words, his mother's smoking has prevented him from reaching his intended birth weight. It is known that such a baby is more vulnerable than one who has reached his full potential birth weight. Being lighter than nature intended affects some organs more than others, particularly the brain, which is growing especially fast in the last weeks of pregnancy. Intelligence tests on children whose mothers smoked in pregnancy show that their intellect is appreciably lower because their brain growth was affected during pregnancy. In this sense, you are not doing your best for your child if, when pregnant, you continue to smoke. The only possible advice about smoking in pregnancy must be that you should stop it for nine months (see also pp. 134–35, 587).

Should You Eat for Two?

Apart from cutting out smoking, you will not make your baby bigger by eating more than you want or by choosing special foods. Nor is it likely that you can keep your baby's size down in the hope of having an easier birth by eating less in the last weeks of pregnancy; in any case, other effects on the baby make this undesirable. A baby seems to take what he needs from the nourishment available, leaving his mother's body to suffer from the consequences of too much or too little nourishment. Your own teeth will suffer before the baby's are affected by insufficient calcium in your diet. But there is no need for your teeth to decay; the old saying that one tooth is lost for each baby should no longer apply.

These generalizations about the effect of diet cease to apply below a certain level of nutrition; the baby born to a mother who is literally starving or chronically undernourished during pregnancy will be underweight at birth. It is also possible that chronic borderline starvation damages the growing fetus and can be responsible for mental or physical deficiency. Experiments suggest that a lack of certain vitamins in pregnant animals leads to malformations in their young, but this finding cannot be automatically applied to human beings. These experiments are interesting for the light they may throw on the problems of malnutrition in developing countries but they have little relevance for pregnant women with enough to eat.

Vitamins and Iron

Provided your diet is reasonably normal, your baby will not suffer from vitamin deficiency or become stunted from lack of the right food. But in any case do drink a pint of milk a day so as to ensure you take in enough calcium for the proper development of your baby's bones and teeth. This also ensures that calcium is not drained from your body to feed your baby.

If you are given extra vitamins and iron during pregnancy, this is to make doubly sure that your own needs are covered too. Some women are anemic before pregnancy and need extra iron to bring them back to normal. Others tend to become anemic unless given extra iron. Perfectly healthy babies are born all over the world to women whose diets seem outrageously "unbalanced" from a Western point of view. A vegetarian is not depriving her baby because she fails to eat meat or fish, so long as there is some source of protein in her diet and enough of it.

A Good Diet

But don't be discouraged from eating well or choosing your diet with care; this is all part of doing your best for your baby and, since you are building his body, eating body-building protein foods such as meat, fish, cheese, and eggs is more valuable than filling up with cookies. However, there is no need to be overanxious about what you eat or drink. Living entirely on cake would certainly be bad for you and your baby, but unless it make you too fat, you can eat cake in moderation. The same applies to alcohol, which can damage the fetus if taken in excess.

Keeping your weight under control is important; you do not have to "eat for two," as the old saying ran.

If you have a craving for a particular food, indulge it moderately unless it is for something that also makes you ill. For example, you may suddenly crave very hot, spicy food, which, nevertheless, disagrees with you. Burning curries are a normal food for pregnant Indian women, but if they give you indigestion, they are not suitable for you.

Thinking Beautiful Thoughts

Do your thoughts or moods affect the baby in the uterus? No one knows yet, and until we do, you can only be yourself and hope for the best. Experiments on rats show that extreme and prolonged anxiety in pregnant animals results in jittery baby rats, but there is no proof that this is relevant to human beings.

If you have an anxious temperament, your baby may be similar, but it does not follow that this was due to your mood during pregnancy. A severely depressed woman will not necessarily produce a more difficult baby than someone without a care in the world. The depressed mother's baby is liable to suffer from the effects of her depression after birth, not before it.

It is inevitable that parents may hope for a boy or a girl rather than just "a baby," but whatever the outcome I only hope the child never learns later that he or she was the "wrong" sex.

Preparation Classes

You can help to prepare yourself and your husband mentally and physically for labor and for parenthood by attending prenatal classes. If, like an increasing number of mothers, you want to know how to help yourself and how to make the most of the help you are offered during delivery, you will not be content to wait till the first contraction starts to discover what labor is all about. Ignorance is rarely bliss as far as childbirth is concerned.

Preparation classes vary in quality and in the methods taught. Teachers explain the various stages of labor and give practical advice as to how to work with those processes that are beyond direct control, by breathing, relaxation, and other techniques that are within a mother's control, especially if helped by her husband. If you know what to expect, you will be able to co-operate with nature, rather than fight against it because of anxiety and tension due to ignorance. It helps to talk about contractions rather than "pains."

No amount of preparation can eliminate the sheer hard work, the labor of labor, or guarantee you an easy delivery. But classes should help you to make the best of whatever happens. There are side benefits too. A sympathetic and experienced class teacher has more time to answer queries than a busy doctor, and you may feel you can ask her things that seem too trivial to ask the doctor. The company of other expectant mothers and fathers is a comfort in the last weeks of pregnancy. Friendships start at prenatal classes, and if you are new in a neighborhood, this is a good way of meeting people.

Involving the New Father

Fortunately, an increasing number of hospitals believe in preparing fathers as well as mothers for parenthood, hence my emphasis on their role. Husbands can help their wives positively through pregnancy and labor by attending special classes with them and by being present at the birth (see below).

Choosing a Hospital

More and more babies are being delivered in a hospital, because it is safer than delivery at home, particularly for someone expecting her first baby, as well as for a mother who has already had several children. Circumstances can change during a normal labor. Only in a hospital is everything immediately available for the best method of delivery and for starting the baby's breathing and keeping it going mechanically by artificial respiration if necessary.

Provided home conditions are suitable and both you and your baby are well, it is ideal if you can leave the hospital within forty-eight hours. This means you will learn about your baby in the more natural surroundings of your own home, with the help of a midwife or visiting nurse. The modern midwife is as interested in helping mothers of babies delivered in a hospital as those whose babies she has delivered at home.

Ask if your husband can be present during labor. Find out about visiting arrangements and whether children are included. Ideally, visiting should be unrestricted for your husband and children. Can the baby stay with you all day and all night, if you want? Can you decide when to feed him rather than being governed by hospital regulations?

The Father's Part

It is ideal if your husband can be with you throughout labor. This is a crucial experience for both of you, and it should be shared. However, it is not enough to find a hospital that merely allows your husband in the labor room, almost on sufferance; such a hospital will not appreciate his needs. A father has to be trained for his role in labor just as much as a mother. Being admitted to a labor room is likely to be very disturbing to a father who has not been prepared for the event.

In choosing a hospital, you should therefore check that there is at least one shared prenatal class for fathers and mothers. At such a class you will be taught what happens in labor as far as the body is concerned—in other words, the normal physiology of labor. You will also be taught how to relax and breathe effectively during labor and how your husband can help you to do this (see pp. 14–15).

If a complication develops during labor, your husband may be asked to wait outside but he will be allowed back as soon as it is over. Some obstetricians are prepared to deliver a baby by forceps with the father still present and to undertake a Caesarean section under epidural anesthesia in his presence (p. 36). Obviously you must respect the wishes of the obstetrician in this matter; he knows the circumstances under which he can perform at his best.

Whether or not your husband wishes to see his baby born, he will feel more of a father and less of a helpless bystander if he knows what to expect during the later stages of pregnancy and during the delivery of his baby. He is likely to become emotionally involved with his child sooner and more easily than a man who remains on the sidelines while his wife and the professionals are producing a baby on his behalf. An involved father tends to be more sympathetic about late meals, an untidy house, and a wife who is preoccupied with their child.

But you cannot force your husband to take an interest beforehand, let alone go to a fathers' preparation class. If he won't, he may be one of those fathers who switch on instant love and attention once their baby actually arrives. However, many fathers, like some mothers, take time to learn to love their babies. The comparatively indifferent father of a newborn baby may later turn into a devoted parent.

Visiting by Children

If you have other children, you should check whether they are allowed to visit the hospital. The rules about children visiting are much stricter in the United States than in Great Britain. This is a useful measure of the humanitarian aspect of the hospital, since those that permit visiting by children are likely to be less authoritarian. It used to be argued that children should not be allowed to visit because of the risk that they might introduce infection. This is nonsense. It is the doctors and nurses who are far more likely to bring in infection, because they are perpetually in contact with infected patients in the hospital, and a hospital infection is more likely to be resistant to some of the antibiotics, such as penicillin (pp. 392–93).

Keeping the other children away from their mother and her new-born baby increases the risk of subsequent jealousy (p. 148). Children should be as much involved as possible in the arrival of their new brother or sister, and it is asking for problems to separate them from their mother, even for a day. Some hospitals are now permitting children to be present during labor if their parents wish.

"Rooming-in"

A most-important question to ask is whether the hospital provides for "rooming-in." This means that your baby will be able to spend the day, and I hope the night as well, in a crib beside your bed. You will be able to look after most of his daily needs, with help from the nurses. Hospitals where rooming-in is the rule are also likely to be more flexible about visiting, feeding routines, and fathers' rights.

I encourage mothers to have their babies in bed with them if they would like to do so. This is so obvious and natural and there is no danger that a healthy baby will be smothered by his mother (p. 110). These babies seldom cry, and I am astonished that hospital staff, at first, find this a surprising suggestion.

Why is rooming-in an advantage? The time you spend in the hospital after your baby is born is a chance to learn as much as you can about him, while still in the sheltered atmosphere of the hospital, where expert guidance and advice are readily available. It may seem ideal, in theory, that these days should be spent in resting and recuperating from the birth, in preparation for the hard work waiting for you at home. This argument might persuade you to favor a hospital using the old system, whereby babies remain day and night in a central nursery looked after by nurses, only being brought to their mothers at set feeding times. This sounds restful, but you will not learn much about your baby before he is handed over to you when you go home, and he will have been missing you. One demonstration bath and one diaper change are insufficient to give you confidence in handling your baby. Nor is the system as restful as it sounds, because you will tend to think and worry more about your baby if he is not by your side, particularly if he is your first.

Having Your Baby at Home

Advantages

Much depends on whether you can arrange for satisfactory help for the two weeks or so after your baby's birth. If you can relax while at home, there are certainly some advantages. A baby born at home has no sudden break in routine when leaving the hospital (see p. 53). You gradually take on his complete care and household jobs. A midwife or nurse calls daily, twice a day at first, providing expert advice and practical help, and hands over slowly as you become ready for it. Your baby's day and night routines can be arranged to suit him individually. He is the only baby to be fed, and it is easier for you to follow your instincts about this than it is in the hospital, where you are surrounded by the activity of the maternity unit and other mothers and babies, who behave differently.

If he is not your first baby, you have more confidence in your own methods. If you enjoy reading a book and eating chocolates while breast feeding and know your baby is perfectly happy, you can do so without incurring disapproval, real or imagined—although this might not be so if someone with strong opinions on baby care is helping with the housekeeping. However, you will probably have sufficient confidence to make it plain that you have your own way of doing things. Such "critical" remarks are the well-meant result of enormous interest in your new baby, not a reflection on you as a mother, but it can be difficult to remember this at the time.

Having stated all these advantages, it still must be said that it is safest for all babies to be born in a hospital, and to be taken home afterward as quickly as possible.

Choosing a Name

You are more likely to be satisfied with your choice of name if you begin the selection during pregnancy. I am sometimes surprised to find parents with a new baby but no plans for his or her name. Perhaps they have chosen either a boy's or a girl's name only, and a baby of the unwanted sex arrives. It is better not to choose the sort of unique and bizarre name that, while satisfying your urge for your child to be different, will make him feel isolated. For the same reason, keep to standard spelling; otherwise he will get tired of having to correct it or of having to put up with the wrong spelling.

The Birth

The ideal arrangement, which exists in a few hospitals, is for the husband and wife, on arrival during the first stage of labor, to be given a room of their own and not to be moved later to the delivery room for the actual birth. This is a carpeted room with easy chairs and a table as well as a bed—very different from the clinical appearance of the usual labor or delivery room. It should be called the "birth room."

The expectant mother is free to sit or walk about until she decides it is time to get up on the bed for the delivery. After the baby is born, she is not hurried to a postnatal ward by herself, often in the middle of the night, but she and her husband are left alone in the same room to get to know their new baby together. This gives parents confidence that it is safe for them to care for their baby, and is the exact opposite of the inhumane approach whereby babies are bundled off to nurseries immediately after birth to be cared for by a nurse.

Although it is usual for the mother to be lying on her back on the bed for the delivery, more and more obstetricians are leaving mothers to choose "alternative methods," such as the birth chair or a semistanding position supported by husband and doctor. Mothers who walk about during the second stage of labor seem able to guide the baby down the birth canal by their own body movements, so that his head comes out correctly and without causing a tear. Fundamental to this approach is that the mother makes the decisions and is in charge.

As soon as the baby is delivered, he is given to his parents and lies on his mother's abdomen or at her breast, where he can feed if he wishes, and the cord is cut. Most important, the parents are not denied the excitement of discovering for themselves the baby's sex. So many mothers have told me of their disappointment at having the sex shouted out by the doctor or midwife, especially if it was not the sex they wanted. Their major concern is to know if their baby is normal.

Soon the mother should turn on her side with the baby facing her at eye level, also on his side. Babies keep their eyes open particularly during the first hour—an essential time for parents to be left alone with their baby and for a mother's senses not to be dulled by being given a sedative. I still hear midwives talk of the need for a mother to have a rest as soon as she is delivered, whereas what she needs is her baby. In any case, mothers have told me that they were far too excited to go to sleep.

2

Preparing for Your Baby

However busy you are before your baby arrives, you will be busier afterward, so it is sensible to make as many preparations as possible in advance. This applies to anticipating problems in housekeeping and generally thinking of ways to make life easier, as well as buying baby things and equipment (pp. 24–35). Something that would have taken a few minutes to settle before the baby is born may seem impossible to fit in afterward, particularly if you are a mother with no backlog of experience or well-tried baby-sitters to help you. Start planning ahead before the very end of pregnancy, when many women tend to tire quickly and because some babies arrive unexpectedly.

If it will be difficult to leave the baby and go out alone, try to do anything that would be easier without him while you are still alone. For example, if you use a hairdresser, get your hair done shortly before the baby is due. A major shopping expedition to buy new furniture is no fun with a hungry, tired baby in tow. Even something that involves mental effort rather than physical energy is better done beforehand, if possible; it can seem far more of a nuisance once you have an unpredictable baby to look after. A woman with a full-time job may think that being at home all day with a baby cannot be as time-consuming as people suggest, but it is a round-the-clock job at first, and it will be less tiring and more enjoyable if you can avoid unnecessary worries or work.

Housekeeping

Unless your husband enjoys shopping and cooking or you have some-one to help you, stock up with food for easily made meals to see you through the first days at home with your baby. A number of complete meals are more useful than snacks. If these preplanned meals are not needed, the extra stores will still save time later. Start stocking up before the end of pregnancy, when heavy shopping is a strain, and remind your husband not to eat it all while you are away!

It also helps to arrange for regular household necessities to be delivered. Delivery is more expensive than going to the supermarket, but in the early weeks the extra expense is worthwhile if you can afford it. If you have a telephone, you will be in the lucky position of being able to order things from your house.

These weeks are a time of extra expense, quite apart from any drop in income because you may have stopped earning money. Easily prepared foods like chops, steak, and frozen vegetables cost more than cheaper cuts of meat and fresh vegetables. There are additional expenses such as extra heating and laundry. In cold weather, a new baby's room must be kept heated and, at any season, his washing is mountainous. You may have to pay someone to do things you previously did yourself.

This type of expense is temporary and justified. The more time and energy you save at this early stage the more contented your baby tends to be. Consequently, he settles down to a reasonable routine sooner, allowing you and your husband to get back to a more normal life. In fact, making life easier reduces the chance of months of tiredness and depression following childbirth (pp. 152f.).

If you are harassed, you cannot enjoy your baby, and anything that increases your enjoyment of the baby helps your whole family. A washing machine, a refrigerator, and a freezer are among the most useful mother's helps, although they won't in themselves guarantee a relaxed mother.

Reducing Housework

Before your baby is born, try to think of ways of cutting down work. One of the best ways of reducing housework is not to do it. This does not mean you and your husband should live in squalor and abandon yourselves entirely to your baby, which would depress most families so acutely that their children would be neglected too. But it does mean that, without extra domestic help, it is impractical to aim at the same standard of thoroughness as before your baby arrived. Put away the silver candlesticks if the sight of tarnish is going to upset you. Rearrange your living space if this would make things easier; for example, eat in the kitchen temporarily, or cut down the number of rooms in regular use and therefore in need of regular cleaning by firmly shutting the door of a spare room. If too little space is your problem, try to eliminate unwanted furniture and make the best use of the space available; bumping into a table each time you park the baby carriage will be infuriating.

Furnishing Your Child's Room

There is no need for a young baby to have his own room (see sleep, pp. 109f). When he does have a separate room, it need not be a traditional nursery. You need only provide special nursery furniture, wall-paper, and floor coverings if you enjoy them yourself. Until he can play outside his crib, all that is essential is that his room can be heated in cold weather. A heater with a thermostat enables the room to be kept at a constant temperature during the cold weather; this need not be more than about 70°F (21°C).

A piece of furniture with a flat top on which you can change his diaper or clothes is useful. A low chest of drawers or steady table can be used for this, if padded with a folded towel or special waterproof mattress. A comfortable chair for feeding is necessary if you feed him in his room. In fact, try to work out what the room will be used for before buying a particular piece of furniture: there is no point in buying a feeding chair for the baby's room if you always feed him somewhere else.

Safety

When your baby can move about, particularly when he reaches the stage of being able to climb out of his crib, safety is the most important feature of his room. Make sure that the furniture cannot be pulled over. Windows must be guarded with bars—vertical, not horizontal; otherwise they will double as a climbing frame. Alternatively, windows can be fixed so that they cannot be opened far enough for your baby to fall out.

Heaters must be adequately guarded. Free-standing heaters should preferably be of the convector or blower type. A fire must be completely screened by a fixed guard with small mesh through which a child cannot poke his fingers or a stick. Electric outlets should be covered. It is best to have the plugs sited in inconspicuous corners or to have a piece of furniture in front of them, even if this is more inconvenient for you. Avoid trailing wires (see accidents, p. 623).

Decorating the Room

If your child will play and sleep in the same room, you would be wise to paper the walls with a pattern that does not show every fingerprint, or to paint them with washable paint. The floor is sure to be stained with spilled drinks or paint water and crushed crayons, so the covering should be a washable material such as vinyl. Cheap carpeting is warmer, but will need replacing sooner.

Your child will be happy playing in his room only if he can relax and enjoy himself there; this is impossible if you are always worrying about untidiness, dirt, and damage. As a child reaches middle childhood or puberty he, and particularly she, will take an interest in the room, although this may not take the form of keeping it tidy and clean —it is more liable to be shown in a determination that all his things are arranged, and remain, just as he wants them, even if this is on the floor, and that his precious belongings are not touched by anyone.

This can be a problem if children of different ages or sexes share a room. It is hard to encourage tidiness in one child when another is always moving his things. Different corners of the same room for each child or at least a drawer or locker of his own for each child may help.

Equipment for Your New Baby

Apart from clothing (pp. 31f.), your new baby needs somewhere to sleep and some kind of transport so that he can go out with you. He must be washed in some receptacle, but a baby bath is not essential (p. 99). A bed, bedding, and baby carriage or carry-bed are his basic needs.

Shopping for baby things can be bewildering, so it is a help to visit the baby departments of large stores, where several different makes of equipment are on display and assistants can give expert advice. There are also specialized shops dealing only in baby things; these give good value but limited choice if they sell only their own products. Mail-order catalogues are another source of information.

It is not essential to buy new equipment. If you wish to economize on items that are soon outgrown, your local children's health clinic may have a bulletin board on which secondhand baby carriages, cribs, and almost anything else babies use are advertised. Local newspapers and news vendors' boards also carry advertisements of sales and wants. The Salvation Army and yard sales are also good places to check. (See points to check, p. 30).

The Baby's Bed

Crib A new baby can sleep in a full-size crib from the start, but it is less easy to make him feel secure and comfortable in a big crib than in a small cradle, carry-bed or basket. You can move him about more easily in a small crib, and small sheets and blankets are quicker to wash and dry than large ones. Another reason for his sleeping in this type of crib at first is that its sides protect him from drafts better than the barred sides of a full-size crib, although it is possible to pad the sides and ends of a crib satisfactorily.

When your baby can sit up, he is no longer safe in a small crib and, anyway, will be outgrowing it and need a larger one. By about six months he will be better at keeping himself warm and he will not need the comfort of a small crib to the same extent. When buying a full-size crib, check that it has a safety catch to prevent him from letting down the sides when he is older.

Carry-beds These are not as attractive as wicker baskets or wooden cradles, but are more versatile. A carry-bed with a waterproof hood and cover allows you to take your baby out in the rain: this is useful even for a short walk from your front door to the car and essential if you take the baby on public transport. With a wheeled stand and a handle, a carry-bed can double as a baby carriage until your baby is too active and too large to be left in it safely (see baby carriage, p. 28). Even if not his only baby carriage, a crib with wheels comes in useful in the house, because you can move the baby from room to room without disturbing him. Check the weight of the carry-bed and the position of the handles to make sure you can carry it easily.

Being lined with plastic or similar material, carry-beds are easy to wipe clean. However, nonporous linings can be dangerous: if the baby rolled to the side of the carry-bed, so that his face was right against the plastic, he might not be able to breathe. Tragedies have occurred in which babies suffocated in this way. The danger arises if the carry-bed is unsteady on its stand and tilts so that the baby slips against the side or end. If you are in any doubt about the stability of the stand (new stands are covered by safety regulations), place the carry-bed on a firm surface, such as a chest top instead, and don't use the stand. To remove the risk of suffocation caused by the baby's face coming up against the plastic, line the carry-bed with a blanket.

If the mattress provided with the carry-bed is thin, you can make your baby more comfortable, and warmer, by placing a folded piece of blanket on top of it and covering this with waterproof sheeting.

Wicker Cradles A basket with handles is lighter than a carry-bed but it has no hood or cover and is not waterproof, which makes it less practical for outings. Some of the cheaper baskets are roughly finished, so your baby might scratch his hands unless you line the inside.

A wickerwork cradle should be lined to keep drafts from the baby; if this is frilled it looks like the traditional idea of a beautiful crib. A wheeled stand makes the cradle easier to move if it is heavy and awkward for one person to carry. If the cradle has no stand, place it on a sturdy table or chest top rather than on a stand that fits imperfectly.

You need not panic if you don't have a crib when your baby arrives; a drawer makes an excellent temporary bed!

Mattresses Your baby's comfort is more directly affected by his mattress than by his crib or carry-bed. It must be firm, so although you can improvise a satisfactory mattress with folded blankets, do not use a soft pillow as a mattress, because the baby could bury his head in it and suffocate. The mattress should fit the crib so that when your baby rolls he cannot become wedged in the gap at the side between mattress and crib. Many mattresses are sold with fitted waterproof covers; otherwise, protect the mattress with waterproof sheeting. Cover the whole mattress, not just the area under his hips—it is amazing how wet a baby's bed can become after an unbroken night's sleep (pp. 27–28). However carefully you cover it, a mattress eventually needs cleaning, so ask whether it can be cleaned. Some modern stuffings cannot be washed or cleaned and have to be thrown away. Foam mattresses filled with nonallergic materials are available.

If you make a mattress yourself, be sure it is thick enough to keep your baby warm. A baby in a carry-bed put down in a cold place with only a thin mattress between him and the ground can get very chilly.

Bedding A pillow is unnecessary for the first twelve months and could be dangerous if the baby were to bury his head in it. This could block his breathing, although it is now believed that a healthy baby can always move his head so that his nose is not obstructed. Even so, it is not worth the risk of giving him a pillow in the early months of life—he doesn't need it.

Small sheets and blankets for crib, carry-bed, and baby carriage can be bought or made from full-size bedding. The more sheets your baby has the better. Sheets get damp frequently in the early months, so, as well as those bought specially, you will find extra sheets made from your old ones useful. Pieces of cloth too small for sheets can be used as draw-sheets under the baby's head or bottom to protect the sheet beneath. Full-size crib sheets can be used, but this means more to wash.

Flannelet sheets are warmer than cotton but take longer to dry. Fitted bottom sheets save trouble but are more expensive than ordinary ones.

A new baby does not need a top sheet, since he is swaddled in a shawl or thin blanket for his first few weeks. You can wrap him in a sheet and tuck him in with blankets instead—a sheet is easier to wash than a shawl or blanket.

Blankets These should be light but warm; cellular ones are both and are easy to wash and dry. Cotton cellular blankets are warm because of the air trapped in the "cells"; they are suitable for swaddling the new baby and are machine washable and even boilable. Some woolen blankets are machine washable.

Avoid blankets with fringes, which your baby will suck. Satin or nylon binding protects his face and neck from irritation if the blanket touches his skin. A firm, close pattern is better than an openwork, lacy blanket, in which the baby catches his fingers and toes. A loop of wool wrapped round a baby's finger can cut off his blood supply, thereby damaging the finger.

Old blankets, cut up in suitable sizes, can be used provided they are not too heavy. Blankets should be large enough to tuck in properly. Crib-sized blankets can be folded and used double in the crib or baby carriage.

You can buy clips to hold blankets in place and to prevent your baby from kicking them off. A sleeping bag may be the answer to this problem, once he is a few weeks old (see below). The number of blankets a baby needs depends, of course, on how warm his room is. Do not pile them on him at night when you would sleep happily under only a sheet, but bear in mind that the temperature drops at night. An underblanket is warm and comfortable; a flannelet sheet will do and is easily washed.

Blankets as well as sheets get wet from urine or dribbled milk, so you must have sufficient to change them whenever necessary.

Sleeping Bag The newborn baby is happier if wrapped securely in a light blanket than in a sleeping bag, but these can be useful, especially if you worry about your baby kicking off his bedcovers at night.

Make sure that a sleeping bag is easily washable. It is liable to get damp after a long night's sleep, even if your baby is wearing plastic pants. If you are relying on a bag to keep him warm at night, you will need more than one. A bag is particularly useful for traveling or for visiting friends when you do not want to take lots of blankets. Some bags convert into robes later—if they are still fit to be worn.

Make sure that a bag is large enough to allow your baby to stretch his legs inside, and that it is not too tight around his neck or at his wrists.

Waterproof Sheets A mattress may be sold with its own fitted waterproof sheeting, but this will not last long if it is made of thin plastic. An unprotected mattress must be covered with a rubber or plastic sheet even if your baby wears plastic pants, since the pants should not be too tight to stop the urine escaping altogether. The baby carriage mattress needs protecting too, and a spare waterproof sheet is useful; you will probably need three. The whole mattress needs to be covered, not just the patch under the baby's buttocks. Urine can leak and spread farther than this.

It is worth buying one really comfortable sheet for the bed where the baby spends most time. A quilted sheet is warmer and not as clammy as a plain sheet when very wet. Waterproof sheets smell unless washed regularly. The quilted type are easy to wipe and then pat dry.

Your baby will be more comfortable if there is a thin underblanket or flannelet sheet between the waterproofing and the bottom sheet of the bed. Otherwise, the wet sheet directly on the waterproofing can get cold and will squelch when soaked.

The Baby Carriage

The baby carriage is usually the baby's most expensive single piece of equipment, although it is possible to buy a good secondhand one cheaply (see p. 30).

More and more parents are using a cloth pouch-type baby carrier (p. 112) in the early days for outdoor and indoor carrying, combined with a carry-bed in the early days and a modern stroller when the baby is older. There is no need to buy a baby carriage before he is born; a pouch-type carrier will serve your purpose while you decide whether you really need one.

Different Types Which kind of carriage is best? There is no clearcut answer as far as the baby is concerned, but different types suit different families. A baby carriage with large wheels and good springs will give a smoother ride than a low one with small wheels and poorer springs, which transmit bumps more easily. Baby carriages with small wheels at the front and larger ones at the back are easier to push up a curb. However, a baby does not seem to notice the difference, while the amount of jolting he receives depends also on the baby-carriage driver and on the mattress. So do not buy a large, expensive model just because you feel your baby needs it, unless you want one anyway.

If you have limited space in which to keep a baby carriage, will have to pull it up steps, or wish to take it on journeys, you need a lightweight model with a detachable body. The chassis itself should fold up and the handle fold forward over the wheels, so that it can be taken in a car or train while the baby sleeps in the body of the carriage.

How to make the best of whichever type you choose is discussed on pp. 112–14.

Carry-bed and Stroller The baby carriage can be used as a carry-bed until the baby has grown out of it. By the end of his first six to twelve months, the baby is too big and too active to be left in it safely; you will then need a proper carriage or stroller for outings. A carry-bed can be folded for storage or can be wheeled from room to room inside the house. The baby can sleep and go out in the same carry-bed, which is worth remembering if you are short of space.

Points to Check When Choosing a Baby Carriage

There are certain points to look for whichever model you choose. You will do most of the pushing, so don't let the salesman or your husband blind you with technical details; insist on having the final say.

Stability   Safety is the most important point. Test the brake. It must be efficient and easy to reach when you are holding the handle with one hand—you may have to do this if stopping on a slope. A brake is more effective if it acts on two wheels instead of only on one.

The baby carriage must not tip over when rocked by an active toddler or by the baby himself, although some light models rock alarmingly, yet remain safe. But remember that the manufacturer cannot guarantee that it will never tip if a toddler is sitting in one end, or if the baby is not harnessed to the carriage to prevent him from standing up and tilting it. The stability depends on the way it is used as well as on the way it is made. Consumer studies can help if you are in doubt about whether a model is safe or a good buy. Well-known makes sold by specialized stores should be reliable if sensibly used.

Safety Harness   Check the fittings for a safety harness. Some baby carriages are provided with a strap to go around the baby's waist but this alone is quite inadequate for an active baby. He needs a full harness over his shoulders, attached to the sides of the carriage and fastened so that he cannot stand up; this requires attachment points.

Is It Easy to Use?   Is it easy to clean, inside and out? Does the hood go up and down easily and fix securely in intermediate positions? Is it easy to push? Remember it will be heavier when carrying a baby and shopping. The smallest, lightest models are not necessarily the easiest to push; larger, heavier models may have well-balanced wheels with ball bearings which compensate for their extra weight. The handle must be the correct height, or be adjustable to the correct height, for you. If the carriage is to last for your next baby, with the older child sitting on a seat at one end, make sure it can be used with such a seat.

If the chassis detaches from the body, check that you can do this simply and quickly. Some firms make a range of interchangeable chassis and bodies, enabling you to choose the combination that suits you best.

Care of the Baby Carriage   If it gets wet, dry the chrome parts when you get home and keep the hood up until it dries, wiping off the excess water if necessary. It will need oiling occasionally; squeaky carriages annoy other people even if you and your baby get used to the noise, and well-oiled wheels make it smoother to push.

Mend small defects, such as holes in the cover, as they arise; it is vital to repair at once anything affecting safety, like a faulty brake. Even those with dark inner linings need to be wiped clean with a soapy cloth at intervals. When your baby is old enough to play and eat crackers in his carriage, parts of toys and crumbs collect in the corners under the mattress and should be removed periodically.

Points to Check When Buying Secondhand   When buying secondhand, remember that an item like a crib frame, which must be safe, may not be covered by the latest safety regulations; a repainted item of furniture could have been painted with a lead paint, which, if chewed, could poison your baby (see p. 625). Look out for splinters on wooden furniture. Baby carriages must be carefully checked for every point that you would check in a new model, as well as for signs of wear. Make sure the hood goes up and down properly and that the cover fits: it is sometimes possible to get a new hood and cover for a model in otherwise good condition. Test the brake and see if any nuts are loose or missing. Look at the rubber tires for wear and replace if necessary.

Carry-bed handles and linings may be wearing out. When buying a full-size crib, see if the drop side can be raised and lowered easily and that the bottom does not sag. Check that the bars are spaced closely enough so that the baby cannot get his head stuck between them. A mattress sold with the crib is likely to be in worse condition than the crib itself, but it may be worth buying it and getting a new mattress.

In general, look for all the safety points expected in new equipment, in addition to making a thorough check on the effects of wear and tear. Something used by a small, immobile baby, such as a cradle or baby carriage, tends to be in better shape than something belonging to an active toddler; strollers are particularly likely to be damaged. However, it is possible to get real bargains, in good condition, and shabby equipment may be worth repainting or repairing if basically safe.

Chairs and Bouncers   A baby can lie back in a chair from the age of a month or two—in fact, as soon as he is able to enjoy himself by looking at the world around him. Don't be frightened that he will harm his back if lying in a canvas or plastic chair; it is better for him to be propped up so that he can see around than to be left lying in a crib and having to stare at a ceiling. Some chairs are made so that the baby can gently bounce himself. The baby-bouncer is a different piece of equipment, which most babies love using when they are ready for it (p. 296).

A highchair, to bring the baby to table level for meals, is not essential. Many small baby chairs can be safely fixed to an adult's chair for the same purpose. The modern baby chair is attractive and easy to clean; quite different from the old-fashioned highchair, with all its corners and crevices.

Baby Clothes

These are a matter of personal taste, adapted to a family's budget and the local climate. The baby is happy so long as he is comfortable and warm, provided you enjoy him—but then, pretty clothes could increase your pleasure in him.

The New Baby's Needs A new baby spends most of his time asleep. He does not need different clothes for day and night, although you may prefer to change his clothes after a morning bath.

With a limited amount to spend on baby clothes, it is better to keep most of it for later on, when he can move about; he will then get dirty and cold much more easily during the day and will need his clothes changed at bedtime. Once he can sit up in his baby carriage and kick off his blankets, he will have to be warmly dressed in cold weather, whereas the new baby remains tucked under his blankets and does not need such warm clothes. He should be dressed in several layers of light clothing rather than a few bulky garments.

Sweaters help to keep a baby warm inside and outside the house and at night in cold weather. But it is not always necessary to add a sweater; dress your baby by the day rather than by the season. Remember that most babies in the U.S. are overclothed, rather than the reverse. Judge his requirements broadly by your own—he will not need several layers of woolen clothes on a day when you are warm enough in a cotton dress.

The number of basic garments needed depends partly on how often you are prepared to wash and dry your baby's clothes and partly on whether you wish him to look spotless all the time. Some babies regurgitate milk after every feeding, so that they look grubby and smell of stale milk even when their clothes are protected by bibs (pp. 436–37). They bear no resemblance to the immaculate babies who advertise infant foods, and there is little point in their mothers aiming at this kind of perfection all the time.

In general, the more clothes your baby has, the less often you need to do the washing. Three to four shirts, three to four nightgowns or an alternative, such as all-in-one stretch suits, plus three sweaters, are usually necessary, according to the season and climate. Although it would be possible to manage with only two of each if you washed one lot while your baby wore the other, this would not allow for extra changes of clothes if he were sick or damp, as new babies often are, or if you could not do the washing on time.

Bootees, mittens, and caps are unnecessary except for outings in very cold weather (see using the baby carriage, pp. 112–14).

Choosing Different makers use different methods of sizing. Baby clothes are sometimes sized by weight and sometimes by age. If you buy the smallest size, a heavy baby may outgrow them quickly, but the larger size swamps a smaller baby. It is a good idea to buy the second size, since the new baby is wrapped up and the fit of his clothes does not matter much. Nightgowns should last for the first year at least.

If you intend to use a washing machine for all the baby's clothes, it is obviously helpful to buy as many as possible in materials that require a similar washing cycle. Baby clothes are made in a wide variety of man-made materials, and many woolen garments are machine washable. Drip-dry clothes cut down the ironing.

To discover the variety available and to compare styles and prices, look around before deciding. There are constant improvements in design and materials that simplify dressing babies and washing their clothes, which you may miss if you rely entirely on the advice of mothers whose babies were born even a few years ago. Mail-order catalogues are useful.

Shirts Since these go next to your baby's skin, it is important that they are soft and nonirritating.

Baby shirts either go over the head or are wrapped around the chest and tied with tapes. If you choose the former, buy the envelope neck type, which fits snugly once on, but which you can stretch when putting it on, so that your baby is not frightened by having a tight garment pulled over his face. Clothes should always be put on and taken off in the direction that avoids their completely covering a child's face. Wrap-over shirts avoid this problem, but the tapes can be difficult to tie and sometimes get knotted when you are in a hurry. If your baby's nightgown fastens at the back and the shirt at the front, he has to be turned over during dressing, so try to buy shirts and gowns both of which fasten at the front or the back. Some shirts have tabs inside at hip level to which you can pin the diaper; this helps to keep the shirt in place.

Long-sleeved shirts are mainly needed in countries with extremely cold winters. A long-sleeved gown and a sweater over a short-sleeved shirt are warm enough for most temperatures.

Long Gowns Gowns come in various sizes and shapes, some opening all the way down and some only a short way from the neck so that they have to be put on over the baby's head. Tapes are generally used to fasten a gown. Some gowns do up with snap fasteners, which are easier to manage than tapes, but these generally have to go over the baby's head. Some fasten at the hem to stop them riding up, leaving the baby's legs uncovered; others have concealed mittens at the ends of the sleeves. If a gown has elasticized wrists, check that they are not too tight, and if they are, snip the elastic to make them looser. A gown in a shift style without snaps, tapes, or elastic slips on easily and is practical.

If you make your baby's gowns yourself, a pattern with raglan sleeves is more comfortable for a baby than set-in sleeves. A sash to tie behind his back looks pretty but can be bulky when he is lying on the bow. The simpler the style the better.

Nightgowns can be bought or made in a variety of materials.

Stretch Suits Until your baby is kicking off his bedcovers, his clothes do not have to keep his legs warm—the bedcovers will see to this. However, all-in-one stretch suits, which expand as he grows, cover arms and legs, feet and body. They are outgrown eventually, so take care they do not later squeeze your baby's feet.

These suits can be worn day and night and are made of soft, stretchy cotton material combined with nylon or some similar fiber. If you decide to dress your baby like this from birth, be sure to buy suits that undo sufficiently around the legs to allow diaper changing with the minimum of undressing. Some kinds are especially made for tiny babies, having no collar, because a new baby's neck is so short, and with mittens incorporated into the ends of the sleeves, to be used if needed. Stretch suits are also made with short sleeves and no legs for use in hot weather.

Stretch suits are easy to wash, need no ironing, and can continue to be worn when your baby is crawling, if they still fit. But they are more expensive than ordinary nightgowns, and many mothers prefer a tiny baby in a traditional gown. Two suits and two nightgowns would be a compromise between tradition and convenience.

Short Dresses and Tops A newborn baby is under the bedcovers most of the time, so just a short top over his diaper and shirt will keep him warm, although when he is picked up for feeding his legs can get chilly.

Short dresses or tops are practical for crawling babies, who are hampered by long trailing gowns. If worn instead of a nightgown from the beginning, three or four will be needed. Long sleeves are more practical than short.

Sweaters and Jackets Small babies look sweet in openwork, lacy frills but they tend to catch their fingers in the holes of the pattern and to suck satin ribbons. You will probably be given some jackets of this type, but for everyday wear sweaters made in stockinet stitch or a similar closely worked pattern are more practical. Sweaters that button all the way up are warmer than those with a single fastening at the neck or a V-shaped front opening. Pullovers look neat but have to be put on over your baby's head; so until he sits on your lap and knows better what is happening, it is best to avoid them.

Many sweaters are made of machine-washable man-made materials, but these are usually less warm than hand-knitted woolens.

Bootees, Mittens, and Hats   A newborn baby's feet keep warm under the bedcovers. When he is picked up, wrapped in a shawl or blanket, his feet can be kept covered on a cool day. His hands and cheeks may feel cold but if he is otherwise warm, this does not matter. When you take him outside, his head is well protected by the sides of the baby carriage and by the hood too if it rains (pp. 112–13). So there is really no need to buy any of these items unless you wish to do so.

Very short bootees come off more readily than long ones. Neither bootees nor mittens should be made in openwork patterns; your baby's fingers and toes will get caught in the holes. Long tapes and mittens are usually sucked. Slippery satin or nylon tapes come undone more easily than cotton ones. Nylon thread is extremely strong and if it becomes knotted around a baby's finger, the blood supply is cut off—so nylon should not be used for mittens or bootees.

Do not use mittens just to stop your baby from sucking his hands; he will only suck the mittens instead, which is not half as satisfying as sucking his own fingers, or he will take the first chance to suck his fingers when you remove the mittens. Mittens help to prevent a baby from scratching his face by accident when his hand spontaneously brushes across his cheek. However, his nails can be kept short to stop this happening, and, in any event, he will soon be able to control his arm movements and put his hands where he wants them—in his mouth (see thumb-sucking, pp. 229–30, 547).

Diapers

There are several kinds of diapers available but, basically, the choice is between washable and disposable ones. You can buy washable diapers for everyday use and disposables for occasional use, when they are more convenient, or disposables can be used the whole time.

Washable Diapers   Diapers are usually sold by the dozen or half-dozen. Three to four dozen are needed, unless you can wash and dry them daily. You should have a sufficient number to change your baby whenever necessary, without worrying about the supply running out.

The initial expense seems large for such a boring item, but diapers have to last for about two years and to stand up to continual washing. Good-quality diapers can sometimes be used for a second baby, and, finally, they make admirable rags for housework.

Disposable Diapers   You can avoid buying ordinary washable diapers altogether and use only disposable ones. This reduces the initial financial outlay and also the time and money spent in diaper laundering; but when calculating the cost of using disposable diapers, bear in mind that you will often need two disposable diapers where one ordinary diaper would do.

There are several brands available, varying in shape and degree of absorbency. Some kinds tend to fluff and to stick to the baby's skin or to disintegrate when wet. This is less likely to happen with the type that is covered with netting; the netting helps keep the diaper in shape. Try several types and find out which works best.

Plastic Pants

Protective waterproof pants, worn over the diaper to keep bedding and clothes dry, are now made of plastic or similar materials instead of rubber. So long as they are not used as an excuse to leave your baby for hours on end in a soaking diaper, and so long as they do not fit so tightly that no urine can evaporate from a wet diaper, plastic pants are a good way of reducing work. Because you do not have to change his sheets and clothes every time your baby wets his diaper, you will be less anxious to start toilet training early in order to save laundry and more relaxed about it when you do begin. You can let someone hold your baby without worrying that he will soak them as well as himself, and sit him in a chair without protecting it first.

Ideally, plastic pants should be worn only on special occasions, when it is important that your baby does not wet his clothes, since they do reduce evaporation of urine, and therefore the baby's skin remains wetter than if he wore just a diaper; this situation encourages diaper rash to develop, and misusing plastic pants can lead to a severe rash. Therefore, if your baby wears plastic pants regularly, make sure that you change him at reasonable intervals. You will be advised to leave the pants off when the baby has a rash, using them only for outings until it clears up (p. 431). Whether or not your baby tends to get diaper rash, his plastic pants should not be tight around his legs or waist. It is better to have loose pants that leak slightly than close-fitting ones that allow no evaporation and dig into his skin.

Waterproof pants come plain and covered with nylon, with frills for girls and with snaps, so that you can change the diaper without removing the pants. Sizes vary, but even the smallest are huge on a newborn baby, who can do without them if you fold his diapers in the proper way. Try to find pants with soft edges, and look out for dirt traps: although most pants are easy to wash and pat dry immediately, some have grooves which become impregnated when the baby soils his diaper. Don't go on using pants when they become hard and brittle.

3

The Newborn Baby

The Routine after Delivery

As soon as a baby is born, his mouth and nose are gently cleared to remove any mucus blocking his air passages. This can be done when he is in your arms.

First Contact with Your Baby

You should be given your naked baby to hold during the final stage of labor, while the placenta (afterbirth) is coming away and before the umbilical cord is cut. Nature made the cord sufficiently long for the baby to be held to your breasts while still attached to the placenta in the uterus. It is natural for you to want to see and hold your baby at once, after nine months of waiting, and indeed for the baby to need contact with you during his first moments in a strange world. Even after a long or difficult labor, a mother usually has a special energy to respond at once to her baby. If his father is there too, the moment is perfect. You will immediately want to know if the baby is normal, but discovering the sex for yourselves is an excitement you should not be denied (p. 19). Not every woman is elated at this point, and you would not be abnormal just to be relieved that labor is over, rather than feeling full of joy.

After a time, and well within the first hour, move the baby from your abdomen or breasts to lie beside you, turning yourself to face your baby. In this "en face" position your eyes can click together, a vital cue to bonding.

If a general anesthetic was needed so that you were unconscious during delivery, you miss the first sight of your baby in his original state. He may be clean and clothed when you meet, and you may be surprised by his thinness and fragility when you see him undressed.

Umbilical Cord

The umbilical cord is clamped and cut; this does not hurt the baby at all. Some obstetricians, having clamped the cord, ask the father if he would like to cut it—a very sensitive and symbolic gesture. An elastic band is commonly used to tie the cord, since the elastic, by keeping a constant pressure on the cord as it shrinks, reduces the risk of bleeding from the stump. A dressing may be applied but not a binder,

3

although there is a tendency for doctors in some countries to leave the cord stump exposed to the air, thereby hastening its drying and shrinking. The remains of the stump drop off within a week or ten days (see navel, p. 102).

Caesarean Section

The decision that delivery must be by Caesarean section is made by the obstetrician. Problems in pregnancy might lead to this being planned before labor starts; alternatively, events during labor could necessitate this method of delivery.

A baby born by Caesarean section often looks more attractive at birth than a baby born the normal way, because his head has not been squashed as in a vaginal delivery (see p. 38), unless it had already entered the birth canal when the operation started. In many hospitals it is routine for babies born by Caesarean section to have the contents of the stomach sucked out through a tube, since, not having been tightly compressed during delivery, the stomach still contains blood and amniotic fluid that have been swallowed. If left in the stomach, these can sometimes cause the baby to vomit.

Many mothers whose babies have been born by Caesarean section experience a sense of failure at not achieving a normal delivery (p. 123). This can be greatly reduced by delivery under epidural rather than general anesthesia. This consists of a prick in the back, leading to the development of numbness in the lower half of the body while the mother remains fully conscious. She can therefore still see the baby being born and touch him as he is lifted out of her abdomen.

Records and Examinations

The baby's birth weight, length, and head circumference are measured and recorded. He is labeled at the wrist or ankle to ensure that there will be no chance of mistaken identity. In many hospitals there has been a return to the routine administration of silver nitrate eyedrops approximately 30 minutes after birth to prevent the possible transmission of gonorrhea to the baby's eyes. The baby is checked by the midwife or doctor as soon as he is born to make sure there is no obvious abnormality. He will have a complete examination by a doctor within twenty-four hours of delivery. I hope the doctor will want you to be present when he carries out this examination, so that you can watch and ask questions. I like to do it on the mother's bed. It is reassuring to know your baby has been thoroughly checked before you leave the hospital. If the examination is done without you, don't be afraid to ask about it. Sometimes a new mother does not realize her baby has had this early check and worries unnecessarily about something being wrong.

The examination includes a check to make sure the baby's hips are not dislocated. If detected at birth, this very serious condition can be cured (p. 426). On the sixth day all babies should have a blood test (PKU test) to exclude phenylketonuria—a rare but preventable cause of mental retardation (p. 586).

Common Anxieties

Most parents are exhilarated by their newborn baby, however different he may look, immediately after birth, from the glossy magazine pictures, but some are disappointed by their baby's appearance. This is usually because they have not seen a newborn baby before. Therefore they do not realize that temporarily he may not look very beautiful because his head has been a little molded during delivery and his face may be a little swollen.

These are the main reasons why you may be concerned:

The Proportions of His Body

A newborn baby's head is large in proportion to his total size. So is his abdomen, which may look distended and may move surprisingly as he breathes. This is normal. In contrast, his arms and legs probably look sticklike and fragile.

The Shape of His Head

A newborn baby's head is usually misshapen, lopsided, or swollen in one or more places. However alarming this looks, it does not mean his brain is damaged. Nature has made the baby's head soft enough to permit it to be squeezed into a shape that allows for easier delivery. The effect lasts only a few hours and is due to unequal pressures in the birth canal during labor. After two or three days you won't recognize him and you will have forgotten how alarmed you may have been by his first appearance.

Caput During birth, a baby's head is molded to let it pass more easily through the birth canal. The extra pressure on the part that goes down the canal first causes a swelling (caput); this disappears in a few hours.

Cephalhematoma This is a swelling that lasts longer than the one due to molding, and is caused by bruising during birth; the bruise is not the result of mismanagement of labor, but is caused by natural strains. The swelling is outside the skull and therefore does not press on the brain or harm it in any way. There may be one such swelling on each side of the head, but these never meet in the middle because each collection of blood remains confined to the area of one bone; it cannot cross the gap between the bones.

Sometimes a cephalhematoma turns to bone around its edge, so that it feels hard. It is still harmless and will always subside within a few months.

Marks Due to Instruments   Use of forceps or the vacuum extractor during delivery may leave marks or swellings on the head. These disappear within a few days. It is important that you should not look on forceps as instruments that damage the baby. They are used in order to ensure a safer delivery by protecting his head from dangerous pressures.

The Fontanel   Because the baby's head is still growing, the bones on the top of the skull are not joined at birth. The gap left for growth is diamond-shaped and is called the anterior fontanel (soft spot). Sometimes you will see this fontanel pulsating; this is perfectly normal. Don't worry that you will harm your baby if you touch or wash his head at this spot. The gap is covered by a tough membrane and no amount of washing will damage the brain underneath. Failure to wash over the soft spot, however, will encourage "cradle cap" to develop (p. 430).

The fontanel varies in size at birth in different babies and also in how long it takes to disappear. It should have closed by about 12 to 18 months.

Occasionally, you may just be able to feel a similar but much smaller gap at the back of your baby's head. This is the posterior fontanel, which has usually closed by the time he is born.

Miscellaneous Swellings

Even if his head looks normal, a newborn baby may look oddly swollen elsewhere.

Enlarged Genitals   The genitals of both boys and girls are proportionately larger at birth than at any other time before the beginning of puberty. This is because chemical substances (hormones) from the mother can cross the placenta and enter the baby's bloodstream. The effect wears off in a few days. Maternal hormones may also cause a whitish discharge from a baby girl's vagina for a few days. Less often the hormones cause vaginal bleeding, like a menstrual period; this lasts for a day or two and is also perfectly normal.

Enlarged Breasts   The same maternal hormones may, in either sex, cause swollen breasts. The enlargement of the breasts occurs when the baby is about three or four days old. Don't be alarmed if you notice this happening and never squeeze the breasts to try to reduce the swelling or to get rid of the milky substance that is sometimes formed. Nothing needs to be done, and everything returns to normal as the level of hormones in the baby's blood falls.

The Baby's Skin

The Vernix   At birth, the baby's body is covered with a greasy film called "vernix caseosa." It is usual nowadays to leave this on the skin rather than wash it off, since it is thought to give some protection against infection. Generally, only the baby's face and hands are washed after birth; if there is a large collection of vernix in the skin folds of the groin or armpits, it is removed. So don't be surprised if your baby is not bathed after birth, or at all while in the hospital. However, since some parents dislike the idea and sight of the vernix, some hospitals continue to give a routine bath after the delivery. In that case, care must be taken not to make the baby cold. Drying must be scrupulous, since evaporation of water from the skin surface causes the baby's temperature to fall.

Dry Skin   Whether or not he is bathed, your baby's skin at birth may look like the "before" stage in an advertisement for ointment. Dry, peeling skin and blotchiness are common (see urticaria neonatorum, p. 429). This does not mean the baby will be dry-skinned for life; it has nothing to do with eczema, and is usually caused by the baby being overdue. The dryness and the blotchy rash will be gone in a few days.

Red Marks   There will often be red marks on the baby's eyelids, on his forehead just above the nose, and also at the hairline at the back of the neck. These are sometimes called the "stork's marks" and are a kind of birthmark. Fortunately, these marks usually disappear in a few months. Before this happens you may notice that they change color whenever the baby cries and gets red in the face. The marks at the hairline sometimes stay, but they will be hidden when the baby's hair grows. Permanent birthmarks are much less common (pp. 419–21).

Veins   A newborn baby's skin is so fine and transparent that you may see the veins beneath, particularly between the eye and the bridge of the nose.

Lanugo   If the baby arrives early, his body may still be covered with the fine downy hair (lanugo) which is normally shed during the last two weeks in the womb. It comes off by itself soon after birth.

Spots   Many babies have small yellowish-white spots (milia) on the face, particularly on the nose. They are due to blocked openings to the oil glands in the skin, and they disappear of their own accord in about a week. Do not squeeze them.

Inside His Mouth At birth, there may be small grayish-yellow spots near the middle of the palate. These are called "Epstein's pearls," and they disappear within a few weeks.

Epstein's pearls are not caused by sucking, but little sucking blisters often appear on the lips soon after the baby starts feeding. They do not need any treatment except a cold cream if they look sore.

Tongue-Tie You may think your baby is tongue-tied because his tongue seems closely tethered to the bottom of his mouth. However, it is normal for the fold of skin that tethers the tongue to the floor of the mouth to vary in length from baby to baby. Since the growth of the tongue is mainly in the tip in the first year of life, your baby will soon be able to stick out his tongue like everyone else. Even when he can't, no harm is caused, and today most doctors believe that neither feeding nor speech is affected. So don't be worried if your baby seems to have tongue-tie—it will right itself and it doesn't affect eating or speaking.

The Eyes

Sometimes a red spot appears in the corner of one or both eyes. This is a small hemorrhage, which is often crescent-shaped, like a new moon. These are often not noticed until the baby is one or two days old, but when a mother sees her baby with his eyes open in the early minutes of life they are already visible. They result from tight pressure on the neck during delivery—sometimes from the cord being around the neck, but more often from a tight fit causing the shoulders and neck to be squeezed together. The mark will disappear in a few days and causes no harm to the eye.

The new baby may squint until he gets binocular vision, that is, the ability always to use both eyes together, when he is one to two months old. If the baby goes on squinting after the age of three months, he should be seen by an eye specialist, in case there is defective vision that could become permanent if not treated early (see pp. 468f.).

A discharge from the eyes is abnormal and needs treatment (see sticky eye, p. 473).

Other Worries

Some of the things your new baby does and the noises he makes in his first few days may puzzle you, at least until you notice that many other babies behave in the same way.

Hiccups   A new baby tends to hiccup frequently. This does not seem to worry him, nor does it mean his milk disagrees with him. You need do nothing special to stop them, though they sometimes stop when he is given a feeding.

Many babies have hiccups while still in the uterus. Most mothers have no difficulty in differentiating these from arm and leg movements, because they are regular and sharp. Mothers have told me that fetal hiccups sometimes occur at the same time of day and continue the same rhythm for a few days after birth.

Sneezing   Unless accompanied by other signs, sneezing does not mean your baby has a cold. He is simply clearing his nose. A baby has a very sensitive lining to his nose, and sneezing is his way of blowing his nose, thereby preventing dust in the atmosphere from getting to his throat and lungs.

Shallow Breathing   A baby's lungs are small compared with his total size, so his breathing is shallow, and to compensate he breathes at a faster rate than we do. You may be frightened by the faintness of his breathing, but this faintness is normal: he won't fade away. His breathing pattern becomes more regular and stronger as he grows.

Color   Babies often frighten their parents because they look so pale when asleep. This pallor, taken with the shallow breathing, may lead you to prod him to make sure he is alive. You need not feel stupid if you find yourself doing this—many mothers do it.

Snuffles   Some babies make a continual sniffing noise when breathing, so that you think they have colds. However, the vast majority of these babies have a low bridge to the nose, and the sniffing is merely the noise of the air going through small nasal passages. As the bridge gets larger, the sniffing stops; this usually happens by the end of the first year. No treatment is needed unless there is also difficulty in breathing that interferes with the baby's ability to feed. In this case, the doctor may prescribe nose drops to be used before feedings.

Hair   Many mothers are worried to find that their baby's hair falls out in the first few weeks. This is common, and it will always grow again, though sometimes the nature and color of the second hair is different. I am unaware of any consistency of pattern of hair loss— dark hair seems to come out more than fair but this may be because the change is more obvious. I would be interested to hear mothers' experiences as to whether some types of hair fall out more than others and how often the color changes.

Tremors and Trembling   You may notice occasional quivers while your baby sleeps; for example, his lower lip sometimes wobbles. This is normal in the early weeks. More dramatic is the automatic way he flings out his arms and legs in response to sudden noise or handling (see reflexes, pp. 219–23).

His First Few Days

Feeding your baby is dealt with in Chapters 5, 6, 13, and 14 (pp. 55, 82, 185 and 196). You may also be concerned about what is happening at the other end of his digestive system. This is a mistake, although it is understandable in view of the mystique that once surrounded, and still lingers around, a baby's bowel functions. Mothers were encouraged to peer at soiled diapers as if the color, consistency, and number of stools provided an infallible guide to the baby's well-being. This misguided preoccupation caused a lot of unnecessary worry. Still, because the idea lingers on, and because you cannot help noticing the contents of your baby's diapers when you change him, here is an explanation of some of the things you may see.

Urine

A newborn baby may not pass urine for up to forty-eight hours after delivery. The first time he does so, there may be so little that it evaporates before his diaper is changed. Your doctor or midwife will want to know that a baby boy, in particular, has passed a normal stream of urine in the early days, in order to confirm that there is no obstruction to its flow. A pink spot on the diaper can be produced by the normal uric acid crystals in the urine; it is of no importance (see p. 446).

Bowel Movements

A baby's bowels generally work within twenty-four hours of birth, whether or not he has eaten anything. The first stools consist of meconium, a blackish-green sticky substance with no smell, made up of digested mucus from glands in the bowel and digested cells, which are continuously being shed from the lining of the bowel. Gradually, over the next three to four days, the bowel contents change color, becoming brownish-yellow as they start containing the residue of milk feedings. The stools of a breast-fed baby differ from those of a baby fed on cow's milk, because of differences in the composition of the milks.

The Breast-fed Baby's Stools

The stools of a baby fed entirely on breast milk are always soft. Breast milk leaves an acid residue which hardly smells and which does not irritate the skin of the baby's buttocks.

Stool Color   The stools are usually yellow but may vary in color. There may be green patches in a yellow stool or a stool may be entirely green. Contrary to whatever grandmother may say, green does not stand for danger; it does not mean your baby is under- or overfed or that your milk disagrees with him. It is just a sign that his digestion is still settling down. The green color comes from the bile, a digestive juice that acts on the food during its journey through the bowels; the green color changes later to yellow, though some green may remain if part of the stool has passed rapidly through the digestive system. But unless your baby also loses his appetite, runs a temperature, or is otherwise off-color or failing to thrive, ignore the color of his stool. Pieces of slime or mucus in the stool are also insignificant in his early days.

Frequency   It is usual for a baby to pass several small stools each day for the first few weeks. His diaper may be dirty at every feeding or more frequently. This is a nuisance but it does not mean he has diarrhea.

After the first few weeks there is a change in bowel habit and he passes fewer stools; one per day or even one every few days is normal for some babies. Breast milk contains so little waste that there may literally be nothing to pass for several days; therefore, infrequent bowel movements in a breast-fed baby do not mean he is constipated, but are an indication of the high quality of breast milk. Genuine constipation, that is hard stools that are uncomfortable to pass, does not occur with babies fed only on breast milk (see pp. 57–58).

Diarrhea is also uncommon since the acid residue left by breast milk in the baby's bowels encourages the growth of a bacillus that fights against the organisms responsible for gastroenteritis. Some normal babies pass what seem to be very loose stools and yet are perfectly well, so you can disregard them. Watery stools are usually abnormal and should certainly be reported to your doctor, but the main thing is whether your child seems well or ill. If you think he is ill, and particularly if he has lost his appetite, as well as having loose stools, call your doctor at once (see diarrhea, pp. 478–80).

The Bottle-fed Baby's Stools

The stools of a baby fed on cow's milk are firmer, browner, smellier, and less frequent than those of a baby fed on breast milk; in fact, they are more like an adult's stools.

Frequency At first, the bottle-fed baby may pass two or three stools per day, later settling down to one a day. Since the baby has to digest a feeding that is not tailor-made for him, as breast milk is, there is bound to be more waste; thus, failure to pass a stool each day can be due to constipation. Missing a day now and then does not matter, but if the baby's stools become hard and infrequent, you can assume he is constipated (see pp. 484f.). Persistent constipation is sometimes caused by underfeeding, so consult your doctor about this.

However, most babies, if given bottles containing the correct strength, thrive on cow's milk and do not get constipated. You can try adding a little more sugar temporarily if the baby's stools seem too hard; when beginning mixed feeding (p. 190) offer fruit and vegetables rather than large quantities of cereal.

The artificially fed baby's stool is alkaline, not acid like the breast-fed baby's, and this can affect the skin around the anus and encourage a diaper rash to develop (pp. 431–33). This can be prevented by applying a barrier cream from the start at each diaper change for babies who are not breast fed. The baby's skin tends to get used to the alkaline stool after the first few weeks.

There may be curds in the stool. This is undigested protein from the cow's milk and is of no consequence.

Care of the Penis and Circumcision

Circumcision is the surgical removal of the foreskin, which covers the tip (glans) of the penis. Parents sometimes assume circumcision is necessary, particularly if all the males in their family are circumcised, and are surprised that the operation is not readily available. Circumcision is no longer common in the United Kingdom, as it was until a few years ago, because it is now widely considered that the operation is never a medical necessity for newborn babies and will never be required if the care of the penis is undertaken correctly (see below). Doctors are reluctant to operate without a good medical reason, since any operation carries a slight risk.

Circumcision started as a tribal and religious ritual; in Jewish families it is performed on the eighth day of life. Muslim boys are circumcised between the ages of three and fifteen years. The practice grew popular among non-Jewish families of the upper and middle classes in the U.S. and the United Kingdom during the last century, becoming fashionable in rather the same way as did the removal of tonsils and adenoids. Encouraged by prevailing medical opinion, parents who could afford these operations thought them desirable "to be on the safe side," for reasons that are now known to be false. Although there has been a decline in the frequency of circumcision in Britain, it is still fashionable in other countries, particularly the

United States and Australia, although there is a strong move against the operation in the United States.

The evidence for the supposed increased incidence of cancer of the cervix in the wives of uncircumcised men has been shown to be faulty, so this argument for circumcision is no longer tenable.

Tight Foreskin   More than thirty years ago, research showed that the foreskin and tip of the penis are united at birth, having developed from a single bud. Thus there is no reason to try to "cure" this natural condition by circumcision. Separation of the foreskin from the tip of the penis occurs gradually and is usually complete by the age of three or four; this is nature's way of "circumcising." Consequently, the term "phimosis," indicating a foreskin so tight that it cannot be pulled back, is a meaningless phrase when applied to the early days of life, and it is not a valid reason for early circumcision, as was once believed.

Forcing back the foreskin before it goes back easily by itself is likely to tear the skin, causing bleeding. This tear heals with scarring, which permanently joins the foreskin to the tip of the penis, so that correction by circumcision does become necessary. Paradoxically, therefore, ignorant management of the foreskin causes a problem where none existed.

Why were parents and doctors so anxious to remove what is, after all, a natural form of protection for the most delicate part of the penis? Apart from the belief that a tight foreskin, even in young babies, was abnormal, it was thought that irritation and infection would be caused by unremoved smegma, the white grainy secretion that collects between foreskin and glans. In turn, this risk of irritation was believed to encourage the baby boy to handle his penis and thus discover masturbation: adults needed an explanation for what is now accepted as a normal and harmless practice. Boys enjoy handling the penis whether they are circumcised or uncircumcised (see masturbation, pp. 337f.).

Function of the Foreskin   In fact, the foreskin protects the glans from the irritation of wet diapers and reduces the consequences of infection. A circumcised baby is more likely to develop a small sore at the opening of the penis, because he lacks this protection (see meatal ulcer, p. 447).

Care of the Foreskin   Clearly, therefore, the best thing to do about your newborn son's foreskin is nothing; leave it alone until it has separated and can be pushed back easily. You could try to do this, gently, when he is about four years old. During his bath is a good time to try. Don't persist if the foreskin does not go back easily; it's not an urgent matter.

Once the foreskin goes back easily, it should be gently pulled back during bathing so that any smegma that has collected is washed away. You should gradually accustom him to the idea of keeping this part of himself clean, leaving it to him once he is capable of bathing himself.

Parents sometimes suggest that circumcision should be undertaken in a baby in case it becomes necessary later. But this approach is no more rational than suggesting the early removal of all organs, such as the appendix or tonsils, which could possibly cause trouble later.

When Is Circumcision Medically Advisable?   Occasionally, repeated infections under the foreskin make circumcision advisable. This is something for a doctor to decide. Infection here is unusual unless the foreskin has been pushed forcibly back.

It is difficult to fix an upper limit for the age at which a tight foreskin becomes undesirable. When a child starts school, the foreskin may be checked at his school physicals, or you could mention it to your doctor when seeing him about something else. It's not urgent.

If circumcision is necessary, the best time for the operation must be considered from the child's point of view. A little boy is possessive and proud of his penis and finds it hard to accept that cutting off the foreskin will not injure him permanently. It is wise to wait until a child is over six and can understand better what is involved and why it is necessary. It may help to remind him of friends who have been circumcised and to point out that they are perfectly all right.

A child can now go into the hospital for this operation as a day patient, that is, without having to stay overnight, so that the additional strain of being away from his family is avoided. You will be told how to care for the wound.

Circumcision in Infancy   After a baby has been circumcised, a gauze dressing is put around the end of the penis. You will be told how to deal with this. There are often a few drops of blood from the wound, but these are nothing to worry about. However, any sign of infection or continued bleeding should be shown promptly to your doctor.

4

After the Birth—Looking After Yourself

Difficulties in the Hospital

You are liable to be worried by minor annoyances (which may seem major at the time) such as noise, indifferent food or hospital routines that interrupt your sleep. Lack of sleep can be particularly trying. If you have lost a night's sleep during the birth, it can be more difficult to catch up in the hospital than it would be at home. Even if you are told to sleep during the first day it is more difficult to sleep in a hospital, surrounded by activity. Sleeping pills help, but you may be awakened very early in the morning for your baby's first feeding of the day. Anyway, try to ignore the noise and activity; sleep while you can during the first days of your baby's life. He spends a great deal of his time asleep for these few days and will probably sleep through the first two or three nights without wanting a feeding. This gives you a chance to catch up on your own sleep so that you are feeling more active by the time he becomes more wakeful. Fitting in with each other is easier at home than in the busy atmosphere of a hospital, which must be geared to the needs of several mothers and babies.

Other worries may later seem magnified and absurd. A nurse may handle a baby in what seems to be a brusque and unsympathetic way; her hurried efficiency may look very much like roughness. How the staff handle your baby is naturally very important to you, and most nurses and doctors realize this and try to make their concern obvious. If someone does seem unduly brusque, it is probably due to overwork and because a nurse knows a new baby is not quite as fragile as he looks; it is your feelings that are hurt, not the baby. If you are really upset, it is worth saying so, as unaggressively as possible.

Upsets are most likely to arise over feeding. Sometimes a nurse tries to help with breast feeding in an inappropriate and insensitive way. She misunderstands a mother's needs and intervenes when all that is really wanted is reassurance that you are doing all right. Babies vary in their readiness to begin feeding, but hospital staff may be so anxious to get routines settled before a baby goes home that they try to hurry the process. For example, a baby may be offered a complementary feeding which his mother instinctively feels is unnecessary (see breast feeding, p. 75). If something like this happens, it is best to explain that you are happier than you look and that you feel you can manage. It can be difficult for nurses to distinguish between those mothers who really want and need advice and help, and those who have strong and reasonable ideas of their own; the staff will usually respect these ideas once they know you hold them, and provided your baby is all right too.

Learning about Your Baby

If your baby has been born in a hospital, I hope you are permitted to keep his crib beside your bed, where you can see him all the time (see rooming-in, p. 17). Having your baby with you is not as exhausting as it sounds. A newborn baby spends much of his time asleep, especially for the first day or two after birth, when your need for rest is greatest. However, countless mothers have told me that they hardly slept the first night because they were so excited by their baby's arrival. Nurses are on hand to demonstrate how to change diapers and are ready to take over completely if necessary. Obviously, if having your baby beside you during the day worries you, you could ask for him to spend part of the day in the nursery, but I think it unlikely you will want this. The essential approach is to take each day as it comes, rather than to plan too far ahead. Each one is different, especially the early days.

Feeding times are generally flexible where rooming-in is the rule, though hospitals vary: some encourage mothers to feed their babies whenever they seem hungry, while others discourage feeding except at fixed times. However, even under the more rigid arrangement, you should discuss your baby's needs with the staff if you are concerned; they can help you decide whether his crying is due to hunger. Under a flexible system, you are likely to be feeding the baby when he wants to be fed, rather than only when he is brought to you for feeding; he will therefore be more responsive and easier to establish at the breast or bottle than a baby who is unsettled by crying from hunger. The more confidence you build up during the early feedings in the hospital, the better the outlook for continuing success at home—although you may find you can relax and feed more successfully once you are back at home.

Rooming-in also helps you to get used to all the normal but possibly alarming characteristics of newborn babies. For example, as your baby lies in his crib, you may see him quiver or you may notice small spots (milia) (see newborn baby, pp. 40f.). You are able to ask at once if something worries or puzzles you—don't think any question is too silly. You will be shown how to wrap up the baby (swaddling) and how to put him down to sleep, how to change a diaper and how to bathe and dress him. You will worry less about your baby if you can watch him; in fact, since he is your reason for being in the hospital at all, it would seem strange to be separated from him. It is natural to want to be close to the baby with whom you have spent the past nine months; rooming-in provides the most natural situation possible within a hospital routine. Moreover, it has been shown that earlier independence results from greater contact in the first year.

Nighttime

In most hospitals in the United Kingdom babies can sleep in their cribs beside their mothers. In many, such as my own, babies sleep in their mother's bed if she so wishes and has not had a sedative. I hope this will gradually become the practice in the United States.

If your baby is in the nursery, there are bound to be occasions when you imagine that all the distant cries you hear are coming from him. It will be a few days before you can recognize your own baby's cry for certain, but you will be amazed by the speed with which you develop this ability. Meanwhile, there should be no problem about your going to the nursery to check for yourself whether it is your baby who is crying.

Your Feelings in the Early Days

The first few days can set the tone for months to come: a mother who has had an upsetting time in the hospital and who has not begun to understand her baby may take longer to feel closely involved with him than she would otherwise have done. But in any case don't be surprised if you don't have the burst of maternal feelings toward your baby that everyone has led you to expect. It takes time to fall in love with your baby, and many mothers feel unnecessarily guilty because they don't love their babies totally at first. Later on they seem to forget this point and fail to pass it on to new mothers. Presumably, this later total love for the child suppresses the earlier feelings. The main thing is for all expectant mothers to know that it is normal not to feel fully maternal toward the new baby the moment he arrives, even though some mothers do (see feeling depressed, pp. 152f.).

Maternity Hospital Life

You may have chosen to have a single or a shared room, but you will learn a great deal from other mothers in the hospital. Talking about and looking at each other's babies is instructive as well as fun; in fact, you will probably feel a pang of regret when you leave them all and miss the companionship when you get home. Permanent friendships often start in a maternity hospital.

Besides the fun and the reassurance of learning that other mothers also lack confidence and know nothing about babies, there can be emotional hazards in maternity hospital life. It is as well to be prepared. Having a baby is an emotional as well as a physical experience; you may easily find yourself involved in other people's problems. Someone may be worried about her baby. You can help, perhaps by encouraging her to discuss her worries with the staff, but you may also become miserable yourself—far more upset than you would be normally, because your emotions are influenced by physical and psychological changes following the birth of your baby. A few days after having a baby, many mothers feel tearful and depressed for a day or two (see feeling depressed, pp. 152f.).

An unmarried mother, worried about her baby's future, can affect the rest of the mothers. General misery will be caused if one mother has a handicapped or a stillborn baby. However, meeting these problems, which may reflect some of your own unspoken anxieties, can help you to get your own difficulties into perspective.

Staff members have to work out very carefully the special needs of mothers whose babies have problems, and the relationships between them and the mothers of normal babies. This is a particularly acute problem if a mother has a stillbirth or a child with a severe handicap (spina bifida, for instance) who possibly has to be transferred to another hospital for surgical treatment. The mother whose baby has to be transferred to another hospital for treatment ought to go with him and be cared for in the same hospital. The mother of a stillborn baby needs very sensitive handling (see pp. 655–56).

Visitors

Husbands and Children

I am very conscious that the rules against children visiting hospitals are unfortunately much more stringent in the United States than in the United Kingdom. I can only hope the vital reasons given for allowing children to visit parents and siblings will influence the authorities.

Ideally, your husband and family should be able to visit you at any time during the day except the afternoon period, when one hopes all mothers are given a rest. This should last about an hour and will be easier if the room is darkened.

The handling of your other child's first visit is very important, and the staff should be specially trained to cope with it. Remember to tell your husband to let the staff know when it is the first visit. This gives the nurse a chance to go in first to tell you, thereby ensuring that your baby is in the crib beside your bed and not at the breast when your child comes into the room. You then have both hands free to greet him. In this way, a child is less likely to feel usurped by finding a new baby at his mother's breast.

Probably your child won't notice the new baby immediately. It's often a good idea to let him find the baby for himself, because he may choose to ignore the baby to begin with; it is much better not to fall into the trap of making him take notice before he is ready. If you are prepared beforehand, you can have attractively wrapped presents ready in the crib as gifts from the new baby to the other child. It also helps if your husband has provided the older child with presents to give to the new baby (see minimizing jealousy, pp. 148f.).

Other Visitors

It is reasonable for hospitals to make some restrictions on visiting friends; otherwise the unit can become so swamped by people that mothers become very tired, the staff cannot do their work properly, and the babies are subjected to a needless risk of infection.

There is a great art in visiting a patient in the hospital. Your visitors should never exhaust you; your pleasure at showing off your new baby to friends should never be marred by the exhaustion of having to cope with them. Have a word with an understanding nurse so that she can keep an eye from a distance on how you are feeling. It is not a bad idea to have a secret signal between you so that she knows when you want her to get rid of visitors who stay longer than you want them to.

The problem of tiring visitors arises at home as well as in the hospital. Unfortunately, in your own home you won't have a nurse to help you get rid of those who stay too long.

A Short Trip Outside with Your Husband

Hospitals should encourage your husband to take you out for a walk or a meal unless you are going home within forty-eight hours. Being alone together gives you a better chance of re-establishing your relationship. It also helps to leave your baby in expert hands so that when you get home you will more easily accept that a baby-sitter can take over for a short time; this will help you to avoid becoming housebound. It is our experience that parents are helped greatly by this opportunity to be alone together.

Restoring Your Figure

Postnatal exercises, to help your figure return to normal, should start a day or two after your baby is born. Practicing is easy under the supervision of the physical therapist in the hospital or the midwife at home, but it is tempting to forget to practice once you are on your own; the baby's welfare seems so much more important than yours and there is so much to do. However, try to go on with the exercises. They do help your figure and your sense of well-being.

Your baby needs a healthy mother, so it is also important to eat well, to get out of the house as much as possible, and generally to look after yourself (see baby-sitters, pp. 156f., feeling depressed, pp. 152–56).

Leaving the Hospital

If you go home from the hospital within forty-eight hours, there is no major break in your routine. But on leaving the hospital after a longer stay you may feel the break acutely; you have only been in the hospital a few days but you have settled down to the routine and have come to depend on the companionship of the other mothers and on the presence of the staff. The situation seems unreal when total responsibility for your baby and for housekeeping is suddenly thrust upon you.

Many mothers who find it difficult to deal with this abrupt transition notice that their breast milk is reduced temporarily, and they feel depressed. Some babies seem to notice the difference between hospital and home and they also behave differently: it is probable that in addition to feeling hungry because the milk supply is less, they also sense their mother's lack of confidence.

I hope your husband will have taken a vacation to coincide with your return. I am in favor of fathers receiving paternity leave as a routine. Coming home with a new baby can be very lonely, especially if you live in an apartment and don't know your neighbors.

The Postnatal Examination

You and your baby will be asked to return to the clinic or doctor's office for a postnatal examination six weeks after the birth. Your family doctor carries out the examination after a home delivery, and sometimes when the baby was born in the hospital.

The reason for this checkup is to make sure all is well with your health, and to put right any small things that are easy to correct at this stage but that might cause trouble if ignored. The doctor will also look at your baby and check his progress.

The postnatal examination gives you the chance to mention any worries about yourself or the baby. Write down your questions beforehand if you are frightened you might forget some. You will also get advice on contraception if you need it. Don't rely on breast feeding to prevent conception (see breast feeding, p. 81).

5

Breast Feeding

Deciding Whether to Breast Feed

Can You Breast Feed Your Baby?

Although the trend toward bottle feeding continues in many parts of the world, this is not because present-day mothers are less capable of breast feeding than previous generations, or because today's babies are any less willing to breast feed. A woman who decides during pregnancy that she will breast feed her baby seldom needs to give up the idea because her breasts cannot produce milk, or because her baby cannot feed from them. Even a preterm baby who is too weak to breast feed at first can usually manage later if his mother has expressed her milk in the meantime (see low birth weight baby, p. 138). A normal baby always thrives on breast milk. He likes the taste and it agrees with him.

Very occasionally, a woman is advised in pregnancy not to try breast feeding for medical reasons such as severe heart or kidney disease. The size of the breasts is irrelevant, so far as producing milk is concerned. Inverted nipples may make it difficult for the baby to suck, and these should be treated during pregnancy (p. 59).

What then is responsible for the comparative unpopularity of breast feeding? Does it matter anyway, since babies thrive on cow's milk and can be equally well loved whichever way you feed them? Why bother to try to understand the complexities of breast feeding when bottle feeding is a perfectly good alternative and when breast feeding seems to be so exhausting, restricting, and difficult? If breast feeding is the natural way to feed babies, why doesn't it come naturally, instead of needing so much discussion and explanation?

To begin with, breasts are more complicated than bottles, and they are attached to human beings whose emotions may interfere with the workings of the machinery. Many of the hazards associated with breast feeding can be reduced or eliminated altogether provided you know what is happening and have been told what to expect in advance. These difficulties are not an inevitable part of breast feeding but are a cultural overlay. Just as "natural" childbirth now involves learning deliberate techniques and unlearning acquired anxieties, so breast feeding in an industrialized society may require more than putting the baby to the breast and letting it all happen.

Until recently the swing to bottle feeding made it seem to be the natural way to feed a baby. But the enormous swing back to breast feeding has led mothers who had decided to bottle feed to tell me they changed their minds in the postpartum unit because they felt left out of things. For this reason I hope doctors will not give a mother drugs to suppress her breast milk (p. 82).

Why Bother to Breast Feed?

The effort is worthwhile because breast feeding is not just a way of nourishing a baby; it is the final stage in the reproductive cycle that began with conception and resulted in birth. The real end of that cycle is when the baby is weaned, not when he is born. It has been shown that mothers who breast feed return more easily to their former weight and figure, because a period of lactation completes the using up of food stores laid down for the baby in pregnancy. Your body expects to produce milk and has to be tricked into stopping, by not being used, when no baby feeds to stimulate the milk supply (p. 82). Breast feeding helps the uterus to return to its normal form (p. 61) and gives both mother and baby emotional and physical pleasure. It is not meant to be a one-way sacrifice by an exhausted mother to a demanding infant. If it were, it would have died out altogether long ago.

In a modern, urban society it is not surprising that many women find it hard to acknowledge how drastically life is changed by motherhood. Bottle feeding seems to offer more freedom and a better chance of remaining oneself, whereas breast feeding is an immediate commitment and an acknowledgment of new responsibility that may seem to doom you to months of dedication to milk production.

In fact, your life changes whether or not you breast feed. Breast feeding, when it goes well, can help you to feel close to your baby and therefore makes it easier to enjoy being a mother and to enjoy the changes. "When it goes well" is the operative phrase, because there is no doubt that many mothers feel as depressed by "failing" as they feel elated by "succeeding." The advice that follows is to help you to decide whether you want to try, and to help you if you do. It may sound as if the argument goes, "Breast feeding is best, but if you bottle feed, that's just as good," because, in a sense, that is the situation. The baby does well either way. It is to help you do well, either way, that explanations are necessary.

Making up Your Mind

Some mothers will decide during pregnancy whether they wish to breast feed. My plea to doctors, midwives, and nurses is that they should not try to extract a decision, which is then recorded in the prenatal notes. A pregnant woman is bound to feel threatened if suddenly asked whether she intends to breast feed and may decide against it on the spur of the moment. I hope that members of the staff will talk all about breast feeding on the assumption that mothers would like to feed their babies themselves, but of course answer questions on bottle feeding as they arise.

To make up your mind about breast feeding you may want to know more about the pros and cons of bottle feeding. Certainly, bottle feeding is satisfactory in countries with a high standard of hygiene. However, bottle-fed babies run a higher risk of gastroenteritis (p. 83), which is rare in breast-fed babies, so that bottle feeding can be positively dangerous in countries with a poor standard of hygiene, particularly where there is no piped water supply. Any young mother who expects to travel abroad while her baby is young would be wise to breast feed him, thereby avoiding the difficulties involved in preparing bottles in unfamiliar surroundings (see bottle feeding, p. 82). Even in a modern home, preparing and sterilizing all the equipment needed for bottle feeding does take time that could be used for rest or for playing with your baby, if you are breast feeding him.

Differences Between Cow's Milk and Breast Milk

Most babies do well on cow's milk, though a few develop an allergy and have to be fed on a substitute made from the soya bean. Breast feeding reduces the liability to eczema (p. 507). Cow's milk is intended for calves and differs from human milk in several ways. It has a higher percentage of protein and this protein has a higher content of casein. Since casein is the least digestible part of cow's milk for human babies, it forms curds, which are visible as little lumps in the stool. Cow's milk puts a greater load on the kidneys of a newborn baby. This is not a problem for a baby in perfect health, but for an unwell baby it could be. The particular hazard in cow's milk is its higher sodium and phosphate content, which can overload the newborn baby's kidneys. For this reason all milk preparations for feeding young babies must be modified (p. 85).

The fat content in the two kinds of milk is about the same, though the fat droplet in human milk, being smaller, is more digestible. Breast milk contains more sugar than cow's milk. The amount of minerals and vitamins is also different.

Weight for weight more calories are obtained from breast milk because the human baby is unable to digest cow's milk completely. This is evident from the baby's stools (see pp. 44–45). Babies fed on breast milk produce comparatively odorless stools and may digest their food so completely that stools are very infrequent. This is not the same as constipation, since, however infrequent, the stool is always soft, whereas a constipated stool is hard. So mothers who breast feed their babies have no need to worry about constipation or about indigestion. In addition, breast-fed babies' stools are less likely to contain the bacteria that cause ammonia dermatitis, the commonest cause of diaper rash (see pp. 431–32).

Breast-fed babies do not get too fat, so you won't have a problem with obesity (p. 207). All this seems adequate compensation for not knowing exactly how much your baby takes at each feeding, which in any case carries its own anxieties (see bottle feeding, p. 84).

However, the main reason for breast feeding, even in a developed country where bottle feeding is safe and satisfactory, is that it is still the best way for you and your baby to develop a close and loving relationship. A bottle can be given lovingly if you cuddle your baby and enjoy relaxing with him, but the hard impersonal bottle does not feel and smell like your breast. Milk from a bottle always flows at the same rate, whereas breast milk flows fast at first, taking the edge off the baby's hunger, then slows down, as his hunger decreases, allowing him to satisfy his sucking urge without overeating (see pp. 68, 547).

Pressures on the Nursing Mother

Nearly all the problems that arise during breast feeding are caused by outside pressures on you and your baby to conform to the routine of the well-run hospital or the well-organized home and by misunderstandings about how breast feeding works. Discomforts and difficulties that are normal at the beginning are more worrying and disillusioning if unexpected.

It may be argued that an African mother in some cases doesn't know about the mechanics of lactation and yet feeds her baby successfully for months or even years. But she doesn't begin with the disadvantages of living in a society where failure to breast feed is common and success surprising. It does not occur to her that she may not have enough milk to satisfy her baby—the Western mother's main concern. Her relationship with her baby is direct; no one will tell her how and when to feed him. Her breasts are readily accessible to the baby whenever he is hungry. She need not plan when and where to feed him —any time and anywhere is normal. The baby decides, and his needs dictate the amount of milk she produces for him.

By contrast, a mother in a "developed" country has to start making decisions about feeding almost from the moment her baby is born. Having decided to feed him herself, she is unlikely to have enough confidence to leave it entirely to the baby to fix his feeding times. She probably feels he will starve if not fed a certain number of times a day, or will become "spoiled" and "demanding" if she assumes that every cry means hunger. At a time when she should be relaxing and getting to know her baby, she is already worried about routines, schedules, and whether he will ever fit into a civilized house-hold.

If your baby sleeps in a crib by your bed, it is easy enough to pick him up and feed him when he is hungry. But in a hospital he may be brought to you only at fixed intervals, and he may sometimes be worn out from crying or half asleep. If you are at home, you may be told to feed him "on demand" but, at the same time, it is often implied that there should be no more than about six feedings in twenty-four hours. If you do feed him whenever you think he is hungry, you may feel guilty and believe he will never learn to wait longer between feedings. Unlike the African mother, carrying her baby with her as she works and letting him feed when he wants to, you know you will have to make decisions at every feeding: decisions to stop whatever you are doing and half undress, and to take him out of his crib, perhaps changing his diaper, before the feeding can even start. An essentially spontaneous relationship between you and your baby somehow has to be adapted to the demanding daily routine of the modern home.

Understanding Breast Feeding

The Breasts

You will be less afraid of having too little milk if you know something about the way the breasts work. For example, it is unlikely that your breasts will be physically unable to make enough milk for your baby's needs. Size alone has no significance. A small breast may contain as many milk-producing glands as a large one, the difference in size being due to fat; in fact, large, pendulous breasts may contain fewer milk glands than smaller breasts.

The shape of the nipples is more important than the size of the breasts. It is difficult for a baby to grip a flat or inverted nipple with his lips; if possible, this should be corrected in pregnancy by pulling out the nipple between the finger and thumb every night and morning. Breast shields worn inside the bra during pregnancy may also help to draw out the nipple. However, the vast majority of women have nor-mal nipples.

Changes in the Breasts during Pregnancy

Hormone action during pregnancy causes changes in the breasts. Tingling and enlarging breasts are sometimes the first signs of preg-nancy. The nipples and the areola (the surrounding pigmented area) darken, and a sticky discharge called "colostrum" may form crusts on the nipple for some weeks before the baby's birth. Wash these off gently.

Colostrum

During the first two or three days after the baby's birth, the breasts continue to make small quantities of colostrum. The baby, therefore, receives some reward for sucking before the milk comes in, whereas he might be discouraged by sucking at an empty breast.

The exact purpose of colostrum is uncertain but it has a high protein content and is therefore nourishing, and it contains antibodies that help to increase the baby's immunity to certain diseases his mother has had (see immunization, pp. 259f.).

The breasts start producing milk as a result of hormonal changes occurring at birth. The baby's arrival is thus the signal for your blood, which for nine months has nourished him through the placenta, to start nourishing him through the breasts instead by forming milk.

The milk takes a few days to "come in." Two or three days after the baby's birth, milk is secreted with colostrum. This mixture is rich and yellow, whereas breast milk alone is thin and bluish, which may be the reason why some mothers believe their milk is no longer good for the baby. But it has not "gone off"; breast milk always looks watery.

The Let-down Reflex

Hormonal activity not only starts milk production, it also influences the "let-down" reflex that controls the flow of milk from the breasts.

When the baby starts sucking, a message is passed from the breast to the pituitary gland in the brain. This causes the pituitary gland to release a chemical called "oxytocin," which is carried by the bloodstream into the breasts. Oxytocin causes muscle fibers surrounding the milk glands to contract so that milk is forced into the ducts behind the nipple. Milk begins to flow from both breasts—the one that is not being sucked as well as the one that is.

If you have breast fed before you may be aware of the sensation of milk rushing in from the first days of breast feeding. On the other hand, you may not feel it until some time later, and some mothers never seem to notice it.

The let-down reflex is not caused by the baby's act of sucking alone—his mere presence can be enough to set it off. It is an emotional as well as a physical reflex. This is one reason why it is important for a mother and her baby to be together from the first (see also p. 68).

When your breasts have become accustomed to the rhythm of feeding, you may feel the milk rushing in when a feeding is due. This illustrates how as a breast-feeding mother you need your baby, as he needs you; you may have to express some milk if you cannot feed him.

Afterpains

The hormone oxytocin, produced by the pituitary gland through the stimulation of the let-down reflex, also causes contractions of the uterus, or "afterpains." These contractions, which ensure that the uterus returns to its normal size, are more vigorous during breast feeding, which therefore has an added advantage over bottle feeding. They last only a few days.

Understanding the mechanism of afterpains is important, since otherwise you might be disconcerted by feeling colicky pains in the lower part of your abdomen for the first few days, whenever you feed your baby.

Avoiding Tension

The let-down reflex is automatic when you and your baby are relaxed and happy, but it can be stopped by anxiety or embarrassment, or by fear of afterpains or of sore nipples. No one can stop being tense to order, but it usually helps to rest or relax for a few minutes before a feeding. Techniques of relaxation learned during prenatal classes are useful methods of easing tension at any time. If interruptions while feeding put you off, admit it and ask to be left alone at feeding times.

It is easier to relax if you realize that the problems of early breast feeding are common and will soon stop. It is good to know that a healthy baby will stimulate the breasts to produce sufficient milk for his needs, however busy and tired you may be. Paradoxically, the knowledge that cow's milk nearly always suits a baby can also help you to breast feed successfully, because you know there is a satisfactory alternative, if needed.

Nursing Bras

It is important to support your breasts during pregnancy and lactation by wearing a really efficient and well-fitting bra. Breasts increase in size whether or not you subsequently breast feed. It is being pregnant rather than feeding a baby that can spoil your figure if your heavier breasts are not well supported. Some husbands do not want their wives to breast feed for fear that they will lose their figures. These should be told that breasts change more as a result of pregnancy than lactation and that breast feeding sometimes improves the shape of the breasts.

When milk first comes into the breasts, they usually feel tense and swollen. Adjust or change a bra as soon as it feels uncomfortable, and wear it at night also. If the nursing bras you bought during pregnancy do not suit you or do not fit properly once you are actually feeding, get another kind. Cotton bras are preferable to synthetic ones, since these may become lax with the frequent washing needed at this stage.

If circumstances permit, it is ideal for you and the baby to be topless when you feed. Skin contact between you and your baby feels nice and encourages the flow of milk. Bras can get in the way. However, a nursing bra that allows one breast only to be exposed by unbuttoning a flap will be useful when you are feeding outside the privacy of your own home.

During feeding, especially in the early days, there will be a flow of milk from the other side as a result of the let-down reflex (p. 60). A soft towel held against the breast not in use will prevent your clothes from getting soaked with milk. This flow may also occur from both breasts about the time a feeding is due, causing your clothes to become damp. You may be tempted to wear waterproof pads inside the bra to soak up leaking milk, but never use these for long, since they make the nipples soggy and more liable to crack when the baby sucks. Better to buy several bras, so that you can change them frequently and avoid the depressing smell of stale milk. This early messy stage is only temporary and is due to the fluctuations in milk supply while baby and breasts adjust to each other.

You might also find useful a simple maneuver commonly used by mothers in developing countries. Since they breast feed in public, they often find themselves in a situation in which they wish to stop feeding before the baby is ready to stop—for example, because they have reached the end of their bus journey. After taking the baby off the breast, they give the nipple a sharp inward push with one finger, which seems to stop the flow of milk completely.

Swollen Breasts and Engorgement

As a nursing mother you may be elated at the sudden enlargement that shows that your breasts are starting to make milk, but the elation quickly wears off unless you also realize that they will soon get smaller. There will also be a reduction in the tenderness that accompanies this sudden enlargement. Breasts are far bigger and feel tighter when you start feeding than weeks later when they are producing three times as much milk for a hungrier and larger baby. The enlargement is due to hormonal activity.

Although some degree of swelling and tenderness is normal, it should not be allowed to become severe. Serious engorgement causes serious discomfort and makes it difficult for your baby to feed. You can relieve mild engorgement yourself by feeding your baby, but tell your doctor if it becomes severe.

If the areola—the darker area surrounding the nipple—has become swollen, so that the nipple is difficult for the baby to grasp, you should express a little milk before putting him to the breast. To do this, first massage the breast lightly, moving your hands from the outer rim of the breast towards the nipple. This maneuver is not intended to squeeze out the milk but to stimulate the let-down reflex, which automatically makes the milk move to the ducts at the base of the nipple (see let-down reflex, p. 60). The second step is to compress the base of the nipple at the edge of the areola regularly between finger and thumb, thereby closing the ducts and forcing out the milk. Once the milk begins to flow, the breast becomes less taut, making it easier for the baby to hold the nipple in his mouth.

Applying either heat or cold to swollen breasts sometimes relieves discomfort, so hot towels or ice cubes wrapped in a cloth may help. If these methods fail, a breast pump is sometimes used.

Feeding Your Baby

Engorgement is uncomfortable but it is a sign of breast activity, and is less discouraging if you know it is only temporary. One reason for putting your baby to the breast regularly, even before the milk comes in, is to accustom him to sucking while the breasts are still soft and supple. Practice will enable him to deal more easily with the breast when it is swollen with milk and the nipple harder to grasp.

How Your Baby Sucks

It is a help to know how your baby draws milk from the breasts. He does not suck only the nipple, but takes into his mouth as much as possible of the areola—the darker area surrounding it—since the nipple has to touch the palate. Most babies manage this on their own, but some need a little gentle guidance to prevent them chewing at the nipple alone. This is achieved by offering the breast, not just the nipple, which is like giving the baby the nipple on a bottle. You will notice that his ears start to move when he is sucking properly as opposed to playing with the nipple.

If you hold the breast behind the areola so that the nipple stands out, your baby can grasp it more easily. He should not be pushed onto the nipple, but should be allowed time to root around and find it for himself. To do this he has a built-in reflex: as soon as the nipple touches his cheek he turns his head and automatically opens his mouth. He then presses the areola between his gums, squeezing the milk from the ducts inside it.

The arm on the same side as the breast in use should be placed right around the baby to support his bottom as well as his head. To help him fix on the nipple, a little pressure on his back from the other arm to press his chest toward your body will help. On no account should the back of the head be pressed against the breast since this causes the head to flex so that he loses the nipple and reacts by pulling himself away from the breast. Once he is sucking, the free hand can be left to play with his toes. There is no need to press the breast in, in order to leave the nostrils free, since these point downward, not forward, thereby allowing normal nasal breathing even when the nose is being pressed into the breast.

Although the baby's suck and swallow reflexes are well co-ordinated, the rush of milk, initiated by the let-down reflex, may be overwhelming at first. If he cannot swallow quickly enough, remove him from the breast till the flow is gentler; otherwise he may be discouraged if choked by mouthfuls of milk.

The First Feedings

Your baby can be put to the breast immediately after birth, unless he is very premature or has had a difficult birth, so that he or you need to rest. It used to be common practice to limit his time at the breast, in the early days, for fear of causing sore nipples. However, I am increasingly aware that mothers who enjoy breast feeding seldom complain of much soreness. I therefore advise mothers to decide for themselves how long to leave their baby sucking. Obviously a mother should stop the feeding if it is hurting her.

There is no need for you to wash your breasts before feeding. It is now realized that a baby recognizes his mother's special smell within a few days of birth. This attracts him to feed, so you don't want to wash it away! Equally, there is no need for the routine application of cream to the nipple, but only to those that feel sore (pp. 71–72).

These first experiments at the breast are important for both of you. Most babies have a strong impulse to suck at birth, and if this is ignored for too long, they may become less enthusiastic and then may have to be "taught" how to feed. Although the ability to suck is inborn, early practice helps to make the baby competent and so con-vinces him it is a pleasurable activity, which he wants to try again. Your baby is easier to feed, you are more relaxed, and the chances of successful breast feeding increase. Because you know there is only colostrum in the breasts at first, you will not worry about how much he is taking.

Evolving a Timetable

When your baby is newborn, don't worry about his future timetable. If you are allowed to get to know each other, with the minimum of interference, a timetable will evolve naturally. I cannot overemphasize the need to let your baby decide on the frequency with which you breast feed him, particularly in the early days. Don't leave him to cry because you feel it is too early for his feeding and don't be frightened lest you are "spoiling" him by frequent feedings—that is impossible. Babies who are being breast fed need more frequent feedings than those who are fed on cow's milk, because breast milk contains less protein than cow's milk. Research, involving different mammal species, has shown a correlation between the protein content of their milk and the interval between feedings. The protein level of human milk places human babies in the group of mammals requiring more frequent feeding, whereas calves, being provided with a higher-protein milk, can go for longer intervals. Since breast milk produces finer curds than cow's milk (p. 57), the stomach empties faster; another reason for a baby wanting to be breast fed more often. By understanding the physiology behind the behavior of your baby you should have no difficulty in agreeing to provide for his needs.

This approach to feeding is commonly called "demand feeding." But I dislike the term, since many mothers are frightened that they won't be able to cope with their baby's demands. If you or I want food, we either go to the kitchen to get it or we ask for it. I therefore prefer the term "ask feeding."

Try not to worry about how much your baby is getting at these early feedings. It is not up to you but up to him to fix the amount of milk produced. There will be enough milk if you relax and allow the physical process of supply and demand to establish itself.

The main point of the first feedings is to help you to get to know each other, not to nourish your baby. By the time the milk does come in, you will have found out, perhaps with guidance from the doctor, midwife, or nurse how best to hold the baby and make him comfortable as well. You may prefer feeding him in bed, supporting his head and making sure the breast is not impeding his breathing; or you may prefer sitting in a low chair, perhaps with a footstool. When the milk comes in, you will already have discovered a lot about how to feed your baby, and feeling confident will help you to succeed.

Allowing your baby to eat when he is hungry does not mean there can be no routine in your life—but it is a routine suggested by him, rather than one planned by you in advance. He will soon fall into a rhythm and increase the interval between feedings, provided you let him set the pace. In the early days he may feed as often as every twenty minutes. The worst thing is if your nurse or midwife believes in "ten minutes each side." This only makes you and your baby tense, in case you don't get the feeding finished on time. The effect is to make your baby into what I call a "clock gobbler"! He is trained to feed fast by your clock-watching, this being one cause of sore nipples (p. 72).

Leave him undisturbed in your arms on or alongside the breast for as long as it suits you. On no account interfere with his comfort by stopping to burp him (see pp. 68–70). As long as the baby continues to suck, milk will be produced by that breast. Consequently, he can remain on the same breast for the whole of one feeding unless you wish to change sides for comfort. Use the other breast at the next feeding to prevent yourself from becoming lopsided. The concept that a baby can empty a breast is unphysiological and does not fit the facts, since milk can still be expressed.

You will be surprised how soon you gain the confidence to know that you are dealing with your baby perfectly. The problems usually arise from conflicting advice being given to you by nurses and doctors as well as friends, but don't let them interfere with your natural instincts for doing what is right for your baby. It is not surprising that it takes time for most women to feel they know best what their babies want. Fear of doing the "wrong thing," due partly to inexperience and partly to conflicting advice from all sides, can stifle a timid maternal instinct.

The Slow Starter

A baby who seems sleepy and unwilling to feed at first should not be jogged about in an effort to make him do so, nor should the nipple be pushed into his mouth. You can encourage him to feed by stroking the cheek nearest the breast, so that he turns his head toward the nipple. He can then be gently guided toward it. He should not be hurried (see sleepy feeder, p. 74).

Babies "root" toward the nipple; they smell the milk and find their own way to it. These minutes at the breast provide their first opportunity for play and learning, as well as nourishment, and should not be regarded as just a time to fill them with milk. A baby who goes on being too sleepy to feed will need to be examined by the doctor, though usually there is no need to worry, since he will be more awake when his appetite increases.

A baby usually feeds more slowly from the breast than from the bottle. Since breast feeding is the natural method, this slower feeding, with rests in between periods of sucking, is the pattern of feeding preferred by a baby. I suspect that part of the reason for faster feeding by bottle is that mothers (and nurses) coax him to get a move on as soon as he stops or when they see no movement of the milk in the bottle.

This is not in the baby's interests, since he suffers two possible disadvantages. First, he may be forced to take more milk than he wishes, thus accounting for the greater risk of obesity in bottle-fed babies. Secondly, he spends less time in your arms.

The only inconvenience is to the busy mother, who has to spend more time over the breast feeding than she feels able to, but this exactly fits the baby's needs for extended contact with her. Every mother knows that when she tries to hasten her baby on the breast, things go wrong; most often he won't take any, possibly because her haste is inhibiting the let-down reflex, and he often starts to cry.

Developing an Appetite

Babies usually become hungrier about the time when milk starts being made instead of colostrum. If, at this point, you let your baby satisfy his hunger when he wants to, he stimulates the breasts to produce enough milk for his increasing needs. It is no accident that babies tend to want several feedings on the very days when the milk is becoming established. Between the third and about the sixth day, a baby may want ten or twelve feedings instead of the six or seven you might have anticipated. Many babies ask to be fed every half hour at first. By responding to his wishes you encourage the milk supply to adjust to his needs.

Of course, feeding at all hours of the day and night, in a society where this involves undressing and getting out of bed, would be intolerably tiring if it went on for more than a very few days. But this frequent feeding, related to the hormonal activity in the breasts, does not continue. It is useful to know when and why it is likely to occur, because, intelligently handled, it stimulates the milk supply, relieves engorgement, and thus indirectly leads to fewer feedings in the days that follow. The baby is not getting into "bad habits" at this stage.

Weight Loss

All babies lose weight at first, whether breast or bottle fed; but if you are breast feeding, you may watch other babies dispatching bottles from the beginning and wonder if your baby is hungry or thirsty. Since breast feeding is the natural way to feed a baby, it would be surprising if lack of milk for the first day or two were a mistake by Nature that made the baby suffer. The sequence of producing colostrum, then colostrum and milk, before milk alone, entirely satisfies the normal baby under normal conditions.

If the weather or the hospital is very hot and your baby seems thirsty, he should simply be given the breast again, not a bottle of water or milk. In fact, the first lot of breast milk to flow during a feeding is more dilute, as though it had been designed to quench the baby's thirst.

Larger babies tend to lose more weight than small ones in the week after birth. They may be able to wait longer between feedings because they can drink more, but, on the other hand, a bigger appetite may cancel out the advantage of a larger stomach capacity.

In general, once a baby starts making good his initial weight loss, usually between the sixth and tenth day, he begins to show signs of settling down to some sort of feeding pattern. It is not essential to keep watching the clock. When your baby's rate of sucking has slowed down and the breast feels softer and empty, put him to the other breast.

The Need to Suck

The breast that is offered to the baby first is alternated with each feeding, to ensure that each breast is stimulated regularly. This is important, at least until breast feeding is well established. Some babies want to suck longer than others because they particularly enjoy the act of sucking for itself as well as for the nourishment it brings. No harm comes from their remaining at the breast.

When your baby learns to suck his thumb, some of his urge to suck will be satisfied in this way. However, it is believed that thumb-sucking is less common in breast-fed babies because feeding at the breast gives greater pleasure than sucking the rubber nipple of a bottle. At this stage it is through contact between his mouth, head, and hands, and his mother's breast that he receives positive sensations of pleasure; he enjoys the whole experience, not just the sucking, so don't put his hands in mittens or pin down his arms in a shawl. The movements of the baby's hands to caress the breast encourage the flow of milk by stimulating the let-down reflex still further (see pp. 60, 293).

Burping

Babies swallow air while they feed, just as adults do when they eat. If you look at an X-ray of the abdomen of a baby or an adult, the picture is the same—the intestines contain air and solid matter, probably in about equal amounts. Air swallowing is therefore inevitable and normal; it leads to no digestive problems.

Unfortunately, for reasons that are not clear to me, people in Western countries have become obsessed by a need to get the gas out of their babies. Mothers in primitive tribes have never heard about gas, and there are also some Western countries where the fetish of bubbling does not exist. I often think that if only burping failed to make a noise, there would be less concern about it.

None of this would matter if the erroneous ideas about gas caused no harm, but unfortunately they do. In the first place, many babies, while feeding happily, have their meal interrupted in order to be burped. This in itself is enough to make the baby cry, but he is even more likely to do so if his mother is on edge until she has heard that magical burp. The other, more serious, mistake, is to ascribe a baby's crying to gas. Of course it is so much nicer to have a ready mechanical explanation every time your baby cries, but since gas is rarely if ever the cause of crying, you must not allow yourself the luxury of such a facile explanation. You must work out whether he is crying because he is hungry—this is very likely if you have stopped him in the middle of a feeding—or whether he is bored, or whether, and this is the most likely cause of all, he is lonely and wants a cuddle. Less often, but essential to recognize, he will be crying because he is ill.

The extraordinary fact is that so much of a baby's crying and other imperfect varieties of behavior are ascribed, during the first six months of life, to gas. Around six months of age the first tooth emerges, which provides another mechanical explanation to take the place of gas. From now on, teething (pp. 247f.) is given as the explanation of those troubles previously ascribed to gas.

How then should you tackle the question of gas? So long as your baby is feeding contentedly, there is no reason to do anything about it. He may be so keen on feeding that when you change from one breast to the other he resents even the second without the nipple in his mouth. Another baby may want a short rest and during that time he may or may not bring up gas; it doesn't matter either way.

At the end of the feeding you should cuddle your baby—he certainly does not want to be put straight back into his crib. While you are cuddling him, he may burp; if he doesn't, then your approach should be that he has not swallowed enough air to need to bring any up. Probably few babies really bring up much gas; and you must never become one of those mothers who believe they must not put their babies down until the magic noise has been heard. It is only a short stage from there to deciding whether he has brought up "enough" gas—though how you measure it is beyond me!

Cuddle your baby in whatever position seems most natural to you. If you like to have him looking over your shoulder, you would probably be wise to have a cloth there in case he regurgitates a little milk while burping. Don't be afraid that your baby will not settle unless his gas is brought up; he is less likely to settle after feeding if kept up when he longs to go to sleep. Struggling to burp only makes mothers and babies exhausted.

I presume that the baby who sucks greedily swallows more air than the placid feeder, but I don't know whether this is really true and certainly nothing special needs to be done about it. Babies who swallow a lot of air may be more liable to regurgitate, but healthy babies who regurgitate do not need any treatment. All that is needed is an explanation (pp. 436–37) for their mothers as to why they do this and a warning to take extra care to protect their own and the baby's clothes.

The question of burping is closely bound up with "three-month colic," which is discussed on pp. 123f.

Night Feedings—Are They Necessary?

Although a baby may sleep through the night for the first night or two after birth, until he gets an appetite, he cannot be expected to last eight or so hours without wanting to be fed. The most that you can hope for is that he sleeps for one long stretch of perhaps five or six hours during the twenty-four, and that this happens to be at night. In any case, once your milk comes in, you may wake up with swollen breasts in the middle of the night even if the baby sleeps on. Milk is being made throughout the twenty-four hours, and both you and your baby need the night feeding at this stage, until the breast milk is well established and less dependent on regular demand. Because you have slept beforehand and are warm and relaxed, it is likely to be a satisfying feeding for the baby and with luck he will sleep till morning.

Any tendency to sleep longer between feedings should be encouraged. There is no need to wake up your baby for a night feeding unless it happens to suit you to do so at a particular time. For example, it is obviously more convenient to wake the baby last thing at night, before you go to bed, and feed him then, rather than to go to bed and have him wake up half an hour later. Everything is much simpler if he is allowed to "sleep-feed," meaning that he sleeps alongside you in bed and feeds when he wants, often without waking you. This is a controversial practice in both the United States and the United Kingdom, but in fact it is perfectly safe provided the mother has not had a sedative. In the hospital where I work we have practiced the method for years without any problems. Many mothers have told me they cannot sleep if the baby is not in the bed. Many others have had their babies in their beds for years but felt guilty until recently, when told it is safe.

In the hospital, you may be asked whether you wish to be awakened to breast feed your baby when he wakes in the night or whether you wish the nurse to give him a bottle of milk. Unless you feel

desperately tired, it is always better to choose to be awakened; you
will probably wake up with swollen breasts anyway.

Catching up on Your Sleep

If you return home from the hospital already tired, you may easily be
depressed by the thought of continual broken nights. There is more
to do during the day than ever before and it seems most unfair that
you should get less sleep. You may be lucky enough to have a baby
who sleeps from his last feeding at your bedtime until 3:00 or 4:00
A.M., so that you can get two reasonable stretches of sleep. But a new
baby may want more than one feeding during the night, whether
breast or bottle fed. It is sensible, therefore, to take every opportunity
to rest during the day. You cannot get through the chores in any case.
It is difficult to make oneself ignore nonessential housework; organizing the day often seems to take more energy than plodding through
it—but it is worth trying to work out the priorities and letting everything else lapse for a few weeks until you can get more rest at night.
Try to avoid lying awake on tenterhooks, waiting for your baby to cry
and wondering if he is all right. A healthy baby will be all right and
does not need to be looked at while he sleeps to check that he is still
alive. Remember that it is normal for a healthy baby to be very quiet
and very pale while asleep.

Problems

Some aspects of breast feeding that might cause problems if misunderstood have already been discussed, such as afterpains and engorgement, which are really normal stages in the establishment of
feeding. There are, however, some problems that need more than just
simple understanding and that can make breast feeding difficult or
jeopardize it altogether.

Sore and Cracked Nipples

The start of each feeding may be accompanied by a slight nip as the
baby first uses his gums. Mothers tell me they soon get used to this
and that soreness is seldom a problem. Some mothers who complain
to me of soreness include a number who have not yet fully made the
emotional change needed to allow the baby to suck at the breast.
During the examination, such mothers complain when the breast is
pressed as well as the nipple touched, while their facial expression is
one of emotional distress.

    Fair-skinned women with pinker nipples are those most liable to local soreness of the nipple, which could lead to a crack. Cream applied to the nipple after feedings may help.

Pads worn inside the bra to prevent milk staining your clothes should be changed as soon as they become sodden; waterproof pads should be used only for special occasions, because the skin of the nipple is weakened if it is left damp for a long time.

Your baby must not be allowed to chew on the nipple; the whole of the pigmented area (areola) must be guided into his mouth. If he refuses to let go and is hurting you, break the vacuum set up through sucking by inserting your (clean) finger into the corner of his mouth. Never hold his nose to make him let go—a very unkind way to end a nice breast feeding. Pulling him away forcibly can result in a cracked nipple. Do not allow him to chew on a nipple that is difficult to grasp because of engorgement; express a little milk before putting him to the breast in order to make the nipple more accessible (see engorgement, pp. 62–63). Babies brought up on a rigid time schedule, thereby being trained to become clock gobblers (p. 66), are much more likely to cause sore nipples than those in whom the approach to feeding is placid and timeless.

Treatment   If a nipple becomes sore, a crack is almost certainly present, though your doctor, midwife, or nurse may need a magnifying glass to see it. Treatment is the same in either case: the nipple must be rested. This can often be achieved without stopping breast feeding by the use of a nipple shield. This artificial nipple prevents the baby from sucking directly on the crack and yet permits the flow of milk from the breast. If this fails, milk can be expressed from the affected breast by hand and given to the baby by spoon or bottle. Normal feeding is resumed when the crack is healed. This usually takes about forty-eight hours, but the nipple should be rested for longer if any pain is felt on feeding.

It is often worth trying a simple trick to alter the site on the nipple where the baby always sucks. The baby lies alongside his mother in the same position as for feeding twins (p. 146). His abdomen is under her armpit and his head cradled in the palm of her hand on the same side while his legs point backward.

You can distinguish the pain of a cracked nipple from the sharp pain sometimes felt when the baby first begins sucking because, in the latter case, the pain disappears after a few seconds, once the milk starts to flow. A cracked nipple goes on hurting.

Breast Abscess

This is almost always a complication of an untreated cracked nipple. Part of the breast, often one-quarter, is inflamed, looking red and feeling sore and lumpy. At the first sign of infection, seek medical help. If the infection is caught early, and immediate antibiotic treatment given, your baby can go on feeding at the breast. Even if he has to be taken off it temporarily, while you are treated, he can continue to feed at the other breast, and restart on the affected side when the abscess has healed.

Breast abscesses are discouraging and painful, but they need not stop you from breast feeding if you want to go on.

Difficult Babies to Feed

Not all the difficulties in breast feeding are due to a mother's inexperience or her lack of milk. Successful breast feeding depends on a satisfying relationship between two individuals, a baby and his mother. Your handling of the baby can affect him; for example, if you are anxious, your anxiety can be transmitted to him, and because he senses it he does not settle during his feeding. However, it works the other way around too: there are certainly some babies who are so difficult to feed that their mothers become tense, and this can affect the let-down reflex and the milk supply. But although your baby may react to your anxiety, this is not inevitable; he may be able to take it in his stride.

The Restless Baby

There is the occasional baby who seems to be born restless. He takes a few sucks at the breast—enough to set off the let-down reflex—and then turns his head away while the milk gushes out. It may be the rush of milk that annoys him at this point, but he tends to go on stopping and starting throughout the feeding. He may scream when he releases the nipple, needing to be calmed before he will begin again. This is maddening if you are already feeling tense, because you know the feeding will take twice as long as it would if he concentrated, or because your baby seems to be taking only half the amount you think he should. Breast feeding is not the peaceful, relaxing experience you anticipated. You may have less milk because of tension, the child does not gain as much weight as a less active baby, and a vicious circle sets in. When the baby can focus his eyes better and turn his head, he becomes even more difficult to feed, because of the competing attractions around him. But by this time you have probably devised a way of feeding him satisfactorily, and are less worried because he has survived despite the restless feedings.

The excitable baby is best held firmly and the feeding begun before he is wide awake or crying. He can be picked up from his crib or baby carriage still lying on the mattress and then wrapped in his shawl. Diaper changing and other handling before feedings should be kept to the minimum. Feed him away from a bright light and without interruption, if possible. Resist the temptation to try to hurry him; it won't work anyway. If he slept like a log from one feeding to the next, you might feel less anxious but you should console yourself with the knowledge that such a baby is usually brighter than the average, that his activity is the sign of an intelligent interest in his surroundings, and that extra wakefulness gives him extra time for learning. One mother, who had been led to believe that normal babies slept immediately after feedings, told me that she was so worried by her baby remaining awake that she changed to the bottle, only to find that his pattern of behavior remained unaltered.

The Sleepy Feeder

Some babies, far from being too active, are slow to wake up and start feeding, or fall asleep in the middle of a feeding (see p. 66). Preterm babies tend to fall asleep at the breast at first, and many other babies are sleepy for a day or two after birth. This is normal.

It used to be said that babies would be exhausted by being left too long at the breast. This is nonsense; a baby falls asleep as soon as he is tired of sucking, but that is no reason to put him down. He will wake up after a temporary rest and is only relishing his time at the breast. Don't you enjoy those gaps between courses at big dinners?

Insufficient Milk

Stimulating the Supply

If you feed your baby when he seems hungry and know what to expect in the early days of breast feeding, you are less likely to worry about or to suffer from lack of milk. You know that if he is unsatisfied on any particular day, he will wake up for food more often, thereby stimulating the breasts to make more. You will not want him to be given a bottle of milk before his first breast feedings or after them, nor will you want him "test weighed" (p. 78) to check how much he has drunk. Ideally, you and everyone concerned will take it for granted that you will produce enough milk, given time and encouragement.

If your baby seems unsatisfied for long, despite being fed more often, you are removing him from the breast too soon. Such a baby will soon wake up and start to feed again if you let him.

Lack of Confidence

Unfortunately, many mothers start breast feeding doubting that they can produce enough milk for their babies. It is so often the reason given for abandoning breast feeding. This initial lack of confidence may be increased during the lying-in period by the hospital's well-meant attempts to ensure that the baby's feeding schedule is "settled" before he leaves. He may be given a complementary feeding (p. 49) and test weighed. However, a week or ten days is not long enough for most mothers and babies to settle down to a regular feeding pattern, or for all babies to make up their weight loss (pp. 67–68).

Getting Advice

Any mother who is still anxious about feeding her baby when she leaves the hospital can get help from her own doctor or from a visiting nurse. There is no need to fear that if your baby leaves the hospital fully breast fed, but not always entirely satisfied, he is going to starve unless he has a bottle too. If he is already having cow's milk as well as breast milk at this stage, he is more likely to be fully bottle fed within a few days. However, if you leave the hospital with your confidence intact and without being obsessed by "average" weight gains, you have a good chance of continuing to breast feed, despite the additional work of keeping house.

The birth-control pill may reduce the supply of breast milk. You can discuss alternative methods of contraception with your doctor before resuming the pill.

Fatigue

A common worry is that once a nursing mother gets up and has housework to do and her family to look after, she will be too tired to make enough milk. Yet rest and relaxation, though desirable, have never been essential for successful breast feeding. Women all over the world work hard, become tired, and continue to feed their babies. Of course, it is sensible to rest as much as possible, to relax before and during a feeding, and to abandon unnecessary work. But it is perfectly possible to lead a busy life, feel tired, and breast feed. Breasts go on making milk in response to the baby's demands. If fatigue does temporarily affect the amount of milk, the baby wakes more often, and if he is fed more often, the supply will be stimulated and increase again. If tiredness were fatal to breast feeding, it would have died out long ago.

Adapting to Home Life

Many women do have less milk when they first come home, but this is due to anxieties about feeding and looking after the baby, and the problem of fitting him into everyday life, as well as to fatigue. The let-down reflex may be inhibited when visitors call, or are expected, so that although there is milk in the breasts, your baby cannot get it. There may be the problem of dealing with a jealous toddler. He may want to sit on your lap during feedings and even to suck at the breast —the novelty soon wears off if he is allowed to try it. Or he may try to annoy you deliberately while you are feeding the baby. He may even throw a tantrum regularly at mealtimes. It is difficult to deal with all this and to feed a baby calmly at the same time. Whenever possible, feedings should be given while another adult or older child is in the house to distract the child. Some feedings can coincide with children's television or radio programs; play a record, or try telling the child a story while feeding the baby. The child must be made to feel welcome although he is being infuriating, because only when he feels secure again will he leave you alone. Remind him that he is bigger than the baby, with the implication that he is therefore more important, though the helpless baby takes up so much time. It probably won't work, but with luck he will soon get bored with hovering over the feeding baby (see jealousy, pp. 148f.).

Common Difficulties

These can be enough to discourage you when you start ordinary life again and the day can no longer revolve entirely around your baby. The baby who was "good" in the hospital now becomes fretful, and you may blame it on your milk or lack of it. If when next weighed he has failed to gain as much as the charts say he should, you worry more.

Spots on the face are common in the early weeks and seem to appear just as relatives and friends arrive to meet the baby. He looks most unlike the thriving beauties that advertise artificial milk products, and he probably cries twice as much as he did in the first week or two. You, and perhaps your friends, may blame all these worrying developments on the quality and quantity of your milk. You should tell yourself, and your friends, that spotty faces are normal at this stage, and that cow's milk might possibly be mixed incorrectly and so disagree with a baby but that breast milk cannot. Crying cannot be due to indigestion caused by breast milk, which always agrees with babies, but is probably because he is now becoming more wakeful and wants more attention. He seems to demand extra attention just at those times of the day when you are overworked, especially when you are trying to tidy up before your husband gets home in the evening; but this will only be a temporary stage (see three-month colic, pp. 123–25).

Encouraging the Milk Supply

Diet Apart from trying to relax and rest as much as possible, what can you do if you suspect your milk supply is diminishing? You should express any milk left in the breasts at the end of each feeding to give them maximum stimulation (p. 74). Eat and drink well, though your appetite will normally see to this. A mixed and varied diet will ensure the best of health. And try not to worry about your figure; many women become thinner rather than fatter while breast feeding. You certainly should not diet while breast feeding, because this can result in the production of insufficient milk.

Extra Drinks There is no proof that drinking special preparations increases the amount of milk, but they do no harm and may help by giving you confidence. There is no point in drinking enormous amounts; apart from making sure you quench your thirst, do not drink more than is comfortable. Studies have shown that drinking too much tends to reduce the quantity of milk made, presumably because this is nauseating; it also has the added disadvantage of increasing the number of visits to the bathroom. However, it is a good idea to have a drink ready before beginning a feeding, because you may feel thirsty then and will not want to interrupt the feeding to fetch one. There is, in fact, no need to become obsessed about food and drink, beyond aiming at a balanced diet and not going hungry and thirsty for long periods.

There is no evidence that particular foods ought to be avoided; alcohol and smoking in moderation do not seem to affect the milk, and if they relax you, may help breast feeding. Few medicines are known to affect the baby through the milk, though the doctor has to take breast feeding into account when prescribing.

Giving Extras

Complementary Feedings Should your baby continue to seem hungry although you have tried in vain to increase your milk, he can be given a complementary feeding. This is an extra feeding of a cow's milk formula taken at the end of whichever feeding or feedings leave him most unsatisfied. It is wise to avoid complementary feedings in the first three weeks or so, while the breast milk supply is fluctuating and while it needs the stimulation of a hungry baby, but there is obviously a point at which your worry and the baby's hungry crying set up a vicious circle, which must be broken.

Test Weighing   Your doctor or a visiting nurse may decide to "test weigh" your baby to learn how much milk he is taking and so to discover how much extra to offer him. The baby is weighed before and after a feed; no change in clothing or diaper is made between the two weighings, so the gain in weight indicates accurately the amount of milk he has taken.

Test weighing is much less often practiced today, since it means creating an artificial situation that may in itself upset a mother and reduce her flow of breast milk during the test feed itself and afterward. It is simpler to calculate the probable amount of milk that the baby is short of and to offer this extra milk until he seems satisfied.

Avoiding Pitfalls   One pitfall of complementary feeding is that, if frequent, it jeopardizes breast feeding by interfering with the supply-and-demand mechanism on which it depends. Another pitfall is that the baby may come to prefer the bottle because he likes the taste of cow's milk and the continuous flow of milk from the nipple. In extreme cases, this can result in a mother expressing her own milk and giving it to the baby by bottle; unfortunately, this only increases the baby's preference for the bottle and his tendency to refuse the breast, although it contains enough milk to satisfy his hunger.

These pitfalls can be avoided by making sure that complementary feedings are not made a routine part of feeding and are discarded as soon as you and your baby are happier. Give him the chance to empty the breasts before offering him the bottle. Giving the complement by spoon avoids the possibility of the baby's coming to prefer the complementary feeding to the breast feeding. Even the smallest baby can be fed in this way, but it takes time and it is more comforting for him to suck.

The milk mixture given should not be too sweet. If your baby will take it unsweetened, so much the better. A feeding of solids instead of milk alone may satisfy him and eliminate the need for complementary bottles (p. 187).

In theory, there is no objection to feeding a baby indefinitely by a combination of breast milk and bottle feedings. He would continue to get the benefits of breast milk, where he might otherwise have to do without them altogether. In practice, you will probably find it tedious to prepare and give complements for a long time; nearly all mothers seem to give up one method in favor of the other within a month.

Breast feeding is not threatened by giving an occasional complement if for some reason the baby seems hungry, or by a bottle given regularly after one feeding, usually in the early evening when the baby seems particularly discontented. But continually relying on complements soon leads to weaning the baby from the breast altogether.

Perhaps complementary feeding is sometimes started because a mother is losing her enthusiasm for breast feeding, as well as her milk. However, if you use it carefully and want to go on breast feeding, complements can tide both of you over a bad patch and help you to continue breast feeding.

Supplementary Feedings

One objection to breast feeding is that it ties a mother to the baby's feeding times. Is it all right to get over this by giving a bottle feeding instead of a breast feeding once or twice during the day? (This technique is known as supplementary feeding, since, unlike complementary feeding, the whole breast feeding is replaced by cow's milk.) Could you go back to work and continue breast feeding if your baby was bottle fed at midday? This might work once breast feeding was well established, but if started early it is seldom satisfactory, since it discourages the milk supply by providing too little stimulation.

Occasional Bottles   However, if you want to go out for a day now and then, your baby can be fed with a bottle of cow's milk, or of expressed breast milk. If you expect to be just a little late getting back and think he may wake up hungry, he can be given a drink of boiled water or fruit juice instead.

If your milk is not yet established, express some milk at the appropriate time to stimulate it; this may be necessary for your own comfort in any case. Once the supply is reliable, you may need to express only enough milk to relieve the tension; the let-down reflex may have taken place and done this automatically.

Starting Solids

When the baby is a few weeks old and getting hungrier, he used to be given feedings of milk mixed with cereal, or other puréed foods, rather than just milk. Today's approach is that by increasing the frequency and length of the breast feeding the need for solids can be deferred until six months of age. The trouble with cereals is that they are a major cause of overweight babies.

Drinking from a Cup

You continue to provide him with most of his milk and can go on doing so until he is ready to drink out of a cup at some time between three and nine months. Most breast-fed babies can make the gradual change from breast to cup without ever having a bottle.

When you first offer your baby a cup, don't expect instant success. Let him take his time and allow him to suck at the breast or bottle for as long as he derives pleasure from it (see mixed feeding, pp. 186f.).

Stopping Breast Feedings

This is entirely up to you and you can do it whenever you want, knowing that your baby will gradually learn to drink cow's milk from a bottle or cup when the time comes. If you are enjoying breast feeding, there is no reason why you should not go on until he is twelve months or older and you will be able to make the transition direct to cup feeding without ever using a bottle. Your problem will be the loss of enjoyment from breast feeding and perhaps the peaceful pleasure of reading a book while doing so. Many mothers find they keep putting off the last feeding because they enjoy it so much. You may find it easiest if you gradually give up all but the last feeding in the evening, so that you still allow yourselves the luxury of a close feeding together at night for quite some weeks after you have stopped daytime breast feeding. Don't be put off breast feeding by the arrival of teeth and the fear of being bitten. Most mothers tell me their babies never bite them, and few give up for this reason. This is due to the fact that the baby places his tongue between the lower teeth and the nipple; biting would therefore cause the baby pain.

Difficulties If You Fall Ill

Apart from abandoning breast feeding because of lack of milk, are there any other reasons why a breast-fed baby should change to bottle feeding? What happens if a nursing mother becomes ill?

Each illness must be assessed as it arises. A cold or bout of flu may make you wish you could go to bed and forget your baby, but your breasts go on making milk and, unless there is someone to help, it will be easier to breast feed than to make up a bottle. Your close contact with the baby before your symptoms appeared means that any infection is likely to have reached him already, whether you breast or bottle feed, so there is no point in stopping breast feeding on these grounds. An acute infection might mean that the milk must be expressed and given by bottle for a few days, but an ill mother is unlikely to have the energy to express her milk regularly. Your doctor will decide how to deal with the situation.

If your baby does have to be bottle fed suddenly, he may protest, especially if he has never had a bottle before. But he will co-operate as he gets hungrier, or he can be fed by spoon instead.

Menstruation and Pregnancy

Menstruation is usually delayed by breast feeding, but if it does start, breast feeding can continue as before. Pregnancy is less likely while you are breast feeding but it is an uncertain method of birth control. A mother who conceives while she is still breast feeding can continue to feed her baby if she so wishes.

Distaste for Breast Feeding

Sometimes, a mother who planned to breast feed finds the whole process distasteful enough to wish to give it up. She may not always admit this to herself or to others and she will probably blame a lack of milk.

It is not surprising that some women find it difficult to regard breast feeding as a normal activity in our "civilized society." Up to the point of childbearing, a woman's breasts are thought of as a sex symbol, and it may be hard to make the switch from thinking of them as such to regarding them as a source of a baby's food. Some husbands dislike the idea. And it is often implied that, to breast feed, a woman must become "cowlike," dedicating her entire time to producing milk. Naturally many women resent this implication. Some who think this before having a baby change their minds when the baby is born, later discovering that they enjoy breast feeding, and find it entirely compatible with feeling normal and living normally.

Other women are surprised by, and resent, the sensuality of breast feeding. It is a pleasurable experience, particularly when it is going well, for the mother as well as for the baby. This is natural; indeed, it is one of Nature's ways of ensuring that babies get fed, but you may find it hard to accept these feelings. Although the baby is the result of "sex," he is meant to arouse only purely parental feelings; any hint that a baby feeding at the breast arouses sexual feelings can be a shock.

The reasons why some women find breast feeding distasteful are therefore deep. A woman can be helped to understand them but she should never be forced to breast feed against her wishes. One of the main benefits of breast feeding should be the close relationship it creates between you and your baby. If this is in any degree jeopardized by your feelings, it is better to give a bottle lovingly.

A mother should respect the feelings of those around her who are embarrassed by seeing a woman breast feed. This can be achieved by subtlety of dress so the fact that the baby is being breast fed is hardly apparent.

6

Bottle Feeding

Instead of breast milk, babies can be fed on cow's milk, using a modified dried preparation ("formula"). Not all mothers are aware that "formula" milk is made from cow's milk.

Goat's milk is not recommended for babies because it has a high level of sodium and phosphate, similar to fresh cow's milk, and a protein content higher than unmodified cow's milk.

Although cow's milk differs from human milk in several ways, needing modifications to suit the young baby's digestion, most babies thrive on any appropriate mixture. The brand of milk, therefore, depends on suiting the individual mother as well as the individual baby, whose age, progress, and rate of weight gain have to be considered.

Bottle versus Breast

It used to be routine for mothers who decided against breast feeding to be given hormone treatment to stop the milk from coming into the breasts. This is now regarded as unnecessary, since the flow of milk is so dependent on the baby's sucking that if this does not happen, the milk mechanism switches off. One advantage of this is that you can change your mind in the first two or three days and still be able to breast feed your baby.

How Safe Is Bottle Feeding?

Although babies thrive on cow's milk, is it as safe as breast milk? In countries with a high standard of public hygiene in services such as drainage and water supply, bottle feeding is safe, although each feeding must still be sterilized. In developing countries, the risk is much greater. Clean water and adequate milk cannot always be taken for granted. The standard of hygiene in a household is determined by its least careful member; she may handle something connected with the baby's food, even if she is not directly involved in preparing feedings. For these reasons, it is safer to breast feed if you live in or visit hot countries. For the same reasons, in these countries early weaning puts a baby at greater risk, since any kind of food may become contaminated; so, within reason, the longer breast feeding continues the better.

Bottle-fed babies in developed countries are not exposed to such a degree of risk, but infections like gastroenteritis still do occur more easily among bottle-fed than among breast-fed babies. Apart from this hazard, bottle feeding is a safe way to feed a baby in these countries.

How Satisfactory Is Bottle Feeding?

Is it also as satisfactory as breast feeding in every other way? As far as is known, the answer is that it can be, although, as with breast feeding, the method of feeding is as important as the quality of the feeding. The problem in both cases is to satisfy your baby's need for comfort and play as well as his hunger. It is perhaps easier to forget or ignore this with bottle feeding than with breast feeding, when you have to hold the baby close to you to feed him at all.

Bottle Holders Bottle holders, which enable a baby to feed from a propped bottle without his mother holding him, are not only danger-ous (see pp. 93, 457), but have the disadvantage of depriving him of the comfort he needs as much as food. It is true that a baby can be held and cuddled at other times instead, but he needs food, comfort, and the presence of his mother together whenever possible. Bottle-fed babies can be held and fed in a relaxed and sympathetic way, making up for the possible disadvantage of the bottle, which, because it is hard and impersonal, is a less satisfying plaything than the breast. Tension caused by feeding troubles, whatever the reason, makes a barrier between mother and baby; if bottle feeding reduces tension, it can bring you and your baby closer.

The Normal Way to Feed?

Because bottle feeding is so general in many developed countries, to some mothers it may feel a more normal way to feed a baby than breast feeding. If it feels natural to you, you will convey that feeling to your baby, and the feeling you convey to him is as important as the food you give him. This relaxed relationship can be spoiled if you feel guilty that you are not breast feeding; your baby then gets the worst of both worlds.

Medical advisers or friends who try to dissuade a mother from bottle feeding, on the grounds that breast feeding forms a stronger bond between mother and baby, can make her feel uneasy without changing her decision. The reasons for preferring to bottle feed may be obscure and private as well as obvious; doctors have to distinguish between mothers who are determined to bottle feed and those who are really hoping for help and support in establishing breast feeding. Your baby will thrive on either kind of feeding if you as his mother are happy.

Anxieties: Is Your Baby Getting Enough?

Paradoxically, bottle feeding produces its own worries in the mother who chooses it so that she can see how much milk her baby is taking. Perhaps she stopped breast feeding because she did not know how much her baby was getting. Now she worries because she does know. Although her baby is contented, if he wants more or less than the "average" amount, she thinks she is over- or underfeeding him. Whichever method of feeding she uses, this mother feels responsible at each feeding for giving her baby the "right" amount. She has not learned the lesson, as relevant to bottle as to breast feeding, that a baby does not feel equally hungry at all meals, and that different babies have different appetites. The breast-fed baby sometimes takes twice as much at one feeding as at another, varying his intake to suit his appetite; the bottle-fed baby should be allowed to do the same, leaving some of his milk or being offered more if he seems to want it (see pp. 94, 199–200).

Does the Milk Agree with Him?

Again, an underconfident mother who is afraid her breast milk "does not agree with the baby" is also likely to worry about whether a particular brand of cow's milk suits him if she bottle feeds. She changes from one variety of milk to another, ascribing any minor troubles of the baby's to the type of milk. Feeding can become the focus of all worries about the baby who is bottle fed, just as it can with the breast-fed baby. Some of these worries can be avoided or reduced if you have been told what to expect: that your baby is likely to thrive on any brand of milk, that his appetite will vary, and that it is not your role to try to make him eat any "average" amount.

Cow's Milk Compared with Breast Milk

Cow's milk contains more protein but less sugar than breast milk, these constituents being of different types as well as in different proportions. Cow's milk protein contains much more casein than the protein in human milk, and forms curds in the stomach, which are visible in the stools of a baby fed on cow's milk (see pp. 44–45). Casein is the least digestible part of the milk, from the human infant's point of view.

The fat content of both milks is about the same, but the fat droplets in cow's milk are bigger and a little less digestible than those in breast milk. Both milks provide sufficient vitamins A and B. There is sufficient vitamin C in breast milk but not enough in cow's milk, and in any case this is destroyed when the milk is boiled. Measurements used to show an apparent lack of vitamin D in breast milk, although breast-fed babies do not get rickets (p. 182). However, newer methods of testing show sufficient vitamin D in breast milk, although there is not enough in cow's milk. (See also breast feeding, p. 56.)

Choosing a Milk Mixture

Whereas a newborn baby can use all the nourishment in breast milk, he cannot digest cow's milk completely and would need to drink a greater volume of fresh, undiluted milk to obtain the same amount of calories. This difficulty is overcome by drying the milk to make it more digestible; water is added so that the baby receives diluted milk, sugar being added to bring up the calorie content. The water must be boiled, unless you are using the terminal method of sterilization (see p. 91). Ordinary granulated is perfectly adequate; there is no special virtue in using brown sugar or glucose.

This mixture is sometimes called a "formula." The one essential for all preprations of cow's milk used for young babies is that they should have been modified to reduce their high levels of sodium and phosphate so that these approximate to the low levels found in breast milk (p. 56). This is stated on the label and should be checked at the time of purchase.

Dried Milks

The advantages of dried milk are that, being powdered, it is light to carry, keeps well when opened, and is easy to store. There are many different brands on the market, at different prices and with various modifications, all being fortified with vitamin D. Some need additional water only, since sugar and all necessary vitamins are included in the powder. This saves trouble but costs more than giving the vitamins separately. There is nothing magical about those milks that are described as "humanized," since it is impossible to convert cow's milk into breast milk; and they are likely to be more expensive. Modification of cow's milk as described above has removed the necessity for half-cream milks, which used to be given to very young or preterm babies.

Some brands mix very easily, only needing to be shaken in the bottle with water to form a smooth, lump-free liquid. Others are more difficult to mix and need straining. In general, you pay more for those that are easiest to prepare, but your baby will do equally well on any brand, provided it has been modified to be low in sodium and phosphate. One firm producing a modified dried milk also produces the same formula as a concentrated liquid for diluting with warm, previously boiled water. Some mothers find this more convenient, especially for vacations and traveling.

Do some research for yourself by reading labels and leaflets on the various varieties, and talk the matter over with your doctor or visiting nurse, who will also advise on preparing and giving the feeding. Full instructions are always given with the milk. These are based on the "average" baby and may need modifying so that the individual baby is given more or less according to his appetite.

Don't Change Around

Once you have settled on a brand, you need not worry that it will not suit your baby. Any problems he has are most unlikely to be due to the brand of milk, and changing around usually only makes you, and perhaps the doctor also, feel that something has been done about the problem—if it makes you feel better, perhaps it has, but from the baby's point of view it is seldom if ever necessary to change brands. If anything is at fault, it may be the way the feeding is given (see feeding your baby, pp. 92–95).

Evaporated Milk (Unsweetened Condensed Milk)

By common usage the term "evaporated milk" refers to unsweetened condensed milk. Sweetened condensed milk should not be used for babies, since it contains too much sugar and too little protein. Most preparations of evaporated milk contain too much sodium and phosphate to be fed to young babies. Only recently has it been appreciated that this high sodium content in evaporated milks in the United States and the United Kingdom makes it unsuitable for young babies. Unmodified evaporated milk is suitable only for older babies. It is widely available, sterile and easy to mix, but it is heavier to carry and bulkier to store than dried milk. You prepare it by replacing the water and adding sugar. The amount of water and sugar added decreases as the child grows until the mixture is the same strength as fresh milk; directions for this are given on the can. The milk itself is sterile in the can, so need not be boiled; the danger lies in contamination after opening (see methods of sterilizing, p. 91). Most brands have added vitamin D.

Fresh Milk

Fresh milk should not be used for feeding newborn babies, because of its high sodium and phosphate content.

Developing Countries

Emphasis has been placed on the need to be meticulous about sterility in the preparation of bottle feedings, and the problem this poses in developing countries, where piped water supply is available only in towns.

In such countries, the need for educated mothers to breast feed has a relevance to the health of the country, as well as to the individual baby. The native population is bombarded with advertisements recommending different cow's milk preparations. If, in addition to this, native mothers see educated women (both native and expatriate) choosing to bottle feed, they will be still more convinced that bottle is best.

Preparing the Feeding

The main points about preparing a feeding are that the proportions and measurements should be exact, and that the feeding should be sterile when it reaches the baby.

How Much to Make

If your baby is completely bottle fed, you may find it easier to make up all his feedings once a day instead of one or two at a time. This is satisfactory provided the feedings are kept in a refrigerator; if they are left at room temperature, any bacteria present will multiply.

It is better to make up more than you think your baby will want and throw away what he leaves than to find he needs more than you have prepared. Whether you make up his bottles once a day or individually, always throw away any milk left over unless he wants to finish a bottle within a few minutes.

Equipment: Bottles and Nipples

The number of bottles and nipples needed for a baby who is completely bottle fed depends on whether you wish to prepare his feedings once a day only; if you do, you will need at least half a dozen bottles and nipples. If you prefer to make up each feeding separately, you could manage with only one bottle and one nipple, though it is wise to have a replacement: a glass bottle may break, and a nipple may get lost or worn out.

Different Types of Bottle

The type and shape of the bottle are unimportant as far as your baby is concerned. All bottles are now the upright kind with an opening at one end. Glass bottles are easy to clean, and you can see clearly how much they contain, but they are breakable and are heavier to hold than plastic bottles. Plastic bottles are light and unbreakable but are not always easy to see through; this makes it harder to be sure they are absolutely clean. It is safer to give a baby who is old enough to sit and hold his own bottle a plastic one, which will not break if he drops it.

Some bottles are made to go with a particular type of nipple. One kind has a wide neck so that the nipple can be inverted into the bottle and covered with a cap to keep it clean and airtight; this is convenient for storage and when traveling.

Supermarkets usually stock several types of bottle. You could buy different types—a wide-necked bottle with inverted nipple for traveling, perhaps, and a small 4-ounce (125 ml) size for giving your baby drinks of fruit juice or water.

Nipples: The Importance of Hole Size

Nipples come in various shapes and sizes, some resembling the human breast more than others and some claiming to be "anticolic."

The size of the hole in the nipple is the most important factor. It may be labeled small, medium, or large, but in any case you should test it to see if the milk comes out at the correct rate when you turn it upside down; this should be a series of rapid drops but not a continuous stream.

If the hole is too small, your baby may swallow a lot of air in his efforts to get the milk; he may also tire and fall asleep before his hunger is satisfied. If the hole is too large, the milk pours out so fast it can choke him or allow him to feed so fast that he vomits afterward. Even if his hunger is satisfied, his need for sucking may not be satisfied if he has taken his food too quickly.

The large-size hole is not usually too big when the nipple is new; but it may become enlarged after much use, so you should check before each feeding that the milk is coming out at the right speed.

Enlarging the Hole

A hole that is too small can be made bigger with a red-hot needle. Stick the blunt end into a cork, heat the point until it is red hot, and push the nipple onto it. Do not do this too abruptly, or the resulting hole may be too big. It is better to push the needle in two or three times, till the hole is the correct size, checking as you go along.

Suiting the Baby

So long as the hole is the right size, most nipples suit most babies, although a preterm or very small baby may need a softer type of nipple; some nipples are made of thick rubber, some of thin. Sometimes the nipple may seem to be too long for the baby; if so, try a shorter one.

It is best to buy one variety of nipple at a time until you are sure a particular kind is suitable, but have more than one in the house, since a nipple may wear out.

Unless the baby is fed as soon as his feeding is prepared, or the nipple is inverted and the bottle then capped, you need to cover the nipple with a small medicine glass. If you store the day's feedings already bottled, you will need an appropriate number of covers.

Other Equipment

Other equipment you need will depend on how you prepare the feedings. Powdered milks can sometimes be mixed in the bottle, but some brands have to be mixed in a bowl and then strained into the bottle. A funnel is needed if the bottle neck is small. A two- or four-cup graduated measure, made of glass so that you can check the measurements at eye level, is useful for measuring milk and water.

Powdered milks often come with their own measuring spoons. Ordinary eating spoons can be used to measure the sugar but they are less accurate than measuring spoons. And these should not be overfilled. The correct amount is level and this can be achieved by scraping off the excess with the flat of a knife. The powdered milk must not be compressed into the measure or the feeding will again be too strong. This would make your baby too fat and could cause indigestion. More dangerous than this is the excessive amount of sodium given (p. 86). Obviously it would be even more serious to give the baby an extra spoonful of dried milk.

Everything used in preparing feedings should be kept together and covered. You then know it is all at hand when needed and do not have to look for and wash things as you go along. For example, it is better to buy a glass measure especially for preparing the feedings than to have to empty and wash one each time you want to mix the baby's milk.

Sterilizing the Formula or Feeding

Why It Is Necessary

Bottles must be sterilized to make them free of bacteria. There is no such problem with breast feeding, since breast milk is fresh and taken directly by the baby from its source. Your own nipples may not be sterile but the bacteria present are unlikely to harm the baby. In contrast, dried cow's milk has to be mixed with water and sugar, transferred from one container to another, and given by bottle through a nipple. Any bacteria in the milk itself, on the equipment, or on the hands of the person making the feeding multiply at room temperature. Bacteria that are harmless to older children or adults may make a young baby ill with diarrhea; he is not yet efficient at fighting the germs or the symptoms they produce.

Sterilizing should be automatic for the first year. It is not worth taking chances while your baby is young; any time saved by being less than thorough will probably be paid for in anxiety, even if he stays well. As the baby grows, he builds up resistance to infection, so that milk feedings need not be sterilized after his first birthday, although a high standard of hygiene is always necessary in preparing his food.

General Preparations

Everything involved in preparing a baby's food must be clean and dry, including the working surfaces and your hands. Bottle, nipple, and milk must be sterile at the end of the process and remain so until the baby is fed.

Cleaning Bottle and Nipple

After each feeding, rinse bottle and nipple in cold water immediately, because the film of milk inside becomes harder to remove if left. The rest of the cleaning and sterilizing can be done when convenient. Wash the bottle with hot water and detergent or soap, using a bottle brush to get in all the corners. The brush should be used for this job only and must be absolutely clean. Rinse the bottle in running water to remove all traces of remaining film and suds.

To clean the nipple, sprinkle it inside and out with salt, rubbing it between your fingers until no stickiness remains. The salt acts as an abrasive to clean away the globules of fat. It is a good idea to turn the nipple inside out, using the handle of a spoon to do this, so as to clean the inside thoroughly with the salt. Squirt water through the hole to make sure it is not clogged.

Bottle and nipple are now ready for sterilizing.

Methods of Sterilizing

There are two sterilizing techniques: the terminal method, in which they are sterilized together with the milk already in the bottles, and the aseptic method, whereby the milk and feeding equipment are sterilized separately.

The Terminal Method

It is difficult to use the terminal method without special equipment, since bottles full of milk are liable to rattle about if boiled in an ordinary saucepan. However, if your baby is to be completely bottle fed for some months and you wish to make all his feedings once a day, you may decide it is worth buying the necessary equipment. You will need at least six bottles, with caps and nipples. It is essential to have sufficient refrigerator space to store the prepared feedings till needed, there being no point in terminal sterilization if the milk is recontaminated before the baby drinks it.

Calculating Quantities The first step is to work out how much food the baby needs over twenty-four hours. Your doctor calculates this on the basis that a baby needs 2½ ounces (75 ml) of fluid per pound (500 g) of body weight, provided he weighs the expected amount for a baby of his age and build. On this basis, a 10-pound (5 k) baby would need 25 ounces (750 ml) of milk mixture per day. You won't need to be as scientifically accurate as all that because a healthy baby knows best how much he wants. These figures are just to give you a guide as to how much you can expect your baby to want.

Because the milk is sterilized after bottling, you need not use boiled water to mix the feed; utensils used in preparation should be clean but need not be sterile. Divide the mixture between the number of bottles the baby takes during twenty-four hours. Put a nipple on each bottle, followed by a plastic, metal, or paper cap. Place the bottles in a sterilizer rack or a deep kettle and boil for twenty-five minutes. The nipples must remain covered by caps until used. Transfer the bottles to the refrigerator when cooled, warming them up if you wish to before each feeding (see temperature of feeding, p. 95).

Nipples Since there is no chance to strain the milk after boiling, nipples are more likely to become clogged with particles of milk with this method of sterilizing, so make sure the holes are unclogged by vigorously shaking the bottle before feeding your baby.

An alternative is to sterilize the nipples separately, putting them on the bottles before feedings. Provided the nipples are properly sterilized and are kept sterile until use, this is satisfactory in a private household but, technically, the method cannot be called terminal sterilization, which means sterilization of all the feeding and equipment together at the very end of preparation.

The Aseptic Method: Boiling or Soaking

Wash all equipment as described in the previous paragraphs. Boil the bottles, nipples, caps, and utensils (including the measuring cup) needed for preparing the feedings for five minutes and then boil water for the formula for five minutes, allowing a few extra ounces for evaporation. Remeasure the water and add exact amounts of other ingredients. These can be mixed in the utensil used to boil the water. After this, pour it into the sterilized bottles, put on the nipples and caps. Be careful not to touch the inner surface or the tips of the nipples. Refrigerate until ready to use.

Feeding Your Baby

The First Feedings

A newborn baby is offered his first feeding between four and eight hours after birth. The exact timing will depend on the individual baby; a hungry baby will be fed early, whereas one who is still sleeping should be awakened after eight hours, since it is time by then for him to have some sugar, which he will get in his feeding.

The first feedings are given by the mother or the nurse. You may worry that your baby is taking too little, thinking that the milk does not agree with him. It helps if you understand that this is normal, since newborn babies' appetites develop slowly. The breast-fed baby is satisfied with colostrum only for the first two or three days of life, becoming hungrier and sucking more vigorously as the breasts fill with milk (see breast feeding, p. 60). It is natural that a bottle-fed baby should follow a similar pattern, taking very little for the first few days. After this, when he is hungrier, the question of how often to feed him arises. A flexible four-hourly routine suits most babies, though some are happier if fed every three hours at first.

The advice on demand feeding and night feedings given in the chapter on breast feeding (pp. 65f. and 70f.) applies also to bottle-fed babies.

Giving a Bottle

It is as important to feel relaxed and unhurried when giving a bottle as when breast feeding. If you are really comfortable, you will be more responsive to your baby's mood during the feeding and will feel rested at the end of it; if you are uncomfortable, your baby will probably be uncomfortable too. Physical comfort depends on sitting in the right chair. You will be holding the baby and the bottle for perhaps half an hour and may find a low chair with a sloping back, plus a footstool, more satisfactory than a higher chair. A chair with arms of a suitable height may help support your arm, which has to keep the baby's head raised throughout the feeding.

Holding Your Baby

Hold your baby as if he were to feed at the breast but slightly lower, so that you can reach his mouth with the bottle without having to hold your arm up in the air. Always keep the bottle tilted at an angle so that the nipple remains filled with milk; otherwise the baby would be swallowing a lot of air (see pp. 94–95, 436). The baby's head must be raised to reduce the risk of choking. It probably also reduces the risk of milk running back up the Eustachian tubes, which lead from the back of the throat to the middle ear, and setting up infection there. This is more liable to happen with babies than older children, since their Eustachian tubes are wide and short (see ear infections, pp. 456–57).

The danger of ear infection is one reason a baby should never be left lying alone to suck from a propped bottle. Another, even more serious, danger is that while feeding he might choke or inhale regurgitated milk. For these reasons, and because he needs handling and comfort as well as food, a young baby should not be expected to feed himself, even if his mother intends to cuddle him later. The only exception is when the mother of twins or triplets uses a propped bottle to feed one baby while she feeds the other; in this case, she would be watching the baby feed, helping him if he lost the nipple, and she would feed that baby herself at the next feeding (see p. 146).

Responding to the Baby

Giving a bottle is easy, but you do need to give your baby your full attention. As you become more experienced you will respond instinctively to his changing needs during the feeding. He may want a certain amount of guidance at first, just like the breast-fed baby. He may feel frustrated or miserable if not helped. He will set the pace of the feeding if allowed to do so.

The tempo of a breast feeding varies because the flow of milk from the breast changes, as well as the baby's rate of sucking, flowing very quickly at first, so that he gets his milk with very little effort, then slowing down, so that he must suck harder. This variation in the speed of milk flow satisfies the baby's urge to suck as well as his hunger. The bottle-fed baby also tends to take his feeding greedily at the beginning, then slow down, but the rate the milk flows from the bottle depends entirely on how hard he sucks. He can get his food just as easily at the end of the feeding as at the start, provided the hole in the nipple is not blocked and there is no vacuum in the bottle. The build-up of a vacuum is prevented by stopping every now and then to allow air to flow back into the bottle or around the edges of the nipple. Sometimes, with a tightly fitting nipple, you have to lift up one edge to let in the air.

Quick and Slow Feeders

A very hungry baby may finish his milk so quickly that his wish to suck is only half-satisfied. However, your baby usually manages to satisfy both needs if you understand him, allowing pauses for him to play during the feeding when he is older and not expecting him to take the whole bottle at an even pace. You should let him take his own time within reason. You can remind him of the main business of feeding if he forgets it for long, but don't urge him to continue if you judge that this is a sign that he has had enough.

Some babies concentrate hard throughout the feeding, whether on breast or bottle, while others appear to lose interest after a few gulps. Much that applies to the easily distracted breast-fed baby is also relevant to the bottle-fed baby (see breast feeding, pp. 73–74); but when bottle feeding such a baby you know for certain how little he has drunk, and so may spend an unreasonable amount of time trying to make him take more. The baby will win, since he cannot be forced to drink, so after giving him the chance to go on feeding, it is better to assume he has had enough for the time being.

Is He Still Hungry?

If he cries when put in his crib and you think it is because he is still hungry, you can offer him the rest of the bottle; however, do not keep the bottle standing about for more than a few minutes, in case he seems hungry again, because of the risk of bacterial contamination (see preparing the feeding, pp. 87–92). With bottle feeding you can be sure he has been offered enough, so you can be fairly certain he is crying for another reason (see crying, pp. 118f.).

Gas

Please read pages 68 to 70 in the chapter on breast feeding for a discussion on gas. The problem is no different for the bottle-fed baby except that there are two things you should do to prevent excessive swallowing of air. First, the hole in the nipple should be the correct size (pp. 88–89). If it is too small, the frustrated baby may take in excessive air as a result of his vigorous attempts to get milk through the hole, although he is more likely to go to sleep. Second, see that the bottle is tilted to fill the nipple with milk while your baby sucks; if you hold the bottle horizontally he will be swallowing half milk and half air, thereby being bound to blow himself up like a balloon.

Temperature of the Feeding

It used to be thought that babies should always be fed with milk warmed to body heat. However, many mothers have found that their babies have drunk cold milk if necessary, for example, on a train journey, when they have been unable to warm the bottle. Although they may have felt uneasy about this, in case it was harmful in some way, it is in fact not harmful. Most adults prefer cold milk, and even the youngest baby will take a cold feeding as readily as a warm one; this has no ill-effects. Bottles can be taken straight from the refrigerator and the baby fed at once, making electric bottle warmers and pans of hot water unnecessary. But although it is not essential, most mothers will probably continue to warm their young babies' feedings, feeling happier that they should have their milk at body heat, as breast-fed babies do (see travel, p. 366).

Whatever you decide, it is useful to know that a feeding need not be interrupted to reheat the bottle if it gets cold; a night feeding can be given without the trouble of warming it up in the middle of the night, or the necessity of keeping it warm in a Thermos for several hours, with the increased risk of bacteria multiplying in the warm milk. Some babies who are used to having their milk warm refuse a change to cold bottles. Similarly, babies brought up on cold feedings may refuse a warm one. This has been found with babies originally cared for in those premature baby units where it is no longer the custom to warm feedings; when sent home these babies have refused to take warm feedings and are only prepared to accept cold ones! This is a salutary warning to those dogmatists who say babies must have feedings at the same temperature as a breast-fed baby. I suspect babies, being conservative people, may insist on keeping to any regime to which they have become accustomed.

To test whether a feeding is too hot, sprinkle a few drops on the back of your hand, taking care to avoid touching the nipple itself. If it feels hot, then it is too hot and could hurt your baby's mouth. The bottle should be cooled in cold water; holding it under a running tap is the quickest way. If you want the feeding to be at body heat, the milk tested on your hand should feel neither hot nor cold.

7

Looking After Your New Baby

Help and Advice

Visiting Your Doctor's Office or Clinic

If you go to your pediatrician's office, he will know you already. This cuts out preliminary explanations and you won't have to fill in your baby's background. Another advantage of attending your doctor's office is that you won't receive conflicting or overlapping advice on baby care, which can easily happen if there are two doctors in your baby's life. Doctors, like everyone else, have differing opinions on the best ways of bringing up a baby, so it is not surprising if they sometimes give different answers to the same question. For example, "When shall I start the baby on carrots?" may get the reply "Today" from one doctor, and "The month after next" from another. This is because there is no exact answer to this or to many other questions a mother asks; but a new mother may wish there was, so a doctor tends to give her a cut-and-dried answer. If you are ever confused by apparently contradictory advice, it is best to ask your own doctor how important it is to stick exactly to what he says.

If he belongs to a group practice, one member of the group may run the clinic for all the children in the practice. The exact arrangements and scope of the well baby clinic vary from practice to practice.

Weighing Your Baby

As part of his assessment of progress, the doctor may weigh your baby, but the scale should no longer be the centerpiece of the office or clinic. Too many mothers worry needlessly over their babies' weight. The automatic weigh-in, which places far too much emphasis on weight as a guide to a baby's progress, is being discouraged by doctors and nurses.

The ideal arrangement is for mothers to be able to weigh their own babies at the office if they wish to. You can then discuss your baby's weight if you are concerned. This removes the old emphasis on weighing and saves valuable staff time. Obviously, if the doctor or nurse is concerned about the weight of your baby—and this will more often be because he looks overweight (p. 190) rather than underweight—he or she will weigh him.

Of course, you may enjoy plotting your baby's weight curve, and weight can be a useful measurement for a doctor to make. But don't forget that there are other, far more important, measurements. A baby's health and progress should be judged by his energy, his progressive development, and his appearance, not by how much he gains in any one week. The opposite also applies: if he has gained the "average" amount but you are worried about him, then don't take the evidence of the scales as proof that everything is all right. Occasional weighing is interesting as a record for the baby book, but it should not dominate your opinion of your baby—or your opinion of yourself as a mother (see growth, pp. 208f.).

Immunization

At the office you will be advised about immunization, which can be given there. Alternatively, if your family doctor is not a pediatrician, he may still be prepared to give the immunizations at his office. It is important to keep an up-to-date record of your baby's immunization program (see immunization, p. 261).

Fringe Benefits

There are plenty of fringe benefits that make going to the doctor's office or clinic worthwhile, particularly for an inexperienced mother. As well as talking to the staff, you may be able to buy vitamins and brand-name foods. There may be a bulletin board, with advertisements of sales and needs, bargains in secondhand baby gear, and offers of baby-sitting exchanges (see p. 24).

The clinic is a good place to meet other mothers and their babies and to pick up tips about play groups, shopping for baby things, and how to simplify life with children generally. Everyone at the clinic is interested in babies, and this in itself is comforting if you live far away from relatives and friends and feel rather alone with your new responsibility. It is a social occasion, so although you can ask advice of a visiting nurse, you may find yourself looking forward to visiting the clinic.

The Daily Care of Your Baby

Bathing

In some hospitals, babies are bathed just after birth and regularly afterward. The practice of waiting until the umbilical cord stump has dropped off before bathing the baby is now known to be unnecessary; if the navel is dried gently after the bath, no harm can result.

If your baby is not bathed during his first week in the hospital, it is because the vernix caseosa, a greasy substance covering the skin at birth (p. 40), is thought to act as a protection against infection and so is left on the skin for a few days. Another reason for washing his face and bottom only, instead of bathing him during the first week, is to avoid the possibility of chilling.

How Often?

It is usual, but not essential, to bathe a baby every day once he is a week or so old. If you are nervous about bathing your new baby or find it hard to fit a regular bathtime into the day, you can compromise by "topping and tailing" him; that is, washing his head, face, and bottom only, every day. You can wash him all over every two or three days.

A very young baby dislikes being bathed; the freedom to kick and splash, which he later enjoys, seems to frighten him at first. So it is important to hold him securely, cradling him in one arm while using your free hand to wash or rinse his body, and to get the bath over as soon as possible. He gets cold quickly in the early weeks, while his body-temperature regulating mechanism is inefficient.

An older baby enjoys playing in his bath; you will probably bathe him daily because he enjoys it so much, as well as because he gets dirtier once he starts moving about.

When?

This is entirely up to you. There is no need to fix a time of day unless you want to. A new baby has no sense of time and does not know if it is morning or evening. A popular bathtime for young babies, because it suits their mothers, is midmorning, when fathers and older children have left. In some families, the baby is bathed in the evening, when father is at home and can help.

Should your baby be bathed before or after a feeding? Either time is all right, but one or the other may agree with him better. If bathed before a feeding he may be so hungry that he screams throughout, which is nerve-racking for both of you, and may tire him so that he feeds less well afterward. However, after a feeding, when all he wants is to sleep, the bath may wake him up or make him sick. You will have to find out which time suits your baby. Sometimes, giving a bath when the baby wakes up but is not urgently hungry is best; a bath can help you both through a time of day when he is wakeful or restless because he wants company and play.

The time of the bath can be changed as your baby's pattern of sleep and wakefulness changes. A baby who is awake and playing for much of the day tends to need a bath or thorough washing in the evening before going to bed.

Where?

It is uncomfortable bending over the family tub to bathe a small baby, so, although once he sits up the baby enjoys playing in the big bath, a small bath or bowl is more convenient for a new baby.

Rigid plastic baths come with or without plugs. Plugless baths are generally cheaper but have to be emptied by baling out or at the sink. An ordinary plastic bowl will do as a baby bath as long as the plastic is strong enough not to bend and spill the water when it is carried. If you have to carry water some distance, a bath with a plug, which empties the bathwater directly into a bucket, is easier to manage than a plugless one.

Some baths are sold with stands; you sit on a low chair to bathe the baby. There is no particular advantage in using a stand, and some are a bit flimsy. The alternative is to place the bath on a table or chest and either stand or sit on a high stool.

Your baby can be bathed in an ordinary sink or wash basin, but it is a nuisance having to clear and clean out the sink first, and the faucets may bump or burn him. Tie some cloth around the faucets to prevent this happening.

Giving the Bath

You will be shown how to bathe your baby before leaving the hospital, or at home by a visiting nurse. But although you will probably bathe the baby at least once under supervision, it is very different when you are alone. You may feel everything ought to be done just as you were shown, in a particular sequence, and worry if it is not. However, the bathtime ritual can be as elaborate or as simple as you like, given a few essentials.

Keeping Your Baby Warm

The first essential is that your baby must not get cold, so the room should be warm and the water the right temperature, about as warm as his body. Test the water with your elbow; it should feel warm rather than hot. A bath thermometer is unnecessary, since you do not need to know the exact temperature of the water; however, if you feel unhappy without one at first, it should register about 29.4°C (85°F).

If you wash your baby on your lap before putting him in the water, it will be cooler by the time you put him in, so have a small pitcher of hot water ready, to heat up the bath water. However, it is safer not to do this if you have another small child who might knock it over and burn himself. Always pour the cold water into the bath first; hot water first can make the bottom of the bath scald the baby. Get into this habit from the beginning, since when the baby is older he may scald himself if left alone for a moment. An older child who got into the bath thinking it was ready could scald himself fatally.

Advance Preparations

If you keep your baby waiting once he is undressed, he gets cold and unhappy. Everything necessary for washing, drying, and dressing him should be at hand before you undress him, arranged so that you do not have to grope for them while holding the slippery baby on your lap. Arrange his clean clothes in a pile in the order in which you will want them, with shirt and diaper on top; you will then save time when dressing him.

Special soap or towels are unnecessary. Any brand of toilet soap is suitable, provided it is thoroughly rinsed off with clean water. Towels should be soft and kept separately for the baby's use only. Use a soft washcloth for his face.

Your baby can be undressed on a bed or table or on your lap. A waterproof sheet or apron topped by a towel is needed to protect you or the bed. Leave his shirt and diaper on while you wash his face and scalp, keeping him wrapped in a towel unless it is very warm.

If he is to go to bed after the bath, prepare his crib or baby carriage beforehand. In fact, don't fill the bath or undress the baby until everything is ready. At first you will probably forget something, but it soon becomes automatic.

The Face

Wash his face with plain water for the first few weeks, using a soft washcloth and gently wiping from the middle toward the sides. Do not cover his whole face with the washcloth, because this will frighten him. Dry by blotting rather than wiping. The closed eyelids should be wiped gently.

It is unnecessary and dangerous to poke things into his nose or ears to clean them, or to wash inside his mouth. Cotton-tipped swabs are useful for cleaning outside and behind his ears, not inside them. You could damage the delicate lining of the nose and ears by attempting to clean them inside. Your baby's nose is kept clean by sneezing, and the wax in his ears (see below) moves naturally toward the opening of the ear canal. Never put drops into his nose or ears without your doctor's advice. His mouth should be left alone until tooth cleaning begins, when his first tooth arrives (pp. 253–54).

Wax in the Ear

Wax is made inside the ear in order to remove the dust, which sticks to it, from the ear canal. The amount of wax made varies from one individual to another and is increased in dusty atmospheres. Never be tempted to try to clean out the wax from inside the canal; all you need do is to clean away the wax that you can see coming out of the canal.

The Scalp

Wash your baby's scalp with water at each bathtime, using soap or shampoo once or twice a week. A special baby shampoo stings the eyes less than ordinary shampoos, but be careful to keep it away from his eyes in any case.

With his body wrapped in a towel, hold him so that his head is over the edge of the bath and wet his scalp with your free hand. Don't be afraid to wash the soft spot (see fontanel, p. 39). Many babies get patches of cradle cap (p. 430) in this area because their mothers are afraid to touch the soft spot.

All traces of soap or shampoo must be thoroughly rinsed away, so if you wash his hair at the end of bathtime, have a pitcher of clean water ready for the final rinsing. Dry his head with the end of the towel he is wrapped in. The older baby with long, thick hair need not have his scalp rinsed so frequently but should have his hair washed at reasonable intervals.

The Body

When your baby's face and scalp are clean and dry, take off his shirt and diaper, first getting off the worst of the mess with a clean part of the diaper if he has soiled it. Wash the rest of him, beginning at the top. You may prefer to soap your baby's arms and legs and body before putting him into the bath to rinse him, because it is difficult to hold and soap a slippery, and often crying, new baby while he is in the water. He could be bathed entirely on your lap, being rinsed with a washcloth wrung out in clean water, but make sure all the soap is off. You may find it more convenient to use one of the new special liquids you put into the bath instead of soap. This way you just rinse your baby all over with the bath water.

Start by washing his neck. This can be tricky, since young babies have short necks with creases that easily become moist and sore unless washed and dried properly. Running a soapy finger inside the crease and then rinsing is perhaps the best way of cleaning between folds.

Wash under the arms by gently flexing the elbow and moving it backward so that his armpit is exposed. Be sure to dry here, since this is another spot that easily becomes moist and irritated. Don't rely on powder to soak up dampness. You must wash and dry the folds and creases in his groins and thighs thoroughly for the same reason. If you do notice redness in any crease, your doctor or visiting nurse may give you a cream to deal with it (see pp. 430–31).

Turn the baby over and wash his back and bottom. You need not soap him all over if you bathe him every day, particularly if he seems to have a dry skin. The diaper area, face, and hands should be washed every day.

Genitals

If your baby is a girl, you should not wash inside the lips of the vulva. Some mothers become obsessional about washing the vulva; this is a mistake (see Chapter 32, pp. 447–48). The only point to remember is that a girl's genitals must be washed and wiped from the front toward the anus, never the other way around; this is to prevent infection reaching the vagina or bladder from the bowels.

Do not pull back the baby boy's foreskin to wash the end of the penis. Just wash the outside of his genitals in the normal way, being sure to dry gently in the folds (see care of the foreskin, pp. 46–47).

Nails

Nail cutting is best done while your baby is asleep, since small fingernails are difficult enough to cut without the added problem of movement. Later, it will probably be most convenient to cut his nails immediately after his bath, with him on your knee. Cut his nails straight across with scissors. Avoid using nail clippers, which shatter the delicate nails of young children.

Navel

It does your baby no harm to be bathed before his navel has healed. Dry it thoroughly after bathing him. If the navel seems a little moist, it can be cleaned with a cotton ball soaked in alcohol, but any redness or discharge should be seen by your doctor or visiting nurse.

Holding Your Baby in the Bath

If your baby is already washed, you will have both hands free to lower and hold him in the water. You will feel more confident at first with only a few inches of water in the bath.

Put one arm under his shoulders, supporting the back of his head, with your hand holding him under his armpit. Your other arm can go under his legs while you lower him into the water; once he's in, you can use this hand to swish water over him. Some baby baths slope at one end to support your arm as you hold your baby's back and head.

Keep him in the bath for only a few moments at first. When he is older and not so liable to become cold quickly, he will begin to enjoy splashing deliberately and can stay in longer. Many babies begin enjoying the bath after the first few weeks. It will be easier by then to soap and wash him in the bath, since you will have acquired the knack of holding him and washing him at the same time.

Drying

Lay your baby on a towel and blot him dry, or wrap him in one towel to dry off most of the moisture and have another ready to use if needed. Keep him covered with a towel while you dry his arms and legs. You may have to turn the baby on his side to get him dry between all the creases. Dab him dry gently with a soft towel, rather than rubbing him.

The towel he lies on is liable to become damp, so move him to a dry area to dress him. Put his shirt on first to keep him warm while you deal with the diaper.

Talcum powder is not essential, but it makes the baby smell nice. If you do use it, make sure his skin is quite dry before applying it, otherwise it gets soggy and irritated. Shake it gently into your hand to prevent clouds of powder floating about near your baby's face; it is bad for him to inhale it.

Safety

Once your baby can sit up, he can be bathed in the family tub. Never leave him alone in it even when he can sit steadily, because he could topple over and be unable to get up again or he might turn on the hot-water faucet and scald himself. It is better to ignore the doorbell or telephone, or to wrap him in a towel and take him with you to answer it.

A diaper or a special mat in the bottom of the bath helps to prevent a baby slipping over and also makes it a warmer place to sit. You may feel safest of all if he shares his bath with you, lying supported between your legs.

Let him play in the bath. He can safely pour water from cup to cup; if he drinks some, it won't do him any harm.

Washing Diapers at Home

It is unnecessary to boil diapers every time, although you may need to when you want to whiten them or remove stains. At other times you should always wash them in very hot water and rinse thoroughly.

Use only pure soap flakes or powders. Detergents are unsatisfactory because they are more difficult to rinse out completely than soap products and they cause more irritation than soap particles if traces remain in the washed diaper. "Biological" stains will respond to soaking in any washing powder. At a launderette use your own soap powder instead of the detergent provided.

If diapers are always put right into water as soon as they are taken off, they will be easier to wash and remain softer and whiter for longer. If your baby dirties several diapers each day, have two pails with lids, one for soiled and one for wet diapers. Plastic pails are light, but make sure the handles are reliable. Put soiled diapers into soapy water and wet diapers into ordinary cold water. Remove the worst of the mess from a dirty diaper by holding it firmly under the flushing water in the toilet; sometimes you need to scrape off the mess first with a knife. It is also worth swilling a very sodden wet diaper in running water before dropping it in the pail of cold water; otherwise the water in the pail quickly becomes concentrated and smelly.

Before washing diapers, wring out as much moisture as possible, in a spin drier if you have one, so that the hot soapy washing water is not too diluted when you put them in. If a diaper is very stained, rub it with soap before putting it into the washing machine, or boil it separately. Don't use bleach to remove stains; boil or soak instead. Rinsing is as important as washing, since particles of soap, and particularly of detergent, irritate a baby's skin. The spin drier of a twin-tub machine may be too small to allow for thorough rinsing; if so, remove the diapers and give them a final rinse in the sink (see diaper rash, p. 431).

Special products to soften diapers can be added to the final rinse but these are unnecessary unless toweling diapers have become stiff. (Never iron toweling; this hardens it.) Diapers feel softer if dried outdoors.

Changing the Diaper

When to Do It

There is no need to wake a baby just to change his wet or dirty diaper. Babies sleep quite happily in wet or dirty diapers and only dislike it when they also feel cold. Occasionally, a baby cries when he soils his diaper, but this is soon discovered when you investigate the reason for the crying. It is always worth changing a wet diaper if your baby wakes and cries, since the activity and handling in itself may comfort him. In general, he should not lie for hours in a wet or dirty diaper, since this encourages diaper rash (p. 431), but there is no need to change him unless he is awake for some other reason, such as feeding. A larger baby produces more urine and may need changing more often for this reason, and because he gets cold more readily when moving around on the floor.

It is generally sufficient to change a young baby after each feeding, unless his wetness makes you uncomfortable while feeding him. A small baby may be so hungry that he needs immediate feeding far more urgently than a clean diaper. If changing his diaper after feedings seems to wake him up when he is falling asleep, you could change him before feedings instead—but he is likely to be wet, and probably dirty too, in the early weeks before the end of the feeding, so you will have to change him again if you want him to go to sleep wearing a clean, dry diaper.

How to Do It

Get everything you need together before you start. It is better to expect every diaper to be dirty at first than to have to look for the necessary things while your baby waits. The diaper can be changed on your lap or on a flat surface. Protect your lap with toweling or a plastic apron; protect furniture with a towel or special plastic-covered pad. The baby can be changed in his crib or carriage if you can reach him easily and the bedding is protected.

Cleaning the Baby

There is no need to wash your baby's bottom every time you change a wet diaper. If he is dirty, you should clean him gently with cotton balls soaked in warm water. Some of the mess can first be wiped away with a tissue or a clean corner of the diaper; be especially gentle if this is toweling.

Soap is unnecessary, provided your baby is bathed daily. You may prefer to use mineral oil or baby lotion instead of fetching warm water; some babies' skin gets sore if washed too often with soap and water. You could use a soft cloth kept specially for cleaning the diaper area, but absorbent cotton or tissues that can be thrown away are simpler.

Wipe a baby girl in the direction away from the vagina and toward the anus (see p. 102). Use dabbing movements when washing and drying your baby's skin. Be sure to wash and dry thoroughly in the groin and the folds of flesh in the thighs. It is not necessary to use baby creams or powders at each diaper change, unless you want to or your doctor has advised a particular cream for diaper rash or soreness. Ordinary Vaseline or zinc oxide suits most babies as much as the more expensive brand-name baby products.

8

Sleeping and Crying

Sleep Requirements

I am often asked how long a child should sleep at night. The answer is for as long as he wants to—and not any fixed number of hours. In the past, doctors and others have given the impression that a child requires a certain quota of sleep according to his age. Some have even created tables to indicate these sleep requirements. This is all nonsense; a child no more needs a fixed amount of sleep than he requires a fixed amount of food. Individual variation is enormous. On the whole, it seems that bright children need less sleep than others and often less than their parents! No harm comes to the child from this; in fact, if he spends his time at night playing, instead of sleeping, he is opting to work overtime and will learn more. His parents have problems but he does not.

There is no truth in the idea that if a child doesn't sleep his brain will tire, or that he needs his sleep in order to grow. The only reason a child needs to go to sleep is to give his parents a rest—a very sound reason. Whether he has enough sleep should be judged by his energy during the day rather than by the number of hours he sleeps at night.

This individual difference shows right from the start. One young baby may need less sleep than another older one, just as one adult needs eight hours a night while another functions well on five. Some babies sleep nearly all the time at first, waking briefly for feedings. This kind of baby makes his mother feel she is doing everything right, whereas a baby who is frequently wakeful from the beginning tends to make her feel that she is doing something wrong, and that he would sleep more if only she fed him or managed him more efficiently. This mother needs to be given confidence that she is handling him well and that his behavior reflects his different temperament.

Reasons for Wakefulness

It is more convenient to have the first kind of baby; for one thing, it is easier to finish the housework and catch up on your own sleep. But the amount each baby sleeps reflects his inborn sleeping pattern as well as the way he is handled by his mother. Feeding and sleeping patterns are to some extent independent (see pp. 118–19), and filling a baby with food does not guarantee so many hours' sleep. Hunger is not the only reason a small baby wakes up and stays awake.

Don't feel that wakefulness always needs an explanation, or that you should try to get him back to sleep as quickly as possible. A baby needs to be awake to register and respond to impressions and stimuli, that is, to learn. If a crying baby stops crying when picked up and remains contented when carried about and entertained, he is showing that he is already a bright, active person who wants to be up and doing, not lying around in bed all day.

Such a baby often makes up for being extra time-consuming at the beginning by learning early how to occupy himself when awake: he watches the movement of his hands and fingers, sometimes putting them in his mouth; he listens to noises and looks around, sometimes trying to copy the noises in return.

Sleep Rhythm and Feeding

A new baby takes time to settle into a feeding and sleeping routine that suits adults; that is, a routine consisting of long periods of sleep interspersed with infrequent demands for food. When he is eating larger quantities and sleeping longer stretches, his total amount of sleep in the twenty-four hours may be higher than it was in his first month. This does not mean he slept too little at the beginning, but merely that he has settled down into a routine. On the other hand, a baby may sleep progressively less as he grows older, so that by the time he is six months old he is awake all day except for one or two short naps. Both patterns and all the variations in between are normal. There is no need to tot up your baby's total sleeping time, any more than you should measure the amount of food he eats.

Putting Your Baby to Bed

Swaddling

In developed countries like the United States it is usual for a baby to be wrapped up securely for the first month before being put in his carry-bed or crib to sleep. A newborn baby placed unswaddled on a flat surface will cry and flail his arms and legs about as a reflex reaction (see development, p. 221). Placing your hand on his stomach to fix his body stops the reflexes and the crying. The hand makes him feel secure. Wrapping him up has the same comforting effect; it stops him rolling about and seems to help him make the adjustment from the confined space of the uterus to the limitless outside world.

Babies in developing countries have the good fortune to spend much of their time wrapped up on their mothers' bodies, not alone in a crib, and this is probably even more comfortable. After a few weeks, a baby dislikes being wrapped up tightly, preferring to move his arms and legs and, perhaps, suck his fingers.

Sleeping Position: Side, Back, or Front?

Until your baby can turn himself over, you have to decide for him whether he sleeps on his side, back, or front. You could start him off sleeping on his side, but when swaddling is discarded he will roll over if put in this position and should be put on his back or stomach. Babies seldom stay sleeping on their side until about six months old. If he sleeps on his stomach, any milk brought up will trickle out of the side of his mouth rather than run back down his throat to choke him, as might happen if he were flat on his back. It is now felt to be safer for babies to sleep in the prone position, on their stomachs, when young. For the first year, do not use a pillow, because it is just possible for this to impede the breathing of a young baby (see p. 25).

Many babies prefer sleeping on their stomachs, with their heads turned to one side. In this prone position they maintain their body heat better and have been shown to sleep longer and rest better. One later disadvantage of this position is that when the baby is old enough to lie awake happily looking around and amusing himself for a while after waking up, he will be able to see only the sides of his carry-bed or crib. A baby reaches this stage before he can turn over by himself, so he may cry from frustration and boredom until someone arrives to help. However, by this age he may be sleeping on his side.

Where Should He Sleep?

Babies in developing countries share living space and sleeping space with their mothers, and often with the rest of the family as well. Such a baby rarely disturbs the other sleepers with prolonged crying in the night, since, if he wakes up hungry, he feeds at his mother's breast and goes back to sleep. His mother is not worried about "training" him to last the night without a feeding, since feeding him at night is not inconvenient.

In developed countries such as our own the situation has been different, but times are changing. It used to be considered ideal for a baby to have a room to himself and automatic that he slept in his own crib. This was based on the belief that a baby should be trained from the start to sleep by himself. However, you will find it easier and your baby will be more content if for the first two or three months you have him sleeping in a crib in your room, even if he has a room of his own, so that he can be picked up and fed in the night with the least possible effort. Place the crib beside your bed, so that you need not get out of bed unless his diaper needs changing.

Don't be frightened about having your baby in bed with you all
night. There is no risk of overlying (see below), and it brings him
closer to you and your husband if he sleeps between you. I used to
be concerned that the baby might fall out of a bed in which his mother
only was sleeping, but this does not happen. A baby snuggles up to
his mother, not away from her.

Overlying

The practice of feeding the baby in bed has been frowned on in the
United States and the United Kingdom because of the possibility of
overlying, should mother and baby fall asleep together afterward.
The idea that a baby suffocates if his mother lies against his face and
prevents him breathing is incorrect; a normal baby wriggles if he
cannot breathe, until he can breathe easily again; so if you and your
baby do happen to fall asleep in bed after a night feeding, don't feel
guilty about it—"sleep feeding" is natural.

One important safeguard. Do not have your baby in bed with
you if you have taken a sleeping pill or are under the influence of
alcohol, since these dull a mother's normal reactions, which guard
her baby.

Minimizing Disturbance

If you find it difficult to sleep because of your baby's sniffing and
grunts, or if you tend to keep looking in the crib to check that he is
still breathing, you may be one of those mothers who prefer to have
their baby sleep out of earshot at night from the start. This is perfectly understandable. Another point to remember is that your baby
may wake some time before he demands a feeding. If you wake up
as soon as he first stirs, you miss the extra sleep you might have had
if he were in another room. Once you know he is awake and will
probably want a feeding before he goes back to sleep, it is hard to go
back to sleep yourself. When this happens more than once a night, as
may well be the case at first, you can lose a good hour's sleep. It also
takes you longer to go to sleep after feeding your baby if you lie
awake until you are sure he is fast asleep.

Alternatives to His Own Room

When there is no separate bedroom for your baby, any other room,
or even a landing, will do as a sleeping area, provided he is not in a
draft. You can let him have the living room for his bedroom by starting off the night with him in your bedroom and moving him out when
you go to bed. This is simple while he is in a small carry-bed, but

becomes more of a problem once he has graduated to a full-size crib, which cannot be moved around so easily; in addition, he will by then be old enough to notice the move and may be awakened by it. A more satisfactory solution, once your baby has reached this age (about six months) is to give him a permanent corner of a room for the whole night; perhaps this could be curtained off, partitioned, or screened from the rest of the room.

The Family Bed

There is a growing tendency to return to the family bed. Single beds and separate bedrooms are part of a social custom that grew up during the eighteenth century. Prior to this the family shared the same bed. Family beds and co-family sleeping is still the practice in many parts of the world.

Those families in a Western society who have reverted to the family bed speak warmly of its advantages to the whole family. New bonds are created, and father, although away most of the day, is no longer a remote figure, because he spends the night close to his children.

The question of sexual relations is always raised, but those who share a family bed say this is not a problem, although other rooms may need to be used at times. Bed wetting is also not the problem that might be imagined.

I always used to advise parents against bringing their children into bed with them, but I have now changed. When it is clear that a child is too frightened to go to sleep by himself, no harm results from bringing him into the parental bed, and parents will not be creating a rod for their backs, as commonly feared.

Children brought up in a family bed decide to leave it at a variable age. Some are ready to take to their own bed around the age of two years, but others want longer. Sometimes they decide to vary the pattern, choosing their own bed some nights and the family bed on others. Sometimes they decide to share with an older sibling who has already left the family bed. Knowing that they can come into their parents' bed in the middle of the night makes the transition easier. It is all so natural that many parents cannot remember exactly when each child decided to make the change.

Many parents say that they sleep better in a family bed because they are not frightened about what is happening to their young children. One mother told me she could not sleep unless her baby was beside her. Parents who are particularly frightened about "crib death" (p. 650) have been relieved to have their babies in bed with them.

The crib is probably still the best place for the daytime rest, when the child faces none of the fears of the dark and is ready for sleep.

Using the Baby Carriage

Is a baby carriage essential (p. 28)? A baby can sleep outside in the fresh air in his carry-bed and can be taken farther afield by car, but most mothers have to walk and to take their babies with them. In developed countries, carrying a baby in a cloth pouch-type baby carrier or in a carrier in a frame on the back is becoming more popular as a substitute for pushing him in a carriage. It certainly stimulates the baby to look around and see what is going on. If you do carry your baby this way (and it can be a useful method in crowded shops and narrow streets), ignore the disapproving looks you may occasionally get from the older generation: the baby enjoys seeing the world from up high, and it will not strain his back or impair his posture. However, a baby carriage is more suitable for regular expeditions in an unreliable climate.

A baby enjoys being pushed in a carriage. It sometimes soothes him if he is restless, and when he can sit up he loves watching the changing scene as well as being able to see his mother or father. A stroller has the disadvantage that in many models the baby can only look away from his mother. For the first month a baby may sleep better if kept quiet, but if you have to take him shopping in the baby carriage the day after getting home from the hospital, the movement will do him no harm.

A baby can sleep outside in his carriage from birth in hot countries and from the age of about one week in cooler climates. Fresh air is good for him so long as he is not too cold or too hot, but there is no need to feel that he must have a set amount of time outdoors, whatever the weather or circumstances. In freezing weather or fog keep him inside for as long as necessary; if this is impossible, ensure that he is warmly covered and make the outing brief.

If your baby is sleeping outside, make sure he is getting some fresh air. There is no point in his being outside if he is lying at the bottom of a high-sided carriage with the hood up and carriage cover on, so that no fresh air can reach him. It will be stuffy inside the baby carriage, and he would get more air sleeping in his crib in a well-ventilated room. When the sun is bright, it is better to protect the baby with a canopy than with the hood, since a canopy provides shade while allowing air to circulate around him. When buying a canopy, take the carriage and make sure that it fits securely. If you park the carriage without a canopy in the shade, check that it remains in the shade. Some baby carriages are provided with little net curtains attached to the hood to protect the baby from heat and glare.

Park the baby carriage away from drafts in all weathers, and in cold weather dress your baby warmly and give him sufficient blankets. He doesn't need a hat, because he is well protected by the sides of the carriage, unless it is so cold that you feel he must have one. Mittens can be used once he is no longer swaddled, if his hands get cold, but by the time he has learned to suck his thumb and fingers he will probably be happier without mittens. Cold hands seldom matter so long as his body is warm, but obviously if his hands get red and puffy, you will have to revert to mittens for a time.

A cat net is essential if there is any risk of cats wandering near the baby carriage. A fine mesh insect net is useful if insects are a problem and it doubles as a cat net.

Finally, your baby should not be left in his carriage for hours on end once he has started to crawl and move about. Even if he is content to sit in the baby carriage for much of the day—although most babies are not content to sit there once they have discovered the fun of exploring—he needs the chance to try out his arms and legs and play elsewhere for at least part of the day. He learns a lot in his carriage once he is a few weeks old, watching moving leaves, shadows, and clouds as well as his own hands, and later, when he can sit up, looking at other babies and his surroundings when you take him out. He may try out his voice to match the rhythm of the baby carriage along a bumpy road and seem to demand to go out when he sees you put on your coat. But there is such a thing as a "carriagebound" baby, one who is left in the carriage all day, except for feedings; some babies are even given a propped bottle in the carriage, because this is less trouble. His mother may ignore his protests, or he seems content, so she leaves him there. Of course, there is no need to pick him up when he is perfectly happy. You can usually rely on a baby to let you know when he is bored and has exhausted the possibilities of amusing himself in the baby carriage, but don't ignore him if he is bored. If he seems content to sit in his carriage all day, he should be encouraged to enjoy himself more actively by having the chance to play elsewhere as well. Spending too long in the carriage reduces the opportunities for learning other activities.

On the other hand, you may have one of those babies who resolutely refuse to stay in their carriages for a minute longer than an outing lasts—even when fast asleep, they wake up the moment they reach the front door. This type of baby sleeps better in his crib; let him do so and don't worry about lack of fresh air. Open

his window and take him out when you can and this will be sufficient.

Sharing a Room with Other Children

Waking Each Other

Should a baby sleep with older brothers and sisters? This can be a
success, depending on the children and baby concerned. Many children sleep through a baby's crying, night feedings, and diaper changing. Others wake up and have more trouble falling asleep again than
the baby. If a child is worried by the arrival of a new baby, he may
seem to force himself to wake at night whenever the baby does, in
order to snatch some of his mother's attention and be like the baby.
Perhaps he needs more attention during the day or would respond to
extra attention at bedtime, such as a few minutes alone with his
mother or father, instead of sharing a general putting-to-bed. In any
case, bedtime should be staggered according to age so that older
children are given the privilege of staying up later than younger
brothers and sisters. Children usually accept this approach and unnecessary jealousy can thereby be reduced.

If your baby has to share a room with an older child or children,
assume this will work but feed the baby in another room or wheel
his bed out temporarily if his crying disturbs the others. Most children sleep soundly through activity nearby, especially if noise is kept
down and there is not too much light: use a dim lamp, or light
from the landing, to attend to the baby. Toward dawn, when sleep
is lighter, the baby's noises tend to wake the children more readily, with the result that they get up earlier than they would
otherwise. Try to persuade them to play in another room if the
baby wants to go back to sleep, or move the baby so that they can
play.

Sharing when Older

Once the baby is sleeping through the night, and provided the other
children have similar sleeping habits, sharing a room usually presents
few problems. But sooner or later the children want their own rooms
for other reasons—mainly stemming from an increasing desire to
organize their own possessions in peace (see furnishing your child's
room, pp. 22–23).

There is no harm in children of the opposite sex sharing a room
until they near puberty, but the children themselves often object as
their tastes in activities, furnishings, and friends begin to diverge.

Children of the same sex may also object to sharing, particularly if the gap in age or temperament is wide (p. 23).

Avoiding Problems

Influencing His Attitude

Although it is impossible to make a baby or small child sleep longer than he wants to, it is possible to influence his attitude toward sleep, bedtime, and the right of the rest of the family to peaceful nights. Some children are undoubtedly more difficult to influence than others, but how you handle the situation can make the difference between a problem being short-lived or long-lasting; other problems can be avoided altogether.

Accustoming Him to Noise

From the start, accustom your child to sleep through noise. If you like to have the radio or television on, don't feel you must keep it soft because of the baby. The worst thing you can do is to adopt a "Hush! Don't wake the baby" approach, since he will then start to wake at the slightest noise and you will probably be setting his pattern for life.

Most babies can sleep through a high level of continuous noise, provided they are not brought up to expect total silence when going to sleep. Some children, used to sleeping near a busy road, complain of the quietness when on vacation in the country. Sudden noises are more likely to wake your baby than continuous sounds—another child crying out in the night, for instance. He will probably fall asleep again easily if the crying child is dealt with promptly; if not, a drink of water may soothe him, or a diaper change. One drawback of children sleeping together is that when one child cries his parents' first aim is to stop him from waking the others. This means you tackle the problem more sensitively from his point of view than you would otherwise; perhaps you should give the child the chance to go back to sleep without going to him. You may take him into your bed in order to stop him from making a noise, which you might not otherwise do (see crying at night, p. 121).

A young child may wake the baby by trying to play with him. If this is a regular problem, the baby could begin the evening sleeping in another room and be moved when the older child is asleep.

Nights Are for Sleeping

New babies alternate between sleep and wakefulness with no notion of day or night. Gradually, a baby responds to the rhythm of the family, eating and playing mainly during the day, sleeping mainly at night. But an interval of months, or even years, elapses before his sleep pattern matches that of his parents.

You can help this process along by conveying the impression from the start that you expect your baby to spend his nights sleeping; not because he needs so many hours of sleep per night (pp. 107–8), but because parents need a rest from children. Unless you live by night, not by day, and want your children to do the same (difficult once they start school), unless you are ready to spend your evenings in their company or are prepared to work round-the-clock shifts in child care, assume from the beginning that they are not going to occupy your nights as well as your days.

Crying in the Early Days

The first weeks at home with a new baby may be idyllic—if your home is effortless to run and if he turns out to be the ideal baby, eating at the right times and sleeping between feedings, as a newborn baby is reputed to do. But more often than not it isn't like this, particularly with a first baby. However carefully you have planned in advance, there seems far too little time to keep house as well as look after your baby: this alone takes most of the twenty-four hours.

Why Does He Cry So Much and Sleep So Little?

Your baby seems to be programed by the wrong computer. Apparently he does not know he is expected to sleep most of the time between feedings. He wants feeding, or something, far more frequently than any reasonable baby. Even when he is asleep, you begin to wonder when he'll wake up and what he'll want next, so that, after a few days, you may feel as if the whole of your life will revolve for evermore around the insatiable needs of a perplexing infant.

You are tired from interrupted nights and overworked days, and everything is made worse by a tendency to blame yourself for your baby's unpredictable behavior. Surely if you did the right thing, fed him correctly and soothed him in the proper motherly way, he would sleep peacefully, waking only to take feedings at reasonable intervals? There seems to be no time to enjoy him, and you are ashamed that you feel relaxed only when he is asleep (see feeling depressed, pp. 152–54).

Expecting Too Much of Yourself

Why are the first few weeks alone with a baby, whose arrival was so eagerly awaited and welcomed, often filled with despair and exhaustion rather than with the contented elation mothers, and fathers, are supposed to feel? There are several possible answers, some or all of which may apply to you.

First, you are probably expecting too much of both yourself and your baby. Although you know that looking after your husband and house and your other interests must take second place to the baby for some time, you may be unable to accept this as serenely as you had hoped (see pp. 151–52). You are, subconsciously, expecting yourself to remain unchanged although your life has totally changed.

Paradoxically, for most women the best hope of emerging from the early months of motherhood with their personalities unscathed is to "give in" and devote themselves to the baby. You will find that this helps your baby to become independent more rapidly and removes some of your feeling of being pulled in several directions at once, which takes up so much emotional energy, leaving you feeling a failure on all fronts. It is really a question of consciously aiming not to work to become the perfect mother. Don't be put off by all those friends who seem to be the perfect mother, wife, and housekeeper all rolled into one. They have their problems. It is much better for you to swim with the tide than to force yourself to be perfect.

This period of adaptation to the new baby may seem at the time as if it will go on forever, but remind yourself frequently that all of you are getting better every day at living together. Your baby is growing and cannot help evolving some sort of routine for himself, however inefficient a mother you may think you are. Your maternal instinct is there, somewhere, and is doing its best to emerge from the layers of confusion and inexperience, which are only masking it. It is not unreasonable to feel anguished when your baby is crying and you can't stop him—if a mother did not react emotionally when her baby needed her, Nature would have made a grave mistake.

Babies Need Physical Contact

It helps to remember how much we expect of a newborn baby, how quickly we expect him to adjust himself to life outside the security of the uterus. A young baby in an advanced society is expected to live a pretty artificial life. Almost as soon as he is born his body is covered with clothing, and from then on he hardly ever enjoys the comfort of direct skin-to-skin contact with his mother. He sleeps alone in his hygienic crib, and we are surprised if, when he wakes, he dislikes being alone and starts crying. Much of his discontent may be a yearning for the physical comfort of his mother's body. When he can feel and smell her, he instinctively feels back where he belongs, at home. Home for a baby is next to his mother, not his lonely crib. He cries to be picked up, not necessarily to be fed. He has to live in a way that suits adults in a civilized society—but we should not expect every baby to find the adaptation easy.

Understanding His Cries

Your baby should be given the comfort he wants; any idea of training or fear of spoiling needs to be forgotten in these first few months of his life. Do not give yourself the unnecessary problem "Ought he to be allowed this or that?" but ask yourself, "What does he want and how can I give it to him?" Concentrate on discovering his needs. It is so much simpler and more accurate if you regard his cries as calls and think of him as an asking baby rather than a crying baby. At this age you cannot make him do anything directly, but by repeatedly answering his calls for help you make him feel safe and you can begin to understand each other.

Crying from Boredom

Of course, you will not always be able to interpret your baby's cries and satisfy his wishes—he may not always have a definite need, but may just feel vaguely uncomfortable and unsatisfied. This is perhaps an early feeling of boredom. After all, there is nothing to do except eat, sleep, and cry, at least until he has learned the amusement of sucking his fingers.

The baby who will later be an interesting and active child may be bright and alert at an inconveniently early age. This kind of baby is far happier when he is carried about and can watch what is going on around him than lying in his baby carriage being expected to sleep. Babies who are carried about on their mothers' backs, as in Africa, cry little, not only because they are fed quickly when hungry, but also because they are comforted by being near their mothers.

If your baby seems like this, let him sit propped in a baby chair on the floor at the earliest moment, which may be as early as a month old. It will not hurt his back. You will find that he will sit and watch you contentedly when he might otherwise be howling from boredom in his bed. He enjoys activity and movement much sooner than you may have anticipated (see play, p. 294).

Sleep Patterns and Feeding: Crying from Hunger

But ought not a new baby to sleep most of the time when he is not feeding? Will he grow properly if he's awake so much? Surely he would sleep more if you fed him correctly? Unfortunately for parents but understandably for babies, the amount of sleep and the number of feedings a baby needs vary enormously between individual babies right from the start (see sleep requirements, pp. 107–8).

Mothers tend to believe—and they have been encouraged in this —that a baby with a full stomach will sleep peacefully until he needs his next feeding. If he does not, his mother feels he has been wrongly fed or underfed or that she has failed to shift his gas (see gas, pp. 68–70). In other words, she blames herself for doing something wrong, and perhaps partly blames her baby for being unusual. But she has done nothing wrong and the baby is not at all unusual. He is reveling in the pleasure of feeling comfortable and enjoying himself taking in the world around him. He may occupy himself in this way for an hour or more.

A baby won't eat more than he wants to, however much he is offered and however convenient it would be if he took large feedings infrequently rather than small ones frequently. Although a baby with a full stomach may sleep for four hours, his stomach may empty considerably sooner than this, or he may wake up for a different reason. It seems that a baby's sleep pattern is not entirely decided by his eating pattern; in fact, well-fed babies sometimes sleep less than underfed ones.

So if your baby sleeps less than you would like, this probably has more to do with his inborn sleep pattern than with his stomach. If he looks well, is filling out and growing, he is likely to be getting enough milk. A breast-fed baby will suck harder and stimulate a larger milk supply if he is hungry (p. 67), and a bottle-fed baby who is allowed to drink as much as he wants of the correct-strength milk mixture is also unlikely to be chronically underfed and to cry for this reason. Your baby may cry for a feeding earlier than is convenient, and this erratic demand for food may continue for a month or so, until you have worked out a routine that satisfies both of you.

Does He Need More Food?

How do you know if your wakeful, crying baby is hungry rather than bored? If he stops crying when you pick him up and looks relieved and interested and stays contented for more than a minute or two, you can assume that what he wants is company. Do not assume there must be gas troubling him and ruin your session with him by waiting on tenterhooks for him to burp. He might well burp while being held in your arms, but this does not necessarily mean it was gas that made him cry (see pp. 68–70).

Picking him up, or changing his diaper, may be enough to break his tension, so that he can get back to sleep when you put him back in his crib or baby carriage. Check that he is not too hot or cold or uncomfortable. He may be too hot or too cold because he is dressed for the season rather than for the actual day (see pp. 31, 112–13).

If it is a couple of hours since his last feeding and he remains unhappy, you could try feeding him again, but do not feel you have to feed him or pick him up twenty times a day because he cries twenty times a day. This will drive you mad after a few days even if he seems to like it. You have to accept that you cannot always interpret his cries. It sometimes helps if you give him the feeding before he wakes and cries.

Pacifiers

I always used to be against pacifiers on the grounds that they were dirty and unhygienic. This is no longer my reason for being against them. I dislike pacifiers because I would far prefer a baby who requires extra sucking comfort to do it the natural way—by sucking his thumb.

A thumb is no cleaner than a pacifier but it has one great asset —it can feel. The baby is able to explore his mouth with his thumb, and this is the normal way in which he learns about his mouth. So important is this step, that if a child is paralyzed—a spastic, for example—the physical therapist should teach him how to suck his thumb, thereby discovering his mouth.

If your baby has already got used to a pacifier or if he has not yet found his thumb and obviously needs the comfort of extra sucking, no harm will arise from his using a pacifier. I would merely recommend that you try to transfer his affection from the pacifier to his thumb when practical.

It is much better to give a baby a pacifier than to leave him crying, but mostly a crying baby who is soothed by a pacifier would be better soothed by a cuddle from his mother or father. The only harm a pacifier can do is if it is dipped in honey or some other form of sweetener, since these rot the teeth (p. 253).

Security Blankets

Many young children become attached to a shawl or piece of blanket, which they will not allow out of their sight, especially at bedtime. Psychoanalysts refer to this as a "transitional object," which helps the young child to make the transition from being part of his mother to being outside and separate.

It helps him to cope with anxiety and loneliness, especially when going to bed or facing strange places like hospitals. No one is allowed to wash the security blanket, and the child will complain bitterly if his mother ever achieves this, since it then feels and smells quite different. Eventually the child will give up his blanket for a toy or a teddy bear, but only if allowed to grow out of his need for it by himself.

Crying at Night

A new baby is bound to interrupt his parents' sleep for the first few weeks of his life, and again at intervals when he is ill, uncomfortable, or upset. But there are ways of reducing these interruptions, and making sure they do not become permanent. If you always deal promptly but *briefly* with nighttime feedings, toilet training, and minor crises such as bad dreams and toothaches, refusing to throw in a social bonus of conversation, stories, prolonged cuddles, or a visit downstairs, your child will register your lack of interest in playing with him at night (see pp. 115–16). You should not cut short the time needed to comfort a frightened child or rush night feedings, but as soon as you have dealt satisfactorily with something that was keeping your child awake you should leave him.

A crying baby who has been changed, has had a short cuddle, and is not ill should be put back in his crib, not carried about for hours in the middle of the night. If he stops crying while being held but starts as soon as he is put down, he is only trying to convey that he prefers sleeping in your arms—very reasonable, but very inconvenient. Taking him into your own bed might solve the problem (see family bed, pp. 111–12). What is needed is a cuddling technique that gets him back to sleep but does not cause him to wake up as soon as cuddling stops. Try, therefore, to avoid picking up your baby from the crib. If you cuddle him in his crib, so that although he is sitting up, his bottom is still touching the mattress, you will find it much easier to lower him back down without his waking up and crying again.

The main point about settling the normal child during the night is to handle him in a relatively unemotional and silent manner, so that he soon learns there are no special rewards for waking up parents in the middle of the night.

Leaving Him to Cry

You want him to stop crying or, as second best, you want to be reassured that it is all right to leave him crying, sometimes while you get on with something else. It is all right to leave your baby crying at times, particularly if you feel so fraught and tense that you need comforting yourself and feel incapable of giving him any comfort.

Some babies do cry an awful lot—it seems more when every wail grates on your nerves. It is far easier to deal with your baby when he cries comparatively little, because you are in a better mood yourself and therefore more responsive to him. If he cries "all the time," you become less and less receptive, and more and more wound up. You switch off and become less sensitive to his cries out of sheer self-defense, although, logically, a better form of self-defense would be to relax and try to increase your sensitivity to the baby, thus becoming better at comforting him and stopping his crying. It is only too easy to set up a vicious circle.

The baby who keeps on crying is reflecting a problem that needs the help of your visiting nurse or doctor. I am concerned by the number of mothers who feel they shouldn't trouble doctors about their crying baby, whereas doctors and nurses should be experts in dealing with this problem. If dealt with early, greater difficulties can be prevented from occurring later. Persistent crying may be related to maternal depression (p. 154), since a baby is a most sensitive barometer of his mother's feelings.

Why Are Second Babies Easier?

The vicious circle arises far less often with a second or subsequent baby. This is not because every second and subsequent baby is inherently more contented and placid than every first baby. They probably cry just as loudly and just as often. But second time around a mother is not so concerned that every cry means grave undernourishment or some significant failure on her part. She is more confident in herself as a mother and in her baby's ability to survive a few trifling mistakes. Her first one survived, didn't he? And besides, the ex-baby, now a boisterous toddler, is so good at pushing his own demands that the new baby's crying seems an almost soothing background noise. The baby either stops crying, because his mother has given him a chance to stop and the passing discomfort has gone away by itself, or he goes on until the most hardened mother could not ignore him any longer. He too survives.

Keeping a Sense of Proportion

You cannot expect yourself to be the perfect, relaxed mother figure first time around, however many books you have read and however adequately you have been prepared for motherhood. Sympathetic help before the birth and following it can be a great help, so can practical help from friends and relations, but the hour-by-hour, day-after-day responsibility of caring for your first baby cannot be made an altogether painless and easy job.

Remind yourself that, at first, most new mothers are probably feeling more depressed and inadequate than they admit. Tell yourself there are better times coming—because there are. There will be difficulties and problems but you will take them more easily in your stride; you won't be so tired, and everything will seem much simpler. So hang on!

Above all, remember that it takes time to fall in love with your baby, just as it did with your husband. Love at first sight can occur with future husbands and babies but both are relatively exceptional.

Don't feel guilty that you don't immediately love your baby totally. Few mothers really do. I would like to see a notice hung up in all labor rooms: "It is normal for you to need time to fall in love with your baby." The difficulty is greater if your baby has been born by Caesarean section, since you will have been denied the satisfaction of feeling and seeing him born unless you had epidural anesthesia (p. 37). You may also experience a sense of failure since you did not achieve the expectations you set for yourself during pregnancy. Many mothers have told me of their feelings of unreality when they came to from the anesthetic, feeling that the new baby was not really theirs. A similar situation occurs when a baby is separated from his mother in a special-care nursery. Doctors and nurses have to be especially aware of these very normal feelings experienced by a mother who has had a Caesarean section.

Don't be put off by the efficient mothers you meet who seem to be so expert at mothercraft—the technical side of looking after a baby. All you need at this stage is a good mothering instinct, which will grow as your baby grows. If you are able to mother your baby, you will have no difficulty in acquiring the technical skills of mothercraft. Mothering is something that you will have inherited from the way you yourself were mothered. It is an inestimable gift, which you are now passing on to your own child.

Three-Month Colic

The term "colic" is often used as an explanation for a baby who screams. The word is used far too loosely by doctors and nurses, and because of this it is understandable that mothers get the idea that gas is caught up in the bowel, which is certainly not the case (see also pp. 480–81).

Some babies cry regularly for a longish stretch at one time of the day, generally in the evening. The usual remedies—more food, comfort, a change of diaper—do not seem to make much difference. By the time the baby is three months old, these regular crying marathons tend to stop, which is why the term used to describe this nuisance is "three-month colic."

The baby draws his legs up when he is screaming because this is the natural position for a baby to adopt when screaming. While doing this he is quite likely to pass gas from his bottom, but this is not because of colic: it is because the increased abdominal pressure during a bout of furious crying forces gas out of the rectum. The intestines contain as much air as food, so it is not surprising that air is forced out in this way.

Causes and Cures

There are several likely reasons why the crying usually takes place in the evenings, and if one of them seems to apply to your baby, knowing the reason for his screaming may help you to prevent it or at least to reduce it.

Tension?   The early evening is the time in the day when you are even busier than usual. You want to get your husband's supper ready before he gets back, you want the baby fed and asleep in bed before he arrives, and you want to look your best for him. There is a lot to be done in a very short space of time, and it is hardly surprising that your baby senses you are in a state as you rush around the place with much less time for cuddling him than usual. Once he senses all this he starts to scream, and if someone calls it "colic," you believe that this refers to the cause of the trouble, whereas in fact it is merely another name for screaming.

If this description fits, ask your husband whether he really minds if your baby is still up and supper only half ready when he gets home. Most fathers would willingly take over the baby's evening feeding, or help cook the supper, or put another child to bed if they were asked and if they realized the baby was crying not from colic, but from tension—or boredom.

Boredom?   This may be an important factor in many cases of three-month colic. Sooner than many parents suspect, babies need company. Your baby may have slept between feedings all day, so that by six o'clock he is ready for a long session of amusement. He does not yet know that bedtime is bedtime. The remedy may be to encourage a wakeful period at a time of day more convenient for you than early evening. Of course, you should not prevent a tiny baby from going to sleep after a feeding if he wants to, but often a baby would stay awake and enjoy himself if he were not put firmly down to sleep after every feeding. He may wake up after a short sleep wanting fun rather than food. If you respond during the day, you help him to get the idea that daytime is for activity and nighttime for sleeping.

However, if despite everything you try he obstinately prefers to be up rather than in bed during the evening, it is obviously better to have him downstairs happy instead of upstairs crying. He is too young to get into a lifelong habit of ruining your evenings—he will not expect to sit on your lap during dinner for the rest of his days because you let him do so for his first three or four months. In summer, he may enjoy going out in his baby carriage. In a sense, your evenings are less restricted by a baby of this age than later, when it becomes more important to put him to bed at a regular time so that he gets into a convenient routine.

Hunger? Suppose he is crying from hunger? There is never any harm in offering more food, but you will probably have tried this without success before deciding the baby is suffering from colic. However, if you are breast feeding, thre may be slightly less milk at the early evening feeding because you have been rushing around and have had no time to relax before the feeding.

Whether you are feeding by breast or bottle, hurrying may make you less sensitive than usual to your baby's rhythm of starting, stopping, and starting again during the feeding. So it may be an unsatisfying feeding from several points of view. More food given in an equally hurried way may only make the baby scream louder.

Gas? Could it be due to gas (pp. 68–70)? Provided your baby has sat on your lap for a minute or two after his feeding, so that any gas that wants to come up can, why should he scream because of gas at a particular time of day only? Consult your doctor if you think your baby is in pain, but remember that furious crying can look remarkably painful. Your doctor may prescribe an anticolic medicine, but if it works, I believe this is more likely to be due to your becoming relaxed than to any direct effect of the drug.

Occasionally, you may be advised to put the screaming baby out of earshot and ignore him. But I think most mothers find this impossible. Wondering how your baby is usually makes you just as tense as hearing him cry. A better remedy, if you feel caught in a vicious circle of crying and tension, is to try to get someone else to listen instead of you—go out in the evening for a change. Even if your baby screams for only a short while, it will seem far longer to you than to a competent baby-sitter, for whom it is much less nerve-racking. Part of the treatment of colic is to think of ways to take the pressure off yourself.

Get rid of the feeling that you are to blame for the crying. Your baby may be screaming because you are feeding him hurriedly or failing to comfort him, but this applies to all mothers at one time or another; moreover, some babies cry more than others whatever their mothers do or don't do.

Evenings Out and Regular Bedtimes

While a baby is still having a night feeding, and still fits his carry-bed, it is easy to take him out in the evening. You can take him home again in his carry-bed, feed him if necessary, and put him to bed for the rest of the night. Most small babies settle down quite happily after an evening out. But the time arrives when it pays to keep to a routine at bedtime, to put your baby to bed in his own bed, in his own room, at approximately the same time each evening. By the time he is about six months old (though it may be earlier or later than this) a baby is more easily disturbed by evening journeyings; he may find it difficult to get back to sleep, or, alternatively, may enjoy himself so much that he wants to share every evening with you, not just the ones that suit you. The benefits of regular bedtimes are that they encourage babies to develop predictable habits at night, which ensure adequate rest for parents. A baby can make up for interrupted sleep in the daytime, but parents cannot.

However, children brought up to respect their parents' rights to uninterrupted evenings and nights will not lose their respect because the general rule is sometimes broken. Staying up late and going out in the evening are fun for children and can be fun for you if you stop worrying about disapproving glances implying "poor little thing, being kept up by those selfish parents." A really tired child will fall asleep anywhere, but keeping himself awake when tired will do him no harm, unless it happens night after night and he has no chance of making up his sleep.

British tourists tend to look with horror at French parents out at night in restaurants accompanied by their small children. But how much nicer it is for a child to be with his parents than to be left at home with a baby-sitter—and the experience is good for him too. He will put his head down on the restaurant table and go to sleep when he wants to, and no harm can possibly result.

The Schoolchild: Late Nights

The particular problem with the schoolchild is that if he stays up late he will be too tired to get up for school in the morning. Obviously this is true, although it interests me that children staying up late during holidays are often up with the lark. It is always easier to get up early when you are going to do something you especially enjoy.

The approach to late nights during the school year must be a compromise to suit the individual family. Clearly, your child must get up in time for school, but provided this is agreed and kept to, a late night now and then does not matter, even if it is only to stay up to watch an interesting television program.

Avoiding Anxiety about Sleep

Children are quick to sense the anxiety of their parents in every field of activity. Your anxiety about your child's lack of sleep will soon be sensed by him, and he will then become worried that he cannot get to sleep. An air of nonchalance about the subject will do much to relieve his anxiety, so that he stops "trying" to get to sleep. Should he call down to you saying he cannot get to sleep, tell him he can have a quarter if he can stay awake all night—he'll be asleep within five minutes!

Unwinding

Don't expect a child to switch off immediately from an exciting game or a cowboy movie and go right to sleep. Give him a chance to unwind, best of all by a bedtime story when he is in bed. Try not to be rushed over his bedtime and enlist his father's help with stories—it will keep them both occupied while you are getting dinner.

Playing in the Night

The main problem is the bright toddler who wakes in the early hours of the morning and wants you to play with him. If he has a room of his own, he will not disturb you so much and you can leave him a few toys to play with on waking. But in the end you may be forced to get up and play for a bit, the consolation being that it is the bright child who behaves in this way, and you are helping him to learn.

Sleeping pills have no place in the treatment of such children. You would need to anesthetize them to put them to sleep. The only answer is to try to work out some compromise for a time and to snatch what periods of sleep you can during the day.

Sometimes giving your child a clock helps, if he is old enough to understand its function. In an attempt to get him to remain playing in his own room until the time when you are prepared to have him in your room (and probably your bed), you could try the effect of an attractively designed arrow to stick to the clock face, leaving this pointing to the position to be reached by the hour hand before invasion of your territory is permitted.

Broken Nights

If you try all these different approaches and, above all, are not over-concerned about your child's need for sleep, you should find that nights broken by his cries are not unbearably frequent. However, if despite all these maneuvers your baby still persists in waking at night, what else can you do? In the early days the cause is likely to be hunger. He cannot know that you will accept a four-hour feeding regime for him in the daytime but expect him to go eight hours at night! Therefore, if hunger is the reason for his crying he must be given a night feeding. Find out whether you get more sleep by going to bed very early and delaying the last feeding until he wakes or by waking him for it. Having him in a room of his own is likely to give you those precious extra minutes of sleep, because you won't be awakened by the early whimpers that precede his real cries (see p. 110). Once your baby has awakened, you go right to him; he needs you and you will hate lying and listening to his cries. The idea that you should leave a baby to cry in case he goes back to sleep on his own is contrary to all normal maternal feelings; I am always surprised how often I am asked whether or not a mother should leave her baby to cry. The fact that the question is asked at all makes me feel that the rigid Victorian attitude that you might "spoil" your baby is far too much with us still.

Naps and Rests

Most young children need to sleep or at least to rest for some part of the day. The nap revives energy and, unless it occupies most of the afternoon, does not make a child less likely to sleep soundly at night. On the contrary, fatigue may be the reason a child finds it difficult to get to sleep at bedtime; a rest during the day may actually make him sleep better at night.

You do not have to make your new baby sleep during the day. At first he sleeps off and on during the twenty-four hours anyway (p. 108). Later a fairly predictable pattern emerges, so that you know approximately when he wants a nap during the day. It may be right after breakfast, which seems strange when he has been asleep all night—but he knows best. The pattern tends to change frequently: every few days, every few weeks, or every few months—all are equally normal. No tables here, because babies are so different in napping habits.

It is best to be flexible about mealtimes and outings, since there is no point in fixing lunch at midday if your baby is too sleepy to eat it then, or if waking him from his nap makes him grumpy for the rest of the afternoon. Of course, once you know about how long he usually sleeps and when he has had his ration, you can wake him if it suits you to do so. There may be times when he has to miss his nap to fit in with your plans; even if this means he is bad-tempered for the rest of the day, it may be worth it occasionally and it won't do him any permanent harm. Babies have to be flexible too.

Although, on the whole, you can leave it to your baby to decide when and how long he wants to sleep during the day, after the first weeks try to avoid the situation in which he sleeps solidly through the afternoon and then wants to be up all the evening. If you see this pattern starting, try to encourage him to sleep more in the morning and to stay awake in the afternoons by making these more entertaining. For example, if he stays awake during shopping expeditions, shop after lunch rather than before it. Or give him his lunch earlier so that his nap ends earlier too. If he insists on an afternoon sleep, wake him up after an hour or two so that he has time to play and get tired again before bedtime.

Individual Variations

The age at which babies give up daytime rests altogether varies enormously. Some babies fall into the "awake all day, asleep all night" pattern well before their first birthdays. Their parents do at least have peaceful nights, so constant contact with their babies all day is not so bad. A few babies sleep little at night and are wide awake all day too—bad luck! But nearly every baby will consent to spending some time alone in his crib or baby carriage, giving his mother a rest even if he is not asleep.

Occasionally a baby resents any attempt to put him to bed during the day, and if you persist, starts hating bedtime as well. It is not worth jeopardizing your general aim of making him regard his bed as his haven and castle, not as a place of banishment, in order to get him to "rest" when he will not. This kind of baby needs little sleep (see sleep requirements, pp. 107–8) and he will not tire his body or his brain (just yours) by being awake all day. He probably switches off mentally and physically when he needs to, so don't force him to take a rest in the day if he doesn't want it.

Sometimes a baby does need sleep but is reluctant to give in. If you know your baby, you will recognize these times and can decide for him that he needs a nap. He may cry at first but he will usually fall asleep, despite himself, after a few minutes. Another baby may take a short while to "come to" after his nap; he may cry when he wakes, as if temporarily disoriented, particularly if you have awakened him. Give him time to revive before plunging him into social activity. To sum up, naps are a convenience to parents and a necessity to most babies. However, provided you give him the opportunity to take his nap at the time he seems to need it, you can trust him to fix its length and to know when he has grown out of the need.

The Schoolchild

A different problem is the child who continues to need a daytime rest after starting all-day school. He comes home exhausted unless his school allows the children to rest after lunch. Something to eat and drink as soon as he gets home may revive him, but he probably needs a restful afternoon and an earlier bedtime until he gets used to the new life.

Dealing with Sleep Problems

Night Fears and Bedtime Rituals

From the age of about twelve months a baby may dislike going to bed because he dislikes being alone and having his mother out of his sight. He is just as anxious on light summer evenings as on dark winter ones, so leaving lights on and doors open, which help a child who fears the dark, may not work for this baby.

At about twelve months the process of falling asleep is becoming less spontaneous. Your baby may need the help of little rituals such as taking a cuddly toy or security blanket (p. 120) to bed with him, or sucking his thumb. Alternatively, your presence may be part of his presleep ritual. Although it is wise to avoid giving him the impression that you are on call indefinitely, it helps him to settle down more quickly if you indulge his need for a ritual. This may mean returning once to reassure him that you are around, producing one drink of water, spending a few minutes on lullabies or stories, or just sitting with him for a short time. The idea is to show him you recognize his very understandable need for comfort, since the more secure he feels, the more quickly he will grow out of the need. However, by setting limits to the amount of time you spend and the number of times you return, you also show him that you are not prepared to spend the whole evening with him.

Reassurance

A child who is frightened of the darkness and silence of night needs all the reassurance you can give him in the way of night lights and open doors. You will not toughen him by dismissing his fears and refusing to help. Telling him there is nothing to be afraid of is only helpful if you also tell him you sympathize with him and acknowledge that his fear is real. Leaving his door open so that he can hear household noises may make a difference. Having a dim lamp on in his room or the door ajar with the landing light on is often sufficient reassurance to enable a child to get to sleep.

It is not wrong to take a frightened child into the bed you and your husband share (see family bed, pp. 111–12). This is much less exhausting for you and much more comforting for a very scared child. It is infinitely preferable to the practice of many parents, who choose to lie down with their child on his bed until he chooses to go to sleep and lets them off the hook. Such a child could be put to bed in his parents' bed and would probably fall asleep without any problem.

When away from home your child is likely to be more afraid, so do not be ashamed of his fear and refuse to let him have a light on at night. Explain that your child is used to having a light on all night if necessary. Tell baby-sitters about it in case they switch off the light.

Insomnia

This expression is inappropriate when applied to young children, since it means lying awake for hours when you would rather be asleep. An older child, worrying about his exams, who wishes desperately to get to sleep but is unable to do so is probably suffering from insomnia. But the small child who is still awake an hour or two after being put to bed, the baby who sleeps less than his parents think he ought to sleep, the toddler who wakes up at dawn—all may be problems to their families but they are not suffering from insomnia (see sleep requirements, p. 107). They want to be awake, and do not worry about going to sleep unless adults put the idea into their heads.

If you are worried by an older child's inability to sleep "normally," or, rather, if he is worried by it, it is worth discussing with your doctor.

Nightmares and Night Terrors

When a child wakes up in the night wide-eyed with terror, panic-stricken, and screaming, you can assume he has had a nightmare. Nightmares are commonest after the age of four, when the imagination is becoming especially active. These children are usually brighter than average, and it is wise for them to be restrained from excessive excitement immediately before going to bed.

Your child may be able to tell you what he has been dreaming about, particularly if it is related to a frightening incident or movie he saw the day before. Sometimes a terrifying sensation, such as a feeling of suffocation, rather than the disturbing content of a dream, is responsible; this may be due to a stuffed-up nose during a cold. Some children have nightmares at the beginning of an infection. It is unlikely that eating certain foods, like cheese, leads to nightmares.

A child who has had a nightmare feels better as soon as he wakes up and realizes he was only dreaming. If you go to him promptly and reassure him, he is quickly comforted and can go back to sleep. On the other hand, a night terror causes the child to scream for about two minutes, and he cannot be comforted because he cannot hear you. All you can do is to hold him close until he comes back to reality and will let you tuck him in. Night terrors always occur between fifteen and ninety minutes after going to sleep.

Some children have nightmares quite often, while others never seem to. There is no need to worry unless a child is waking up terrified nearly every night; then his nightmares are clearly more than the result of an exciting day or an active imagination, and you should investigate the cause of his anxiety with your doctor.

Restless Sleep

Individuals vary as much when asleep as when awake. Everyone moves about during sleep, however peacefully they appear to be sleeping. Some children always sleep restlessly, tossing and turning, making grunting and sucking noises, so that you wonder if they are asleep at all if you have to share a room at night. But they wake up refreshed even if you do not. Tooth grinding and talking in sleep are also harmless, and should be disregarded.

Sleepwalking

Sleepwalking is rare in preschool children. It most often affects children between ten and fourteen, but it is uncertain how common it is, since doctors do not usually see children for this reason. However, a child who sleepwalks is showing a strange pattern of behavior, and you have every reason to discuss the problem with your doctor. It is as if he were able to keep his worries under control while awake but not while asleep. A child may therefore go through a sleepwalking phase while worried about exams, for example; the phase disappears with the cause of the worry. The episode usually occurs shortly after falling asleep, when sleep is particularly deep. Some sleepwalkers have a history of night terrors when younger.

The sleepwalker rarely injures himself, but he does not undertake complicated forms of activity. Almost all the normal protective mechanisms that safeguard him during the day still work, but it is wise to shut his bedroom window all the same. The best way of dealing with a child found sleepwalking is to lead him gently back to bed. It is unnecessary to wake him up unless it seems the right thing to do; for instance, if he is in the middle of a nightmare.

Sleeptalkers do not produce intelligible conversational speech.

9

The Low Birth Weight Baby

In developed countries, such as the United States and the United Kingdom, the average boy baby weighs about 7 pounds (3.17 kg) at birth, the average baby girl slightly less. Any baby who weighs 5½ pounds (2.49 kg) or under used to be called "premature." This term only considered the baby's weight, taking no account of whether he arrived before the end of the normal forty weeks of pregnancy, or of why he weighs less than the average. Therefore, a more accurate term than "premature" is "low birth weight" baby.

Causes

There are three major causes for a low birth weight: being born early (preterm); being made small, usually because the parents are small; and being small as a result of insufficient food while in the uterus. For each baby, the doctor has to find the cause and to assess the baby's degree of maturity as compared with that of a full-term baby. The answers are important, since they indicate the baby's ability to cope with living in the outside world; they also determine how he should be managed.

The Preterm Baby

The reason for the premature onset of labor is often not known. Sometimes the waters break for no apparent reason and this starts it off. Accidents and shock may produce premature labor, though much less often than is thought. Twins, by reason of their combined size, may set off early labor. Because there are two babies, each one is likely to be smaller than average. Premature labor may be brought on by illness, such as toxemia of pregnancy. This also has the effect of causing the baby to be small, as a result of starvation. A malformed baby may be born earlier than expected.

The Genetically Small Baby

Some small babies are not immature at all. They are small for genetic reasons—their parents are small. A genetically small baby arrives on time and is as capable as a heavier baby of adapting to an independent existence. Being a full-term baby, he has no need of the special management that is essential for the low birth weight baby who is immature. He leaves the hospital at the normal time, and at home should be cared for and fed in the normal way.

The "Small for Dates" Baby

Not every baby who arrives on time but weighs less than 5½ pounds (2.49 kg) is following the family pattern. Sometimes a baby is small because he has been malnourished in the uterus. This baby is known as "small for dates." The reason for the malnutrition in the uterus is not clear-cut; most often it is due to a combination of circumstances. It occurs much more commonly in lower economic groups. In addition to the effects of poverty, this is also the result of less regular prenatal care, a higher rate of smoking (see pp. 12–13 and below), longer working hours, a general lack of knowledge about health and diet, leading to maternal malnutrition.

The Effect of Diet

The standard of the mother's own nutrition has a bearing on that of her baby: if she has suffered from lack of proper food over a long period, he may well be lighter in consequence. On the other hand, except under extreme circumstances the nature and quantity of her diet during pregnancy have little effect on the growth of her baby, because her nutritional reserves protect him. A healthy woman who eats normally during pregnancy need not worry about producing a baby who is smaller than he should be; she does not have to "eat for two" to make sure her baby grows (see pregnancy, p. 13).

The Effect of Smoking

Smoking during pregnancy leads to lack of nutrition in the uterus. It reduces a baby's birth weight by an average of 6 ounces (170 g) because it causes the blood vessels in the placenta to narrow, so that less blood and therefore less food and less oxygen reach the baby.

The seriousness of this is not the mere fact that the baby is light in weight, but that he weighs less than intended, owing to partial starvation. The most grave effect is on the brain, since starvation, in making it lighter, also makes it less efficient. It has been proved that the babies of mothers who smoked heavily in pregnancy are less intelligent than those who did not smoke. The brain is growing particularly fast during pregnancy; to grow to its full extent it must not be starved during this crucial time, since the loss can never be made up later.

With these facts now available, it is small wonder that doctors are so emphatic about mothers not smoking in pregnancy. My wonder is that mothers should dare to continue, and I believe that many of them do so because the facts have not been given to them straight. The habitual smoker has to give up her habit for only nine months, for her baby's sake. Smoking before or after pregnancy doesn't affect the baby (see also pp. 12–13).

The Individual Baby

In each case the doctor must discover whether the baby is the expected size for the length of pregnancy. By this means he can decide whether the baby has been starved before birth and is therefore small for dates, whether he has simply been born prematurely or whether he has inherited his small size. The genetically small baby needs no special treatment (p. 139), but the preterm baby and the small for dates baby present special problems; they must be looked after in the hospital until they are strong enough to go home.

Parents' Problems

This is a difficult situation for parents. First, there are practical problems—grandparents have to change their arrangements if they were planning to come and help with the house and the other children. More serious is the fact that you and your husband may not yet be ready psychologically for the baby's arrival. A mother may blame herself for delivering early.

Apart from normal concern for your new baby, you have the additional anxiety of his small size; you are also missing the early contact with him that is so important for the development of your relationship. This is all the worse if your baby has to be moved to a special-care baby unit in another hospital and there are no facilities for your accommodation.

The situation is less of a strain if the hospital lets you see your baby and pick him up from the earliest possible moment. Even if he is in an incubator, it is often possible to take him out and nurse him for a short time. If this would be bad for the baby, doctors now accept that it is good for both mother and baby if she slides her hands into the incubator to touch him. Turn your head so it is aligned in the same plane as your baby's so that your eyes can click in together. If you are breast feeding or expressing milk for your baby, you have more chance of getting to know him. Fathers sometimes use their interest in the machinery of the incubator as their way of getting involved with their babies in a special-care baby unit.

It is up to the medical and nursing staff to watch your feelings carefully if your baby is in a special-care nursery while you are in a room with mothers whose babies are beside their beds. Many hospitals provide you with a photograph of the baby; if not, ask if your husband can take one. However, don't hesitate to voice your feelings if they seem to go unnoticed; ask if it is possible for you to have your baby with you in a single room, if you would be happier with that arrangement. Some hospitals are prepared for the incubator to stay beside the mother's bed if it is needed solely to provide extra warmth. One of the problems is that when a baby is so small that he requires care in a special unit, you are bound to feel incapable of caring for him and therefore, to an extent, inadequate. It is also natural to be fearful of visiting him until you feel sure he will survive.

The fact that he has to be placed in a "special-care" baby unit makes you feel you must give him special care when he comes home. This is one reason for the finding that such babies are brought to the doctor by their mothers more than average in the first year.

If you have to leave your baby in the care of the hospital staff, you go home empty-handed. However much you appreciate the chance to rest and get things ready for your baby, whose arrival may have taken you by surprise, it can be a tense and unreal time. Ideally, whether you are breast feeding or not, you should stay with your baby in the hospital until he is ready to come home, getting out of the hospital as much as possible between feedings. This should be the practice in the United States, just as in the United Kingdom.

I must emphasize that staying in the hospital with your baby does not mean being confined to the hospital. Just as I encourage mothers of full-term babies to go out for walks and meals with their husbands, I do the same with the mothers of small babies—only, with even greater emphasis because their stay is longer.

Coming Home

In the past, babies were required to have reached a certain weight, such as 5 pounds (2.27 kg), before they were allowed home. The tendency today is to judge each baby individually, so that fewer are moved to special-care baby units and babies are discharged earlier.

Problems Caused by Immaturity

A preterm baby faces all the normal hazards of birth plus others caused by his immaturity. Being born is not only more difficult if you are small, it is more dangerous.

Delivery   Hospital delivery is safest. If your baby arrives unexpectedly and is delivered at home he may have to be moved to the hospital.

The baby's small head moves rapidly through the birth canal without being molded (p. 38), so that it reaches the mother's perineum, the area between the front and back passages, before this has had a chance to stretch and soften. A collision between the soft unmolded head and the hard perineum can cause brain damage or other injury. This is why you will probably have an episiotomy to enlarge the opening of the front passage (vulva) if your baby is born early. This will often be combined with the use of forceps, which by enclosing the baby's head during delivery can protect it from damage. Do not think of the forceps used by the obstetrician as being damaging to your baby—on the contrary, they are used for his protection.

Breathing   A baby who is born early has an immature respiratory system and a poorly developed cough reflex, and he is therefore not as efficient at breathing and at clearing his air passages as a full-term baby. This increases the risk of lack of oxygen, both during labor and afterward. He may need the help of special apparatus to maintain his breathing.

Resistance to Infection   The preterm baby has even less resistance to infection than the average baby, so conditions during delivery have to be scrupulously clean. This is easier to achieve in the hospital. During his early weeks, special care has to be taken to protect him from infection. People with colds should always be discouraged from going near babies, but must be positively prevented from visiting preterm babies.

Keeping Warm   A preterm baby changes temperature easily because his temperature regulating mechanism is immature and because he lacks an insulating layer of fat beneath the skin, having missed the last weeks of pregnancy, when this fat is laid down. Moreover, the top layer of the skin is much thinner. Therefore the delivery room must be especially warm, with a heated crib ready to receive the newborn baby with the minimum of delay. An incubator will be available in case he needs the extra heat and humidity that can be provided by incubator nursing. It is usual for a pediatrician to be in attendance.

Other Problems   The preterm baby goes on needing special care until he reaches the stage of maturity he should have reached at birth. The problems that increased the danger during delivery continue to operate until this time. There are other dangers also. Because his liver is immature and not yet working fully, he is liable to become jaundiced (see jaundice, pp. 439f.). He may suffer from low blood sugar within two or three days of birth, because his body missed the normal opportunity for storing sugar in the liver, since this takes place during the last weeks of pregnancy. These problems are detected and treated early in order to prevent brain damage and subsequent handicap. The immaturity of his lungs may result in difficulty in breathing—the "respiratory distress syndrome."

Overcoming a Bad Start

Hospitals are equipped to deal with all these problems, and they need have no permanent effects on the baby. His chances of growing healthily and developing normally are directly related to the skill with which he is cared for in his first weeks.

Given optimum hospital conditions for delivery and aftercare, the outlook for preterm babies weighing 3 pounds (1.36 kg) or more is almost as good as for full-term babies. For babies weighing less than 3 pounds (1.36 kg) the chances of survival are less, and there is the risk of brain damage leading to mental handicap and to physical handicap, particularly cerebral palsy. However, even for the very smallest babies the results of all the recent advances in treatment have greatly improved their chances of surviving and of being normal.

Feeding

Why a Routine Is Necessary

A preterm baby sleeps more than a full-term baby and cannot be trusted to wake and cry when he needs food. You cannot be sure he is well fed because he seems contented, although this is normally a reliable enough guide (pp. 118–19). Therefore he has to be fed according to a schedule and not simply by demand (see breast feeding, pp. 65f.).

Three-hourly feedings are the usual routine. The number of calories the baby needs has to be worked out. Not only does he need the correct amount of the right food, but also he must be fed in a way that reduces the risk of losing the food again through choking, vomiting, or diarrhea. His head must always be raised during feedings, to lessen the risk of choking or breathing in milk. He may be able to feed from the breast from the start; a baby who cannot suck or swallow well enough to do so is fed by bottle or by tube till he is stronger. If you are willing to express your milk, it can be given to him by bottle or tube until he is strong enough to breast feed. This is tedious for you but it is worth doing, since preterm babies do best on breast milk.

Alternatively, the baby can be fed with milk from a supply donated by mothers with a surplus (the milk bank). A modified cow's milk preparation (pp. 85–86) is a suitable alternative to breast milk.

Feeding Your Baby at Home

However your baby is fed, you will be given detailed instructions when you take him home and have to organize his feedings yourself.

Vitamins and Mixed Feeding

Follow your doctor's advice on when to start mixed feeding and vitamin supplements (pp. 180f. and 185f.). The preterm baby needs extra iron to minimize the risk of anemia (p. 518), because he missed the last weeks in the womb, when iron stores are laid down in the liver. Extra iron is given from the age of four weeks or earlier, and is continued until the baby is eating a mixed diet, at least until the age of six months (see mixed feeding, pp. 186f.). Vitamin C and D supplements are needed from the age of two weeks. They are given first as a concentrate, since the preterm baby cannot manage cod liver oil and orange juice like the full-term baby. He requires 25 mg of vitamin C and 400 units of vitamin D daily, but your doctor will make sure you are kept up to date on his vitamin requirements.

Coping with the Low Birth Weight Baby at Home

If you are fortunate enough to be able to adjust your life so as to stay in the hospital for the longer period demanded by your small baby, you should have few extra problems of adjustment when you return home. On the other hand, if you have had to leave him in the hospital, it may be more difficult to adjust to his arrival at home, and you will need all the help your husband can give you as well as the professional help from your doctor or visiting nurse.

Treating Him Normally

Once your small baby is thriving, try to remove, as far as possible, any idea that he is different from other babies of the same age. This will not be easy, especially since you will probably have to see your doctor more often than the mothers of normal-sized babies. But it is still very important to make the effort, so that the baby who needed special care in his early days in the hospital, when he was probably nursed in the special-care nursery, does not become labeled by you as a special-care baby, thereby being overcoddled and overprotected (see also development, p. 218).

10

Twins

Twins multiply the pleasures and pains of parenthood. Everything that applies to twins applies to triplets, only more so. If the prospect of one baby is daunting, the prospect of two is overwhelming. One baby makes a lot of work; two can make more than double the amount. On the other hand, the bonuses are good. If you dislike being pregnant, there are two babies for the price of one nine-month stretch. If life is to be restricted by having one baby, it might as well be restricted by two. Although caring for two babies at once is initially more exhausting than caring for one, there are compensations later. Twins are used to each other's company; they occupy themselves better than one small child playing alone or two children of similar ages.

As well as the normal anxieties of prospective parenthood, parents expecting twins are often apprehensive about problems arising from the very fact of twinship. Apart from the practical details of coping with and providing for two babies at once (pp. 143f.), you may worry about the relationship between the twins themselves and their impact on the family.

It is different to be a twin. To arrive in the world with a constant companion is undoubtedly different from arriving alone. A twin baby seldom has his mother to himself; he seldom has himself to himself. He has to learn to share people and objects from the start. Before he can become aware of his own individuality he must discover, like every baby, that his mother is a separate person, but he must also discover that the other face in the baby carriage belongs to someone else.

Parents compare him not only with the "average" baby and the neighbor's baby, but also with his twin. This makes for built-in complications to the ordinary growth of relationships. However, twins also have the advantage of feeling close to another human being, combining togetherness with individuality—a state most people have to work hard to achieve.

There are many other factors, which have nothing to do with being a twin, that influence a twin baby's development, including the temperaments of the two individuals concerned and of the rest of their family, the way problems are handled as they arise, and the emotional support and physical help the mother of twins receives during the early months.

Fraternal and Identical Twins

Fraternal twins are no more alike or unlike than any other pair of children in the same family. They are two babies who have shared the same pregnancy, but they have only half their genes in common, like ordinary brothers and sisters; identical twins have identical genes.

Should Closeness Be Discouraged?

Whether twins are fraternal or identical, you should not feel you must stop them from being close, or, on the other hand, that they should be encouraged to be closer. The right degree of interdependence for a particular pair will evolve naturally in an ordinary family where the most important thing about the twins is not their twinship but their individuality.

However, because all twins spend so much of their early life in the same place doing the same things, from sitting in the double baby carriage to starting school on the same day, fraternal twins may end up in much the same position as identical twins—with more in common than most children and in danger of being treated as if they had everything in common. This is particularly likely with fraternal twins of the same sex who happen to look alike. Neither of these facts, nor the sharing of early experiences, necessarily makes two children interchangeable.

Fraternal twins are more likely to suffer as a result of being treated as a pair rather than as individuals, simply because identical twins really are alike in physical and mental characteristics and tend therefore to share tastes and inclinations. But how identical twins use their potential differs as with any two individuals; they should not be expected to achieve equal success.

Dressing Alike

Does it matter whether or not twins are dressed alike, are put in the same class at school, receive the same treats, toys, and discipline? It's not so much what you do to your twins as why you do it that matters. If twins are always dressed alike because their parents' main pleasure is to parade them as an irresistible double act, then it probably does matter, because it helps to convince the twins that the most important thing about them is being twins, and that taken separately they are pretty insignificant. Parents who dress twins identically for this reason tend to reinforce the impression by giving them very similar names and by treating them continually as a pair. But if twins are dressed alike because it is simpler or cheaper or because it's fun, and they are allowed to dress differently when they want to, then it does not matter at all.

Separating Twins at School

Twins who play together most of the time and who get on well will suffer if they are separated when starting at a play group or primary school. Each misses not only his mother, like any child, but also his twin. Starting school of any kind can be a strain, so unless you feel your twins need to get away from each other for a while it is kinder to let them get used to school together, leaving it to their individual progress and wishes to decide later whether they continue together. Even identical twins may come to need different classes or different types of school because of variations in intellectual or social development. Sometimes one twin does all the work. He learns to read, so the other does not bother—why learn the same things? It is called "division of labor" but unfortunately is not appreciated by parents and teachers.

Twins may suffer at school from insensitive comparisons between their performances and results, so that one begins to feel hopeless and overshadowed by the other. Instead of healthy rivalry, comparisons can produce a lack of confidence and fear of failure which effectively stop the child doing better, as everyone keeps urging him to do. This can happen to any child at school, but a twin is more likely to have all his problems ascribed to his twinship, while his real needs are overlooked. Being a twin should be only one aspect of his life, at school or anywhere else.

Fair Shares for Both

The question of distributing toys and treats need not be much greater than between any two children in the same family. A child is bound to feel that his parents are being unfair some of the time; the situation to avoid is one where the same child has this feeling most of the time. Twins have early practice in learning to share possessions, so they may share one new toy between them.

It is better not to make a policy of always giving them one toy each or always giving two of the same at the same time: there is no point in falling over backward to be fair, since you will not be able to keep it up forever, and children who are always given presents together seem no more contented than those who realize early that temporary disappointments are a part of life. Twins, like other brothers and sisters, should have some toys in common and some of their own. The same applies to treats and friendships.

Discipline

It is equally impossible to aim at 100 percent fairness in discipline. You have to try to be just and tell off the right twin, but it is not disastrous to be wrong occasionally. One child may be more wicked than the other but so good at covering up that, unless you are careful, you blame both twins or the wrong one. Twins may work together to outwit their parents; this is hardly surprising and it is just one aspect of their loyalty to each other.

If one twin is punished, the other may feel affronted and hurt too, so you have to think of the effect on both of them. But twins may keep each other out of trouble as well as get each other into it. Most problems of discipline with twins will probably have little or nothing to do with the fact that they are twins (see discipline, pp. 265f.).

Twin Language

Some twins learn to communicate with each other by using a "language" that is gibberish to everyone else. This may happen because they have been left alone in each other's company a good deal, or it may happen anyway, parallel with the development of ordinary speech. Normal language is usually delayed in twins because of their mutual special language.

Unless the use of twin language persists so long that the twins find it difficult to communicate with anyone else, the habit need not be discouraged. But make sure that people continue to talk to them in the ordinary way.

You could also show you are bored with twin language by ignoring requests made in it and generally showing that you prefer to be addressed with words you understand. The need to make other children understand may be a better incentive than the need to please parents.

The Effect on Other Children in the Family

It is probably harder to share your parents with twins than with two other brothers and sisters. Twins attract attention, twins stick together and don't want to play with you, twins make a family special —all these facts can easily make another child resent twins rather than feel proud of them.

This is more likely to happen if the twins are identical, if the other child is younger than they are and the same sex, and if there are no other children. An age gap of several years tends to reduce resentment and the impact twins have on another child, while if he is older, at least he has a start over them.

Avoid gearing family life too obviously to the needs of the twins; it is important not to let any child feel displaced by another, and especially by two others (see minimizing jealousy, pp. 148f.).

Twins as Babies

Prematurity

Twins are often born prematurely, usually for the straightforward reason that they have outgrown the space available for the two of them in the uterus. Although they may be small and fragile at first, it is a mistake to go on treating them as if they were particularly delicate (see low birth weight baby, p. 139).

Different Habits

One baby may be larger than the other, even if they are identical twins, because one has received more of the available blood supply from the placenta. Identical twin babies are similar in temperament, so tend to share a similar pattern of sleep and feeding, which makes life easier for parents. Fraternal twins may be maddeningly dissimilar in their demands for food, comfort, and sleep; they may tread on each other's toes in every way from the start—or they may not. Twins may get on well to begin with, then less well, then better again. Parents are often given advice on how to manage "the twins" when what they really need is individual advice on each baby.

Differences in Progress

Problems that could arise with any baby hit twins especially hard if they are expected to behave as a unit when they are developing at different rates. One example is toilet training. The fact that one twin is willing to use the potty does not necessarily mean that the other is —however convenient that would be. Even identical twins, whose physical maturation is parallel, may disagree over when and how to use their new skills. Imitation plays a part, and one twin may encourage the other to copy unless nagging parents put him off the idea (see toilet training, pp. 240–41). A girl may copy her twin brother and urinate standing up—or vice versa. This does not show morbid closeness but a natural tendency to copy the person you spend most time with.

It is a mistake to get annoyed with the slower twin over toilet training or any other sign of progress. Continually comparing twins prevents you from seeing each one's problems for what they are. It is useful only if it throws light on what the individual child needs; for example, if one of a pair who have been identical in development and health suddenly lags behind the other, you have an early warning system that something may be wrong, which you lack with a single child.

Practical Problems

A twin baby who is small at birth needs the same care as any other low birth weight baby (see low birth weight baby, pp. 133f.). Preterm babies need more routine than full-term babies and the same applies to twins, both because they are likely to be small (p. 133) and because the mother of twins is so busy that keeping to a routine is the only way she can care for twins by herself and preserve her sanity. Even though you are sure you know your babies apart, it is a wise precaution to keep identification tags on them for a few days after leaving the hospital.

It is essential to prune the nonessential aspects of baby care. The daily bath is a luxury for any baby—a bath on alternate days is the most any twin should expect (see bathing the baby, p. 98). Clothes and diapers need to be plentiful and practical rather than beautiful (see clothes, pp. 31f., diapers, pp. 34f.). Borrow as much equipment as possible, since you will never need two of everything again—with luck. Get as much help and as much efficient laundry equipment as possible. Fortunately, multiple births jolt friends and relations into special generosity and efforts to help.

Feeding

It is difficult to feed two babies at once or to feed one when another is howling in the background. A pacifier may help to occupy the waiting baby. There are problems whether twins are breast or bottle fed.

Complete demand feeding is almost impossible unless you have someone to help. Two babies wanting feedings at various times of the day and night means an awful lot of feedings (see night feedings, p. 147). So although there is something to be said for sometimes feeding one baby between official feeding times, thus giving him an opportunity to have you to himself for once, in general it is easier to feed both babies at one session. Feed the baby who wakes up hungry, and then wake and feed the other. If they both scream for food at once, you can try feeding them simultaneously (see below) or they will have to take turns.

The pros and cons of breast and bottle feeding are the usual ones (see breast feeding, pp. 55f.; bottle feeding, pp. 82f.), plus some added hazards.

Breast Feeding

If you wish to breast feed, do not be put off by the idea that you cannot possibly produce enough milk for two babies. Breast feeding depends on supply and demand (p. 67), and two babies are even better than one at creating demand and thus ensuring supply.

The real difficulties lie in when and how to feed them. You may have ample milk but you won't have ample time, although at least you do not have to make up double quantities of bottle feedings. Complete demand feeding is difficult if one baby is much smaller than the other, because he will need feeding at shorter intervals, making it impossible to get both feedings over at once.

Simultaneous Feeding You can try putting both babies to the breasts simultaneously. It can be done with the help of cushions, armrests, and ingenuity, but it needs experimentation and the help of your midwife or a visiting nurse. Each baby's head is propped on a pillow beside the breast while his body is under your armpit and his legs behind you. An additional hazard is that one baby may start to suck hard before the other has started and set off the let-down reflex; the slow starter is then overwhelmed by a strong flow of milk before he is ready to begin feeding.

Feeding Separately If you feed the babies one after the other, feed each at a separate breast. Otherwise, the first to feed has the easier time, obtaining most milk with least effort (see breast feeding, p. 68).

Bottle feeding

Bottle feeding twins (pp. 93f.) has many of the problems of breast feeding, as well as the additional one that it is more difficult to hold two babies and feed them with two bottles at the same time. However, some mothers have told me they have achieved simultaneous bottle feeding in the same position as for simultaneous breast feeding. Alternatively, each baby lies with his head on her lap and his feet pointing out sideways.

Propped Bottles It is practical to feed twins together if you prop up the babies and the bottles (but see p. 83), supervising both but giving each baby individual attention as he needs it. However, this deprives them of the contact with you that should be part of feeding. You can try to make up for this at other times of the day, but as a mother of twins it is unlikely that you will have time to spare for this.

A Helper at Feeding Times The best solution is to have someone to help you at feeding times. A young brother or sister is capable of giving a bottle competently if shown how and kept under supervision; the baby can be propped up in a padded chair if necessary. But few children enjoy being summoned several times a day to feed the baby, and the novelty soon wears off. Shifts of friends may help out. Husbands who might have opted out of helping with one baby may agree to help with two.

If you have a refrigerator, it is much simpler to make up enough milk for the whole day's feedings at one session (see bottle feeding, pp. 90–92). If one or both twins are very small or if any difficulty arises, your doctor may advise you to keep a record of how much each twin takes at each feeding. This is probably essential with triplets unless you have an exceptional memory. Otherwise follow the normal method of allowing each baby to decide how much milk he wants at each feeding (see bottle feeding, p. 94).

Mixed Feeding

Since you will be extra hard-worked with twins, there need be even less compulsion than usual to get started on mixed feeding. Your doctor will have advised you on appropriate vitamin or iron supplements to their milk diet. If they seem contented with milk, they could continue on milk feedings only for as long as five to six months (see mixed feeding, pp. 185f.). Follow the ordinary guidelines for mixed feeding (pp. 190f.).

With twins it is particularly desirable to encourage self-feeding at the first opportunity. Rather than spoon feeding them, let them pick up small pieces of bread and butter, cheese, apple, etc., and eat crackers and toast. Some twins find it easier to feed each other than themselves.

Sleep

One of the major difficulties with twins can be sleep, or the lack of it from a parental point of view. One crying baby may wake the other, but you need not worry that either will go short of sleep, since young babies cannot help sleeping enough for their needs (see sleep, p. 107). However, if twins wake at different times during the night, this can add up to an awful lot of lost sleep for parents.

Night Feedings Since they may be small as babies, twins may continue to need night feedings for longer than the average baby. While both want night feedings it is usually best to wake and feed the second baby after feeding the one who woke first. Otherwise you will need to get out of bed just as you are dropping off to sleep again.

One solution is for parents to work shifts, each dealing with crying and feedings up to an agreed time of night, for example, before and after 2:00 A.M. Another is to harden one's heart, feed both babies when the first wakes, and refuse to get up till the early-morning feeding. The parents of twins need more routine at night as well as during the day in the interests of their own survival.

11

Effect of the New Baby on Family Life

Minimizing Jealousy between Children

Preparing Your Other Children

Whether a baby is born in the hospital or at home, the way you introduce him to brothers and sisters is important, particularly if an elder child is under five years old. There is nothing parents can do to prevent a child feeling a certain amount of natural displeasure at the arrival of a new baby, but you can make it easier by preparing him in advance and by avoiding situations that emphasize his changed position. For example, see that any major changes in his life, such as starting nursery school, do not coincide with the baby's arrival, otherwise he may "blame" the baby for the new situation. The same applies to moving out of a familiar room or crib or even from baby carriage to stroller.

Of course, you will tell your child that a new baby is expected, but don't tell a small child too long beforehand or he may get bored by waiting; when he starts noticing your size and the preparations at home is early enough. Let him pat your tummy so that he can feel the baby inside; if he's lucky he may feel the baby kick, which will make the experience all the more real. Show him some young babies lying helpless in their carriages, so that he does not expect a fully grown playmate from the start.

Introducing the New Baby

The first meeting with the new baby is an important occasion; it needs careful preparation and handling. However pleased you are to see your other children again for the first time, they may not see it that way if the new baby seems to dominate the room. It is easier for a small child to appreciate that you have missed him if you greet him with open arms—not with arms filled with the new baby. Make sure the baby is in his crib when they first meet. Spend a few minutes concentrating on the child and listening to his news, however far away it seems; don't be too eager to introduce the baby to him—they are going to have plenty of time to get to know each other.

The new baby will probably be surrounded by presents from friends and relations, few of whom will have remembered an older child, so it is a good idea to put an attractively wrapped present in the crib as a present to him from the new baby. You will have to avoid the impression that every visit automatically means a reward, while showing that he is appreciated and loved. Giving a present instead of your time and attention is no good (see also visitors, p. 51).

Reactions to the Baby

A small child's first reaction to his new brother or sister may disappoint his parents. He may say something uncomplimentary or just seem indifferent; this is probably intentional, so leave him to "find" the baby in the crib, rather than pointing him out. Don't try to force a comment if he does not react spontaneously. He may be so overwhelmed that he doesn't know how to behave, or seeing the baby may mean little to him at first. It is his long-term relationship with the baby that is important, not his early reactions. If he tries poking the baby, try not to sound shocked and angry, even if it seems malicious, but restrain him gently. It helps if his father or someone else is there to provide a quick distraction.

Handling a Jealous Child

Initial reactions to a new baby are often misleading. Because a child has appeared delighted, you should not assume he can do without extra reassurance and evidence of your continuing love and interest. For every child who shows his jealousy of a new baby and accuses his mother of no longer loving him, there is another who says and does nothing out of the ordinary but feels just as jealous and insecure and needs to talk about his feelings.

Listen to his outbursts; then tell him you understand and perhaps that you felt like that about your little brother. Help him to understand that you love him as much as ever, even though you have less time to spend alone with him. Involve him in the baby's needs because the baby is so small and helpless. Discuss, on the lines of joint responsibility, what you should both do for the baby.

Research has shown that brothers and sisters handled in this manner respond to a remarkable extent and exhibit much less jealousy.

Degrees of Jealousy

Children are usually most jealous of the baby born directly after them; a small child who already has a younger brother or sister is unlikely to be as jealous of the next baby. But it is impossible to predict the degree or effects of jealousy among children in any family on the basis of their ages or the size of the family. Endless combinations occur, relationships changing as the children grow older.

You cannot shield your children from experiencing jealousy altogether. It is impossible to do so, because learning to share with others the people you love is difficult. It is a valuable lesson to learn as part of growing up. Many an older child has to learn it later in life, after marriage perhaps. All that parents can do is to avoid giving a child any additional and unnecessary reasons for jealousy, making allowances for behavior that may be caused by it.

Dealing with the Symptoms

A child should be given the benefit of the doubt for annoying behavior following the birth of a new baby, but this should not become the excuse for and the explanation of everything that happens. For example, a child of two may behave in the negativistic way characteristic of this age whether or not a new baby arrives to complicate the scene.

How you deal with specific events is not as important as your general warmth toward your child. For instance, a child might put a stone or stick in the baby's dinner; his mother is understandably furious and shows it. But she does not go on being furious or making the child feel small all day. They both recover; she knows he was acting mainly through jealousy and partly through devilment, and he knows she was angry with him only temporarily, that it was for a good reason and not because she dislikes him now that she has a new baby.

Some of the annoying things your child does may be meant kindly —the stones or sticks in some dinners may be presents from child to baby! The baby's feeding times, particularly if he is breast fed, may need ingenious planning. It helps to feed him while the other child is watching television or has something special to do. He may want to try to feed too—one try is usually enough (see breast feeding, p. 76).

Emotional Problems

A child who begins wetting his bed, biting his nails, or showing other signs of emotional strain at a time when he could be feeling jealous of a new baby should be handled with this in mind. But remember that there may be a different cause, such as starting nursery school. The problem should be tackled indirectly: give your child more time and obvious affection, and take any other measures your common sense or your doctor, nurse, or your child's teacher suggests.

Older children may show jealousy indirectly—by trying to compete for attention through behaving outrageously, in contrast with the good behavior of the supposed favorite. Your attitude to your other children is bound to shift slightly with any addition to the family. Apart from the work and time involved in baby care, a baby's arrival affects emotional relationships in the family and also, perhaps, the balance of power among the children and between children and parents.

Spacing the Family

Can jealousy be minimized by spacing one's family closely so that each child is too young to mind the arrival of a younger sibling? Probably not—even a baby of twelve months will notice another baby, but you cannot explain things to him as you could a year later. He will notice if his baby carriage or crib is abruptly taken over. Any such changes should be made well before or after the birth of the new baby. Even if he feels less resentment than an older child, the one-year-old may suffer in other ways. His mother generally has less time to spend with him during his second year, when he begins exploring and speaking. If she is harassed by things in general, she is more likely to take it out on him than on the baby.

There are advantages and disadvantages in any age gap between children, and it is better to deal with jealousy as it arises than to plan one's family around this consideration alone. Whatever the gap between children, there are special problems and joys at each age; the best way to stop a child resenting his brothers or sisters excessively is to show him how much you value him.

Keeping House

A new baby introduces extra work in the form of laundry and time taken in feeding and attention, but he does not make the house dirty and untidy in the way a small child does. If the house is fairly clean and tidy when you arrive home with him, his mere presence will not cause chaos, given some reorganization and provided you don't set yourself impossible standards in baby care (see crying, pp. 116f.).

Unless you positively enjoy having evidence of your baby all over the house, keep his things together as much as possible. Keep one room respectably tidy, so that there is somewhere to take visiting aunts without feeling apologetic. Concentrate on those undone jobs that really worry you, like unmade beds or an unswept floor, and leave others, those you can ignore happily, whether these are washing up after every meal or emptying wastepaper baskets.

If you find housework a relaxing contrast to motherhood, and if shutting yourself in the living room with the vacuum cleaner helps you through a bad patch of the day, don't feel you ought to be sitting by the crib instead. Some mothers probably feel they ought to devote themselves constantly to their babies when really they would prefer to keep as near to their old standards and routine as possible. Do whatever suits you; so long as your baby is loved, fed, and washed he will be all right.

Feeling Tired

If you can keep the house immaculate without feeling exhausted, this is admirable. But if, as is far more likely, neither your baby nor the house is immaculate and you still feel tired, remember that it is more usual at this stage than the idyllic family life you feel you should be leading. Rest or sleep during the day if your nights are disturbed.

You may find it helps to practice the relaxation you learned at prenatal preparation classes; five minutes of proper relaxation can be more valuable than half an hour of uncomfortable "rest." Another lesson taught for labor is to deal with each contraction as it comes, instead of worrying that worse is to follow. This is sound advice to apply to the first hectic weeks at home with a new baby. In other words, don't worry about how and when the house will ever be tidy again, whether you will be able to cope next week or next year, or whether you will ever have a full night's sleep again. Try to live each day as it comes.

The weeks when your baby is adapting himself to the world and you are adapting yourself to him can seem long and confused, particularly if he is not a model of regular sleep and feeding. You may feel that you will never have any time to yourself again and that life will be forever devoted to meeting the insatiable demands of an unpredictable infant. But babies grow up and mothers grow more efficient. Just as cooking meals and washing shirts may tire a new wife, but are later done almost automatically, so looking after a child becomes a part of a mother's life; always an important part, but not the millstone it can seem at first.

Feeling Depressed

You are very likely to feel a bit depressed a few days after your baby is born, especially if no one has warned you that it often takes time to fall in love with your baby and to feel maternal (p. 50). For example, whereas most mothers enjoy cleaning up their babies after they have passed a stool and making them feel comfortable again, some mothers find the whole business of stools very distasteful at first. This depressed feeling is so common that it has many names, such as "postpartum blues." It may be partly that the physical and chemical changes that follow birth can make you less stable emotionally. This is not surprising considering that the much slighter changes in chemical balance during the monthly cycle make many women moody, tense, and easily upset. But lack of understanding, especially in the hospital, with consequent guilt feelings that you are a failure plays the largest part. It is all too easy for a mother to feel "bad" when really it is because no one has given her a chance to share her fears of failure.

Mothers in the hospital together can affect each other, so that if one gets the blues, the others may cry as well. Something small can start it—one mother going home, a baby being slow to feed, a rough gesture from a nurse, a husband being two minutes late at visiting time. This is the time when a mother is liable to feel inadequate, therefore relatives and friends must be sensitive to this possibility.

Reasons for Depression

The big point about postpartum blues, as opposed to true depression, is that they are short-lived. As a new mother you may be upset not only by bodily changes, probably increased by the effects of fatigue or of drugs during labor, but also by a sense of emotional anticlimax. Nine months of waiting, culminating in the climax of birth, are followed by reality. Your baby can be positively ugly at first, or the "wrong" sex, and it can be overwhelming to realize that you have produced another human being who is entirely helpless and almost totally your responsibility. A husband may suddenly feel the weight of fatherhood but he doesn't have to face the immediate day-to-day care of his baby. He has longer to adjust than his wife, who is supposed to act like a mother at once, even if she doesn't yet feel like one.

These forebodings flit through most parents' minds or are uppermost for a few days and then pass. Naturally, the sense of responsibility for your child, the feeling that you will never be entirely safe again because of this responsibility—not just for your own life but also for the development of another, unpredictable, person—are emotions that can recur at any stage of the growing relationship between you and your child. But normally they do not become permanent, dominating, or disabling worries.

Severe Depression

But don't be under the impression that feeling low and tired for months is an inevitable consequence of childbirth—this is not so. A mother who does find herself constantly anxious about her baby and exhausted and depressed by her responsibilities, or just by the everyday work of motherhood, is suffering from more than the usual postpartum reaction. She is not just "tired"; she is depressed and needs help for her depression.

I suspect that "tiredness" in most people is more often caused by depression than by physical exhaustion. Tiredness from hard work or exercise that has been enjoyed provides you with good sleep and finds you elated on waking. The depressed person is still tired on waking and has no wish to get out of bed.

What should you do if you suspect that you are depressed? Sometimes you can counteract the state by identifying the things that seem to contribute to it and taking steps to change your routine (although a characteristic of depression is that it seems hopeless to attempt anything). For example, chronic fatigue can make depression worse so that becoming less tired, in itself, makes life seem more manageable. Exhaustion from lack of sleep because your baby cries at night should be tackled through the baby himself. Your doctor or visiting nurse can help by suggesting changes in his feeding or sleeping routine that ought to hasten the time when he sleeps better at night. If having him in your bedroom at night worries you, move him out (see p. 110). Although there is no substitute for a good night's sleep, take any chance of short sleeps or rests during the daytime. Practicing relaxation helps you to make the best of these rests (see p. 152).

Counteracting Boredom

Continual tiredness can be due to sheer monotony as well as to lack of sleep. Having a baby makes it difficult for you to go out and cheer yourself up by doing something different. The gloom settles instead of dispersing in a change of scene. Any tendency toward bouts of depression is encouraged by the life you may be forced to lead, especially with a first baby, and if you have few friends or relatives living nearby.

Diaper washing and housework are dull substitutes for a job, which, however routine, at least provided adult company and an extra contribution to the household funds. No outside job goes on for twenty-four hours a day, but before your baby has settled down to some kind of rhythm of sleep and feeding you can become so tense and tired that you feel perpetually on duty and unable to relax even when you get the chance. You may never actually enjoy your baby except when he is asleep. You can feel physically unattractive, uninterested in sex, and mentally blank.

It is natural to feel like this to some extent at this stage, since with a new baby to care for, you must act primarily, if only temporarily, as a mother rather than as a wife. You have to be a maternal rather than a sexual figure or an intellectual force, because this is the role nature means you to play for the benefit of your child.

As the child grows you regain some of your lost independence and your interests widen again. If you understand that some loss of independence and individuality is normal and necessary for your baby, you are less likely to remain depressed by the changes in yourself and you will know that you have not lost your self-confidence for good.

Getting Out of the House

Some narrowing of outside interests and activities is inevitable for most mothers; staying at home all the time with a young baby can reinforce tension and anxiety, but it is still possible to reorganize your life to beat depression if you feel it threatening. It is important to try to get away from home and from your baby, especially if his crying gets on your nerves.

If there are no baby-sitters available, a husband who notices his wife's gloom must persuade her to go out while he takes over. A mother may be afraid to ask someone to baby-sit, because although she is in despair over her own lack of competence with the baby, she is too anxious to trust him to anyone else. Alternatively, she may think that everyone else will find him as difficult and tiring as she does. If you feel like this, remember that looking after a baby, however fretful he is, does not seem so tedious to someone who doesn't have the responsibility all the time. People can always refuse to baby-sit if they dislike the idea (see baby-sitters, p. 159).

Take reasonable care in choosing and briefing the sitter, then you can forget about your baby for a few hours, or try to: it may take a conscious effort to forget him after spending weeks or months looking after him. Try to arrange to get out during the day sometimes as well as during the evenings. After a long day at home with a small baby you may not want to move in the evenings—but make the effort, because you will feel better for it. However tired you are from broken nights, fatigue may be due partly to monotony; at least you will be tired for a different reason after a night out.

Telling Your Doctor

You should always tell your doctor or nurse if you feel perpetually tired, dismal, and unable to enjoy anything. I am appalled by how often I hear mothers who have been depressed say that it did not occur to them that their doctors could help them over their feelings; they think of their doctor only in terms of what they regard as real illness.

Don't expect your doctor to notice automatically if you are depressed; you may be concealing the fact admirably, or you may cheer up as soon as you see someone, so that no one realizes how dreadful you really feel. His advice may be that you will feel all right as soon as your baby has settled down to a reasonable routine and you are more used to him; give this a chance, but if it proves wrong, let him know. Occasionally, acute depression descends like a bombshell and you will need immediate help.

How a Husband Can Help

Your husband can help by being useful with the baby and sympathetic about chaos in the house; by not expecting you to feel like a mother overnight when your past life has been spent in a totally different way; and by taking the initiative sometimes to prevent you from becoming a drudge who never wants to leave the house. When a woman does need help from her doctor in adjusting to the new life, it is disastrous for her husband to scoff. His role is to try to understand the stresses she feels when she suddenly becomes completely responsible for their child, and to offer her practical sympathy. Arranging for domestic help, buying her a washing machine, taking her out regularly—all can help.

Going Back to Work

If you want to continue with outside work, part- or full-time, this must be discussed rather than dismissed out of hand. Your baby will not automatically be happier with his depressed mother at home all the time; a suitable mother substitute, plus a happy mother at home some of the time, is a better compromise (see working mother, pp. 162f.).

Baby-sitters

There is no need to wait until your baby is a certain age before feeling you can leave him with a baby-sitter. It is all right to go out the day you arrive home from hospital, if you can find someone responsible to stay with him. Some hospitals may encourage parents to go out for a meal together before mother and baby go home. This helps a mother adjust to leaving her baby in someone else's care for the first time. It also reminds a couple that they are still husband and wife, as well as new parents, and are entitled to enjoy themselves without their baby when they can. It is a pity if this is their last outing for a long time because they cannot find a baby-sitter or feel they should not leave the baby.

Leaving Your New Baby

You may be dubious about leaving your baby at first, for several reasons. While his feeding times are very erratic, especially if he is breast fed, it may seem impossible to go out for long enough to make it worthwhile. But a full-term baby will come to no harm if he is kept waiting for his next feeding. If you are worried that he will starve, or if you want to stay out later than his normal feeding time, prepare a feeding of cow's milk (see bottle feeding, p. 85) or of breast milk, expressed and decanted into a bottle.

Some sitters feel uneasy unless they have something to offer the baby if he cries persistently, in which case you could leave a bottle of boiled water or fruit juice. If a breast-fed baby won't take a bottle, your baby-sitter could try offering the drink by spoon.

Briefing the Baby-sitter

Anticipate some of the sitter's possible problems and give her some idea of your baby's temperament. Does he usually sleep peacefully between feedings or is he likely to wake up? Do you want her to change his diaper? Does he have a pacifier or does he go back to sleep if turned on his side? If you have only just brought him home and have very little idea how he will behave, confess this to your stand-in and let her feel you trust her to cope. Don't feel guilty that the baby may cry and interrupt her knitting. She won't mind pacing the floor with him for half an hour if he does. Most people enjoy soothing a crying baby; it's only when he's your own, and the situation crops up several times a day, that the novelty wears off. Show her where your baby's things are kept.

How thoroughly you brief a baby-sitter naturally depends on her experience of babies and on how much she has to do besides just sitting. A grandmother might resent being shown how to pin on a diaper, but someone unused to small babies needs to watch you changing a diaper and giving a feeding. Ideally, a sitter with common sense but without experience of babies should spend some time helping you to look after your baby before being left in charge.

It saves time, and prevents a sitter feeling you lack confidence in her personally, if you give her a list with telephone numbers and general information. Tell her where you are going and leave the telephone number, even if it's a restaurant. Your doctor's telephone number should be listed as well as the number of a friend, neighbor, or grandparent who could give advice if you cannot be reached. Leave the name and address of a neighbor if you have no telephone. The chances are this information will never be needed, but you are both less likely to get jittery if you know she can get help quickly if necessary.

Leaving the Older Baby

As your baby settles into a routine, between three and twelve months, you will be happier about leaving him, but it becomes more important for a sitter to know his routine and for the baby to know her. If you are going out before his bedtime, she must know what he expects; preferably she should help you to put him to bed once or twice. It is unfair to your child and to her if you forget to mention that he won't go to sleep without his old piece of blanket to suck, that his door must be left ajar, or that he needs to go to the bathroom at 10:00 P.M.

It is always a mistake to hurry a small child's bedtime routine because you want him in bed before the sitter arrives. Start putting him to bed earlier than usual, rather than rushing him by cutting out his bedtime story, or forgetting to kiss him good night.

Reassuring Your Child

Should you tell a child who is old enough to understand that you are going out and that someone else will look after him, or should you slink out and leave her to deal with the consequences if he does wake up? Parents who feel sure the child won't wake up and who are also sure it would upset him to know they are going out are sometimes tempted not to tell him and to hope for the best. This probably works nine times out of ten, but if the child does wake up and finds them out, he will be suspicious in future and may even try to keep himself awake to make sure they stay at home. On the whole, honesty is best.

As the child comes to realize that you do return and that it's not too bad being left with a baby-sitter, he will not mind so much, even if he still goes through the motions of minding. If he fusses whenever you are going out and tries all kinds of ruses to stop you, you have to react gently but firmly—that tricky combination—and go anyway.

Introduce your child to the sitter, preferably before the evening when you go out. Even if he screams at the sight of her, he will most likely settle down the moment you go. Don't hover anxiously, or he will think there really is something to worry about. A small child may be reassured when left with someone he does not know already if you talk about her beforehand and mention some familiar characteristic or connection which makes her less anonymous—for instance, perhaps she knows or baby-sits for a friend or lives on a familiar road.

Once he is used to a particular sitter, a child is usually quite happy to be left with her, although he may still protest when you start to leave. When a child is old enough to understand, you can explain that parents enjoy going out and doing something different just as much as he does. It's your turn, in fact.

The Terrified Child

What should you do if your child seems genuinely terrified at the idea of your going out? If this happens suddenly and unexpectedly there may be some special cause for his anxiety, perhaps connected with the last time you went out: he may have had a nightmare that the sitter couldn't dispel or he may have wet the bed. Remembering and telling you about it may be enough to reassure him at once, or it may take longer for his confidence to build up again.

A child who is used to his parents leaving him and returning safely, with no harm coming either to them or to himself, does not often become really afraid of being left unless this is part of a deeper and more general anxiety about other things. The underlying cause needs finding and tackling (see problems affecting behavior, pp. 546f.).

A baby or small child who is going through a phase of clinging to his mother and resenting other people may temporarily hate her going out, but if he is used to it he will not be desperately frightened. It is good for a child and for his parents to keep in practice over these temporary partings.

Choosing the Ideal Baby-sitter

The ideal baby-sitter is the one your child likes. You can go out and enjoy yourself and know he is enjoying himself too. Obviously, for the very young baby, the sitter should have reasonably hygienic personal habits and some understanding of infants, since she may have to handle or feed the baby. But you can always prepare his food yourself, and unless someone is obviously dirty, a healthy baby is unlikely to suffer from a few hours of her company. So perhaps warmth, reliability—she must turn up when arranged and stay put till you get back—and common sense are the most important qualities for a sitter whatever the baby's age.

Strangers

Are there any precautions to take when choosing a sitter? It is safest to interview a stranger who answers an advertisement before employing her for the first time. If you are uneasy at the interview, don't employ her. But don't feel uneasy just because at first sight she is not your idea of a mother figure. One teen-age girl may love babies and prove an entirely reliable baby-sitter, while another may want to baby-sit just to find somewhere private to meet her friends, or a free telephone for lengthy conversations. You should explain what you expect of her. You may be happy about one or two friends, but if the evening becomes too much of a social event, the baby may be forgotten and left to cry. Someone old and slow-moving is not the best person to chase a toddler around the house, but may be all right for a small baby. A hard-faced lady who believes that crying is good for babies is not the ideal baby-sitter, however experienced she is in "mothercraft."

Male Sitters

An impecunious male student may make a good baby-sitter, particularly if he comes from a large family and is used to small children. Obviously you do not employ a strange man to baby-sit without checking his suitability and his motives, but men should not be discriminated against in the baby-sitting market just on grounds of sex. A male lodger often proves an excellent baby-sitter; his bedtime stories may be especially gripping! Renting a room, with regular baby-sitting as part of the agreement, has solved many families' baby-sitting problems.

Agencies and Clubs

Sitters from well-established agencies are selected by the agency and so should be reliable, but they are often expensive. Try to get the same person regularly. A cheaper solution is to join or to start a baby-sitting circle with local parents. Health clinics sometimes have details. Parents baby-sit for one another and it costs nothing but your time.

Relatives

Relatives make natural baby-sitters and have the advantage of an inbuilt interest in your child. But they don't like being overworked or taken for granted. However delightful her grandchildren, a grandmother has other interests and can find small children more tiring than a young parent does; she dislikes it if her daughter assumes that she is always available (see grandparents, pp. 171f.).

Daytime Baby-sitting

When you leave your children during the day it is important to make sure that the sitter knows your house and yard well, and is briefed on the children's habits and foibles. If a child is a terror crossing streets, tell her in advance. Accidents happen more frequently when there is an unfamiliar ingredient in a situation—which could well be the fact that the sitter does not take the precautions you take automatically because you know the child and his surroundings (see accidents, pp. 621–22).

You cannot cover every possibility or insure against everything that could go wrong, any more than you can when in charge yourself.

But find someone you like, tell her everything she wants to know and whatever you feel would be useful—then go out and try to forget what is going on at home.

Choosing a Mother Substitute

Qualified Nursemaids

A trained nursemaid has the advantage for her charge of providing constant and consistent care. Since this is her career rather than a stopgap or a way of learning the language, she is likely to stay with a family as long as she is needed. Her professionalism and expertise put parents' minds at rest so far as the child's everyday care and well being are concerned but, paradoxically, these very qualities contain a major snag which some mothers fail to recognize when deciding to employ a nursemaid.

Because her job is to look after children and not to help out generally, it can easily happen that a nursemaid becomes the mother figure in a child's life. To avoid confusing her child by competing with the nursemaid in the nursery, a mother may find herself withdrawing from the role she would like to fill in her child's life: a woman usually wants to be a full mother, even if she cannot be a full-time one. If she is at home all day, she has to busy herself with household matters while the nursemaid looks after the children; if she is at work, she may find the nursemaid's influence remains dominant even on her day off.

This situation is more liable to arise with a nursemaid of the old school, who in the past was expected to take full charge and still expects to. A young nursemaid is often more adaptable, and willing to help outside the nursery while parents look after the children.

Parents who want help with their children and can afford a nursemaid ought to consider carefully the kind of help they really want. It might often be better to opt for more domestic help, plus some general help with the children from a mother's helper. This is possible to arrange even if you go out to work full-time, although admittedly in return for remaining the first woman in your child's life you have to expend more energy in organizing help.

Qualities to Look For If you decide to employ a nursemaid, you should look further than her paper qualifications or other employers' recommendations, however ecstatic. It is important that you and your husband like her as a person and agree with her basic approach in bringing up children—if your child or children are old enough to have an opinion, this is important too. If the nursemaid is a rigid disciplinarian who believes that a baby must be clean, tidy, and presentable at all times, while you are happy with less perfection and more fun, your child will become confused and the nursemaid will probably leave quite soon. On the whole, a young nursemaid is less likely to have this approach.

A nursemaid, like a mother, should be good at mothering as well as at mothercraft. You can assume that a trained or experienced nursemaid knows how to change a diaper and give your baby his bottle, so concentrate on finding out more about her as a person.

Sharing Your Child Occasionally, a nursemaid forms a barrier between a mother and her child by making the mother feel inadequate and inefficient. The nursemaid conveys the impression that there is only one way of doing things—her way—so the mother surrenders more and more of her child's care, both physical and emotional. In fact, the nursemaid takes over. This is to some degree inevitable and understandable. A nursemaid who did not feel slightly possessive about a child when she had so much responsibility for him would not be successful at her job in other ways. But a good nursemaid is on the lookout for this and does not allow it to happen. She knows a child should feel comfortable and natural with both mother and nursemaid in the same way that he can accept and give affection to relatives and friends. But if he senses rivalry for his affection, or, rather, for power over him, he will either use it to get his own way or become unhappy trying to reconcile the two women in his life.

Disagreements However efficient your nursemaid, if you really disagree with something she is doing it is best to talk it over with her. She may have better reasons than you realized, because she knows the child intimately and from a different angle. But ultimately your child is your responsibility, and a parent cannot abdicate this responsibility over something that really matters. You do not stand by and say nothing if, for example, your child wets his bed and this is treated as straightforward naughtiness by his nursemaid. You would be right to feel uneasy and right to insist that another approach is worked out, if necessary enlisting your doctor's help.

Working Mothers

Choosing to Work

Some mothers have to work, some are determined to work, but many others are torn between their desire to be good mothers and their need for the outside interest of a job. If you worked before your baby was born and enjoyed working, you will not necessarily find it easy to hand over your job to someone else, or to make the mental and physical leap into full-time housekeeping and motherhood.

No one would be surprised if a man found it difficult to adjust himself overnight to a life revolving around the home and caring for a helpless infant, after spending the first twenty or thirty years of his life at school and earning his living. True, a man would have no maternal hormones and instincts to help him make the adjustment, but in a civilized society these are in strong competition with other forces—like the individual's right, almost his duty, to use his talents, to enjoy himself, and to achieve a high standard of living. Giving birth to a child does not automatically wipe out these rival pressures or enable you to adapt smoothly to this phase of marriage: you are likely to feel guilty when you realize that even though your baby is everything to you, he is not yet enough.

If you feel like this, should you draw the conclusion that you are not one of nature's mothers and hand over your baby to someone who is, while you go back to work? Or should you grit your teeth and stay at home because you feel every child needs the sole care of his own mother? There is no easy answer: each family has to work this one out for itself—but some guidelines may help.

Work and careers go on but babies grow up. They grow up surprisingly quickly, and however long the early months of motherhood may seem, time starts flying by; soon babies are schoolchildren and there is time for mothers to work.

The Effect on the Mother/Child Relationship

Babies and small children need loving individual care from one person who handles them most of the time. This is important from the very beginning, when the feel and smell of his mother, or mother figure, is becoming familiar and reassuring to a baby. From about four to six months a baby begins to recognize and depend on this one person more strongly; soon afterward he becomes temporarily suspicious of other people. The baby with a working mother is all right if he has someone else to provide this focus and interest, as long as she is warm, understanding, and permanent. For his parents, finding and keeping the right person can be difficult and nerve-racking. Also it is sometimes forgotten that a mother is "identifying" with her baby as well as the baby with his mother in these early months.

The fact that your baby spends most of his day with someone else would not lessen your basic love and affection for him or prevent him from developing a special feeling for you as his mother; a child is able to cope with more than one woman in his life. But the relationship between the two of you might be less intimate, more of a "special relationship" than the deep friendliness that develops between two people who are constantly together. Mother is probably a more romantic figure if she is not always available and is not associated with the kitchen sink, but she is also a more remote figure. She may find herself being more indulgent than she knows is good for the child because she is anxious to enjoy him while they are together. However, the opposite can happen—a mother falls over backward to avoid "spoiling" her child and ends up by being stricter than comes naturally to her.

If your child goes to his nursemaid for comfort and appears to be on easier, more spontaneous terms with her, you cannot help feeling resentful as well as relieved that they get on together (see nursemaids, pp. 161–62). The nursemaid's day off can seem more of a strain to a working mother than a whole week with the child to a mother at home; this is not necessarily because being a mother comes more naturally to the full-time mother, but because she is in practice. On the other hand, a few mothers become so depressed when they are at home all day that they would find it easier to enjoy their children if they worked and the children were only a part-time responsibility (see postnatal depression, pp. 152f).

Working Part-Time

One solution, if you have a new baby but feel reluctant to give up all ideas of a career, is to accept that there will be little time for outside work for the first few months. If you have the energy and are lucky enough to find work to do at home, you may be able to fit it in. But it is normal to feel intellectually rather lazy for a year or so after having a baby. You may not feel like doing anything more demanding than reading magazines, yet worry that you are neglecting your mind. Don't force yourself to take on work because you feel it is expected nowadays; don't feel that you are wasting your time and education or that your brain will wither from disuse; if it was active before, it will be active again. You are likely to be happier if you take a short-term view of life for a while after your baby is born, regarding his care as your present job and letting your future career look after itself.

As your baby becomes more independent, so will your mind; inconveniently, his physical and intellectual agility coincides with the return of your mental agilities! You are on full-time duty keeping him out of trouble and responding to his demands for you to play with him just as you feel capable of thinking again. From about eighteen months to three years a toddler expects to have the undivided attention of his mother. You may resent being unable to read a book or write a letter until he is in bed, particularly because you are probably too tired to do either by then; but if he demands your attention you should give it. This is such an important learning period that you should be involved in his play even though at times your role is to sit quietly observing (p. 299). But that does not mean you can read your book—the intelligent toddler will soon complain about that!

Some mothers manage to fit part-time work or interests into their baby's sleep periods during the day. Alternatively, it does a baby no harm to be cared for by someone else for a few hours a day. If this is begun before he is six months old, he probably won't mind, but if the change coincides with a phase of clinging to mother, which is normal at around six months, it can be more difficult at first. It is best if he is looked after in the familiar surroundings of his own home, and has a chance to get used to a stand-in while his mother is nearby.

Day-Care Nurseries

A large nursery with a few staff to care for several babies is not the ideal place to park your baby while you work; even the most devoted staff cannot give each child the individual attention he needs until the age of two or three, when he begins to play with other children. It is a solution some mothers have to accept because they are poor or alone. In any case, for mothers who are not in desperate need of them and must work, free or cheap nursery places for babies are a rarity. For mothers to whom work is a luxury, or at least an optional extra, employing other women as stand-ins is the best answer (see pp. 161f.).

Once the child is two years old and is happy to leave home, a day nursery can be quite a different place, provided it is run by well-trained staff and is not overcrowded. At its best it can be as good as a nursery school (p. 317).

Play Groups

Once your child is old enough to attend a play group—that is, at about three years—you can at least have some free time each day, if you can get him into one (see preschool, pp. 314f.).

If there is no play group, you and other mothers can sometimes help each other out by taking turns looking after the children, thereby freeing several mornings (see p. 316).

Working When Children Are School Age

Once your children have started school you may want to work even if you did not want to before. The difficulties are school vacations, the couple of hours after school, and illnesses. You have to make arrangements in advance to cover these events. Paying someone to stand in domestically may make it not worthwhile financially for a mother to work. The solution may be part-time work, best of all (as far as making arrangements is concerned) work that can be done at home. Again, each family has to work out its problems, financial and personal.

It is beyond the scope of this book to advise you how and where to find this ideal work, but if you make a start—even voluntary work or a job unworthy of your qualifications—it may lead to something better, and at any rate it gives you confidence.

Do Children Mind Mothers Working?

Will your children feel deprived when they compare you with other children's mothers who are always available to bake and sew? Someone who longs for a career probably wouldn't be baking or sewing even if she were at home all day, unless she happened to enjoy these things anyway.

Schoolchildren like a mother who enjoys herself and is fun; they like her to be a person in her own right. You may find that the stimulus of an outside job releases more, not less, energy to spend on home and family. Your children won't much like it if your work makes you continually harassed and bad-tempered, and leaves you no time for them even when you are at home. But they will probably be proud of you if you manage to be reasonably good-tempered, reasonably unhurried, and reasonably interested in them as well as in your work. At least they avoid the kind of mother who clings on to her children and wants to know their every doing when they are old enough to lead a life that is partly private and independent. If you work, your relationship with your children will be different from the one you would have had otherwise, but it won't necessarily be a worse one. However, remember that children at school like to think of home as the place that contains their mother while they are away. So discuss all this with them and do all you can to be back at home when they return from school.

Mothers Who Must Work

Unfortunately, many women with small babies have to work whether they like it or not and even if they are unhappy about the arrangements made for the care of their babies. The shortage of free or cheap day-care nursery places in most industrialized countries is particularly serious because it is in these societies that relatives who could help are least likely to be living nearby. Few places of work organize facilities for preschool children, however desperate they are for female staff. Let us hope it will not be long before establishments such as factories and hospitals develop a feeling of responsibility for the preschool children of the women they employ, and begin to provide suitable day nurseries for them.

Regulations in the United States provide a greater safeguard for the rights of working mothers to keep their previous job. No longer can a pregnant employee be dismissed on the basis of pregnancy.

The Importance of Individual Care

Individual care is of little value if all it means is that a baby is not shuttled about. He must also be played with, talked to, and enjoyed. Without this, he is not much better off than the "institution children," whose apathy drew attention to the importance of individual care for even the smallest babies. These children are brought up not only without mothers but also without stimulation provided instinctively by loving and interested parents, but this is not the alternative for many babies—the alternative is poverty-stricken, harassed parents or inadequate substitutes. In either case, the result is understimulation and its sequel, underachievement. The baby who lies in his crib all day, ignored in the back room of a private house, is no better off.

The importance of providing as much individual care as possible for each baby is now recognized, but because costs must be kept down, the ratio of staff to babies in nurseries is inevitably low. It is impossible to organize individual care for every baby whose mother works, but it is possible to organize stimulating surroundings.

Group Care

Recent research has shown that with the right kind of stimulation, group care can give babies a very good start. It may not be as ideal as the stimulation provided instinctively by loving and interested parents, but this is not the alternative for many babies—the alternative is poverty-stricken, harassed parents, or inadequate substitutes. In either case, the result is understimulation and its sequel, underachievement. This pattern can affect the whole of a child's life, particularly when his home, his neighborhood, and his school are all impoverished. It is these children who are most likely to get a bad start in life, unless something is done about it.

There is nothing "cold-blooded" about using deliberately tested and planned methods to enrich a baby's environment (see development, pp. 214f.). The aim is not to start him on the rat race earlier, but to prevent the large-scale loss of individual potential resulting from a failure to accept the true situation—that more and more babies are going to be cared for by a group of professionals while their mothers work.

The argument that to provide a practical alternative to minding their own babies will tempt more mothers back to work earlier is not valid: more women want or need to work anyway, for economic, social, and personal reasons. Children are a country's investment for the future, and governments are slowly acknowledging the preschool child's right to a stimulating environment. They need persuading by determined mothers, educators, and doctors that the investment should start earlier and that the right facilities should be provided for even the youngest infants if they are in need of them.

All Our Loving?

Favorites

Parents with more than one child are bound to hear, sooner or later, an indignant voice claiming that another child is their "favorite." No parent admits this, protesting instead equally loudly that he or she loves all the children the same. In denying you have favorites you are trying to convince your child that there is no need to worry, that basically he is utterly safe and loved as much as any other child in the family.

At the most profound level, this is true: you probably do love all your children equally deeply and without reserve. You have probably noticed that however emotionally distant you may have felt from one of your children, a threat to his health or happiness instantly reminds you how much that child means to you and puts your feelings for him into perspective. But on a more superficial level it is impossible to feel the same degree of love for each child all of the time. Loving your child does not mean you will always get on with him.

The Child You Don't Get on With

It is comparatively easy to accept that you will find any child aggravating and unlovable at times; it is harder to acknowledge feeling permanently cool toward a child, to like him less than the others. But since parents cannot choose their children's personalities and looks, and it would not guarantee a successful relationship if they could, it is not surprising that each child arouses a different emotional response, making you a different parent. You have only got to hear different grownups reminiscing about their childhood to realize that one man's warm, loving mommy is his brother's cold, dragonlike mother.

It is natural to feel more sympathetic and appreciative of some individuals than others. Discovering that this applies in your own family should not make you feel an inadequate parent or an unusual one. It is normal and need not lead to an emotional divorce between you and your child or to an emotionally disturbed or deprived child. However, it does mean that you have to recognize when this relationship needs hard work and conscious effort, and to accept that you may never achieve an easy intimacy with a particular child. You may have to let him know you love him, making it obvious in ways that are unnecessary with another child, who happens to be on the same wavelength as yourself. But you may end up learning more from each other and giving more, just because you have had to try harder to understand each other.

When you are worried because you lack spontaneous warmth for a child, it can be helpful to try to work out the reason for it, but very often it needs a doctor's help. Sometimes it is because the child himself seldom responds openly to affection. As a baby he may have been restless whenever cuddled or held quietly. This may have been due to separation from your baby at birth and a lack of understanding of its effect on you and your baby by those in charge. You may have become depressed (pp. 152–53) but no one realized what you were going through—except your baby, by his reactions. Consciously or unconsciously you have felt rejection of your love. When we call a child "lovable" we usually mean he is "loving"—and therefore easy to love back.

A perfectly normal child may seem cold and unaffectionate compared with other children in the family. It is far better to accept him as he is than to try to force him to display affection. Real mother love consists in giving a child what he needs: this child may not need much cuddling, but like every child he does need to feel and to show love indirectly, through mutual appreciation and consideration.

Getting Over a Bad Start

There are so many reasons for a bad start—the important thing is for doctors and others to be aware of them and to help you understand them. They must help you from feeling it is your fault when the "fault" lies in circumstances or the rigid "system." Examples are: guilt feelings arising from attempts to terminate the pregnancy, or even merely the thought of doing this; mismanagement of the lying-in period under a rigid hospital routine with lack of contact between mother and baby in the vital first days, when they need to be together—much can be done to prevent this even if your baby is premature and has to receive special care (see Chapter 9, the low birth weight baby, pp. 133f.); unhappy early feeding experiences, leaving a mother feeling she has failed as far as her baby is concerned; postpartum depression, forming an emotional barrier between them so that the mother feels alienated from her baby. The baby may have been the "wrong" sex, have arrived at an inconvenient time, been shockingly ugly—anything that got him off to a bad start may mean that one or both of his parents never feel quite at

home with him. He begins to feel the outsider in the family: someone else is always the favorite.

A bad start of this kind is sad, but lost ground can be made up.
As the child grows up, the feeling of emotional alienation can diminish
and finally disappear by helping him to understand its reasons. Children never cease to amaze me by the depth of their understanding
when complicated matters are explained in simple language. A
mother who found her child a tremendous strain as a young baby, who
despaired of herself as a mother, can enjoy him later on. She may turn
out to be better at mothering older children than someone who was
an instant success with her new babies but less at ease with ten-year-
olds. Mothering goes on all the time—no one is the ideal mother for
every child at every age, but nearly everyone is very good, or at least
promising, for much of the time. The baby you could not enjoy except
when he was asleep may turn out to be your favorite companion—and
vice versa.

Sharing Your Feelings

Sometimes the child you get on with most easily is like you, but not
always. Believing a child is "just like me" can mean that when you
notice your own faults appearing in him you stamp on them extra hard
—which tends to lead to cries of "Unfair!" and "Why do you always
pick on me?" Your child may work out the reason before you do and
know that your exasperation over his forgetfulness is really because
you are so absent-minded yourself. He won't despise you for admitting this; in fact, a child appreciates his parents' confessions of fallibility, particularly if this means that they are going to try to reform too.

"Smother Love"

Just as it is hard to accept that all children do not want the same kind
or degree of demonstrative mother love—the kind that leaves you
warm and happy—it may also be difficult to adjust your mothering to
the developing needs of each child. The phrase "smother love" accurately describes this kind of overdemonstrative, overwhelming
"love," which is not so much an expression of affection for the child
as an expression of some need on the part of the parents. Paradoxically, a smother-loved child may be deprived of the kind of loving he
really wants, love that is sensitive to his changing needs, that brings
him his meals on time as well as a surfeit of kisses.

Take your cue from your child's behavior. The amount of demonstrative love demanded by each child varies. The one who asks for a
lot should be given it; he is showing you that he needs more than the
others, possibly because he is less secure. Get rid of your fear that
you are spoiling him—this is loving, not spoiling.

Untying the Apron Strings

The small boy who sits on your lap will, eventually, dislike being cuddled, at least in public. He will also want you to let him go in other ways, to understand that he needs his gang of friends as well as his family, and other people's ideas as well as yours.

He does not stop loving his parents and he still needs their love, but he has changed and he needs a different kind of loving—a recognition that he is growing up, and away. He is more likely to get this in a large family, where parents are far too busy with his successors to go on babying him. But in a small family, it is not so easy to lose the "baby" to growing independence; you may need to remind yourself deliberately that your child is growing out of dependence on you; otherwise your emotional development may not keep pace with his. This does not mean that you must stop cuddling a child at a given age, but just that the timing and amount of demonstrative affection should be related to his needs as well as to yours.

Regaining Your Independence

Luckily, today, mothers tend to increase their commitments and widen their interests outside the family as their children grow older; this takes the place of successive pregnancies in ensuring that each child is allowed to untie the apron strings. Adults do not stop developing at the point when they become parents. Normal adults continue to grow up throughout their lives, and the happiest families are the ones that grow up together. The parents accept that their children will want different things from them at different times, because they themselves are still changing and wanting different things from life. It is only frustrating to watch everyone else running when you are standing still.

Your grown-up children will continue to need the comforting reassurance of parental love and support, to be relied upon whatever happens, independent of their successes and failures. If they have been shown that love in childhood, they will know that it is always there. It will enable them to give the same love to their own children. A happy childhood in the widest sense is the best preparation for parenthood.

Grandparents

Nowadays grandparents less frequently live with or near their married children, but the birth of a grandchild often brings a closer relationship between the generations. They see more of each other because of their new common interest—the baby. A daughter who felt independent of her parents during her working life and early marriage wants her mother's support and advice again when she becomes pregnant.

You may find that having your own baby makes you appreciate, perhaps for the first time, the nature of your parents' feelings toward yourself: apparent possessiveness and exaggerated concern about your activities, health, and happiness are more comprehensible once you understand what it feels like to be identified with the well-being of your own child. It also becomes easier to sympathize with a mother-in-law, to realize that what seemed like interference and a slight on yourself as a wife is really just continuing love for her son.

So the grandchild's arrival tends to provide a focus for family affection and interest and to revive the intensity of relationships, particularly between the new grandmother and her daughter. This may mean that the prickly areas, where any antagonism previously flourished, also revive, complicated by the difficulties of adapting to being a mother for the first time, not to say a grandmother.

For some weeks after your baby's birth you are liable to be touchier and more likely to burst into tears than usual (see postpartum depression, pp. 152–53). This may cause you increased concern if one of the grandmothers is living in to help you, but it is something that she will understand. She will make allowances for it and will not take offense for long—if she does, your husband should help explain things to her. At the same time, he could tell her how grateful he is for the sheer hard work and physical help she is contributing.

If you feel in advance that you will be unable to get on with either grandmother if she actually lives with you to help with the new baby, try to find someone else, who is less emotionally involved with you. The grandmothers may be temporarily offended—or secretly relieved —but there are always other ways in which they can help and feel involved.

Taking Advice on Your New Baby

As a mother, you may desperately want advice from your mother or mother-in-law and approval of your methods, but you may also desperately resent any hint of criticism. What you really need is confirmation that you are doing the right thing; it is because you are not sure of yourself that you mind criticism so much. Once you feel more confident with your baby, you will be able to deflect or laugh off the kind of remark that upset you in the early weeks.

It is also a difficult situation for a grandmother, since she may be asked for her opinion several times a day when what she is really being asked for is emotional support. If she tries to give this support uncritically and to suppress any doubts she has, criticism will probably be sensed or imagined anyway. If her opinion differs from that of the doctor, nurse, or anyone else, it may be dismissed as old-fashioned —yet you may feel an emotional tug toward accepting your mother as the final arbitrator, as you did in childhood. You will resent the tug and be crosser still. If grandmother disapproves of demand feeding or disposable diapers, even if she does not say so outright, since she knows she should not contradict the doctor and confuse her daughter, she may be unable to resist the temptation of offering her explanation of your baby's restlessness or sore bottom. It is natural for grandmothers to feel strongly about the right way to look after their grandchildren. They have probably noticed the pendulum swing in the field of child care more than once since they brought up their own family, and it would be too much to expect them to believe wholeheartedly that the current opinion is the final word on the subject. Ask yourself if you will find it easy to abandon the ideas you now have if, as is quite possible, your grandchildren's upbringing contradicts them. If your policies seem to work with your children, you will see no reason why they should be replaced by "new-fangled nonsense."

Sticking to Your Guns

One way of reducing irritation is to remind yourself that opinions and comments are an expression of interest, concern, and love for the child, rather than criticism of you as a parent or part of a game of "who knows best." Refuse to join in this game if you suspect it is being played. Don't argue over the superiority or otherwise of some aspect of baby care; it is better either to say you are following your doctor's advice or to admit that it is a matter of opinion between adults, but not a matter of life or death for the baby. You are doing what you think best.

Looking after a baby is not a science but an art, which means that there may be several "right" ways of doing things. However, since you are his mother, your baby is mainly your responsibility, so you have to make the decisions. Don't do anything you feel is wrong from the baby's point of view for the sake of politeness to a grandmother or anyone else. For example, if you want to pick up the crying baby, pick him up, telling grandmother that the only way anyone really learns is from firsthand experience, much as you appreciate her advice.

Making Sure You Are Right

The trouble is you will not always be 100 percent sure you are doing the right thing; some of the "professional" advice you receive may vary (see pp. 96–97) and you may worry that perhaps you are harming your baby by doing the wrong thing. Check with your doctor or visiting nurse, not with your mother or mother-in-law, if you are seriously worried, since there are some areas that are not a matter of conjecture and about which grandmothers tend to be genuinely out of date.

Once you are sure of your facts, you can say so politely, getting your doctor to confirm your opinion if necessary. For instance, we know that breast-fed babies who fail to pass a stool every day are not constipated (see breast feeding, pp. 57–58). Grandmothers may stop worrying about this only if they know what you know, so tell them. They may urge you to begin toilet training. You cannot truly toilet train a baby before he is physically mature enough to exercise some control over his bladder and bowels (see toilet training, p. 240), so although holding a small baby over a potty may save a few wet diapers, if you think it is too soon to begin, explain the scientific reason for your decision; this will convince grandmother sooner than heated arguments.

All this may give the impression that relations between new mothers and grandmothers consist of a constant rejection by the former of misdirected advice from the latter. Of course, it is not like this for most of the time and is never so in some families, but I have concentrated on the areas of battle because you need advice only when things are not going well. Moreover, relationships go more smoothly when people are aware of their motives and can recognize and avoid emotionally charged and recurring situations.

Disagreement over Upbringing and Behavior

Confidence in yourself as a mother grows with your baby. You learn to play it by ear and to trust your instincts. His grandparents see that he is thriving, and if they disagreed with some of your ways, they begin to realize that he is surviving despite them. His social development—that is, his growth into a "civilized" human being—now becomes the area in which parents and grandparents differ.

Your baby's behavior, when and how you should try to influence it, looms larger and larger as he becomes mobile and starts to have an impact on his surroundings. You may start to hear phrases like "You're only storing up trouble for yourself if you let him get away with that, dear" or "It's never too early to start teaching him table manners" or "A little smack and he won't do that again." You may be criticized for inconsistency. Your mother may consciously be comparing you with the nursemaid she may have had to help her. But this nursemaid had only the children to look after; she had time to be consistent, to see that they always ate their food and washed their hands.

You may be criticized for putting your child to bed too late, for giving him "unsuitable" food, for letting him dabble his fingers in his cereal. On the other hand, the rules you do keep, for example not letting him have candy between meals, may come into the category of "being too hard on him." Point out that he is happy and healthy despite his strange regime.

These differences occur because grandparents and relatives are anxious to do their best for the child, and this may not coincide with your views. If a grandmother suspects that you are too harsh or too soft, she may begin interpreting your every move in this light. Since she is not with you all the time, she does not see the whole relationship, only isolated incidents. If you always tend to be tense when you feel your family is being judged, meetings with grandparents tend to be tense too. It may be better to arrange meetings when grandparents and grandchildren can be left alone together to enjoy themselves.

How Children Benefit from Grandparents

It does not matter if grandparents' standards differ slightly from those of parents. The children will not be molded overnight into different beings, but will profit from a relationship with loving adults that makes different demands on them and gives them something back. Grandparents may, instinctively or calculatingly, provide just what is missing from a parent-child relationship. They have time to be good friends in a way that busy parents may not have. They provide another sympathetic ear and another interpretation for a child's difficulties. He may confide in them when he cannot bring himself to confide in you. Grandmother may be the first to know that your child is worried about school; she can provide you with an early warning system and him with a safety valve. When parents are divorced, grandparents can be doubly valuable to a child.

Living with the Family

When grandparents live with the family they can also help by keeping an eye on the children. A grandmother can make her daughter's life very much freer by relieving her of the necessity of being with her children twenty-four hours a day, even perhaps enabling her to work (see working mothers, pp. 162f.).

Whether they live in the same house or nearby, grandparents are the best possible baby-sitters, because they have a genuine and continuing interest in their charges that no one else can provide. Young parents who live far from their families often feel they are missing something by not having relatives at hand to support them in bringing up their children. Good friends are not quite the same, since they cannot have this built-in concern that grandparents share with parents.

Don't Take Grandmother for Granted

But don't forget that older people find children tiring, and that no one likes being taken for granted or feeling "used." Grandmother may not always feel like baby-sitting just because she loves her grandchild. She may enjoy taking over while you go on vacation one year but not every year. Don't overload her with work and responsibility and assume she has no life of her own apart from being a grandmother.

Serious Policy Differences

Grandparents who live with the family but who continually disapprove openly of parents' methods irritate the adults and confuse and worry the children. If talking it over does not improve things, you can only try to avoid direct confrontation in the most provoking situations; for example, if mealtimes are a nightmare of criticism of your child's diet and manners, stagger the meals. Try to enable grandparents to have an independent life in their own part of the house if the children, by being boisterous and noisy, are too much for them.

The Effect of Divided Loyalties

A child can accept some degree of contradiction in the way the adults in his life treat him but if, when he is trying to become a sociable being, he is pulled in two directions at once, hearing one say "Eat up" and the other "Why should he, poor little thing" at every meal, then he is going to end up overwhelmed by the conflicting approaches. He will not know where his loyalty lies and may decide it is safer to have none and disobey both. Alternatively, he may play one adult off against the other, being good with granny and naughty with mommy, or vice versa. It is essential to be firm and insist that since you have the final responsibility, you also have the final say. Again, husbands or grandfathers may be more successful than mothers at persuading grandmothers to stop interfering. A husband may need to point out to his wife that she is allowing herself to be bullied against her better judgment, and help her to stand up to a grandmother.

As your children get older, grandparents may offer advice about education, friendships, manners, and other matters about which you feel differently. It may annoy you, but you can at least explain to an older child that people can hold different opinions and that they are entitled to express them and to agree to differ.

"Could I Hurt My Baby?"

Normal Exasperation

Nearly every parent, at some time or other, feels capable of battering his child. It is normal to wish, to the point of desperation, that your baby would stop crying, or that your toddler would behave himself. However, the moment you feel like shaking your child you know it is time to ignore him for a while, and to occupy yourself in some other way until the feeling passes. It is normal under these circumstances to put your baby in his crib and go and make yourself a cup of coffee. The abnormal reaction, found in mothers who batter, is to be unable to separate themselves from their crying babies. Such mothers feel compelled to make their babies stop crying.

If you become uneasy because this kind of intense exasperation with your child is occurring too often, you should feel able to tell your doctor about it. He will take you seriously, realizing what you are trying to tell him, although not every mother admits it outright; it is natural to ask for this sort of help in a roundabout way. You may be unaware of your inner fears but a doctor can understand what you are trying to say.

Danger Signals

Unfortunately, a small proportion of mothers and fathers are unable to recognize that their feelings have become unreasonable and may become dangerous. Such parents cannot "switch off" fury with their baby, but feel compelled to force him to do what they want. Because the baby cannot "obey" in the way they expect, he is "battered": in this way he is silenced if he has been crying, or is punished if he has been "naughty"—if he has wet his bed, for instance.

"Battered Babies" or Child Abuse

The baby or small child is brought to the doctor or emergency room with bruises, fractures, or other injuries. His parents explain that he has fallen out of his crib or highchair, or down the stairs, or perhaps that he has knocked himself against the side of the crib. Babies can sometimes hurt themselves in these ways, but unfortunately a proportion of "accidental" injuries are not really accidental at all: they are inflicted by a parent.

The doctor's suspicions may be aroused because the small child is brought in repeatedly; a mother keeps bringing her baby for advice about apparent trivialities when she is really asking for help before she loses control and damages him. The doctor has to distinguish this mother from mothers who are anxious about their babies because of inexperience and natural concern. The doctor and other people in a position to help must prevent such incidents by recognizing those parents who need help before they harm their babies. They must create the right atmosphere so that parents who feel the need for help are given the opportunity to ask for it beforehand, not afterward.

A mother does not hate the baby she has battered, nor is she indifferent to him, but her love is like the demanding love of a spoiled child who must have what he wants the minute he wants it. This parent is in need of the very kind of love she is failing to give her baby —unquestioning, undemanding, and patient devotion—the sort of love that does not ask for instant "results" or good behavior in return. In fact, she needs someone to mother her until she is ready to mother her baby. The need has probably arisen because she lacked normal mothering in her own childhood, and as a result felt herself to be a wicked or unsatisfactory daughter; now she finds herself an inadequate mother. When her baby cries she may be feeling that he is accusing her of not making him happy. She projects her sense of inadequacy on to him, feeling that he must be "no good," like her. Until she likes herself better, she cannot love her child.

Overcrowded houses, where children's noise and crying are always on top of the parents, and poverty, resulting in a lack of labor-saving equipment to lighten the chores of motherhood, push some parents over the edge, and they become child abusers. But decent housing with "room to escape" is in itself no guarantee that a baby is safe, since the problem is primarily an emotional one. Better-off parents are also liable to harm their children in this way, though they may be able to reduce some of the stresses on themselves by better living conditions and by employing nursemaids and other helpers. It is for this reason that the battered babies we read about in the papers tend to come from the poorer sections of society.

Emotional Battering

Not all babies who suffer in this way are physically assaulted. Some, by being deprived of normal maternal affection, are emotionally assaulted. The original term "child abuse" was used to cover both forms of assault. The change in term was largely made because no one took any notice when experts wrote about child abuse. Once they wrote about the battered child, society had to take notice.

Emotional battering is often more harmful than physical battering. The child becomes withdrawn, passive, and silent, so that he not only loses his interest in life but also fails to grow and to develop.

How can these babies be saved from injury, and even death, and their parents be saved from unhappiness and guilt? Not necessarily

by taking the babies away from the parents. I have already emphasized that the battering parent does not hate, ignore, or neglect the
child, and is not indifferent to him: he or she wants to be a good parent
but needs help to become one. The mother does not need mothercraft
classes—she may be excellent at this already—but she must be identified and helped before the stage of hurting her baby. Mothering and
mothercraft are not the same. Mothering is learned in childhood on
your mother's knee, as a result of the love given to you by your
mother and your father. It enables a mother to care totally for her
baby twenty-four hours a day without expecting gratitude in return.
Mothercraft is the technical skill of child care, which can be practiced
without love. Fortunately, most women have the ability to mother and
to practice mothercraft.

Getting Help

A new mother (or father) who shows that she expects her baby to
"behave," who thinks that babies who wet their diapers after being
introduced to the potty at an early age are "naughty" and need punishing, and who thinks that a baby "must be made to obey" does not
necessarily end up by twisting his arm so hard that she breaks it, but
this is the kind of attitude that can lead to battering. She needs help
toward a more understanding view of the development and needs of
babies. She must know that someone is always available to give moral
support. The telephone can be a lifeline between such a mother and
her doctor or visiting nurse. Sometimes an understanding friend who
can mother the mother and on whom she can lean heavily makes all
the difference as to whether she batters her child.

Visiting nurses and doctors are as interested in how a mother is
feeling as in the baby's progress. A "professional" who makes a
mother feel incompetent in minor matters, like bathing her baby, only
causes her to be more anxious lest the baby is reflecting badly on her
as a mother.

Few mothers love their babies totally as soon as they are born;
it takes time to fall in love with your baby, just as it takes time for
adults to fall in love. Understanding this fact may make all the difference if you have mixed feelings toward your baby and feel guilty
about not loving him as much as you think you ought.

12

Vitamins

Everyone needs regular daily vitamins in tiny quantities. Sufficient vitamins are present in most ordinary diets because they are present in natural foods and are added to many processed foods. The healthy adult, therefore, has no need to calculate the amounts he receives in his meals or to supplement them with additional vitamin pills.

In the case of vitamins, more is not better—it is useless and can even be harmful (see p. 183). Infants should be given vitamin supplements because they are growing fast; this makes their vitamin needs proportionately greater for their size than is the case with adults (see p. 182).

The Main Vitamins

Different vitamins are distinguished alphabetically, the most important being:

Vitamin A   This is found in dairy products like milk, cheese, and butter; also in eggs, liver and kidney, fish liver oils and fatty fish like herrings; green vegetables, especially watercress; carrots, tomatoes, and dried apricots. It is added to margarine.

Vitamin A keeps the linings of the urinary, bronchial, and intestinal systems healthy. In this way it enables the body to resist infection. However, since an ordinary diet contains enough vitamin A, there is nothing to be gained by taking more in the hope of warding off infections more effectively.

Vitamin A also protects part of the eye; one of the first signs of deficiency is night blindness. But, again, eating extra carrots will not enable you to see better unless you really are short of vitamin A.

Vitamin B   This is really a group of vitamins known as the vitamin B complex. Although they have different names, such as thiamin, riboflavin, and niacin, which are liable to be listed confusingly on cereal packages, the B vitamins are found mostly in similar foodstuffs, so there is no need to try to calculate exactly how much of each your child is receiving.

The B vitamins are found widely in natural foods such as dairy products, meat (especially pork), liver, potatoes, brewer's yeast, whole-meal bread and flour, wheat germ, cereals, and eggs. It is added to some products, like white bread and breakfast cereals, having previously been removed by refining processes.

Vitamin B in its various forms is necessary for every part of the body. The effect of its deficiency can show up in many ways, but this is not a problem in developed countries.

Vitamin C (Ascorbic Acid) Vitamin C is present in many fruits and vegetables. Excellent sources are citrus fruits, such as oranges, lemons, and grapefruit, and also black currants, tomatoes, and green vegetables. Potatoes also contain vitamin C.

Vitamin C is a delicate substance, which is easily destroyed by heat, as in cooking, and by long storage. Freshly gathered and quickly cooked vegetables and potatoes contain more vitamins than those that have been stored for a long time and cooked slowly in lots of water with the lid off the pan; most of the vitamin C in greens cooked this way escapes into the cooking water. It is well worth cooking vegetables in the minimum of liquid, soon after you have bought them, and serving them shortly after cooking.

Frozen fruit and vegetables and some canned foods contain as much vitamin C as fresh foods. Because frozen foods are frozen very soon after picking they may, in fact, contain more vitamin C than food from the supermarket, which may have taken a long time to reach the shelves and finally the table.

Lack of vitamin C causes scurvy; this may occur at any age but is mainly found in babies between the ages of seven and twelve months. The symptoms are irritability and pain due to bleeding within the bones of the arms and legs; bleeding may also occur from the gums, provided the teeth have arrived, and into the skin, to produce bruising.

Vitamin C helps the body resist infections and this has led to the idea that colds can be prevented or cured by taking large extra quantities of vitamin C, either as pills or by eating oranges. Probably in cold weather people tend to eat more puddings and forget about fruit, so eating extra oranges does nothing but good. However, eating half a dozen oranges will not stop or cure the common cold (see p. 394).

Vitamin D This is soluble in fat like vitamin A and is therefore found in a similar range of foods (see Vitamin A). The chief source is fish liver oils. It is added to margarine and evaporated milk and is present in milk and butter in variable quantities, according to the amount of sunshine enjoyed by the cow.

Humans also manufacture vitamin D in their skins through the action of the sun's rays. Ultraviolet light in the sun's rays acts on a complicated chemical in the skin to change it into vitamin D, which is then absorbed into the body. In the early days of vitamin D research there was a violent argument between those who said rickets could be cured by giving fish oils (which contain vitamin D) and those who said you should give the patient sunlight. Both were right! It follows that a child is less dependent on his diet for vitamin D in a warm, sunny climate where he wears fewer clothes than in a cold, gray one where this source of vitamin D is practically nil.

Vitamin D is required by the body to help it absorb calcium and phosphorus from the diet. This ensures that the bones and teeth are strong and healthy. Growing children need it in large quantities. Lack of vitamin D causes rickets, a disease in which bones and teeth are soft. The soft bone in rickets leads to bowing of the legs if the child has reached the walking stage. If he is at the crawling stage, pressure on the soft bones of the wrists causes them to bulge (see p. 534).

Whereas excessive vitamin C is harmless, excess vitamin D can be harmful; it disturbs the delicate balance of calcium in the body of a young child.

Vitamin Supplements

Your Baby's Needs

Your baby, like anyone else, needs vitamins A, B, C, and D in his daily diet to keep him healthy. Breast milk contains enough of all the vitamins, but cow's milk does not contain sufficient vitamin D for human babies. There is also insufficient vitamin C in cow's milk for a human baby's requirements. This is not the cow's fault, because her body, unlike ours, can manufacture the vitamin so that a calf will never go short. Modern preparations of dried cow's milk contain sufficient added vitamins so that no vitamin supplements are required until the baby is six months old.

Why Extra Vitamins Are Necessary

Why are babies given these extra vitamins when in the past they survived without them and often lived healthily on milk alone for more than a year? The answer is that not all of them lived healthily —many suffered from vitamin deficiencies, especially scurvy, resulting from too little vitamin C, and rickets from too little vitamin D. We hear little of scurvy and rickets in affluent societies, both because mothers and children have a varied diet and because of the use of vitamin supplements for babies. Even so, rickets still occurs in some areas. In poorer countries it is by no means uncommon.

Giving Vitamin Supplements

Vitamin C Orange juice is the most popular choice, although tomato and apple juice are also good. Fruit juices must be diluted with boiled water, which is cooled before mixing so as not to destroy the vitamin C. Never boil fruit juice, for the same reason. All vitamin C preparations or fresh fruit juice should be mixed and given to your baby immediately, not prepared in advance and kept, since vitamin C is rapidly destroyed by exposure to air.

It is easier to use preparations specially made for babies to begin with, since these give you precise details on quantities. If you like using fresh orange juice, you may find your baby prefers it to be strained.

Canned and frozen orange juice contain vitamin C and can be used for babies.

Fruit Juices and Tooth Decay Concentrated fruit juices are a good source of vitamin C. However, they are very sweet and can be responsible for tooth decay in young babies if given undiluted or in a strong concentration via a miniature feeder—a tiny bottle with a nipple designed to keep a baby sucking happily. When filled with sweet juice this is equivalent to a tooth-destroying version of a pacifier. If the juice remains in contact with your baby's gums for long periods, it can weaken his teeth and they will begin to rot soon after they appear.

So if you use a sweet juice, remember it can cause tooth decay; those pearly milk teeth can only too easily end as black stumps. Give your baby his fruit juice as a straight drink and follow it with water to help rinse away the sugar.

Vitamin D This vitamin, together with vitamin A, is found in fish liver oils and can be given to babies in the form of cod or halibut liver oil. However, concentrated drops of vitamins A, C, and D are more popular and just as good. Moreover, the concentrated liquid is preferred by mothers because it does not smell fishy.

If you forget to give the vitamins one day, do not give your baby a double dose the next day. Twice as much is not twice as good, and he won't fade away if you forget once in a while. In addition, with vitamin D it is possible to give too much, and a sensitive baby can become ill. A few years ago it was found that certain babies became ill through too much vitamin D. Their fortified milk feedings, plus extra vitamins, and perhaps also baby cereals with vitamin D, all added up to an excessive dose.

When to Stop Giving Vitamin Supplements

For total safety, vitamins should be given to children up to the age of five years. In practice, most mothers gradually stop giving their children vitamins long before the age of five for the good reason that, once a child is eating a mixed diet, he receives sufficient for his needs through his meals. A child who takes about one pint of milk, in any form, a helping of fresh fruit, fruit juices, or vegetables, and meat, fish, or egg daily, no longer needs vitamin supplements. But remember that a baby who is weaned early to strained foods, which replace some of the milk in his diet, may not be taking a really balanced diet for some months and still needs his extra vitamins.

If you are worried about the small amount or the limited variety of your child's diet, it is a good idea to continue giving daily vitamins after babyhood. Even if his diet is more adequate than you realize, provided you stick to the correct amount you will not be "overdosing" him with vitamins, and the fact that you know he takes his vitamins will help you worry less about his eating habits (see feeding problems, pp. 204–6).

13

Mixed Feeding

Before their first birthdays, most babies are well on the way to eating a mixed diet based on normal family meals. But although we never meet children or adults who are still existing on a solely milk diet, you may find yourself worrying, almost as soon as he has settled down to breast or bottle feedings, that your baby will never make the change from milk feedings to mixed feeding. You may have the idea that babies need to be encouraged to the point of forcing them to make the change, whereas, as with many situations involving the developing child, it is really an inevitable part of growing up. When to start introducing the first "solid," which food to give first and which second, how to give it—all these questions tend to assume alarming proportions, which may make you feel as if your baby's life literally depended upon eating the right things at the right time.

A Golden Rule: Be Flexible

It is a pity if this happens, because mixed feeding is not nearly as complicated and scientific a subject as it is sometimes made to sound. Babies thrive on countless different diets and, given a few common-sense precautions (pp. 190f.), you do not need to follow any exact scheme. You may feel more confident following a chart, such as those issued by some baby-food manufacturers listing foods to start at certain ages, and this does no harm provided you do not forget that no chart includes the most important factor, the individual baby's reactions. It is impossible to start giving carrots at a specified age if your baby refuses to eat them. So bend the "rules," which are nothing more than convenient guidelines, and be adaptable; otherwise, following a chart will produce more problems than it solves.

In dealing with this changeable and opinionated person—your baby—you will find an experimental approach works best. He will do most of the work if you let him and don't expect too much of him. He does not have to be taught to progress to mixed feeding; he will want to try something new, even if it is not at the exact moment you choose to get him to try it.

There are some general points to remember when you embark on mixed feedings, and, of course, your baby's rate of progress, your own inclination, together with the opinion of your doctor or visiting nurse, if needed, all enter into it. Try to look on the introduction of mixed feeding as a gradual enlarging of your baby's diet and experience, with no prizes for speed and no clear finishing line. The whole process will then become less intense and less urgent. Some general approaches are described here as guidelines, rather than as instructions.

When to Start

Milk is a baby's main food, and his only essential food, for the first few months of life. A baby who is contented with milk can be started on mixed feeding when he is about six months old.

Starting Late: A Warning

It is unwise to wait longer than six months because by this time the store of iron in the baby's liver is running low and neither breast nor cow's milk contains enough iron for his growing needs. The practice of feeding a baby on milk alone for the greater part of the first year, or longer, which is still followed in many parts of the world, can lead to his becoming anemic in the second half of his first year. Foods rich in iron are green vegetables, meat, liver, and egg yolk.

The Happy Medium

Under controlled conditions it has been shown that babies can eat different things in different ways at a very early age. But that does not mean that the average baby would benefit from starting mixed feeding so young. He would not grow or develop more quickly if fed on a more grown-up diet; milk supplies all his nutritional needs in the most easily digested form at this stage. So you should be in no hurry to begin mixed feeding in the hope of "improving" your baby's rate of progress or weight gain (see pp. 196–98, 208–9).

Although there are some valid arguments for starting to vary your baby's diet before he is as old as six months and beginning to need the extra iron in foods such as egg yolk, meat, and vegetables (see above), there are also some mistaken ones. For example, don't start mixed feeding early in order to make your baby sleep more. A baby sleeps through the night when he is ready to, provided he has enough milk during the day. There are many reasons babies don't sleep (pp. 115f.), and giving a baby more food does not automatically ensure he sleeps longer. Don't start spooning food into your contented baby, who is longing to sleep after a satisfying milk feeding, merely because your neighbor's baby started early.

To sum up, there is seldom any need to start mixed feedings before your baby is two or three months old, since, if he is hungry, extra milk usually satisfies him in his first weeks.

The Breast-fed Baby

For the first six months a breast-fed baby needs nothing else to cover all his nutritional needs. After this age, breast milk, like cow's milk, contains insufficient iron, so that extra foods that contain iron (p. 186) are needed. A mother who breast feeds her baby has supplied all his nourishment since birth and so it can be quite a blow when he takes his first food from an outside source. If you have been enjoying breast feeding, you may find yourself reluctant to make this move, which acknowledges that your baby is becoming less dependent on you.

Complementing Breast Feedings with Mixed Feedings

If a breast-fed baby continues to seem hungry, despite efforts to stimulate the supply of milk (see breast feeding, p. 77), starting mixed feedings can be a way out of the difficulty; you can give extra food by spoon rather than extra milk by bottle.

Why is this a better idea than offering a complementary milk feeding, which is quicker and easier to manage than starting spoon feeding? The answer is that giving a bottle regularly after breast feeding tends to undermine confidence in breast feeding and may also encourage your baby to prefer the bottle to the breast. Once you start each breast feeding with a bottle ready by your side, it is easy to begin thinking of the complement as the "proper" feeding and to hurry the breast feeding. A bowl of cereal and a spoon does not have the same bad effect on your morale, but gives you confidence instead; you know your baby will have enough to eat, and you yourself will have supplied his milk, the most important part of his diet.

The Bottle-fed Baby

A bottle-fed baby who is given enough milk of the correct strength (see pp. 85f.), with added vitamins, does not need new foods any sooner than a breast-fed baby. But because you are already planning and mixing his food, giving him new foods will seem a more natural step than when you are breast feeding. You will probably want to start earlier, especially if you feel he is taking too little milk. Remember that this is unlikely, although like a breast-fed baby he may take less at some feedings than at others (p. 84).

Milk is your baby's main food, so do not hurry him on to a mixed diet because you are getting bored with mixing milk feedings, or because you hope that the more he eats the longer he will sleep—it's not as simple as that (pp. 118–19). However, you should start the change to a mixed diet before your baby runs the risk of becoming anemic, which means before the age of six months.

Giving Extras by Bottle

A bottle-fed baby can be given a thickened feed of cereal and milk by bottle at first, if you want him to start cereal without the effort of feeding by spoon. Start gradually (p. 190). It is unwise to carry on for long giving food via the bottle, since your baby may resent it when you want to start using a spoon.

A baby who seems hungry for more than milk can start having extras when he is a few weeks old, but first make sure that his milk mixture is the right strength for his age and size and that he has the chance of taking as much milk as he wants (see bottle feeding, p. 84).

Learning to Eat

Suppose your breast- or bottle-fed baby is thriving and seems contented with milk. He is not yet six months old, so his diet is adequate. Is there any reason to bother yourself with spoon feedings until the second half of his first year? The answer is that you can do whatever suits you best.

Biting and Chewing

A baby begins to bite and chew before he is six months old, which is a good reason for introducing him to new foods before this age. By about his fourth month he bites on anything that reaches his mouth; he shows the first signs of chewing at about six months. Being toothless is no deterrent.

It may be sensible to take advantage of your baby's enjoyment in his mouth by introducing him to food with a more interesting texture than milk at about four months. His reaction may be excitement, suspicion, wariness, or apparent indifference; even if he would like to help, he will find it difficult, since eating from a spoon is quite a different process from the suck-and-swallow rhythm to which he is accustomed. At first, a baby tends to push against the spoon with his tongue, and if something goes into his mouth and down his throat, it is more or less by accident.

If you look on these first spoon feedings as an experiment, a way of playing rather than of making him absorb vital nourishment, there is more chance that you will both enjoy them and become efficient quickly.

Finger Foods

Your baby soon enjoys practicing his biting on a piece of toasted bread or cracker; he will hold it himself at around six months. Never leave him alone while he is eating, because of the danger of choking—a cause of accidental death at this age. If he manages to bite off a large piece, remove it before he gets into difficulties trying to swallow it whole. If he does begin to choke, immediately hold him upside down by his legs and smack his back until the food is dislodged. Usually, however, the toast or cracker dissolves gradually as he bites on it, and is swallowed without trouble (see also p. 624).

Progress from crude biting with toothless gums to efficient chewing with a set of milk teeth is not complete until your baby is about three years old. Until then, the texture of his food must match his ability to chew, gradually becoming like the ordinary food eaten by the rest of the family (p. 193).

Learning to Taste—and to Disagree

Another good reason for choosing about four months to start mixed feedings is that your baby's taste buds have not yet fully developed. At this stage he may spit out food because he has not mastered the technique of eating, but he is less likely to spit it out because he dislikes the taste or because he enjoys watching the effect this has on you. By the age of six months, though, he is discovering the fun of not doing what you want; so you have his growing assertiveness to deal with as well as the mechanical problem of helping him to eat from a spoon.

Of course, accepting new tastes at four months does not guarantee that a baby will never refuse them or change his mind later. Learning to eat a mixed diet is seldom a smooth and steady progression; it is more likely to be a case of two steps forward and one back, varying with your baby's mood and appetite.

Appetite This is connected with the rate of growth, which slows down after the first six months of life (see pp. 199, 208). It can also be affected by other people trying to make him eat when he is not hungry (see feeding problems, pp. 198–201).

General Principles to Follow

Whether a baby is breast or bottle fed, there are certain points to remember when you start mixed feedings. These are not rigid rules but suggestions to help make things easier for you and safer for your baby.

Start Cautiously

The order in which you give new foods is unimportant but it is best to try only one at a time, waiting a few days before starting another; this applies until your baby is accustomed to mixed feeding. If something has disagreed with him, you will then know which food to suspect and can leave it out of his meals for a while.

Do not, however, blame a new food for a severe stomach upset; this needs diagnosing and treatment by your doctor. Avoid introducing unfamiliar food when your baby is off-color or in very hot weather, when he is less likely to want it.

Quantities: Avoiding Obesity

It is wise to start with small quantities, a teaspoonful or two at first, building up gradually to as much as your baby wants—with the proviso that if he is getting fat, he should not be offered unlimited helpings of fattening foods, especially cereal. Fat babies grow into fat children and then into obese adults (see p. 207). While a baby's diet consists of milk alone he is unlikely to get too fat, but once he is eating a mixed diet containing fattening foods, he may eat too much of these and become overweight. Put away the cereal and cookies and offer vegetables, fruit, and protein foods such as meat, fish, cheese, and eggs.

Self-feeding

It is a good idea to let a baby try feeding himself as soon as he shows any inclination to try, which may be as early as five to six months. It is doubly important if your baby is fat, because this is an excellent way of helping him slim. At first, more food goes down his front or into his hair than down his throat, but his figure will improve!

Unless a baby is becoming too fat, there is no need to measure quantities and helpings, but it is better to put too little on his plate and give him more if he finishes it than to risk putting him off with a large, unappetizing heap of food. Let your baby eat as much or as little as he likes, giving him time to eat at his own pace (see feeding himself, p. 202).

The Slowpoke

He may take a long time and this can be irritating if you are standing over him, anxious to get on with something else; it is much easier to have a baby who opens his mouth like a little bird and bolts his food as quickly as it's offered, but not all babies are like this. Some babies dawdle, just as they dawdled at the breast or bottle. You cannot wait forever, and it is not worth waiting half an hour for another spoonful to disappear. Your baby does not know you want to get to the stores before they close; nor does he understand that meals are meant to be over and done with in a certain space of time. So if your baby eats slowly, try to approach his mealtimes in an unhurried frame of mind; he will probably eat more and you will probably be less frustrated. A good idea that should help both of you is to provide two teaspoons. One is for the use of your baby, who can experiment as slowly and as messily as he wishes. The other is for you; you will probably find he accepts food from yours while playing about with his own.

Timing of Mixed Feedings

It does not matter at which end of the meal you give the solid food. At first, it is best to offer it after the milk feeding; your baby is more likely to accept it when his hunger pangs have been partly soothed in the familiar way with milk. Some babies who refuse food from a spoon eat well if given solids in the middle or at the end of the meal.

Nor does it matter at which feeding of the day you start giving extras. Ten in the morning or midday is popular; this is a convenient time in many households, since fathers and older children are out of the house. Your baby does not know if a meal is meant to be breakfast or supper and will not mind having meat for breakfast and cereal for lunch. However, if you want him to eat normal family meals as soon as possible, it is sensible to base his meals on these as soon as he is eating a variety of foods.

Preparing Your Baby's Foods

Hygiene

It is unnecessary to sterilize everything connected with the preparation of mixed feedings, in the way that it is essential with bottle feedings—milk provides an ideal medium for the growth of harmful organisms. However, any food for a young baby should be carefully prepared, so all utensils, strainers, bowls, etc., must be clean. It is easier if things for the baby are kept separately; then you won't find the strainer is dusty and the can opener sticky with cat food.

Wash your hands before preparing your baby's food or before giving it to him. Food that is made some time before his meal should be kept cool and covered. Cans and jars of baby food are sterile until opened, after which they keep fresh for as long as similar fresh foods; advice about preparation and storage is usually given on containers. If you know your baby will want only part of the contents, transfer the lot to a clean dish and warm up only enough for that meal. Do not warm it all up and rewarm the remains later.

Food from a family meal that you save for the baby must be thoroughly recooked, not just warmed through, to kill any organisms that may have multiplied in the warm food. When traveling, it is safer to give food cold than to keep it warm for several hours (see bottle feeding, p. 95). Milk and water used to mix with food should be boiled until your baby is at least six months old.

As your baby progresses to meals more like the rest of the family's, you will probably find yourself relaxing and taking less special care in preparing his food. This is logical—as he nears his first birthday he is better at coping with organisms that might have caused infection when he was younger and, by the time he is crawling about the floor, he will be in contact with plenty of dirt no matter how conscientious you are. However, there is no age at which you can safely stop preparing his food with care. The safest way is to have a high standard of hygiene in preparing food for the whole family—then your baby will be safe too.

Consistency of Food

A baby is a conservative individual, and the more his first new food resembles milk, the more likely he is to accept it. It is probably for this reason that a special baby cereal mixed with milk is the most popular first "solid" food, although soup, milk puddings, or strained food would be equally suitable. No particular variety of cereal is best.

Special baby cereals are easy to prepare, they need no straining, and they are fortified with vitamins and minerals. You can compare ingredients by studying the packages. Directions about mixing are given on the packages but it may be worth trying a thinner mixture than recommended if your baby dislikes the original version.

Babies tend to dislike sticky mixtures and, with any type of food, it may be the consistency rather than the taste that puts yours off; so experiment and find out if he prefers a runny mixture. You can change the consistency of canned baby food by adding a little boiled milk, water, or stock.

Until your baby is six or seven months old, his food should be smooth and free of lumps. Make it into a purée by putting it through a strainer or a blender. When buying baby food in cans and jars, buy strained food, not the "junior" kind, which is chopped and lumpy.

Junior foods are intended for the second half of your baby's first year, when he should be encouraged to chew. Don't wait for teeth to appear before you offer him chopped and mashed food, because he may become so used to eating the easy way that he refuses to try anything different. But don't expect him to make the change from strained to lumpy food overnight. Keep trying at intervals and do not be concerned if he refuses anything but strained food when you first give him something different. Do you know any adults who still live on purées?

Diet

Fresh or Canned Food?

Babies thrive whether fed entirely on special "baby foods" or entirely on fresh food prepared by their mothers. His health will not suffer either way. But it seems sensible to give your baby as consumer, and yourself as cook, the benefit of both fresh and prepared foods. The latter may be in cans, jars, or packages.

The main point to help you decide on fresh or canned is your own convenience. Choose the method of feeding that is easiest and least emotionally frustrating for you (see below). One point in favor of giving him the food you have cooked is that you are not later faced with the possibility of your child refusing your food because he has become accustomed to the cans and jars and objects to a second period of weaning.

If you would prefer your baby to eat mainly fresh food but he obstinately prefers "baby foods," you can deceive him by adding something fresh to his meals: for example, he may dislike tomato, but if you strain a fresh tomato and mix it with his favorite canned dinner, he is unlikely to notice. Finely grated cheese is a valuable addition to any savory food, and eggs can be incorporated into cakes and puddings.

Developing Good Taste

You may protest that you want him to like tomatoes, eggs, and cheese, and wonder how he can develop a sense of taste if he's confused by such tricks. For one thing, his ability to discriminate between different tastes is developing only gradually; for another, there is going to be plenty of opportunity to steer him toward whatever you consider good taste in food, or a taste for good food. It is a mistake to try to do everything at once—getting him used to eating from a spoon and accepting new tastes and consistencies are quite enough as a beginning.

Adapting Family Meals for the Baby

There are many family meals that can be adapted for the baby. Meat and vegetables, milk and fruit puddings, soups, etc., can be strained and served as part or all of the baby's meal. This saves expense and takes some of the mystery out of mixed feeding.

It is sometimes inconvenient to plan a family meal suitable for the baby also, but spending half a morning making meat or vegetable broth is only worthwhile if the baby eats it. If he does not, his refusal will upset you far more than if he refuses a can of soup it took you ten seconds to open. So while you are unsure of your baby's likes and dislikes, you may find it less demanding in emotion as well as in time to use ready-made baby food. The better you are at avoiding frustrations at mealtimes, the smaller the risk of meals becoming a battle or a bore.

Unsuitable Foods   Some things adults and older children like are obviously unsuitable for a baby, but it is unfair to the rest of the family to expect them to eat only meals that can be adapted for the baby. So when you are eating, for example, spicy food, twice-cooked leftovers, or bought pies, give your baby his own special baby food. However, foods considered unsuitable for babies are much fewer than was once assumed—for instance, cheese is excellent.

A Balanced Diet

During his first year, your role is to help your baby to enjoy eating new foods in new ways, at first supplementing and then gradually replacing his milk diet. It is far more important that mealtimes are pleasant than that any particular food is eaten in particular quantities. No foods, even ones that are especially "good" for a baby, like meat and eggs, are indispensable. A baby brought up on a vegetarian diet is neither more nor less healthy than other babies, provided he has enough protein sources in his diet, such as milk, eggs, cheese, and beans. On the other hand, not eating vegetables does not cause deficiency disease if a baby eats other foods that contain iron and minerals—meat and fruit, for example.

Try not to regard mixed feeding as a battle to make your baby eat a "desirable" range of foods. If you assume he will enjoy cheese as much as ice cream, he probably will; if he does seem inclined to prefer a diet of crackers and cookies, which are easy to eat, fill him up, and provide energy but little body-building material, buy fewer of them and offer him a variety of more valuable protein foods.

Snacks

Don't give him candy or crackers between meals because you are sorry for him and afraid he'll go hungry. A piece of fruit or cheese makes a better snack. Even if he eats only a quarter of the things you offer, he will not allow himself to starve (see feeding problems, p. 199).

Likes and Dislikes

Comfort yourself with the remainder that you cannot predict future eating habits at this stage. Many children come to enjoy a food they hate at first, provided they are not put off it for life by continually being badgered to eat it. Try to avoid the words "Eat it up; it's good for you." Young children often do prefer a diet of fish sticks, hot dogs, baked beans, and other foods that give mothers little scope as cooks. But the same children later develop a more sophisticated taste in food if their families eat well.

Children do not have preconceived ideas about which foods they ought to like and they should not be expected to show concern about which are good for them. Given a variety of different foods and allowed to choose for himself, a child takes a balanced diet over a period of time, even if he eats nothing but tomato sandwiches one day and cereals the next.

The problem is that you cannot know what a baby feels like eating on a particular day, nor can you provide a large choice at every meal so as to make sure he can pick what he wants. Babies have to take it or leave it. Most babies will take it if they are hungry enough. In a few cases, a mother has to show considerable ingenuity to encourage her baby to eat what is considered a balanced diet (feeding problems, pp. 199–201).

The Real Problem

In countries where there is enough food to go around, doctors seldom see deficiency diseases caused by a baby's failure to eat, though they do see numerous mothers who are convinced that their babies are about to suffer from some nutritional deficiency or to starve themselves because of "feeding problems" (pp. 196f.). Some babies and children in developed countries do have an unsatisfactory diet: this is not because they refuse to eat good food, but because the adults looking after them have failed to provide it for them through ignorance, thoughtlessness, or poverty.

14

Avoiding Feeding Problems

The only feeding problem that makes children ill, leading to under-nourishment and even death, is a shortage of good food. Possibly as many as two-thirds of the world's children go to bed hungry every night. In a country where there is insufficient food to go around or in an extremely poor family, parents have a genuine feeding problem: how to fill their children's stomachs. Under these conditions, there is no question of children refusing to eat whatever is offered. "Feeding problems" in the sense of a child being a "difficult" eater are luxuries of affluence, because every child is born with a will to survive; this means eating enough to stay alive and to enjoy life.

How Much Is Enough?

From what I have already written about mixed feeding, I hope you will accept that it is not vital for your child to eat any particular food at any particular age. Provided he is energetic he is getting sufficient food; only if he is getting enough for body building will he have spare calories for running around. Underfed children waste no energy on nonessentials. They just sit or lie. So long as your child is energetic and looks well, his actual weight gain does not matter. Do not be concerned because he eats less than other children.

The New Baby

Trust Him to Eat Enough

Put out of your head the possibility that your new baby may eat too little for his needs. Because he is so helpless, and so much your responsibility, it is natural to feel that it is up to you to see that he eats enough of the right food. But don't confuse your job of providing the food with his of eating it. You cannot make him drink more than he wants from the breast or bottle, and what he wants happens to be the right amount. You may wish he would take a large feeding and then sleep a long time or grow an extra ounce, but it is not as simple as that: sleep and growth cannot be matched with ounces of milk drunk (see sleeping and crying, pp. 118–19).

Therefore, if your problem is worry over the amount he takes at his feedings, remember that a full-term baby never voluntarily starves himself or eats too little for healthy growth provided that he is offered enough milk of the right strength in his bottle or that his supply of breast milk is sufficient (see below and breast feeding, p. 74, and bottle feeding, p. 84). He may take two ounces rather than six but if this is the amount he wants at a particular feeding, it is the right amount. Don't you ever leave food on your plate? Unless you are on a special diet you would not dream of measuring your own intake; treat your baby in exactly the same way.

The Bottle-fed Baby

If your baby is bottle fed and takes only two ounces, there is more chance that you will sit there for another twenty minutes hoping he will take more because you can see all the milk he has left in the bottle. He may drink another ounce eventually, but is it really worth it? Overlong feedings are tedious for you and exhaust your baby; they do not make him grow or sleep better. He drinks most of what he needs in the first minutes of a feeding so if your problem is long, boring bottle feedings, just stop when he has lost enthusiasm, however much is left in the bottle. It might be easier if all bottles were opaque, just as the breast, so their contents were invisible. Moreover, persuading babies to finish the bottle is probably the chief reason they are more liable to be too fat than breast-fed babies.

The Breast-fed Baby

With breast feeding it should be easier to judge when your baby has had enough on the basis that he seems satisfied, loses interest in feeding, and wants to go to sleep. Certainly, in communities where breast feeding is the rule, mothers do not waste time wondering and worrying how much their babies have drunk. It is in societies where the breast-feeding mother is surrounded by other mothers discussing how many ounces have disappeared from the bottle that you are liable to lose the advantage of not knowing how much your baby has had.

Since your baby obtains most of his milk in the first minutes at each breast there is no more point in lengthy breast feedings, from the point of view of intake, than in long sessions with the bottle. If you worry about having too little milk, take the advice of your doctor or visiting nurse. The supply will increase again, and your baby can be given extra milk to tide him over, if needed (see breast feeding, pp. 77–79).

Slow Feeders

Some babies are certainly more difficult to feed than others in the sense that they don't "concentrate" or "get on with it." These are usually the brighter babies, who are more interested in their surroundings than in their food. This kind of baby takes longer to feed than one who bolts his milk, and it takes more skill on a mother's part —gentle reminders of the task in hand are necessary. But again, there is no point in spending an hour, or even half an hour, with your dawdler, because he too will have taken most of what he needs in less than this (see breast feeding, pp. 73f., and bottle feeding, pp. 94f.). Do not add long periods of waiting for the gas to your difficulties (see gas, pp. 68–70).

Does His Milk Suit Him?

Perhaps you worry that your baby's milk does not agree with him and that indigestion is the reason he cries. Breast milk is better adapted to a baby's digestion than anything a computer could formulate, while nearly every baby can digest any reasonable artificial milk mixture— so changing brands of milk is seldom necessary (p. 86). Discuss the reason for your baby's crying or apparent indigestion with your doctor if it is really worrying you, but remember that babies cry for a number of reasons (pp. 116f.), and that gas or "colic" is more often the result of crying rather than its cause (see colic, pp. 123–25).

Loss of Appetite

A sudden loss of appetite in a baby whose appetite is usually good, or any change in feeding pattern, is a sign of illness, usually an infection. If your baby loses his appetite, you should always consult your doctor (see infections, pp. 433–34).

The Older Baby

Slowness to Accept Spoon Feeding

It is mothers, doctors, and nurses who decide when to start babies on mixed feeding, but babies vary in their readiness to try new foods and new ways of eating. Therefore it is not surprising that some babies take longer than others to graduate from milk to a mixed diet. Your baby may be so slow to enjoy eating from a spoon that you begin to feel the instructions printed on the label, "gradually increase the amount until baby is taking a full can," will never apply to him. Have you a feeding problem on your hands? Not yet! Your baby will come to no harm—but *you* may become increasingly frustrated. This is less likely to happen if you follow the general principles outlined on pp. 185 to 191 and give him the chance to get used to the idea.

Will He Starve?

Meanwhile, your baby has his milk feedings and vitamin supplements, so his nutritional needs are being met. He is no more likely to starve himself voluntarily at this stage than earlier and, as so often with feeding, the real problem is to stop yourself worrying about this possibility and not to attempt the impossible task of making your baby eat more.

It is more important to change your attitude rather than his, both because it is a waste of energy to worry about this particular problem and because the more you worry and badger your baby to eat, the more likely he is to refuse. This increases your frustration and completes the vicious circle. Mealtimes can become a real problem in this way, although, paradoxically, your baby is as healthy and well nourished as ever. So stamp on your anxiety early.

Here are some of the reasons he may eat less than you expect him to or less than the other babies you know.

Small Appetite

Your baby may have a naturally small appetite, which nevertheless is large enough to enable him to grow at the rate that is normal for him. He is not indifferent to food but to too much food. Frequently, a baby whose mother complains he eats too little is being expected to eat too much. Being used to measuring his bottle feedings and seeing how much he drank, she now expects to measure and see him eat so many ounces of solid food.

This emphasis on quantity is encouraged in a bottle-feeding society, and can lead to the real "feeding problem" of affluence—overeating—because once a baby is offered palatable, fattening foods he may easily eat more than he needs, and go on eating after his hunger is satisfied. So there are advantages in a child having a small appetite, even though he is more of a nuisance to feed. He was probably not a particularly eager feeder at breast or bottle and is now equally uninterested in new foods. He looks away disdainfully after only one or two spoonfuls, and you begin to feel that every mouthful he takes is a matter of pitting your ingenuity and will power against his indifference.

Again, the real problem is to stop yourself worrying rather than to "make" your baby eat. Attack the worry by asking your doctor to confirm that your baby is healthy and making satisfactory progress, then try to resign yourself to a baby who is, where eating is concerned, not unsatisfied but unsatisfying—from your point of view. It may not always be like this. Sometimes a child who seems uninterested in food for months or years turns into the child who always wants a third helping.

Appetite and Rate of Growth

Another factor is that the rate of a baby's growth slows down in the second half of the first year. It's bad luck that this is the very time when he is expected to eat ever-larger quantities of a widening variety of foods, the time when you are most likely to be concerned that he eats a balanced diet in sufficient quantities. Unless you realize that appetite does not go on expanding as he grows, and that he does not need more because he is bigger, a "feeding problem" can easily arise.

Parents all over the world are concerned that their children should be taller and heavier than they are. They are seldom concerned that they are too heavy, although in countries like the United States and the United Kingdom this is becoming a serious problem (see pp. 206–7). Doctors have graphs that show the average normal curve of growth at all ages, for both height and weight, and also the highest and the lowest limits of normal. If you are still worried whether your child's height and weight are within normal limits, ask your doctor to plot his measurement on one of these "percentile" charts. You are almost certain to find he falls well within the normal lines on the chart.

Temperamental Complications

As he approaches six months, your baby's sense of taste and his sense of himself are developing fast (pp. 189, 193–94). He has more idea about his likes and dislikes but he cannot yet tell you about these. He may prefer apricots but you provide prunes. If he is really hungry, he will eat the prunes; otherwise he fills up on something else or eats more at the next meal, provided you don't fill him up with snacks.

If pressed to eat, he may swallow a bit more or resolutely refuse, depending on his personality and his mood at the time. Some babies who are "difficult" to feed are just showing their forcefulness at the most effective occasion open to them at this stage—mealtimes. The mother who is anxious for her child to eat, wants him to show his appreciation of the food she has prepared with such love and care. Meals are a good time for her to show love but they are also a good time for him to show he is growing up. This complicates the business of eating.

Avoiding a Battle of Wills

A bright baby enjoys the sensation of power as he watches the effect on his mother of his dawdling and refusing to eat. The more interesting the effect, the more determined he becomes. He may even leave something he would rather like to eat.

In fact, perpetually coaxing your baby to eat can make a small appetite even smaller; his natural degree of hunger is blunted by the prospect of another emotionally exhausting session with a fussing mother. An adult easily loses his appetite if something unpleasant or dramatic interrupts a meal. Nobody enjoys eating in the middle of an upsetting argument or can sit down happily at the table when already feeling apprehensive. However delicious the food, you would probably feel sick in advance if your hostess announced she would make sure you ate everything.

Your job as cook and waitress is to provide a reasonable range of wholesome food and to help create a relaxing atmosphere during your baby's meals. He can then decide how much he wants to eat without the complication of holding his own in a battle of power. You will find you are much less concerned about his eating up manufactured food as opposed to food you have spent all morning preparing for him (see pp. 193–95). Reduce your emotional attachment to his food by giving him something you have not spent hours preparing—this should work wonders with your reactions and may break the vicious circle.

The Child Who Won't Eat

As your baby grows into a toddler it becomes even more important to avoid battles over meals. The small child is disturbed because, on the one hand, he wishes to please his mother and clear his plate of food, and, on the other, he wants to choose for himself. If his choice is to leave his food, these wishes clash. This conflict can make him feel sick and actually be sick. If his parents then accuse him of "doing it on purpose," since he probably looks relieved that the issue has been settled for the time being, he will be even more confused, miserable, and lacking in appetite at the next meal. He may reach the stage when he faces each meal wanting to eat, but unable to. The help of your doctor may be needed to untangle the situation.

Encouragement without Bullying

Inevitably, there will be times when you encourage your baby or small child to eat up his vegetables, or hurry up and finish the meal. Sometimes a child is slow when you want to clear away; sometimes you can urge him into trying something he is refusing out of habit. If you use your natural instinct, this happens without much thought and no harm is done. Trouble starts when admonitions to hurry, eat up, not leave any vegetables, stay at the table till every scrap has been eaten start to dominate mealtimes, leading to continual battles, which nobody wins.

To sum up: if your baby eats slowly or eats less than you want him to, deal with your concern by seeking your doctor's opinion of his health. The doctor will probably be able to reassure you by an explanation of what is happening, so that you can stop worrying about the risk of potential starvation and ill health. Offer your child good food, with as little anxiety about his acceptance or refusal as you can manage. Letting him feed himself as early as possible and forgetting about "manners" can also help.

If you are still worried about your child's eating despite assurance from your doctor that he is well, a different kind of help may be needed. Deep personal feelings that a child needs more food when, in fact, he is healthy, may have originated in a mother's own childhood because she was pressured to eat. Such feelings need to be talked out at depth with someone especially qualified.

Feeding Himself—Signs of Readiness

A baby may feel frustrated because his food is spooned into him when he wants to try to feed himself; he may react to this by refusing to eat. This is sometimes because his mother does not realize he is ready to try to feed himself.

As soon as he starts to put his hand on the handle of the spoon and helps to guide it toward his mouth he is showing that he is ready to start helping. You may notice him doing this but discourage him because you think he is too young or because of the mess he will undoubtedly make; also, perhaps, because you fear he may eat less if he feeds himself.

Babies are messy self-feeders for a long time, but it is still wise to let them try as soon as they want to. This is when the urge is strongest: even though your baby's control over his movements is weak, his desire is strong, making up for his lack of skill. Later, when you judge that he is competent enough to try, he may no longer want to bother, and another potential difficulty has arisen. Therefore, it is always worth giving a baby the chance to feed himself, at least for part of the meal. It may make all the difference to his enthusiasm for meals. If he eats a bit less, this will not be enough for him to go hungry—he can be trusted to see to this.

Table Manners

Teaching table manners is a waste of energy until your baby has some idea of what is expected and why. Demanding "good manners" too early can be as effective a method of reducing his appetite and causing mealtime dramas as expecting him to eat too much. To a baby, putting his hands in the food, squeezing it between his fingers, even throwing some on the floor, are all just as much a part of the meal as the actual eating.

What about your point of view? Should you start the way you mean to go on by expecting a certain minimum standard of behavior at the table, by restraining your baby when he wants to play with his food, and by removing the plate promptly if he tries? What about the mess, and what will grandma say?

Because you allow your one-year-old baby to use his food as a plaything, it does not follow that he will go on behaving the same way forever. On the contrary, it is the child who is never allowed to experiment when a year old who still hankers after this enjoyable experience when he reaches the school cafeteria. He is more likely to be the bane of the cafeteria supervisor's life, the boy who always throws the peas, than the revolting one-year-old who became bored with throwing food long ago.

However, if you are one of those parents who find the sight of your baby's dinner going down his front and over the floor too much to bear, you will get on with your baby better if you try to stop him from making a mess in the first place. It's no fun playing with your carrots while your mother looks more furious every second and your father is shouting at your mother. If you find this happening, it is wiser to recognize that you or your husband won't change; give your baby less opportunity of infuriating you but remind yourself that if he does manage to outwit you, it is curiosity, not wickedness, that makes him put his hands in his food.

When to Start

During your child's second year, you can discourage the use of food as a play material by showing that you are becoming tired of clearing up the mess. He wants to please you as well as to enjoy himself. Once he eats his meals with the rest of the family, they tend to make plain their disapproval of flying cereal; also, he will want to copy what he sees going on around him. Provided they are reasonably well mannered, he may even be helped by his friends, whose shocked looks can have a more dramatic effect on his behavior than the familiar protests of his family.

Meanwhile, his experiments—and remember they are no more

than this—will be less of a nuisance if you put newspaper or a plastic cloth under his chair and an all-enveloping bib around him. A semi-rigid plastic bib, with a shaped pocket to catch the food that misses his mouth, can be wiped clean and used again at once.

Dealing with Critics

If there are still complaints from relatives and friends that your baby will "never learn," or that you are making work for yourself, point out that washing machines, whether in the home or in the launderette, are more efficient these days, so it is no longer as urgent to keep children clean. Remind the critics that whereas nursemaids had only the children to look after, mothers have everything else as well and must work out their priorities: table manners are not a priority at the age of one, but keeping on good terms with your baby is.

Phases

Let Him Change His Mind

Feeding troubles can start because mothers don't let babies change their minds. A baby sometimes refuses food he previously enjoyed or refuses to eat from a spoon or drink from a cup, or wants only puréed food again after starting on lumpy food. This looks like a step backward, and it is disheartening to feel your baby is going backward, particularly if you feel, mistakenly, that every step forward depends on you rather than on him. If you regard it as a major disaster when, for example, he wants a bottle of milk again instead of the customary boiled egg and bread and butter at suppertime, this greatly increases the chances of his demanding a bottle for the next six months rather than the next six days. It is better to let him have the bottle for a while than to spend hours over the boiled egg. He stays happy, the supper bottle fulfills whatever function it has to fulfill, such as gratifying his sucking needs, and then—back to the egg.

Refusing Solids

Occasionally, a small child goes off eating, as opposed to drinking, and refuses anything "solid" at all. There may be a dozen explanations, and if you think it is due to jealousy of a new brother or the strain of starting nursery school, then pay attention to this side of the problem. But let him have his way and give him food in liquid form, by bottle, if he wants it. It's inconvenient and potentially shaming if your snootiest friend arrives just as he is having his lunchtime bottle, but tell her it won't lead to bottle feedings for life.

Fruit juice, beaten egg in milk, milk thickened with cereal, meat and vegetable soups can all be drunk rather than eaten and are just as nutritious this way. Give your small child vitamin supplements and ask your doctor to judge if the diet is adequate, if you are doubtful about it. Once you feel confident he has enough to eat, you will be more relaxed, and when you judge the time has come to get out the spoon and cup again, you will be more likely to convince him it is a good idea.

Food Fads

Many children go through phases of liking only a few foods. Provided these are not solely in the category of nonbody-building and less valuable foods (pp. 194–95), nearly every child-chosen diet is more satisfactory than his mother fears. The fact that your child dislikes chewing meat, only enjoying hot dogs and canned luncheon meat, can be tedious when you are planning his meals, but if he eats a larger helping of what he likes, rather than one reluctant mouthful of "real" meat, he gains more nourishment in the end. If he hates all meat and enjoys only baked beans and fish sticks—well, these are both protein foods. Apples may be the only fruit he enjoys, but this is fine. The chances are that a child who will not eat vegetables and is not wild about fruit will take copious vitamin C drinks. Don't worry about the effect of lack of vegetables on his bowels—luckily, bowel actions do not depend on a daily consumption of greens (see also balanced diet, pp. 194–95).

Of course, it is unreasonable for a child to expect instant obedience to his commands over food. If he suddenly changes his mind about the hot dogs you have already cooked, he should not expect an immediate alternative—but the cook will bear his request in mind, next time.

Feeding Problems and the Schoolchild

In this age group your first concern is likely to be that your child isn't eating enough for all the activity he is undertaking. But, once again, the golden rule applies that if he is energetic, you can be sure that his body is getting the amount of food it needs even though he seems to eat less than all the other children you know. Children differ in their needs as far as food intake is concerned, in just the same way as cars differ in their gasoline requirements. For children, it is a matter of different metabolic rates; for cars, it is the question of difference in the number of miles per gallon.

Is a Hot Breakfast Essential?

A common anxiety is that the child does not eat enough before going to school, particularly if he does not eat any hot food. A mother so often feels that "he must have something warm inside him before he goes to school." But there is nothing magical about warm food—cold food becomes warm (i.e., reaches body temperature) in a matter of minutes once it is inside the stomach, whereas hot food soon cools down to the level of body temperature.

Many children do not like a large breakfast, and it is perfectly all right to send them off to school with nothing inside if that is what they want. An analogy with cars is again reasonable, to reassure those of you who still feel anxious. A car that is half full of gasoline does not have to be filled to the brim before it leaves your own garage. You can fill it whenever you want to, but you must make sure it doesn't completely run out. Exactly the same with a child, only he has the advantage for you that he will never let himself run out of food, whereas your car might let you down!

Of course, you can reasonably point out that if he has no breakfast he may find himself very hungry during class, when he won't be able to fill himself up. An apple in his pocket to eat during the morning break may help, but perhaps your discussion about the possibility of feeling hungry in the classroom may make him decide to have some breakfast after all. The big thing is not to nag him over his breakfast but, rather, to help him work out his own needs.

The Child Who Eats Too Much

The main cause of malnutrition in the United States today is overeating. The early introduction of solids, particularly cereals (see below), has caused a major problem by producing thousands of overweight babies. Does this matter?

We now know that fat babies are very likely to grow into fat adults. The reason for this is that giving too much food to young children not only causes the fat cells (adipose cells) in the body to increase in size, but also causes them to multiply. The baby may be left with millions more fat cells than he should have. Consequently, for the rest of his life these fat cells are clamoring to be filled up with fat. This explains why it is so difficult to make a fat child thin.

Don't make the mistake of calling a fat baby a "healthy" baby —he is nothing of the sort. In fact, if anything he is a sick baby, or at any rate he is more likely to pick up infections, especially bronchitis (p. 464). When you see a fat child, don't say, "Poor kid, he's got something wrong with his glands." Obesity is almost always due to overeating and only very rarely to glandular trouble. The idea that adolescents develop "puppy fat" as a natural part of growing up is another misconception. The adolescent who becomes too fat is eating too much.

Fat Babies   The prevention of obesity in babies is largely a matter of not giving them too much to eat, particularly cereals. There is no special value in cereals and they should be cut out altogether from the diet of a baby who is overweight. Similarly, don't start your baby on cereals early, since this may create an obesity problem.

Treating obesity is always more difficult than preventing it. You will need to concentrate on the protein foods—meat, fish, cheese, and eggs—while cutting down on carbohydrates. This means cutting out sugar, cereal, crackers, and cake. Give as little potato and bread as possible and don't give more than one pint (approx. 500 ml) of milk in the day.

Let your baby feed himself, in the hope that less food will go into his mouth than when you accurately spoon it in (see pp. 190, 202). Use every trick you can in order to reduce the amount of food going into his mouth. See if you can get him to miss a meal altogether, without noticing it, rather than sticking to your previous timetable of meals. He may become so absorbed in his play that he falls asleep, without demanding his usual drink of milk. Alternatively, you may be able to substitute orange juice for that drink of milk or dilute it by half with water.

Fat Adolescents   The adolescent who becomes too fat is certainly eating more than he should, but there may be an emotional reason for this. Eating is a pleasure, and overeating may occur in someone who is unhappy, as a subconscious search for happiness. The reason for this unhappiness, which is often associated with loneliness, may be easy to discover but it is often deep-seated, requiring professional help for its solution.

Since eating is associated with emotions, some adolescents develop an abnormal lack of appetite (anorexia nervosa). This usually results from an intense desire to be thin and very often requires medical help.

It is chastening to realize that fat people tend to have fat dogs; that the chances of a teen-ager being admitted to college are halved if he is obese; and that a fat executive is paid less and is less likely to advance as fast or as far as a thin one.

15

How Children Grow and Develop

It is natural for you to be concerned about your baby's growth and development during his first two years. By the time he can walk, he has passed the major physical milestones, and you will find you relax, taking it for granted that he is healthy and developing normally. Your attention will then shift to his behavior and how he reacts to the world. In other words, your concern relates to the most obvious aspects of your baby's progress; it is centered on growth while he is growing at his fastest and on his developing skills as he gains control of his body. Once he is moving about and learning to fit into his environment, you will find your main concern is that he does so smoothly and happily.

To bring up your child successfully, you need not know exactly how and when he should reach various stages of growth and development, but understanding the usual sequence will help you to avoid unnecessary worry, so that you enjoy your baby more.

Growth

Growth and development differ, though they are related and affect each other. Growth is increase in size, whereas development means increase in complexity. Growth is easier to measure than development.

Rate of Growth

Your baby is growing at his fastest when he is born, and although he still grows very fast during his first two years, the rate is falling sharply all the time. From three to ten years, growth is comparatively slow and steady, being slowest just before adolescence. At adolescence there is a sudden growth spurt; this is the only time after birth when an acceleration in the rate of growth occurs. At the end of adolescence, when the child has become an adult, all growth in height ceases.

Your child's appetite will reflect his rate of growth; in his first six months a baby needs more calories for each pound he weighs than an adult doing heavy work. Not until puberty, when the growth spurt occurs, is he likely to have such a large appetite again. For this reason, don't expect your child's appetite to increase steadily with age; rate of growth is one of the many factors that influence it.

The Baby's Weight Gain

Your baby's size at birth is determined partly by inheritance—tall parents have larger babies—and partly by factors operating during his life in the uterus. These prenatal factors include your health and social circumstances, your age, whether you have proper prenatal care, and whether you smoke—smoking makes smaller babies (see pregnancy, pp. 12, 134).

In the first week of life it is normal for babies to lose a few ounces. The reason for this is that they do not immediately settle down to full feedings, so that the loss in weight from stools and urine passed is not yet compensated for by the amount of food taken in. Large babies lose more weight than small ones, the average weight loss being 4 to 7 ounces (113 to 198 grams). A full-term baby usually regains his birth weight by the tenth day. After this, the average weight gain is 5 to 6 ounces (142–170 grams) a week, so that a 7-pound (3.17 kg) baby weighs about 21 pounds (9.52 kg) at one year. However, it is perfectly normal for many babies to gain less than these amounts; energy and contentment are better guides to progress than a baby's weight, and frequent weighing is not only unnecessary but often causes needless anxiety.

Normal babies do not gain weight steadily in a straight line on the weight chart; their progress is more like a staircase, with flat periods as well as gains. The more frequently the baby is weighed, the more obvious are the flat periods.

The average child gains about 7 pounds (3.17 kg) in his second year and 5 (2.27 kg) in his third. Thereafter, his weight increases comparatively slowly until the adolescent spurt occurs.

Height and Proportions

The different body materials, fat, bone, and muscle, grow at different rates, and a child's proportions change as he grows. A newborn baby needs a large brain, so his head is very big in proportion to the rest of his body. In the first year of life, the size of the head, as measured by its circumference, increases by 5 inches (12.7 cm), from an average of 13 inches (33.02 cm) at birth to 18 inches (45.72 cm) by the first birthday. This rapid increase in the first year is remarkable when compared with the next eleven years, when there is an increase of only 3 inches (7.62 cm) (Fig. 1).

As with weight gain, a baby's increase in height (or length) is greatest in the first six months; it then slows down gradually. The prenatal factors that help to decide a baby's size at birth continue to affect it for the first two years of life. It is only after this that a child's own growth hormones control his growth; so it is difficult to predict future adult height accurately in the first two to three years. After this age it becomes increasingly possible to calculate a child's future height by X-ray studies of his bone development, assessment of the

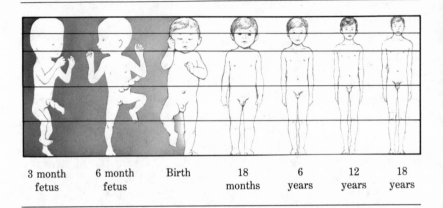

| 3 month fetus | 6 month fetus | Birth | 18 months | 6 years | 12 years | 18 years |

Fig. 1. The changing shape and proportions of the human body from embryo to adult. Head and trunk are approximately the same size in the three-month-old embryo. At birth, the head is a quarter of the total body length, while in the adult it is only one-eighth. The size of the arms and legs in relation to the rest of the body also changes dramatically.

child himself, and family trends. This may be useful if, for example, a child wants to be a ballet dancer, and it is necessary to know whether she is likely to grow too tall for success.

Adolescent Growth

The steady, comparatively slow rate of growth during middle childhood becomes much faster as the child reaches adolescence. Since girls mature physically about two and a half years before boys, their growth spurt occurs earlier. On average, girls are 6 inches (15.24 cm) shorter than boys when they have finished growing. Puberty begins in girls with development of the breasts; don't be surprised if one side starts to grow before the other—this is common, and they often end up not quite symmetrical. This is followed by the growth of pubic hair and then of hair in the armpits, together with enlargement of the genitalia; menstruation is the last development (see sex education, pp. 336–37).

Parents with a tall girl who has only just had her first period may be worried that she will be excessively tall by the end of adolescence. They can be reassured that a girl has already passed her maximum growth by the time menstruation starts. The girl with an early puberty may seem tall for her age but is likely to end up smaller than her contemporaries, since an early growth spurt means an early end to growth.

Puberty in boys begins with the appearance of pubic hair and is followed by enlargement of the genital organs and breaking of the voice. The beard then begins to grow and hair appears in the armpits (see sex education, pp. 336–37).

Education for Adolescence

Since both boys and girls are reaching adolescence earlier—indeed more than one girl in ten now begins menstruating while still at elementary school—it is important that they should be prepared for these changes. Sex education should be regarded as "growth education," and should be started as soon as your child shows interest in the subject—which may be as soon as he can talk. If your child does not ask questions himself, it does not mean he is not interested; you should introduce the subject gradually and naturally as the opportunity and need arise. Further help on sex education comes in later chapters (see pp. 310–11, 330–41, 353–54).

Can Growth Rate Be Influenced?

A child getting an adequate diet in a favorable environment is likely to reach his full potential size as dictated by his genetic make-up. Endocrine glands under the control of the pituitary gland regulate his growth.

Severe malnutrition or a severe illness can affect growth. How much and how permanent the effect depends on the severity and length of the interruption and the age at which it occurred. The earlier the interruption to growth occurs, the greater its effect. A child who seems to you to be eating an unbalanced diet over a short period of time will not suffer; in any event, his diet is probably far less inadequate than you fear (see feeding problems, pp. 204–6).

Rate of growth is affected by the seasons, being faster in spring and slower in autumn. For this reason a child has to be studied over a whole year to see the effect of any treatment aimed at altering his growth. The reverse happens with weight; children gain more weight in winter than summer, since they are less active in colder weather but eat more.

"Catch-up" Growth

If a child's normal rate of growth has been slowed by illness or starvation, he will adapt with a period of "catch-up" growth, when the rate may be two or three times faster than normal. Once he is back to his normal rate it slows up again. How the signal to stop growing so fast is given is not known; and it is not certain how long or how severe an interruption must be to affect a child's size permanently. Catch-up growth is comforting evidence of the body's ability to overcome setbacks.

A child does not need to be made to rest in the hope that he will grow faster. There is no truth in the belief that sleep is needed for growth. Nor should the thin, healthy child be "rested" in the hope that he will put on weight.

The Child Who Is Small for His Age

If there is serious concern that a child is too small for his family pattern, a doctor may arrange for tests to check that growth is proceeding normally. He takes into account the child's general health and any illness he has had, together with the height of his parents and family. Sometimes there is a family tendency to slow growth followed by an unusually intense growth spurt in adolescence.

Emotional Consequences of Being the "Wrong Size"

The child who is too big or too small for his age is often treated by adults as if his mental age matched his size; a small child talked to in a babyish way sometimes reacts by behaving that way; a large three-year-old may be expected to behave like the five-year-old he resembles. The strain of living up, or down, to these inappropriate standards can interfere with a child's natural development; the large child may take refuge in regressing and the small child may enjoy being babyish, using his power to gain extra privileges.

Older children may suffer agonies of doubt about their size, being teased by their school friends and perhaps misunderstood by their teachers. If you really are concerned about your child's size, do seek advice. But do reassure him about the wide range of normal size and tell him of a similar pattern of growth in other members of the family, if there is one. Above all, a child should be treated appropriately for his age and not his size. It is often the confusion arising out of other

people's manner toward him that creates a child's difficulties, rather
than worry about being too tall or too short.

Growth of Other Systems

So far I have concentrated on growth in height (skeletal growth) but
mentioned that not all the body systems grow at the same rate
throughout childhood (Fig. 2).

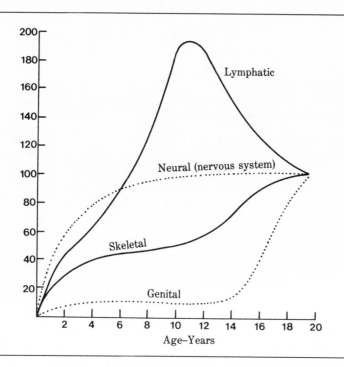

Fig. 2. Graph showing variation in growth rates of different body systems
from birth to puberty. The curves are drawn to a common scale by comput-
ing their value at successive ages in terms of their total postnatal incre-
ments. (After Scammon, R.E., *The Measurement of Man*, 1930)

The early growth spurt of the brain is well shown, accounting for
the baby's large head. The late growth spurt of the genital organs is
also obvious. The growth of the lymphatic system, which protects the
body from infection, is instructive. Part of this system can be seen by
looking at the tonsils at the back of the mouth and by feeling the
glands in the neck and groin (pp. 454 and 460–61). The tonsils cannot

be seen in a newborn baby but grow to be very obvious by five to six
years of age. In the past this has led to their removal, when in fact
they were working very hard as the body's front line of defense
against infection. This also explains the larger neck glands, which can
easily be felt in a child's thin neck at this age and sometimes unnecessarily alarm parents.

Development

A baby's physical growth is easy to see and measure. His general
development—that is, all the other ways in which he is changing—is
much more difficult to assess.

Sequence of Development

Babies show their individual characteristics right from the start; each
one develops at his own pace. However, all children keep to the same
sequence of development, reaching the major milestones (better
called "stepping stones"), such as sitting up and walking, in the same
order. The attainment of one step is usually essential for the achievement of the next; for example, a child cannot sit up until he has
developed head control. On the other hand, an unnecessary stage, like
crawling, may be left out altogether without ill-effect (see p. 228).

Development is continuous, from conception to maturity, but
does not unfold smoothly: it tends to go forward in spurts, with
plateaus during which a baby seems to make little progress. While
concentrating on a new skill, your baby may temporarily neglect
something he has already achieved. This does not mean it is forgotten
but merely that he is using his energy in the most efficient way.
You have to remember the number of different fields in which he is
developing: these include control of movement and manipulation,
emotion, social relationships, understanding and memory, speech,
seeing and hearing, play and feeding behavior, bowel and bladder
control.

Don't be surprised then if for a time your baby does not seem to
be developing as fast as he was. He may be in a plateau between two
spurts. Sometimes, a change of environment, such as going on vacation, may be a stimulus that sets off a spurt in his development.

A child develops literally from head to toe. Just as at birth, the
head is large compared with the rest of the body, the legs being short
in proportion, so development follows a similar pattern: control starts
at the head and moves down the body to the arms, trunk, and legs.
Movements are at first crude, gradually becoming finer.

Setbacks and Holdups

A child does not develop at an equal pace in all fields. Backwardness in any particular area is probably caused by his individual blue print or sometimes by lack of stimulation in that field. Sometimes illness is responsible for interrupting or delaying progress—for example, the child just beginning to walk may go back to crawling for a while after he recovers from an illness.

Reverting to an earlier stage of development is known as "regression"; it is particularly likely to occur to a child under stress, perhaps due to illness or to emotional pressures, such as jealousy of a brother or sister. The toilet-trained child may wet his pants again, or the child who can feed himself may sit back and wait for his mother to do it for him. Thumb sucking may reappear. If this happens to your child, don't be cross with him but recognize that what he is really doing is asking for extra love and attention until he feels secure enough to go back to his normal behavior (see jealousy, pp. 150–51).

Preterm (Premature) Babies

Babies born before term are a little later in reaching the various stages of development than those who were born at the right time, because they have to make up the development they missed in the uterus. Usually, however, the added stimulus of adapting to the outside world hastens the process so that their achievements are a little ahead of what they would have been had they been born at the correct time. For example, the baby born six weeks early, instead of being six weeks late in smiling is likely to be only four weeks late (see also pp. 219–21, 468).

Keeping a Baby Book

If you keep a record of your baby's development in a baby book you will probably notice that after weeks with no major changes there is suddenly a great deal to enter. Actually he will have been practicing and co-ordinating the skills he has already acquired, thereby preparing for the next stage of development. The three-month-old baby lying in his carriage opening and closing his hands is practicing for the time when he will be able to use his hands to grasp objects. He does not wake one day suddenly able to grasp, but practices and anticipates the "new" skill for weeks beforehand.

The baby book will also show how your new baby's progress compares with your older children or with other people's children. Such comparisons usually confirm how difficult it is to generalize about development—any table of average development is, in some respects, hopelessly inaccurate for the individual baby. Record the details of your baby's development as they happen; it is so easy to forget and then later to substitute the age at which you think he ought to have achieved one of his new skills.

Can Development Be Stimulated?

Every baby's rate of development in any particular field depends on the growing maturity of his nervous system. This is an inherited pattern and it cannot be hastened by outside factors. You can encourage your baby to sit up by offering him a hand to pull on when he seems to want it, but you cannot make him sit alone before he is ready. You can provide a comfortable rug for him to crawl on, but he will not crawl unless he has the ability and urge to do so.

On the other hand, since babies are stimulated by their surroundings, lack of stimulation can delay and discourage a baby from using his new skills; for instance, he cannot pull himself up if there is nothing to hold on to, or learn the shapes and sizes of objects if he is given nothing to handle. An added incentive, unquestionably, is your delight in his activities, which he soon notices. Babies brought up without the love and interest of sympathetic parents do not thrive physically or develop their full potential; this applies particularly to emotional development, but it also affects the rate of learning in other fields, such as speech (see p. 592).

A stimulating environment is therefore essential, but this is very different from directly stimulating the child to go faster in order to achieve more than his optimum and may well have the opposite effect. Children are not like cars, which go faster with superchargers. In fact, mothers should imitate their babies rather than stimulate them, thereby encouraging their own spontaneous activities.

Parents should also be aware that for the first six months everyone has been a friend. By the age of six months, babies appreciate that there are people who are "strangers," who differ from their parents. Consequently, they cling to their parents and shun strangers, who must be aware of the need to approach babies at this stage very slowly, while the parents provide the extra confidence being asked of them.

This can be a very trying time for the mother, since her baby won't be left with anyone else, sometimes not even with the father. The stage lasts for two to six weeks, varying in intensity with different babies, and gradually making way for the social behavior expected, provided the baby is allowed to achieve this feeling of safety at his own pace and that no one rushes him into trying to make him be friends with a stranger until he is ready. Fathers may feel very hurt by this temporary behavior of their babies, unless forewarned.

Encouraging His Sense of Achievement

Provide your baby with ways of entertaining himself during the periods when he must be left to his own devices. A baby smiles and vocalizes not only at people but from a sense of achievement; he is happy if he recognizes something or can make something happen.

The most successful toy is neither too novel nor too familiar; familiarity gives a baby little sense of achievement, while something that is beyond his capabilities altogether overwhelms him, so that he gives up and ignores it. An activity that stretches him but can be mastered with effort—or sometimes an object to look at which is half-familiar—is the most enjoyable because it gives him most sense of achievement. Even babies brought up by the best of parents have been found to make faster progress in using their hands, for example, and to become adept at amusing themselves earlier, when given specially devised toys.

We now know that even the youngest babies are far more aware of their surroundings than we once thought, and need things to look at and listen to from their earliest days. This has been proved by experiments measuring the rate of a baby's heartbeats while trying to attract his attention with something. When is he is paying attention, his heart beats faster even if his face gives nothing away. So if there is nothing happening around him, he is missing something from a very early age. (See pp. 167, 294.)

Surprisingly, it appears that he is also missing something if there is too much happening around him. Stimulation must be distinctive. A baby in an overcrowded home with a constant barrage of noise and movement may be overwhelmed by the bombardment and therefore unable to start learning to distinguish between the different stimuli surrounding him. He may be handled and fed by so many different people that his mother remains an indistinct figure among them.

Critical Periods of Learning

It is believed that there are certain quite short periods when a child is especially ready to develop in the various fields. These are termed the "critical periods of learning." If he is not given the proper opportunity at the right time, he may falter over this particular piece of learning or may learn it in an inappropriate way. For example, if as a mother you never respond to your toddler's signals when he is about to wet his pants, he may give up trying to take the initiative himself and will probably be less co-operative with your efforts at toilet training. The whole process may take longer because you did not take advantage of his readiness to learn, using it to reinforce your own attempts to teach him. Equally, you might try to train him long before he is physically capable of controlling his bladder, and by provoking his resistance make him less co-operative when he does become capable of it. Either way you missed the critical period of learning.

This does not mean that you must know exactly when the "average" baby has reached each stage of development. All you need to do is to respond to your own baby, taking your cue from his progress, not from a table of averages or the example of other babies. This happens naturally in a normal relationship between a baby and his mother. Worry interferes with this relationship, spoiling your enjoyment of your child without making him mature more quickly; indeed, as with the example of toilet training, it may delay his progress rather than encourage it.

Is My Baby Developing Normally?

If you are worried about your baby's development, particularly if he is backward in *several* ways when compared with other babies, tell your family or clinic doctor or the visiting nurse. These professionals have been trained to assess a child's development, comparing it with the range of normal development for his age. The whole child is studied, his general alertness and the way he responds being just as important as his actual performance in any special tests. Since babies, like adults, have their off days, if there is any doubt about a child's performance, he will be checked again on another day.

Parents often worry most about delays in sitting up and walking, but doctors take less account of variations in these fields, which often follow a family pattern, than of a baby's reactions to his surroundings. Does he respond normally to his parents with a smile and obvious pleasure? Can the doctor make contact with him? Does he use his hands normally to grasp objects? Does he show a natural curiosity? Is he beginning to babble? The doctor will check that there is no physical cause for any backwardness—deafness, for instance, would delay the development of speech. (See handicapped child, p. 592.)

It may turn out that your baby's development is perfectly normal and that your concern with the major milestones, like sitting up, has made you overlook his general alertness and development in other fields. Possibly this is because other people usually ask if a baby is sitting up or standing, rather than whether he is friendly or plays a lot. Other mothers are naturally proud of their own babies' development and focus on their best points—which may be quite different from your baby's. Mothers need to share the pleasures of their own babies as much as they need to share the anxieties.

The Newborn Baby

Creating a Bond

A newborn baby seems helpless and entirely dependent on others for survival. His hunger and thirst cannot be satisfied without help, although many of his basic bodily needs, such as breathing, getting rid of waste, and temperature regulating, are met automatically.

At first sight, he appears to be at a disadvantage compared with other newly born animals which can move toward and cling to their mothers from birth. However, the human infant is not utterly helpless; there are even certain advantages in his dependence on others. He cannot go to his mother himself but he can cry, thereby unconsciously attracting her attention. He cannot cling to her as she moves around, like the young chimpanzee, so he makes sure that she comes to him. He soon begins to smile and show pleasure when she appears, thus increasing her love and reinforcing the bond between them. In fact, a baby has to become a social being from the start, communicating in more subtle ways than physical clinging. Tests have shown that, given the opportunity (pp. 19–20), a baby focuses on his mother during the first hour after birth. Mothers have known this for years but have been hoodwinked by the ignorance of doctors and others who made out that babies didn't focus till four to six weeks of age, thereby preventing the mothers from believing what they saw.

Although a baby's communication is at first unconscious on his part, the resulting food, comfort, and handling he receives gradually build up his impression of the world; he is learning from the beginning, though at first he cannot respond. The long, sheltered years as part of a family and of wider social groups such as school give him the time to gain experience and the opportunity to develop in a far more complex manner than the young of faster maturing species.

Bonding and Attachment

These are two separate processes. Bonding is the flow of feeling from parent to child and remains with the parent for life. Attachment describes the child's feelings for his parent. It increases throughout childhood but then lessens as the child lets go in becoming an adult.

Reflexes Present at Birth

Your baby is born with certain primitive reflexes, automatic reactions to changes in his surroundings, which later disappear as voluntary movements take over. Some of the reflexes are protective, being necessary for survival; some reflect behavior that can only have been appropriate at an earlier stage in human evolution. If a cat falls from a height, he lands on all fours because of these primitive "righting" reflexes. A baby is endowed with similar righting reflexes, so that most of his early movements are automatic.

There is a general tendency for these reflexes to disappear by the age of three months. This is the age when your baby begins to take over his movements on a voluntary basis because he is starting to understand what he wants to do and has reached the stage when he is just beginning to be able to do it. Around the age of three months there is something of a lull in his movements, since automatic movements are dying out and voluntary movements only just beginning to take over.

Sucking, Swallowing, and Rooting Reflexes   These reflexes enable your baby to take food actively as soon as he is born, when he is no longer being nourished through the afterbirth (placenta). They are present in full-term infants and in all but the smallest preterm

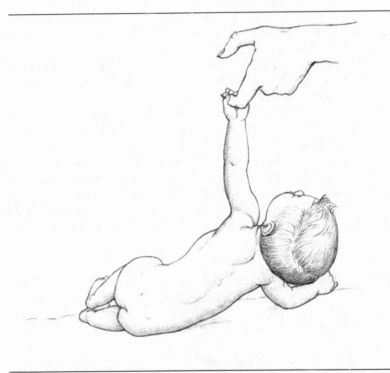

Fig. 3. Grasp reflex. This is lost by about three months. As the baby grows older he gradually learns to use his hands deliberately.

babies. Sucking movements are practiced in the uterus during the last weeks of pregnancy when some babies suck their thumbs, and may even cause "sucking blisters" on the back of the hand.

Since a newborn baby not only sucks and swallows but can also "root" to search for his food, he does not need to be pushed onto the breast or the bottle. When touched gently on the cheek, he moves his head in the direction of the touch, which is the mechanism whereby he searches until he finds the nipple. This basic instinct to feed is gradually strengthened as his nervous system matures, and as he begins to connect sucking with food and satisfaction, and handling with comfort and the possibility of food.

Reflexes That Vanish

The "Grasp" Reflex At birth your baby has a "grasp" reflex, which makes him automatically clench his fist around any object placed in his palm. This is strong enough to support his weight; if you were to let him grasp one of your fingers in each hand, you would find you could lift him off the bed (Fig. 3). The grasp reflex disappears by about the third month; it is a relic of the primitive need to cling physically to mother or to the branch of a tree for survival. It is not the direct forerunner of deliberate grasping, which develops separately (see using his hands, pp. 229–33).

The "Walking" Reflex This is produced when a baby is held upright with his feet touching a firm surface and propelled gently along; it vanishes after a few weeks without leading directly to standing and walking. But that need not stop you from enjoying the excitement of watching him make this first automatic walk by holding him up on a table during his first week or two (Fig. 4).

The "Startle" Reflex Your baby responds with various set patterns of movement to sudden changes in position or surroundings. Some of these reflexes seem to be an attempt to protect himself and to keep his balance. You will probably notice the "startle" reflex, his reaction to sudden loud noises—he flings his arms and legs outward and his head back. This set reaction to shock is later replaced, as your baby's repertoire of voluntary responses develops and he begins to assess each situation separately.

Doctors can use these different reflexes to assess a baby's development, since they know the ages at which they normally disappear. They are also used to assess the degree of prematurity of a baby born before term, since the age at which they first appear in the uterus differs for each reflex.

Conditioned Reflexes and Habit Training

Nature does not provide automatic responses to meet every possible situation, and one way a child widens his range of behavior is by acquiring new reflexes as a result of his experiences. These are termed "conditioned" reflexes. They were first described by Pavlov, the Russian scientist, who conditioned dogs to anticipate the arrival of food whenever he rang a bell. In a short time the dogs would salivate to the sound of a bell, even though no food had appeared.

A conditioned reflex occurs naturally but it may also be used by parents, both deliberately and unconsciously, to encourage habits that help children fit into family and community life. For example, the reflex emptying of bladder and bowels when full can be "conditioned" to become associated with sitting on the training seat. This use of a conditioned reflex is convenient but it is not the same as real toilet

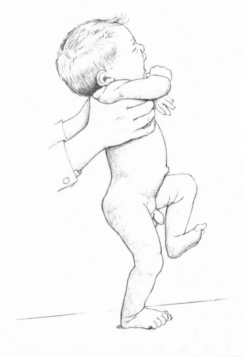

Fig. 4. Walking reflex. A two-day-old baby stepping out, with help. He will lose this ability by about three months but regain it when he begins to walk on his own.

training, which is possible only when the child is physically capable of control and emotionally ready to participate in the training (see toilet training, p. 240).

A child can also be conditioned to pass a motion at the same time every day, commonly after breakfast, if his mother encourages any natural tendency in this direction. Similarly, a baby is at first hungry at frequent intervals throughout the day and night, but as he grows larger and capable of taking more at each feeding he is encouraged to wait longer for food and to do without it overnight, so becoming accustomed to the widely spaced mealtimes normal in most societies.

Thus some of a baby's reflexes can be conditioned to become habits: shortcuts to socially convenient behavior. This does not mean the early reflexes have to be repressed, but merely that basic tendencies are modified by experience. It is one of the ways a child learns naturally for himself all the time. For example, very soon after birth he opens his mouth and makes sucking movements as soon as he is picked up—before his lips are touched. He is already learning that being handled heralds food, so handling alone is enough to stimulate his basic instinct to suck. What is more, he comes to realize, soon after, that he will be fed only when held in a certain position. As a result, he no longer makes sucking movements whenever he is picked up, but only if he is held in a feeding position.

Stages in Learning to Sit

Achieving Head Control (Figs. 5 a–d)

A newborn baby has no control over his head or posture. If you sit him up, his back is quite rounded and his head falls forward; if you pull him up by the hands, his head will drop backward—so support it. Whether on his back or his front, he lies with his head turned to one side. When lying on his front he humps up his buttocks, bending his arms and legs under his body. By the age of about seven weeks, his head does not lag completely when you pull him up to a sitting position and, once upright, he can hold it up for a moment. By about sixteen weeks, increasing strength and control of his head and his back make it possible for him to raise his chest and head himself, when lying on his front. His buttocks are now flat on the bed. A baby's ability to lift up his head first when lying on his front is the reason why this position, which shows him to best advantage, is often chosen by photographers for pictures of young babies. By about six months he can roll from his stomach to his back, later learning to roll the other way.

Sitting Unsupported (Figs. 6 a–c)

As his back and neck muscles get stronger, your baby learns to sit, at first with support and later alone. You will not harm his back if you let him sit propped up as soon as he seems to enjoy it, which may be as early as one month. Adjustable chairs are useful; they help him to look around and prevent him from being bored. By six months, a

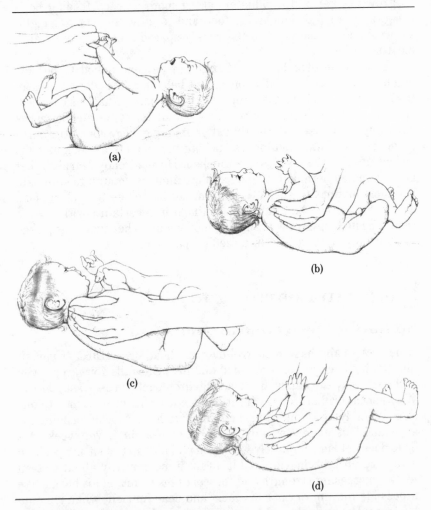

Fig. 5. Learning to sit—achieving head control. (a) The first four weeks. If you pull the baby up to a sitting position his head lags completely. WARN-ING: this is *not* a game to play with your baby. Always support his head when lifting him. (b) Seven to eight weeks. Less head lag. (c) Four months. No head lag. (d) Five months. The baby lifts his head to help.

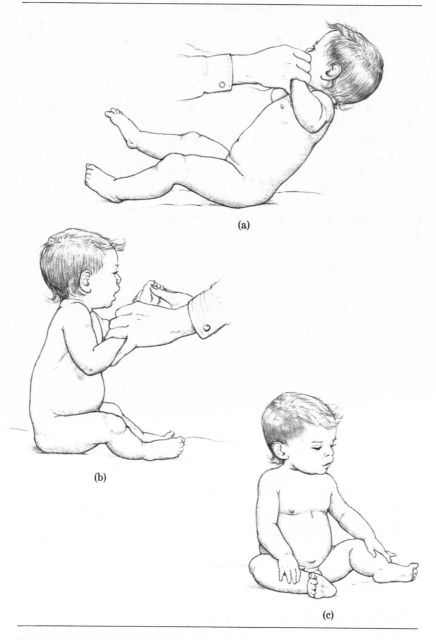

Fig. 6. Learning to sit—unsupported. Six months. (a) He braces his shoulders and assists; there is now no head lag. (b) At the end of the movement his back is straight and his head firmly erect. (c) He can sit for a moment without support.

baby usually braces his shoulders as if trying to help when pulled up to sit; there is no lagging of his head, and his back is straight once he is sitting, though this only lasts momentarily without support.

The age at which a baby sits alone varies greatly, depending more on his inbuilt pattern than on intelligence or practice. Most babies manage it between seven and ten months, but the range of normal is much wider than this. If your baby is nearly a year old and you are getting impatient, ask your doctor to check.

When your baby first sits alone, he can only lean forward, but by his first birthday he can probably twist around while sitting, without toppling over (Figs. 7a and b). He pulls himself up to sit before learning the knack of lying down again. You may sometimes find him sitting up and crying because he is tired but has not yet learned to lie down without help.

Widening His Horizon

Once your baby can sit, many more activities open up. His range of vision widens, and seeing things nearby makes him want to pick them

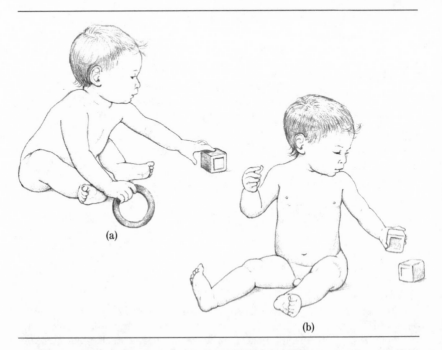

(a)

(b)

Fig. 7. Learning to sit—nine months. Enough confidence to (a) reach forward and (b) twist around while sitting unsupported.

up and test them for himself by putting them in his mouth. This desire encourages him to practice reaching out at various angles without overbalancing—an example of how different aspects of development mesh together and stimulate each other.

In the same way, once your baby can sit and pick up objects within reach, he soon becomes ambitious to get at things farther away. This incentive reinforces his maturing capacity to move about by rolling, crawling, shuffling, or walking. The more opportunity you give him to move about and play, the more likely he is to make full use of his developing abilities. This is what is meant by giving him a "stimulating environment."

Your Baby Becomes Mobile

Stretching His Legs

Legs and feet come last in the main sequence of movement development, since a child must have control over head, arms, and body before he can balance and therefore stand, crawl, and walk.

As with other aspects of development, your baby anticipates the final stage by exercising his legs long before he can use them to stand or walk. Although the walking reflex disappears during the third month of life and he stops bearing his weight and "walking" automatically, he soon starts using his legs in other ways: at about two months he stretches them out; between three and six months he tries his legs more and more, kicking and playing with his toes. At first, kicking is merely spontaneous and random; then he begins to enjoy the movements and they gradually become more deliberate and controlled. He kicks his legs for fun and to express emotion, just as he waves his arms about when angry or happy.

Finding His Feet

By about six months your baby likes feeling the ground with his feet and may bear much of his weight if supported. He loves bouncing and will enjoy himself in a baby bouncer (see play, p. 296). This kind of exercise does not strain him or make him bowlegged; as with other activities, a baby will not try it unless he is ready.

Learning to Walk

Around seven months, your baby may start pulling himself up to stand and before his first birthday perhaps walks around the room holding on to the furniture. From walking with support, he progresses to walking alone, generally between twelve and eighteen months. But remember—the age when children stand and walk varies enormously. As with sitting up, lateness is usually due to the individual blueprint; only seldom is it connected with poor intelligence or weak legs.

Crawling and Shuffling

The rapid crawler has less incentive to walk than the baby with a slower method of moving about. On the other hand, many babies skip the crawling stage altogether, and this does not matter at all. The year-old baby is an explorer; he wants to get around and is quite unaware that walking is a more advanced method of travel than crawling or shuffling.

Helping Him Walk

A walker may encourage your baby if he is physically ready to walk, by showing him the delights of upright movement and by giving him useful practice. Of course, it has the snag that he may find this such a good way of moving that he is reluctant to leave it and walk alone. In the same way, one child may gain the confidence to walk alone if offered a supporting hand at first, while another comes to rely on it and is unwilling to let go and try by himself. Try to strike a balance, giving enough help to prevent your baby from getting discouraged by continual falls but not intervening when he is ready to experiment alone.

If he is wearing a diaper, fold it so that it is not bulky between his legs, because this would make walking more awkward. The bulky diaper not only exaggerates the normal degree of bow legs at this age but can also exert enough pressure to encourage abnormal bowing (see bow legs, p. 532).

Delay in Walking

Sometimes a child takes a few steps by himself and then several weeks pass before he tries again. As with other skills, walking is anticipated before the child is fully ready to use it—he may be physically ready but mentally hesitant about discarding an old and tried skill like crawling. Even when he is walking well, he may go back to crawling if he wants to go somewhere quickly. It does not matter when your child starts walking, so long as he is developing in other ways and has the opportunity to practice if he wishes. If he is nearly two and you are worried by the delay in walking, ask your doctor to check that there is nothing wrong. There is usually no need to worry, since the range of normal is so wide, but your doctor can advise you about handling and play.

Increasing Confidence

When he starts taking a few steps alone your child is bound to be unsteady and topple over easily; he will gradually become more adept, and when he no longer has to concentrate entirely on walking will be able to pull or carry things at the same time. When he is two, he will begin to walk up and down stairs, but you will notice that he puts both feet on each step at first. He will bend over to pick up a toy. Next he runs, and soon he will learn to walk on tiptoe. By the time he goes to school, he will be jumping, skipping, and generally agile, whether he started walking early or late.

Footwear

There is no need for your child to wear shoes until he walks; moreover, when he first starts to walk, let him go barefoot whenever possible, so that he can feel the ground until he is better at balancing. When he does have to wear shoes, make sure they are comfortable. Fit is more important than quality at this age, since shoes are outgrown rapidly, and there is less temptation to hang on to them a little too long if they were inexpensive. Tight socks are as harmful as tight shoes. (See acquired bent toes, p. 534.)

Using His Hands

A newborn baby has a strong grasp reflex and for the most part keeps his hands tightly closed. He progressively opens them more frequently as the grasp reflex becomes weaker, and during the third month, when the grasp reflex disappears, the hands usually remain open.

Learning to Suck His Fingers

Your baby's hands first become important to him as objects to suck and watch. If, when he waves his arms, one of his hands accidentally bumps his face and touches his mouth, he immediately starts sucking his fist, cramming in his thumb or fingers if he can. The random arm movements stop and he settles down to enjoy sucking until his hand falls out of his mouth, to his obvious displeasure.

At this stage he is not deliberately putting his hand in or out of his mouth, but, encouraged by the pleasure of sucking, he soon learns to do so. This has nothing to do with teething (pp. 247–49), so don't think your baby has a toothache because he puts his fingers in his mouth.

It is fascinating to watch how he does not move his hand deliberately to the other parts of his face, since they give him no particular pleasure; pleasure is a powerful incentive to learning, and out of the myriad of experiences bombarding your baby's senses, he concentrates on those that are most satisfying. He has now entered the oral phase of development, when he puts everything in his mouth because it is the focal point for his pleasure. He is also able to learn more about objects, because by placing them in his mouth he is testing their feel.

This is the age when he drools a lot—as one mother put it to me, "his mouth seems to run like a faucet." Although this stage may last for months, and many mothers are distressed by how smelly and messy it makes their beautiful baby and his clothes, it always stops in the end. Continuously dabbing at his mouth makes the drooling phase last longer, because this adds to his pleasure (see will he starve? p. 437).

Watching His Hands

For weeks before he can grasp or play with other objects a baby will lie in his carriage looking at and sucking his hands. Most babies watch the back of their hands before the front.

Learning to Grasp

Between three and four months your baby can hold a rattle if you put it in his hands, although he cannot yet pick it up for himself. He pulls and lifts up the hem of his clothing, studying it as if it were the most interesting object in the world. He is learning to co-ordinate eye and arm movements, this being essential before he can pick up what he sees.

By about five months he is trying to reach out and take something he wants, provided it is large and easy to grasp. At this age he uses both hands together. He will not begin to show a preference for one or other hand until the second half of his first year and often much later. He is likely to be two or three years old before obvious dominance of one or other hand has shown itself. Obvious dominance in the first year could mean there is something wrong with the other arm, and this needs checking by your doctor.

At first, a baby's efforts are clumsy and fumbling; he closes his whole hand around the object, grasping with his palm rather than with his fingers (Fig. 8 a). More mature finger movements and another three or four months of practice are needed to achieve sufficient control to pick up small things between thumb and forefinger (Figs. 8 b, c; 9 a, b). Once he can grasp, he occupies much of his walking time manipulating objects, putting them in his mouth, learning what they feel like, look like, and in general, what to expect of them.

By six months he no longer gazes at his hands—his range of amusements has widened. From feeling the breast or bottle as he feeds, he progresses to using his hands to help feed himself, holding the bottle or cup without help. At about six to seven months he is

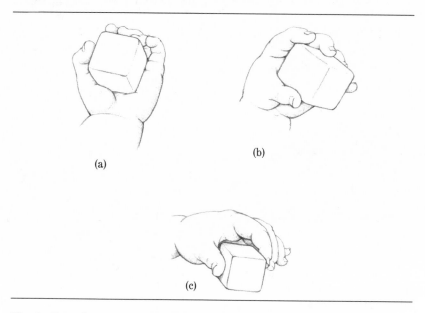

(a)

(b)

(c)

Fig. 8. Grasping a cube. (a) At six months the baby uses his whole hand like a scoop. (b) At nine months he uses several fingers and his thumb. (c) At one year he uses only one finger and his thumb—like a pair of pincers. This is the most efficient and economical way to grasp an object of this size and shape.

starting to chew, even if he has no teeth, so he enjoys feeding himself with toasted bread or cracker (see mixed feeding, pp. 188–89). He plays with his toes, learning where his body begins and ends. You will see him transfer things from hand to hand and begin to bang on the table.

Learning to Let Go

At around eight months your baby offers you something he is holding but does not know how to let go and give it up; this is something he cannot do until he is nearly a year old, but he more than makes up for it then, dropping things deliberately over the side of his baby carriage or highchair, until you wish he would unlearn this particular skill.

This kind of repetition is part of learning all new skills, and is not done to annoy you, at first, although later on he may seem to relish the sense of power in making grownups bend over continually to pick up his toys. In addition, this game requires that he understand that objects that have fallen down have not disappeared forever. Up to the age of eight months a toy that has fallen to the ground is forgotten by a baby, as though it has fallen off his world and no longer exists, but around eight to ten months he starts looking down for a fallen toy.

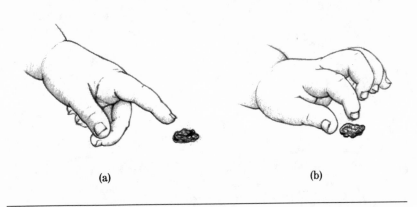

(a)   (b)

Fig. 9. Using the index finger and thumb to pick up a small object. (a) Pointing at the object as a preliminary to picking it up. (b) Picking up the object—note the fine pincer movement.

New Games: Using His Hands

Growing control of his hands gives your baby plenty to do, and he amuses himself for long spells with activities like taking things out of a basket one at a time. He wants to play with everything, including his food, and it is hopeless to expect him to make an exception of that at this stage. He dabbles his fingers in it, smears it, and squeezes it between his fingers. He picks up the spoon but turns it upside down as it goes in his mouth. If he is too fat, you should be relieved that more is going on the floor than into his mouth, but even if he is not, do not try to stop his attempts to feed himself between nine and twelve months. The urge is strong and it is quicker in the long run to allow it full rein, accepting the mess and the slow mealtimes. If left until you think him old enough to feed himself, he may not be so interested in doing so.

Increasing skill in manipulation coincides with waning interest in mouthing things. The year-old baby no longer automatically puts everything in his mouth. Other senses are replacing mouthing as a way of finding out about things. The ten-month-old baby uses his hands to play games like pat-a-cake and to wave bye-bye; he is becoming more and more sociable and at the same time has more and more ways of showing his sociability.

The rate at which he reaches the various milestones in the use of his hands varies, as with other abilities, but the average child can place one brick on another at fifteen months and can build a tower of four bricks at eighteen months. When he is two he can turn the pages of a book singly and his scribblings may now contain tentative imitations of vertical and circular strokes. He will probably be three years old before he copies a circle successfully and four and a half before he can copy a square or cross.

Dressing and Undressing Himself

Between four and five years your child has the ability, if not the will, to dress and undress himself, managing all but the buttons, ties, and laces.

About the age of twelve months children usually start holding out their arms and legs to help while being undressed; a few months later they begin pulling off their socks. Having learned to take things off, they begin, about the second birthday, to put them on, and your child may surprise you by appearing fully dressed one day in an odd assortment of clothes. However, not many children will dress themselves as a matter of course simply because they have the ability. It depends on their own feelings, the incentive or otherwise provided by brothers and sisters, and how important it is to their parents that they dress themselves at an early age. The mother with older children to get to school, and younger ones to feed and dress, obviously needs and expects her four-year-old to put on his own clothes.

Right-handed or Left-handed?

Most children are right-handed, but about 10 percent of boys and slightly fewer girls are left-handed. Others are ambidextrous, using both hands with equal facility; some use the right hand for certain activities and the left for the rest.

You may wonder whether you should keep an eye on your baby, if necessary trying to steer him toward right-handedness, so that he is like the majority and will suffer none of the minor inconveniences of left-handedness. The answer is no, leave him alone. In the past, left-handed children were often encouraged or even forced to use their right hands, particularly when writing. Apart from the unnecessary emotional conflict and wasted energy this caused, it sometimes resulted in stuttering and difficulties in learning to read and write, since the centers in the brain that control handedness also control these activities. To interfere in one area is to risk confusion in others.

Learning to Talk—and to Listen

Learning to talk starts long before the first word is uttered. Feeding, sucking fingers, and exploring things with the mouth, smiling and laughing, crying and babbling—all are necessary preparations for recognizable speech, which give your baby practice in the use and co-ordination of lips, tongue, and vocal cords.

Before he can talk, he must be able to tell one sound from another —to listen to what he hears. From the bombardment of different sounds assailing him, he learns to pick out the significant ones: the ones that mean food and comfort.

Hearing Before and Just After Birth

Some of these sounds are already familiar before birth. Tests have shown that the baby in the uterus reacts to sounds during the last two months of pregnancy. Put your head on someone's abdomen to get an idea of the noises. He is able to hear his mother's voice and her heartbeat and bowel sounds while still in the uterus; therefore, at birth, he already associates these sounds with warmth, security, and a continuous supply of food, because he has been fed via his mother's bloodstream.

Beginning to Listen

He continues to associate the sounds his mother makes with feelings of satisfaction. You may notice that your baby, soon after birth, becomes calm as you approach and before he can see you, apparently because he has heard you coming. He does not yet understand that you are a separate person but he does know that your presence equals comfort.

For some days after birth your baby may react only to loud noises, perhaps because fluid remains in the middle ear, but within a short time you will notice him beginning to listen for sounds that mean something to him. At two months he will turn his head toward a speaking voice, but before he can turn his head, he will watch you while you speak to him.

Stages in Vocalizing

At about six weeks of age, your baby starts smiling and then goes on to make little sounds—grunts, murmurs, and coos; this is a form of dialogue with you and it is also a sign of contentment. Even before he actually starts to vocalize he may seem to be trying to do so by opening and closing his mouth as he looks at you.

Vocalizing begins as a form of verbal play. By about three

months your baby will have found he can make different sounds, such as squeals, gurgles, and hums, by moving his lips and tongue while emitting a noise. He enjoys the vibrations and sounds in his throat and mouth that occur while he makes these sounds. He also enjoys listening to himself, and this encourages further experiments. It is this verbal play that starts off his learning of speech. The deaf baby, lacking the auditory satisfaction of verbal play, is at a grave disadvantage in the long process of learning to speak (see speech problems, p. 567).

The First Recognizable "Words"

At six months, your baby will tend to spend less time vocalizing than he did at three to four months, but the sounds he does make are becoming more sophisticated, some being the monosyllables needed for speech. Between six and nine months, sounds like "ba," "da," "ma," and "pa" appear, which when combined to make "dada" and "mama" will convince you and your husband that your baby is addressing you. You will naturally show your delight by repeating his "word," and this encourages him to say it again.

This is the next stage in speech development—imitation. You imitate the meaningful sounds your baby makes and then he imitates you. Babies of all nationalities produce similar sounds at first, despite the different languages spoken by their parents. This is why variations of "mama" and "dada" have come to mean "mother" and "father" in so many parts of the world. Children starting to speak learn all languages equally easily. They are not bothered by the problem of acquiring the correct accent, as adults are, since they learn to speak it as they hear it.

Beginning to Understand You

Your baby has now cooed, babbled, and made a variety of noises—but when is he going to talk, using recognizable words and applying them with the correct meaning?

By nine months, your baby is beginning to understand that some sounds always mean the same thing, particularly the sound of his own name and words like "no" and "bye-bye," which you will tend to emphasize with physical gestures, such as altering the expression on your face and hand movements.

As with all kinds of learning, your baby learns most effectively when his feelings are involved. His own efforts at communication are emotional—expressing pleasure, displeasure, and urgent needs, often intense enough to make him wriggle his body and wave his arms. The whole baby is involved, not just the parts necessary for voice production.

Using Words with Meaning

The "average" one-year-old uses two or three words with meaning but mostly he is still holding babbling conversations involving plenty of gestures; his highchair is his soapbox. His first words are what linguists call "holophrases," a single word being equivalent to a phrase or sentence. For example, "mama" can be a command, or a request; it can mean "Mommy, I want that toy" or "Hurry up with my dinner" or just "Come here." A word like "dog" can be applied to any animal at first; it may mean "Look what the dog is doing" or it may be used to express any other thought about the dog.

In contrast, at this stage, a phrase such as "all gone" is used like a single word. The baby hears speech as blocks of sound, not as a series of words. He reproduces the parts of the block that he associates with certain things; if he always heard the words "all gone" together, they equal one word to him, and you cannot really claim he is yet joining words. True word-joining, such as "Daddy come," begins around the age of eighteen months, although it may occur later (see late talker, pp. 565–66).

Sentences

This stage of word-joining at around eighteen months is how your baby starts to construct his first real sentences. Somehow, he manages to select the two or three words most relevant to his purpose. He will repeat your sentence by picking out the most important words, so that if he hears "Mommy is going out now," he repeats "Mommy out." If he wants a drink, he cannot manage "John wants a drink," so he selects "John drink," which conveys his meaning well enough.

These two words are by no means a random selection. Your baby may know every word in your sentence and be able to say any one of them separately; however, since he cannot yet string them all together as a long sentence, he chooses the most important ones up to the number he can manage. This is quite a feat for someone who has not been taught grammar. In fact, his phrases now have a valid grammatical structure, appreciated by linguists even if not obvious to the rest of us (see p. 238).

Growth of Vocabulary

Putting two words together in this way opens up endless possibilities: "John" will not only "drink" but can do many other things. From now on his vocabulary accelerates rapidly, although there may be lulls and spurts in progress.

Growing up Bilingual

You may want your child to grow up bilingual because you are yourself or you are living abroad while your baby is learning to speak. Your child will be less confused if you always speak to him in the same language, whether this is to be his "first" or "second" language. It seems that children can learn two or more languages simultaneously provided that they learn each from different people, so your husband should speak to him in the other language. Having a mother who tries to teach you two names for everything at once leads to confusion and rebellion. Given the opportunity it is always worthwhile helping a child to be bilingual. But remember that it is normal for him to be a little slower than a child who has to learn only one language.

Encouraging Language Development

Talking to Your Baby

How can you help your child to learn to talk, and talk well? First, by talking to him yourself. Talking and singing to babies comes naturally, but some people stop themselves from doing it, thinking it must sound ridiculous, as well as being unnecessary and unappreciated by the baby. It is almost as though the mother is embarrassed by talking to her baby—a mother once told me she could talk to her dog but not to her baby! However, your first instinct is right: your baby needs to be talked to—not nonstop chattering, but spontaneous responses to his efforts to communicate with smiles and noises. He does not have to understand a word you say but he does need to feel you enjoy him from the beginning; and he needs practice in learning to listen (p. 234). It is not words he hears but nice noises coming from the person who means most to him.

Later on, when starting to associate some noises with particular things, your baby learns words more easily if he hears them frequently. You do not need to limit your vocabulary, or to keep repeating the few words he knows, or to reduce your conversation completely to his level. You will probably find yourself adopting instinctively the most helpful conversational level, which is not right down at his level but slightly higher, so that it stimulates and expands his speech but is not so complicated as to be meaningless to him. This is the way he learns best in other fields also (see p. 216).

Your baby picks out from your sentences the words he needs to express himself (p. 236); you can do the opposite for him, putting flesh on the bare bones of his basic expressions. For example, his remark

"Mommy coat" becomes "Yes, Mommy is putting on her coat." It will become more interesting still if you add, "It's red."

You teach him by catching his interest, not by endlessly repeating the same boring words. The aim is not to cram more words into your child or to improve his grammar but to achieve the essence of any dialogue, namely an exchange of feelings and ideas. Vocabulary and grammar will look after themselves if your baby hears plenty of talk and is not always left out of the conversation.

Singing and Reading to Your Baby

Babies as young as one year enjoy the sound and rhythm of stories, nursery rhymes, and songs whose meaning they cannot understand, in the same way as small children enjoy listening to older children's bedtime stories (see stories and nursery rhymes, pp. 323f.). Reading aloud to very young children is not a waste of time: experiments with a control group have shown that by twenty months, babies who were read to for a few minutes each day from the age of twelve months were ahead in language development. But again, reading aloud and singing to your baby should be done because it is fun rather than as a deliberate lesson or because it is good for him.

The telephone, either real or toy, is a valuable instrument for encouraging your child in natural conversation. Most children love to talk on a real telephone, but whether or not you have one, let him have a toy one with a dial. Better still, have two, so that he can talk to his friend across the room. When she is alone, you may be surprised by the breadth of his conversation with an imaginary friend on his toy telephone—you may also learn some of his thoughts you had not known about before.

Do "Mistakes" Matter?

There is no need to worry that early "mistakes" in grammar and pronunciation will continue indefinitely if unchecked. Children's grammar has its own validity, and some of the apparent mistakes made by small children are really the results of logical reasoning. Saying "I growed a bean" instead of "I grew a bean," or "sheeps" instead of "sheep," shows that the child is applying rules that work most of the time. Learning the exception to the rule is a matter of imitation, not logic, and obviously takes time, particularly in a language like English, where exceptions are so numerous. Your child will get there in the end without continual prompting, although the occasional correction is useful.

In the same way, it is unnecessary to stop him from using his own words instead of the proper ones. Some of these show considerable invention and are adopted by the whole family—until the "baby" grows older, becomes embarrassed, and demands that they use the correct ones.

A Parent's Role

It is natural for you to compare progress and to be worried if your baby seems slow to develop in some directions. Your concern is part of your absorbing interest in your child's development, helping to ensure that you are alert for any signs that he needs help and that you give him the encouragement he needs in order to develop fully. However, remember that your role is not to try to make him grow and develop, but, rather, to provide a sympathetic and stimulating environment in which his inborn potential can unfold.

The more interest you take in studying your baby's developing abilities, the more absorbing you will find it. And it is so much more important than his weight, though sadly this still seems to be the thing on which mothers often concentrate. Moreover, by concentrating on learning about his development, you will unconsciously be encouraging him and will be providing the optimum stimulus, so that he learns at full speed.

Don't be unnecessarily worried if he is developing less fast than some of your friends' children, because individual variation is so great. On the other hand, if you have any fear that his degree of variation is outside the normal, ask your doctor to check his development. For some milestones the individual variation can be very great; for example, a normal child may start to walk at any age between ten and twenty months. On the other hand, while the average age at which a baby smiles is six weeks, it would be unusual for this to occur more than a week or two earlier. Equally it could be serious if he were not smiling by ten weeks, though this might be because no one had smiled at him.

16

Toilet Training

When Should You Start?

If you are the mother of a new baby, you may soon find yourself being asked whether you have started toilet training. You will hear stories of babies who were "trained" at a few months, the implication being that it is vital to start early to get a baby into good habits. You are also likely to hear the opposite: that any attempt to encourage your baby to use the potty will have disastrous emotional consequences. Be skeptical about both types of advice.

A baby cannot be properly taught to use the training seat until he is old enough to control his bladder and bowels voluntarily, just like an adult. When he reaches this point, usually during his second year, he will be helped by relaxed encouragement from his mother and father, and a total lack of concern from everyone else, especially grandparents.

Before this time a baby may perform as a reflex when the cold rim of the potty touches his bottom; if he has bowel movements at particular times of the day, you may feel it worthwhile to hold him over the training seat, or to sit him on it when he is older, at these times. There is no harm in this, provided you are quite clear that you are merely doing it to save laundry and not to teach him to be "clean." Your baby is merely responding to a reflex. You should not be "encouraging" him to have his bowel movements by making straining noises; if you do, you will become obsessional. It is essential that you understand and accept this so as to be prepared for the day when he refuses to co-operate (see also discipline, p. 278).

Most babies who have been using the potty in the early months start refusing it when they get old enough to have opinions, around nine to twelve months. It may be galling to go back to washing extra diapers, but this refusal is natural, and indeed practically inevitable. If you try to insist that your year-old baby sit on the training seat, you are delaying rather than hastening the day when he responds to the signals of his own maturing bladder and bowels and co-operates with you.

On balance, I think you will find fewer problems if you delay putting your baby on the potty until he is physically capable of beginning to control himself. This will be around the age of two and never before the first birthday.

Relax

Whatever the age of your baby when you start to toilet train him, it is essential to relax about the whole business. A long time may elapse between the first occasion you produce the training seat and the day when you can rely on your child to ask for it or go to the bathroom himself. But this day will come, however unco-operative he seems; if you are casual about it, it will probably come sooner. He will want to be like everyone else and use the bathroom. If you are the mother of an eighteen-month-old baby and are thinking he will be going to school in diapers, you are worrying unnecessarily; for reassurance, go and look at the children arriving at your local nursery school. Are any still in diapers?

Stop comparing your baby's progress with the supposed achievements of other babies and stop worrying about the effects of your "mistakes" in training on his future mental health. If you are ready to encourage him when he seems ready, he will probably be clean and dry at whatever age nature decided for him. There is nothing disgraceful about being "late," though you may long for the day when he looks less bulky from the rear and there are no pins to find or diapers to wash.

Helping Your Child Train Himself

Your child will notice you looking pleased when he used the potty, but there is no need to be too effusive or to imply that he is being especially good; this may make him feel that failure is "naughty," and it overloads the whole episode with emotion. When he is pleased with himself, he likes to share his pleasure and interest, but, in general, try to be as unconcerned as possible about his progress, or lack of it. Think of yourself as being there to help in a natural and inevitable development, which you are far more likely to hinder than to encourage by fussing and interfering (see also pp. 488–89).

During the second or third year, it is wise to be on the alert for signs that your child is about to need the bathroom. He may clutch himself or signal to you in some way, but he may be so busy playing that you have to remind him.

Introducing the Training Seat and Potty

It is up to you to let your child know that there is such a thing as a potty. If he is a second child, he obviously sees other children using one and will begin to realize what a potty is for. With a first baby, it is a good idea to buy a training seat and produce it occasionally, telling him what it is for and letting him try it. On no account should you hold him down on the potty when he wants to get off. The idea is to let him know that potties exist and that you would be quite pleased if he felt like using one.

There are many different and attractive types of potties on the market now. You may find your child feels safer on one of the solid seatlike type—he is much less likely to tip over if he uses one of these. In addition, being more solid, it is less mobile, so that there is less likelihood of his using it as a tricycle and roaring around the room, instead of remembering the purpose for which he is sitting there.

Discarding His Diaper: Training Pants

Taking off your baby's diaper and putting him into training pants for part of the day may be useful by making him aware of being wet or dirty, thus helping him to anticipate his need for the potty.

Having worn diapers all his life, a baby may hardly realize when he is wet or dirty. He may like or dislike the sensation of urine trickling down his legs, but at least if he is wearing pants instead of a thick diaper, he can feel it happening. A child associates wearing a diaper with being wet and dirty—after all, that is why he wears it; so it is not easy for him to understand suddenly that he should not wet his diaper, particularly if a younger baby is allowed to do so. Being in a diaper is likely to encourage him to feel that he is still a baby and therefore could be a factor in delaying the feeling that he is grown up and should be dry.

It is best to try him in pants in the summer, when he can be outside instead of indoors wetting the carpet, though of course it is not always summertime when the appropriate stage is reached. Training pants with a waterproof backing and toweling inside offer some protection to your carpets.

The Child Who Learns Suddenly

Although some babies start letting their mothers know when they need the potty early in the second year, others give no sign. You may feel that your child is never going to begin to co-operate, but try not to start worrying. It is not uncommon for a child who seems totally unconcerned suddenly to take to sitting on the training seat, even demanding it; thereafter, he may train himself in a matter of days. This tends to happen about the age of two.

By the use of modern psychological learning techniques, embodying the principles of "behavior modification," a child who is ready to learn—usually by about twenty months—can become dry and clean in one day if the whole of a mother's time is set aside for teaching that

day. Behavior modification seeks to praise "good" behavior and ignore "bad." In this way there is reinforcement for the behavior that
it is desired to bring out of the child. This is toilet education rather
than toilet training.

Bowel Control

Most children learn to control their bowels before they can control
their bladders. It would be unusual for a child to gain control over
both functions at the same time, so don't nag him because he does not
use the training seat for both. Nagging could lead him to the idea of
using his newly acquired skill to annoy or please you; he might deliberately choose to keep it as a weapon, rather than follow his natural
inclination to become fully toilet trained.

A child who senses his mother's excessive concern about his
bowel movements—whether he passes them and what they are like
—is likely to develop the commonest variety of constipation at this
age, "stool holding." This arises from his reaction of not doing what
his mother wants. He refuses to give in to the need to evacuate and
holds on instead of letting go.

Helping Him Stay Dry at Night

Anxiety can also prevent a child from staying dry at night. It is
usually some months before a child who is clean and dry during the
day can be relied on to stay dry while asleep. He may even wet the
bed during a short nap because he has not yet learned to respond to
the signs he recognizes when awake. It helps if he is "toileted" before
his rest. If your child still tends to wet himself at night, put on diapers
when he goes to bed until he is usually dry when he wakes. It is better
to keep diapers on longer than to get in a state about wet sheets and
convey your anxiety to him.

It is not a good idea to stop him having a drink either before his
daytime rest or in the evening, although there is no need to remind
him if he does not ask for one. Refusing if he does ask only gives him
an immediate raging thirst and may make him anxious about staying
dry.

Make sure he empties his bladder before he gets into bed and sit
him on the potty again just before you go to bed, or earlier if he tends
to get wet before this. There is no need to turn on the light and wake
him right up, or to take him to the bathroom. He will pass urine as
a reflex when he feels the cold potty, without necessarily waking up

fully, and will probably not remember it next morning. Some children still need to be toileted after starting school. It is better to continue if your child tends to have frequent accidents, since several in a row can start you and him worrying about wetting the bed, and so prolong and increase the tendency. Prevention of a bed-wetting problem is far easier than a cure.

Children tend to become dry overnight some time during the third year, though many need toileting during the evening for another year or more. Some also need to be put on the training seat first thing in the morning, since early-morning noises can rouse a child without waking him sufficiently to get on the potty himself. It is a good rule for the first adult up to sit the child on the potty as soon as he gets up.

Delays in Achieving Control

There is no need to worry if your child still wets at night, despite toileting in the evening, until around his fourth birthday. The fact that some children become dry before others possibly relates to the size of their bladders and to family traits. It has nothing to do with intelligence. Bed-wetting appears to be commoner in boys, but there is no obvious reason for this except that members of the female sex seem to be able to hold on for much longer than boys and men.

During the day a young child can go to the bathroom as often as he wants to, but his bladder may be incapable of holding a whole night's urine. Although some children do wake up when they need to urinate, others sleep heavily and do not, so that they wet the bed in their sleep.

If your child is still showing no sign of becoming dry at night when four years old, and you are concerned, go and see your doctor (see bed-wetting, p. 554).

Using the Bathroom by Himself

When your child can be relied upon to use the training seat, he will gradually imitate the rest of the family and want to go to the bathroom alone. Help him by making sure that he can reach the toilet seat and the handle or chain by himself. Put a platform by a high toilet, and add a length of cord to the chain if necessary. A child's seat which he can fit over the toilet seat may make him feel safer; this provides an incentive for him to use the "grownups'" bathroom.

Some mothers make the mistake of accompanying their children to the bathroom and wiping their bottoms for far longer than necessary; this is partly out of habit and partly out of fear that the child would not do it properly. It is much better to let your child be independent, even if this does mean slightly soiled pants. By the time he starts going to school he should be able to use the bathroom without your help; this gives him confidence and means one thing less to worry about (see p. 319).

Helping Him Avoid Accidents

When your child is first trained, expect occasional accidents. It helps if you suggest he go to the bathroom before an outing, even if he could last a little longer. When he is so absorbed in play that he has forgotten to go, it is reasonable to remind him, provided you can manage to do it without starting a battle. If he always uses the same potty, take it with you on vacation and even on short visits. However, it is less trouble to get him used to sitting on different potties and toilets from the beginning. The child who is used to one potty in a particular room may refuse to use one in a strange place. So although it may be useful in training to appeal to your baby's love of routine and pride in his own potty, bear in mind the possible consequences (see travel, p. 367).

Accepting Your Baby's Enjoyment of Excretion

Throughout the time when your baby is beginning to notice his bowel and bladder movements and is learning to use the training seat, it is important that he is not made to feel "dirty." Reacting briefly with adult distaste at some of the sights and smells he enjoys is natural and helps him to understand that not everyone shares his pleasure. However, making him feel he revolts you is different.

A small child regards disapproval of any part of function of his body as disapproval of his whole self. If the mother he loves and depends upon is constantly disgusted by his accidents during toilet training, and by his childish disregard of smells adults find unpleasant, he feels rejected and guilty. These feelings of guilt may be transferred to other activities also. He may become afraid to play with water and sand, and of making any kind of mess. A child may arrive at nursery school or even primary school reluctant to join in this type of play. It can take a long time to reassure him that it is not wrong to handle messy materials.

Such children are also in danger of later confusing their disgust of excretion with their sexual feelings, thinking of these as "dirty" too.

Of course, no mother is likely to feel or look indifferent when she finds her child's crib smeared with feces: a stage some young children go through. There is no point in feeling guilty if your reaction is the natural one of immediate disgust, but it is best to be matter-of-fact, and not to go on about it. Reduce the chances of repetition by removing him promptly for his crib when he wakes after a rest.

Similarly, you cannot expect to conceal your displeasure every time your child wets the carpet; at the right moments, appealing to his wish to be grown up does no harm. He should become aware that it is a nuisance for you to be continually cleaning up after him; he is more likely to co-operate and to try to control himself if toilet training has not already become an emotional battleground (see also pp. 488–89).

Your baby will probably go through a stage of intense interest and pride in anything he produces in the potty and will want to look at it and expect you to admire it too. He may be reluctant to see you empty the potty down the toilet. If you overdo the amount of praise you give him for producing a stool in his potty, he may understandably get into a muddle when a moment later he sees you carelessly throw it away. This is a normal stage and, if regarded as such, soon gives way to other interests; using the training seat becomes a boring necessity.

17

Teething and Looking After Teeth

Don't waste time worrying about when your baby's teeth will come through. This is one of the things decided by his own genetic blueprint, and with teeth, as with so many other things, very little can affect the working of this blueprint. However precocious or backward a child may be in other ways, his teeth come through at the time and in the order preordained by nature. Illness and malnutrition, which would affect general growth, have little effect on the rate of teething.

A few babies have a tooth already through at birth. This sometimes has to be removed because it is loose and therefore might be inhaled. It would not matter if it were swallowed, since it would pass easily through the intestine. If it is well fixed in the gum it should be left alone, since removal unfortunately means there will be a gap for years, until the second dentition appears. The presence of a tooth is not a contraindication to breast feeding (p. 80).

At the other end of the scale, it is normal for some babies to be toothless at the age of one year. This does not mean they have been poorly nourished before or after birth, or that you have done something wrong. A dentist can advise you if teeth fail to appear within a reasonable time. You can do nothing to hurry up or slow down the process of teething. Nor do you have to teach your baby to bite or to chew; these are built-in reflexes (pp. 188–89).

Teething takes a long time. To some parents it seems like an eternity! It starts while the baby is in the uterus and goes on till his wisdom teeth come through, usually during his teens, but often later. By the time he is born, all the milk teeth are present inside the jaw and the permanent teeth are starting to develop (Fig. 10).

Is He Teething?

There is no point at which one can say for sure that a baby is teething or is not teething, but when at around six months the first tooth appears through the gum, it is tempting to blame it for any unexplained crying or irritability. Teething is often used to explain a baby's behavior for some weeks before a tooth actually appears, and from then on "teething," like the "gas" (pp. 68f.) which preceded it, is a convenient scapegoat for anything that goes wrong.

Teething and Illness

There is little harm in blaming teething for your baby's bad moods, but it is really dangerous to use it to account for an illness. Sadly, doctors are always having to deal with cases of serious infection brought late because the symptoms were at first put down to teething.

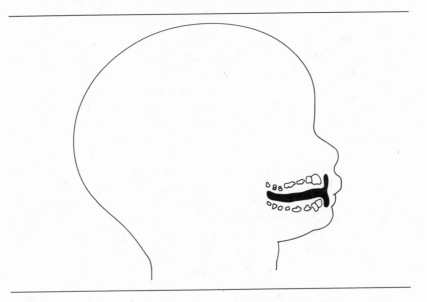

Fig. 10. Teeth already formed in the gums of a newborn baby.

Since babies cannot tell you where they feel pain, the first sign of a sore throat or urinary infection will be loss of appetite. If your baby suddenly goes off his feedings at a time when you think he may be teething, never consider that to be the reason. Let your doctor decide. Another dangerous belief is that teething causes convulsions (p. 615). This is never true.

Nor is it true that some babies "cut their teeth with bronchitis." A baby may have bronchitis, diaper rash, or any other complaint while cutting teeth, but this is hardly surprising, since he is cutting teeth throughout most of babyhood. Bronchitis needs treatment whenever it occurs; it should not be ignored in the hope that it will "go away" when the tooth is through. However, many cases of supposed bronchitis turn out to be false alarms; the extra saliva produced by the eruption of a tooth may make a baby cough and gurgle so that you think he has bronchitis.

In fact, during the period between six months and two years, when teeth are appearing fast and furiously, your baby may suffer from a number of symptoms that need diagnosing and treating; the fact that the natural process of teething is also taking place is irrelevant.

Varied Reactions to Teething

What difference does teething make? There is a great deal of truth in the saying that teething only produces teeth. In most babies it causes no trouble. But babies vary in their tolerance of the minor local discomfort caused by an erupting tooth. One baby may have a slightly red gum and a pink patch on his cheek in the region of the tooth, but his mother may not even notice it, because he makes no complaint. Another mother may notice the swollen gum because her baby's grumbling makes her look for the reason. Most of the village mothers in developing countries know nothing about our sort of teething, so their babies do not "teethe" in our sort of way.

Does He Need Medicine?

If you can accept that teething is not the reason for a baby being difficult or miserable, then it goes without saying that no medicines are required for teething. But it is still important to discover the reason for his symptoms.

Teething Rings

Babies start putting their hands in their mouths as soon as they find out how, usually at the age of a few weeks. They do it not because their gums hurt and teeth are coming through but because they enjoy it (see development, pp. 229–30, thumb sucking, p. 547, and pacifiers, p. 120). So do not think your baby's gums are painful because he keeps putting things in his mouth.

I sometimes wish Nature had not planned the oral phase of development (pp. 229–30) to coincide with the sudden eruption of a number of teeth! If babies had been born with a full set of teeth or their appearance delayed until, say, the age of three years, parents would not believe a baby's normal stage of putting everything in his mouth was due to teething.

Fingers are the best teething rings, but a baby may enjoy having a hard ring, or something similar, to chew upon as well.

Teeth in Order of Appearance

The first tooth to appear is a central incisor, usually a lower one. By the time he is one year old, the average baby has six incisors, the front teeth he needs to bite the end of a cracker. The teeth he needs for chewing, the molars or double teeth, start coming through soon afterward. The first molars appear before the canines, or eyeteeth, so don't be surprised by a gap in his set of teeth. The last to come through are the second molars, at around two to two and a half years. There are twenty milk teeth in a full set, compared with thirty-two permanent teeth.

Some babies cut a batch of teeth one after another, but often there is a time lag of weeks or months between teeth. It all depends on the pattern a baby has inherited.

The following table gives average times at which teeth appear, though your baby will not necessarily keep to it (Fig. 11 a–e):

Milk teeth (deciduous dentition)

6–12 months	incisors
12–14 months	first molars
18 months	canines
2–2½ years	second molars

Second teeth (permanent dentition)

6 years	first molars
7–8 years	incisors
10–11 years	premolars
9–12 years	canines
10–13 years	second molars
12–25 years	third molars (wisdom teeth)

The permanent teeth start to come through at six years, though it is interesting that no one ascribes a six-year-old's bad moods to teething. The first permanent incisors often look crooked and may appear behind the baby teeth, before these have come out. This usually rights itself, but you should be taking your child to the dentist regularly and he will deal with anything unusual.

Care of the Teeth

You started caring for your baby's teeth during pregnancy. Before birth, all his teeth have started developing, except for the second and third permanent molars; the crowns of his milk teeth are almost

completely filled with calcium. By the time you are six months pregnant the enamel is completely formed on all his first teeth. So eat well
during pregnancy, including plenty of food rich in calcium, such as
milk and cheese. Vitamins A, C, and D are important too, but these
are bound to be present in a mixed diet (see pp. 180f.).

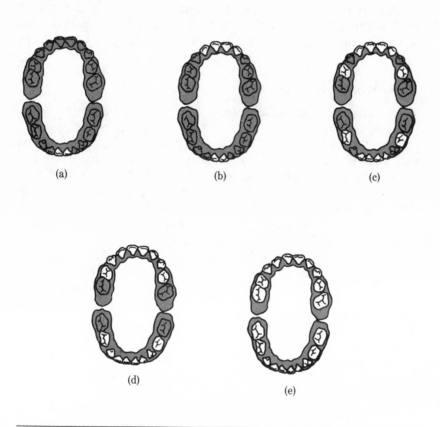

(a)   (b)   (c)

(d)

(e)

Fig. 11 The usual order of appearance of the milk teeth. (a) Six months. (b)
Eight months. (c) Ten to fourteen months. (d) Eighteen to thirty months. (e)
Second molars complete the set of milk teeth.

The Importance of Diet

A young baby's milk plus vitamin supplements if needed (pp. 182f.)
provide the raw material for continued healthy development of his

teeth. When he starts eating other foods, remember that, in general, foods that are valuable for general growth also help the development of strong teeth; these foods are unlikely to leave a residue that encourages decay.

Less valuable foods, such as candy, sticky buns, puddings, and presweetened soft drinks, provide little raw material for development of the teeth and they do leave the harmful residue that encourages decay. A sensible general rule is to make these foods part of a normal meal, not between-meal fillers. This means you can see that teeth are cleaned promptly afterward, or at least that your child drinks some water or eats an apple, orange, or pear, which cleans his teeth as he eats it.

How Decay Starts

The enamel covering each tooth is hard and it protects the softer material beneath, but the surface of the tooth gets covered with plaque. This is an almost invisible sticky film that harbors bacteria and coats the teeth, thereby setting the stage for dental decay and gum disease. The bacteria that live in plaque, reacting with food residues, produce an acid, which by being held against the teeth in this sticky film goes to work to invade the dentin (the body of the tooth). If we could get rid of plaque, most of our problems would be over, so it must be carefully removed every day.

Candy and Decay

It is the candy bar or lollipops on the way to school and the package of candy sucked at intervals, all day, that do most damage. Do be firm about daily candy at school, even if this makes your child the only one who does not have candy in the playground. Chewing gum is a possible substitute, which may satisfy his need to be like the others, but help your child to understand that looking after his teeth matters and that no one else will have his toothache for him.

It is seldom easy to deny candy to children altogether. Everyone else eats it, and once your child mixes with other children it is unfair to expect him always to refuse candy, although it is wise to discourage regular candy sucking and nibbling sweet things between meals. Ration his candy and try to see that teeth are cleaned afterward.

Try to discourage aunts and uncles from giving candy as presents or rewards. Many visitors want to give children something, and candy is the easy answer; but try to persuade them to give fruit instead.

Pacifiers and Decay

The most disastrous thing you can do for a child's teeth is to dip a pacifier in honey or, worse still, give him one of those "comforters" made like a miniature bottle containing concentrated orange juice or sugar water. These rot the teeth and cause rapid decay. (See vitamins, p. 183.)

Fluoride

If fluoride occurs naturally in your water supply, or has been added by the state, your children's teeth will have additional protection against decay, because fluoride makes the enamel less susceptible to attack by acid. If this is not the case, fluoride should be given as drops for the very young or as daily tablets. In addition it should be applied direct to newly erupted teeth in the form of fluoride toothpaste.

Teeth Need Exercise

If a diet contains plenty of food that needs chewing, in fact that uses teeth as they are meant to be used, most of the food particles sticking to the teeth are removed. The gums are massaged, saliva flows, and the teeth and mouth are clean at the end of the meal. This partially explains why primitive people who eat natural, unprocessed foods tend to have perfect teeth without the help of toothbrushes, toothpastes, or dentists. Once introduced to sweetened, refined, "easy-to-eat" foods, their standard of dental health drops dramatically.

Teeth need exercise. Chewing hard and tough food never hurts teeth, because their roots are not in direct contact with bone but are attached by a resilient membrane that cushions the shock of hard chewing. This membrane needs exercise too and may deteriorate if underused so that teeth become loose in their sockets and gum troubles start. So don't try to "protect" your child's teeth by giving him only food that is easy to chew. Once he has the equipment to chew, he should use it to the full.

Cleaning His Teeth

Are cavities inevitable? No, they can be prevented by a strict program of preventive care starting at birth. This comprises dietary control, plaque control, fluorides, regular scaling and polishing, flossing, and fissure sealing (see p. 255).

When to Start

When should you start to clean your baby's teeth? Modern dentistry recommends that mothers start cleaning as soon as the first tooth arrives. The gums should be kept clean as well as the teeth, so that you remove food residue and keep down the acid, thereby ensuring that his first teeth arrive in a clean plaque-free environment.

Cleaning is undertaken with a piece of gauze about two inches (5 cm) square. This is held between the thumb and forefinger and wiped vigorously over the teeth and gums. Fluoride toothpaste can be used on the gauze. Cleaning is carried out twice daily and the easiest position is for you to have the baby lying in your lap with his feet pointing away from you.

Encouraging the Habit

By the age of two years you can graduate to a toothbrush, which should have a small enough head to reach every tooth and a large enough straight handle to be held easily. The bristles should be soft, straight, small, and even; they should be made of nylon, so that they have rounded ends. By the age of seven years the child should be able to take over the tooth brushing, though he will have been helping you before this.

Teach your child to brush up and down, not from side to side—just as you should be doing—and remind him to go around the corners and to the back. Encourage him by letting him choose his own toothbrush. Remind him to clean his "six-year-old molars," the back teeth that come through at this age and that have to last all his life.

The important thing is to encourage a lifelong habit; this won't happen if you put him off the whole idea.

How Often?

It is important to brush teeth after the last food or drink of the day so that your child at least goes to bed with clean teeth. The flow of saliva slows down in sleep, so this natural way of washing the teeth is less effective at night. It is ideal to clean teeth after other meals also, but one usually has to compromise. Your child will not appreciate being the only child who takes a toothbrush with him everywhere he goes—better to give him an apple to eat after lunch.

Going to the Dentist

How a child reacts to the prospect of visiting the dentist and behaves when he gets there depends on the build-up "going to the dentist" receives in his family. If he has observed other people cowering at the thought, heard them speaking of their ordeals in the dentist's chair, and had the impression that the dentist is an ogre who always makes the worst of a painful job, it is hardly surprising if he takes no notice when his mother tries to convince him there is nothing to worry about half an hour before his first visit.

If your experiences at the dentist's have been unpleasant, never talk about them in front of the children. If they have been good, talk about them a lot. But, either way, don't wait till the last minute to introduce the idea. It is wise to talk about going to the hospital even though your child may never have to (p. 404): it is essential to talk about dentists, because he must visit one.

The First Visit

It is a good idea to take your child for his first visit to the dentist before there is likely to be anything wrong. Don't wait until he complains of a toothache or you can see signs of decay before making an appointment. Take him before the age of two years, since dental decay can begin before then. This first visit may be only to have a look at your child's mouth, to teach you the proper way to brush teeth and how to use floss to remove food caught between teeth, and to talk about diet. This will often be undertaken by a dental hygienist, who will be employed by any dentist keen on the preventive aspects of tooth care for children. Fissure sealing, a method of putting a layer of plastic on the biting surface of newly erupted teeth, is carried out by a dental hygienist.

Choosing a Dentist

Try to find a dentist who likes dealing with children; he will usually provide comic books in his waiting room and make his office less forbidding to a child. It makes all the difference if the dentist takes time to talk to a child. Ideally, he will show him the frightening-looking instruments and explain something about them; by making the largeness of the chair and the noise of the drill something interesting, he can create a new and exciting experience rather than an overwhelming one. Your son may become really interested in the modern gadgets he is shown. If the dentist gives your child a ride up and down in the chair, the next visit can become something he anticipates cheerfully.

Your Child's Reactions

Should your child become frightened by the atmosphere and equipment, don't force him to stay long; neither of you should pretend he
is not frightened. Try again later.

Your child may refuse to open his mouth on his first visit. It is
his mouth, after all, and it is still a source of pleasure and enjoyment
and not something he shows to everyone. He needs time to get used
to the idea of a stranger delving about in his private property. If you
have brought him along for the experience rather than for treatment,
there is no hurry. He will open his mouth on another visit. The dentist
will probably offer him a small reward—not candy, but perhaps a tiny
sample of toothpaste or a pamphlet for children with pictures to color
or advice on tooth care in the form of a comic strip.

A child who is very upset may need the prospect of a reward from
you to help him through the experience. However, don't assume he
will need it unless he is upset, because this may put the idea into his
head that visiting the dentist is awful.

Your Own Reactions

If treatment is needed, try not to wince and feel every pain for your
child. Milk teeth hurt less during drilling than second teeth, so the
chances are your child is not suffering as much as you imagine. In
fact, of course, if you start your children on a preventive program
from birth, they should emerge at sixteen years of age without ever
needing any fillings.

Look After Those Milk Teeth

Do not delay a visit to the dentist in the mistaken belief that because
milk teeth are not permanent, they are therefore not important. Loss
of a milk tooth alters the relationship of all the surrounding teeth,
because each tooth keeps the next one in position, ensuring that the
second teeth come through in their allotted places. The balance of
power in the mouth changes whenever a tooth is removed.

The sooner a cavity is detected—and it needs a dentist's skill to
detect a small cavity—the simpler it is to drill and fill. Provided your
child's first experience of treatment is comparatively painless, he will
not dread the next time.

X-rays

The dentist may take an X-ray if he is unsure whether decay is present. This is carefully controlled and quite safe. By the time a hole in
a child's tooth is visible, decay may have progressed quite far—an-

other reason why you should take him regularly to the dentist instead of waiting for obvious signs of a hole.

The School Dentist

If your child attends a public school, his teeth may be inspected as part of his school physical checkup when he starts school and at intervals in his school career. Treatment can be carried out by the school dentist or, if you prefer, by your own dentist. But it is a confession of neglect if the need for dental treatment is discovered only at a school physical checkup. Don't put off taking your child for regular checkups to your own dentist.

Problems with Permanent Teeth

When the permanent teeth replace the milk teeth, problems of over-crowding and crooked teeth may arise. Your dentist may arrange for specialist treatment by an orthodontist if their position requires correction. The treatment might consist of extracting some teeth to make room for the rest, or fitting an appliance that gradually corrects the trouble. Unpleasant and uncomfortable as an appliance can be at first, your child will get used to wearing it and will usually agree that it is worth suffering for the sake of future beauty.

Protruding or jumbled teeth can cause him to be the subject of teasing and make him hate his own face, and will probably affect his ability to chew efficiently. Overcrowding encourages decay because the teeth cannot be cleaned properly, so it is important not to ignore the problem.

Damage to Teeth

Your young child, usually while still a toddler, may shatter you one day by falling over and seeming to have lost a tooth as a result. But all may not be lost—the tooth may have been pushed back into the gum, from where it will emerge again. You may just be able to see or feel it, but if in doubt, consult your dentist. Usually the tooth is not affected by this injury, but if the nerve has been damaged it will become dull gray. However, this is not too serious in a first tooth.

Much more serious is the tooth that is broken by injury, since the result is disfiguring. The sharp edge may also prove a hazard to your child's tongue or lips when he is eating. Fortunately, the dentist of today is very skillful in cosmetic dentistry, and broken teeth can be repaired. He can also give a child a single artificial tooth if necessary.

If your child knocks out a tooth in an accident, you should immediately wash it and then replace it in the empty socket. Keep it firmly in position for a few minutes and all should be well—but speed is essential.

18

Immunization

Why Immunize?

The aim of immunization is the prevention of disease. Unfortunately, the number of diseases against which immunization has been developed is relatively small. The main ones for the United States and the United Kingdom are: diphtheria, whooping cough, tetanus, polio, measles, German measles, and tuberculosis. In the United States, immunization against mumps is routinely offered. Added to these are a number of tropical diseases, such as yellow fever and cholera. The protection is not always complete, so that a child immunized, for example, against whooping cough might still get the disease, but in a much milder form than if he had not been immunized.

Immunization programs vary from country to country, according to their pattern of disease, but the guiding principles are always the same: protection against each disease must be as strong as possible, the number of injections as few as possible, and the risk of reaction as slight as possible. Despite the fact that only a few diseases can be prevented in this way, you may still feel that much of your baby's first two years is spent in being injected. You may wonder if it is all necessary, especially for an illness like diphtheria, which has almost vanished from Western countries. Less persuasion is needed with a disease like polio, which is still remembered as a crippling illness.

The answer to this question is that it is only by immunizing all children in a community that these diseases are prevented from reappearing in epidemic form. The recent severe outbreak of whooping cough in the United Kingdom, resulting in thousands of severely ill infants and a number of deaths, emphasizes the ever-present risk when the level of immunization throughout the country is allowed to fall. Immunization programs aim to protect the whole community as well as its individual members. As parents you have an obligation to the community as well as to your own families in seeing that your children are immunized. But this is also in your own interest, since a high level of community protection means greater safety for each individual.

How Immunization Works

The Antibody Mechanism

Immunization is based on reproducing the body's fight against infection. When it is attacked by a germ it produces either antibodies against that germ or antitoxins against the poison produced by the germ. If the germs attack a second time the body is prepared, having already made the appropriate antibody or antitoxin to prevent the infection taking hold. In this way, the body prevents itself from suffering a second attack of an infection such as measles.

There are two types of immunization: active and passive.

Active Immunization

Active immunization involves the giving of a weakened form of the germ so that the body forms antibodies without having to suffer a first attack. Its protection usually lasts as long as that following the actual illness. It may be lifelong, as in the case of diphtheria, or as short as a year, as with influenza. This short protection in the case of influenza limits its value because it has to be repeated each year. Moreover, there are many types of influenza, and protection against one type is no safeguard against another.

Passive Immunization

This involves the giving of serum (a part of the blood) from another person or animal that already contains antibodies. Passive immunization has two disadvantages: it lasts only a few weeks and the body may react against the serum. This is particularly liable to occur if the serum has been obtained from an animal—for example, the horse in the case of antitetanus serum (ATS).

Protecting Your New Baby

Passive immunization of the newborn baby occurs during pregnancy: antibodies in the mother's circulation pass across the placenta into the baby's circulation. Antibodies also reach the baby via the colostrum (see p. 60). These antibodies protect the baby for a few weeks before they disappear; they also block his ability to make the same antibody if he is immunized before they have gone. These facts influence the timing of the vaccination program, which is a compromise between giving the vaccine as early as possible for protection and not giving it so early as to be only partially effective. Health authorities make recommendations to the medical profession with regard to immunization procedures, but the final decision lies with the child's doctor.

One exception to the transfer of antibodies across the placenta is whooping cough—the antibodies are too big to make the journey.

What Is Vaccination?

The term "vaccination" covers immunization against all diseases and not only smallpox, for which the word was originally coined. The route for vaccination varies with the disease. For measles, it is by injection; and for polio, by mouth.

Keep a Record

It is essential for a vaccination record to be kept both by the parent and by the pediatrician, so that you know when next to bring your baby, and the doctor or nurse knows what to give. This record is also very important when your child has an injury, in order to help the doctor decide whether to give an extra tetanus immunization booster. This is an easy matter if he has once been fully immunized against tetanus, since it involves active immunization with tetanus toxoid and no risk to the child. On the other hand, if he has not been immunized against tetanus, the only immediate protective immunization available is passive immunization, involving the giving of horse serum (ATS), which has a high risk of reaction.

Types of Immunization

Diphtheria, Whooping Cough (Pertussis), and Tetanus Immunization (DPT or Triple Immunization)

Protection against these three diseases is conveniently combined in a triple vaccine. The vaccine is given as an injection, three doses being needed to build up the necessary protection. In the United States the recommended ages for these three shots are two, four, and six months.

Boosters

A booster dose is given at the age of eighteen months and again at four to six years of age. The booster is also against diphtheria, pertussis, and tetanus.

Make sure that your child's protection against tetanus is maintained by a further dose when he leaves school. After this, it is ideal for tetanus immunization to be repeated every ten years.

In countries where tetanus is a problem in newborn babies, because the umbilical cord is cut with a dirty instrument or covered with dirt or dung, the baby can be protected by immunizing his mother during pregnancy.

Timing the Shot   As well as deciding the timing of the DPT vaccine, your doctor will judge whether your baby is well enough to be immunized on a particular day. If your baby has a cold and fever, he is likely to postpone the shot for two weeks, but if he keeps getting coughs and colds, it is wise to go ahead with immunization; it won't make his symptoms worse and such a baby is in extra need of protection.

Unpleasant Reactions   If your baby has a reaction—if he becomes irritable, especially if he cries inconsolably and in a different way from usual, or feverish or off-color—let your doctor know. He may then decide to omit the whooping cough component from subsequent injections, since this is the most likely to cause reactions. Recent publicity has caused great anxiety among parents over the risk of brain infection (encephalitis) from whooping cough immunization. However, provided there are no contraindications (see below), figures have shown that the risk of this complication in the first year of life is less than the risk of catching the disease; this can be very serious in young babies and is sometimes fatal.

Do not ascribe any symptoms to immunization beyond minor irritability, since they may be due to a quite different illness, for which your doctor's help is needed. It is common for a small lump to be felt at the site of the injection; this always disappears by itself in time.

Briefing Your Doctor   Your doctor needs to know if your baby suffered any brain symptoms at birth, such as may follow a delay in taking his first breath. He must also know if your baby or any near relative has ever had a convulsion. Either of these might lead him to omit whooping cough vaccination because of the increased risk of complications.

Poliomyelitis

Vaccination against poliomyelitis used to be given by injection but is now given by mouth; a live, but weakened virus is used. It is given by dropper. Your child will have this vaccination on the same day as his triple immunization against whooping cough, diphtheria, and tetanus. A booster dose is given at eighteen months and again at four to six years of age.

Although immunization against polio is not a legal requirement before visiting tropical countries, anyone (adults as well as children) going to a developing country, where the disease is much more widespread than in Western countries, should be certain to be immunized beforehand. If only this were a legal requirement many tragedies would be avoided.

Measles

Immunization against measles is achieved by a single injection of live weakened virus. It is given, with immunizations against rubella and mumps, at fifteen months of age. By this time the passive immunity passed on from mother to child has waned.

In developing countries, where vaccination is not yet fully available, measles will continue to be a serious and sometimes fatal disease for many years. In Western countries, immunization is already ending the two-yearly epidemics that used to affect nearly all vulnerable children under five. This means that children who have not been immunized will be more liable to catch the disease later in life, since they are now less likely to come in contact with it when very young. Obviously, it is particularly important to immunize children who travel to developing countries, owing to the increased likelihood of their meeting children who have measles.

Reactions It is common for a baby to be feverish and to produce a mild rash a week after the measles injection. It is wise to bear this in mind when arranging the timing of the immunization shot. Although the child may look as if he is having a mild attack of measles, he is not infectious to others.

There is a small risk of convulsions following measles vaccination but this is less than the risk of brain reactions as a complication of natural measles. A child with a history of convulsions is at a greater risk of brain reactions. Consequently, the doctor will only recommend vaccination if he gives a protective dose of gamma globulin at the same time. A family history of allergy is a contraindication to measles immunization because some preparations of the vaccine have been grown on egg, to which the child might be allergic.

Mumps

Routine immunization is offered at fifteen months.

German Measles (Rubella)

The latest form of vaccination to be developed is that against German measles. The only reason for wanting to protect anyone against this mild disease is that if it occurs in the early months of pregnancy the virus can damage the developing fetus (see p. 10).

In the United States all children are offered a combined shot against measles, rubella, and mumps at fifteen months of age.

BCG Vaccination (Tuberculosis)

This form of vaccination gives protection against tuberculosis (TB). It is a protection against the type caught from human beings and the type caught through drinking infected cow's milk. The abbreviation BCG is derived from the names of its discoverers. Where the tuberculosis rate is high, as in most tropical countries, all newborn babies should be vaccinated.

The policy varies in different countries. In the United States tuberculosis testing is routinely undertaken at twelve months of age. The majority of babies are negative, and no further step is taken. However, if later circumstances make retesting a necessity because of possible contact with a patient, a change to a positive result in the child is of vital importance.

The policy in the United Kingdom is to give BCG to all children between the ages of eleven and thirteen years, if negative when tested.

Smallpox

Routine smallpox vaccination of babies is no longer recommended in the United States and many other countries, since the world has been pronounced free of smallpox. But vaccination is still required for travel to some countries, so you should check the local laws about this with your travel agent. It is hoped that this requirement will soon be stopped. Countries that require smallpox vaccination usually waive this requirement for infants under twelve months.

The reason for stopping routine vaccination is that even the very low level of complications, particularly the minimal risk of inflammation of the brain (encephalitis), is a greater danger than the risk of catching smallpox. Individuals who expect their children to travel to countries requiring vaccination should wait till the occasion arises—some of those countries demanding certificates of vaccination now may no longer do so in the future.

Vaccination gives immediate protection to the individual, so that if a person with smallpox inadvertently entered your country, the possible contacts could still be completely safeguarded by immediate vaccination.

Travel to the Tropics

If you are going to the tropics, ask your doctor or Public Health Service about immunization against such diseases as typhoid, paratyphoid, yellow fever, and cholera. (See living in the tropics, p. 373.)

19

Discipline and
Punishment

Although I have devoted one chapter to "discipline" as such, I want
to emphasize that what I have to say on this subject is inherent
throughout the whole book. How to discipline your child can only be
understood in the context of understanding normal development and
the stage of development that your child has reached (Chapter 15). In
fact, discipline has been well defined as the way you show your understanding of your child's development. If a young baby of ten months,
sitting in his highchair, knocked over his cup of milk, it would be more
than absurd if his mother were to smack him; it would indicate that
she herself had a problem for which she needed help. Even more
would this be true if she were to smack her baby of three months for
crying. Such a mother is in urgent need of help (see battered babies,
pp. 177f.).

You will, therefore, find the subject discussed in many different
places in the book, for example in the sections on bedtime (pp. 125–26,
129–130), meals (pp. 203f.), and toilet training (pp. 240f.). By seeing
discipline in terms of your child's development you should find that it
proves to be a much smaller problem than you might anticipate.

Stating your views on discipline becomes increasingly difficult as
your own children grow up, because you give fewer direct disciplinary
orders as you learn more subtle ways of handling them. Fewer orders
usually mean fewer reasons for punishment. If it were possible to
measure the amount of punishment inflicted on children, I think that
first children would be found to receive the most, because with increasing experience parents find the need for punishment becomes
less.

Grandparents are frequently said to spoil their grandchildren,
and I think they often do, but part of this apparent spoiling is, I
suspect, due to a more subtle handling of the child. Knowing more
about child behavior, the grandparents can be in a better position to
get a child to obey without the need for strict disciplinary methods.
Of course, another reason for children obeying grandparents rather
than parents is that, being less closely involved, the grandparents
have a more relaxed attitude. The fact that his mother is closer to him
means that a child is more likely to react negatively to her requests.

To a very large extent how you start to discipline your child will
be based on how you were handled by your parents. If you were

smacked a lot as a child, you will probably find yourself doing the
same to your own children. It is as well to remember that the way you
handle your children will largely influence the way they handle their
own later on. The child from a happy home is given a head start in his
ability to create a happy family himself. The child from an unhappy
home, perhaps a broken one, is sadly bound to have greater difficulties
in relationships with other people when grown up, and will have far
more problems in the handling of his or her children. An unhappy
childhood is the most catching of problems, and it is likely to be
repeated in the next generation. It is only by understanding this fact
that steps can be taken to improve the situation. Doctors and other
specialists, such as social workers, can help here (see pp. 546f.).

The Difference between Discipline and Punishment

Direct "teaching" of behavior and actual punishment play only a
minor part in bringing up children. You teach your child indirectly
through living with him, and only rarely will it be necessary to think
consciously about "discipline."

You will want your children to grow up capable of self-discipline,
of behaving considerately, because they want to, not because they are
afraid of the consequences if they do not. Forcing a child to behave
as you wish, by punishing or threatening to punish him if he does not
obey, is only effective as shock treatment or as an occasional sharp
reminder. Fear will not help a child to learn how to behave well; it will
merely alter his behavior temporarily (see punishment, pp. 288f.).

Is Learning by Trial and Error Enough?

How then can you help your child to develop from a self-centered baby
into a sensible child and a responsible adult, without losing his individuality and spontaneity on the way? How does a child learn to fit
in with others? How does he recognize that his immediate impulses
and his long-term needs are sometimes incompatible and that he has
to find a balance between them? Can parents sit back and rely on the
natural development of a child's own intelligence and conscience to
enable him gradually to evolve a workable code of behavior for himself? Do you let him sort out right and wrong for himself or should
you constantly intervene to make sure that right is winning?

The answer is that it is not enough to rely on a child's soaking
up the atmosphere of his home and learning by what he sees going
on around him, if only because the adult example is seldom consistently good. Why should a child copy only what is good and ignore

anything doubtful or dishonest? Becoming a parent does not make you wiser overnight or mean that you have ironed out all your own imperfections. Your child will notice white lies and petty dishonesties, so don't pretend to be perfect. Moreover, such a policy would involve a dangerous amount of learning by trial and error.

Understanding Your Motives

Obviously, therefore, you will have to exercise some authority over your child. A knowledge of normal child development and behavior at various ages, together with an understanding of your own motives as a parent, can help sort out some of the problems that arise in exercising this responsibility. For example, by knowing that temper tantrums are common between the ages of two and four, and that a small child lacks the self-control to stop a tantrum to order, you should avoid punishing your child for disobedience when he goes on screaming (see discipline at different ages, pp. 275f.). If you do punish him, you must recognize that what you are really doing is giving vent to your own annoyance, rather than trying to help him. This knowledge should improve your general relationship with him even if it is not much use to him at the time. Understanding yourself is as important as understanding your child; indeed the two are often inseparable.

Behavior Modification

From time immemorial young children have been modifying the behavior of their parents. Only recently have parents been encouraged to learn how they can modify the undesirable behavior of their children while encouraging good behavior. The principle is to reward your child's good behavior while disregarding the bad. Parents of a child who is always shouting may suddenly become aware that, much as they dislike his noise, they have in fact only been responding to his calls if he shouts. It is as though they have rewarded his shouting. Once they disregard his shouts but praise and encourage his quiet periods with play and attention his behavior changes dramatically.

The Influence of Your Own Upbringing

How you exercise your authority as a parent cannot easily be altered by deliberately adopting a particular theory of child management, since your basic attitude toward discipline is rooted in your own upbringing. Memories of the roles of father, mother, and children during your own childhood remain to influence your new family. Even when an adult reacts against his parents' methods by adopting the opposite approach, perhaps allowing his children maximum freedom in contrast to the strictness he disliked as a child, his attitude still stems mainly from his own childhood experiences.

This does not mean you are doomed to make the same mistakes as your parents or that it is hopeless to try to do better. Your new family will not be a carbon copy of your old one since every family is a unique mixture. Husband and wife, coming from separate backgrounds, have to adapt to each other and work out a common approach to discipline.

Parental Disagreements Over Discipline

A slight degree of difference in parental approach does not affect a child; in fact it may be an advantage to a child that his parents see things from a slightly different angle. But a child becomes confused if his parents demand totally conflicting standards of behavior, expecting him to adapt so as to behave differently with each of them. It is unhealthy for him, and for his parents' marriage, if a child can enlist one parent as an ally against the other. Deep-seated difficulties between parents may be brought into the open by problems that occur in the management of their children. Should this occur, the problem is not the disciplining of the children but the need for the parents to work out their own differences. For example, a mother who constantly leaves all discipline to her husband, the "wait until daddy comes home" approach, needs to recognize that her problem is not her unmanageable and boisterous son but her need, for whatever reason, to shelve responsibility and to lean heavily on her husband.

Each new baby adds a new ingredient to the family mixture. This affects the relationship between the parents themselves, and between the parents and each child. The same family seems quite different to each member when they discuss it in later years. The impact of the children at the receiving end always upsets, to some extent, any decisions about how to bring them up. Your children will change you and your ideas, so any attempt to "bring up the baby by the book" is complicated not only by your built-in attitudes to family life, but also by the baby.

Fitting into the Community

Another complication is that discipline inside the home is affected by attitudes outside, both in the local community and in society at large; this can both help and hinder parents' relationships with their children. Children are expected by outsiders, even if not by their own parents, to behave like the other children in their community. As a child becomes more independent of his immediate family circle and more involved in activities outside the home, he becomes aware of this, and wants to be accepted by other children and their parents. He will modify his behavior accordingly, whatever your attitude, because he does not like feeling different. Consequently, most children are happier if their parents' views on discipline are moderate rather than extreme and if they match those of the majority of their friends and neighbors (see extreme attitudes to discipline, pp. 284f.). In practice, this usually happens, since despite superficial differences, most families share the same basic standards as their friends because they probably come from similar social backgrounds.

Influence of Social Class

Methods of discipline and punishment vary according to the social class of the family. Used in this official sense, "class" is determined by the father's occupation; it has nothing to do with how much he earns. Parents belonging to the same social group expect similar standards of behavior. It is not a question of "good" or "bad" behavior, or of "high" or "low" standards, but of different interpretations of these terms. You may think yourself strict or permissive, compared with other mothers you know, but probably you are strict or permissive about the same issues, considering the same type of behavior "naughty" and the same kind of play "valuable." For example, parents from the professional classes are likely to consider childish interest in sex as natural curiosity, whereas working-class parents tend to discourage or punish evidence of this interest, considering it to be "naughty." To question an order given by a parent is more often considered impudent in a working-class family than in a professional family (see explaining discipline, pp. 271f.). A working-class child who paints a series of unrecognizable blobs might be told off for wasting materials and time, whereas the professional-class child would be praised for his "action painting."

Similarities of attitude, which most parents can take for granted because they probably live among people of the same social background, simplify the problem of helping children to get on with friends and neighbors. They can help you to sort out why you expect your children to behave in certain ways and whether these are reasonable or just conventional within your stratum of society. For example, faced with the problem of children who refuse to go to bed on time, one could ask oneself: does the working-class child come to any harm from staying up later than the average professional-class child? Is it necessary to insist on an early bedtime because this is good for the health of the children or is it because parents need a peaceful evening or want the children in bed before the baby-sitter arrives? If children could play until they were tired, putting themselves to bed when they felt like it, without parents feeling ashamed of what the neighbors thought, possibly the problem of getting the children to bed would dissolve (see bedtime, pp. 125–26, 129–30).

Faced with a problem of discipline, it is always useful to try to work out whether the rule you are insisting upon is really necessary or whether it is just a family, social, or individual custom.

Parents' Rights

Children must fit into the family's way of life and the family includes adults. Adults are perfectly justified in wanting some privacy, quiet, and time to themselves and in expecting children to respect their possessions (see forestalling trouble, p. 272). You do not have to feel guilty if you are angry with a child who, having persistently refused to leave something alone, finally breaks it; the child would be angry with you in the reverse situation. He is quite capable of understanding justifiable fury over one of his actions, and prefers this to continued feelings of tension.

Feeling Loved: The Most Important Ingredient of Discipline

Your reaction to any one misdemeanor is much less important to your child than the general feeling and atmosphere of your home. If a child lives in a basically happy home where he knows people are fond of each other and of him, a quarrel, an "unfair punishment," or a bout of bad temper won't seem a threat to his security or proof that he is unloved. He takes them in his stride, regarding them as temporary troubles which soon clear up. You need not feel that every decision about discipline is vitally important to the future development of your child; your mistakes will balance your successes. So long as a child feels loved, he can cope with his parents' imperfections and will gradually learn self-discipline despite them.

On the other hand, a child whose family life is basically miserable, so that he cannot take affection and security for granted, may feel that every punishment is a proof that he is not loved. He will find it much harder to trust others and to sympathize with their motives and needs. He may learn a veneer of good manners, but this is unlikely to be based on an understanding or an appreciation of other people's rights, as are genuine good manners.

Added to this is the essential need to be aware that children vary in the age at which they feel secure. They learn to be independent by being allowed to be dependent for as long as they need and this varies from child to child.

Explaining Discipline to Children

Children should grow up feeling that authority is based on mutual responsibility and participation in decisions. It is better to reason with them than to expect blind obedience. Children are interested in motives and are more likely to do what you want if they understand why you want it (see pp. 561–62).

Striking a Balance

On the other hand, do not ignore the dangers of overburdening a child with responsibility for his own conduct (see extreme attitudes to discipline, pp. 284f.). Some parents, without realizing it, are so sweetly and continuously reasonable, talking over every decision and never just telling their children what to do, that the children have absolutely no legitimate excuse for feeling resentful or for being naughty. A simple order is often easier on a child than yet another "Don't you think you ought to do so and so?" Remember that a child cannot always live up to the standards set by his parents; his conscience may then make him feel that he is to blame for this.

Explaining to the Young Child

The age of your child will help you to decide how much explanation is reasonable. In general, the younger the child the less you need to explain yourself: a young child is bored and confused if given every reason why it is necessary to go out immediately or why he has to wash his face. He may retaliate by endlessly keeping up the game of "Why?," although he is as bored with it as you are, if his apparent interest in detailed explanations is taken too literally.

On the other hand, you cannot take it for granted, as you can with an older child, that he understands why certain rules are necessary and convenient; for example, why meals should be more or less on time. The two-year-old needs a warning that he will soon have to stop playing and start eating. You can't just shout "Dinnertime" and expect him to drop everything. Despite the warning you may still have to back up words with action, by gently propelling him toward the table, but he will appreciate having been given a warning and will be less likely to react against your command.

Learning to Make Choices

Talking things over with your child gives him an opportunity to make a choice; he needs practice in this as in any other skill. Your aim should be to give him some opportunities to decide for himself without overburdening him with choices. You should make the decisions when it is simpler for both of you if you do so or when there is only one choice that suits the rest of the family. It is pointless to let a child think he can have a real say in some family decision when the result is a foregone conclusion. He prefers honesty, and is quite capable of seeing that adults do not always have much choice either.

Is Arguing Impudent?

Some adults think that explaining the reasons for their decisions to a child undermines their authority, considering that a child who questions and discusses their decisions is impudent. This approach is more prevalent among working-class families than among middle-class families. It has been suggested that it contributes toward fundamental differences in class attitude to authority in adult life. If you allow your child to talk things over with you, making him feel responsible for disciplining himself rather than expecting him to obey blindly, he will grow up aware of the value of persuasive argument. As an adult he is likely to assume that people in authority are approachable and open to argument, taking it for granted that most differences can be settled by talking.

In contrast, a child who thinks it is useless to say what he thinks, because arguing is only taken as further evidence of his naughtiness and gets him nowhere, seldom has the chance to understand the reasons behind decisions taken by adults. In practice, he will sometimes disobey but he seldom disagrees with them openly. Experience with schoolteachers may do little to change his opinion that talking to people with power over him is a waste of time; nor may his education equip him with the language to argue confidently. He is likely to grow up regarding authority as "Them" and himself as "Us," feeling that the gulf is unbridgeable by words and that discussion of disputes on equal terms is impossible. Feeling like this is frustrating at the least; in the extreme, it can lead to violence.

Forestalling Trouble

To get away with the minimum of formal discipline and punishment, you need to learn the art of forestalling trouble. To achieve this you do not have to possess particularly saintly children or particularly low standards. The behavior you expect of your children should be reasonably appropriate to their ages and personalities and to the life they lead inside and outside the home. You have to become adept at spotting trouble in advance, at preventing clashes, at providing distractions, and at finding honorable solutions that leave everybody involved in a disagreement feeling better rather than worse (see playing with friends, pp. 301–4).

Forestalling trouble is not especially difficult. As you get to know your child's reactions, you can avoid head-on collisions by being one step ahead of him. This is not the same as taking the easy way out and giving in to all his demands, or letting the needs of the rest of the family take permanent second place. It means coming to a satisfactory compromise in living together based on actual circumstances rather than ideals; the size of your house and how much noise you can tolerate are relevant factors.

Balancing Children's and Parents' Rights

The adults in a family need a certain amount of time to themselves; some of their possessions cannot be used as playthings without being ruined. But young children are boisterous, noisy, and full of curiosity. They do not appreciate "peace and quiet" or the comparative value of your various belongings. Unless you live in a vast house where no one's activities get in the way of anyone else's, and where the children can rampage safely but out of earshot, you have to devise a workable compromise between the children's right to behave like children and the rights of the adults. Working out this compromise is the responsibility of parents, not children.

Respecting Possessions

Children need help in understanding that some objects are spoiled if used as playthings. A young child cannot know that a camera is in a different category from a saucepan, that it is naughty to drop one but not the other. A child soon learns that there is some difference between them, because his parents are furious when he smashes the camera, but do not mind him dropping the saucepan. Their reactions probably seem illogical and teach him little except that parental fury is a strange and unpredictable thing. It is much better to avoid this kind of situation by keeping valuable or delicate belongings out of a child's reach until he is old enough to appreciate that some things must be looked after and used only in the correct way. The age at which a child can accept this varies, depending on the family's attitude to individual possessions, but if you respect your child's own possessions and help him to use certain tools or gadgets properly, he will learn to take care of things more rapidly.

Leaving Each Other Alone

A child needs help in distinguishing between adult activities that can be interrupted and those that should not be; otherwise his parents end up making frequent pleas of "Go away and leave me alone," with escalating threats of punishment. A three-year-old cannot know that you are more irritated by his chattering when you are trying to decipher your tax form than when you are reading a bad novel. However, he is more likely to accept that some of your occupations need comparative quiet and freedom from interruption if given your undivided interest and attention part of the time; also, if you respect his right to play without constantly interrupting him.

Every child needs somewhere to play in his own way without annoying others (see his own territory, p. 298). Some games are ruined by parents interrupting thoughtlessly at the vital moment. If a child refuses to stop playing and to do what his mother wants at once, he is called naughty, but really he is only showing that he is interested in what he is doing (see play, p. 299).

One way of forestalling trouble is to make it easy for your child to play happily. If he goes to a play group or nursery school for part of the day, you can get on with your own work without him and enjoy him more when he is home again (see preschool schooling, p. 316).

Leading Your Own Life

The more easily a child can play within the household without annoying everyone else in it, the more quickly will he come to accept that parents too have lives of their own to lead which cannot be entirely shared with him. A child does not appreciate parents whose lives revolve around his or whose main interest is his doings. This concentrated attention is suffocating after babyhood; it results in obsessive interest in his progress and the nagging that often goes with this.

An older child wants to be proud of his parents, to feel that they are interesting people in their own right, not just two adults whose only role in life is being his parents. If you are still interested in learning new things, and doing new things yourself, instead of living only through your child, he is able to develop and learn at his own pace. A child needs to feel your interest in his progress but not that all your hopes for the future are invested in him.

Parents who continue to develop their own new interests encourage similar development in their children. This atmosphere of interest and learning is the probable reason why the children of parents who have been to college are more likely to go to college than children whose parents have not.

You will find you get on best with your children when your own life is going well. It is in the dull patches or when you are worried about other things that your children will get on your nerves. When depressed you may notice yourself disciplining your child for behavior that you accept as normal boisterousness when happier. Sometimes, anxiety about a child's behavior turns out to be exaggerated; the problem is to improve the parents' tempers rather than the child's manners. Therefore, another way of reducing or avoiding friction and the need for discipline is to keep yourself happy.

The main way of preventing trouble, rather than relying on discipline to cure it, is to understand your child's varying abilities and needs at different ages and to consider whether these correspond with your expectations of him.

Discipline at Different Ages: The First Six Months

Some parents are worried about discipline, although they are probably unaware of it, as soon as their baby arrives. They apply words like "naughty," "greedy," and "spoiled" at a stage when these terms are completely unrealistic. They feel they ought to be disciplining him, in the sense of training him, from his earliest days, because if they do not, he will "get into bad habits," "never learn," and grow up completely irresponsible. Occasionally, a young baby is smacked for wetting his diaper or for not finishing his feeding.

Can You "Spoil" or "Train" Him Yet?

Such parents are not necessarily cruel or stupid, but they seriously misunderstand the young baby's nature and needs. They are rightly aware that he can be influenced for good or for ill from the start and that how he is treated is important; a baby's first impressions of the world are determined by how he is fed, handled, and generally cared for in the early weeks. He is influenced by loving parents who guide him toward confidence but he cannot be "spoiled" in the usual sense of the word, since he is dependent on his mother for all his needs. It is impossible to spoil a young baby by meeting these needs promptly. What he needs at this age is food when he is hungry and comfort when he cries (see sleeping and crying, pp. 116f.). A baby's impression of the world is spoiled if he is repeatedly left to cry, is often cold or hungry, and is seldom cuddled or talked to: the world must seem a lonely and uncomfortable place.

A baby cannot begin to control his behavior until he recognizes his mother as a separate person who is pleased by some things he does and not by others. This stage does not arrive until about the end of the first year and is a very gradual process.

Trying to Make Him Behave

Even if you are well aware that you cannot yet train your baby, you will sometimes feel exasperated and want to try to make him behave. Most parents who find themselves shaking their small baby, because he will not stop crying or refuses to feed, are just expressing this exasperation. They quickly come to and stop when they realize they are treating him as if he could respond to orders, as if he were being deliberately disobedient and should be punished. A mother who does not realize what she is doing and who has an abnormal compulsion to control her baby may not stop and may hurt him (see "Could I Hurt My Baby?," p. 177).

Six to Eighteen Months

By the age of about six months your baby is beginning to respond to you as an individual instead of just another smiling human face, and this development increases his incentive to please you. He will know whether or not you are pleased with him by the expression on your face and by your tone of voice, which he is able to interpret long before he can grasp the actual meaning of words. You can now teach him in a direct way as well as indirectly through the way in which you handle and feed him.

Showing Him You Disapprove

Your baby will notice when you disapprove of his behavior. It is important to convey the impression that you dislike something because it is a nuisance, or is making life difficult for someone else, not because it is "bad" in itself. For example, you want him to stop pulling your hair because it hurts, not because it is a wicked thing to do at this age. You want him to learn that people dislike being pushed and pulled, not that he was wrong to try the experiment. So instead of looking furious and calling him a "bad boy" in a deadly serious voice, remove his hand gently and tell him he is hurting you. It does not matter that he cannot understand the words; he will see you dislike what he is doing. Give him something else to do with his hands. Distracting his attention can solve many potential disputes throughout childhood.

Even a young baby senses the difference between his mother's various reactions. He is more likely to howl if you are really furious with him than if you are calm and gently restrain him. He learns more from the second approach, and this helps him gradually to discover that people resent being pushed and pulled. In this way you will convey to him that it is his behavior you dislike, not himself: babies are very good at sensing what their mothers are feeling and at spotting the differences in their reactions.

Keeping Him Out of Trouble

Once your baby is sitting up, is beginning to pick up objects, and is trying to act independently, he gives you far more reason to correct and restrain him. You have the responsibility of keeping him safe; you have to stop him from falling out of his chair or putting beads into his mouth, and you have to show him that some of the things he wants to do upset other people. You cannot let him find all this out for himself by trial and error (see extreme attitudes to discipline, pp. 284–87, accidents, p. 626).

There is far less need to correct him if you have planned in advance. If he is strapped safely in his chair, if there is nothing small enough to choke on within his reach, and if he has the space and opportunity to play without annoying others, you can avoid a great deal of direct interference with his activities.

Is He Being "Stubborn"?

You may overestimate the degree to which your baby can control his actions because he seems bright in so many ways; you may begin to wonder if his persistence in repeating actions you have disapproved of is due to "stubbornness" that should be punished. You are right to begin the gradual process of helping him to modify his behavior, but remember how gradual this process must be. Your baby seems to be learning very fast in the second half of his first year, yet he cannot learn to be sociable and unselfish overnight, nor can he profit from formal training.

Expecting Appropriate Behavior: Table Manners

For example, there is little point in trying to teach table manners to a baby who is just beginning to feed himself. Appropriate table manners for a one-year-old consist of enjoying meals, getting better at manipulating the spoon, and feeding himself. This involves dabbling in the food, making a dreadful mess, and perhaps taking a long time to finish the meal—or not to finish it. No problem of discipline arises if you accept that this is normal behavior and that he will pass through this stage more quickly if allowed to enjoy it at the appropriate time. If you or your husband is unable to bear the mess, it is better to acknowledge this and to feed your baby separately, so as to give him less chance to upset your mealtime (see feeding problems, pp. 203–4).

On the other hand, having his meals with you will help him to learn manners more quickly by copying you.

Toilet Training

The same applies to other aspects of development you may find tedious, although you know they are normal stages. If you know why you are irritated, it is less likely to lead to trouble; for example, your approach to toilet training will be based partly on a knowledge of normal development, but it will also be influenced by the attitude with which you grew up (see toilet training, pp. 240f.). You will not beat your baby for wetting his pants if you know he is too young to be fully toilet trained, and if you acknowledge that you have discarded his diapers early because you cannot resist training him before he is really ready for it. So long as you know what you are doing, and understand that your baby's slowness to respond is not due to naughtiness, you will avoid creating unnecessary problems of discipline.

Will He Behave?

As soon as a baby sits up, his activities begin attracting attention; you tend to become more conscious of the effect of his behavior on other people, of the impression he is making. If he cries or is irritable when you are with friends or relatives, you feel you must defend him, and yourself, by ascribing this to "teething" or to his being "off-color." You may try to explain his behavior to prevent him from being thought an unsatisfactory baby and yourself an unsatisfactory mother. This could be because the people you are with seem to believe that a baby is always happy unless his mother has done something wrong, and that there always has to be some physical explanation for a baby having an off-day. Either way, if you are extra anxious about him, he is liable to notice and to be more than usually restless or miserable.

Social occasions often cause a baby to miss his familiar routine; he is not ready for the strain of social gatherings if these mean he has to be especially quiet and undemanding for long intervals. Some parents expect a different standard of behavior when they take their baby out; but it is unrealistic to be cross with the child or with yourself if he is not the perfect guest. If you can find something to attract his attention and occupy him, you will soon find he behaves better.

Eighteen Months to School Age

Once your child can walk and talk, you will probably take him on longer and more ambitious family outings. The same problems arise as with the younger baby, since the walking, talking two-year-old is still a baby in many ways and may still embarrass you. This happens particularly when he irritates the kind of people who do not realize that toddlers are messy and noisy by nature and may have temper tantrums, and that this does not mean they are badly brought up.

Keeping Him Out of Trouble

This is a tiring age for parents, because the child is so active and energetic, needing constant watching; even if the household is organized for his safety, you cannot make the rest of the world equally safe. He is as yet too young to have more than a rudimentary understanding of what is and is not acceptable behavior.

You will be busy keeping him out of trouble, helping him to discover that fire burns, and knives cut, before he finds out accidentally (see preventing accidents, pp. 620f.). The age at which children can be trusted not to touch the carving knife or get too near the fire is very variable. Keeping the knives out of reach and guarding the fire efficiently avoids the need for constant nagging not to touch. Parents who are continually anxious that their baby is about to hurt himself have to keep saying "no," and then the word loses its significance. The less you have to correct him, the greater the impact when it is necessary.

In the meantime, you can help him to learn that some things and activities can be dangerous; for example, let him watch you use the knife; show him the sharp edge and demonstrate how it cuts meat, so that he sees it would cut his finger equally well. You can let him feel how uncomfortably hot his hand becomes when he puts it near the fire. This helps him to learn to avoid trouble for himself but it will not guarantee he will remember all the time; you will still have to protect him with automatic safety measures.

Temper Tantrums

The two-year-old has little judgment and a strong will—a powerful combination that can lead to frequent clashes with his parents. "Temper tantrums" are the climax of some of these clashes. They do not mean the child has an exceptionally bad temper, but are a sign of the lack of control that is normal at this age; he really cannot help himself when he is in the middle of a tantrum, so it is little use ordering him to stop or punishing him afterward. The problem is to keep calm, so that he catches your mood, instead of becoming so exasperated yourself that your rage feeds his. It is much better to walk out of the room, leaving him to work himself out of the temper, than to stay with him and shout at him. No one performs well without an audience; the child in a tantrum is likely to calm down more quickly if left on his own, but be sure to leave the door open and do not go far away.

Steer around trouble as far as possible and try turning his attention in another direction, but don't feel you have failed if your small child sometimes becomes enraged. The more frequent tantrums of some children may be due to differences in temperament or to differences in the number of provoking occasions in their day-to-day lives. Tantrums become progressively fewer as a child gets better at making choices and putting up with delays in getting his own way (see forestalling trouble, pp. 272f.; playing with friends, pp. 301–4; breathholding, p. 552).

Reluctance to Share

As a child becomes more sociable and starts playing with others, there are bound to be quarrels, often over sharing toys. Unwillingness to share without a tussle or an argument is not a sign of deep-seated selfishness or insecurity during the first two or three years of learning to play with other children. It may simply be a sign of a strong measure of will power—useful in later life—so do not be too ashamed of him or too quick to reprimand him. A child who always meekly hands over his toy to another is the one who stands out as unusual at this stage, and he may need to be helped to feel confident enough to stand up for himself. (See also play, p. 293.)

Children Learn from Each Other

Sometimes, suggesting an alternative activity or producing another toy may solve the problem, but for the most part it is wiser to let children sort things out for themselves and not to keep intervening in disputes unless someone is being hurt (see playing with friends, pp. 301–4). Children learn much from each other, and you may spoil a valuable lesson in the art of getting on with others if you interrupt with your interpretation of the rights and wrongs of a dispute, even among young preschool children. At all stages of childhood, you can safely leave some of the responsibility for disciplining your child with his friends.

If he goes to a play group or nursery school he will learn not only from the other children but also from his teachers. It is good for him to see that he is not the only child in the world who has to be corrected or thwarted by adults. It is good for parents to share some of the responsibility for discipline with another adult whom their child knows well (see play groups and nursery schools, pp. 316–19).

Five Years and Onward

Discipline at School

When your child goes to school, you start sharing the responsibility for discipline in earnest, whether you like it or not. Home life is still the most influential factor but outside influences become increasingly important. Your child wants to please other adults and children, and has more opportunity to compare his behavior and achievements; this is an added incentive to behave considerately and to conform.

Conforming to some degree is inevitable and does not necessarily stifle a child's individuality: this usually stands up well to the routine of present-day school life, especially if you choose a school where the aim of education is to bring out the child's own qualities rather than to push in information. At such a school there are likely to be few rules and little direct discipline, and certainly no corporal punishment (p. 290). The pupils are likely to be happy and to behave well because they see the point of doing so.

In Trouble at School   A child who is being punished frequently at school is perhaps being expected to fit into too formal a routine; his "naughtiness" may be no more than normal liveliness, which would be acceptable in a more relaxed school. Do not assume your child is exceptionally difficult until you have found out the exact nature of his offenses. It is always wise to try to co-operate with teachers and see their point of view, but do not be afraid to discuss the problem with them.

Inconsistent Behavior   It is not unusual for a child to be "good" at home and naughty at school, or vice versa, so that parent and teacher seem to be discussing a different child. This may happen because the child finds it too much of a strain to conform all the time, so he protests by behaving badly at one or the other. When he is more accustomed to school and finds work and making friends less of a strain, his behavior will become more consistent. However, some children continue to show different sides of their characters at home and at school throughout their school careers. Unless the child, his parents, or his teachers find it a serious problem, it can be ignored. If someone does, then discuss it together and with your child. Sometimes the trouble turns out to be a minor one, but occasionally it is big enough to make changing schools a solution worth considering.

Discipline at Home

Becoming a Responsible Person   During these middle years of childhood, your child is becoming increasingly responsible for his own behavior. He is developing a reliable conscience that usually knows the difference between right and wrong and makes him feel guilty when he chooses the latter. But he is still a child and no more capable than most adults of behaving well consistently. Sometimes he will act maturely, sometimes he will seem a baby. He will respond to reason nine times out of ten, but the tenth time may fly into a temper reminiscent of the tantrums of a two-year-old. Do not expect too much of him and keep your sense of humor to help you through bad patches.

Do not always wait for your child to be the first to "make it up." A child does not despise his parents for admitting their share of responsibility for a family row or for helping him not to lose face; he likes them for it.

Living Together

Tidiness and Helping in the Home

Tidiness, or, rather, untidiness, is a good example of an area where family friction can easily and frequently develop, and to which a vast amount of superfluous discipline is devoted. The same could be said of several disciplinary problems that really have nothing to do with right or wrong behavior but with convenience. Much that is written here applies equally to other areas of behavior, from feeding to toilet training.

It helps to regard tidiness not as a self-evident virtue but as a useful quality which makes living together simpler. As such it is a useful habit for a child to acquire, both for his own sake and for yours. It is important to keep a balance between the need for some order in the household and the need for children to play without constant interference (see play, pp. 298–99).

However, it is also wise to acknowledge that few adult tempers are improved by living in chaos and that there is little point in letting children do as they please on one front if this means friction on several others. Someone's untidiness may be a daily annoyance to another member of the family, cropping up so often that there is little chance to think of a better method of tackling it. It is also one of the areas where parents' imperfections make it harder to deal reasonably with the children's.

Trying to Hide Your Inconsistency

If you are untidy yourself, it is no use hoping your children will not notice the muddle behind the closet doors; it is difficult to convince children of the virtue of hanging up clothes each night if they know very well that your own are discarded in a tangled heap. You will have a nagging feeling that children ought to be "trained" for later life, or at least for their visits to Aunt Mary. A familiar pattern is to demand bouts of tidiness from the children, then to give up the effort for a while because fundamentally you sympathize with them. It will be hard not to be hypocritical about tidiness unless you are prepared to live in total disorder—and most untidy people do not really enjoy disorder.

If you are like this, your children will notice and probably resent your inconsistency and trade on it. But having an inconsistent mother does less harm than living with an obsessively tidy mother, who hates disorder so much that she organizes life to avoid it. This is impossible with children in the house unless something more important is sacrificed—play, the most creative and enjoyable of the children's activities. Being creative frequently means creating chaos, at least in early childhood. You can minimize the chaos by forethought—newspaper under the paint pots, easily washed clothing, a bargain with the children that they keep their mess within a certain boundary—but you cannot eliminate it without making children worried, or rebellious, or, in the long run, unimaginative.

Learning from Experience

Children do like their surroundings to be comparatively orderly, although they dislike spending their time and energy in actually helping you make them so. A preschool child may quite enjoy helping you put away his toys, if he has finished that particular game. Later, he grasps the idea that people trip over and often break things that are left around in the wrong place, and that if he wants to keep his plastic tank in one piece it had better be put away.

Appreciating His Effort

A school-age child understands that it is unfair for his mother to have to pick up his things all the time, but may still find it hard to remember to help without regular reminders. He will probably make the occasional dramatic gesture like clearing out a kitchen cabinet, and may even criticize your standard of tidiness, while remaining exceedingly untidy himself. He may do regular chores without grumbling, but will resent it if you try to take advantage of his willingness by adding to them in the hope that he won't notice. It is better to suggest doing something together than to overwhelm a child with an order to do a long and tedious job alone. Children like helping as long as they feel it is strictly fair and that the help is really necessary and appreciated. Remember to notice your child's efforts and to thank him.

It may be easy to help one child to acquire the habit of tidiness but another child, while seeing the point, may never actually feel like tidying up at a given moment. It is impossible to generalize and to say that by a certain age every child should, for example, keep his own room tidy. If you decide your child is old enough, or if he hates you touching his things, shut his door in the mornings and try not to have a daily row about it. He will certainly point out that it is his room and he does not mind if it is untidy. You can accept this, but ask him to keep his things tidy in rooms that belong to the whole family. He will probably find out for himself how inconvenient it is to lose things in the muddle.

Going Through Stages

A child may go through stages of tidiness. A small girl of nine who positively enjoys arranging her belongings in her own room may turn into an adolescent who appears to revel in total personal disorder. Nagging makes the room no tidier but sours relations between you. By the time she is a parent herself, the untidy adolescent may be well organized again. So do not decide you have failed on the tidiness front at any particular age. What you are trying to encourage is consideration for other people, rather than tidiness for its own sake—and if your child shows consideration in other ways, then you have succeeded. Even a child who seems thoughtless at home can be most helpful when he is away. He remembers that other people should not have to clear up after him, and he has obviously grasped the fact that tidiness is a desirable social grace, even if he completely conceals this understanding from his parents.

Extreme Attitudes to Discipline

Extreme attitudes to discipline tend to spring from an exaggerated idea of the extent to which any one "system" of bringing up children can influence their development, for better or worse. At one extreme are the parents who believe that it is only constant discipline and the threat of punishment that prevent children from becoming uncontrollable demons; they believe that a child cannot grow up into a responsible adult unless prodded every step of the way. At the other extreme are the parents who believe that it is only adult intervention that prevents children from growing up into perfect human beings. Utopia would be around the corner if only a generation of children were allowed to develop unspoiled by the hang-ups of their elders; therefore, children should learn entirely by trial and error and should never be checked or corrected.

Both extremes underestimate the importance of the individual child's temperament and needs, and how these interact with the rest of the family. Every child's natural tendency is to develop from a self-centered infant, oblivious of other people's rights, into a sociable person who tries to modify his own impulsive behavior in order to be liked and accepted and to live a reasonably balanced life. Every child needs some help and encouragement from his family and friends in gradually achieving this compromise.

Parents who anticipate a child's every move, to make sure he behaves correctly, give him no chance to behave well of his own accord. On the other hand, parents who let their child behave exactly as he likes at home lose the opportunity of helping him in his early attempts at self-control. Both kinds of parent make their children's attempts at self-discipline far harder and more bewildering.

Effects on the Child

Too much or too little discipline tends to have the same result—an insecure child who shows his insecurity either by behaving exceptionally badly or by being exceptionally "good." Many children survive their parents' extremes because their temperaments are sufficiently resilient to withstand them and because outside influences counteract what goes on at home; but in other children the effect can become obvious.

The Overdisciplined Child

Present-day children suffer less from excessive discipline than their predecessors. A greater understanding of children's needs and how they develop, and a respect for their individuality, together with a general decline in the degree of formal behavior expected socially, at school and at work, make it easier for parents to relax and to let their children behave like children.

However, everyone knows a few children who are expected to behave like little adults. Their parents worry about discipline almost from the moment of birth, showing this in their concern that their baby will become "spoiled" if fed when hungry instead of at fixed times, or if he is picked up and cuddled when he cries (see discipline at different ages, pp. 275f.). When the baby starts to feed himself there is constant worry about his future table manners, and when he crawls he soon finds that most activities and places are taboo (see discipline, pp. 277f.).

If the baby is a gentle, mild character he may give up experimenting and abandon this natural desire to touch and play with things. He may soon become wary even of activities that are not forbidden, perhaps becoming afraid to play with modeling clay as well as mud, because the latter is always regarded as dirty and messy in his family. He may transfer his anxieties to another, quite unrelated area, so that he becomes afraid of the dark or of animals as well as being afraid of doing the "wrong" things.

If the child's disposition makes it hard for him to give in meekly and obey, he may react to too much ordering about by having temper tantrums or becoming deliberately destructive; he behaves like a "spoiled" child because he has been spoiled—by lack of understanding of his need to play and behave like a child of his age. His parents should relax and trust him to develop and become more grown up in his behavior without constant interference. Observing other children and learning more about normal development helps.

The Underdisciplined Child

The completely undisciplined child gets into a muddle as he grows older; he cannot help noticing that his behavior often annoys other people, although it is apparently all right at home. He compares himself with other children, even if his parents do not.

A child's happiness depends partly on his ability to get on successfully with other children and adults. The child who rampages through the neighbor's house, bullying the children and disregarding any reprimand, may be momentarily enjoying himself, but he will not remain happy once he realizes how unpopular he is becoming. You have to help your children to be friendly and unselfish, as well as to express their individuality, because they need to develop in all these ways to be happy in the long term.

Even if you start off believing that children develop best if allowed to learn entirely by trial and error with the minimum of interference, you will find it difficult not to modify your approach in practice when your baby becomes mobile and begins to endanger himself and the family's possessions, unless he is restrained and guided (see pp. 273f.).

Feeling Angry   A child who is never openly checked has no legitimate reason for anger; but it does not follow that he will never be angry. He is bound to feel cross sometimes, because things will go wrong, however efficiently you try to shield him from disappointment. Toys will break or refuse to be manipulated as he wants; he will be frustrated because his own smallness and lack of skill stop him from doing many of the things he would like to do; and he will notice that people sometimes become exasperated with him, even if they feel it would be wrong to admit it. The resulting "bad" thoughts and aggressive fantasies about his parents and others may not be expressed openly but may nevertheless make him feel guilty. It is better for you to behave naturally with him, and for him to feel naturally cross with you at times.

A child who is allowed to behave outrageously by the standards expected in his society soon knows he is going too far and should be stopped. He notices that other children are not permitted the same "freedom" and wonders why his parents never admit to being cross with him. He knows they must feel annoyed sometimes—they probably cannot help showing this in their faces anyway—and he begins to wonder if they are storing up some gigantic future punishment to pay him back for all the trouble he has caused. Unlike children who are occasionally told off by their parents and sometimes prevented from doing what they wish, he has no peg on which to hang his resentment or guilt. He may begin to worry far more about his behavior than a child who is reproved, forgiven, and can then stop feeling bad about an incident.

Antisocial Behavior If adults take none of the responsibility for his behavior, a child has to bear it all himself. He may find this burden so overwhelming that he gives it up altogether, continuing to behave like a demanding toddler. Unfortunately, once past the toddler stage this is called antisocial behavior. The child's antisocial behavior conceals a plea for help, for reassurance that he is loved. But the kind of love he needs is not shown by more kisses and more presents—he needs to be relieved of some of the responsibility of trying to behave sensibly all by himself. His parents can help him partly by forestalling trouble (pp. 272f.) and by telling him when to stop, instead of forcing him to find out everything for himself by testing other people's patience.

Of course, this child will not benefit if he is suddenly forced to behave differently, or if he is punished for behavior that was formerly tolerated. What he needs is to feel that his parents care how he behaves; that when they ask him to do something or to stop doing something, they mean what they say; and that there is a reason for their decision, though this may merely be that they too have needs and rights. In practice, this change in attitude usually comes about gradually, before a crisis point is reached, as parents begin to see that the policy of "anything goes" is disrupting family life and is failing to make the child happy.

Too Good to Be True The child who reacts to too little guidance by becoming naughtier at least feels secure enough to misbehave; otherwise he would not risk losing his parents' love and might react in another way, by becoming excessively obedient, as if this were the only way he could be sure of being loved. He would still benefit by knowing how far he could go, thereby feeling safe enough to be more adventurous.

Enforcing Discipline: Punishment and Threats

Methods of Punishing

It would be convenient if there were an effective and suitable punishment to fit every childish crime. In theory, the punishment should fit the individual child, his age and his misdemeanor. In practice, even if it were possible to recommend this neat solution, actual punishments would continue to be influenced by variable and unpredictable factors, such as the circumstances leading up to the showdown and how tired the parent was, the relationship between the naughty child and the angry parent, and the family tendency to practice a particular brand of punishment. For example, a mother who smacks her child at the end of a long day is punishing him because she is tired and for all the irritating things he has done that day, not just for the trivial offense that finally provoked the slap. An outsider who saw only the isolated incident might think her harsh and unreasonable, but the child himself probably understands that the penalty covers a multitude of sins, and that his mother always gets bad-tempered around this time after a busy day. If he has a normal, affectionate relationship with her, he may feel resentment, but he will not feel as unhappy about the punishment as the critical outsider fears.

Keeping a Good Relationship

How you punish your child is not nearly as important as your general relationship with him, and the punishment itself is less important than the spirit in which it is given. If he feels secure and you feel confident, punishment will seldom be necessary; when given, it will usually achieve its aim of correcting the child and clearing the air. The aim should never be to humiliate your child or to force him to behave through fear. He cannot learn this way.

Sometimes, even a basically happy relationship between a parent and a child suffers because the child is punished too much or the punishment is inappropriate for his age or misdeeds; his behavior then becomes worse, not better, and he becomes unhappier. If this applies to your child you must find out what it is that is wrong, and consider why so much punishment seems necessary. You can no longer afford to take it for granted that your child still acknowledges your basic good will toward him. It may help to think about punishment and discipline from a different, objective angle or to try a different approach.

Spanking

This form of punishment is a good illustration of the fact that the type of punishment is insignificant in the context of the total relationship between two people. It is a good rule to avoid spanking or any other kind of physical punishment if you have time to think of anything better, but don't feel too guilty if you do find yourself giving the occasional light whack. Most parents feel guiltier about spanking than about other ways of punishing children but find it difficult to avoid altogether.

You may sometimes find it more effective and less upsetting to a small child to give him a quick spanking rather than a lengthy explanation (see explaining discipline, p. 271). It is possible to be vindictive using any method of punishment. A child senses your effort to humiliate him whether this is through a slap or by making him seem ridiculous in a verbal onslaught. Spending hours thinking up the best way to humiliate a child or to make him too afraid to behave that way again is far more harmful to parent/child relationships than an ill-considered but nonvindictive punishment. The aim of punishment is to improve your relationship with your child so as to get through to him in the far more important discipline of living together.

Spanking is at least quick and direct and it sometimes works when everything else has failed. It is more useful as a way of expressing and getting rid of your bad mood than as a corrective for your child; but you may urgently need to relieve your feelings and your child may benefit indirectly from the better atmosphere afterward.

In general, if you have time to think of another way of correcting your child it is better not to spank him, but if you do spank in the heat of the moment, or to get through to a child temporarily impervious to argument, this probably does no more harm than any other type of punishment. But once you notice that a child feels humiliated by spanking, stop it. The older the child, the more likely he is to react this way.

When Spanking Becomes Dangerous The trouble is that since moods can change as well as punishments, smacking can escalate; it has to become harder and more frequent to have the same effect. While the occasional spanking from a harassed mother does most children little harm and may be less upsetting than a cutting remark, it is worth hesitating if you find yourself spanking more often or with more force than you intend. Many parents become frightened by their own anger, and afraid that they may really hurt their child. Those who are able to recognize the reason for their fear are likely to be wise enough to stop spanking altogether; alternatively, their anxiety may take them to their doctor, who must recognize its cause even if the question is not put directly. Less often, the danger signal is not recognized and the result is a battered child (pp. 177f.).

Corporal Punishment

There is a long distance between a quick slap and a desperate beating, but both have origins in the intense emotional relationship between parent and child. It is because parents, particularly mothers, are involved in an intense day-to-day intimacy with their children that they are likely to spank them. Corporal punishment administered in a classroom is far more horrifying than a spanking from a parent, not just because it is more painful physically for the child, but because it is given in cold blood, with an implement, some time after the event, by someone who cannot have a parent's love for the child. A parent who organizes a formal beating as a punishment for his child is only proving that might equals right, is doing nothing to help the child evolve a conscience of his own, and is helping to open up an emotional chasm between them that will make future discipline more difficult.

The Law of Diminishing Returns

A child who is frequently spanked, often more as a reminder than as a punishment, may cease noticing or reacting to spanking and is much more impressed by a change in his mother's tone of voice. A child who has never been spanked will be far more shocked on the first occasion and may even remember it for the rest of his life. Any kind of punishment or threat of punishment is devalued by overexposure. A bad-tempered shout from a usually patient mother has an instant effect, while another roar from a mother who roars all day goes unnoticed. No intelligent child takes any notice of a threat to deprive him of candy or television if the threats are a kind of background noise and are never carried out. This may do little harm, but it adds to the irritations of family life. If a child feels you mean what you say, he usually obeys.

The Verbal Approach: Threats and Appeals

There is a distinction between threats, bribes, and appeals to reason in persuading a child to do as you want. "If you don't put your toys away, I'll spank you" is a threat that bullies the child into obedience. "If you don't put your toys away, you'll get no allowance" is an attempt to bribe him into obedience. "If you don't put your toys away, they'll get broken" appeals to reason, so that the child is learning something; it may also work. If it does not, it is easy to find yourself using the bribe technique, then the threat—the final stage of actual punishment is seldom reached. It is best to avoid all the stages or as many as possible, forestalling trouble by thinking ahead (see forestalling trouble, pp. 272f.).

How the Child Fits the Punishment

How a child is punished depends to some extent on the child himself. Some children are never spanked or threatened because they obey verbal requests or even a change of expression on their mother's face. The mother of this kind of child does not need to spank him but she may spank another of her children, who never does what he is told.

A small boy who usually shrugs off quite hard spankings may occasionally dissolve into tears when tapped lightly or told off, if he sees someone is really angry with him.

Feeling Sorry

Although it is difficult to generalize, spanking tends to make a child cross with you rather than sorry for what he has done. This means that it is less effective than explanations and reasoning, or punishments such as withholding privileges—which give him time to think over his misdeed—in the long-term aim of helping him achieve self-control.

On the other hand, it is sometimes better for a child to be punished at once with a spanking and have it over and done with, than to involve him continually in feeling guilty and responsible for his behavior; he may be cross but his anger will be turned outward not inward. Too much anger with himself and a feeling of personal unworthiness depress a child and make him give up trying to discipline himself—the opposite of the true aim of discipline (see explaining discipline, p. 271).

I have gone into spanking at length because it is naturally a subject that concerns parents greatly. The more you think about it, the more convinced you should become that spanking is a poor and possibly harmful way to punish your child. It is an aggressive act, which could reasonably be expected to get a child to retaliate in kind —perhaps not with you, because you are too big, but possibly with his younger brother or sister. If a child finds himself being spanked by his parents, it is understandable that he may sometimes spank the baby. You have licensed him to spank.

Alternative Punishments

What alternatives are there to spanking? I have referred to the powerful effect of the altered tone of a mother's voice and to the expression on her face. Used well these can be very effective, but it is important not to shout. Removal of privileges, such as allowance, the dessert after meals, or a favorite television program, can be effective if used only occasionally; but if you make a threat of this nature, it must be put into action—otherwise it is meaningless.

Should You Send Him to Bed?

Whatever you do, don't make the mistake of sending your child to bed as a punishment. Bed is a castle where he feels safe, cozy, and warm at night. It must not serve the dual purpose of castle at night and prison cell during the daytime. For similar, though less strong, reasons, I do not like the idea of sending a child to his room as a punishment, though I accept that there are occasions when you and your child need to be separated in order to take the heat out of a situation. The ideal arrangement in such circumstances is for you to go off to another room, leaving the door open between you so that he can come in for a cuddle when he wants to.

In practice, the long-term and short-term aims of discipline must be balanced; punishment should be used only as an occasional weapon in the much longer process of discipline.

20

Play

The Importance of Play

Play is an unsatisfactory word because it stands for so many varied activities and because it still implies a frivolous and unimportant pastime. For a child, play is work but, to an adult, play suggests relaxation. An adult often plays when he should be working. The expression "child's play" also underlines this misconception. A playing child is not just idling away his time until the next important event organized by an adult, such as dressing, eating, or helping in the house. To play is to make the very best use of his time. Play is a vital process in growing up.

Nor is it a question of the child's playing because he is not yet old enough to do anything else—not mature enough to work. In a small child's mind, no gulf exists between play and work. A child who plays hard shows he is capable of hard work in the adult sense, whatever his progress in school subjects. Nursery-school activity is all play. Enlightened elementary school teachers acknowledge that children learn best when enjoying themselves, and try to delay the sad day when the break between play and work becomes obvious to the child. Once this has happened you may have to teach a child how to work, how to achieve, whereas you never have to show a normal child how to play.

Playing with Your Baby

Playing and Feeding

Play starts at the breast. Your baby soon begins to do more than just suck and take in food; he pauses and looks around with enjoyment, he strokes and even pummels the breast. This serves the biological purpose of encouraging the flow of milk by stimulating the let-down reflex (pp. 60–61) and makes you feel happy and relaxed; but if you watch a baby feeding, it is clear that he is also enjoying these activities for their own sake. Through playing he is learning what the breast feels like and how doing different things with his hands produces different sensations.

A baby feeding at the bottle will also stroke and feel it, but the bottle remains inert; it is not comfortable and yielding like a breast, so it does not make such a good plaything (see breast feeding, p. 68). On these grounds, it might be said that the first way you can help your child to play is to breast feed him, and to allow him to linger over his feedings. Equally, if you bottle feed you should give your baby time to experiment and play during feedings (see bottle feeding, pp. 93–94).

Play During Wakeful Periods

After the newborn period, your baby begins to stay awake for increasingly long periods during the day. He has to be awake if he is to absorb impressions, that is, to learn, so don't think there is something wrong with him, that he must be hungry or discontented, if he is not asleep all the time between feedings. Don't feel you must add cereal so that he remains asleep.

He is less likely to spend these wakeful intervals crying if he has something to look at, and if his hands and arms and legs are free to move. As early as a month, or as soon as you think him ready, let him lie on the floor on a clean towel, to enable him to move his arms and legs about. Sit him in a special baby chair, which can be adjusted to support him at the correct angle for his age, so that he can watch what you are doing or at least look around at a less restricted view than the one from his crib. Prop him safely in the corner of an armchair with cushions if you do not have a special chair. It is far better for him to be sitting up happily than lying bored and crying in his carriage, and it does not harm his back.

However, do not feel you must entertain him all the time he is awake, because he will often lie contentedly. At all ages, a child needs to be left to himself sometimes; a sensitive parent recognizes and respects this need, even in a baby.

Something to Watch

When your baby is lying in his crib or carriage, make sure that there is something moving for him to watch. A mobile above his crib is much more exciting than a boring ceiling; the leaves of a tree blowing in the wind are much more interesting than a boring sky. Toys strung across his carriage or crib within arm's reach create a similar interest. These should comprise objects with different textures and shapes, making different sounds when moved. In this way he will learn how to be contented even though he is alone, and how to become independent.

We now realize that many babies brought up in institutions where they are left lying in cribs with closed sides and only the plain ceiling to stare at suffer from lack of stimulation. They become used to being alone but do not have the advantage of learning how to occupy themselves without supervision (see development, p. 216).

Responding to Your Baby

Playing with your baby means talking and singing to him (see stories, p. 323). It means acting spontaneously and cuddling him, giving him something to respond to and being ready to respond to him. You do not have to think about it in advance, nor need you feel uneasy that you will not know exactly when he will want you to play peek-a-boo or to count his toes. Your baby will show by his response which kind of game he is ready for, and he will also let you know when he is tired of a game and wants to extend his repertoire.

He Does It Only to Annoy

Remember that some of the games your baby enjoys most may not seem like play at all, but more like annoying habits; the "dropping things over the side of the carriage" game is one of these. It starts at around nine months and goes on far too long, but it shows he has learned to let go and follow falling objects down to the ground and that he still needs to practice this skill and to see how he can use it. He is not doing it to annoy because he knows it teases, although this negative aspect may come into it later, particularly if you look annoyed. But this too is teaching him something—how people react to his actions (see development, pp. 231–32).

Dabbling with food and playing at mealtimes may also seem undesirable habits (see table manners, p. 203), but a baby does not divide his day up into play periods and times for serious activities; anything may be play and everything is serious. You have to find the right balance between letting him play and helping him to fit in with the rest of the family. This gets more difficult when he starts to move about. He needs to crawl and explore but you must keep him safe (see accidents, pp. 620f.) and also keep your house in one piece (see his own territory, p. 298). You have to restrict his activities and reach a compromise, but you won't go far wrong provided you recognize that his needs are serious and that he really must have some opportunity to explore in safety.

Playpen

Your baby won't stay in a playpen for long at this stage, nor should he, since it would then become a cage restricting his natural need to explore. A playpen is mainly useful to pop him into while you answer the door and to keep him safe in the kitchen while you get on with the cooking (see p. 627).

Baby-bouncer

This is a useful piece of equipment for stimulating your baby's developing skills by providing new experiences. A baby is usually old enough to use a bouncer by about six to seven months. You will probably find that he is ready to give it up by the end of the first year. Babies will sometimes bounce happily for hours but, as with all forms of activity, it is not a good idea to go on for so long that it becomes monotonous and stereotyped. Always stay in the room when your baby is in the bouncer, in case he bumps himself.

You can adjust the height of the bouncer so that it is correct for your baby—his toes should just be able to touch the floor. Do not use the bouncer as a swing; it is not made for this.

Which Type of Play Is Best?

All types of play have importance and serve a purpose in a child's development, physical, emotional, intellectual, or social. It is a mistake to regard one type as less valuable than another and therefore to try to discourage it. If your child wants to spend hours playing an apparently monotonous and unimaginative game with his toy cars instead of playing "creatively" with his construction set, then let him. His imagination may be working overtime and anyway he is playing the way he needs most, at this particular moment.

Let Him Decide

Therefore, provided your child has the opportunity to play in different ways, you can trust him to organize his play in the most fulfilling way possible for him. Sometimes, this will involve concentrated activity and close attention; at other times, it may seem an undemanding recharging of batteries—more soothing than stimulating, repetitive rather than challenging. You cannot expect him to be flat out the whole time.

Expressing His Feelings

Play helps your child to know himself by giving him the chance to explore his own mental and physical capabilities and to use his imagination. Play also enlarges his horizons, but at the same time helps to reduce the world to manageable proportions, enabling him to make sense of the flood of impressions pouring in from the outside world. Play is the medium through which he can express positive emotions and channel negative ones; it provides a safe outlet for emotional stresses. A vague fear can be attached to a specific "bogy man" in play; taking different roles in a game can help a child adjust to difficult relationships. For example, acting out violent jealousy of a brother or fury toward a parent in a dramatic game may help him to cope with the problem in a safe setting, at the same time dispersing some of his aggression. A game is only a game; the real people remain unscathed and therefore do not become angry with him. They may even join in themselves, temporarily changing places with the child. Forbidding fathers and harassed mothers can relax—you too can be safely silly or frighteningly fierce under cover of play. Your child can be boss, and you, as his parents, take the orders.

This type of play gives a child a chance to feel what it would be like to be someone else. Although his conception of the life of a cowboy or a doctor is limited, games of "let's pretend" show the beginnings of sympathy with other people, interest in their activities and in the world of work, and at the same time make this world more comprehensible. Language develops under the stimulus of sociable and imaginative play, since the participants in a game often need to communicate ideas and express more than basic demands. Since good speech is the foundation for further intellectual growth, it is obvious that this kind of play is a useful preparation for formal education as well as being enjoyable in itself.

Learning through Play

How does a child learn through play? Playing helps him to develop control of his body, to perfect physical skills and muscular co-ordination, and to refine the use of his sight, hearing, and other senses (pp. 213–39). When a baby plays with his fingers he is learning how to get them where he wants them, what they look like, what it feels like to suck and to chew them, and eventually how to use them as tools. Primarily, he is doing these things for pleasure, because it's fun; the learning is a by-product of play. Without this opportunity to play— if his arms were swaddled and his fingers in mittens all the time—he would lose essential learning time as well as valuable playing time (see p. 167).

The four-year-old, running and jumping and full of boisterous activity, is not just expending surplus energy, he is becoming a more competent runner and jumper. He is also bringing these skills under control so that he can use them without thought to play even more interesting games, rather than as accomplishments in themselves.

Building a tower of blocks or fitting the pieces into a jigsaw puzzle are not a different class of activity from holding a pencil in order to write. A child who has lacked the chance to use his hands in play has to catch up in manual dexterity before he can use them for work. The impatient parent who wants his child to stop scribbling and start writing is making a dividing line where none should exist. Scribbling is the beginning of writing and drawing; it is fun in itself and also a useful preparation for these activities.

How to Help Your Children Play

His Own Territory

If you respect your child's need to play, it follows that you try to give him good "working conditions": somewhere safe to play in comparative freedom from unnecessary interference or interruption, but with the understanding that help is on hand if required. The toddler will probably refuse to play for long alone in his room, and young children also tend to use their bedrooms only on the occasions when they want to do something alone. Preschool children want to play where the action is—probably near the kitchen or living room.

If there is a place for children to play near the kitchen or wherever you spend most of your time, it will be easier to keep them out of the room you use for your own entertaining. It depresses most adults to have every part of the house invaded by children's paraphernalia. Parents are more relaxed about mess in some rooms if they know that part of the house is tidy, or at least untidy with adult activity. Open-plan living has its advantages—you can see what your children are up to and they can see you—but perhaps you would all rather be alone some of the time. If the whole family does spend its waking hours in one open-plan area, you will need to encourage the children to play in one part of it, unless you are happy to give in and share it all while they are young.

A Little Help

You can help by giving practical aid—putting together the rails of a train set your child cannot manage himself, for example, or with suggestions for expanding or improving a game when his own ideas are running out. But don't be too eager to help. This makes a child feel incompetent and stifles his imagination, encouraging him to rely on someone else to think of his next move and to work out his problems. Too much help takes away his sense of achievement.

Your child needs reliable equipment (see toys, pp. 304f.) and suitable colleagues (see playing with friends, pp. 301f.). But although play is hard work and a serious business, you do not need a diploma in order to provide good conditions, friends, toys, and suggestions. Common sense and observation of your own child are sufficient. The more you watch him at play, the more you will understand his needs.

Don't Interrupt but Don't Go Away

Concentrated play should not be interrupted, though your presence may be making it possible for him to concentrate—so don't go away. One of the commonest mistakes is expecting a toddler or even an older child to play by himself and then to get annoyed with him or worried about him because he needs you to play with him or to watch him play. It cannot be emphasized too strongly that this is entirely normal.

You have to be old enough to be self-sufficient to play by yourself and the age at which this stage is reached varies with each child. It takes longer if the child is insecure, especially if he has had to make his demands (and anxieties) very clear in order to get his parents to understand his needs and to stay with him.

It is to be hoped that when he was a baby, you always responded to his needs without resentment. Now that he is older he still needs you, but in a different way. You can be sure he will make it very plain when he is grown up enough to play by himself—probably by telling you to go away!

Play has to be interrupted for meals and sleep but try not to make these interruptions too sudden and be prepared to compromise when your child is obviously gaining a great deal from his play. Don't make him clear up his game in order to provide space for a meal, but somehow ensure that there are separate areas for play and meals, even if this means careful placing of chairs over the toys that have been so assiduously arranged on the floor.

"Helping"

All children enjoy "helping in the house"; the child who is allowed to help you with the housework or cooking is playing and learning in a valuable way. Although your speed and efficiency decline dramatically, it is worth letting him join in, whenever practical. This is easier to manage, and less frustrating for you, if your small child spends part of his day elsewhere (see preschool schooling, p. 315). Then, when he "helps," you will be less irritated by the way he slows you up; moreover, your child is more likely to feel he is being really useful—a good feeling for anyone to have, and something every young child needs.

Understanding Your Child through His Play

It requires training in psychoanalysis to interpret the play of an emotionally disturbed child in order to use the findings to help him; but any parent can learn a great deal about his own child through

watching him play, observing his choice of games and how he plays
them. In other words, you can learn to understand your child's play,
even though you cannot interpret it in an analytical sense.

Your child's play may show you sides of his nature that are
usually dormant: open tenderness in a child who seems rather aloof,
a tough streak in an apparently meek child, the concentration of the
perfectionist in a child who "won't pay attention" at school, co-operation and obedience in a child who normally finds these difficult. The
fact that these qualities come out more in play than in his direct
dealings with people does not make them a less genuine part of his
character. It indicates that he finds it easier, at this stage, to express
them indirectly through play; he will continue to do this until conditions in his development and in his relationships at home and outside
allow him to show these aspects of himself openly.

Obviously, you should be concerned if your child always assumes
a totally different character when playing—if, for instance, he is always aggressive whereas normally he is the opposite. The kind of
contradiction needs thinking about; if you are really worried, mention
it to your family doctor.

Understanding your young child's play helps you to understand
him better. He plays all day long whether happy or unhappy. How he
plays when he is unhappy or frightened gives you a unique opportunity to know more about his feelings. By knowing that he learns all
the time he is playing and only stops when asleep, you may find
yourself more sympathetic to his noisy play in the early hours of the
morning. Play is his form of work and therefore he is opting to work
overtime!

War Games

However, aggressive play—enjoyment of mock warfare and blood-
curdling deeds—is common and normal. Boys, and girls, manage to
play at war even if never bought a toy gun; the right-shaped stick does
instead.

Fortunately, the opposing armies and characters involved usually
come from the past rather than the present; children tend to play
cowboys versus Indians rather than Russians versus Chinese, and
their games are full of energy, not hate. If you bring up your child
to recognize that war is destructive, not romantic, playing war games
will do him no harm.

Play in the Hospital

Because play can absorb stress and since, through play, a child can
be helped to understand what is going on around him, play groups
should be organized in all children's wards. They are essential if a

child's special needs in a hospital are to be met and satisfied and if the staff are to learn and understand as much as possible about their child patients. Through play, a child can be helped to understand what is happening to him and what is going to happen. For example, a child can be prepared for an operation or other hospital procedure by undertaking the same maneuver on the hospital teddy bear (see p. 412).

Day-Care Nurseries

Play organized by trained professionals in a day-care nursery (pp. 165, 317–18) benefits a child because it gives experience in co-operating with a larger circle of adults and children in a wider range of activities than is possible in the average home. This is a valuable bonus for children who possess understanding parents and good opportunities for play. But it is vital for children who live in overcrowded or extremely poor homes, and especially for those children who would otherwise spend their waking hours without good opportunities; for example, children being "minded" in a toyless back room with neither the space nor the sympathetic understanding necessary for satisfying play (see working mothers, pp. 167–68). Similarly, such facilities are essential for children living in apartment buildings with no opportunities for play. It should, in fact, be compulsory for such buildings to be provided with communal rooms for organized play.

Playing with Friends

Babies do not need other babies to play with, although they enjoy watching each other warily while playing their separate games. You do not have to provide friends deliberately, nor do you have to keep them away if they appear.

In his second year, a baby begins to appreciate other children playing nearby, although as yet he has little idea of co-operating in a game. So if you know no one of his age, it is a good idea to take him to the park and let him play near other children.

Sharing

There may be disputes about ownership of toys—do not expect a child of two or three to share out of the goodness of his heart. If he gives in and hands over a toy meekly, it is because someone else has greater physical strength or will power, or because he is tired of playing with that toy anyway. You have to stop small children from hurting each other in the struggle for possession, and certainly you ought gradually to encourage generosity and the ability to share; suggesting a temporary exchange of toys may work.

But remember how inexperienced children of this age are in human relations; they hardly know themselves yet, let alone how to deal with other people. Moreover, although your two-year-old may seem very advanced in many ways, he is incapable of consistently reasonable behavior and will remain so, to a lesser degree, for a few years yet. So do not be furious with him or worried that he will never be civilized if he refuses to part with his toys. Unless his reactions to other children's overtures are always aggressive or frightened, he is only behaving normally for his age. (See also discipline, p. 280.)

Quarrels

Give small children a chance to work out their disagreements among themselves—intervening to prevent bloodshed, of course. They tend to learn more from each other's reactions than from adult intervention. A child soon realizes that no one wants to play with him if he is continually unco-operative, and will draw the conclusion that he must compromise a bit if he wants friends. He will see the others playing and will want to be one of the group. But he has to work this out for himself; it will then be part of him, and he will not need continual adult supervision to ensure that he is getting on with his contemporaries.

Avoiding Trouble

Where adult intervention does help is in forestalling predictable trouble. For example, do not take your child's favorite toy to the park if you know someone else is likely to demand it. Your child is bound to hang on to it for dear life and the whole afternoon may be spent in disputing the point. Provide two buckets and spades if you want two children to play peacefully in the sandbox. Divert attention and suggest an alternative activity if the current one is reaching boiling point (see forestalling trouble, pp. 272f.).

On the other hand, it is unnecessary to feel you must always provide two sets of toys in order to avoid quarrels, and that you must always be on the alert for trouble. A certain amount of tension is unavoidable, and perhaps an essential part of learning through play; your child sees that he can feel angry and others can be angry with him, that you are not the only mother who gets cross, and that it is still possible for everyone to remain friends and play together again another day.

Shy Children

What if your child is reluctant to play with others? Do not try to make a small child join in. If he is timid, he needs to stay near you until he feels secure enough to leave your side. Pushing him away does not make him brave. He may be the kind of child who takes a long time to warm up socially; once he does, he may be as sociable as the others, if not more so. This is the child of whom strangers say "Isn't he shy!" because he does not smile readily, and stays by his mother at the beginning; later on he surprises them by being the life and soul of the party.

A child who continues to cling and never makes forays toward other children needs his mother to stay with him while he plays near them. He needs his confidence built up in whatever ways his family, and his family doctor, if necessary, can think up, and he needs to feel you respect his reserve.

Imaginary Friends

A child may have an imaginary friend with whom he is on extremely close terms and who seems to provide him with all the companionship he needs. There is nothing sinister in this, provided it does not go on for years. Many children possess such a friend for a while—usually another child, sometimes an animal. The friend may have extremely inconvenient habits, such as slowness in eating, so that meals are held up while he finishes.

It is all right if you get cross with the imaginary friend and demand certain standards of him in order that your child does not use him as an excuse too often. But you need not worry that your child is abnormal and incapable of making real friends. He may have plenty of these and still keep his imaginary friend, who can be manipulated to provide just what your child needs of a friend in a way that real people cannot. Your child may show considerable ingenuity, humor, and imagination in his dealings with his imaginary friend. Be pleased that he is showing these qualities, which will later be integrated into his "real" life.

Choosing Friends

Some children prefer to have one or two "best friends," others from the beginning share their favors more widely. Both are normal, but the child who relies on one friend can be upset if this friend moves away or changes schools. Luckily a child of this kind is usually quick to find himself another "best friend."

"Undesirable" Friends

At some time or other there is bound to be a friend of whom you disapprove, however broad-minded you hope you are. Disapproval may be on the more traditional grounds of social group, manners, or character, or it may be harder to define; you may think he comes into the category of "being a bad influence," or just feel he is the wrong friend for your child.

Whether your objections are logical or not, remember that friendships, like romances, find their own level more quickly if outsiders keep out. Some quality in one child appeals to the other and fulfills a need in him; perhaps the unsatisfactory friend is gaining something from the friendship. A child from a "good" home has little to lose from contact with a child from a "bad" one. Changes for the worse, such as widening his vocabulary of swear words, are generally superficial and transitory. A child who wrecks your house on every visit or who hurts other children ideally needs your help and more friendship, not less.

However, parents do not always have the energy or the good will to provide this. Your child will soon see for himself the disadvantages of this kind of friend. The general rule must still be relax and don't worry. Children need all kinds of friends, and anyway, today's bosom pal is often replaced tomorrow.

Family Friends

Apart from the friends your child collects for himself, it is good if he has others who are friends of the family, the children of family friends who are about the same age and whom a child may see only occasionally but regularly over a period of years. They may never be as close as the current best friends but nevertheless give a child a feeling of security and continuity; there will always be some birthday parties to which he is invited even if he quarrels with his gang and falls out with his schoolmates.

Children often say they do not want to see these family friends, but usually end up enjoying themselves, and get something from the relationship.

Toys

A toy is not necessarily something you buy from a toy store; a child may use as a toy anything he enjoys playing with, as every mother who has parted with her wooden spoon and best saucepan can testify. Kitchen equipment makes admirable toys for imaginative play. They help the child to learn by copying what you are doing. In the same way, play in the hospital includes the use of hospital equipment, which for the time being becomes "toys" (p. 412). The enjoyment and profit derived from a toy are in no way related to its cost, appearance, or to an adult's opinion of its educational or entertainment value.

You cannot predict with certainty whether a particular toy will please your child, how long he will continue to play with it, or in what way and when it will have served its purpose and can be safely discarded. A toy may be needed although it is no longer used because it has become a part of your child's life; its familiarity makes him feel secure and he is still fond of it. Don't scoff and throw it away.

Avoid buying expensive toys if you expect them to be played with for longer than cheaper toys and in the "right" way, thereby giving you value for the money. It is impossible to grade the suitability of toys by age groups or by sex. One child may be ready to appreciate an intricate construction set meant for an older child of the opposite sex, while another may obviously not be ready although he is in the age range specified on the box. The toy manufacturer does not know your child. His generalizations are meant for puzzled aunts who need a little help when shopping for nephews and nieces they hardly know (see toys for different ages, p. 307).

Boys' and Girls' Toys

Do not try to make your son more "masculine" or your daughter more "feminine" by selecting their toys exclusively on the basis of what you think little boys and little girls ought to like. There will be quite enough pressure in that direction from other children, who, for instance, will probably tease a boy who likes playing with dolls. Boys have always liked playing with dolls, and now the toy industry has recognized the fact and made it respectable. Manufacturers have produced a toy manikin that can be dressed up and equipped with all the latest astronaut, military, skiing, and other outfits. These masculine dolls not only help a boy to play in the way he finds most enjoyable and meaningful, but they also help those fathers who think their sons are in danger of becoming effeminate because they want to play with dolls. I have been able to unravel serious conflicts between fathers and sons with this problem by persuading the father to buy an Action Man for his son.

In the same way as it is now possible for boys and men to indulge their natural enjoyment of clothes and to grow their hair long without being thought unmasculine, it is becoming possible for both boys and girls to play in whatever way satisfies them as people rather than exclusively as males and females. You should buy toys on the basis of individual taste, not according to sex and age. If your daughter wants a fort instead of a dolls' house, let her have it.

Not Too Many

Too many toys spoil the game, if not the child. The sheer volume of toys in some households, the rapid arrival of new ones before the virtues and possibilities of the old have been explored, overwhelm a child, who may ignore them and take refuge in demanding yet more playthings. He is dissatisfied and feels that the perfect toy must be just around the corner; his parents then search desperately for this perfect toy—that is, the one that will occupy him silently for longest —hoping it exists and that if only they go on buying, they will find it. Everyone is cross and everyone is bored.

Where toys are concerned, true generosity is not the willingness to spend money or buy everything your child wants; it is willingness to spend time finding out what he would really like—not the latest heavily advertised and overpriced gimmick he is demanding, but the toy or equipment that you know from your observations and from his comments he would most enjoy, with least frustration. Buying something too complicated and then expecting your child to play alone with it for hours is a common mistake.

If your child is longing for something you cannot afford, like a bicycle or a dolls' house, it is worth asking grandparents and relatives to get together and buy this as a joint present, perhaps to cover both Christmas and birthday, instead of giving several smaller presents.

Playing in His Own Way

Once your child has opened his presents, let him play with them as he wishes; don't feel hurt if at first he prefers the box and wrapping paper to the super toy inside! Do not make him feel incompetent by standing over him while he makes a hash of his construction set or uses the toy engine to play traffic jams. You can usually see when help is really needed and when your child wants to know the most efficient way to use something, but don't be surprised if he continues to revert to his old ways of playing when he feels like it. Don't expect him to "finish" every game (see pp. 295–99).

Looking After Toys

A child who is old enough to own a piece of equipment like a bicycle or a camera is old enough to be responsible for looking after it, for putting it away after use and generally seeing that it is kept in decent condition. You are entitled to insist that your child does his share, although it may take plenty of reminders (see tidiness, pp. 282f.).

Storing Toys

Although it is a bad policy to do all your child's clearing up for him, because he never finds out for himself how inconvenient disorder can be and why tidiness is quite a sensible idea, it is worth doing some thoughtful organizing of toy storage. If you ask a small child to put away his toys, he is most unlikely to sort them out first. He will scramble them all together in the toy box, and next time he wants to play with something may abandon the thought after hunting fruitlessly for the pieces. Jigsaws and other puzzles usually come packed in flimsy cardboard boxes which quickly disintegrate; transfer them to stronger tins or plastic boxes. Cheap wastepaper baskets or old cracker cans make good containers for construction sets.

The complaint "He never plays with his toys" is heard less often if toys are easy to find and your child does not first have to hunt through a pile of oddments to find the various parts of a game. It is also easier to persuade a child to put things away in a well-organized toy cabinet. So part of the answer to helping your children to be tidy is to do the preliminary groundwork yourself.

Toys for Different Ages

The list that follows is not exhaustive, since every child breaks the rules, preferring some toys that are intended primarily for children of another age group. A toy first enjoyed at an early age may go on being used for years. But there are a few basic toys that the majority of children start to appreciate at around the same stage of development; some of these are listed below.

Improvised Toys

No one toy is essential and many can be improvised from household materials; for example, building can be done with thread spools and smoothed-down blocks of wood left over from carpentry, or a rattle made from a plastic shampoo bottle containing a few dozen pieces of macaroni or rice. The top must be securely *glued* on. Empty plastic containers and plastic mugs serve for games in the bath. A cardboard box can become a doll's crib, and doll's-house furniture is fun to make. Matchboxes stuck together can make a regal cupboard. Small children enjoy using "the real thing," for example, helping to vacuum-clean with your machine. They make no division between work and play (p. 292).

Safety

This is always important. While your baby is still putting everything in his mouth, make sure that toys are too big to swallow or choke on, are unbreakable, and, if painted, are painted with lead-free paint (see accidents, p. 625). For the same reason, keep a young baby's toys clean. Once he is crawling about the floor, perfect cleanliness will be an impossible aim, but at this age he will be more resistant to infection anyway.

Up to Six Months

Things to Watch Mobiles. Balloons, streamers, or anything that moves in air currents. Toys suspended from a carriage or crib, not too close to his face but within reach of his hands. (See p. 294.)

Toys to Hold and Bite Rattles—in various shapes and producing different sounds, some being easier for a small baby to grasp. An unbreakable rattle enclosing a ball or another shape interests the older baby. Teething ring—not strictly necessary, since fingers or rattle can be used equally well. The purpose of this ring is not to help with "teething problems," but since the age when teeth first appear coincides with an enormous interest in the mouth, it is a good idea to give a child something to bite on, whether or not the teeth have come through (see teething, pp. 248–49).

Six to Eighteen Months

Soft Toys Not too many, since their entertainment value at this age is limited; one or two companions to hold and cuddle are enough.

Baby-bouncer For exercising arms and legs enjoyably and safely (see p. 296).

Household Objects For example, wooden spoon, saucepan, and lid to bang. Thread spools. Wax paper to crackle, crumple, and tear. Basket to fill and empty with safe objects (see safety, p. 625).

Fit-together Toys Nesting boxes. Hammer and pegs.

Building and Demolition Wooden blocks.

Toys to Follow Balls and rolling rattles.

Toys to Push or Pull Baby-walker or wagon—helps in learning to walk and can be used as a wheelbarrow. Animal on wheels.

Bath Toys Plastic ducks and fish. Boats. Unbreakable mugs and pitchers for pouring.

Eighteen Months to Three Years

Fit-together Toys Picture tray. Simple jigsaw with large wooden pieces. Screw toy.

Action Toys Tractor or engine to ride on. Tricycle. Rocking horse.

Outdoor Toys Sandbox with buckets, spades. Wheelbarrow. Jungle-gym, swing, slide.

"Let-go" Toys Mailbox. Bank with very large, pretend coins.

"Playing House" Dolls, doll carriage, crib, and clothes. Doll's house. Miniature cooking utensils. Toy telephone. Toy ironing board and iron.

Drawing and Painting Thick crayons, large sheets of paper (kitchen paper in a roll is cheaper). Water colors or poster paints, big brushes. Easel. Blackboard.

Three to Five Years

Construction Sets With large pieces, firm plastic or wood.

"Playing House" As for younger age group.

Drawing and Painting As for younger age group.

Small Cars, Soldiers, Animals To be used alone or with layouts made with building bricks; or with garage, fort, or farm sets.

Cutting-out and Pasting Equipment Round-ended scissors, post-cards, old magazines, and scrapbook.

First Games Dominoes. Playing cards for "Go fish."

Outdoor Toys Tricycle.

Five to Eight Years

Construction Sets Smaller pieces can now be managed.

Modeling Kits Plastic pieces to be glued together and painted.

Carpentry Sets Tools can be bought separately and put into a carpenter's bag, to suit the individual child.

Games Board games. Card games.

Puppets Glove puppets first, later string.

Outdoor Toys Larger tricycle. Bicycle. Roller skates. Gardening tools.

Eight Years Upward

Realistic Equipment For example, scientific and chemistry sets. Handcraft sets such as loom for weaving; raffia or basketwork sets. Sewing things.

Games Monopoly, chess, checkers.

Theatricals Toy theater. Conjuring and magic sets. Disguise set.

Pets for Children

Should You Buy Your Child a Pet?

To help you answer this question I am going to suggest some of the ways in which your child can gain by owning and caring for a pet. I do not intend to help you to decide which pet to choose, since this is a personal matter, involving your feelings and your husband's about animals, as well as what is practical for your household. The pet chosen should suit the whole family and in a sense belong to the whole family, although one child may be the official "owner."

Learning the Facts of Life

Children brought up in the country, especially if they live on a farm, are usually more knowledgeable about the facts of life—mating, birth, and death—than those who live in town, where they may have nothing to do with animals. Observing and learning what happens to animals in life and death provide a matter-of-fact way of understanding the same processes in human beings. Questions are asked without embarrassment, and it should be an easy matter for parents whose work involves the care of animals to explain the facts of life to their children. Half their work has already been done for them as the children watch normal animal activity on a farm. Of course, this built-in biology lesson does not take care of all aspects of the facts of life. Mating animals do not give a child a picture of human love, and he needs to understand that only the mechanism of reproduction is similar in people and animals (see sex education, pp. 330f.).

Caring for a pet can provide some of the information that comes naturally to the child living on a farm. Clearly, not all pets will provide the opportunity to watch the process of mating and birth, but all give some understanding of life and death. Most fish reproduce by external fertilization, but the child will still be able to see how babies develop from eggs. Some tropical fish in home tanks can be watched in love-play during the mating processes. Internal fertilization occurs in some fish (live bearers); if one of these varieties, such as the guppy, is kept, a child can watch the young growing larger inside the mother.

Other Advantages

Apart from this gain in a child's factual knowledge from keeping a pet, he is also given something on which he can lavish all his natural caring instincts. Time and effort spent on feeding a puppy or kitten are worth hours of explanation about his own behavior at mealtimes and why you care so much that he eats up the food you have provided for him. The fact that you can accept a messy puppy or kitten may also help you to be more sympathetic toward your messy child. In the process, your child may understand and appreciate your efforts to clean up after him.

The puppy or kitten will make it clear to a child when it dislikes having its tail pulled. A nip from the puppy or a scratch from the kitten can be a salutary reminder to a child of the need to accept the wishes of the individual, and of what can happen when feelings or bodies are hurt. From such experiences your child can learn to understand problems involving feelings, which he cannot easily grasp when you try to explain them to him. A young child is busy trying to learn to control his own feelings. To help him to do this he needs to control someone or something. A pet can help him in this process, and can provide opportunities for him to realize that no one likes to be controlled all the time although some control is essential.

A child needs to love as well as to be loved. This should be provided by human relationships, but it is a valuable addition if he can also lavish his feelings on his pet. His feelings will not always be admirable—he will feel annoyance, even hate, for his pet, then love again. But this too is normal. An animal provides an outlet for emotions and tensions. When no one seems to understand you, you can rely on your dog, cat, or even your tadpole to remain loyal.

Losing a Pet

The death of a pet is likely to be your child's first experience of bereavement. Give him the opportunity to grieve, since this is an essential human need following the loss of someone loved. It is part of the natural recovery process following the shock and distress of bereavement. He may suggest holding a funeral and in any case is likely to be helped by holding one (see child's attitude to death, pp. 342–46). Do not make the mistake of immediately rushing out to the pet shop for a replacement to help him forget. If you do this, you may plant the thought that anything lost can be replaced; this does not help a child to accept the hard facts of life and death. Moreover, while your child is mourning his pet he may be unable to accept an immediate "replacement." Should he ask for another pet at once, it is probably what he needs, but be careful that in your haste you do not buy an unsuitable animal.

Nothing can replace a dead loved one, be this a human being or a pet. The new pet is loved for himself, while the dead pet still has his place in the family.

More Work for You

A pet is bound to mean more work for parents, but the gain in enjoyment and experience is well worth the extra effort. Before you go out and buy the pet you must have accepted that you will have to do a lot of the work involved, even though your child has promised to do it all. His promise means indeed that he wants to, but accept the limitations of his age, and when some other activity makes him forget his pet's mealtime, do not always call him back to his duty, but be prepared to do it for him.

Your child cannot be expected to learn all the responsibilities of a mother as soon as he has a pet, and even if he never takes full responsibility, do not make it an issue between you. Remember always that the pet is providing a superb learning experience, whatever the drawbacks for you. The ultimate responsibility for the pet's survival and well-being must remain with you. A young child cannot judge when an animal has played long enough, whether its diet is suitable, or how often its cage needs cleaning. This is your responsibility. Do not give your child an unnecessary lesson in failure associated with recriminations on both sides that neither of you looked after the pet properly.

It is not only in the home that pets have a valuable role. School and hospital can be made more homey by the presence of pets, particularly warm-blooded ones, rather than just fish. For a school, rabbits and hamsters are more suitable than dogs and cats. In my hospital wards we have had guinea pigs for a long time. The question of the risk of infection is always raised by visitors to the ward, but this is greatly exaggerated.

Even if your home is too small or circumstances unsuitable for most pets, your child can keep tadpoles in a jar; even a caterpillar provides a temporary companion.

Diseases Caused by Pets

These are important, but I feel the risks to a child and his family have been overemphasized. The diseases can be treated and you should certainly not be dissuaded from buying a pet on the grounds of the possible risk to your child's health.

The major problems are skin diseases caused by fleas and mites, particularly from dogs and cats. Some of these give rise to a direct infection of human skin, but more often the skin rash is due to an allergic reaction through hypersensitivity of the individual person to contact with the flea (see papular urticaria, p. 510). Such a rash may be due to handling the neighbor's pet. Ringworm can be caught from a dog or cat, though some varieties are confined to humans and, therefore, can only be caught from another person.

These skin diseases are easily treated if only the correct diagnosis is made. Similarly, the fleas can easily be eradicated from the pet, although reinfestation can cause difficulties. Part of the problem lies in the reaction of people to the idea of fleas, which are associated in their minds with dirt and filth and are therefore thought of as a slur on the way the parents are caring for their children. Don't, therefore, have hurt feelings if your doctor asks about your pets and the possibility of fleas.

Worms can be passed from dogs to children, but although most puppies have worms, this does not happen very frequently. In any case, the worms are relatively harmless and can easily be treated with the medicines now available (see worms, pp. 490f.).

Of course, there is the risk of bites from pets, and you must warn your child about this—tell him not to put his face too near. For the treatment of animal bites, see p. 644. Beware of the possible jealousy felt toward a new baby by a dog who shared your house alone with you and your husband prior to the baby's arrival. Some jealous dogs have made dangerous attacks on babies.

Serious Diseases Really serious diseases like rabies, which is caught from being bitten by a rabid animal, are kept out of some countries, including the United Kingdom, by quarantine laws. The United States's extensive wildlife makes elimination of the disease impossible. Therefore it is essential that dogs, cats, raccoons, all mammal pets, be immunized properly and that anyone suffering a bite from a strange animal report the bite to the police and to the doctor. Psittacosis is controlled by reputable bird pet stores by treated bird food and by elimination of infected flocks of birds, such as pigeons. I would strongly advise you to pay the extra cost and to patronize pet shops that provide only safe pets. People should avoid strange animals, their bites and sneezes, their dust, hairs, and feathers, and people should wash thoroughly if they have fondled such animals.

Becoming Sociable and Starting School

Preschool Schooling

So much is heard nowadays about the importance of the preschool years in the development of a child's intelligence and intellectual potential that some parents feel guilty if their child spends these years at home with his mother and receives no kind of part-time "education." If other children are already past the starting point of the rat race, will their child be left hopelessly behind and his IQ be lower than it might have been had he been given preschool prodding? In other words, should any expense or effort be spared to ensure that your child receives the best available expert help for a couple of years before he starts school?

Fostering Intelligence

It is true that the preschool years are vitally important in influencing the intellectual growth and curiosity of a child, and that by the age of five the measure of his intelligence gives a rough estimate of his future performance. But ordinary family life, the encouragement and interest of loving parents, learning through playing, alone and with others, going out, staying in—all provide the raw material upon which intelligence feeds and sharpens itself.

Programs of help devised for babies and small children from impoverished homes are based on professional observations of the real experts—mothers. There is no laboratory-tested secret that they know and you don't. The crash course in normal living provided for these deprived children is a substitute for normal parental encouragement and attention, not an improvement on it.

More fortunate children receive this "head start" at home without their parents having so much as read a newspaper article on the subject of child development. Babies have an inbuilt zest for learning that is hard to stifle; normal parents encourage and stimulate it merely through responding with pleasure to their infants' progress. Learning about life provides sufficient material for mental growth for a great deal longer than the five preschool years. Learning to read or write early is no advantage if it takes up time and energy your child would prefer to spend on other activities; an early start is no guarantee that he will stay ahead at school.

Is Regular Companionship Essential?

It is not essential for a preschool child to attend a play group or nursery school in order to learn to become sociable and to get on with other people. Children brought up on isolated farms, even those living in the middle of the Australian outback and receiving their schooling over the radio, do not grow up incapable of friendship or normal human relations.

Children enjoy playing with or near other children to a greater or lesser extent at different ages and stages; it is ideal if there are other children living nearby to provide regular companionship from the age of two or three years or earlier. However, if there are no other children and no play group or day-care nursery, it is not a disaster for your child, though it can be very tedious for you.

Mothers Need Time Off Too

However much you enjoy your child's company you need some time alone or with other adults. Today there are usually only two adults in each separate household, one of whom, the husband, is out at work all day. Members of the wider family circle—grandparents, aunts, brothers and sisters—are seldom near enough in distance or intimacy to provide daily informal contact and adult companionship for a mother and alternative mothering for her child.

A small child at home all day with his mother is under her feet and no one else's. In this situation it is only too easy for you to become overwrought by the difficulties of keeping house with a constant companion in tow. Far from being allowed to "help" with the housework or cooking, your child is liable to be put off with promises of "next time," or yelled at to go away and play in the next room. If this happens constantly, it is better for both of you to spend some of the day apart.

Therefore, one of the reasons for organizing some kind of preschool social life for your child is to give you a change or a rest. It is a perfectly good reason, needing no justification on the grounds that it is essential for his development; although it does, incidentally, help you to enjoy him better when he is at home and so to provide him with a more stimulating atmosphere. You will enjoy your constantly chattering, constantly moving three- or four-year-old much better when he has been chattering and moving somewhere else for a while.

Play Groups and Nursery Schools

Helping Him Start

The aim of these preschool groups is to widen your child's learning experiences. He should go only when he feels secure enough to leave your skirts, but not before he is about 2½ years old. Even then he may want you to stay with him in the early days to give him confidence. Later on, it will still be a good idea for you to stay for short periods, so that you can learn about his play from his teacher or play-group leader. In a group of this sort he will begin to learn the rudiments of social life; learning to play with other children is an important step.

Organizing a Play Group

If you cannot afford or find a play group or nursery school, discover, by advertising, if desperate, another mother or mothers with children of similar ages and in a similar situation; they will soon admit that they would also like a break sometimes. One of you can look after the children while the others have some free time, or at least can get the housework done in peace. If there are several of you, each can have several breaks per week. It is more fun to spend one morning a week amusing several children than to spend every morning trailing around the stores and the house with one bored child. Some mothers, who enjoy it, end up running their own play-group or helping in one. There are now courses as well as books on the subject. If you become interested in running a play group, your local Public Health Service can give you the names of organizations willing to assist.

Choosing a Play Group

Even if you are lucky enough to have a choice of play groups and nursery schools, it may be necessary to put your child's name down well in advance; so although it seems a far-off day indeed when your first baby will be out of his cradle and off to start his social life, in some areas two or three years ahead is not too early to sign up for a place.

How do you choose? Play groups are generally run by mothers; some are ex-teachers and some are just experienced mothers who have taken a relevant course and done their homework on the subject of caring constructively for several children for a few hours a day. The best play groups model themselves on the best type of nursery school.

Play groups function in rented quarters or private houses and vary in size and scope. A shy child might be happier in a small group of eight or ten children run by a motherly person in her own living room; a boisterous child might enjoy himself more in a larger group run by several staff members with many other noisy children and space for large equipment and letting off steam. On the other hand, you might decide that your shy child needs the more outgoing atmosphere of the larger play group and your boisterous boy needs calming down by the motherly lady. Either child would get something out of either group.

The kind of group to avoid is the one you suspect is being run only to make money, where the aim seems to be to keep the children quiet and occupied at all costs, whether they like it or not. The best way of finding out about the local groups or nursery schools is to talk to mothers whose children attend them, although their requirements may not be the same as yours; and you can learn a lot from other children's descriptions of their activities in a play group.

Play groups are usually held for two or three hours in the morning. It is usually possible to send your child for fewer than five mornings a week, and this is a good idea until he gets used to going. Some children enjoy it so much they want to go every day from the start.

Choosing a Nursery School

Nursery schools are staffed by qualified teachers and are run privately or by the community. They accept children from just under three until the age of five, but most of the children are three or four years old. The schools are usually open from 9:00 A.M. to 3:30 P.M., and have normal school holidays. Many of the children attend mornings only or afternoons only.

Sadly, there are still far too few nursery schools, and it will be a great day when there is a nursery-school place available for every child who is ready to leave his mother's skirts. It must be emphasized that nursery schools exist to meet the needs of the children and do not cater for working mothers.

Because they are called "schools" do not expect your child to start learning to read and write. This is not what nursery education is about, although in some schools the older children are encouraged to take the first steps in this direction if they show interest. Talking to other children helps to widen a child's vocabulary and increases his power of expressing himself clearly; this is the best foundation for learning to read later. As in a play group, the emphasis is on play, with as much stimulus to the child's imagination as possible.

Creative Play

Children in a play group or nursery school can make a "mess" with clay, paints, dough, sand and water, and with finger painting, without interruptions from a mother who is understandably anxious about her carpets and the amount of clearing up that creative play involves. For a child from a home where disorder and untidiness are positively disallowed, this kind of play in nursery school is doubly important. At home this child is never allowed to experiment with materials; he always has an anxious adult hovering over his activities, ready to stop anything interesting at the beginning or to stop it just as it is becoming most gripping from his point of view. He may be so discouraged that he gives up his experiments and resigns himself to interruptions; in this way, he gradually becomes less capable of finishing and rounding these off in a satisfactory way. When he starts school, his parents wonder why he "can't concentrate"! (See play, p. 299.)

Sharing Discipline

Another benefit of preschool school is the experiences a child gains through spending time with a group of children who are not brothers or sisters, under the supervision of an adult who is not one of his parents. He notices that he is not the only child in the world who hears the word "no." He learns that most disagreeable demands made by his parents are not just personal crosses he has to bear—apparently other children bear them too. This makes discipline easier to take and helps him to separate dislike of obeying orders from feeling furious with the person who gives the orders, previously nearly always his parents.

Not many orders are given in nursery schools, but children must be prevented from hurting themselves and from deliberately damaging property. It is obvious to adults that fire can burn and knives can cut, but a child needs to learn these facts through observing that the rules of life apply to everyone; he begins to understand they are not devised to punish him alone for real or imagined wickedness.

Learning to Play Together

Playing alongside and with other children increases the scope of play and helps a child to learn how to get along with others. This is essential because he wants to be liked and approved of; to an increasing degree, as he grows older, the approval of his contemporaries is important to him.

No matter how many times you yourself tell your child he ought to share his toys and not snatch other children's, he may persist in doing so. A few rebuffs from other children bring it home to him far faster. He will gradually learn to curb his first impulses if these prove unpopular, to tone down his bossiness or come out of his shell a little, whatever is needed to make him feel one of the boys. It takes some time, but the year or two before starting school is a good time to start learning.

Will He Lose His Individuality?

It may seem a little sad to see your individualist suppressing part of his individuality in the cause of popularity—but it is an entirely natural and inevitable step for anyone who wants to be reasonably happy in the world. He is adapting rather than repressing himself.

A nursery-school teacher keeps an eye on the relationships between the children; she steps in quietly where necessary, preventing anyone from becoming crushed, and giving gentle pushes in the right directions. Her intention is not to iron out the differences between the children, to make each conform to her idea of a "nice child," but to protect their right to be different from one another and to act as a neutral referee in disputes. The child learns that the adult in authority is to be trusted and is essentially fair; so when he meets his first teacher at school he feels the same way about her.

Going to School

Preparing Your Child for School

If your child has become accustomed to spending part of his day away from home, he will be less likely to feel unhappy and upset during his first days at primary or elementary school, especially if his nursery school was part of his primary school. The groundwork will have been done already—he is used to other children, to your absence, to sharing the attention of the adult in charge with several others.

However, not every nursery-school child settles into primary school without tears. The most confident and independent five-year-old may surprise everyone with his terror at being left at the school door, while another, apparently shyer, child strides in without a backward glance. The opportunity to visit his future class beforehand, perhaps spending an hour or two there, with or without his mother, benefits any child about to start school. At least show your child the school from the outside. Tell him about school routines, meals, recess, anything to familiarize him gently with the idea in advance. And make sure he is capable of dealing with his clothing (see development, p. 233) and going to the bathroom alone. Give him practice in this by going to public bathrooms once or twice before school starts (see toilet training, p. 245). To help him put his shoes on the correct feet, put an arrow inside each pointing inward so that he can tell the left from the right.

An ordinary playground is a good place for your child to learn to mix with others and it will prepare him for coping with the school playground, especially if you have been able to stay in the background while he plays. Playing "school" at home also helps, particularly if you have one or two of his friends to play as well. Try calling the roll, because many children are bashful about answering to their names in public on the first occasion.

Prepare him for the journey by doing it with him once or twice before school starts. If school is not within walking distance, at least accompany him to where he will board school transportation.

Make contact beforehand with the mother of another child starting at the same school on the same day. If the children have already become friends before school starts, they can give each other a great deal of mutual support. To get the names of children starting on the same day, you could speak to the school secretary.

The First Day at School

A child who is not used to being away from his mother is likely to fuss at being left on his first day at a primary school. The most secure and independent child may protest and feel overwhelmed by the sheer number of other children, the noise and the movement they create, and by the alien atmosphere, the very smell of school.

The way you handle the journey and your manner of parting from your child can help enormously in the adjustment he has to make when going to school for the first time. If your husband can take him, parting with you at your front door is easier for him than watching you walk away from school. Having the company of another child also helps him to be brave, and this may be the beginning of shared journeys between you and the other child's mother, so that each of you has to take the children to school only half the number of times.

A sympathetic teacher makes all the difference; if you can literally transfer your child's hand from your palm to hers, all may be well. Such a teacher is likely to have the wisdom to show an apprehensive child the telephone—a link for messages or conversation with his mother if he is unwell, or unhappy. It is a good idea if he takes something with him to school, whether it is some flowers for the teacher or the nature table, or a toy to show off. Try not to let him take his favorite cuddly toy, which he will suck all day, unless this is his only route to comfort and security.

Most small children who scream when arriving for their first day at primary school stop once their mothers have left; after a few days, they come in happily and that is the end of the problem. Others go on screaming at the door for half a year or more but seem perfectly happy once it is shut behind their parent. Some of these children probably go on giving a token scream, almost as if it were expected of them, long after they feel quite happy to be left. Mothers and teachers have to sort out this group from those children who really are unhappy. A child who settles down happily at first may later react and protest, seeming afraid or reluctant to go to school, even to the point of vomiting or looking pale.

Consulting His Teacher

It is impossible to give advice that applies to every problem. The opinion and advice of your child's teacher are obviously important. If she judges that he is basically all right and that the best thing to do is to leave him in her charge, while you depart in a determined way —then leave her to it. If, despite her opinion, you know he is miserable and worried at home too because he dreads leaving you, then it is best to discuss it more fully, with the principal as well. It should be possible for you to stay with him in the classroom for a period. The novelty of having his mother around may soon wear off, and he will want to be left like everyone else once he is confident that you can stay if necessary. Many schools encourage mothers to stay for a time during the first days at primary school, and this is a good idea.

Your child must know who is going to meet him after school. In the early days it should be you and not another mother. Don't be late for him. Once he gets home, allow him to amuse himself as he will, rather than planning afternoon activities; these should come later.

School Lunches

If possible, it is a good idea for your child to stay for lunch; it helps him to adjust to another form of social activity. It is good for him to have someone other than you supervising his behavior at meals.

Helping Him Make Friends

Enjoying, or at least tolerating, school, often depends on what is happening to your child on the playground, rather than in the classroom. Finding a friend may make all the difference to a child who previously disliked going to school. You may be able to hasten the day by asking likely looking children to play at home, and by accepting your child's friends even if they are not ideal from your point of view (see discipline at school, p. 281; choosing friends, p. 303).

If, despite all your attempts, your child remains unpopular and without friends at school, talk over the problem with his teacher. She is probably very clear as to which part of his character is disliked by the other children and should be able to advise you. Children are very discerning, and if your child still cannot make friends, it sounds as though you should have a talk with your doctor. This is a serious problem, and if it continues despite all your attempts to correct it, your doctor may consider referring you to a children's specialist.

Persisting Fear of School

The child who is really frightened of school, especially one who has previously enjoyed going, should not be forced to go to school. School phobia is serious and needs treatment by a doctor.

22

Stories, Nursery Rhymes, and Television

Stories and Nursery Rhymes

When to Begin

Don't wait until your child can talk or until he can understand long words before you begin telling him stories and singing him songs. He may not understand all he hears but he will understand that you are communicating with him. This is why parents have always talked to their babies and sung to them much earlier than seems "sensible."

Rhymes and songs are enjoyed by the youngest babies; rhythm, whether in the form of rocking in a mother's arms or hearing her sing a lullaby, is a comforting sensation. When your baby wakes up you can rock and sing him back to sleep. The lullaby restores the rhythm that was broken, while the action of singing and rocking will relax you as well, so that your own contentment is transmitted to your baby. When you feel the need to sing and talk to your baby don't stop yourself for fear of seeming ridiculous.

As your baby grows, he will respond more actively to nursery rhymes and to the bouncing and clapping games that go with them. You will find that he joins in, in his own way, trying to make his own version, and is obviously proud of expressing himself in a new direction. He will enjoy your performance in a most flattering way! Parenthood offers us the rare chance of being a perfectly adored performer with, after a while, complete audience participation. This is one performance where the quality of the artist does not matter a bit, and where the same old show is demanded again and again.

Nursery rhymes do not date because, however they originated, the actual situations described are simple and dramatic and easy for children to identify with. Even before the words mean anything, the sense of rhythm and drama comes across. Some of today's pop songs and TV jingles have a similar effect, although whether many will remain permanent parts of the parent's repertory is doubtful.

Choosing the Right Story

You may notice your baby listening intently to a story told to an older child. Babies as young as twelve months benefit from hearing stories because the sounds help to develop their sense of language (see language development, p. 237).

There is no need to try to match exactly the level of the story and the level of your child's language and intelligence. A child will absorb what he can understand and what he needs from whatever he hears. You can see if he is bored, but you may be surprised when your five-year-old appears to devour every word of the story meant for his eight-year-old brother with more relish than the story you thought suitable for a child of his age. Vary the level of the material you offer so that your children gain from the level that suits them. If a child demands the same story over and over again, he needs something from that story, and however boring it is for you, it is worth giving him what he needs.

Fairy Tales

Fairy tales, especially, have this effect, as though the child were refining what he hears until his emotional needs have been fulfilled by a particular tale. The form of concentration devoted to a storyteller is quite different from the concentration given to most television programs, which is often a listless and rather uncontrolled surrender to whatever is offered rather than the conscious and active participation in a well-loved story.

Apparently horrifying and frightening fairy tales may seem to reassure rather than to frighten a child, perhaps by giving him something to be afraid of outside himself and his own small world. Exactly why children enjoy scary stories, just as many adults enjoy being frightened to death in the movies, is complicated, but there is no evidence that a child who likes a bloodthirsty tale is bloodthirsty himself or is being encouraged to become so. However, if your child plainly dislikes or is made anxious by a certain type of story, or has nightmares after a gory tale last thing at night, accept the fact and do not try to toughen him up by continuing to tell stories of this kind.

Reading to an Older Child

When your children can read, they will still enjoy being read to or listening to stories you have made up. This does not make them "lazy" about their own reading; rather, it reinforces their pleasure in books. A bedtime story remains a treat long after the age when it has ceased to be part of the bedtime routine. It also gives you the chance to choose the book and introduce something that is new to them while probably having nostalgic associations for you.

The most competent readers need to go back to more childish reading matter sometimes, and most children enjoy comics although they may also like a "good book." Let them relax with a comic book without making them feel guilty. If you give the impression that reading should be reserved for worthy literature, you make it a duty rather than a pleasure.

Reading versus Television

Don't be surprised if your children read less than you did at their age. You probably read to relax, whereas they watch television instead, but not every book is worth more than every television program. It is a pity if your child fails to discover the pleasures of reading because he is always watching television instead, since in reading he can go at his own pace in a way that is impossible with television. However, provided he is given an opportunity to read and is brought up in a family where books are obviously enjoyed, he will discover these pleasures for himself, sooner or later.

It is important not to confuse "interesting" a child in reading with "teaching" him to read. This should be left to his teacher, since it is a highly skilled craft requiring training and experience. Do not use the same book at home as he reads at school, since this can lead to confusion, duplication, and boredom. The important point is to help your child look on reading as an activity with a purpose, so that it is established as a thinking process and not as an exercise in identifying shapes and letters.

A Sense of Proportion

It is a mistake to overvalue reading as an activity. The child who reads a lot is not necessarily more intelligent than the child who would rather be making or doing something. How many adults wish they could still enjoy the artistic and physical skills that seem to fall into abeyance once reading is mastered? Your child will probably spend a great deal of his adult life with his nose buried in a newspaper or a book, consulting other people's opinions and imbibing their ideas—let him continue to form his own for as long as possible.

The perpetual bookworm can be as much of a problem as the television addict: both should be encouraged to vary their activities. A child who seems to be using reading as an escape from unpleasant reality is not reading for pleasure, or for instruction, but because he needs to forget his problems.

Television

Most children like watching television. Sooner or later most parents find themselves taking advantage of this: switch it on and you know where the children are and approximately what they are doing. At certain times of the day when their favorite programs are on you can be guaranteed a child-free period. It is not surprising that television has been called the modern equivalent of the baby-sitter.

Should you feel guilty if you take advantage of your child's willingness to watch television and switch off from him for a while? Obviously not, although parents should not hand over total responsibility for amusing their child. You should keep an eye on the influence your stand-in is having, and intervene firmly if you think the influence is becoming undesirable or unbalanced.

The Need for Stories, Outings, and Friends

It is a mistake to think that television can replace your child's need for stories and nursery rhymes shared with his family (see stories, pp. 323–25). Even the most skilled presenters on children's programs cannot do more than give an illusion of personal intimacy with your child. They cannot judge his individual reactions and tailor-make the material to suit his needs. Your child cannot ask them to repeat the same story nightly for a week.

Although television can widen his world, it can also shrink it. If your child is never taken to the "real thing" because it is "so much better on television—you can see everything," he misses the excitement of events that would remain as highlights of childhood when hours and hours of television viewing have become a blur. Do you remember the fifty football games you saw on television as clearly as the one you saw "live"?

When friends come to play and spend the whole of their visit watching television none of them will remember the afternoon, although it may have been more peaceful for you; but if you limit the viewing to their favorite program and then start them off on some other activity, they will probably enjoy themselves more, despite automatic protests when the set is switched off.

The Compulsive Viewer

However, children sometimes have a way of ignoring the television set and playing happily while it is on, only to stop playing instantly and turn their attention to the screen the minute you threaten to switch it off. Some of the most avid addicts, in terms of insisting on keeping the set on, are the least concerned with what is being shown. It seems to be merely a reassuring noise in the background, particularly needed if mother is out of the room. If it does not annoy you, this probably does no harm beyond encouraging a need for incessant background music in later life.

Children who remain glued to the television set are often bored stiff and in a stupor; their watching is a form of compulsion and may be a reaction to parental nagging about prolonged viewing. Provided you do not force your child to stop watching, thereby becoming involved in a battle, he may quite quickly become bored by boring programs. His length of viewing would then be determined by his interest, and to be interested is good for him. For this reason I am not worried by children staying up late to watch television, since if they are interested, they are learning. Obviously, a compromise must be reached—they should not stay up so late that they are too tired to get up in the morning (see sleep, p. 126).

Reducing Viewing Time

If you want your children to watch less television, you have to suggest alternative activities and must be prepared to spend more time with or near them. Enlist their co-operation by explaining why you do not want the set on from the moment they get home from school till bedtime—because of homework, the noise it makes, their health, eyesight, or whatever your reasons may be. Then let each child choose which programs he wants to watch, provided these are at a time that suits the rest of the family and if you feel they are suitable. An older child enjoys going through the list of programs and marking the ones he really wants to see.

Actually, as far as eyesight is concerned, there is no evidence that prolonged television viewing has any harmful effect on the eyes; it does not cause "eye strain."

Acting as Censor

Trivialities

Which programs are suitable? It depends what is meant by suitable. Much of television is merely trivial. A diet of unadulterated trivialities is unsuitable in the sense of being unrewarding for a child who receives little other stimulus, such as the child parked with a baby-sitter who leaves him sitting in front of a television set all day instead of playing with him, taking him out, or letting him join in her activities (see working mothers, pp. 166–67).

But the child who spends most of his time in the real world and who receives plenty of impressions apart from the flickering images of a television set takes what he wants from the trivialities—it may be only relaxation, and mild enjoyment, but anyway it is an insignificant source of stimulation in his life. He gets the real meat elsewhere, from his relations with other people, from the things he sees and the stories he hears. The child who is busy and happy can safely be allowed his share of trivialities.

Violence

If you ban violence altogether from your child's viewing, you ban much of children's television as well as many adult programs. Fairy stories contain horrors of all varieties. Cartoons are among the most violent of programs, and since they may feature monsters and characters totally unrelated to reality, it is difficult for children to feel sympathy or compassion for the pain and suffering depicted. News and documentaries contain terrifying scenes of individual and crowd violence, and it is not even possible to tell your child truthfully that this is all "made up." You have to admit that life is sometimes ugly.

While it is wise to ban programs known in advance to have a sadistic content, and they usually come on late enough in the evening to prevent children from watching them, it is impossible to stop your children from seeing violence on the screen. What you can do is to explain that violence is frequently used as an ingredient of television productions to increase the sense of drama, and that the blows, shots, and punches that seem to be passed off so easily on television result, in real life, in blood, pain, and often death.

Fortunately, most children seem to appreciate the difference between the world of television and the world in which they live. The carnage of a real road accident makes a deeper impression than a thousand crashes on the screen. A child knows that it hurts when you punch someone because it has happened to him, although he may suspect this is because he is so small, believing that when he grows up he will be magically endowed with limitless strength both to give and to withstand violence, particularly if he identifies himself with the "good guys," who always win—on television.

Watching with Your Child

If you watch with your child sometimes, which you should do, you can take the opportunity of straightening out any false impressions he seems to be accumulating. You will notice when he is getting frightened and can reassure him or switch off. The things that frighten him most may not be the obviously alarming scenes. It may be that he identifies strongly with a character suffering some apparently mild humiliation, or something may strike a half-forgotten chord of fear in him. Anyway, do not dismiss his fear; try to understand and accept it.

Watching television with your child can increase its learning value to him by giving you the opportunity to talk about the meaning of some of the things he sees. Some children's programs actively involve the co-operation of parents—I only wish more did.

Switching the Set Off

Should you leap up and switch the set off if a disturbing, violent, or sexual scene suddenly appears on the screen? Will switching off just increase the children's curiosity when they might otherwise hardly have noticed what was happening, or will it save them from being warped for life?

If your instinct is to leap up and switch off, this is what you should do, since your action reflects your whole attitude to the subject that is disturbing you. Children do not discover their parents' attitudes toward sex, violence, and everything else through isolated actions but through their total approach to life. You will know when it is right to protect an individual child from a particular incident. This is why it is important for parents to have some knowledge of what their children watch, and to use their understanding of each child to judge how much television is good for them and what may be positively harmful.

A Necessity or a Menace?

Finally, if you do not have a set at all, is your child missing something? Or, alternatively, will this give him a head start over his televiewing contemporaries? He may sometimes feel he is missing something, particularly when he has been watching someone else's set and has become attached to a particular program. But if he has never become an addict he won't miss it, and if he has plenty of scope to make his own amusements, he will probably learn to spend his time more profitably than the child who knows he can slump in front of the television until bedtime.

However, you cannot assume that simply not having television will turn your child into an avid reader or make him more conscientious about doing his homework. Don't make television the scapegoat for a child's lack of interest in other activities or for his lack of progress at school. If he wants to do nothing but watch TV, something else is to blame, not the TV set.

23

Talking to Your Child

Sex Education

Sex education has become such a widely discussed and almost technical topic that some parents now doubt their ability to explain the facts of life to their children. But sex education is only one aspect of your child's need to learn to understand everything that goes on around him. The fact that some of his questions may embarrass you is part of the problem. This is because the subject involves your most intimate feelings and those of the people nearest to you. It is all the more difficult because it is colored by your experiences as a child. Because of the greater difficulties experienced by the previous generation in discussing the subject, your childhood introduction to talking about sex is likely to have been imperfect. Added to this is your awareness of the necessity for being truthful and accurate, since incorrect information, or questions only half answered, can lead to serious problems for your child.

Provided your child feels free to talk to you about anything, you will not have to plan your talks on sex beforehand. If you have always answered his questions in a truthful and unembarrassed way it will not occur to him that his questions about sex are different from anything else he has asked you.

Answering His First Questions

Your child is bound to want to know where babies come from and he can be expected to ask this question when he is three or four years old. Keep your answer as simple as possible and do not imagine that at this stage you should be talking about sexual intercourse. All he needs to know is that babies grow in their mothers' tummies. You can point out a pregnant woman in the street to illustrate the point. After this he will want to know how babies get out, not how they got in. If you had your head stuck down a rabbit hole, would you be asking how you got in?

Don't ever put off the opportunity to talk about sex on the grounds that your child is "too young to understand." If he is old enough to ask a question on any subject, he is old enough to be answered; but make sure you answer in language he understands.

At a later stage, which may be years later, he will want to know how the baby came to be in the mother's tummy and you can explain that his father put a seed there. The first time your child asks this question he may be satisfied if you simply tell him that his father gave you the seed: later he will wish to know how. If each question is answered simply and directly he will be getting the information he is seeking. The usual mistake is for a parent to give far more information than the child can understand, because he or she feels that here is an opportunity for a sex lecture. This can confuse the child, though fortunately most children ignore information they are not ready for. Perhaps one of the reasons a parent embarks on a sex lecture is embarrassment, which produces a desire to tell all so as to get everything over as quickly as possible.

It cannot be too strongly emphasized that the answers to your child's questions should be direct and simple. Pitch your answers on the same level as his questions. This is an important subject, but there is no need to invest every answer with a solemnity and significance out of proportion to the actual content of the question.

Because you have been waiting and conscientiously preparing for your child's first question on "the facts of life," you may make the mistake of launching into a lengthy explanation for which he is quite unready. Halfway through your lecture you will be puzzled to notice that his attention has wandered to some more absorbing topic, such as the whereabouts of his teddy bear. You must listen to his question and just tell him what he wants to know. Don't answer supplementary questions unless he puts them to you.

When a Child Doesn't Ask Questions

An apparent lack of curiosity may be due to a child's sensing that the subject is taboo as a topic of conversation in his family. His tentative opening questions may have been stamped on because his parents were embarrassed and did not wish to admit to themselves what he was asking, or because they thought he was too young to know the answers. Should this happen, he will turn to some other source of information—probably a school friend, whose answers are likely to be dramatic and inaccurate.

If a child is discouraged from talking about certain subjects when he is young enough not to be inhibited, he will not become more open about them later. Take advantage of your child's willingness to consult you about everything, so that you and your husband remain the people to whom he feels he can say anything.

Sometimes a child's innate sense of the importance of these questions makes him more persistent in seeking the answers, although more often it will have the opposite effect, of silencing him. If you, as parents, then heave a sigh of relief and put off until adolescence your comprehensive lecture on the subject, which you hope will dispose of it once and for all, you are misinterpreting the situation. Your child is interested, and he needs to be given information even if he does not ask for it. Explanations of each aspect of sex should be repeated and expanded as opportunities arise, so that he can gradually integrate them into his growing understanding of human relationships.

Believing Two Versions

Don't be surprised if your child needs to have the same explanation repeated several times over a long period, or if he apparently accepts your correct version and, simultaneously, another one, of the stork variety. A small child may seem to have grasped how his new baby sister was born and then announce to the world that his father collected her at the station. He may have found the correct explanation too funny to accept, he may have forgotten it, or he may just feel happier having an alternative version to fall back on, because this fantasy version is in harmony with the world of storybooks and imagination in which he lives.

Similarly, an older child may find it impossible to accept, at any rate all of the time and wholeheartedly, that his parents made love to conceive him. Most adults admit that as children they went through a stage of disbelieving that their parents could ever have indulged in sexual intercourse! Therefore, the child also half believes that babies can be conceived by taking a pill or by some other less intimate means, or that he himself was adopted (see adoption, pp. 353–54). A child is likely to go through a stage of believing that if there are three children in the family it means his parents have made love three times.

All these misconceptions and reactions are quite natural; they do not necessarily arise because parents have explained things badly or because a child has an unhealthy view of sex. They are just illustrations of the complexity of the subject and of the way a child needs time and sympathetic understanding before the facts become really acceptable to him.

There is no "right" age to begin sex education or to end it—adults continue to learn about sex all their lives. If a child fails to ask questions but opportunities arise, use them to provoke questions. For example, if you are pregnant again when your child is old enough to talk and understand, you can begin by letting him feel your tummy and the movements of the growing baby, telling him about it at the same time (see p. 148).

Sex Education in School

A child absorbs a major part of his sex education from observing his parents' relationships with each other and with the rest of the family, as well as from their attitudes to all the topics related to sex. Sex instruction in schools is necessary to complement this family influence when it is good and to counteract it where it is harmful. It is particularly important for children whose families fail to teach them the facts or to give them a positive attitude toward sex.

Some parents worry if their children receive group instruction about sex. This is usually the result of a fear of sex and of the possible effects of sexual knowledge, arising from the parents' own childhood experiences. These are likely to have been due to inadequate sex education. Such parents are frightened that sex education will lead to sex experimentation, but this results more from ignorance than from information.

Parents who have been teaching their child about sex as he has been growing up can be glad that he will also learn about it at school, since group discussion is bound to widen his knowledge. If you are frightened at the thought of your child receiving sex education at school, remember that he is being given a learning opportunity that probably never came your way. Bad sex education in a parent's own childhood can easily be passed on from one generation to another; sex education at school is one way of trying to prevent this.

The Myth of Innocence

In the minds of some parents there is still the feeling that a child is "innocent" and should remain that way as long as possible. This arises from the now discredited theory that a child is born sexless and neuter and remains so until taught otherwise, or until he reaches a certain age and stage in development. In fact, a baby is sensual, taking physical enjoyment from the sensations derived through feeding and playing via his mouth, and later, as every parent knows, relishing the joys of excretion (see p. 245).

The Importance of Physical Contact

A baby learns through feeling; he gives and receives pleasure through his body while being cuddled and handled. This is his first sex education. Parents who enjoy touching their baby, continuing to give him the comfort of physical contact through childhood for as long as he wants it, are helping their children to accept themselves as physical beings. They are taking for granted the fact that people who are fond of each other touch each other for reassurance and pleasure, and not only for erotic reasons. Their children will grow up aware of their bodies and of those of other people, neither afraid of the body nor obsessed by it (see nudity, p. 340).

The Latent Period

Children are probably less emotionally involved and interested in sex between the time they start school and the time they approach puberty, so that they can absorb information about sex in a comparatively dispassionate way. Whether this latent period is quite as free of sexual interest as some believe it to be is debatable. Probably some children are always more interested than others, although undoubtedly the physical changes of puberty (pp. 210–11) give a new significance and urgency to this interest in all children.

Admitting You Don't Know

If you don't know the answer to some specific question, admit it to your child. Whatever his age, he will appreciate your admission of fallibility and will learn to take for granted that grownups do not know everything, and that they are willing to admit it and to try to find the answer. You could buy a book to read together, or look it up at the library, or ask someone who does know. It would be wrong to refuse to answer or to say "You are too young to know; I'll tell you later," in reply to an awkward question, or one that you cannot answer. Let me repeat what I have already stressed: when a child is old enough to ask a particular question, he is old enough for a satisfactory reply. There are numerous publications to help parents explain the facts of life in a way appropriate to each age group.

Reluctance to answer a question may be related to an understandable wish to protect your child from knowing too much too soon. For example, perhaps you would like him to have time to absorb the facts of normal sex before he graduates to understanding the less normal. It is a wise rule not to overload your child with explanations of sexual perversions, or of the precise differences between the various forms of contraception or venereal disease, while he is still busy absorbing the straightforward basic story.

Explaining Perversions

Because we are bombarded into familiarity with sexual deviations through newsprint, television, and films, and because it is increasingly difficult to protect children from this bombardment, it is becoming necessary for parents to explain more at an earlier age, and sooner than may be judged ideal for a particular child. If he asks, "Mommy, what's a sadist?" at the age of nine because of something he has seen in the newspaper, he needs an answer. While he does not need to be told the full range of possible sadistic activities, you can help him to understand that pain and pleasure, hate and love, are closely connected in everyone's lives, but that in some individuals the emphasis has gone wrong, so that they can find sexual pleasure only in inflicting pain.

The aim in explaining any of the sexual perversions or oddities should not be to produce fear, hatred, or revulsion in your child; overdramatizing may make them seem unduly important, or even glamorous. The aim is to give him some understanding of subjects he is bound to read and wonder about, divesting them of both fear and glamour. He will then be able to comprehend that perversions are not more exciting than ordinary sex except to those individuals whose capacity for normal enjoyment has gone off course, usually because of unfortunate early experiences. Encouraging your child to be tolerant of deviation won't encourage him to try it for himself.

Child Molesters and Exhibitionists

Both boys and girls need to know about child molesters and exhibitionists. At first, you need only explain that they should never accept lifts or go off with strangers because a few mentally ill people wish to harm little children. A child who has to travel alone or through empty streets or fields to get home from school should be warned more specifically to avoid empty vehicles, buildings, caves, culverts, and friendly overtures from strangers. He must also be told to suspect plausible stories from strangers who may say, "Your father is ill" or "Your mother asked me to take you home." He can seek advice from his teacher, or a nearby policeman, or storekeeper.

It is a pity to have to convey distrust and to risk hurting the feelings of genuinely friendly or lonely people, but a child must be helped to understand that it is not possible to assess a stranger's motives on the spot and not worth taking the risk.

The dangers involved should not be exaggerated, since in the case of exhibitionists and the majority of molesters, no physical harm is inflicted on the child. The degree of psychological shock is less if a child has been warned in advance and is not made to feel in any way guilty about the experience afterward. However, prevention is far better than cure, so help your child to avoid the experience altogether.

Understanding the Opposite Sex

Try not to limit your child's understanding of the "normal" facts of life to the minimum necessary for his own happiness. Understanding the opposite sex's problems helps boys and girls to treat one another with sympathy and a sense of responsibility. Boys should grow up with an idea of girls' problems and feelings and vice versa.

Menstruation

Obviously, the time when information is needed differs; a boy does not need to know about menstruation as early as a girl, who must not be taken by surprise. She needs gradual preparation for this stage in her life, relating it to the part it plays in her development as a woman capable of bearing children, and to the cycle of reproduction. Having a box of sanitary pads stowed away in her closet may help her to look forward to her first period, particularly if it has not been put over as "the curse." Many girls today prefer to use internal protection from the start, and this is perfectly all right.

Wet Dreams

In the same way, a boy should be told about wet dreams before he is likely to be surprised by one, but they can be explained to a girl at some time as part of her general knowledge about the way the opposite sex functions physically. Explain to her what bearing this more urgent need for sexual release may have on her relations with boys.

Preparing for Future Parenthood

By knowing more than the basic facts of childbirth, both boys and girls will be helped to enjoy parenthood and to be good parents. Emotional preparation for childbirth is as important as physical preparation. Ideally, this preparation starts in childhood; it should involve more than a blithe assurance that labor is painless—not true for many women anyway, and certainly insufficient to offset the contrary impression your child will get from other sources. It does no harm to admit that your own labor was painful or painless, but don't leave it at that. Both girls and boys can appreciate that pain is registered differently by different people, that attitude of mind affects the threshold of pain, that techniques to cope with pain can be learned, and that there is a difference between hard work, or "labor," and pain.

It is important to explain to a girl that the outlet of the vagina is specially constructed as a birth canal, and is able to stretch without damage and return to normal afterward. Probably, many girls fear secretly that they are "too small" to give birth, or perhaps even to have intercourse. It is also a good idea to explain that the size of the breasts has no bearing on the ability to breast feed, especially since the opportunity to see babies happily feeding at the breast is missed by many children nowadays. You could also mention that the breasts commonly develop unevenly at first; in fact, one may appear some time before the other. Slight asymmetry in fully developed breasts is common.

Remind yourself regularly that the facts you take for granted have to be learned for the first time by your child. It does not matter if he knows some of them already, and has a little laugh to himself at your concern to tell him about them. This is much better than chancing it and hoping that he has no secret fears.

Virginity

Attitudes toward virginity are something that every family has to work out for itself. Children reflect the views of their parents, and these views are liable to alter as parents get older and possibly wiser.

Try to bring up your children with concern for the feelings of others and respect for the individuality of everyone they meet. In this way they will be less likely to grow up ready to trample on others sexually, or to be trampled on. Selfish or thoughtless behavior is wrong, in the sexual field as in any other (see also pp. 353–54).

Adolescents should know about contraception and venereal disease as part of their education in responsibility. They must also be helped to understand that responsibility in sexual relationships is not limited to preventing an unwanted child, but extends to preventing damage to the other person. Whether or not you expect your children to remain virginal, try to teach them not to use people. However lightly a sexual relationship is taken, the two people involved seldom have exactly the same expectations of it and one of them is liable to be hurt when it ends. Adolescents are bound to learn by trial and error. They will be hurt and will inflict hurt while tentatively discovering the opposite sex and their own identity, but at least if they have grown up with a sense of responsibility and have been adequately informed, there is less danger of one adolescent's fun becoming another's disaster.

By the time children are involved in actual sexual relationships, they tend to be reluctant to share their worries with parents, however open they were previously. Therefore do not expect to be able to help directly in sorting out your adolescent's sexual problems: cross your fingers and hope he or she will come out of each experience wiser. Indirect general conversation is your best hope at this stage; although your children will probably see through your heavily disguised advice, they will be grateful for your concern, though they may not admit it.

Masturbation

This is not a depraved habit indulged in by a few children, but an almost universal practice in both sexes. By now, it can be hoped, most parents must be aware that it does not lead to weakness, insanity, or sexual perversion, but nevertheless it is something they often still feel uneasy about. They would rather their children didn't do it or at least that they did it out of sight.

This uneasiness springs from their own sexual guilt feelings and doubts, hangovers from their childhood, when masturbation was much less likely to have been regarded by parents as normal and, therefore, children were much more likely to have felt like solitary sinners in a sexless world. The fact that childhood is not the sex-free time it was once thought to be is widely accepted in theory but hard to accept in practice (see p. 333).

Touching the Genitals in Babyhood

All babies touch their genitals; boy babies have more to touch so they touch theirs more. One day, sooner or later, your baby finds that handling his genitals is especially pleasurable—it is emphatically not like scratching his chest. At first, the pleasure probably resembles the warm satisfaction he gets from using his mouth and lips to suck, to feel, and to explore. It is sensual rather than specifically sexual. Erections of the penis can be produced by a full bladder and are not necessarily due to masturbation.

Some babies appear to discover earlier than others that stimulation of the genital area is exciting, and therefore worth doing purposely. From the age of a few months, a baby may periodically rub himself (or herself) rhythmically against the crib or rock back and forth. He looks preoccupied: he stares and puffs (he probably goes red in the face and sweats) as if he were working himself up into a climax; finally he relaxes and goes to sleep.

Worries about Masturbation

This form of masturbation, as opposed to "innocent" handling of the genitals, is likely to cause parents more anxiety. They worry that it will do the baby physical harm; that he is abnormally highly sexed and having discovered sexual pleasure so early will fail to develop normal childish interests; and that his activities in public will embarrass others, and themselves. Sometimes the whole situation is misunderstood and the baby is thought to be in pain.

The answers to these natural anxieties are clear-cut: first, masturbation itself does no harm to a child's bodily health or development. Secondly, he is not destined for a life of sexual promiscuity or perversion. Thirdly, yes, it can be embarrassing if your baby works himself up into a state resembling sexual excitement in full view of his great-aunt. On these occasions, it is perfectly reasonable to keep one eye open for signs that he's off and to divert his attention before he gets going, even to interrupt him in the middle, although he will resent it.

The Best Policy

But, in general, the best way to deal with handling the genitals and masturbation is to disregard them. The emotional difficulties produced for children by masturbation are mostly created by adults—by their looks of disapproval, their hasty removal of hands from genitals when the child has not even noticed what he was doing, and their constant attempts to "divert his attention," which the child, as he gets older, sees through immediately. However determined you are not to make a child feel guilty or wicked, if you feel that masturbation is wrong he will sense it. This is bound to make him feel guilty to some degree and, since he will still go on doing it, the idea that sex must be furtive is planted.

Your child has a right to a private sex life, but it is a pity if it has to be furtive. He will learn from the disapproval of others, if not from you, that in a society like ours public sexuality is not acceptable to the vast majority of people; this means that handling his genitals and masturbating in public are taboo. It is not exactly the same as not picking your nose in public, since there are no emotions and only minimal pleasures involved in nose picking, but try to keep the subject in that category.

Even knowing that masturbation is harmless, you will want to discourage it. You may have accepted that you should not punish your child, or even reprove him, but this is not because you don't mind his masturbating—it is because you have been told that the best way to discourage his interest in sex is to ignore it. Adults are embarrassed by sexuality in children, but in addition they probably feel that a child who discovers the power of sex too soon is only adding to his problems in life and will be unable to cope with the energy he has released in himself.

Compulsive Masturbation

However, young children do not become obsessed with the pleasure and relaxation they gain from masturbation unless they need this comfort because life is otherwise disturbing or boring. An addiction to masturbation during early childhood is a symptom to be treated, not ignored, since it means that a child is using masturbation as an escape from reality.

Compulsive masturbation is sometimes the unfortunate result of parents' interfering when a child handles his genitals as part of his normal development. It is similar to interfering with a child's pleasure in sucking his thumb: disapproval only succeeds in having the opposite effect to the one intended. Small boys sometimes clutch their genitals as if afraid of losing them—a word of reassurance from you may help. Frequent masturbation has no harmful physical consequences but only increases the mental anxiety that provoked it in the first place. It is the anxiety that needs tackling, not the masturbation; this will become less obsessive when the child is happier.

Occasionally, masturbation is mistaken for a convulsion, but your doctor can soon put your mind at rest about this.

Sex Play

It is inevitable that some children, both boys and girls, will experiment with these pleasurable games together rather than on their own. They may call it "playing doctor." You will probably be even more worried by this, but the same principles of management hold as for masturbation. It is a good idea to think about the possibility beforehand, so as to be cushioned against producing an unguarded burst of anger when you meet the problem for the first time. On no account should the friendship between the children be broken because you find them playing together.

Nudity

There is no need to have a "policy" about nudity in the family. If it does not worry you to be seen by your children in various stages of undress, then it is unlikely to worry them; but if it does worry you, they will wonder why and feel uneasy too. It might surprise or upset a child suddenly to see one of his parents nude for the first time, but the familiar sight of a parent in the bath is unlikely to become sexually stimulating overnight just because a child has reached a certain age.

Dealing with "Personal Remarks"

Behave in whatever way comes naturally to you. If a child annoys you with unfavorable comments about your figure or by getting the giggles every time he sees a certain part of your anatomy, shut him out of the bathroom and tell him why. But try to answer questions without embarrassment. A child's comments on the adult form frequently relate to breasts and sexual organs solely, because these are the most different from his own. It is not rudeness or premature sexuality that provokes questions on pubic hair or the size of father's penis; having a good look and even touching satisfies curiosity, not sexual feelings.

Knowing what naked people look like at various ages should be something that happens naturally. A child is then far less likely to become obsessed with "rude" pictures or to spend time wondering what mother looks like without her bra on. The human body will lose its mystery; it will become delightfully interesting again when your child reaches adolescence but the interest will be focused on particular individuals outside the family.

Respecting Modesty

The alterations in the body at adolescence tend to make children shy about their own nakedness. You should take your cue from your child. Do not tell him that you bathed him as a baby and expect him to think this a good reason for inspecting him all over now that he is twelve. Encourage brothers and sisters to respect each other's desire for privacy.

If one parent minds being seen naked while the other does not, this need not mean that their children grow up with a warped idea of the male or female anatomy or role in life. They can be helped to recognize that their parents possess different thresholds of modesty and will leave it at that unless a great issue is made of it.

Explain to children that attitudes toward nudity and modesty vary from person to person and from family to family, and that it is safer not to rush about the house naked when you go away to stay. This is just another aspect of fitting in with other people.

Children and Drugs

Teen-age drug taking is a vast subject, which is dealt with in many specialized publications. I do not propose to describe the effects of different drugs but only to suggest ways in which parents can influence their children's attitude toward drugs before they become teen-agers.

"Drugs" should not be put in a special category for discussion, in the hope that a straight talk at a certain age will cover the problem, any more than one explanation is enough to take care of sex. As with all the important "subjects" we should clarify for our children, the question of drugs should be regarded as a recurring theme, to be discussed openly and often as natural opportunities crop up.

Family Attitude toward Medicine

Trying hard or soft drugs and the dangers of addiction are not problems isolated from the rest of life. They are connected with an individual's attitude toward stress and his tolerance of pain—both physical and mental. A child brought up in a family where the slightest ache is the signal for a rummage through the medicine cabinet for the appropriate remedy, who knows that no one in his family ever waits to feel better or expects to recover without taking a pill or a drink to

hasten the process, grows up believing that the answer to life's problems lies most often in "taking something." This is the child who, as
a teen-ager, may come to rely on drugs to change his mood and make
his problems disappear, if only temporarily.

Assessing the Dangers

Most teen-agers will come across contemporaries who take drugs; any
teen-ager may try soft drugs and continue to use them, believing
them to be harmless and no more wicked than his parents' drinking
and smoking. The danger of addiction as a result of taking soft drugs
is disputed by experts; parents, therefore, are more likely to be consulted by their children if they keep an open mind on the subject. A
child who knows about the certain dangers of some drugs and the
probable dangers of others, and who understands that drugs provide
an unreliable and very temporary solution to life's problems, is in little
danger of becoming addicted.

Of course, it helps a child if he has comparatively few problems,
if he has a stable background, friends, and the opportunity to use his
talents. A teen-ager who has none of these things may know the
dangers of drug taking but may almost bring them upon himself in
preference to the dreariness of reality.

So although there is no guaranteed method of preventing drug
abuse by teen-agers, the best answer lies not in lectures and strenu-
ous efforts to prevent contact with drugs altogether, but in the general family attitude toward drugs, medicines, and mood-changers of
all kinds. Tranquilizers, antidepressants, sleeping pills, and pain kill-
ers are all helpful for specific problems, and this can be explained to
your child. But he should not grow up with the idea that agitation
automatically calls for a tranquilizer, gloom for an antidepressant, a
sleepless night for a pill, and a mild headache for an aspirin. If he
does, it is logical that he should use drugs to keep him awake, elate
him, or make him forget his worries.

Talking about Death

A Child's Attitude toward Death and
Bereavement

Every child thinks about death, even in societies like our own where
death and mourning have become private matters that are concealed
as far as possible. It is impossible to prevent a child knowing about
the deaths of relatives, friends, or pets, even if he has never been
directly affected by bereavement.

As soon as a child is old enough to feel attached to another person, he begins to be aware of the possibility of losing that person. Fear of death, originating in the fear of losing something that is loved, is a basic human emotion, which arises spontaneously in a child without being instilled from outside (see above). For these reasons, you cannot shield your children from the idea of death; you can only help them accept it as part of the cycle of life.

Once a child can talk, it is not long before he asks questions about death, although it will be years before he can fully grasp its implications. In fact, most children are probably unable to think about death in a way adults regard as rational until they are eight or nine years old; they do not react to bereavement in a conventional way until this age. Adults are sometimes shocked by a child's apparently callous indifference to the death of someone he loves. But accepting the facts of death, like the facts of life, may take several years and go through several stages; and a child often believes several versions simultaneously.

This is particularly characteristic of the years between five and eight. A child may show by his conversation that he knows a dead grandparent has gone forever, only to ask later if he will be coming back. When a child of this age says he wants to kill his parents, he is only expressing the wish that they should disappear temporarily. The idea that death is irreversible is either too difficult or too intolerable to grasp. But he should never be told that "grandpa has gone to sleep forever," because he may then become terrified of going to sleep in case he too disappears forever. He may also feel guilty because he did not say "good night" to grandfather before he went to "sleep." Similarly, it is unwise to use the expression "God has taken him to live with him." Your child may become frightened in case he too may be suddenly taken away.

Reactions to Bereavement

Death seems to be regarded by the small child as a kind of magical punishment, rather than as an inevitable end to everyone's life. Should someone close to him die, he may suspect that it is the result of his own destructive thoughts about the dead person; this is particularly likely to happen with the death of a brother or sister, of whom the child was sometimes naturally jealous. He then tries to behave extra well, as if trying to reverse the situation and bring the dead person back to life. Another child may behave badly, as if trying to provoke punishment from outside, so as to lighten his load of guilt. His parents wonder why he is reacting to the death without grief— actually he is grieving, but in a way that fits his theory of death. A child may behave in a way that adults think appropriate, that is, with sadness, or he may show conflicting emotions. One father expressed his intense feelings of anger against his teen-age daughter, who did not seem to him to be showing enough grief for the loss of her younger brother. In fact, the father's feelings against the daughter were only making her personal sorrow still harder to bear.

Disturbed Reactions

If your child becomes really disturbed following a death in the family he is usually reacting to other strains as well, strains that existed before (see bereavement, p. 358). So, do not use a bereavement to explain away all a child's troubles.

An older child, with a more realistic view of death, may also feel somehow to blame when someone dies, because from time to time he used to hate the dead person. He may express this anxiety by seeming indifferent; by aggressive behavior as well as by sorrow; or by a mixture of grief and guilt. Such a child needs to discuss and express his feelings and to be helped to understand that although they are not unusual, they are unreasonable and unjustified.

Talking to Your Child About Death

Children of all ages should be allowed and encouraged to talk openly about death, even if their attitudes seem incomprehensible to adults. The fact that children have immature ideas about death does not mean that it should be hidden from them and their questions ignored or glossed over until they are "old enough to understand." Some parents prefer to give any explanation but the truth, on the grounds that the child is not yet ready for it—rather like some people's attitude to questions about sex. The probable reason for this is that many adults are themselves frightened by the subject, and prefer to put it out of their minds. They show by their answers that the questions are unwelcome; the children then stop asking questions but they are unlikely to stop thinking about death and dying.

Adult emotions about death also tend to be colored by fear, guilt, and fantasy, so it is not surprising that it is a particularly daunting subject to discuss rationally with a child, whose interest is based on curiosity rather than on fear. Another complicating factor is that children expect their parents to be certain about things, whereas even the most religious parent will feel some ignorance on the subject of death and a possible afterlife. Fortunately, a child does not need precise answers; he needs to feel that his parents are neither worried nor preoccupied by the fear of death; that they accept death as necessary for change, development, and new life. Even a small child can appreciate that there would be no room for more babies if everyone lived forever.

Accepting the Death of an Individual

It is nevertheless difficult to give an adequate reason for the death of an individual, particularly if that individual is another child. It is sad and unfair and you cannot help conveying this to your child; but so are many other things in life. It is not a parent's duty to deny this fact, but it is his job to help his children accept it without becoming unduly anxious or obsessed. He must help them use their emotional energy to change things that can be changed, not to brood on what is unchangeable; to love life, rather than to fear death.

Explaining to your child what happens after death will depend on your own beliefs. Even if you do not believe in survival after death, you may judge it reasonable to use the idea of heaven or a possible afterlife to help a young child to accept the death of a friend or relative. Older children can be told that an individual life should not be measured by its length alone, but also by its quality. Someone who dies young may have enjoyed more life and happiness than many older people. An animal with a short life span has a different sense of time from a man; its life may therefore feel as long as the life of a human being. This idea may help a child over the loss of a pet, which is often his first contact with death. Your child will soon learn that a dead body disintegrates, but whatever your views about life after death, you can truthfully tell him that the memory and influence of someone who has died live on forever. In this sense, death is never the end of the individual.

None of these suggestions can prevent a child from puzzling over death; this would be an impossible and an unreasonable aim. But they may make it easier for him to bear the death of someone he loved.

Above all, it is essential to help children to share the grief felt by parents. Children of all ages should be allowed to attend with their parents funerals of those they have loved. The idea that this will be bad for the child totally ignores his need to mourn and his difficulty in understanding what has happened if he does not go to the funeral. It helps children to ask what they want to ask and prevents them from feeling that their parents are hostile and rejecting because they don't understand their needs and have often allowed a conspiracy of silence to develop.

Might I Die?

You may need to reassure a young child that the moment of death is usually peaceful, not violent and bloody like the deaths he has seen on television and in movies (see p. 654). A perfectly healthy child may ask if he might die; most children probably consider this in fantasy, or fear their parents may die. It is no good assuring him that only old people die; it is better to be honest and admit that early death is a possibility for everyone, but an unlikely possibility. A critically ill child will need honest answers to his questions (pp. 653–55).

I have the impression that many teen-agers and some younger children admitted to a hospital today with illnesses that are not dangerous to life are frightened of dying. This is understandable when one considers that it is more common nowadays to die in the hospital than at home. The possibility that this fear of not getting better exists in a child's mind must be watched for during conversations in the hospital. Every nurse, including the most junior student nurse working her first day in a children's unit, must know how to answer the child who asks her if he is going to get better. She should always ask him what made him ask that question, in order to understand more of the meaning of his question. After carrying on the conversation for as long as she feels at ease, the nurse should end by telling the child that he is asking such important questions that she is going to ask the head nurse to talk with him.

24

Adoption

This chapter is addressed to adoptive parents. Its aim is to help you with some of the problems you may meet, and which your children may meet as adopted children.

Most of your problems, and theirs, will be ones that could affect any parents and any children: first and foremost you are a family. The difference adoption makes will vary, depending on the characteristics of the members of your family. A good home background will do much to make up for the bad start your baby may have had if his early months were unsettled.

But there is one major difference, since adoptive parents are likely to have had to come to terms with the fact that they cannot have a baby naturally. They have to mourn the baby they cannot conceive. Infertility is possibly the most difficult aspect for adopters to cope with. There are feelings of inadequacy—of not being in full health. Moreover there is no expectation of sharing the grief with friends, because most of the friends don't know. It is a painful secret between the two people. Of course I am aware that some parents adopt when they are still able to have children of their own, the adoptive children sometimes being of different ethnic origin or handicapped.

The Waiting Period

Frequently, there is a long interval between the time when a couple first decides they want to adopt a baby and the point where the possibility becomes a reality. So there is a long period during which the idea of starting a family in this way has time to develop, followed by a short one during which you prepare for the arrival of your baby.

Discussing Your Feelings

As happens in pregnancy, prospective parents have periods of elation, periods of depression, and periods of coasting along. It is natural if you feel more than normally anxious about your role as parents, since you have to think about this consciously in coming to the decision to adopt. You will be in close contact with the staff organizing the adoption, but may feel less eager to share your feelings with relatives and friends than if you were ordinarily pregnant. You may be afraid of criticism or discouragement.

Telling Your Family and Friends

However, it is a pity not to use this interval to involve your family and friends, in order to give them time to get used to the idea and a chance to offer their support and help. When a daughter becomes pregnant, this is often the start of a closer relationship between the generations (grandparents, pp. 171f.), and the same can be true of adoption if you allow parents and friends to share some of your feelings during the long wait. It gives anyone who is uneasy about it time to come around, to understand your decision, and to welcome the baby when he arrives. This is particularly desirable if you are adopting a baby of a different race or color, an idea that grandparents may take a long time to accept.

Second Thoughts: Your Fitness as Parents

During this waiting time, you may find yourself reconsidering and churning over your motives for adopting a baby. You may have second thoughts as to your fitness to be parents. All prospective parents tend to have these doubts, but only those proposing to adopt a baby are selected beforehand. If you have been accepted as adoptive parents this means that, in more than one professional opinion, you will make good parents. You have been passed as physically and mentally fit and your desire to start a family has been interpreted favorably: you want a baby not to patch up your marriage or to fill up an empty life, but to complete a happy marriage and to share an already interesting life. You have had to think of the realities of living with another individual, who will grow from a helpless baby into a demanding child, who will be time-consuming, sometimes a problem, and who will not go away when difficulties arise, any more than a child born to you would.

The adoption worker will have decided from her discussions with you that your attitude to children is realistic, that you understand that your commitment to the child must be for better or worse, and that both you and your husband want a child. She will have made sure that you accept, as some parents do not, that your child's individual development is unpredictable; that he may not turn out as you imagine or as you might ideally wish him to. Ultimately, having a child is a gamble, and you have to be prepared to accept the bad as well as the good.

What Will Your Baby Be Like?

In fact, adoptive parents know more about their coming child than ordinary parents: the risk of unknown handicaps is reduced by thorough examination of the child, and by investigations into his parentage and birth. You will be given any relevant information about their possible consequences.

Every pregnant woman has moments of fear that there will be something wrong with her baby. Adoptive parents have the reassurance that their baby has been screened before adoption. You need have less "blind faith" than the ordinary prospective parent. You would not decide whether to accept your own baby on the basis of whether he was "perfect" or not; but with adoption every effort is made to ensure that you are warned if there are any problems.

Obviously, it would be wrong to delay adoption until you are absolutely certain that the baby is developing normally. Adoption agencies tend to delay the placing of babies for adoption if the pediatrician cannot assure them that they are perfect. This, I believe, is the wrong approach. I cannot recall a single occasion when prospective adopters have decided to hand a child back on learning that he might possibly be handicapped in some way. Moreover, successful adoption is now taking place for children with handicaps such as Down's syndrome (mongolism) and for older children who somehow got left in children's homes.

A child born to you might not take after either of you and might not resemble anyone in the family. Every child at times seems a "total stranger" to his parents: this is not much more likely to happen with an adopted child who has grown up as one of your family. It is the commitment you make to a child's daily care and well-being that makes him your own (see all our loving?, pp. 168f.). The important thing is that you feel responsible for him. It is natural that this responsibility will weigh heavily at times—all responsibility does.

Caring for Your Baby

An adoptive mother may find she is a "natural" so far as day-to-day baby care goes, whereas a natural mother may find looking after her baby a bore. Giving birth is no guarantee of an influx of maternal feeling, nor does it bestow a diploma in mothercraft. The same is true of taking an adopted baby into your home, but you may feel even more responsible for him because he was born to somebody else. So do not feel you are abnormally heavy-handed or incompetent in handling your baby, or worried if it takes time to "love" him. He needs to feel securely held, and to be secure in the feeling that someone will soon come when he is hungry or unhappy. You will get to know him and to do the right thing given time, which every mother needs (see looking after your new baby, pp. 96f.).

You may find that allowing the new baby to sleep between you and your husband in the early days increases the bond between all three of you (pp. 109f.). Some mothers of adopted babies have been able to breast feed although they have never had a baby of their own. Even if the baby does not stimulate lactation, you may discover that allowing him to suck at your nipple brings you closer to each other.

Accepting Each Other

A baby who has spent his first few months with another family, whether his natural mother's or a foster parent's, will take time to accept you. He may look wary, as if sizing you up, and may refuse to respond to your friendly overtures. But gradually—or, more rarely, suddenly—he accepts you. It is as if he is reluctant to give his emotions free rein until he feels sure of you.

Although it is disappointing if you fail to feel instant rapport with your baby, this can be a sign that he has been well cared for and therefore has had a good start in life, which will stand him, and you, in good stead in the future. A baby or small child who has been shifted from pillar to post or brought up in an institution without individual care may be instantly friendly, but this friendliness is superficial and worth less than closeness based on mutual trust, achieved through living with a happy family.

Some adoptive parents do feel their baby belongs to them at once and detect a similar feeling in the baby. But it is normal to have ups and downs, to wonder if this stranger is ever going to fit into your life, and whether you even like his face. Natural parents, if they are honest, may well admit to similar doubts about their own flesh and blood.

Taking Advice

You will continue to have contact with the adoption workers, particularly until the adoption is made final, so take the opportunity to talk over any problems and doubts you have. Your baby will not be snatched away from you because you admit to difficulties. Asking for advice is more likely to be taken as a sign of your confidence and maturity as parents than as an admission of failure.

General Problems of Upbringing

Because the relationship with an adopted child is special and cannot be taken for granted in the same way as a blood tie, parents have a tendency to connect any problems that arise with the fact that their child is adopted. For example, if he is going through a difficult phase you may seek the explanation not only in your knowledge of him and in the current family situation, but you may also wonder if it has something to do with unknown hereditary factors, or with anxiety about being adopted. If he says he hates you, you will probably think he wishes you had not adopted him, whereas this is a phrase any parent can hear from any child.

Of course, there are times when a child's problems are connected with worry about his personal origins or feelings of insecurity about his present situation, but if you are always willing to talk to him about these subjects on the lines suggested below it should usually be possible to discover whether these are the basis of his problems. You should concentrate on making him feel more secure, by clearing up any misconceptions he may have as to the permanency of your feelings and commitment to him, and by the method that works with all children—demonstrating more affection.

Difficulties may arise from other people's tactlessness in making him feel different. He will be able to cope with this if he feels secure at home; you may feel more indignant than he does. A black child in a white community faces this prejudice too, and needs help in forgiving people's ignorance.

Discipline

Parents may fear they are being too hard, or too soft, or unfair on a child because he is adopted, particularly if they also have children of their own. The problem of favoritism arises in most families with more than one child, since it is impossible to be "fair" all the time (see favorites, pp. 168f., and twins, p. 142); but adoption gives it a special twist. Neighbors and friends may seem extra critical of your treatment of an adopted child, or so you tend to imagine.

The thing to remember is that nearly all your reactions and feelings to your child will be toward him as an individual. He will be as naughty and annoying as any child might be on occasions, and in turn you will be as annoyed or fed up with him as you might be with any child born to you. "I can't have produced this monster," thinks the natural parent, feeling guilty a moment later. "I wouldn't have produced this monster," thinks the adoptive parent, feeling even guiltier. Occasionally, all parents wish they could have given birth to a different child, or chosen differently.

Are We the Best Parents for Him?

Adoptive parents may feel guilty if their child is in trouble or un-happy, feeling he might have been better off with his own mother or with other adoptive parents. In fact, illegitimate children rarely do better living with their natural mothers, since illegitimacy is still a stigma; emotional, practical, and financial difficulties remain to com-plicate the lives of an unmarried mother and her child. Studies of children born illegitimate have shown that those adopted into a nor-mal home do better in every field of activity and learning than those who remain in a single-parent situation with their unmarried mothers (see one-parent family, pp. 361–62).

Ordinary parents often come to the conclusion that they them-selves are very imperfect, and so are their children, that family life is not always quite all it's cracked up to be, and that compromise is necessary for living with the people you've got, as opposed to the ones you imagine you might like to have. When adoptive parents feel like this, they do not have the automatic reassurance that their feelings are normal and have nothing to do with the fact that their child is adopted. Once they do realize this, everything is easier. The most difficult time for adoptive parents is during the period between get-ting the child and the adoption order.

Telling Your Child He Is Adopted

When, how, and what to tell your child about his adoption and origins is a major worry to most adoptive parents. It is rather like the ques-tion of sex education, or the facts of death, and my advice would be similar: tell your child the truth when he seems to you to be ready for it, preferably at an early age, and in a manner appropriate to his age, understanding, and needs. Play it by ear; do not expect to give a "once and for all" lecture and then to be done with the subject, but regard it as a theme that needs to recur if it is to be properly assimilated. If your child asks questions, answer them—if he does not, do not assume he has no need for information about his personal origin; give him the opportunity to bring up the subject or, failing this, introduce it your-self.

Will the Truth Make Him Insecure?

Parents often feel it is impossible to give a child a feeling of security and at the same time to convey to him that he is not really theirs. They fear that once he knows he is not their child he may no longer love them. But a child's love for his parents is based on his feelings for them rather than on blood ties, and these feelings reflect theirs for him and the security engendered by a normal parent/child relationship. The danger comes if he learns of his parentage from someone other than his adoptive parents, particularly if it is hurled at him during a moment of anger. Not only is it his right to know the truth; he is safer once he does know.

How these facts are told will vary with the teller; the important thing is to tell the truth. A child can understand that he was chosen by his parents and may become so proud of this fact that he tells his friends at school that he was chosen by his parents instead of simply arriving, as they did. But too much should not be made of the idea that he was "chosen" or is "special," lest he feel he is letting his parents down by not measuring up to such a standard.

Nothing should be said to belittle the love felt for him by his natural mother. You can help him to understand that this love was such that she wanted him to have a happier life than she could have given him.

A child whose background is very disturbing need not be told all the details at an early age, although at adolescence he may demand and need to know them. No child can accept the idea that his natural parents are totally "bad," although he may be able to take the idea that they are "imperfect," particularly if his present family are not perfectionists.

This is your problem, not his. You may have to overcome an inclination to bury his past and prefer to think only of building your future. You may be jealous of his interest in his natural parents, especially if he "puts them on a pedestal." Perhaps you find it painful to think of the tragic or "unsavory" circumstances of your child's birth. But his past will not go away; it may appear to have done so through his childhood years, but the problem is certain to reassert itself during adolescence, when all children are concerned with their parentage and origins.

The Adolescent and Sex Education

For an adopted child, these questions are more closely connected with his need for information about sexual relationships, making adolescence even more of a strain for him. He is trying to find his sexual and personal identity and needs to know the specific facts about his personal origin as well as the general facts of life.

Natural children sometimes go through a stage of imagining that they are adopted, perhaps because they find it hard to accept that the two adults whose imperfections they have now begun to perceive are their real parents. Imagining another set of parents allows scope for fantasy, hopes of inherited genius and riches—and moreover permits the child to escape the inescapable fact that his mother and father must have had a sexual relationship in order to produce him (see sex education, p. 332).

Therefore, an adopted child needs to be told the facts of life even more fully and frankly than an ordinary child, since this is one way he can understand and accept his origins. For example, if he was illegitimate, as he probably was, it is not sufficient to give him the basic facts of conception and birth and tell him that when people love each other they get married and have babies. He needs to know about unmarried love, that love can exist on many different levels, that it is possible for people to love one another sexually without feeling deep affection and wanting to spend their lives together, that such people are not beyond the pale morally, and that babies can equally well be born from such unions. An adopted adolescent cannot be expected to square the idea that long-lasting love and responsibility are the only things that make sexuality acceptable with the obvious fact that his parents' sexual relationship was temporary and, to some degree, irresponsible. They did not make love because they wanted him, but because they wanted each other.

This is easier to accept if your child knows that such behavior is not exceptional, but very usual. One benefit of living in a more tolerant, permissive society is that adoptive parents and their children are going to feel less "judged" morally. The fears of adoptive parents that their adolescent might follow in the footsteps of his "immoral" natural parents seem exaggerated in an era when sex outside marriage is generally accepted, even if it is not universally approved.

25

The One-Parent Family

Divorce

A marriage can be dissolved but parenthood cannot. A couple who separate for their own sanity, health, and happiness owe it to their children to behave toward them with continuing responsibility, that is, with love.

Children must feel they have two parents, whoever they live with after a divorce. Each parent needs to feel that he or she has the support of the other in bringing up their children. A happily married woman bringing up her children is often alone with them, and has to deal with the physical work and the daily problems largely on her own. But she is supported by knowing that her husband is equally concerned and that there is someone to share the burden of providing permanent love for and interest in their children. A divorced parent needs this emotional support even more. Divorce must not mean that one parent signs off emotional responsibility for the children.

Emotional Security

A child may be happy or unhappy within or outside a two-parent family. Whatever the situation, his well-being depends on the knowledge that both parents love him, unquestionably, for himself. He needs to feel that this love is not conditional on how he behaves, or on his parents' moods and attitudes toward each other, or on changes in family circumstances. Even if he has to move house after a divorce and no longer sees one of his parents every day, this awareness can provide him with emotional security.

Is Staying Together Always Best?

Children suffer when their parents dislike each other, whether they live together or not. A couple vibrating with scorn and hate for each other cannot switch on love for their children; they are more likely to find their children nerve-racking. Many a child is bullied by a parent who is really expressing marital unhappiness and frustration, whereas happily married parents are generally good to their children just because they are happy.

For this reason, it is impossible to state categorically that a couple with children should always stay together "for the sake of the children." A couple considering divorce has to work out whether staying together will mean merely living under the same roof, exuding an air of self-sacrifice. If so, "the sake of the children" might be better served by separating.

Parents who want to separate sometimes decide to stay together "until the children no longer need them." But how long is this? Even when children are grown up they need to know their parents are somewhere in the background and available when needed. It is seldom wise for parents wishing to separate to decide to stay together solely because of the children.

The decision is usually far from simple. Many marriages are "so-so," with periods of drifting along in comparative contentment interspersed with periods of desperation at the thought that this emotional dead end is all there is to life. The choice may be between comparative misery together and comparative misery, probably plus poverty and loneliness, apart. A childless couple might reasonably decide to try their luck alone, but a couple with children have to think harder and to try harder.

Having children sometimes shows up the weak spots in a marriage by making diversions more difficult, but it can also prove an overwhelming reason for riding out the bad times. Many couples are grateful that they had this incentive to hang on, because in the long run their marriage has turned out to be good after all. Stamina is necessary both for bringing up children and for staying married.

Parental Quarrels

Quarreling in front of the children, while not recommended, is not as harmful as a perpetually poisoned atmosphere or the sterility of non-communication. Children get used to the tone of their parents' marriage but are quick to spot changes for the worse.

Material Consequences of Divorce

Money raises its ugly head as usual. A comfortably off couple who could afford to part without drastically changing their standard of living is obviously in a stronger position to consider setting up two households. On the other hand, if a divorce means that children will be living with a parent who is made miserable by financial worries as well as by emotional ones, it will clearly be more disrupting for everyone. The children are deprived not only of the day-to-day presence of one of their parents but also of their familiar way of life. A child whose parents have separated but whose daily life continues much as before, who goes to the same school, lives in the same house, and keeps his old friends, has the security of all this familiarity to help him cope with the upheavals of divorce.

This is not to say that divorce is all right for the children of rich parents but never feasible for the less well off. But it would be irresponsible to ignore the potential effects of having to support two households on the same money—or, alternatively, of both parents having to work at a time when the children clearly need more, not less, attention. Fun costs money, and although new clothes, toys, and outings do not in themselves add up to a happy childhood, a child who loses both the presence of one parent and the prospect of any enjoyment that costs money is more deprived than the child who loses only a parent.

Life with Father

This consideration might mean that a child would be happier staying with his father if the alternative were to live in reduced circumstances with a mother who had to work all day to support him. With more flexible attitudes toward the roles of men and women, more divorced women will want to use their freedom to work and to live independently; they will be prepared to leave the children in the care of their father, and will not automatically demand custody. It will help the children and the adults concerned if the mother is not branded as a neglectful, heartless woman because she makes this decision. If a man genuinely wants his children to live with him and is able to make good arrangements for their daily lives, and if his ex-wife knows that she would only be making a gesture toward society's expectations of her as a mother if she insisted on taking the children with her, living with their father could be the better solution for the children as well (see the bereaved child, below).

Keeping Two Parents

If you do decide to divorce, make sure that, in your children's eyes, you do not kill off the other parent. If you are a divorced mother with custody of your children, remember that their divorced father is still their father. It does not help the child to be continually told how bad his father is, because this makes half of him bad. They should still be able to talk about him freely and easily. Even if you do not have his photograph displayed, your children should feel able to do so if they wish, and certainly they should possess some photograph of him. Although he is no longer your husband, he is always their father.

Losing a Parent: The Bereaved Child

It is impossible to generalize about the effects of bereavement on children, since these depend on the age of the child, the effect grief has on a particular child, and to a great extent on the practical results of the loss of a parent on the family's standard of living and everyday life. If a child becomes disturbed after a bereavement, these interacting factors make it hard to assess how far this is due to grief and how far to the disruption of his normal way of life.

Paradoxically, happy families are less strained by the death of a parent than unhappy families. The surviving partner of an unhappy marriage sometimes feels abnormally guilty about this solution to the dilemma; guilt makes it harder to emerge from the normal stages of grief to gradual acceptance of the change. It means that the children suffer additionally as a result of the remaining parent's emotional problems.

This double penalty of bereavement is inevitable to some degree in any family, since a parent cannot help being absorbed by the personal grief of losing a husband or wife. A depressed widow cannot mother her children in her normal way, although she can make herself care for them physically as usual. She may try to hide her grief from them because she thinks them too young for the burden, but silent unhappiness is more confusing for them to cope with than open grief, and it is likely to be longer-lasting. The death of one parent then becomes the loss of both to the child because the survivor is lost in grief.

Children can survive a period of emotional upheaval but they must be helped to mourn their loss. A child needs to share his grief just as much as the surviving parent. They must be allowed to attend the funeral to help them understand what has happened, even though they may be too young to comprehend its meaning fully at first. Mourning does not warp a child's personality, but a continuingly unbalanced relationship with his surviving parent may have a long-term effect. For example, growing up without a father need not in itself be disastrous for a child unless his mother becomes so dependent on his devotion that she makes it impossible for him to break away from her emotionally and practically in the normal way during adolescence. In this case, bereavement can have repercussions that only show themselves many years after the event. Some disturbances in adolescence and later can be traced to the death of a parent in childhood—particularly depression when older.

Children being very protective of their surviving parent can be left carrying far too heavy a burden for their young shoulders. This is where a family counselor can help, so that the burden is not left solely on the child.

Economic Consequences

However, since bereaved families, unlike families disrupted by divorce, are more likely to have been happy than unhappy previously, their long-term problems tend to be mainly economic. When a father dies, a mother may have to work to support her children, and they have to get used to seeing her less than before at a time when they are upset and need her more. This is tragic but usually unavoidable.

Losing a Mother

If their mother dies, children have an even more drastic change to face. Even a comparatively well-off father may find it difficult to afford an adequately paid housekeeper; he may decide they will be better off with relatives. This is most likely to happen when a father is left with a young baby who needs immediate and constant care. Something must be arranged quickly, and the baby's long-term interests may have to give way to short-term necessity.

However convinced his father and relatives are that a baby must have the security of a permanent mother substitute, in practice it can be difficult to find someone suitable at once and he is shuttled about from person to person before being settled into one household. The distress the baby felt at the loss of his mother may harden into a permanent distrust of committing himself to another person; he may become afraid to love deeply because of the disappointment that might follow. It is important to know how a child feels when separated from the main figure of his life—his mother.

Fear of Separation in Babies

Until a baby is about six months old, he does not understand that his mother is a separate person, and therefore does not get anxious if he is separated from her, although he is affected by lack of sympathetic care in her absence. From the age of about six months, until he is about two years old, he literally mourns her absence. Having no idea of time, he cannot know she will come back.

His anxiety has three main stages, which have been compared to adult reactions to bereavement: at first he cries angrily, refuses to be comforted by others, and watches for his mother's return; then he becomes quietly sad and despairing, as if he had given up hope of her returning; and finally he seems to recover, having apparently forgotten his mother and his grief.

When a baby over six months old loses his mother permanently, perhaps through death, although he is unable to distinguish between temporary and permanent separation he inevitably reaches the final stage of grief: apparent indifference to her absence. It is at this point that he can begin to accept a substitute for her and to transfer his love to the substitute. Attempts to make him respond before he has reached this stage are usually rejected, and it is better to allow him to work through his sadness before expecting him to react positively to kindness.

Thus the younger a baby is when his mother dies the less he suffers, immediately, although the long-term effects will also depend on his experience in later childhood. He is happier if he has the same person looking after him all day than if he spends shorter periods with different people (see pp. 163–64).

Choosing a Mother Substitute

When arranging for somebody to look after a baby or small child, it is important to look for warmth and understanding rather than for high standards of housekeeping. A father, or a working mother, should settle for sympathy rather than efficiency, if unable to find someone with both qualities. The child needs someone who is interested in his activities and development, so that he has an incentive to display and practice his achievements: this particularly applies to the process of learning to speak, which can slow down if it is not stimulated during the second year of life. This, in turn, can affect general intellectual development (p. 565). A parent is naturally interested in his baby's progress but if he or she is at work all day, someone else must provide this interest.

A preschool child whose parent is dead or has to work also needs a reliable stand-in to take an interest in his activities. The child who lacks encouragement at home is at a disadvantage when he starts his formal education. This does not mean that a mother substitute must be an expert in child development or education, but she should have an instinctive understanding of a child's interests. He does not need someone to teach him to read before he starts school, but he does require someone who knows he needs to play even if he untidies his room while playing. She must not feel hurt if the child, or the baby, takes some time to accept her.

Losing a Father

A small child tends to react to the death of his father with less open sorrow than to the death of his mother; this is because it leaves less of a gap in his daily life. Some children ignore the event altogether; others react as they do to other kinds of stress, by behaving aggressively or by relapsing to an earlier type of behavior, such as bedwetting.

Long-term Effects of Losing a Parent

The death of a parent of the same sex as the child is more likely to have a continuing effect on his personality if it occurs when he is about three or four years old. This is because at that age he is modeling himself on the parent of his own sex.

A child's needs differ from a baby's in that he asks questions about his parent's disappearance and must be answered truthfully. Since his mother or father will not come back, it only adds to his anxiety if the surviving parent's promises to the contrary never come true.

A school child, especially if he is more than eight or nine, is more likely to suffer grief in the same way as adults. This can affect his schoolwork by making him depressed and unable to concentrate. A bereaved child may also fall behind at school because he misses the dead parent's encouragement and interest in his progress. The surviving parent can help by being aware of this and by taking an added interest, but he or she may be too preoccupied by grief to notice. A sympathetic teacher who recognizes the problem can sometimes fill the gap. Above all, the child's probable feelings of personal guilt about his parent's death must be relieved.

Although bereavement adds to his existing problems and can make him behave badly, the older child has the advantage of remembering his parent. The parent's influence remains, giving the child someone on whom to model himself; he does not have to build up an image of the parent from his imagination like the child who has lost someone whom he no longer remembers. Photographs help, but the main thing is for the dead parent to remain a subject of everyday conversation.

Bringing Up a Child Alone

In many ways this is more difficult for a mother than for a father. A father has to provide a mother substitute to run the home while he is at work. She may be a nanny for the children or a housekeeper for the household. A mother will not have to make this provision if she does not go to work, but if she does she will face the problem of finding someone sympathetic and understanding, who does not try to steal from her the role of mother. The risk of competition between the two women is great (see pp. 161, 163–64).

A mother bringing up her children by herself has to avoid becoming overpossessive and yet, to some extent, she has to assume the dual role of mother and father. She is bound, at times, to feel that there is no one to give her the support her husband would provide. An older brother or sister can go a long way to restore the family balance. For example, an older boy can take a younger one fishing or help him with his carpentry, as his father might have done. The problem is to stop too much of a father's role being thrust on the older boy, who still needs to feel like a son and to have someone male to whom he can appeal for support and help. Male relatives and friends can provide some of the companionship he needs.

Perhaps the mother's most difficult task is to be more available to her children when circumstances inevitably make her less available. However, if you are a widow or a mother alone, it is important to remake an interesting life for yourself, independent of your children; this is both for the sake of your own happiness and in order to avoid living entirely through them. If you base your life on theirs, it will be doubly hard to let them become more independent and break away from the family when the time comes. You may all become too dependent on one another, or the children may rebel and cut themselves right off from you. It will be easier to build a new life if you had outside interests or work while your husband was there, but it is possible even if you were entirely dependent on him, especially if you know it is important for your children's sake as well as for your own (see p. 171).

The children in a single-parent household are likely to have greater anxiety over the possible loss of this parent than are children who have two. Having already lost one parent they are more aware of the possibility of further loss and of the fact that they have only one to lose.

The unmarried mother, in deciding her child's future, has to face the difficult fact that it might be better for him to be adopted into a normal two-parent household, instead of remaining in a one-parent situation (see p. 352).

26

Travel, Vacations, and Living in the Tropics

Journeys

Babies are soothed by movement and they often sleep solidly or stay awake peacefully while traveling, but small children do not enjoy travel for its own sake. A child is not content to watch the scenery go by; sitting quietly for hours on end is physically impossible for him, and unless he sleeps or is provided with amusement, he will find ways of amusing himself which are usually unpopular with parents and fellow travelers—fighting, crying, creating as much noise and movement as possible, or restlessly demanding more food, candy, and reassurances that the journey's end is imminent.

Planning the Journey

Planning the journey means less trouble and more peace en route. Work out beforehand the best ways to feed, occupy, rest, clean, and clothe your children and you will take some of the trauma out of traveling with them.

First, if there is a choice, try to plan the journey so as to cause the minimum disruption to their usual sleeping pattern. It is better to start before normal bedtime so that children can sleep on the way than to wake them up to set off in the middle of the night. Long journeys seem even longer with children exhausted from lack of sleep. Speed and comfort may cost more, but getting to your destination happily sometimes makes the whole vacation more enjoyable.

Air Travel

Most children are excited by the prospect and the experience of air travel, although some may be afraid of a possible crash. Whether or not a child says he is afraid, the best policy resembles that for visiting the dentist—no horror stories and confident parents.

Airlines try to provide amusement for child travelers and also help in preparing babies' feedings. There are sometimes other facilities, such as space for carry-beds. Check the facilities offered beforehand: they may help you to decide which airline to choose. The important point is to warn the airline well in advance so that they can provide the best seat, with room for a carry-bed in front of you, disposable diapers, and help with feedings.

Pressure changes during takeoff and landing cause much pain to children's ears. Listen to their crying next time you fly. Babies can be saved this pain if fed during these times, and this is made possible by the extra strap which attaches to your own, allowing you to hold your baby in your arms. Ask the cabin staff for this.

Also check the time involved in getting to and from the airport and in making any connections. Hours of waiting with tired children in the middle of the night offsets the advantage that the speed of flying offers over other forms of transport. Many airports provide nurseries with trained staff. You should also allow for the effects of crossing time zones, as happens between London and New York, since this will upset the sleep rhythm of both adults and children, and may affect your children's mood (as well as your own) for a day or two after arrival.

Although some entertainment may be provided, from free crayons to a movie, have something of your own ready to amuse your children. Most of the diversions suggested for car journeys are suitable (below).

Trains

Children and trains go well together. There is more space for activity than in a car, although you may not appreciate this after your twentieth chase up the aisle after a determined explorer. Seats next to the aisle are easiest to get in and out of without disturbing other passengers; window seats are best for counting cows. Reserving seats in advance is always worthwhile when taking children on a long train journey.

The novelty of the train itself, stops at stations, visits to the restaurant car and bathroom, all help to break up the monotony of the journey. But one disadvantage is that your children's behavior is on public view. The yelling and bickering, which are at least private in the family car, have to be restrained if you wish to avoid bothering fellow travelers. However, children do tend to behave rather better than usual under the watchful eye of strangers, some of whom will like children and help to amuse them during the journey.

Babies sleep well on trains, finding the rhythm and movement soothing; so crying and disturbing other passengers is rarely a problem. Feeding and changing present problems unless you have anticipated them in advance (see pp. 366–67).

Traveling by Car

On a car journey your children's behavior does at least go unobserved, except in traffic jams, where it may entertain or horrify neighboring motorists. However, for the peace of mind of the driver and the safety of the passengers, a well-organized, comparatively quiet carload of children is essential. You must have safety belts for all children, and special safety seats for babies and toddlers (p. 634).

Total peace means sleeping children; this is possible, if you are driving overnight, but at the price of an energetic first day, when you may want to rest and they do not. Traveling by day means thinking up quiet activities for your children in advance. A pillow and a blanket for each child will encourage them to rest.

Amusements

Suitable occupations naturally depend on the individual children and on their ages. Some of the toys and activities suggested for bedbound children are equally good for journeys (see the sick child at home, pp. 402–3). These include pads and pencils, books and comics, and games that can be played on laps, such as jigsaws, puzzles, threading beads, and hand puppets. A book can provide a useful surface to play on; even better is a small, deep-sided tray—one for each child. Something new, even if it is only a notebook, often entertains for longer than something familiar. Avoid toys with sharp edges, which might injure your child if the car stops suddenly.

The need to make a noise can be channeled into songs, jokes, and stories. If you start them off, the children may take over and you can then relax. Older children can divert themselves in ways suggested by the journey itself: following the route on a map, using a pocket compass, guessing the next motel sign, competitions involving license numbers and different makes of cars, playing I-spy, identifying various road signs. There are several publications available giving more ideas on car traveling with children.

Clear up the debris at intervals, otherwise the clutter will make play difficult and quarrels more frequent. Give each child something to put his things in, to avoid quarrels over possessions.

Breaking Your Journey

How often you break your journey must depend on the driver as well as on the children. Short stops every hour are often recommended, but sometimes fewer but lengthier stops are better, particularly on long trips, when children seem to adapt to the rhythm of the journey and become less restless. Choose places to stop where they can really run about and let off steam. The edge of a busy road or a pull-off with vehicles entering and leaving are obviously not safe and provide little change of atmosphere.

Food and Drink

Picnic meals are more fun and more relaxing than long waits in hot restaurants. Snacks between meals help ward off boredom as well as hunger. Things to nibble that are not too filling are best—chips, apples, and cheese in little packets, for example. Chewing gum is good. Take plenty to drink, since children become extra thirsty on journeys and it may be difficult to get suitable drinks at the right time.

Feeding Babies While Traveling

Breast Feeding The easiest and safest way to feed a small baby while traveling is to breast feed him. Unfortunately, breast feeding in public sometimes causes embarrassment nowadays, or, at the least, surprise, so unless you can find a deserted corner or feel up to explaining the situation to other passengers, you may end up feeding your baby in the bathroom. This may be unpleasant for you, but the "germs" won't kill him. Airlines vary enormously in their approach to breast feeding. Check this point when making reservations and see if they provide a leaflet giving facilities for babies.

Bottle Feeding If you give your baby a bottle in public no one will be shocked but it will involve much more planning, particularly if there are going to be several feedings during the journey.

Your baby's milk or solid food need not be warmed up while traveling (see bottle feeding, p. 95). This will relieve you of the task of negotiating for hot water or carrying a supply in order to warm the feedings. Keeping a baby's milk warm for several hours is dangerous, because any germs in the milk multiply in the heat—it is far better to give it to him cold.

Solid Food If your baby eats solid foods, take his favorite cans with you—enough to last the journey and the vacation as well if you are uncertain about what is available. This is not the right time to introduce new tastes, to worry about eating at the right time, or about the exact balance of his diet.

Let your baby eat directly from the can but throw away the rest if it cannot be kept cold and covered until the next meal. Instant powdered foods can be mixed with boiled water as needed and are light to carry; but do not wait to try them for the first time while traveling.

If your baby is used to eating mashed versions of adult meals, he will enjoy the same in restaurants, but avoid made-up and reheated dishes, since the risk of food poisoning from such foods is greater when they are prepared in communal kitchens. Custards, cream, and cold meats are also unsafe for babies unless freshly made at home (see mixed feeding, pp. 192, 193).

Washing and Changing the Traveling Baby

"Topping and tailing" is all that is essential (see bathing, p. 98). Take something waterproof to lay on your lap while dealing with your baby, and plenty of plastic bags to stow away the debris. "Disposable" is the most useful word to remember. A copious supply of tissues and the special damp cloths now available for baby cleaning are useful whenever soap, water, and clean towels are scarce. Baby lotion and mineral oil can replace soap and water for topping and tailing.

Disposable diapers are the obvious answer to the diaper problem while traveling and on vacation.

Travel Sickness

Nearly everyone is sick when sailing a stormy sea but some people, particularly children, are made sick by the much gentler motion of travel by car, boat, or plane; trains do not seem to have the same effect.

Why do some children suffer from travel sickness? Presumably the balance mechanism in the middle ear is especially affected by the movement and vibration of traveling, so that they feel or are sick, although it would take considerably more violent movement to bother the average adult. A slow rolling movement upsets the balance mechanism much more than a jerky up and down movement. This explains why a child may be sick on one type of journey, or indeed in one type of car, and not another.

Some children show a tendency toward sickness when they are as young as six months; but remember that there are several other reasons why your baby may vomit while traveling. For example, a baby who regularly regurgitates after feedings will also do so in the car. Nearly all children grow out of the tendency completely, sooner or later; relatively few adults are carsick, although many remain bad sailors.

Preventing Sickness

Food and Drink   There are certain things you can do to reduce the likelihood of travel sickness. Do not give your child a large, greasy meal within a few hours of the journey or during it. But an empty stomach does not help either, and may even make him feel sicker. A light meal about an hour before setting off, with not too much to drink, is the best start. Don't ban food while traveling but allow sodas, crackers, and similar snacks if your child wants them.

Keeping Calm   Try not to show anxiety about what your child is eating or how he is feeling, or he may feel he is bound to be sick.

Excitement and apprehension play a part in travel sickness—children are more often sick on outward journeys than on the way back.

Reading a book is supposed to increase the likelihood of sickness, but so does having nothing to do or to think about, so keep your child occupied (p. 365). The front passenger seat is probably the best place for avoiding carsickness, but this advantage is offset by the fact that it is also the most dangerous place for your child to sit, because an adult's seat belt is too large to protect him properly (see accidents, p. 634).

Drugs A surer method of stopping persistent sickness is to give your child a pill to prevent travel sickness half an hour before starting. Antiemetics sold under such brand names as Dramamine and Marezine are effective in preventing travel sickness and are commonly included in the antisickness pills available from the drugstore without a doctor's prescription. It is extremely important that the label or the descriptive literature on the package be read carefully to determine the proper dosage for children and the frequency with which it may be safely taken.

Take something like a plastic bag for your child to be sick in, and something to clean up with, but keep them out of sight unless needed. You will get to know the telltale signs; common ones are going pale, drowsiness, and sudden silence from a talkative child.

Finally, remember that although travel sickness is inconvenient, it does not harm a child's health; it always gets less troublesome, and nearly always disappears as he grows older.

Extra Immunization

Depending on your destination, extra immunization may be needed for both adults and children. Protection against yellow fever, smallpox, and cholera is compulsory in some countries. Vaccination against polio is not compulsory but is very desirable; polio attacks adults as well as children and is still common in developing countries. So is malaria; therefore antimalarial drugs are necessary (see living in the tropics, p. 000). Typhoid vaccination (TAB) is a wise precaution if you are going to any country where the water supply and standards of hygiene are less reliable than those at home, so consider it if you are visiting a Mediterranean country, Eastern Europe, or any developing country (see immunization, pp. 259f.).

Check with your doctor whether extra immunization is needed well before you are due to leave; immunization programs involve intervals between shots and should be started several weeks before effective protection is needed. Your travel agent should be able to give you a leaflet for travelers prepared by the U.S. Department of Public Health Services.

Vacations with Children

Small children in normal families do not need to "get away from it all" at least once a year as parents usually do. Until around school age children prefer home, familiarity, and routine; they have little concept of distance and time, and cannot be expected to appreciate the expense and effort involved in transporting them to far-off places. So don't go on vacation "for the sake of the children." On the other hand, don't stay at home for their sake if you want to go. Unless you are confident that your children will be happy with relatives or friends, it's better to take them along. A vacation with small children is bound to be a compromise but it can be an enjoyable one. Moreover, you will probably worry less about them if they are with you and you may feel far lonelier without them than you had anticipated.

Where you go should be influenced by the realities of life with children; it is no good planning a vacation based on an exhausting schedule of sightseeing and museums if the tantrums of a bored and exhausted two-year-old prevent you from looking at anything. But, equally, a vacation based solely on children's amusements with none for the bored and exhausted adults is bound to be a failure.

At the Beach

Don't expect too much of the beach; don't assume that once you get there, your children will automatically be happy and amuse themselves. It is true that many children between five and ten will be entranced by the sea, enjoying its noise and the fact that no one stops them making a noise too. The sea fights them and they enjoy fighting back.

But the toddler may be very frightened of the sea, especially when he sees you disappearing into this strange thing. He may be too hot (see sunburn, pp. 376–77, 493–94)—or more likely too cold in northern areas—and the sand in his pants may make him itch.

You still have to work to entertain your children at the beach, and you have to guard them even more carefully than in your own home.

Going Abroad

Children of all ages have traveled long distances and spent vacations and lived in all kinds of climate happily, but only you can decide whether you can face a long journey abroad in unfamiliar heat with your particular child. Some families manage it happily, often because they find a way of combining the unfamiliar aspects of going abroad with a degree of familiarity and routine that enables recognizable family life to continue.

Self-catering Vacations

This kind of vacation is easiest in a temporary "home of your own," whether a tent, camper, cottage, or house. There must be space for the children to play, and you should take with you some of their least bulky but most entertaining toys. Cooking and cleaning can be minimized if you are not too house-proud and are willing to eat picnics rather than four-course meals. The great advantage is that you can look after your children in a more or less normal way, unrestrained by the gaze of hotel guests and by the necessity of keeping them especially quiet and abnormally "good," so as not to disturb other people.

Hotels

Trying to keep children amused on a wet day in a hotel bedroom will not add much to the enjoyment of your vacation. Eating in a hotel dining room surrounded by adults trying to hold adult conversations can spotlight the deficiencies in your child's manners and the loudness of his voice, which you may have successfully ignored for the rest of the year. The poor child is suddenly expected to have perfect table manners, to eat strange food, to wait for the next course, not to play around while he is waiting, and not to make personal remarks about the other guests.

Most parents would probably prefer to rent a cottage or go camping until their children reach the age of discretion for life in a hotel. This time may arrive sooner than you expect, since children tend to understand the necessity of behaving and not bothering other people when on public view earlier than they become convinced of the need to behave consistently well at home.

Life with Father

Another aspect of family life that vacations tend to dramatize is any difference between their parents' views on discipline. Suddenly, the children are around for the twenty-four hours of their father's day. He is no longer partially insulated from the reality of life with his children by departing every morning and returning near bedtime. Irritation at the noise and demands they make, together with feelings of guilt that his poor wife endures this all the time, may show itself in criticism of her methods of dealing with them. She will resent criticism but may also feel guilt, because although mothers need vacations at least as much as fathers, the idea that earning the family's living is far more exhausting than actually looking after the family lingers on. At its extreme it ends up with the kind of vacation where father departs with his fishing rod for the whole of each day, leaving his unfortunate wife to hold the babies. Recognizing the symptoms in time should help to achieve a compromise between father's, mother's, and children's rights, and enable everyone to enjoy the vacation.

Vacations with Friends

Going away with another family has many advantages, if you know beforehand that you get on well with them. Whether you are camping or renting a cottage, sharing with another family means you can arrange shifts for cooking, and you can also baby-sit for each other so as to allow husband and wife to have a meal out by themselves. If the men decide to go off on their own for a few hours, the wives, left together, are unlikely to feel neglected.

Taking one of your children's friends on vacation with you can be a great success. The visitor may trigger off new amusements among your own children so that they entertain themselves more successfully than with only the family for company.

Vacations without Parents

Are vacations for children away from their families a good idea? At what age would a child enjoy one of the special vacations arranged by various organizations—a riding vacation or a week at Scout camp? Some children love the idea and are eager to go from the earliest age at which such organizations will accept them, which is usually around eight. Others even dislike the prospect of a week at camp with familiar friends, though they may enjoy it once they get there.

Don't send a reluctant child on an independent vacation to "toughen him up" or in an attempt to make him more independent. He may feel he has been pushed off while you enjoy yourself and he will probably return home loathing the outdoor life and determined never to leave your side again. Wait till such a child shows he is ready for the experience. It is the child who is already comparatively self-sufficient and adventurous who wants to go to camp at an early age and will enjoy it. Going with a friend or a brother or sister gives confidence, particularly the first time away, and may persuade a half-hearted child that it is a good idea after all. A teen-ager will probably enjoy being with people of his own age more than a family holiday.

Sign up for a camp or a trip early while there is still a choice of location and type of activity available; this will give you a good chance of finding one that matches your child's interests or hobbies. Make sure he goes off with all the right equipment, and write to him right away, even if you are busy organizing your own vacation.

Keeping Healthy on Vacation: Precautions

The change of air, routine, food, and scene, which is meant to make everyone feel healthier on and after a vacation, does not always have that result, particularly with small children, who thrive on familiarity. Keeping well on vacation, especially when changes of climate and diet are marked, is largely a matter of taking common-sense precautions before trouble starts. For example, anticipating sunburn rather than having to deal with its effects (see too much sun?, pp. 376–77, sunburn, pp. 493–94); calculating and avoiding the possible effects of too much unfamiliar food and drink before stomachs are upset, not afterward; avoiding the cumulative effects of nonstop excitement and late nights by keeping reasonably close to your child's normal routine—if he is used to a midday rest, he cannot suddenly do without it every day without becoming fractious. Expect a certain amount of adaptability from your children—they will enjoy it—but expect too much and everyone will end up bad-tempered.

Take a first-aid kit (p. 649), adding items like sunburn cream and perhaps a medication recommended by your doctor to deal with minor stomach upsets if you are going to unfamiliar territory (see p. 376). Give plenty of fluids if your child gets travelers' diarrhea. If he feels ill with diarrhea, he may have dysentery and you should see a doctor. Check on immunization well beforehand if you are going abroad (p. 368), and make sure you know how to minimize the effects of travel sickness if this is a family problem. Medical insurance taken out before leaving relieves you of expense and anxiety should medical treatment abroad be necessary.

Living in the Tropics

Your husband has been offered a job in a tropical country: should he accept or should you both turn it down because of possible dangers to the health of your children? Provided certain precautions are taken, there is no reason why any member of the family should be less healthy, although, unfortunately, you will be just as likely to get coughs and colds in the tropics as in a temperate climate.

As a mother you will have more domestic help, which will mean that you will have more time for your children. They will have the benefit of the sun and probably much more space outdoors for play than they have now at home. You will all come back with a store of memories and, provided everything goes well, your children will have a new understanding of racial tolerance. The experience and the broadening in outlook that will come to your children as well as to yourselves will be of inestimable value.

Medical Care

Although the standard of medical care in many large towns is high, doctors in developing countries are in short supply and, consequently, very busy. Few doctors specialize in the care of children. So it helps all around if you know how to avoid common troubles and how to deal with those that do arise. This is largely a matter of foresight and common sense and everyday living: if you eat and dress sensibly, many minor discomforts can be avoided (see below).

Immunization

It is essential to arrive fully protected against all those diseases for which immunization is available. Travelers to the tropics must be inoculated against certain tropical diseases such as yellow fever; the legal requirements vary according to the country visited. However, make sure that your children (and yourselves, where relevant) are also immunized against the more common childhood complaints like measles, whooping cough, and polio. These are still very common in most developing countries, so check that your child's immunization program is up to date (see immunization, pp. 259f.). Tuberculosis is another common infection in developing countries, so your children should be protected against it by BCG vaccination (p. 264).

There is no inoculation against malaria, but if you are going to a malarial area there are appropriate antimalarial tablets to take. These should be started one week before you arrive and continued for four weeks after you return. The tablets must be taken regularly while you are living in a malarial area; they do no harm either to you or to your children. The same medicine is available in syrup form for very young children.

Visiting the Dentist

Before leaving for the tropics, and during every home leave, the whole family should visit the dentist and any treatment should be completed. Dentists are few and far between in developing countries. However, you will probably find it easier to keep your children's candy eating within reasonable bounds, and consequently their teeth reasonably free of decay, because there won't be a candy store and an ice-cream truck at every corner.

Clothing

In many towns there is a variety of clothing available, but the choice of basic children's clothes is not as wide as in chain stores at home and the cost is usually higher. However, you will find plenty of attractive material on sale, so cotton dresses, shirts, and shorts can easily be made at home or by a local dressmaker or tailor.

Cotton is the most suitable material for wearing in the heat. It is cooler and more comfortable than any of the man-made fibers such as nylon, or polyester, which tend to make you feel still stickier. Although short-sleeved shirts and shorts are all a child needs most of the time, some long-sleeved tops and trousers are needed for wearing in the evenings, when the insect population arrives in force to bite uncovered limbs. Cool evenings often follow hot days, so lightweight but warm sweaters are needed. Night clothes should be long, unless your house is bug-proofed or the beds covered with mosquito nets.

Keeping Babies Cool

A baby can get too cold in the tropics when the temperature falls during the night, but the main problem is keeping him cool. A light cotton top and a diaper are all he will need for everyday wear; the top can be discarded if necessary. A long-sleeved nightgown will keep him warm if the nights are cool.

A gauze diaper is cooler to wear than a terry toweling one and is often sufficient, because moisture evaporates quickly in the heat. Plastic pants and sheets are hot, so leave off the pants whenever possible and put a rush mat between the plastic sheet and the crib sheet. The rush mat becomes sodden and needs frequent replacement but locally made mats are cheap.

You can easily get help with the washing and ironing, and the sun solves the drying problem, so it is not as urgent as in a cool climate to keep the laundry to a minimum. It is a good idea to leave off your baby's diaper if there is any sign of diaper rash (p. 35).

A young baby cannot move himself out of the sun if he becomes too hot, so put his carriage or crib in the shade. He will sleep more comfortably in a basket than in a plastic-lined carry-bed, because a basket allows more air to circulate. It is usually easy to get one made to order if you cannot find a suitable ready-made basket.

Feeding Babies

Breast Feeding   It is safer and easier to breast feed a baby in the tropics because of the extra care needed in preparing bottle feedings (p. 82). Some mothers who might not have breast fed at home prefer it here because of the domestic help available and the more relaxed tempo of life in a developing country.

Bottle Feeding   If you do bottle feed your baby, give him the milk mixture you would have chosen at home. There is no need to use a special brand of milk because you are living in the tropics. If it is impossible to obtain your first choice of powdered milk, your baby will do just as well on another brand (see bottle feeding, pp. 84–86). Fresh cow's milk is even riskier in a hot climate, and the chances are that it won't be available.

Extra Drinks   Prepare your baby's food and drinks personally, unless you have complete confidence in your domestic help. A bottle-fed baby should be offered drinks of boiled water as well as his milk feedings to replace the water lost by sweating; this helps his kidneys to deal with the extra protein and minerals contained in cow's milk. A breast-fed baby may also appreciate drinks of water between meals in hot weather.

Mixed Feeding   Introducing mixed feeding should follow the same principles as would apply at home (see mixed feeding, pp. 185f.). Base your baby's diet on whatever foods are available locally. Special baby foods are imported but are expensive for everyday use. Locally grown food is as suitable for your baby as for the rest of the family if prepared in your own kitchen, where you can make sure refrigeration and hygiene are adequate.

Feeding Older Children

Although visitors seldom go over to a completely native cuisine, it is impossible to eat exactly the same diet as at home. The food available is different and there are fewer easily prepared foods on sale at reasonable prices. However, since you can employ someone to peel potatoes for you, saving time in the kitchen is less of a priority in the tropics. The children may miss their hot dogs and hamburgers at first, but they won't allow themselves to starve. They may eat less at first because of the heat.

Boiling Water

It may be necessary to boil all drinking water unless your local supply is entirely reliable. Boiled water tastes better cold from the refrigerator. Add fruit juice if your child is reluctant to drink it plain. When on the move, it is essential to take a supply of boiled water or bottled drinks with you. It is safe to buy fizzy drinks of reputable make.

Extra Salt

While living in your own home in the tropics it is unnecessary to suck salt tablets to make up the salt lost through heavy sweating, as used to be recommended; it is sufficient to add a little extra salt to the cooking.

Illnesses

Diarrhea

Whenever someone, adult or child, moves to another country, he is liable to get diarrhea shortly after arriving. This is due partly to the different food but also to the fact that the bacteria in the food are unfamiliar to him. Bacteria are present in all diets, but whereas those prevalent in his home community become harmless through familiarity, strange bacteria can cause diarrhea at first.

This is rather like a situation that is common among hospital staff. Someone returns from vacation, fit and well, but within a few days gets a cold or some other infection; he seems to have lost his immunity to the hospital germs and has to build it up again. Both the strange food and the strange bacteria become familiar in time and cease to cause trouble.

Do not make your child eat more than he wants. His appetite, like yours, will probably be smaller than usual until he gets used to the heat, but he will want to drink more. If he does have an attack of diarrhea, encourage him to drink copiously, since it is the loss of fluid that is the great danger. Add a little salt to his drinks.

If an attack of diarrhea continues for more than twelve hours, if the stool is watery or your child is obviously ill, be sure to get medical advice. Always report a young baby's diarrhea immediately (see diarrhea, pp. 478–80).

Too Much Sun?

Fair-skinned adults and children need extra protection from sunburn; they may need a sun-screen cream in addition to the ordinary sun creams, and they may also feel happier wearing a hat in strong sunlight. But other people do not need hats to protect them from the danger of "sunstroke," which used to be blamed on sun shining directly on the head and neck.

The symptoms previously attributed to "sunstroke" are really caused by overheating of the whole body, and they are now called "heatstroke." There is no need to insist that your children wear hats when they go out to play; they will move into the shade as they become too hot. Take normal precautions to stop them from getting sunburned at first, allowing them to build up a tan. In fact, you will find it far more difficult to get tanned in the tropics than on your beach at home, partly because you will be more interested in keeping cool than in getting brown, and partly because the sun is so often clouded over in the tropics.

Stock up with sun screens and sunburn remedies before leaving home, because these may not be widely available. (See also sunburn, pp. 493–94.)

Minor Skin Troubles

Insect Bites   Insect bites worry visitors more than the native inhabitants of a country. This is particularly true of mosquito bites. Once you have been bitten, all the bites start itching again at each new bite. Children must be discouraged from scratching, since this may infect the bites. The number of bites can be kept down by bug-proofing the house and by wearing suitable clothing (pp. 373–74). Insect-repellent creams and sprays are effective provided they are reapplied every few hours. This is another item you should bring with you, because you cannot always buy them when you need them. A fly spray for killing insects in the house is another valuable item to be brought with you.

Prickly Heat   This is common in hot weather. It is a very uncomfortable skin condition consisting of itching red spots and minute blisters. All ages are affected, but especially young babies; the spots occur mainly on the face, neck, back, and chest. (See also heat rashes, p. 429.)

Prickly heat is caused by sweating, and both the prevention and the cure lie in frequent changes of sweaty garments and frequent baths or showers. It is unnecessary to soap your child all over, since the bath is merely to freshen up—in fact, too much soap irritates some skins. Prickly heat at the back of the neck is discouraged by cutting or tying back the hair. Calamine lotion soothes prickly heat, and by drying the skin and discouraging sweating, helps to heal the spots.

Foot Troubles   Athlete's foot is encouraged by sweating, so it is common in hot countries. Frequent washing helps (see athlete's foot, p. 500). Going barefoot discourages athlete's foot but can encourage hookworm (p. 492); lightweight sandals should be worn.

Making Friends and Influencing Each Other

Every mother who comes from a developed country to a developing one has the chance to learn from the different cultural methods of bringing up children. She also has the chance to explain and perhaps to pass on some of her own culture's experience and knowledge. Some of this exchange comes through observing, some through conversation, and some through direct help and advice.

You will meet educated women whose ideas and standards of child care are similar to your own, but also women whose views appear very strange and illogical at first. For example, the notion that an illness is due to offended "spirits" rather than to infection seems less strange when one remembers that similar attitudes were held in Europe as little as 200 years ago. These ideas cannot be changed overnight by a headlong attack, but they are altering gradually. Meanwhile, you can help in a direct way by encouraging mothers to have their children immunized. Your own domestic staff will probably have children, and it is here that you can be particularly helpful.

Diet and Malnutrition In developing countries, preventing ill-health in children is closely linked with preventing malnutrition, which is due as much to ignorance as to poverty. Children do not get enough protein, even though there may be a good supply of protein foods available locally, because their parents do not realize its value. Among your own staff, try to encourage mothers to give their children some protein food, such as beans, every day.

The Importance of Play

Another important way in which you can encourage a greater under-standing of children's needs is in convincing their parents of the value of play. The African baby lives on his mother's back. This is a comfort-ing place for a young baby: he is near his mother, he can feed easily when hungry and so tends to cry less than a baby tucked up in his separate crib and fed at special times only. Western mothers can learn from African mothers how much a baby needs contact and comfort as well as hygienic surroundings and a balanced diet. However, living on his mother's back becomes less satisfactory when the baby becomes a crawler and a toddler. At this stage, he would enjoy him-self, and learn more, exploring on the ground.

When the African child does get off his mother's back he may still have little chance to handle and play with toys and objects in the way most children in Western society take for granted. For instance, he does not learn to use scissors or to manipulate an interlocking toy at the age when both his general intelligence and his manual dexterity would be stimulated by this type of play. Such things are just not widely available, nor is the need for them appreciated.

It is possible that this lack of opportunity for learning and prac-ticing manual skills when young affects the individual's ultimate per-formance; this would put him at a disadvantage when it comes to earning a living in an industrialized society. Of course, some children in developed countries are also deprived of the chance of stimulating play in the preschool years, either because their parents are too poor to provide the materials or because they underestimate its value.

The need for education, in its widest sense of enabling each child to develop and use his potential, is being acknowledged all over the world. In developing countries the problem is far more widespread, and there is a large backlog of poverty and parental ignorance to overcome.

Children and Work

Their own children's enjoyment when playing with yours is perhaps the best way of convincing the mothers you meet that playing is not a waste of time, although they may feel, with some justification, that once a child is old enough, he is better off helping adults than playing childish games. This is a valid point and something that has been largely forgotten in developed countries—children do enjoy and learn from the responsibility of "proper" work and tasks helping adults; they like giving genuine help as well as pretending to help. But they need to work at playing too (see play, pp. 296–98).

2

The
Sick
Child

27

Children, Parents, and Their Doctor

Your Family Doctor

Different systems of medical care operate in different countries. It is important that you should understand the system in your own country in order to get the best out of it. In the United States the individual chooses his own specialist. But this presupposes that a patient knows what is wrong with him and therefore knows which specialist to choose. If he should choose the wrong specialist the error might not immediately be obvious, since a specialist is bound to think in terms of his own specialty first and therefore to try to fit the patient's symptoms into his own field. In the United Kingdom a general practitioner, who is an expert in family medicine, looks after the whole family, referring individual members to specialists when necessary.

Having worked in both countries, I prefer the British system because a family doctor is better equipped to pick the right sort of specialist; moreover, because he knows the patient, he is more likely to choose a specialist whose personality suits him or her. This is particularly important when choosing a psychiatrist for a patient.

The family-doctor system does not eliminate a patient's freedom of choice of specialist—a family doctor aims to satisfy this aspect of his patient's wishes. Under the National Health Service there is no restriction of choice of specialist for the general practitioner. He is more likely to choose a specialist from his nearest main hospital because he knows him and because it is geographically more convenient for his patient. But he could refer him to any specialist in the country, provided his patient could make the journey. A patient's or parent's right to ask for a second opinion, though not always easy (pp. 390–91), is not affected by the National Health Service.

Your Relationship with Your Doctor

An understanding relationship between your family doctor—in other words, your general practitioner—and your family is essential if you are all to be able to help each other fully and to get the best out of this working partnership. Asking for your doctor's help with one of your children should not lead to a one-sided transaction in which the doctor is active and you are passive. Seeking your doctor's help initi-

ates a two-way process to which you should be allowed to contribute
as much as your doctor for the benefit of your child and, through him,
of your whole family.

Taking the "Family History"

A doctor has been trained in his side of the relationship both in the
art of communication and in the ability to diagnose and to treat illness.
But you must help the doctor, so that he understands as much as
possible about your problem. This may involve a lot of detailed and
personal questions which may not at first sight seem relevant. But
since everything to do with a child is intimately bound up with what
is going on in his family, a picture of his family background needs to
be built up by the doctor during the course of his first conversation
with you—this is the way the doctor takes the "family history" part
of his clinical history. Once your doctor knows your family, many of
these preliminaries can be skipped at future meetings.

If at this stage in the relationship you were to react aggressively
to the doctor's questions, regarding them as superfluous or imperti-
nent, he might react in one of two ways. The human response would
be to return your aggressive reaction with an aggressive outburst,
thereby starting a verbal slugging match. Alternatively, he might
give up trying to get to know you, reacting to your outburst by closing
up like a clam. Either situation could result in the doctor's treating
your child solely as a medical "case," not as an individual; this might
seriously impede the successful treatment of your child's problems.
It is important for your doctor to have a long talk with you on one of
your early visits, since otherwise he may never know you properly.
Once a superficial relationship between doctor and patient has developed it is very difficult for a doctor to achieve a deeper understanding
of the patient's needs. Again, it would be your child who suffered as
a consequence. Trusting your doctor means accepting that, because
this is a professional relationship, he is not "prying" into your affairs;
he needs to know more about you in order to help your child.

The ideal professional response to resentment of questioning
would be for a doctor patiently and sympathetically to work out why
his questions prompted this reaction, thereby determining its relevance to your child's problems. Such reactions need to be understood
if a good parent/doctor relationship is to develop. Your doctor, having
noticed your resentment, has to keep the discussion at a safe level to
avoid annoying you further. Of course, the reverse may happen: you
have to restrain your remarks to appease him.

Does Your Doctor Always Know Best?

Today's doctors have been trained to communicate in a very different manner from their predecessors. The doctor of old would ask a number of questions and would then, after his clinical examination of the child, give his advice. Parents would usually accept this advice unquestioningly, and even if it did not work, they would believe the doctor had done his best.

This is what I call the "pedestal doctor," who pronounces his advice from on high and expects parents to do exactly what he says. If they do not do as he says, then it is their fault if the child does not get better. Such a form of "communication" is, I am glad to say, becoming increasingly outmoded among doctors, because they are now aware that it is not in their patients' best interests. It is a relic of the idea that "the doctor knows best."

The relationship between doctor and parents must be one of partnership. If you pool your knowledge of your child, your doctor is in a far better position to help. When a doctor was looked on as some kind of god, disasters occurred from lack of communication. It should not be necessary for any parent to have to conceal knowledge and pretend ignorance of medical terms or treatment because of fear of invading the doctor's professional "territory." The general public, parents included, is learning more and more about advances and techniques in medicine, both through the media and because doctors have, quite simply, come down from their pedestals. Since doctors have encouraged this tendency, it is illogical if they resent evidence of parents' understanding, which is only another facet of concern for their children. If a mother feels like asking whether her child's tonsils should be removed, she is anticipating a discussion with her doctor. He would be quite wrong to give her an unqualified "no" without explaining that large tonsils are part of normal growth at a certain stage in a child's life (pp. 454f.).

All this takes time and a lot of patience. It is much easier and quicker for a doctor to hand out a prescription, accompanied by a few words of advice, than to spend a long time listening to a parent and working out the child's problem with him or her.

It is an interesting thought that in the old days, when the bulk of the medicines available did little good and a few did positive harm, the doctor's approach was to prescribe, believing implicitly in the power of his medicine. Today, when doctors have medicines of a power undreamed of by their predecessors, the handing out of a prescription is generally accompanied by much more conversation and much more concern on the part of the doctor as to whether he is prescribing the right medicine.

Getting to Know Your Family

I have already emphasized that your doctor will need to ask you a lot of personal questions to help him build up a picture of your child's daily life. He will probably want to ask at an early stage what your husband's job is and what job you used to do. He will need to know whether you go out to work. This is not to determine whether you are a "good" mother who stays at home looking after her children (this may not be ideal in any case—see pp. 162f.), but to know more about you. To take an obvious example: if a mother has been trained as a doctor or as a nurse she is bound to have a different outlook from someone without this kind of background. It would be a poor doctor who did not learn this important fact at an early point in the interview. In fact, if the doctor fails to discover it, the mother is likely, almost subconsciously, to use technical terms, perhaps partly to let him know that she has been trained in medicine or nursing and needs to be talked to in a more sophisticated way than an untrained parent. Of course, a mother without this sort of training may also use technical words because she knows them and uses them in her ordinary conversation, but I do not find this very common.

Although the need for a doctor to know something about the earlier training of a mother may not always be so obvious as in the example given above, nevertheless such information is essential for building up a store of information about any child's background.

Discussing Worries Frankly

Doctors are aware that patients come to see them complaining of one symptom when really their anxiety is about something quite different. For example, a patient who goes to his doctor for a cough may subconsciously be saying, "Have I got tuberculosis?" or "Is my heart healthy?" Sometimes the symptom that takes a patient to see his doctor may be a subconscious attempt to get the doctor's help for some deep family problem. This is sometimes the reason for a night call when a child is ill. However, and I must stress this, do not let knowing this fact influence you in deciding whether or not to call your doctor at night when your child is ill. If your child is ill, you must call the doctor.

It is the doctor's task to unearth these hidden reasons for seeking his help; if he is tired, busy, or rushed he may miss the clues. If you have insight into the real reason why you want your doctor to see your child, it is better to say so at the outset, since not only does this save time, but it also reduces the chances of the doctor missing the real reason for your visit.

Some doctors are always in a rush, giving their patients (and themselves) the impression that they are very busy. Other doctors are equally busy but give their patients the feeling that they have all the time in the world to listen to their problems—almost as though they have no other patients to see. The first type of doctor is an example of the "busy man syndrome." He is not at ease listening to his patient and therefore has built up a reason why he must rush off to the next one, thereby avoiding an experience he cannot tolerate. Such doctors suit patients with certain temperaments, but doctors and patients are both helped by having insight into the reasons why they behave as they do.

Many parents who go to their doctor because of anxiety about their child are frightened that they may be laughed at if they expose the real reason. Your anxiety may relate to something like a fear of leukemia, or a belief that your child's continuing crying is going to drive you mad or lead you to harm him if the doctor does not recognize your need. Some mothers are aware of what they are asking their doctor, others are totally unaware. If you are aware, it is best to be direct, but if you are unaware it is the doctor's skill that should unearth the hidden reason.

What might be termed "maneuvering" between mother and doctor is lessened if they understand each other. It often happens that a mother brings her child to a doctor because she wants reassurance, not a prescription. All she wants is to find out whether there is something wrong or not. For example, she may not be sure if a cold has affected her child's chest or ears, or is uncertain whether to take a certain symptom seriously. The doctor may misinterpret her motives, feeling that she will not be satisfied unless given a bottle of medicine. Don't be afraid to let your doctor know if it is advice, not medicine, you are after. To do this, you may need as much tact as the doctor is supposed to possess. Provided you (and your doctor) accept that you have to help him to help you to the full, all should be well.

With fewer people attending church today, help of this sort—friendly and serious advice on fears, problems, or anxieties of any kind, which could perhaps be equally well given by a minister or priest—is now coming more and more into the field of medicine. Ideally, whatever their personal beliefs, doctor and clergyman should be working closer and closer together for the benefit of people, whether as patients or as members of a congregation.

Choosing a Doctor

It is as essential for you to have an understanding of how your doctor reacts as it is for him to understand your reactions. You must try to find the sort of doctor who does not make you feel frightened when you have called him for something that turns out not to be serious. A good doctor will make you feel you did the right thing, thereby helping to give you more confidence for the next occasion when one of your children is ill. You cannot have a relationship with your doctor that is based on a constant worry about how he will react if you call him unnecessarily.

To help you in your choice of a new family doctor when you move, you will of course talk to friends and neighbors. Whenever possible it is a good idea to choose a pediatrician, for he will have a special interest in your children. Also, your present pediatrician can look up the résumés of doctors in your new area, or you can telephone your new local hospital for names.

Helping Your Doctor to Help Your Child

Your doctor will be getting to know your child at the same time as he is asking you questions about his illness. To help him he will also ask your child how he feels, and if he is old enough he will ask him to tell him more about the symptoms you have described. Alternatively, he is very likely, right at the start of the consultation, to ask your child some simple question to put him at ease. Don't make the mistake of answering the questions for your child or of telling him to speak up; let the doctor get to know your child in his own way. Such a reaction on your part tells the doctor more about you than about your child, and may have the disadvantage of making your child feel still more uncomfortable and embarrassed.

It is essential to be absolutely truthful when dealing with children; they are not made worse by being told the truth, even if it is painful, either physically or emotionally. I am increasingly staggered by the amount a child will let a doctor do to him provided the doctor is honest. Unfortunately, one still occasionally hears of a doctor or nurse stupidly saying, "It won't hurt" before giving an injection to a child. How could a child treated in this dishonest way ever trust that adult again?

Children are able to understand their illnesses to a remarkable extent if a doctor makes the explanation simple. Using diagrams to illustrate what goes on in the body often helps. Nothing is so complicated that it cannot be explained to a second person, but it needs a clever brain and, particularly, a good imagination to explain a complex process to someone who is a layman, whether it be in medicine, engineering, or anything else. It is vital for parents and doctors never to talk down to children. A child sees through this immediately, and treats the conversation with the derision it deserves.

Children vary enormously in the way they should be handled, and it is up to your doctor to work out how best to get to know your child. With a difficult toddler he may well ask you not to talk while he examines the child on your lap. The child needs the contact with your body to give him confidence to accept the doctor's examination, but every time you speak you bring his emotions up to the surface and make him cry. It is as though your attempts to reassure him by word only serve to remind him of the difficult situation he is in; it is physical contact with you that he needs most to help him cope with the situation (see also p. 406).

Your attitude to your child is all-important in maintaining his health and getting him through his illnesses. The children of anxious parents seem to get more colds than anybody else. Some infections are inevitable in childhood and your attitude to your child's illness should be sympathetic but matter-of-fact. If you are anxious, your child will feel doubly anxious. He will reflect your feelings to an extent you never imagined.

Illness, or going to the hospital, must never be used as a threat in order to make your child behave. Regrettably, some mothers do this, and it makes relationships between doctors and their child patients that more difficult. (See also the sick child in the hospital, p. 404, and the sick child at home, p. 395.)

How and When to Call Your Doctor

Basically, the time to ask your doctor to see your child is whenever you are worried about his health. This does not necessarily mean that you ask him to come to your home, and today's doctors are very reluctant to make house calls: whenever possible take your child to his office or telephone him there.

Visiting the Office

If your family doctor is to be as available as possible to all his patients, he should spend most of his time at his office rather than visiting patients in their homes. Most ill children can be taken to the office. A child with a fever can be taken to the office by car. If this idea worries you, remember that if your doctor calls at your house and then refers your child to the hospital, he will still have to go out in a car or ambulance.

Ideally, the doctor's receptionist is always someone who acts as a link between patient or parents and doctor—not a barrier.

Symptoms Needing Medical Advice

Apart from general anxiety about any aspect of your child's health, what are the major symptoms for which you should call your doctor? Accidents and poisoning are immediate emergencies, and when you telephone your doctor he may ask you to go straight to the hospital's emergency department (p. 391), and he will probably telephone them to say you are on your way (see accidents, pp. 635f.). Difficulty in breathing is of course an emergency (see p. 463).

Loss of appetite in a young child is always serious if it is an alteration from his normal pattern. It usually indicates an infection, which is particularly dangerous in a small baby because infections can attack a baby rapidly and fiercely. If your baby suddenly refuses his feedings you must call your doctor without delay (pp. 433–34).

Vomiting, meaning the bringing up of food (p. 478), could be a serious symptom, particularly if it is unusual for your child to be sick. Constipation (pp. 484–85) is not an emergency unless associated with other symptoms such as vomiting. On the other hand, diarrhea (pp. 478f.) can be serious, and if your child is ill with it or if it persists you should telephone your doctor.

A rise in temperature is not a particularly good guide to a child's health. Normal children may get very hot at times, whereas babies may be very ill with a temperature that is below normal.

A convulsion or fit (the words are synonymous) is always a reason to call the doctor, but not until your child has come around (pp. 615–16). Never leave a convulsing child alone.

Rashes are seldom serious, except for one caused by the meningococcus bacterium, which causes spotted fever. The danger is extreme if mauve patches develop as well as the red spots, and you should rush the child straight to the hospital.

Difficulty in breathing requires a call to your doctor, who may diagnose asthma, croup, or a respiratory infection. The most dangerous cause is when your child chokes after inhaling a peanut or large piece of food. There is no time to call the doctor and you must act quickly yourself (see p. 624).

Urinary symptoms need a doctor's opinion, but try to collect a sterile specimen of urine (p. 444) to take with you.

You should always consult your doctor if your child develops a limp (p. 535).

Second Opinion

You should be able to be frank with your doctor if you want him to refer your child to a specialist for a second opinion. A good doctor will never object to your asking for this; doctors do it for their own illnesses far more than the rest of the public. In fact, a doctor whose rapport with his patients is good will suggest calling in a second opinion before you mention it yourself. He will anticipate that you want to be sure you have done everything possible for your child, and he will suggest a second opinion even if he thinks it is unnecessary.

General practitioners and specialists are well aware—and should not be offended by the idea—that a large proportion of children are referred for a second opinion in order to give parents confidence, rather than for strictly "medical" reasons.

Having said all this, and I believe it most sincerely, I have to admit that some doctors are not as understanding of your needs for further reassurance as one would wish. If they are difficult over your request for a second opinion, it is probably because they have the very human reaction of feeling you are questioning their competence. If you think your doctor may react unfavorably to your suggestion, you could try to help him by saying, for example, that you're sure there is nothing wrong with your baby, but because you're a mother, and worried, you feel you won't be able to rest until you have seen a specialist.

It may happen that the pediatrician to whom your child is referred seems to get to know more about your child's needs than your own doctor, who has been looking after you for years. If this is so it may be because he has the advantage of starting from scratch to build up the relationship.

Hospital Doctor

When you go to a hospital a great deal of personal data may be recorded which, at first sight, may appear to have little relevance. Why, for example, when you bring your child to the hospital should you be asked your religion? But the information helps the doctor in building up his picture of your family background as well as preparing him for those possibilities where your beliefs and his treatment might come into conflict. For example, a parent who is a Jehovah's Witness will not accept a blood transfusion for his child even when told it will be life-saving.

The Emergency Department

Since the general practitioner is becoming a specialist in family medicine it is obviously safer to go to see him first with your sick child than to take your child to a hospital emergency department. The only exception would be for an accident or some other emergency, and even then it would be wise to telephone your doctor before leaving for the hospital. It helps your doctor to know what has happened, and he can alert the hospital about any important family medical matters that may help in your child's recovery.

The name "emergency department" emphasizes to those in charge, and to patients, the proper function of such a department.

Your child is more safely treated by your family doctor or pediatrician for all but the most severe accidents. He knows your background in a way that a hospital doctor cannot, and he is probably more experienced than the younger doctor you are likely to meet in an emergency department.

Is Your Prescription Really Necessary?

The more that patients and parents can understand about one of the basic tools of a doctor's treatment, his medicines, the more they can work together as partners instead of prolonging the kind of situation where the patient seems to be demanding a prescription, which the doctor then writes out even though he knows it will do very little good. It is sad if a doctor uses a prescription to get a demanding patient out of the room, thus failing to discover the real reason why his help was being sought.

There is no harm in having a blind faith in the medicines prescribed for your child; in fact, there may be an advantage if you are that kind of person, since confidence in treatment helps to make it effective. However, if you doubt the necessity for a prescription or question your doctor's motive in giving you one, it is better to discuss this with him. He can then explain why he is giving the medicine—perhaps it is to give your child the feeling that something tangible is being done to make him better. At any rate, it is a good idea for you and your doctor to work out together what you and your child really need.

Cough Medicines

Cough medicines fall into the category of reassuring but chemically inactive medicines. There is nothing magical about the action of a "tonic": it is usually given during the convalescent stage of an illness and it is then credited with helping the natural recovery, which would have taken place anyway. A cough medicine may be soothing but it does not loosen sputum, one of its previously believed actions. On the whole, pediatricians teach mothers simple respiratory therapy to remove sputum from the lung (pp. 466–67).

Antibiotics

At the other end of the spectrum from cough medicines are the modern chemicals, with enormous powers both for good when used properly and for harm when used wrongly. The antibiotics, such as penicillin, are good examples of such drugs. The discovery of penicillin by Alexander Fleming revolutionized medical thinking. Previously, it had been thought that any drug that was powerful enough to kill germs inside the body would at the same time kill the body or part of it. Fleming's discovery heralded a blind faith in the power of the antibiotic, and a number of tragedies resulted. For example, chloramphenicol, a powerful antibiotic, which used to be given for colds, caused several deaths because it was given in what we know now to have been too large a dose and for too long a period.

The next stage was the realization that antibiotics were not the panacea for all ills, since certain bacteria have the ability to resist their action. Take penicillin and staphylococcus for example: this particular germ has the ability to produce an enzyme called penicillinase which destroys penicillin. By this means the life of the germ is saved, leaving it free to wreak havoc on the human body it has invaded.

Not all staphylococci have this property, but self-selection in an environment such as a hospital, where penicillin exists, means that those that have it survive. Thus a patient entering the hospital risks acquiring an infection caused by a penicillin-resistant staphylococcus —a risk that is only slight if he remains at home for treatment. Doctors have to take this danger into account when advising that a patient should be moved from home to the hospital.

Doctors and nurses have to be scrupulous about hand washing; it is now realized that infection is transferred much more often by hand contact than by breath contact (droplet infection). It is for this reason that visitors to a hospital, provided they have not got a cold or flu, are much less likely to transfer infection to the patients than doctors and nurses, who may well be carrying antibiotic-resistant organisms on their hands.

Fortunately, not all organisms have this power of developing resistance to antibiotics. The streptococcus, one of the causes of a sore throat and an important factor in the production of acute nephritis (inflammation of the kidney, p. 446) and rheumatic fever (p. 516), is not capable of producing the enzyme penicillinase. This means that the streptococcus always remains sensitive to penicillin, and therefore that penicillin can and should be given for years to children who have had rheumatic fever, in order to reduce the likelihood of a second attack and the possibility of heart damage (p. 517) The ability of bacteria to develop resistance to antibiotics is one of the reasons for continued intensive research into the development of new antibiotics.

It is in your interests as parents that you should understand these facts. All antibiotics have side effects, some more damaging than others. Because the dangers of antibiotics as well as their blessings are now realized, doctors are much more cautious about prescribing them than they used to be.

Virus Infections

A lot of infections are caused by viruses, against which, at present, no antibiotic is effective. The common cold and influenza are the most common illnesses caused by viruses. You have to accept that your doctor has no magical treatment for a cold, and therefore that there is nothing to be gained by going to see him when you have one. In fact, the only positive result of your visit may be that your doctor catches the cold! Similarly, when an epidemic of influenza is about, it is not necessary to call your doctor if the illness is taking its usual course (p. 531). Let your child stay in bed for a day or two; give him plenty to drink, and don't be surprised that he does not feel like eating. Of course, if he is obviously ill or if the illness does not fit the usual pattern of influenza, your doctor must be called.

Vitamins

The story of the use of vitamins has a certain similarity to the story of antibiotics. Once the role of vitamins was discovered, there was a rush to have more and more in the hope of making the body even healthier. Lack of vitamin C reduces one's resistance to infections. This knowledge has led to the taking of extra vitiamin C in the hope of warding off colds. This is illogical; although a shortage of the vitamin increases the chance of infection, there is no evidence that a superabundance reduces it (see also p. 183).

28

The Sick Child at Home

Caring for Your Sick Child

Any child, however healthy, is bound to be sick at times, but effective modern medicines, particularly antibiotics, have cut short many illnesses that formerly needed hospital nursing. A visiting nurse is often available to help at home on the rare occasions when special nursing techniques are necessary. Today, the trend is for as much surgery and treatment as possible to be carried out on a day basis in the hospital; spending the night in the hospital is often unnecessary. Mothers make excellent nurses and, in fact, often help to nurse their children if a stay in the hospital is necessary.

Is Isolation Necessary?

All this means that children are nursed at home more than in the past, but modern ideas on the management of illness make your role as nurse far easier than before. Sickroom isolation, with your child kept apart from the rest of the family, sterilization of plates and cutlery, separate laundry—all these are seldom necessary. Isolation of a child with measles is unnecessary since the younger children, one hopes, have been immunized; this means that in the unlikely event of their catching the disease it will be much milder (see infectious fevers, pp. 522–24).

Infectious fevers are usually passed on during the first day or two of the illness, often before they are recognized as anything more than a cough or cold. Scarlet fever, just one variety of streptococcal sore throat (see p. 529), is much less serious than it used to be and responds quickly to penicillin. You are not, therefore, involved in endless precautions, with the almost impossible aim, in a busy household, of keeping the sick member of the family isolated.

Giving Medicine

It is usually easy to give medicines nowadays, since they mostly have a nice taste. In fact, your problem may be to resist demands for more. Tablets are best crushed and given in a spoonful of fruit juice, or hidden in jam on a spoon. The reward of candy afterward may persuade a reluctant medicine taker, but the damage done by candy to teeth should reduce this form of bribery. On no account should parents refer to medicine as candy.

Must He Go to Bed?

The attitude toward keeping a sick child in bed has also changed. There are very few exceptions to the rule that if a child feels well enough to be up, he is well enough to be out of bed.

Another exploded myth is that a rise in temperature is the signal for pajamas and bed. I have explained elsewhere that temperature alone is a poor guide to the state of a child's health (pp. 390, 434). A child can be very ill without fever or have a fever without significance. A child with a high fever probably wants to rest without being made to; when he feels better, he wants to get up again of his own accord (see below and p. 403).

It is sufficient to use your common sense and allow your child to decide whether he wants to be in bed, unless your doctor has given you specific advice on the matter. A child who wants to lie down is often happier on a couch in the living room, where he is near you, than alone in his bedroom. It also gives him a chance of joining in the fun with the other children, even if he only feels well enough to watch them. If he looks really weary, he will probably want to be led gently to bed, particularly if someone is prepared to stay with him for a while. A sick child is sometimes grateful to have decisions made for him. If he is happier left alone, this is not necessarily a cause for alarm —it is probably just good sense.

Getting Up Again

A child who has been ill may need you to help him to get up if he has got into the habit of lying listlessly in bed. If he is only mildly ill and stays in bed all day, he cannot be expected to sleep at night in his normal way. It is up to you to vary his day in a sufficiently interesting way to make bedtime, or going-to-sleep time, a special event, not one that merges into an endless wallow in bed. A short session watching television, or at least sitting in a different room, may make all the difference.

Won't your child take longer to recover if he is allowed to be up? No; staying in bed may even prolong the illness by making him feel worse than he really is. When you watch a child in bed who wants to be up, you will notice that he expends a great deal of energy in restlessness, even bouncing on the bed. You are likely to spend your time running to him as he finds more and more excuses to interrupt your housework in order to relieve his own boredom. A child, like an adult, tends to act the prima donna once he is nearly better. You will be able to get on with your own activities if he is near you, and he will be a lot happier.

Must He Keep Warm?

Surely it is important to keep him warm, and isn't it easier to do this if he is safely tucked up in bed? No; a sick child does not need a room like a furnace. He should not sit in a howling gale, but he will be perfectly all right in a temperature that suits the rest of the family and with the usual amount of fresh air.

A feverish child is in far more danger of overheating than of getting too cold. Doctors today find themselves far more often telling a mother to take off some of the child's extra clothes and to cool the room, rather than the reverse. Sometimes it is necessary to tepid sponge a child with a temperature over 103°F (39.4°C) in order to bring down his fever (see tepid sponging, p. 401); this is essential for the prevention of febrile convulsions (pp. 614f.).

Food and Drink

Unless the doctor mentions it, you can assume your child does not need a special diet. There are few illnesses that necessitate an invalid diet. Let him eat what he wants when he wants it, which may be little and often.

The most important point to remember is that a sick child needs extra fluid and should be offered plenty to drink. If your child refuses solid food, as often happens during the acute stage of illness, it does not matter as long as he has adequate fluids. The less he eats the more important it is to use ingenuity in choosing drinks. Added sugar gives him energy and ordinary household sugar (sucrose) is just as good as glucose, since it is changed into glucose in the stomach. So it is unnecessary to buy expensive glucose drinks unless he specially wants them. Fruit juices provide vitamin C (see vitamins, p. 183). Milk contains protein and almost everything else your child needs. Flavor the milk if he dislikes it plain. Children often enjoy beef consommé or bouillon.

If your child keeps vomiting, he will become dehydrated (p. 479) and will have to go to the hospital so that he can be fed by another method—probably into a vein.

The day your child says he wants hamburger is the day he can digest it properly—even if he cannot, it will not be disastrous. A child who has become thinner while ill soon makes it up afterward.

How to Help the Doctor

Your doctor will be daunted by being presented with a detailed diary of symptoms, but he will welcome a concise and clear-cut description of how and when the illness appeared. If you never remember what you want to tell him until he has left, it is worth jotting down some notes in advance. He will ask you anything he needs to know about your child's illness, but your observations are very helpful to him.

Using a Thermometer

When to Take His Temperature

If your doctor needs to know your child's temperature, he can take it during his examination. You will usually be able to tell by touch or by the look of your child whether or not he is feverish, without using a thermometer. I would stress again that temperature is a poor guide to a child's condition, and it should not be necessary for you to know his exact temperature in order to convince your doctor that you are worried.

The times when you need to use a thermometer should be few and far between: for example, when your child is very hot and needs tepid sponging (p. 401) or when your doctor asks you to take it.

Reading the Thermometer

Here are the points to remember if it is necessary to take your child's temperature: all thermometers are marked in degrees, with smaller marks dividing each degree into five. An ordinary thermometer starts at 95° Fahrenheit (35° Centigrade). For babies, doctors use a special thermometer giving a reading down to 77°F (25°C), since babies lose body heat more rapidly and become correspondingly colder than adults. An arrow marks the point of the average normal temperature (Fig. 12), but the average normal temperature fluctuates above and below this point according to what a person is doing and other factors, such as the time of day. Average temperature is 98.6°F (37°C) if taken

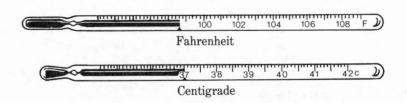

Fahrenheit

Centigrade

Fig.12. Thermometer with arrow pointing to a normal average temperature.

by mouth, and 99.6°F (37.4°C) if taken by rectum. Thus an individual's temperature may be slightly higher or lower than the "average" and yet be perfectly normal for him. The arrow is just for guidance, and you need only be concerned if the reading is at least one degree above or below it.

Temperature is registered by the reaction of the mercury stored in the bulb at one end of the thermometer. The mercury rises up the thermometer in a thin line, which is usually magnified to make it easier to see. You may have to roll the thermometer between your fingers until the line becomes visible. The bulb containing the mercury may be thin or stubby in shape.

Types of Thermometer

The stubby-ended type is intended for taking temperatures by rectum but it can equally well be used in the mouth, armpit, or groin. It is difficult to take a child's temperature by mouth until he can co-operate by keeping his mouth shut for long enough for the temperature to register, and can be trusted not to bite and break the thermometer; so I suggest you choose a rectal thermometer for common use. Keep a separate oral thermometer for use in the mouths of the older children and adults. A thermometer should always be washed thoroughly in cold water after use. Don't wash it in hot water: you may expand the mercury so much that it breaks the thermometer.

Before using a thermometer it is essential to make sure the mercury is below the arrow marking the normal temperature level. If it is not, the reading will be inaccurate. To make the mercury fall, shake the thermometer with a flick of the wrist, as if trying to flip off something sticking to your fingers. Hold the thermometer firmly at the end opposite the stub and continue to shake it until the mercury has dropped below the arrow—it does not matter how far below the arrow it goes.

Taking His Temperature by Rectum

It is hard to keep the thermometer in place for long enough either in a baby's mouth or under his arm, so the rectum provides the best answer. You must take care not to dig the thermometer in too far and hurt your baby; you must also be careful to prevent him from wriggling about, or the thermometer may knock against your arm and break. The best way is to lay him on his front across your lap with his diaper off. Press him down firmly with one arm and gently insert the stub of the thermometer for about an inch (2–3 centimeters). The stub should be lightly greased with petroleum jelly beforehand. Do not hang on to the thermometer for dear life or it may snap off if your baby suddenly twists in the opposite direction; keep your palm resting on his buttocks with the end of the thermometer between your flexed fingers (Fig. 13).

Taking His Temperature by Mouth

When you take your child's temperature by mouth the bulb end should be under his tongue. If you are frightened that he may bite off the end, you could put it between his teeth and his cheek. Don't be too alarmed if he does have the misfortune to bite off the end of the thermometer: the small amount of mercury is not poisonous, and if he has swallowed any little bits of glass he will pass them in his stool.

Whichever method you use, the thermometer must be left in for at least one minute to give the mercury time to settle, and therefore to give an accurate reading. Remember that a rectal temperature is always higher than a temperature taken by mouth. Shake down the

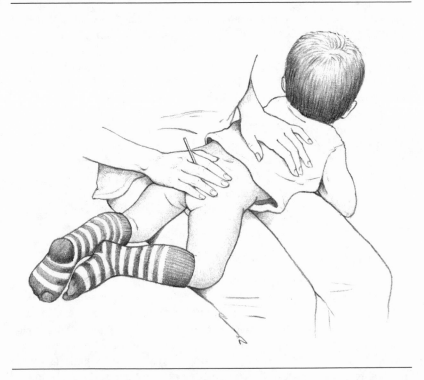

Fig. 13. The easiest and safest way of taking a baby's temperature.

thermometer and wash it immediately after use and then it will be ready when next needed.

Tepid Sponging

This is an effective way of bringing down a child's temperature when it has reached 103° or 104°F (39.4° or 40°C) and is making him uncomfortable and restless. Your doctor will advise you how and when to tepid sponge, but you can also use it to reduce your child's fever whenever you think it necessary, or when waiting for the doctor to arrive. Cooling him lessens the chance of a febrile convulsion resulting from high fever (see convulsions, p. 614), as well as making him more comfortable. There is no danger of chilling a child by tepid sponging if you stop when his temperature falls below 102°F (38.8°C).

It is not essential to tepid sponge every time your child's temperature rises to 103°F; the decision depends on how hot, distressed, and ill he seems. A feverish child will be more comfortable if you just remove some of his clothes and bedclothes. One acetaminophen tablet also helps to reduce the temperature. However, a child may be too ill to take a tablet or may look so uncomfortable that he would obviously benefit from cooling: in this case take his temperature and tepid sponge if it has reached 103°F or more.

How to Tepid Sponge

Undress your child and put him on a waterproof sheet, or in an empty bath. Cool his face, trunk, and arms and legs with tepid water applied with a sponge or washcloth. It is important that the water is tepid, not cold, since cold water contracts the blood vessels near the skin, so preventing the loss of heat from the blood. Tepid water does not cause contraction; the blood vessels remain dilated, so that when the water evaporates from the surface of the skin, maximum cooling occurs.

To increase the amount of cooling you can wrap damp cloths loosely around your child's neck and groin and in his armpits when you have finished sponging him all over. Take his temperature every ten minutes to check the effect of your sponging. Stop when it falls below 101.3°F and cover him lightly with a sheet without dressing him.

The whole process may take a few minutes or up to about half an hour. If his temperature rises again, repeat the sponging.

Amusing the Sick Child

A child is far less likely than an adult to regard enforced "time off" as a benefit. Your husband may bask in bed catching up on his novel reading long after he feels well enough to get back to work. An older schoolchild may similarly enjoy a break from school and the sheer luxury of a rest in bed, until he starts worrying about missing schoolwork; but a young child wants to get back to work, that is, to play, as soon as possible. Even while he feels like staying in bed, he begins wanting to play.

He needs to be provided with suitable amusements, which do not frustrate him by being too complicated or too demanding for his immediate fund of energy. A child who is well can fetch what he wants and so can change activities at will. A sick child may feel well enough to amuse himself gently but not well enough to get the vital component of his construction set, or to think what to do next. His threshold of boredom and frustration will be lower, probably resembling that of a young child, because, like all of us, he wants to be mother's baby until he feels able to face up to the world again. This explains his childish demands for attention and the fact that he may enjoy playing with things you thought he had grown out of ages ago—one reason for not giving away every easy jigsaw or cuddly toy the minute you consider him too old for them.

Even in bed, there are far more things your child can do than might be thought. For instance, if you cover the bedding with polythene or a plastic tablecloth, games involving sand and water, messy paints, and clay are possible. Now that the emphasis on perfect sickroom hygiene has largely disappeared, your child can have his family pets in his room if he wants them. The guinea pig in his cage or the cat on the end of the bed may provide just enough company to save you several searches for diversion. Growing plants is also fun; mustard and cress come up quickly. Attractive mobiles to hang over the bed can be bought or made at home. These tinkle and sparkle, giving the child a variety of shapes, patterns, and sounds to watch and listen to.

For the younger child, a notched broom handle fixed across the crib allows toys to be suspended within reach. The same can be done with elastic tied to the crib sides, but this is more of a nuisance when you need to lower them. For extra storage space a bag on a coat hanger can be hung on the crib.

Your child will enjoy being allowed to do something he is not normally allowed to do, such as looking at the most expensive coffee-table book, or watching television at the "wrong" time of the day, or tidying up your workbox, or using the typewriter. It is a good idea to keep in reserve an assortment of oddments, games, and books, for producing when you are suddenly faced with the task of amusing a sick child. These could consist of any presents left over from Christmas, Christmas cards or old magazines to cut up and stick in a scrapbook, puzzles, scraps of cloth and wool, string, cardboard boxes, and anything that can be turned into dolls' clothes, puppets, or toy theaters.

A new drawing pad and set of crayons may amuse a child, whereas the sight of his old ones provides no inspiration at all. There is no harm in giving him some small present daily to revive his flagging interest, but don't give more than one present at a time; this is liable to end in his playing with none and becoming increasingly demanding at the same time.

It is always wise to remove things as they are discarded and before he is overwhelmed by an avalanche of toys, although if a child seems quite happy in the mess, he probably is.

Obviously, how you deal with your child depends on his age and tastes, how he feels on any particular day, and how free you are to spend time amusing him. Usually, ten minutes of concentrated attention when he really wants it is worth an hour of resentful company from you when you would much rather be doing something else. Moving his bed near the window so that he can look out, or moving him closer to the rest of the family when he is ready for it, may provide as much company as he needs.

Visitors

Unless he has an obviously infectious illness, like mumps, there is no reason why he should not be visited by some of his school friends if he feels like it. Of course, no one with a cold, whether child or adult, should visit the patient if it can be avoided.

Going Out and Back to School

Your doctor will decide when your child is well enough to go out and when he can return to school; don't hesitate to ask him if he has forgotten to say. These stages are now reached much earlier than in the past, when doctors thought differently. In general, once your child is running around the house, he will be well enough to run around the yard. The time for his return to school after one of the infectious fevers is set by the authorities (p. 521).

A spell of illness at home may be a time when your child has never had it so good, because of your almost undivided attention. He can rightly claim more of you than the other members of the family and this can do him good. Bed-wetting may stop and behavior problems improve. Afterward, life may continue with more mutual warmth and understanding.

29

The Sick Child in the Hospital

Nearly every child has to go to the hospital at some time, to visit the emergency department or the outpatient department. Fewer children have to be admitted to a room or a children's unit, since the number of illnesses requiring a stay in the hospital has dropped dramatically, thanks to modern drugs and treatment (see the sick child at home, p. 395).

Preparing Your Child for the Hospital

It is wise to make your child familiar with the idea of the hospital before he has to visit one. Do this gradually and naturally as opportunities arise. Let him know if another child has gone to the hospital and explain why this is sometimes necessary in order to get well. Point out the local hospital in the same way as you do his future school building. If you have a friend who is a doctor, nurse, or staff member there, ask him to show you and your child around. Do not refer to the hospital in awed tones when discussing the subject in his hearing— this is as disastrous as recounting horror stories of visits to the dentist. Never use the hospital as a threat or punishment; the remark "Mommy will end up in the hospital if you are naughty" is as bad as threatening your child with banishment there.

Seize any opportunity you can to let your child visit a friend in the children's unit of a hospital. More and more hospitals in the United States as well as in the United Kingdom are encouraging visits of this sort; it is good for the patient and it can be fun for your child as well as helping him to understand what it is like being a patient in the hospital. In the past, doctors have discouraged visiting by children on the grounds that they may bring in infection. This is grossly exaggerated: they are no more likely to introduce infection than adults. Doctors and nurses are more likely to transfer infection from one patient to another, via their hands. For this reason they have to be scrupulous about washing their hands after contact with each young child.

Obviously, you won't bring a child in as a visitor if he has a cold, or if he has been in contact with measles or mumps. The only real barrier to visiting by children is lack of space in the unit.

If you have to visit the outpatient department with one of your children, bring the others along as well, if this is practical. The doctor can bring them into the picture by showing them what their brother's or sister's mouth looks like inside. All this helps in preparation for entering a hospital and it can help the doctor as well—if a young child is frightened by a stethoscope or by being asked to open his mouth, the older child can be asked to take part and show that it doesn't hurt.

Playing "Doctors and Nurses"

Another way to accustom young children to the idea of the hospital is to encourage games of "doctors and nurses." They don't need elaborate first-aid kits or uniforms; improvised bandages, orange juice medicines, and "dressing-up" clothes do equally well. It is a mistake to interfere when children are playing, but if you do have the chance to make unobtrusive suggestions, point out to an exceedingly bossy "doctor" or to a callous "nurse" that real doctors and nurses are kind and gentle.

Fear of Separation

The more familiar the idea of the hospital becomes to your child, the less frightening it will be if he has to go there. But most important of all is that he should feel secure and trusting and that he should have had some experience of separation from you, in the form of being left with a baby-sitter or friends. Because he knows you come back after leaving him, being left in the hospital should be less of a shock. However, small children, particularly between the ages of one and four, are very likely to be upset by a stay in the hospital, however well their parents and the hospital staff play their parts. This is why surgical operations are delayed until after this age whenever possible.

It is also the reason why hospitals are encouraged to allow unrestricted visiting for parents and to provide rooms for mothers (and fathers) of young children to stay in. This reduces a child's sense of being abandoned in a strange world and lessens the chances of long-term emotional disturbance afterward (see pp. 408–10).

Visiting an Outpatient Department

Keeping Your Child Happy

Take something for your child to play with or a book for him to look at; even the best-organized outpatient departments cannot avoid delays. One patient may take five minutes of the doctor's time but the next may take an hour, so he must allow for some overlap in appointments in order that full use is made of his time.

A well-run department will do its best to keep children happy, leaving mothers to undress their children and help whenever possible. Ideally, a play therapist (p. 412) should be employed to work in the waiting room, so that there is a continuous play group in action for the children while they are waiting to see the doctor. Fathers, grandparents, brothers and sisters, and friends should be allowed to accompany mothers and children, and to go in with them when they see the doctor. This is a chance to accustom your other children to the idea of the hospital before they have to go themselves.

Student Doctors

In a teaching hospital, a student doctor (I prefer this term to "medical student") is likely to take the first history of your child's illness and to examine him. He will then explain his findings to your consultant, who is also his teacher. Other students will probably be present when the child is examined by the consultant. Ask your family doctor if you are uncertain whether or not you are going to a teaching hospital.

The Examination

When the doctor examines your child you may wonder why he is interested in things that have no apparent bearing on the illness. However, he is not wasting time; the more thorough the examination, the happier you should be, since this shows that the doctor is interested in the whole child and not just in his illness (see p. 384). It is particularly important in the case of babies and very young children for the doctor to gain a general picture of the child's development and progress; this may be intimately connected with the illness, and in any case he will want to check on the development of any child he sees.

The doctor knows how to make his investigations with the minimum of discomfort to your child. He will not make the mistake of telling your child to "look the other way" or that an injection will not hurt; don't spoil his efforts to gain your child's confidence by interrupting with remarks intended to divert your child's attention from the unpleasant things happening to him. If he has to give an injection, the doctor is likely to say, "You will feel a prick that will hurt for a moment." Whatever he does he will be watching your child's face for evidence of pain or discomfort; even a phlegmatic child's feelings do not go unnoticed. Try not to sit and suffer for your child. Your help is needed; for example, you can hold your child while the doctor examines him. The illustrations show you the way to hold him for part of the examination (Figs. 14 a, b) (see also pp. 386–89).

A doctor senses when it would be wiser not to talk about your child in his presence and will arrange to speak to you alone, if necessary; but you are the best judge of this, so let him know beforehand if you think your child should not hear a discussion. Jot down questions you wish to ask the doctor—he should not make you feel he is too busy to give you his time, even if he is.

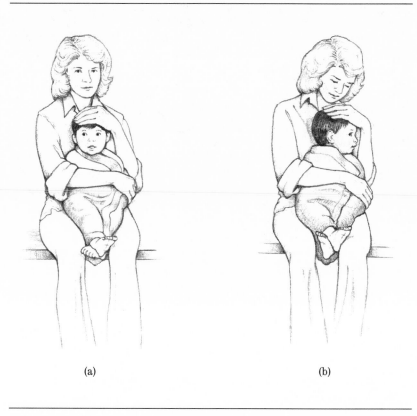

(a)   (b)

Fig. 14. (a) Examination of the throat or mouth. If necessary, you can keep your child's legs still by gripping them firmly between your knees. (b) Examination of the ear.

Tests

As far as possible, the doctor will arrange for any necessary tests to be done on the same visit, saving both of you a second session at the outpatient department. For example, an X-ray can often be brought back for the doctor to see, and he may explain this special sort of photograph to your child.

Admission to the Hospital

Sometimes, after examining a child in the outpatient department the doctor decides to admit him to the hospital. In this case, especially if he is too young for explanations, it is better if you can take him home first to collect his things and give him time to get used to the idea. He will then be much less likely to be frightened on any future visit to the outpatient department. You also need time to accustom yourself to the fact that he is going to stay, so only in an emergency should a child be admitted direct from the outpatient department.

Settling In

If your child has to be admitted to the hospital, be sure to bring with him any of his intimate belongs that he hates being parted from. Hospital staff know that a small child needs his favorite toy or security blanket (p. 120) with him, however dirty and unhygienic this may be. Obviously, a child who takes an old blanket to bed with him for comfort at home needs it all the more in the strange surroundings of a hospital. Similarly, a baby who is used to a pacifier should not be deprived of it on admission to the hospital—although he may be persuaded to abandon it when he leaves (see pacifiers, p. 120).

A child feels more secure if his own clothes remain at the hospital near him, even if he cannot wear them. It is very alarming to be stripped of your familiar clothes and bathed and dressed in strange ones, while your mother carries away your belongings as if she were leaving you in prison.

Happily, not all hospitals insist on a routine bath when a child is first admitted; most children are perfectly clean anyway, and many have been bathed at home immediately beforehand. If it is necessary to bathe or undress your child, you are the person who should do it.

Visiting Your Child in the Hospital

All hospitals should allow parents to visit at any time of the day or night: that is what unrestricted visiting means. Unfortunately, "unrestricted" visiting is not always 100 percent unrestricted; many hospitals still have time limits. It is not always practical for other relatives to visit, and there may not be enough space to allow brothers and sisters to play while mothers and fathers visit the sick child. But a head nurse with modern ideas will let other children visit as much as possible, whether they are brothers and sisters or school friends. It is also good for them to get an inside view of the hospital when they are well.

The atmosphere should be such that you do not feel you have to report to the nurse on duty on arrival, though obviously you will greet her as you go to your child. It is a different matter when you leave.

Then you must tell the nurse in charge, so that she can once again assume total responsibility for your child. She must also be ready to comfort him when you have gone. Always be totally honest about the fact that you are leaving the hospital; some parents make the terrible mistake of sliding out when their child's attention is elsewhere, or say they are coming back soon when they know they won't be back till the next day.

If you wake up at 3:00 A.M. feeling apprehensive about your child and unable to get back to sleep, it is better to go and see for yourself than to spend the rest of the night tossing and turning in a panic. The night nurse should greet you and take you to your child's bed, not look at you in surprise and make you feel neurotic.

Your Child's Reactions

Why is unrestricted visiting a good idea? Because it lessens the emotional stresses on your child. He is less likely to feel abandoned, he is more likely to be happy in the hospital, and he is much more likely not to show disturbed behavior when he comes home (p. 414). If possible, make your visits short and frequent, so that he gets to know that you will play with him at intervals in your work, just as you do at home. He can accept your need to leave him in order to go shopping or to pick up the others from school, especially if you can stop to see him with the shopping or with his brothers or sisters on the way home. Short visits also reduce the boredom you may feel just sitting by his bed. At home you would be fitting in lots of other jobs as well. Of course, this is only possible if you live near enough to the hospital.

I am often asked if unrestricted visiting doesn't make it harder for those children whose parents cannot visit often. I am sure this is not the case; it makes it easier for such children to be visited—in the early hours of the morning, for instance, when father may be on his way home from night work. Moreover, parents who can get to the hospital often will always bring the unvisited children into their activities with their children. In any case the nurses and the play therapists are on the lookout to prevent loneliness and isolation. It was much worse in the days of special visiting hours, because a child with no visitors felt so much more left out.

The increasing universality of the telephone also helps. All children's units should have a coin telephone booth the children can use to speak to parents and school friends.

Don't be surprised if your small child doesn't greet you ecstatically when you first visit. He may seem indifferent to your presence, or sullen and withdrawn; this only shows how lonely he is and how hurt he feels by what he considers you have done to him. It makes visiting all the more important. He is less likely to react like this in a relaxed, happy unit where visits are informal. He will probably cry when you leave, but that is not a reason for not visiting—exactly the reverse. He will gain confidence from your regular visits, knowing you come back often.

The child who seems to adapt best and not to miss his parents is not necessarily the happiest. Sometimes he is stunned into apathy by being admitted to the hospital and separated from them. In the old days, such a child was sometimes described as a "good" patient, because he didn't often cry. Today it is realized that it is much healthier, emotionally, for a child to show the outward signs of the natural distress he feels rather than to react by a stunned silence.

When a child is well enough, he should be allowed to go out for a walk with you. Some hospitals seem to forget to mention this to parents, so suggest it yourself if you think your child is ready for it.

Operation Day

Doctors are divided on the question of visiting on the day of an operation. You may not be allowed to visit your child until he is out of the recovery room; alternatively, you may be involved to the extent of accompanying him into the anesthetic room and staying with him until he starts to go to sleep. I hope that at least you will be allowed to remain by his bed until he goes to the operating room and to be waiting for him when he comes back.

Staying with Your Child in the Hospital

Ideally, every baby or toddler admitted to the hospital should be accompanied by his mother. Whether this is practical in your case will depend on your other commitments at home and on the facilities available in your hospital.

It is debatable whether or not you and your child should share the same room; much will depend on your own feelings and how ill your child is. But I am clear that most mothers who decide to stay in the hospital with their sick child prefer to sleep in the same room rather than in their own. This should be more universal than it is, since even the smallest cubicle can accommodate a folding bed, which can be moved out during the day, if necessary. Similarly, in children's units, there is usually enough space between beds to accommodate a mother or father on a folding bed. Additionally, playrooms can be used as dormitories for parents at night.

One of the major problems faced by a mother staying in the hospital with her sick child is boredom. Try to get out of the hospital for part of the day—you will need to see how things are at home. Your husband can exchange duty with you; I hope the hospital will agree to his sleeping in the hospital sometimes so as to give you a night or two at home.

Talking to the Staff

I hope that the atmosphere in the unit will be such that you will feel at ease in asking questions of any of the staff. Obviously, the consultant pediatrician is not always immediately available, but you should have no difficulty in making an appointment to see him if your questions remain unanswered. The people who are nearly always available are the house physician and the head nurse or, in her absence, the staff nurse in charge of the unit. Above the intern or junior resident is the senior resident, who may be very experienced and will shortly be a consultant.

At least the word "pediatrician" is now sufficiently well known for only the minority of laymen to believe that one is a foot specialist! I have also been asked if the training is shorter, since you only look after children!

Another member of the team whom you may meet is the medical social worker. She is particularly experienced in understanding the stresses and strains that illness in one member of the family produces for the others. You will find her very helpful in explaining the feelings you are experiencing because of your child's illness.

The staff's attitude to the children in their care, their ability to look at hospital life through a child's eyes and to make it resemble home life as far as possible, is much more important than whether or not the hospital building is modern. Consultants have the major role in encouraging this attitude among staff, since they are in the strongest position to do so. Provided the consultant regards parents as partners, rather than intruders, so will the rest of the staff.

You should feel you can ask questions as they arise and the staff should feel they can answer your questions without waiting for the consultant. If they don't know the answer they should say so. In fact, the hospital should be organized to minimize the bewilderment of both parents and children. For this reason you should tell the staff any special words your child uses to describe everyday happenings, such as when he wants to use the toilet or even how he asks for a drink. Ideally, the nurse will make this one of her routine questions when your child is first admitted.

Helping to Look After Your Child

In a hospital where parents are welcome, mothers are encouraged to bathe and undress their children, to help with giving medicines and to watch nursing and procedures, such as an injection. Mothers do not have to take on these responsibilities, but I believe most of you would far rather help than stand by helplessly or go away while someone else takes over your child. Watching the real thing is usually far less nerve-racking than imagining it. An increasing number of fathers are discovering this by being present at the birth of their children instead of pacing hospital corridors.

Play in the Hospital

The Play Therapist

The play therapist is an important member of the hospital staff. She is trained to understand a child's feelings as expressed through his play and she will explain her observations to you and to the members of the staff looking after him. An adult or older child can talk about his fears, but a toddler may only be able to show them through play. However, he needs the appropriate kind of play in order to bring out his emotions, and it takes a trained person to provide this and to know what he is trying to express.

It is to be hoped that play therapists will soon be employed in all children's units and children's outpatient departments. Play is organized individually for very sick children and in groups for those able to take part together. Parents and nursing staff are encouraged to take part; today's children's nurse should be an expert in play, which is as much a part of her skills as a nurse as the more traditional nursing techniques.

The Purpose of Play in the Hospital

Play in the hospital does much more than just keep your child happy and occupied during his stay. Not only is it a safety valve for his emotions; it is a way of preparing him for some of the different things that may happen. For example, a child who is to have an operation can play a game with a teddy bear involving masks and "going to sleep," so that when he is given an anesthetic the procedure is already familiar. The play therapist discovers, in advance, whether any special aspect frightens your child, and then takes time to explain it, using play techniques with hospital objects; this makes it much less frightening for him. She will not only explain the "special sleep" for operations, but will assure your child that the operation will not start until he is asleep. Children also fear that they will not wake up afterward and that they may be put in a different bed, where their parents cannot find them. All this can be discussed.

Play in the hospital need not be limited to clean, quiet, and unexciting activities. Bedding can be covered with waterproof sheeting, making it possible to play games with water and sand. A guinea pig or other pets can be safely kept in the children's unit. Sometimes it helps a child who is apprehensive about an operation to be told that a favorite pet will be on his bedside cabinet waiting for him to wake up when it is all over. Noisy games and songs are not banned, since children who are too ill to stand noise will not be in the main part of the unit. But I find that sick children seldom object to noise in the way that sick adults do; it is a natural part of their life and can be comforting. Being alone and silent is usually more frightening to a child.

Many sick children ask to be moved in their beds to the playroom because they find the playroom atmosphere more natural. A sick child can enjoy playing with his eyes, by watching other children play, when he is too sick to take part himself. Some children, when too tense and upset to sleep in a quiet room by themselves, fall asleep as soon as they are moved to the playroom, because it makes them relax.

Play and Recovery

Active play and even noisy activity are part of the prescription for a more rapid recovery. You may be surprised that neatness and quiet are not the order of the day in your child's unit. You may even worry that he is being "overstimulated" and that there is a lack of hygiene. But the chaos is organized and risks are not taken.

Some parents feel that the opportunities for play in such a unit are greater than can be provided at home and that consequently their child will be dissatisfied when he returns. Talk to the play therapist or to the head nurse if this is your feeling. It is not so much a question of equipment as of understanding about a child's play needs and how he learns through play. By using hospital equipment as "toys" the play therapist helps the child to gain as much as possible from the experience of being in the hospital. Once you understand this you will be able to improve his opportunities for play at home.

The Hospital Teacher

More children's hospitals now employ a schoolteacher as a member of their staff. This used to be just for those children who were going to stay in the hospital for a long time and who would therefore suffer from the break in their schooling. Now it is realized that the schoolteacher has a part to play from the moment a child is first admitted, even if he is not going to stay long. A child who breaks an arm or leg is likely to be very worried about the schooling he is missing, especially if he has an exam shortly ahead. The hospital teacher can telephone your child's schoolteacher to find out what work he should be doing, and if you bring in his schoolbooks can give him private tuition while he is in. Any other information the schoolteacher can give to help the hospital staff know more about your child is appreciated. Such an arrangement also encourages schoolteachers to visit their pupils in the hospital—I only wish more would come. I just hope that pediatricians in the United States and the United Kingdom will increasingly value the help a schoolteacher's visit can provide both to the child and to the staff.

Quite another aspect of a hospital teacher's work, which unfortunately is not undertaken sufficiently often, is to help the child prepare a project for his class so he can explain why he was in the hospital and what happened to him. This makes his admission to the hospital still more a learning experience for him. If he has broken his leg, he should be lent his X-rays for his "lecture" to his class on how bones unite and heal. He could illustrate how they are helped to join up straight by using sticks and plaster of Paris.

The Aftereffects of Admission to the Hospital

The hospital is bound to be an unsettling experience, despite efforts to make it pleasant, especially if your child is feeling ill when he is left there. It is understandable that a child sometimes suspects he is being punished by separation from his family and familiar surroundings. Because of this he may refuse to talk to his parents, especially his mother—his most important person—while he is in the hospital, and sometimes after returning home. He may feel so angry at what you seem to have done to him that he refuses to make contact with you or, reacting the opposite way, becomes very aggressive. Staff members working with children in the hospital are trained to recognize aggressive and other forms of disturbed behavior as an emotional reaction to the shock of being admitted to such a strange place and removed from the security of home.

It is a mistake to argue that everyone, including small children, must learn to put up with a certain amount of hardship in life, and that therefore trying to sugar the pill of the hospital is misguided. Life provides everyone with plenty of practice in surmounting unavoidable difficulties, and we should try to eliminate from a young child's life as many of the avoidable difficulties as possible.

Temporary Behavior Problems

A stay in the hospital may upset a child's progress in toilet training or his rhythm of play, rest, and sleep, and it may be some time before he gets back to his old routine. He may start to wet the bed again or to be difficult over meals. He may be frightened of being left alone in his own bed at night. He may cling to you to the extent of accompanying you into the bathroom, because he is afraid to let you out of his sight. If he is as disturbed as this you must let him stay with you all the time. These will be only temporary problems if you handle them sympathetically and with understanding, realizing that they are totally normal reactions to the mental shock he has had.

By understanding the reason for this behavior you can handle it properly, so that it lasts only a few days. By being involved in the care of your child in a modern setting (not necessarily modern buildings), you and the hospital staff can minimize the chances of your child's exhibiting such behavior; in other words, of his becoming disturbed in the first place.

I hope that the result of your child's stay in the hospital will be not only a cure for his pneumonia or his broken leg, but also that the experience will be a positive gain for him and for the rest of your family. Obviously, some of the methods of care I have recommended are not yet universal, but what is universal is a general move toward a greater understanding of the needs of the child in the hospital and his family.

30

Congenital
Malformations

Most babies are born perfect, but a few are born imperfect. This is not surprising considering the complexity of human development while the baby is growing in the uterus—in fact, the remarkable thing is that, relatively, it happens so seldom.

What Is a Congenital Malformation?

The term covers a wide range of imperfections, from minor blemishes like most birthmarks to a major handicap like spina bifida. There is, therefore, little point in lumping all these conditions together in order to give a general estimate of the risk to any baby of being born with a congenital malformation. Most congenital malformations are present at birth but a small number, such as pyloric stenosis and some forms of birthmarks, do not make their presence known until a few days later.

Causes

For about half the children with these malformations the cause is unknown, at present. For the other half, there are two major groups of causes, the first hereditary, and the second the effect of outside influences—environmental factors. These include the age of the mother when pregnant, infections during pregnancy, and the influence of drugs such as thalidomide; they are described in the chapter on pregnancy (pp. 7f.).

A surprising but very important factor is the mother's socioeconomic state. The poorer she is, the greater the chance that her baby will be malformed. The British Perinatal Survey of 1958 showed that mothers from social class 5 (wives of unskilled workers) had six times the number of malformed babies as mothers from social class 1 (wives of professional workers). This is one more piece of evidence indicating how the health of a nation is bound up with its socioeconomic conditions and emphasizing the importance of their improvement.

Environmental causes of congenital malformations are in some ways the most difficult to control, but enormous strides have recently been made. A few years ago it was inconceivable that some congenital malformations could be prevented, but the thalidomide disaster highlighted the risk from drugs taken by the expectant mother. The liability to malformations from intrauterine infections such as German measles will soon be negligible as the result of immunization of young girls. There is a reduced risk of congenital malformation in the baby of the younger mother.

In older mothers there is a greater risk of congenital malformations in general, but particularly of Down's syndrome (mongolism) (see p. 589). The increasing age of the mother makes the fertilized egg less efficient in the complicated maneuver of development. The age of the father does not appear to be linked with the risk of producing an abnormal baby.

Testing the Amniotic Fluid (Amniocentesis)

It is now possible to test the amniotic fluid that surrounds the baby in the uterus to decide if it is a Down's baby. This is a very complicated test, which involves growing, in a tube, some of the skin cells shed by the baby. It is now available as a routine test for older mothers. Other tests for inherited disorders, making use of amniotic fluid, have also been discovered. The most important is that for the severe form of spina bifida (p. 425) and for the detection of anencephaly, a condition in which the brain is grossly malformed.

Inherited Disorders: Genetic Counseling

If your baby is born with a malformation, you will want to know whether it is inherited, and if so, the risk of repetition in a future child. The giving of this information is termed genetic counseling. You will not be told whether or not you should have another baby—that is something only you and your husband can decide. Genetic counseling is also vital before you start a family if anyone in either your family or your husband's has an inherited disorder. Genetic counseling may be given by your family doctor, by a pediatrician, or by a geneticist —a specialist in genetic disorders.

Abnormal Genes: What Are the Odds? Inherited disorders result from the possession of abnormal genes by one or both parents. Genes are chemical markers carried on the forty-six chromosomes we all possess. There are two major forms of inherited disorder—dominant and recessive. These depend on the characteristics of the abnormal gene.

Dominant Gene A parent who has a dominant abnormal gene suffers from the disorder in question; its influence is so strong that although the other parent is normal, half the offspring are affected. A good example of such a disorder is achondroplasia, the usual cause of short stature in dwarfs.

Recessive Gene   A recessively inherited disorder results from both parents being carriers of the abnormal gene. They do not show evidence of the disease themselves but the overall odds are that one in four of their children will suffer from it. Two in four of their children will be healthy carriers like themselves, while one in four will be totally unaffected. An example of a recessively inherited disorder is cystic fibrosis.

It is probable that all of us carry many abnormal genes, but the chance of our carrying the same ones as our marriage partner is small. The risk is increased when cousins marry. Genes are responsible not only for the inheritance of disease but for many of our physical and mental characteristics as well.

The odds of inheritance of disorders would be relatively small if the genes always behaved in the straightforward manner described. Unfortunately, from the point of view of accurate forecasting, they do not. Genes mutate; that is, they undergo a change, thereby altering the odds. It is when this happens that the advice of the geneticist is often required. In straightforward situations, such as cystic fibrosis, the family doctor or the pediatrician has no difficulty in explaining to parents the chances of future children being affected. In practice, this information is often given by the pediatrician, because the family doctor is likely to have referred the child to him in the first instance for diagnosis.

Acting on Advice   Genetic counseling means giving an explanation of future risks. It does not mean telling parents what they should do; this is something they must decide for themselves once they have been given the information in a manner in which they can understand it. The risk for each future baby remains unaltered however many previous babies have been affected. If a coin is tossed up and comes down heads on three successive occasions, the chance of its being heads or tails the next time is unaltered.

Some Common Malformations

Some of the commoner congenital malformations are discussed here. Others are covered in appropriate chapters (pyloric stenosis, p. 438; Down's syndrome, p. 588; jaundice, p. 442; urinary infections, pp. 443–46).

Birthmarks

There are several varieties of birthmark, all with apt names. The good thing about them is that most disappear with time; the odd thing is that some are not present at birth. Although the occasional mark is disfiguring if untreated, no birthmark is physically harmful.

"Stork's Beak" Mark

The commonest birthmark is a flat red patch on the eyelids. There are often similar marks in the middle of the forehead above the bridge of the nose, and on the back of the baby's head at the nape of his neck near the hairline: just the places where the stork's beak would have gripped the baby when he was being delivered to his mother! These red stains are made up of capillaries (the smallest of the blood vessels) that are wider than normal. They are not bruises or pressure marks made during birth; both of these would disappear in a few days, whereas stork's beak marks do not.

Will They Disappear?   The marks on the face do disappear eventually in almost all babies, although this may take a few months. Until they disappear you may notice that they show up more when your baby cries—this is of no importance. You will seldom see this kind of mark on an adult's face. The marks on the nape of the neck sometimes remain for life but are usually covered by the hair. It is common to be told that other children in the same family were born with similar marks.

Treatment   Stork's beak marks need no treatment and you can ignore them when washing your baby, since the skin here is no more tender than elsewhere. They do not bleed more easily than normal skin.

Strawberry Mark

Though less common than the stork's beak mark, this is still common. It may not be there at birth, especially if the baby is born prematurely. The mark resembles a strawberry—it is raised, soft, and reddish.

How It Changes   Whether present at birth or appearing a few days later, the mark behaves in the same way: it is small to begin with, perhaps no bigger than a pin's head, and gets steadily bigger for about six to nine months. Don't be alarmed—it will go away of its own accord. The first sign of this is when the color begins to fade in the center and pale islands appear. The pale islands enlarge and grow together until a completely pale center with a red rim replaces the strawberry. During this process the mark has gradually become flatter, and finally the whole thing disappears, leaving no sign that it ever existed.

Bleeding   It is exceptional for the mark not to disappear entirely on its own. Occasionally, the surface of the mark may be damaged, leading to oozing of blood; this is never dangerous, and the bleeding can always be stopped by light pressure. Unfortunately, if the surface is broken, a scar will be left when the mark itself has disappeared.

Surgery   It may be difficult to ignore your baby's strawberry mark if it is in the middle of his face, especially as you watch it grow alarmingly larger. But since these marks nearly always disappear of their own accord, surgery is no longer advised except for those rare cases in which the marks do not go away. The disadvantage of surgical removal is that it leaves a scar, which grows with the child, so the doctor will wait until your child is at least seven years old before considering treatment by surgery.

Port Wine Stain

This is the least common but the most serious type of birthmark, since it can be disfiguring and does not fade away. It is dark red or purple and although usually flat it may have a knobbly surface. A port wine stain on the face, especially a mark covering a large part of the face, is obviously a distressing sight for parents, and can make a child miserable about his appearance when he is older (see pp. 556–57).

Remedies   Fortunately, these marks can now be camouflaged by using a special cream, like a pancake base make-up, chosen to match the child's skin. It may take several minutes each day to put it on, but the child will prefer this to being stared at because of the startling mark on his face. The cream is suitable for boys as well as girls.

Moles (Pigmented Naevus)

Many children are born with brown or blackish moles, which may or may not sprout hairs. They may be flat or raised. Often they are too small to worry about or are hidden by clothing. When large enough to be disfiguring, moles are still usually small enough to be removed neatly by plastic surgery. Otherwise nothing need be done, since they are harmless.

Mongolian Blue Spot

This is a racial characteristic rather than a congenital malformation, which occurs mainly in babies of African or Oriental origin but also in Italians, Greeks, and Eskimos. Dark or pale blue areas are visible, particularly at the bottom of the spine.

These spots can be single or multiple, small or large. They may occur all over the back and sometimes on the arms and legs. It is usual for the color to fade during the first year; moreover, since the skin of African babies darkens after birth, the spots become almost invisible. They are sometimes mistaken for bruises if they have not been met before.

Hernias

A hernia, or rupture, is a lump containing intestine that has passed through a weak point in the muscular wall of the abdomen so that a loop of intestine lies immediately under the skin. The two most common hernias in babies and young children are the umbilical hernia at the navel and the inguinal hernia in the groin, which in boys may go into the scrotum.

Umbilical Hernia

Cause When the stump of the umbilical cord comes away, there may be a delay in the closure of the "umbilical ring," the gap in the muscles through which the cord with its blood vessels passed. The result is an umbilical hernia. These are extremely common in babies, and vary in size. They nearly always disappear without treatment before the age of five years.

Is Crying Harmful? Although the swelling may protrude more when the baby cries, distending like a balloon, this is not dangerous. Crying itself does not cause a hernia, nor is the uncomplicated hernia painful. You may think a hernia is painful because it gets larger and tenser when the baby cries, but in fact it is the other way around— crying causes the hernia to distend.

Treatment It used to be common practice for the doctor to apply strapping to an umbilical hernia; this is seldom done nowadays because it was found not to help and sometimes even delayed natural healing. In order to give natural healing every chance it is best to leave the hernia alone until the age of five or older; if this is done, a surgical operation is seldom required.

Prominent Navel You may sometimes suspect your baby has an umbilical hernia because his navel sticks out; usually this is because he hasn't much fat over his abdomen. Later on, his navel will be at the bottom of a valley, not on top of a hill.

Inguinal Hernia

This hernia in the groin or scrotum is less common than an umbilical hernia. It occurs far more frequently in boys, sometimes being associated with an undescended testicle on the same side.

Cause During intrauterine development the testicle moves from inside the abdomen, where it is first formed, into the scrotum. To do so it passes through a canal in the groin (inguinal canal), which normally closes once the testicle has passed through. Occasionally, the canal fails to close and a loop of intestine may be pushed into it.

Although the open canal through which the hernia will pass is present at birth, the loop of intestine may not yet have passed down it; in fact, the hernia is seldom present at birth. It may appear at any age but some time during the first year of life is the most usual time. The swelling caused by an inguinal hernia often disappears when the child is lying down, because the intestine then slides back into the abdomen.

Possible Complications Unlike an umbilical hernia, an inguinal hernia can cause trouble. There is always the possibility of "strangulation," meaning that the intestine becomes stuck outside the canal; the resulting pressure on its blood vessels stops the supply of blood, causing rapid and dangerous damage to the intestine.

Treatment Because the likelihood of strangulation is greatest during the first year of life, it is now the rule to operate on an inguinal hernia as soon as practical after it has first appeared. Therefore, if you notice a swelling in the groin—that is, the area between the abdomen and the top of the thigh—or if your baby boy's scrotum looks enlarged, tell your doctor promptly.

Another advantage of operating to repair an inguinal hernia shortly after it first appears is that there will not have been time for the muscles to become stretched and weak. The surgeon has only to tie the neck of the open canal so that the intestines can no longer go down it; he does not need to repair the muscles as well.

Hydrocele

This is a collection of fluid around the testicle which makes it look and feel larger than normal. It is quite often present at birth, and although one side only may be involved, it more often affects both sides.

No treatment is required, since the fluid disappears on its own, leaving the testicle undamaged. Only in the very rare situation of a hydrocele persisting to the age of about four need an operation be considered.

Undescended Testicle

As part of his routine examination of a new baby, the doctor checks that both testicles are present in the scrotum. The testicles develop in the abdomen but have usually descended before birth in full-term babies. In some babies born prematurely the testicles may descend shortly after birth.

Temporary Conditions   Of all those babies in whom the doctor cannot feel a testicle, the vast majority merely have a "retractile testicle"—that is, a testicle that has been pulled up into a pouch lying just above the scrotum. Provided the doctor can milk the testicle down into the scrotum, nothing needs to be done, even though the testicle may immediately go back into the pouch. Testicles that can be brought down will certainly come down permanently of their own accord before puberty.

Checking Doubtful Cases   If the doctor cannot find the testicle during his routine examination, he will usually arrange to examine the baby again within the first month of life. If one or both testicles are still not in the scrotum, he will arrange to check the boy again when he is about three years old.

Treatment   If the testicle is then still not in the scrotum, the doctor will arrange for a surgical operation at the age of about four years. The reason for such an early operation is to ensure the best possible function of the testicle when the boy grows up.

Movement of Testicles   One last point: you may sometimes notice your small boy's testicles moving up and down, particularly when he laughs or coughs, although they may not disappear altogether. This is absolutely normal and is due to the pull of a small muscle inside the scrotum; the muscle is much more active in younger children than in older ones.

Cleft Lip (Harelip) and Cleft Palate

The upper lip and palate develop in two parts which join before birth. Occasionally the join is incomplete, and a baby is born with a cleft lip, a cleft palate, or both. The cleft lip is more of an immediate shock to parents, because it is so obvious, although it causes less trouble than a cleft palate, which interferes with feeding and speech.

Cleft Lip   If your baby is born with a cleft lip, the shock caused by his appearance will be greatly reduced if you are shown, at once, photographs of babies whose cleft lips have been repaired by surgery. Modern plastic surgery can achieve wonders; the scars are almost unnoticeable.

A cleft lip is usually repaired at about three months. The results are more satisfactory than if the operation is undertaken immediately after birth. A cleft lip alone causes very little trouble with feeding and most mothers find they get used to the disfigurement, knowing that it is going to be removed.

Cleft Palate A cleft palate varies considerably in its degree of severity. A cleft soft palate alone affects the back half only, so it is much less serious than a cleft that involves the hard palate as well. Occasionally, only the uvula is cleft, and nothing needs to be done about this.

Treatment Cleft palate is now treated earlier than formerly. Immediately after birth the baby is likely to be fitted with a plate in the roof of his mouth. The main purpose of this is to ensure that the two halves of the palate come to be of equal size—at birth, one side is usually smaller. The plate is fitted in such a way that the smaller side is helped to grow faster than the larger side.

New plates need to be made as the shape of the palate alters. Once the sides are of equal size—the process usually takes several months—the operation to repair the gap is carried out. The final result is much more satisfactory than if the palate is repaired when the two parts are of unequal size. The plate has the secondary advantage of helping the baby to feed by preventing the milk from escaping up his nose. If the cleft has divided the palate exactly in half, the palate is not required. Repair in such children is carried out when the baby is between twelve and eighteen months old.

Most children with a cleft palate will require special training to overcome speech difficulties resulting from the cleft. The risk of deafness is increased, so that a special watch has to be kept for this.

Breast Feeding This is always worth trying. Despite the malformation, some babies can feed well this way and you will have had the satisfaction of feeding your baby yourself.

Bottle Feeding If breast feeding proves impossible, a baby with a cleft palate can sometimes manage to feed from a bottle using an ordinary nipple; others need a special nipple with a cowl on its upper surface that blocks off the cleft. Alternatively, the nipple may be cut with scissors so as to provide two parallel slits at its end.

Other Methods Some babies can be fed with a spoon whose edges have been bent over to make it funnel-shaped; this makes it easier to pour the milk onto the back of the tongue. These babies need some opportunity each day to try to suck so as to keep them in practice. A baby who has no opportunity to suck loses the skill, and when his palate is repaired he cannot suck the bottle. If all else fails, the baby has to be fed by tube.

Feeding a baby with a lip or palate defect is tiring and depressing. You need sympathetic support and frequent reminders that all will be well in the end.

Spina Bifida

In normal babies the spinal cord is safely housed within a chain of vertebrae which comprise the backbone. Each vertebra has a large tunnel through which the spinal cord passes.

In a few babies the formation of part of the spine before birth goes wrong, and the vertebrae are split into two parts: this is spina bifida. If the skin is intact, the condition is called spina bifida occulta; this seldom causes any trouble and most often is only discovered when a person is X-rayed for some other reason.

Effects on the Baby The serious form of spina bifida involves a gap in the skin overlying the affected part of the spine. This is filled by a cyst, usually a meningomyelocele. Consequently the spinal cord is unprotected, and it is also usually malformed. This causes paralysis of the legs and of the valves controlling the bladder and the rectum, so that urine and feces leak. It is very common for the urine to become infected and for serious infection of the kidneys to develop.

Hydrocephalus The majority of children born with the serious form of spina bifida develop hydrocephalus, or water on the brain. The "water" (cerebro-spinal fluid) is in fact inside the brain, in its normal position in the ventricles (hollow spaces in the brain that are connected to the canal running through the center of the spinal cord). Hydrocephalus results from a blockage of the normal circulation of the fluid inside the brain and spinal cord. It may be present at birth or develop shortly afterward. It causes progressive enlargement of the head and consequent destruction of the brain.

Treatment and the Baby's Future The serious form of spina bifida used to lead to almost certain death during infancy from meningitis, hydrocephalus, or a general failure to thrive. Today, as a result of surgery and of better total care, many children are surviving. The surgeon closes the skin over the exposed spinal cord shortly after birth. This prevents further damage, but it cannot rectify damage that has already occurred to the spinal cord, nor can it correct the malformation of the cord that is usually present.

Hydrocephalus, provided it is not severe, can be successfully treated by inserting a tube which leads the extra cerebro-spinal fluid from the brain to the abdomen or, less often, to the heart. To make sure that the flow of fluid is one way only, there is a small plastic valve inside the tube.

Unfortunately, because nothing can cure the abnormality of the spinal cord, if the child is already paralyzed, he remains so. The management of these handicapped children is one of the major challenges facing pediatric care today, and much can be done to help them. With orthopedic care, including braces and crutches, most will learn to walk.

Because many of these children grow up severely handicapped despite early surgery, doctors are now more selective in their choice of patients for surgery. If the quality of life for the child is bound to be severely impaired, many doctors now feel that such children should be allowed to die without treatment. There can never be a clear-cut answer to this vital but desperately difficult question which is now being widely debated. However, it is essential that parents, as well as staff, are involved in working out the decision for each baby. (See also handicapped child, p. 572.)

One cause for hope in the prevention of spina bifida is that taking extra vitamins before conception is possibly effective.

Congenital Dislocation of the Hip

One of the marvels of our newer understanding of babies is that this very serious condition can be cured if it is discovered when a baby is born. It is now part of the routine examination of every newborn baby for the hips to be checked; it is a relatively simple matter to discover whether they are dislocated. If they are, the baby is put into a simple metal splint for a few months. This keeps his legs in the "frog" position, and by holding the head of the thigh bone in the correct position, helps to mold a normal deep socket for the head of the bone to move in.

More common than the finding of a dislocated hip is the discovery that the hip joint is looser than normal. This is learned by detecting a click in the hip when it is examined. This is quite normal and is due to the hormones that loosen the mother's joints for ease of delivery and have a similar temporary effect on some of the baby's joints.

Thanks to this great step in the early diagnosis and treatment of congenital dislocation of the hip, we should no longer see children growing up with the appalling limp that results from the condition.

Club Foot (Talipes)

This is the condition that affected Byron. One or, more often, both feet are misshapen, the commonest type being the foot turned inward at the ankle. The condition usually results from the position of the feet in the uterus, whereby they were squashed against the rest of the body by compression from the wall of the uterus.

Treatment is by splints or plaster of Paris. These have frequently to be altered as the foot grows, but the final result is usually perfect or very nearly so. In severe cases treatment may be required for some months.

31

Disorders Affecting Young Babies

Skin Troubles in the First Weeks

In the first few weeks of life a young baby's skin may pass through many phases, from peachlike to peeling, from clear to spotty. This does not necessarily mean he is being fed, washed, or cared for incorrectly. It is so common as to be a normal stage (see the newborn baby, pp. 40–41); possibly it represents the reaction of the skin to contact with air after contact with the liquid surrounding him in the uterus.

As a new mother you are likely to worry that your baby's skin troubles mean that something is wrong. You want to know which need attention and which can be safely trusted to go away with time. For example, it is important to recognize a sign of infection like a septic spot (below), and not to confuse it with the little white spots, or milia, on the nose of a new baby, which are normal and harmless (pp. 40–41).

Spots and Rashes

Terms such as "milk rash" and "heat rash" are often used loosely to explain rashes whose causes are unknown. I prefer to admit that I do not know the cause of many rashes I see in babies, though I suspect they result from the change in environment described above. Such rashes disappear on their own and are easily differentiated, by the doctor, from those for which he has to prescribe special treatment. There is no point in changing brands of milk or stopping breast feeding on the suspicion that spots are due to the milk disagreeing with the baby—this is hardly ever the case.

Is It Eczema?

Infantile eczema (see pp. 507–8) affects a few babies but does not usually start before a baby is two to three months old. Many rashes that look like eczema turn out to be the usual temporary scattered spots. Some rashes are due to sensitivity to wool, so it is wise to use cotton clothes next to the skin.

It is safest, with your first baby, to ask your doctor or visiting nurse about any spots he gets, although they will probably reassure you that this is just another normal baby going through his spotty period.

Heat Rashes and Prickly Heat (*Miliaria*)

"Heat rash" is a vague term covering a variety of trivial rashes. Even in cold weather, a baby can get a heat rash if he gets too hot under layers of thick clothing and bedding. In the tropics, "prickly heat" is common (living in the tropics, p. 377).

A hot baby sweats; he cannot take off his coat, or move to a cooler room, and his mother may not realize he is crying because he is too hot, so she feeds him again or, worse still, puts on another blanket. The sweat produces a rash in the areas where sweat glands are most numerous—face, neck, shoulders, and chest—especially in the creases between folds of skin.

Remedies The remedy is to cool your baby by removing some of his clothing and bedclothes. Dress him according to the weather, not the season (see baby clothes, pp. 31–34). Do not put wool next to his skin; in cold weather put warm clothes over a cotton shirt. Keep blankets away from his neck and face, using a top sheet if necessary.

A bath is refreshing and washes away the sweat that causes the rash. A little talcum powder or calamine lotion applied to the rash is soothing, but make sure his skin is quite dry first.

Wheals: Urticaria Neonatorum

A baby in the early days of life sometimes develops a condition called "urticaria neonatorum," which produces wheals as well as spots. It is quite common and looks rather like hives. There are red blotchy areas and small white spots, which appear and disappear on different parts of the baby's body in a matter of a few hours or even less. This tendency to wheals and spots lasts about two or three days and disappears without treatment. It does not mean the baby will suffer from hives later on.

This rash is often called a "heat rash," but a baby does not have to be hot to get it. Possibly it may be the clothes or bedding, to which the baby's skin is sensitive, but since it disappears without any special treatment or change in clothing, it may be a reaction of the baby's skin to the change from the fluid environment of the uterus to an air environment.

Septic Spots (Pustules) and Skin Rashes

Even an isolated septic spot (pustule) or pimple should be taken seriously in the first months of life. Babies seldom get septic spots before the end of the first week, but after this they are comparatively common in maternity nurseries, where staphylococcal infections can spread easily (p. 393). A good treatment is to apply gentian violet, which, although a startling color, works better than an ointment because it quickly dries up the spot. Tell your doctor if you have an important occasion pending, such as the christening, so that your baby isn't covered with violet paint then.

"Cradle Cap" (Scurf, or Seborrhea of the Scalp)

Signs   Many babies develop a thick brown layer of crusts on the scalp. This may cover the scalp or it may appear in patches, commonly near or on the "soft spot" (anterior fontanel), because this tends to be washed less vigorously than the rest of the scalp in the mistaken fear of damaging the brain underneath (p. 39). However, cradle cap may appear on the heads of the best-washed babies, owing to the tendency of some skins to produce too much grease. The trouble can also spread to the nearby skin, causing red scaly inflammation (seborrheic dermatitis). It is particularly likely to cause cracks just above the ears. This generalized form of the trouble can be very alarming because much of the baby's skin becomes inflamed. Fortunately, the condition usually responds well to the treatment now available.

Remedies   If you deal with the flakes or crusts when they first appear, you may be able to wash them away with a solution of one teaspoon of sodium bicarbonate to one pint of water. Alternatively, you may be able to remove the crusts by soaking them overnight with arachis or olive oil to loosen them, then gently lifting them away with a comb. If they fail to come off easily, or if the condition is severe and the skin underneath the crusts is red and inflamed, you should get your doctor's or visiting nurse's advice.

Once established, cradle cap is hard to dislodge with ordinary shampoos and soap, but medicated shampoos are available that can be rubbed in as an ointment at night and used as a shampoo in the morning. This treatment clears the scalp in a day or two, although crusts may reappear, in which case it has to be repeated.

Regular shampooing should keep cradle cap under control once the crusts have been removed.

Sore Creases (Intertrigo)

Heat rash, seborrheic dermatitis, and other skin trouble can involve the creases in which babies abound; if so, your doctor will advise you how to deal with the problem as a whole. However, your baby may have a sore, red crease from skimpy washing or drying. It is easy to overlook some of his folds and creases at bathtime, particularly if he is plump and they are many and deep. You may forget to wash and dry behind his ears and under his arms, and if you forget once too often, irritation and soreness may start here.

Remedies The best way to prevent soreness is to remember that your baby's creases need regular and gentle washing and drying (pp. 101–2). Once trouble has started, protective ointment applied after washing soon clears it up.

Creases in your baby's neck sometimes get sore because of tight clothing around his neck.

Diaper Rashes and Sore Bottoms

Even the best-kept babies get diaper rashes and sore bottoms from time to time. They are extremely common during the diaper-wearing age, since however frequently diapers are changed, it is impossible to prevent the skin from remaining in contact with urine or stool. You can minimize the length of time your baby spends in wet or dirty diapers by changing him regularly, but it is unrealistic to aim to keep him dry all the time; this would involve waking him up to change his diaper and spending half your day laundering (see changing diapers, p. 104). However, prevention is simpler than cure, and a few precautions will cut down the amount of discomfort your baby suffers.

Prevention Breast-fed babies suffer from diaper rashes much less often than those fed cow's milk because their stools differ and are less liable to cause irritation (see below). Thoroughly clean, soft diapers chafe less, so wash them in a pure soap product and rinse out all the soap. Do not use detergents or enzyme powders, which can cause irritation if traces remain in the diaper (see washing diapers, pp. 104f.). Clean your baby's skin gently, using oil or baby lotion if it begins to look sore. Do not misuse waterproof pants by letting your baby wallow for hours in a drenched diaper (see diapers, p. 35). Leave off the diaper altogether and let him lie on a sheet, or let him exercise without a diaper on the floor for as long as possible if signs of diaper rash appear; this is easier to organize in summer. Exposure to air helps the skin to recover, and the less it is covered by a soggy diaper the better. A disposable diaper may help (pp. 34–35).

Applying petroleum jelly, zinc oxide, or other ointments and creams helps to prevent and treat soreness by forming a barrier between the skin and the wet diaper. However, some kinds of diaper rash need to be identified and given more specialized treatment.

Ammonia Dermatitis

General precautions reduce the likelihood of this, the commonest kind of diaper rash, but knowing something about the chemistry involved will help you to understand why the most effective treatment is a straightforward chemical method.

Signs How do you know if your baby's rash is due to ammonia dermatitis? It starts around the genitals rather than the anus and you will probably notice a strong smell when you change his diaper, especially if he has worn it overnight. The smell is due to ammonia and may be strong enough to make your eyes water.

Your baby's urine does not smell of ammonia because his diet disagrees with him, or because teething is making his urine "strong." Normal urine produces ammonia when its main ingredient, urea, is chemically split by germs in the stool. This only happens when urine and stool remain together, so the longer your baby lies in a wet, dirty diaper the more time the urea-splitting germs have to get to work.

These germs are contained in normal stools but they flourish particularly in an alkaline medium. A cow's milk feed produces an alkaline stool, so the bottle-fed baby is more likely to get ammonia dermatitis than the breast-fed baby. Breast milk produces an acid stool, which discourages the chemical reaction responsible for this type of diaper rash.

Unrecognized and untreated ammonia dermatitis can become severe. Having started as a rash around the genitals it can spread all over the diaper area, the groin, and the lower abdomen. At first the skin is spotty red and moist, later becoming thick and wrinkled, then peeling at the edges. Shallow ulcers may form. In circumcised babies, a meatal ulcer is common (p. 447).

The "Chemical" Weapon These added discomforts are not inevitable if you deal with the rash promptly, using a simple chemical weapon, which will also cure the more severe symptoms if these have developed. Apart from the general precautions for preventing and treating soreness (above), you should give the diapers a final rinse in diluted vinegar (acetic acid) after washing them. Use it in the proportion of one ounce of vinegar to one gallon of water—you will soon learn how many drops of vinegar you need to add to your washing water to get the proportion right. Drop the diapers into it, take them right out, wring out some but not all of the water, and hang them up to dry. Enough of the acetic acid will remain in the diapers to prevent the bacteria from making ammonia.

This simple method has replaced the use of boric acid, which had the same purpose but which occasionally led to boric poisoning if absorbed through the baby's raw skin. Boric acid in any form is now avoided for this reason. Preparations are available for rinsing diapers, but the vinegar-and-water method is easy and cheap. Creams such as petroleum jelly and zinc oxide help by forming a barrier between the skin and the ammonia, but do nothing to counteract the basic cause of ammonia dermatitis. Special creams containing safe ingredients which neutralize the ammonia are available.

Since the ammonia is formed outside the body there is no reason to give your baby extra fluid to dilute the urine, as is sometimes suggested. Nor are medicines required to alter its composition.

Diaper Rash Caused by Thrush

When a baby has thrush in the mouth (p. 434) his stools contain the thrush fungus. This can cause a rash around the anus; the rash is usually on the buttocks only, unlike ammonia dermatitis, which starts around the genitals.

Whenever a baby has a buttock rash, the doctor looks in his mouth to see whether he has thrush; to check the diagnosis, a microscopic examination of scrapings from the rash may be needed. A solution of gentian violet clears up the rash and is often tried in doubtful cases.

Seborrheic Dermatitis

Diaper rash is occasionally caused by seborrhea, the brownish dandruff babies tend to get on the scalp (see above). Flakes may fall from the head and spread the condition to other areas, such as the cheeks and around the ears; it causes cracks behind the ears. A seborrheic diaper rash is extensive; it is found in the armpits and in the groin as well as on the genitals and buttocks, and is a brownish-red color.

The doctor looks for seborrhea elsewhere on your baby's body to help him decide the cause of the rash. He will probably prescribe a medicated shampoo to deal with the scalp and an ointment to clear up the diaper rash. Leave off your baby's diaper whenever possible, and follow the general rules for dealing with soreness in the diaper area (see above).

Infections

A newborn baby is not as resistant to infection as an older child; infections in the first weeks of life are therefore serious and need prompt treatment. He has some resistance to the streptococcus, the common cause of sore throats, but little to the staphylococcus, the organism that can cause sticky eye (p. 473), infections around the umbilicus (p. 102), septic spots (pp. 429–30), and genital infection.

General Signs

Loss of Appetite The most important symptom of infection in young babies is loss of appetite. If your baby has been feeding well and then refuses feedings, you should tell your doctor. Infection must be regarded as the cause of loss of appetite until proved not to be.

Vomiting If you try to make your baby feed when he is suffering from an infection, he will probably vomit, and this loss of fluid may lead to his becoming dehydrated. A dehydrated baby is restless for fluid, but later becomes apathetic. Long before this stage, you should have recognized that your baby is ill and needs your doctor's help.

Fever Don't make the mistake of thinking your baby is all right because his temperature is normal—I have stressed on page 396 that temperature alone is not a reliable guide to a child's state of health. A baby with a general infection may have no fever; in fact, a fall in temperature is not uncommon and is more serious.

Preventing Infection

In the Hospital Because infection carries such risks in the newborn period, every effort must be made to prevent it. This is easier in your own home than in a large maternity nursery, where the risk of cross-infection among babies and adults is greater. This is one good reason for going home early when your baby is born in the hospital (p. 15).

It is safer for babies in the hospital to be nursed by their mothers under the "rooming-in system" (pp. 17–18)—the babies' cribs are left beside their mother's beds instead of all being close together in a large nursery. Single rooms are ideal from the point of view of preventing infection, but they are lonely for mothers, and in any case there are not enough of them.

At Home What can you do to minimize the risk of infection for your baby? Be scrupulously careful in preparing his feedings if he is bottle fed (see sterilizing the formula, pp. 90f.). Wash your hands before handling him in the early weeks, taking particular care if you have a boil or diarrhea. But don't overdo it—it is no good wearing a mask if you get a cold, since you have probably already infected your baby, and in any case a mask is worse than useless without proper training in its use.

Thrush (Candida Albicans)

Thrush is caused by a fungus infection—candida albicans. It occurs mainly in babies, partly perhaps because they are less resistant to infection but particularly because the fungus is more likely to reach the mouth at that age. It arrives there on incompletely sterilized nipples or during the baby's passage through the birth canal if his mother has vaginal thrush. In the hospital, it occurs particularly in premature baby units because the fungus likes the heat and humidity. It is your job to sterilize your baby's bottle and nipples. Your doctor will need to check you for vaginal thrush and give treatment if it is present.

Symptoms

Thrush appears mainly on the inside of the cheeks but may be found on the tongue and palate as well. You will see white patches, which can be easily mistaken for milk but, unlike milk, thrush does not wipe off easily. Scraping thrush away needs force and will cause bleeding. Thrush on the tongue causes a thick white fur.

Thrush makes feeding painful, and because you know your baby well you will realize that he wants to suck but is forced to stop and cry. He may also vomit. Most infections cause a loss of appetite, but with thrush it is mainly the pain caused by the condition that makes a baby stop feeding.

Treatment

Thrush can be treated by applying gentian violet to the patches. This is messy but has the advantage that you can see where you have painted and your doctor can check that you have done it. You have to continue painting the patches for a week after the last one has gone, because there may still be fungi present in the mouth.

An alternative treatment is an antibiotic called nystatin, supplied as a clear liquid, which is dropped into the mouth. It is less messy than gentian violet and is without the disadvantage of gentian violet, which may make the baby's mouth sore, especially if he is a preterm baby.

Diaper Rash

Thrush fungi may affect your baby's bottom, since the fungus is present in the stools. If these are left in contact with the skin for long the diaper area can become infected. Thrush is therefore the cause of one type of diaper rash (p. 433).

Vomiting

"Mucusy Baby"

Vomiting is a common symptom in newborn babies. If your baby is sick in the first few days of life, the most likely explanation is that he is a "mucusy baby." He is vomiting mucus that has accumulated in his stomach as the result of irritation of the stomach lining by blood and amniotic fluid swallowed during birth. This vomiting is not caused by illness or by his feedings disagreeing with him.

Your doctor has to exclude other possible causes of vomiting, particularly obstruction of the intestines and infection, before making a diagnosis of "mucusy baby."

Other Causes of Vomiting

Gulping Air Taking his feedings too greedily and gulping down lots of air with the milk may cause a baby to vomit, though this has probably been exaggerated as a cause of vomiting in the past. The problems of gas and colic are discussed on pages 68–70 and 123–25.

Bottle Feeding A bottle-fed baby may be sick after a feeding because the hole in the nipple is too small and he has to suck extra hard, drawing in air around the edges of the nipple. If the bottle is not kept tilted while he feeds, the nipple will contain air as well as milk, and this too can lead to vomiting. Too large a hole in the nipple can cause a baby to feed too quickly and bring up his milk afterward. Such mistakes are understandable and not disastrous—you have to learn how to give the bottle feeding correctly (see bottle feeding, pp. 87–89, 92–93).

The "Wrong" Milk Do not blame the brand of milk for your baby's vomiting; as long as the feeding is mixed correctly at the right strength for him, it is most unlikely that his feeding disagrees with him. Vomiting from an allergy to cow's milk is rare.

Breast Feeding A breast-fed baby may be sick because of the way he takes his feedings, not because his mother's milk disagrees with him. He can gulp his feeding too quickly either because of hunger or because of the overwhelming flow of milk for the first seconds after the let-down reflex starts (see breast feeding, p. 60). Sucking for long periods at an empty breast is sometimes blamed as a cause of vomiting, but this would be more likely to make a baby fall asleep or else cry because he was still hungry. As you and your baby get used to breast feeding, and the breasts become attuned to his sucking, he is less likely to vomit for these reasons.

Regurgitation

Some babies tend from the very beginning to bring up a mouthful or two of milk during or after a feeding—other babies never, or hardly ever, do this.

Is It Harmful? It is absolutely normal and harmless, and you need do nothing about it, apart from protecting your baby's clothes and your own from the overflow. A baby who regurgitates is hard to keep clean and sweet-smelling, but don't be persuaded that this is anything more than a nuisance—it does not mean he should be fed less or differently or that he will become undernourished. It sometimes helps not to bounce him on your knee at the end of a feeding, though usually he will regurgitate however gently handled because it is a habit he has learned and he enjoys it.

The Older Baby   Your baby may regurgitate less when he is taking a more solid diet. On the other hand, this type of baby often becomes the happy extrovert who, in the second half of his first year, vomits for the fun of it. Being sick does not distress him in the least—he positively enjoys it. I often describe them as "happy vomiters"! Perhaps he finds exceptional pleasure in his mouth. Every baby enjoys his mouth intensively from the age of three or four months, when his fingers are frequently crammed into it and most of his play centers on it. Bringing up part of his feeding, then perhaps "chewing the cud" or ruminating, as it is called, is just another pleasurable activity. Some babies start this habit when they are taken off the breast. I suspect this is because they miss the more peaceful and prolonged pleasure of sucking at the breast.

One compensation, if you are fed up with rubbing stains from the carpet and sending your clothes to the dry cleaner's, is that this kind of baby is likely to be bright and happy, and to cry less than the average.

Will He Starve?   If your baby is thriving, there is no need to worry that he is not getting enough food because of the vomiting. Above all, don't spend your time trying to stop him from being sick. You won't be able to and in any case he enjoys it! He will eventually stop when he is about two years old and has other things to enjoy. Meanwhile, all you can do is to take evasive action to save your own clothes and put polythene covers on the carpet if you haven't got a linoleum-type floor. Don't keep dabbing at his mouth—this only adds to his pleasure and prolongs the habit.

I always wish I could keep a record of the subsequent development of babies with this problem, because I suspect they are more cheerful and extrovert than the average. I sometimes wonder if their enjoyment of their mouths (and speech) increases their chance of becoming politicians!

Vomiting as a Serious Symptom

Obstruction of the Bowel and Infection   A baby with an obstruction of the bowel may vomit, and so may a baby with an infection such as a cold or inflammation of the ears. But in both these cases, the baby is ill. The baby with bowel obstruction develops abdominal distension and becomes constipated. The baby with an infection refuses his feedings; he is often miserable, crying in a continuous whimper, quite different from his usual sounds.

Calling the Doctor

If you are in doubt about the cause of your baby's vomiting, please consult your doctor. If being sick distresses the baby—if he retches uncomfortably, if he is plainly miserable afterward, if he has diarrhea as well, or brings up a large amount more than once, take his vomiting seriously. Copious vomiting and diarrhea can lead to dehydration, or drying out, which needs prompt treatment (see also pp. 478–80).

Pyloric Stenosis

If at the age of two or three weeks your baby suddenly starts being sick and this develops into violent vomiting, so that he seems to be "pumping it up," you should tell your doctor at once. This "projectile vomiting," in which a whole feeding is brought up and may be shot across the room, can be the symptom of a fairly common disorder called congenital pyloric stenosis.

The disorder is not congenital in the ordinary sense of the word, since it is not present at birth, but the tendency to it is decided before birth; the fact that it tends to run in families also points to an inherited cause. By the time the baby is two or three weeks old, whether he is full term or preterm, something triggers off the predisposition to the disease.

The trigger that provokes the actual illness is feeding. The baby is now using his own digestive system instead of being nourished through the placenta as he was before birth. If he is predisposed to pyloric stenosis, feeding causes the muscle of the pylorus (the channel at the end of the stomach) to thicken. This narrows the channel and leads to vomiting. The condition is much commoner among boys.

Other Symptoms

The baby has a good appetite, which is a useful aid in the diagnosis of pyloric stenosis, since if he were vomiting from an infection his appetite would be poor. He is likely to be constipated, since not enough food is getting through to fill the rectum. The doctor makes the diagnosis by feeling the thickened pyloric muscle while the baby is feeding.

Treatment

The baby is usually treated by a surgical operation and the outlook is excellent; digestion is normal afterward. It is possible to give treatment by drugs, but because this takes longer it is now seldom used.

You do not have to worry about the possibility of pyloric stenosis in a baby who starts vomiting only after the age of six weeks.

Jaundice (Yellowness) of the Newborn

There are several reasons why newborn babies become jaundiced. The three main categories are: physiological ("normal") jaundice; jaundice from rhesus (Rh factor) disease; and jaundice caused by infection.

Physiological Jaundice

The liver lies in the abdomen under the ribs on the right side. One of its many tasks is to deal with the red blood cells when their life span is over. Normal red cells live for about three months. At the end of this time they are dissolved; the hemoglobin they contain is liberated and then converted into bile in the liver. Bile is a liquid that passes from the liver to the intestine and then out of the body. It also contains substances known as bile salts which help to digest the fat in the diet.

When the liver is working at full capacity it can deal with the breakdown of red cells as fast as this occurs. But if the liver is not working to full capacity there is an accumulation of the yellow coloring matter formed from the red cells, which is recognizable, in the skin color, as jaundice. Because the breakdown of red cells is a normal bodily process, this type of jaundice is known as "physiological."

Since it is related to the efficiency of the liver, this cause of jaundice is more common in the preterm baby whose liver is working less efficiently than that of a baby born at full term.

Treatment Physiological jaundice usually disappears without treatment within a few days. Apart from making the baby drowsy and slow with feedings, it seldom causes any serious problem. However, since severe jaundice can damage the brain, this possibility is prevented by a number of different forms of treatment. In the first place the doctor will ensure that the baby has enough to drink, giving milk by tube if necessary.

Light Treatment A high level of jaundice can be lowered by exposing the baby to natural (cool blue fluorescent) light. This form of treatment is termed "phototherapy." He is undressed, his eyes are bandaged to protect them from the bright light, and a special box is placed over his crib. The baby is taken away from the light for feedings and the eye bandages are removed so that you can watch each other. The fact that his eyes have to be bandaged while under the light is sure to distress you but the treatment is much less drastic than an exchange transfusion. Babies seldom need the light treatment for more than two to three days; it is stopped when blood tests show that the level of jaundice is falling. The light treatment cannot harm your baby, but you are bound to miss picking him up whenever you want to. However, there is no reason why his incubator should not be placed beside your bed. The treatment sometimes causes mild diarrhea.

If the jaundice becomes very severe—something that nowadays is usually prevented—the baby can have his blood changed (see exchange transfusion, p. 441).

Jaundice Caused by Rhesus (Rh Factor) Disease

During birth, some of the red cells from a baby's blood may cross the placenta (afterbirth) and enter his mother's blood. This is because there is only a thin membrane in the placenta separating the baby's blood from his mother's blood. When the placenta is tightly compressed during labor some of the baby's red cells can be squeezed through this membrane.

No harm results from this mixing of the two sets of cells provided the two blood groups match. If they do not, the mother forms antibodies to her baby's cells because they are foreign to her. These antibodies stay in her blood, doing her no harm, but if she becomes pregnant again, they cross the placenta and enter the new baby's circulation. Again, no harm results if the baby's blood matches his mother's, but if it does not, the antibodies will destroy many of his red cells. This leads immediately to anemia—lack of hemoglobin. The excessive destruction of red cells increases the work of the liver by increasing the number of red cells it has to deal with; consequently, jaundice may occur (see above).

This problem arises only in women who are Rh-negative. In the United Kingdom, they make up about 15 percent of the population. On the other hand, only about 1 percent of women of African origin are Rh-negative, so that the condition is much less common in their babies. When an Rh-negative woman marries an Rh-positive man, some of their babies will be Rh-positive. The proportion depends on the man's degree of "positivity," which may be full or half. If he is fully positive, all his babies will be Rh-positive, but if he is half positive only half the babies will be positive. The problem only arises when an Rh-negative woman is carrying an Rh-positive baby, and then only after she has formed antibodies. Since antibodies are formed only after the red cells have crossed from the baby into the mother, something that occurs mainly during labor, it is largely a problem of second and subsequent Rh-positive babies.

Prevention Rh disease causes babies to become jaundiced and anemic. It can cause death, or brain damage in babies who survive. However, it is possible to prevent the disease by stopping the formation of antibodies. This is done by destroying the baby's red cells immediately after they have entered his mother's blood by giving her an injection of Rh-antibodies (RhoGAM) within seventy-two hours of delivery. These antibodies have been made in the blood of another person; they have no effect on later babies, since they disappear within a few weeks.

The effect of this injection is to prevent the mother from forming her own antibodies, since the baby's red cells are destroyed before they can trigger off this mechanism. If all Rh-negative mothers were treated this way, the problem of Rh disease would be wiped out.

Prenatal Tests The blood of all pregnant women should be tested to detect those who are Rh-negative. If you are found to be Rh-negative, you will be tested to see if you have antibodies. If so, your baby will be very carefully checked during pregnancy and must be delivered in the hospital. As soon as he is born, his blood will be tested to see if he has Rh disease.

Exchange Transfusion If your baby has Rh disease it may be necessary to change his blood by an exchange transfusion. This washes away most of the antibodies that have reached him from you while he was in the uterus; the use of Rh-negative blood supplies him with blood that is not vulnerable to any remaining antibodies. Changing the blood reduces the level of jaundice, thereby lessening the chance of brain damage. It also raises the level of hemoglobin by supplying blood that is not anemic. It is impossible to change all the blood, so the exchange transfusion may need to be repeated the next day if the level of jaundice rises again. Once the baby's liver can cope with the burden of dealing with the breakdown of extra red cells, so that the level of jaundice no longer rises, no further transfusions are needed.

In addition to an exchange transfusion, or sometimes instead of it, the baby can be given phototherapy (pp. 439–40).

Jaundice Caused by Infection

Infection of the liver (hepatitis) is a rare cause of jaundice in the newborn, and is usually due to a virus. Although it may be very serious, fortunately the risks to a baby when a mother catches infectious jaundice are not as great as it was once feared. Isolation of the baby from the mother is largely useless, and only makes a mother who is already depressed by the jaundice feel even worse. The incubation period for infectious hepatitis varies with the different viruses, but is so long that whether or not the baby is going to catch it has already been determined by the time the infection is diagnosed.

Although infection of the liver itself is a rare cause of jaundice, other infections are a more common cause. Babies with an infection of any organ may become jaundiced because infection impairs the ability of the liver to work efficiently. Before developing jaundice in this way the baby will already have refused his feedings and will usually be seriously ill. Antibiotics have reduced this problem enormously by dealing with infections before they reach this stage.

Rare Causes of Jaundice

A rare type of jaundice, termed "breast milk jaundice," is caused by the presence of an unusual chemical in breast milk which does the mother no harm but reduces the efficiency of the baby's liver in dealing with the normal disposal of old red blood cells. Fortunately, it never causes a dangerous level of jaundice, so it is perfectly safe to continue breast feeding. The doctor makes the diagnosis by excluding all the other causes of jaundice. As the baby gets a few weeks older, the jaundice gradually disappears even though he is still being breast fed.

A very rare cause of jaundice is a congenital defect whereby the baby is born without the channel (bile duct) that leads the bile from the liver to the gall bladder and so to the intestine. If this defect involves only the channel outside the liver, a surgeon may be able to effect a repair. Unfortunately, it is more often the minute channels within the liver that are malformed and therefore obstructed. This cannot be cured, and the baby dies after a few months. Jaundice from this serious cause does not appear until the baby is about ten days old.

32

Urinary and Genital Problems

Trouble can start anywhere in the urinary system: kidneys, bladder, connecting tubes (ureters) or urethra, either because bacteria have entered the tract or because an abnormality somewhere in the system has made it easier for bacteria to set up infection.

Girls are more likely than boys to suffer from infections caused by bacteria entering from below, because in girls the urethra (the tube leading from the bladder to the outside) is shorter. In addition, germs can reach the bladder more easily in girls because the opening to the bladder is nearer the rectum.

Infection in the urinary tract in children is more often in the kidneys than in the bladder, since a child's bladder is resistant to infection. When cystitis (inflammation of the bladder) does occur in children, it is usually due to an obstruction to the flow of urine.

Diagnosing Urinary Infections

It is more difficult to diagnose urinary infections in children than in adults because the symptoms are less obvious. It would take a very astute mother to notice that it was painful for her baby to pass urine, or that he was doing so abnormally often; if the baby is in diapers, such symptoms can seldom be detected. The symptoms you would notice—loss of appetite, vomiting, fever, fretfulness, and failing to thrive—could have many other causes.

When a doctor can find no explanation for a baby's symptoms, he has to investigate the possibility of a urinary infection by checking the urine. This will also be his first move when treating any child who has pain or difficulty in passing urine, is doing so too frequently, or whose urine looks bloodstained. If your child has any of these symptoms take him to the doctor: don't wait for the symptoms to go away.

Any baby boy who from birth is unable to pass a normal stream of urine must be checked immediately for a congenital blockage. Dribbling of urine, as opposed to a normal stream, is always serious.

Testing the Urine

For a laboratory test to be accurate, the urine specimen must be clean. If after leaving the bladder it is contaminated by contact with the foreskin or the vagina, urinary infection can be wrongly diagnosed. This has probably happened frequently in the past, and children were sometimes treated for urinary infections they did not have.

Obtaining a Specimen of Urine

There are several tricks that help in obtaining a clean specimen. For example, babies tend to wet on waking or feeding; if a sterile container is ready and the diaper area has been washed beforehand, a clean specimen can be caught. Only a small quantity is needed. Sterile plastic bags are used to obtain specimens from both boys and girls. The least contaminated specimen is that passed in the middle of urination (midstream urine). It must be collected into a sterile container, which the doctor or hospital can provide. Pouring scalding water into a jar or pot does not sterilize. You will be told exactly how to use whatever method your doctor favors.

If your doctor is unsatisfied with the sample, he may decide to obtain urine by inserting a needle directly into the bladder. This sounds frightening but it is no more painful than having a prick to obtain blood straight from a vein. A bladder puncture can be done in the outpatient department, without having to admit your child.

You may wonder why checking the urine to find out if it contains anything unusual is necessary when drugs are available to deal with infection. The answer is that a drug may clear up the symptoms but it also removes the evidence needed for a more accurate diagnosis, and thus may prevent discovery of an underlying problem that needs correction at an early stage.

Checking the Urinary System

Ideally, after one urinary infection has been proved by tests, a child should be investigated to see if anything is wrong with his kidneys, bladder, or connecting tubes.

A congenital malformation anywhere in the urinary tract makes the system more liable to infection. Early discovery gives a much greater chance of cure. This will usually require surgery. Delay in diagnosis can lead to irreparable kidney damage.

X-ray Methods

X-rays are used for these investigations. An "intravenous pyelogram" (IVP) checks the kidneys and ureters, and necessitates a prick in the arm. A "micturating cystogram," taken during the passing of urine containing a radio-opaque dye, shows whether the bladder and urethra are normal. This test requires a fine catheter to be passed into the bladder. If your child needs these tests, the doctor will explain to him what he is going to do.

Treatment of Urinary Infection (Pyelonephritis)

When it has been proved that your child is suffering from a urinary infection, treatment with drugs is continued for weeks or months to clear it up completely. Once the urine is normal you still have to take samples of urine for checking at regular intervals for a year or two.

Your doctor will probably arrange for a urine test to be sent to the laboratory whenever your child is ill, and before starting him on antibiotics; he will do this even if there is something obvious to account for the illness, such as acute tonsillitis, in case there is also a hidden flare-up of the urinary infection.

Abnormal Bed-Wetting

Occasionally, there are physical explanations for a child's failure to become toilet trained. It is for this reason that a child who continues to wet the bed after the age of four should be checked by a doctor (pp. 554–56).

Changes in Urine Color

Urine is paler than its usual straw color when diluted from copious drinking, and darker when concentrated. Urine formed during the night is more concentrated than daytime urine and therefore darker. This is Nature's way of ensuring longer periods of sleep without the disturbance of having to get up to pass urine. Dark orange urine is a normal result of fever or heavy sweating. A child with a feverish illness will pass darker urine, but apart from offering him extra drinks, you should not be overconcerned. It is his illness that must be treated, not the color of the urine.

Strong Urine

The usual reason why urine has a strong smell is that it is giving off ammonia. There may be enough to make your eyes water when you change your baby's diapers. This problem arises only with the baby who is still in diapers, because it is the prolonged contact between urine and stool that leads to the formation of ammonia outside the body. Urine contains a substance called urea, which can be chemically changed by certain germs in the stools. These split the urea, thereby liberating ammonia. The ammonia may be strong enough to burn the baby's bottom, causing the variety of diaper rash called "ammonia dermatitis" (p. 431).

Since the ammonia is formed outside the body there is no logic in giving the baby more water to drink in order to make the urine less strong, or special medicine to change the chemistry of his urine. All that is needed to prevent the formation of ammonia is to rinse the diapers in vinegar (see p. 432).

Cloudy Urine

Urine that has been standing may go cloudy. Urine that is cloudy when passed is abnormal. Take a sample in a clean bottle to your doctor if you are doubtful or worried.

Red Urine

Red candy can make the urine red. Beets have this effect in some families. If your child produces reddish urine, the first thing to consider is whether something he has eaten could be responsible.

A small amount of blood in the urine may be invisible except under the microscope. A larger quantity makes the urine look smoky; there has to be a great deal of blood to make it look red. The usual cause is nephritis, a condition affecting the kidneys, which can develop two to three weeks after a streptococcal sore throat in certain individuals (pp. 455, 530). This is an uncommon complication now that such infections are treated with penicillin. Bloodstained urine would not be the only symptom of nephritis.

Pink Spot on the Diaper

This occurs occasionally with babies and is due to the normal uric acid crystals in the urine. Its only importance is that it may be mistaken for blood, but this would leave a brown stain. It is commoner in boys, since their stream of urine is more likely to be aimed at the same area of the diaper.

Ulcer on the Tip of the Penis (Meatal Ulcer) or Stenosis

A circumcised baby boy has no foreskin to protect the delicate knob-like end (glans) of the penis from contact with wet diapers. As a result, he may get a tiny ulcer on the edge of the glans, particularly when he already has a diaper rash (pp. 431–33). The ulcer goes down into the urethra, causing him to scream with pain when passing urine. The scab formed on the ulcer is repeatedly wiped off when he passes urine, and this can cause scar tissue to form at the opening of the urethra, so that the opening becomes progressively narrowed. Be sure to let your doctor see your baby if you think he may have this problem.

The aim of treatment is to shield the ulcer from the abrading urine while it heals by covering it with protective ointment. The ointment is applied on a tiny glass rod which is inserted into the opening of the penis; this also helps to widen the opening, thus preventing it from shrinking during the process of healing. Avoid rubber pants and expose the penis to the air as much as possible.

Vaginal Discharge

A normal newborn baby girl may have a white vaginal discharge caused by chemical substances (hormones) from her mother that are still circulating in her blood. As the hormone level drops, the discharge ceases (see enlarged genitals, p. 39).

Until a year or two before puberty, the glands of the vagina produce only a small quantity of mucus, which is not normally noticeable. A small girl who does suddenly produce a copious vaginal discharge should be seen by her doctor. He has to make sure that there is no foreign body in the vagina, since a small girl sometimes experiments in this way and is too shy to admit it. Another possible reason for the discharge is infection.

It is normal for a vaginal discharge to occur for a year or two before the start of menstruation. A nonirritating discharge at this time is quite usual and is evidence of activity of the mucous glands at the beginning of puberty. It has nothing to do with poor hygiene and is not "catching."

An irritating, offensive, or colored discharge causing a sore vulva is abnormal and needs diagnosis and treatment. The doctor takes a swab to help identify the trouble. Occasionally, such discharge is due to threadworms entering the vagina from the bowel.

On the whole, the problem of vaginal discharge is much less important than mothers think. I see many girls every year because of vaginal discharge or pain "down below" resulting from obsessional "washing down" by their mothers. The amount of discharge is within the range of normal, and the pain is due to hurt feelings. This type of obsessional cleaning can lead to frigidity and other marital problems.

33

Coughs and Colds

The Common Cold

The common cold is a virus infection, not the result of wet feet or of sitting in a draft. The shivery feeling sometimes blamed as being the cause of a cold is more likely to be its first symptom.

Symptoms

The cold virus infects the mucous membrane lining the nose, causing a clear discharge. Your child may complain of a slight sore throat, but children experience less pain in their throats than adults (pp. 454–55). The cold becomes worse because the virus has lowered the body's resistance, making it easier for other germs to attack and cause secondary infection. The clear nasal discharge becomes thick and yellow, perhaps spreading to the bronchial tubes in the lungs. The tonsils and adenoids may enlarge to help protect your child from a deeper spread of the infection. In an older child, the sinuses may be affected (p. 462). There will probably be a cough because the extra secretions irritate the back of the throat.

Unfortunately, catching one cold does not give protection from others, since different viruses can be responsible; moreover, immunity from any particular virus is short-lived. Children are likely to catch extra colds in their first winters at school and they will probably bring back the infection to the younger ones in the family who are still at home.

Can Colds Be Prevented?

Children tend to get fewer colds as they get older, so some resistance builds up. Some children do undoubtedly catch colds more easily than others, without being any less healthy in other ways. A child eating a normal diet is not helped by extra vitamins (p. 181), nor is an effective vaccine available. Removal of tonsils and adenoids is not the answer either.

Excessive anxiety about colds, and about health in general, seems to increase the frequency of infections in a family. Children are likely to get a number of colds whatever their parents do, and too much protection does more harm than another cold. Wearing too many clothes tends to increase the liability to colds, so judge the number of layers of clothing your children need by what you feel is comfortable for yourself; give them the same number.

The Baby with a Cold

A young baby is much more seriously upset by a cold because he cannot breathe easily through his mouth at any time and particularly during a feeding. He is also more likely to get lung complications, such as pneumonia.

Preventing Infection   No visitor with a cold should be allowed near a baby. A mother with a cold is going to infect her baby whatever she does, and has probably done so before she realizes she has one. I would not recommend using a mask to feed or handle your baby, because even if you learn the complicated techniques required for it to have a chance of success, and change the mask frequently, it is unlikely to stop the infection from reaching him. It is probably hopeless to try to keep brothers and sisters from infecting him, but it is still worth trying in the case of a very young baby.

Treatment   If your baby does get a cold and cannot breathe easily, the most effective treatment is to use nose drops, which allow him to breathe through his nose temporarily. They are particularly useful before a feeding, to enable him to suck.

   The seriousness of the cold should not be judged by whether or not your baby has a temperature. As with other infections in babies, the temperature may not rise and yet he can be quite ill. Consult your doctor if your baby seems ill, whether or not he is feverish, and always if he refuses his food (see infections, pp. 433–34).

Colds in Older Children

An older child's cold may not be bad enough to keep him away from school, though it is perhaps selfish to spread the infection. The first signs of a cold can be more dramatic than the cold itself: the child may lose his appetite, vomit, and look feverish. These symptoms may herald more serious complaints, but many children begin ordinary colds in this way.

When to Consult Your Doctor   There is no need to consult your doctor unless your child has a high temperature, deafness, earache, or a very sore throat, or if he is obviously ill.

Treatment   You should not give your child aspirin as a routine at bedtime to help him sleep, unless there is high fever; it is better to make him comfortable with a hot-water bottle and a warm drink. Nose drops give only temporary relief and are unnecessary in the older child who no longer relies on sucking to feed, though a child who sucks his thumb may be more upset by a blocked nose. Show him how to blow his nose effectively by blowing one nostril at a time, pressing the other shut with a finger (see allergic rhinitis, p. 453).

Coughs

Causes

Coughing has many possible causes. These are usually obvious; the child will already have some infection, such as a cold or rhinitis. When the mucus from his nose trickles down the back of his throat, the irritation makes him cough. This is more likely to happen when he is lying down, so he will probably cough more at night. When he wakes in the morning he may have a bout of coughing to bring up the mucus that has accumulated at the back of his throat during the night. He will probably swallow the mucus, but this does not matter. You may think he has a bad cough, but he may cough very little for the rest of the day, although running may bring on a cough because exercise shifts the mucus, causing irritation.

Tonsillitis may be accompanied by a cough; a child with asthma will cough (see pp. 504f.). Coughing is necessary in wheezy bronchitis in order to bring up the matter irritating and blocking the bronchial tubes. The more effectively a child coughs, the better he will clear the obstruction, thus helping to clear the infection (see pp. 463–64, 466–67).

Inhaled Foreign Body

A sudden prolonged bout of coughing from a healthy child probably means he has inhaled a hard piece of food or a small toy. If he goes blue from choking, apply immediately the emergency treatment described on p. 624. If he then seems well and you can identify the whole of the object he inhaled, there should be no further trouble. But if you are in any doubt, and especially if his cough persists, please take him to your nearest emergency department.

Impress on the doctor at the hospital that there may be something stuck down in your child's lung, so that he has the chest X-rayed. A foreign body made of plastic will not show up, but its effect will be obvious because some of the millions of balloons that comprise the normal lung will be deflated, causing a shadow on the X-ray. Removal entails bronchoscopy, whereby a special tube (bronchoscope) is passed into the lung under an anesthetic, so that once the surgeon has seen the object he can remove it with long forceps. Permanent damage results if the object is left in the lung, and its immediate removal is essential for the lung to return to normal. Your child will probably be given respiratory therapy to ensure that the lungs re-expand completely. NOTE: Never give peanuts to a young child (p. 624).

Cough Medicines

Coughing to bring up matter in the bronchial tubes is useful and necessary; cough medicines designed to suppress the cough should not be used. Sometimes a child is worried by a continual tickling throat, which makes him go on coughing. Although a cough medicine has no appreciable effect and certainly cannot cure any cough, a spoonful may comfort your child by soothing the back of his throat; it also helps him feel you are sympathetic.

Coughing may be a matter of habit. A child who has had whooping cough may whoop with each of his next few coughs (see pp. 526–28).

Persistent Rhinitis

There can be several explanations for nasal rhinitis (catarrh). The term, which technically refers to a nasal discharge, is often used loosely to describe any blockage of the nose.

Reasons for a Runny Nose

The sniffly baby usually has a low nasal bridge and therefore particularly small nasal passages; this makes him sound as if he has a perpetual cold. But he is not ill and his "sniffing" is due not to a cold but to the air passing through narrow passages. The baby is not harmed and the noise disappears by the end of the first year, when the passages have grown bigger.

A young child may have a persistently running nose because he has not yet learned how to blow his nose. The age at which this skill is acquired varies, but you should try to achieve it by the time he goes to school. Teaching a child how to blow his nose must not be done aggressively, otherwise he will react against doing it. Worst of all is the constant nagging from a mother who is particularly sensitive to the sight of a running nose.

Adenoids

The site of infection may be the area at the back of the nose, which can be blocked by enlarged adenoids, so that secretions cannot drain away properly. In the schoolchild sinusitis may be present but this seldom needs separate treatment (p. 462). Your doctor may treat the infection with antibiotics and prescribe nose drops to reduce the swelling of the lining membrane of the nose. He may also arrange for your child to be taught breathing exercises by a respiratory therapist. Exercises will help him to breathe correctly through his nose, thereby clearing the nasal passages. This enables the body to fight the infection more effectively and allows mucus to drain away, preventing further infection. (See also tonsils and adenoids, pp. 454–56.)

Blowing the Nose

Blowing the nose efficiently prevents the accumulation of mucus. One side should be blown at a time, a finger pressing on the other nostril to keep it closed. If both nostrils are blown at once, it is possible for material to be forced up the Eustachian tubes, setting up infection. These tubes lead from the back of the throat to the middle ear on each side (see Eustachian tubes, p. 457). If infected material from the nose passes up one of the Eustachian tubes, an infection of the middle ear results (see otitis media, p. 459).

Allergic Rhinitis

Occasionally, a persistently runny nose is caused by allergy. Allergic rhinitis (hay fever) can occur at any season, since the allergen—the substance to which the child reacts sensitively—is not always pollen. When he inhales the allergen, the lining of his nose swells and it starts running; he may have bouts of sneezing. Some asthmatic children begin an attack of asthma with symptoms of allergic rhinitis, which causes a clear discharge. Asthma is the more likely cause if other members of the family suffer from allergic complaints (see allergy, pp. 502f.).

The Effect of Climate

Nasal rhinitis is not confined to people living in a damp climate. It commonly affects people in hot countries; but a child's rhinitis should not be blamed on living in a particular district of the United States, since local geography makes little difference. Dampness in a home has probably been overrated as a cause.

Consulting the Doctor

A child with rhinitis is often perfectly well, and the discharge clears up in time without any treatment. There is no need to treat your child as if he were "run down." However, if he complains of earache, he should be taken promptly to the doctor, since otitis media can be started by infection from the nose passing up the Eustachian tubes (see otitis media, p. 459). Your child should also be

seen by the doctor if he seems unwell in addition to having persistent rhinitis.

Tonsils and Adenoids

Their Function

Why do we have tonsils and adenoids? They are often regarded as
troublemakers which cause ill-health and should therefore be
removed as soon as possible, In fact, their job is to protect us against
infection. Tonsils and adenoids are both composed of lymphoid tissue;
this acts as a filter to trap harmful organisms. Both are sited in the
best places to provide a first line of defense against germs entering
by the mouth or nose. Unlike the tonsils, the adenoids cannot be seen
by looking into the mouth; they are at the back of the nose. They are
visible to the doctor through a small mirror he places at the back of
the throat and directs upward.

Are Large Tonsils Harmful?

Since the tonsils, one on each side of the back of the throat, are visible,
it is tempting to look into your child's throat to try to judge the state
of his health by the size of his tonsils. However, peering down
his throat will give you little information. Although his tonsils become bigger after his first year, this is normal (pp. 213–14). Babies
always have small tonsils and adenoids, and do not get tonsillitis
(acute inflammation of the tonsils); in a baby a throat infection tends
to involve the whole throat, not just the tonsils. But during
early childhood tonsils increase in size, in common with the rest of the
lymphoid tissue throughout the body. Your child's neck glands therefore become more noticeable at this time too (see glands, pp. 460–
61).

This natural enlargement is related to the fact that these are the
years when a child is most likely to suffer from acute infections, such
as the infectious fevers of childhood (p. 521). So this is when children
need the strongest defense—and strong defenses need to be big. In
addition, tonsils and adenoids may get temporarily larger when en-
gaged in their job of fighting infection.

Acute Tonsillitis

Symptoms   Acute tonsillitis can be caused by a number of different
germs. The tonsils become inflamed and the throat red but, surprisingly, a young child seldom complains of a sore throat even when his
tonsils are very inflamed. In fact, he is more likely to say his stomach

hurts, perhaps because he only knows it hurts somewhere and he cannot quite identify the place, or because the lymph glands in his abdomen are also inflamed. The reason acute tonsillitis does not cause a painful throat in a child is not clear, but it is the reason doctors have to check the throat every time a child is unwell, whether or not he has a fever. Sometimes an inflamed throat causes pain in the ears when there is nothing wrong with them. This is called "referred" pain, and it happens because the throat nerves and the ear nerves share a common pathway.

Other symptoms may include general aches and pains, headaches, vomiting, and fever. An additional symptom may be neck stiffness, caused by "meningismus" (see p. 465). This can lead to confusion with meningitis, and a lumbar puncture (p. 614) may be necessary to decide from which of them the child is suffering.

With the welter of symptoms and the fact that a child with tonsillitis may not complain of a sore throat, it is not surprising that you may not suspect what the trouble is, and that your doctor can make the diagnosis only when he looks inside the mouth.

The symptoms may come on quite suddenly, or tonsillitis can follow another infection, such as measles. It is infectious, and because the immunity gained from an attack is very short-lived, it is worth keeping other children away from the sick child if practical.

Complications   Tonsillitis sometimes settles without trouble, but in some children tends to lead to the complication otitis media (p. 459). If the attack is due to the germ streptococcus ("strep throat"), there is the additional risk of this organism later causing acute nephritis (p. 446) or rheumatic fever (see p. 516). This happens less often nowadays because antibiotics kill the streptococcus while it is still in the throat.

Treatment   Your doctor will assess whether an attack of tonsillitis should be treated with antibiotics. To help him come to a decision, he is likely to take a throat swab for culture, to check what germs grow from it when it is tested in the laboratory. He may advise giving acetaminophen to relieve pain or fever. Gargles are seldom recommended nowadays for the treatment of a sore throat—tests with dyes have shown that the fluid gargled does not come in contact with the back of the throat during the process of gargling.

Removing the Tonsils

An increase in the size of the tonsils does not automatically mean they should come out; on the contrary, enlargement is a sign of efficiency; it is tonsils that have become small and immobile through scarring, due to repeated infections, that sometimes have to be removed, because they are no longer effective barriers against infection. The large wobbly tonsils that almost meet across the back of a child's throat, even when he is quite well, hardly ever seem to obstruct his breathing or worry him in any way, though they worry mothers a great deal unless their function is explained.

When should tonsils be removed? The final decision lies with the ear, nose, and throat specialist. No operation, however minor, is advisable purely as a precautionary measure—after all, you would not want your child's appendix removed just in case it caused trouble later. Moreover, if this first line of defense is removed, infections go through to the second line, the glands in the neck (pp. 460–61).

If a child has repeated attacks of severe tonsillitis, it may be necessary to take out his tonsils because they are no longer functioning efficiently, and are causing trouble instead of stopping it. However, many children get fewer attacks of tonsillitis as they grow older, whether or not their tonsils are removed. In coming to a decision, the doctor and surgeon study the whole picture, the child's general health, which is far more significant than the condition of his tonsils alone.

An operation to remove tonsils only is hardly ever carried out before the age of four, because up to this age the tonsils are still performing some useful function. Should it become necessary after this age, the chances are that the adenoids will be affected too and will need to come out at the same time.

Removing the Adenoids

Adenoids do not cause mothers as much concern as tonsils, since they cannot be inspected, but they may nevertheless be wrongly blamed for stuffy noses, or an apparent tendency to breathe through the mouth.

Breathing through the Mouth

It is easy to make a mistake and label your child a "mouth breather" when, in reality, he only keeps his mouth open from habit. When tested, the majority of "mouth breathers" are found to be breathing through their noses.

Ear Infections

The most serious effect of enlarged adenoids is that by preventing free drainage of matter from the nose, and by partially blocking the openings of the Eustachian tubes (which lead from the back of the throat to the middle ear), they can cause otitis media, cr inflammation of the middle ear (see below). So if a child has repeated attacks of otitis media, and the doctor judges that enlarged adenoids are contributing to this, he may decide the adenoids should be removed. Repeated ear infections, not large adenoids in themselves, are the main cause of deafness; thus if adenoids are partly to blame, they must come out without delay, before hearing is permanently damaged.

It is not advisable to wait in the hope that they will cease giving trouble, or for your child to reach a more suitable age for a stay in the hospital away from you. Operations to remove adenoids only are usually done before the age of four. After this, if either tonsils or adenoids need to come out, both generally have to be removed.

Large, infected adenoids may also be responsible for persistent rhinitis, but in this case respiratory therapy aimed at teaching the child to breathe correctly through the nose is the answer, rather than an operation. Once he breathes through his nose the airways are kept clear, and matter can drain away instead of continually building up and causing inflammation (see rhinitis, p. 453, respiratory therapy, p. 466).

Ear Troubles

In order to understand the ear troubles that are common in childhood it is necessary to know something about the anatomy of the ear. The opening of the ear leads by a passage called the outer ear to the membrane, or eardrum, on the other side of which is a little box called the middle ear. Inflammation of the outer ear is called otitis externa, and that of the middle ear otitis media.

The Eustachian Tubes These are small tubes leading from the back of the throat to the middle ear, one on each side. Their purpose is to equalize the pressure on either side of the eardrum. When you go up in an airplane you feel discomfort in your ear because the pressures are unequal. Tell your child to swallow, so that he can equalize the pressures again.

Why Babies Get Earache Otitis media is commonest in babies and young children because their Eustachian tubes are short, straight, and proportionately wider than an adult's, and because they spend a great deal more time lying down. Both these facts make it easier for bacteria to travel to the middle ear from the throat or nose, or for part of a vomited feeding to pass along this route. If a baby is fed from a propped bottle while left alone lying in his crib or carriage, there is a very serious danger of milk going up his Eustachian tubes as well as down his throat. Never feed your baby this way, since there is also danger of suffocation from inhalation of vomit.

Enlarged adenoids block the openings of the Eustachian tubes, thereby preventing proper drainage of the middle ear. This increases the liability to middle ear infection, and is the main reason for removing adenoids.

The Outer Ear

Sometimes a child develops an inflammation of the external air passage because he has pushed a stick or some other foreign body into his ear.

Wax in the Ears   Wax is a natural secretion with a cleansing function; it removes dust from the canal and reaches the edge of the ear of its own accord. You can then wipe it away without prodding around in the canal, an unnecessary and potentially dangerous practice, which encourages your child to do the same thing.

Water in the Ears   Although you should avoid cleaning inside the ears, there is no need to fuss about water getting in during bathing or hair washing, unless your child already has an ear infection. Water will not get beyond the eardrum, and any that enters the canal will soon drain out again.

Otitis Externa (Inflammation of the Outer Ear)

This is relatively common in children. It can be due to swimming, especially in chlorinated pools, and it can result from poking things into the ears (see above). Sometimes it just happens for no apparent reason. It is very painful. The doctor differentiates otitis externa from otitis media (inflammation of the middle ear) by the fact that moving the ear is painful in otitis externa—the middle ear, being inside the skull bones, is unaffected by movement of the ear. The canal may look red and there may be a discharge. The essential point is that if there is any discharge apart from wax, or any pain in the ear, you should contact your doctor without delay.

Swimming should be forbidden while your child has an ear infection.

Boil in the Ear

The outer canal of the ear is lined with tiny hairs, so it is possible for a child to get a boil here, but this will never happen beyond the eardrum.

A boil in the ear is very painful. It may be connected with otitis externa (see above) or there may be no obvious cause. Your doctor will advise on treatment (see boils, pp. 494–95).

Otitis Media (Inflammation of the Middle Ear)

Symptoms A baby who is ill with fever, vomiting, diarrhea, and loss of appetite may give his mother no reason to suspect his ears as the source of infection. But a doctor will always examine the ears of a child with these symptoms when there is no obvious explanation for them.

Sometimes a baby with otitis media pulls on his ear lobe, so that you suspect his ears are aching. The pain may be severe enough to make him shriek, but even if he is old enough to tell you about it, he may not complain of earache.

Some children with otitis media have no fever and may not seem ill, but when the doctor looks into the ear with a special instrument called an otoscope, he sees that the eardrum is red.

Runny Ear A "runny" ear should never be disregarded. If it is due to pus breaking through the eardrum from a middle ear infection, urgent treatment is needed to prevent later deafness. If you are uncertain whether a runny ear is due to pus or wax, take your child to your doctor. He won't mind giving the quick look in the ear that can decide the matter, and if it turns out to be wax, he will be as pleased as you are.

Causes Middle ear infection is started by bacteria arriving from the throat or nose. Violent nose blowing can push the discharge from the nose along the Eustachian tubes; this is why you should teach your child to blow each nostril separately, closing the other one with a finger while doing so (p. 452).

As explained on page 457, a child's short, straight Eustachian tube makes it easier for infection to penetrate the middle ear, while enlarged adenoids can partly block the canal so that secretions accumulate in the middle ear and infection starts.

Otitis media can also be the sequel of another infection, such as measles or even a bad cold. This means that if your child seems deaf during a cold, he must be checked by a doctor, since the probable cause is inflammation in the middle ear. Children sometimes insert objects, such as beads or sticks, into the ear passage. If not immediately removed, otitis media results. Worse still, they may puncture the eardrum causing otitis media.

Sometimes a child complains of earache but the doctor finds that his throat is infected, not his ears. A child's ears sometimes ache when he has mumps. These are examples of the way children tend to feel pain in the "wrong" place, due to what is termed "referred" pain. Warm compresses applied to the ears relieve this kind of pain.

Treatment The doctor will prescribe an antibiotic and very probably nose drops as well. You may think it strange for him to prescribe nose drops for inflammation in the ear, and you may even imagine you have misheard. The reason for giving the nose drops is to keep the Eustachian tubes open in order to allow proper drainage of the middle ear. Ear drops are seldom used for infections in the middle ear, since they cannot reach it if the eardrum is intact. An operation to pierce a hole in the eardrum (myringotomy) is only seldom needed nowadays, because of antibiotic treatment.

"Glue Ear" (Serous otitis media)

This is becoming increasingly common in Western countries, whereas the old type of otitis media, leading to a runny ear with pus, is now much less common. The change is believed to result from the wider use of antibiotics for infections in general, and the fact that in the case of ear infections the course of treatment is often not completed. It may also result from the inherited shape of the middle ear and Eustachian tubes, since it is more common in some races than others.

There is often no earache, but a slow realization that the child is partially deaf. The doctor finds that the eardrum does not move normally when tested, due to the sticky gluelike material in the middle ear.

Treatment   A simple decongestant medicine may first be prescribed but if this fails, an operation is required. Simple incision (myringotomy) of the eardrum is insufficient to let out the sticky material. Instead, a grommet, which is a little plastic tube, is inserted into the eardrum and left in place. This is an air tube to allow immediate equalization of pressure on both sides of the drum. It is not there to drain the "glue," since this blocks the grommet if it gets inside. After a few months the grommet drops out by itself; if the doctor finds the grommet is still in position after eighteen months, he usually removes it to allow the drum to heal.

Some doctors ban swimming, but more now allow the child to swim provided ear plugs and a bathing cap are worn. However, diving and jumping into the water must be forbidden, because these could cause water to enter the middle ear through the Eustachian tubes.

"Swollen Glands"

The small lumps that you may be able to see or feel in your child's neck are part of a system of lymphatic glands sited at strategic points throughout the body; each area has its own set of glands, which give protection by filtering out harmful germs before they spread and cause further trouble. There are lymph glands in the armpits, the abdomen, and the groins; tonsils and adenoids are composed of lymphoid tissue.

Why Glands Swell

Wherever there is an infection, the nearest lymph glands swell as they cope with it. For example, a swollen gland at the back of your child's neck will make the doctor look for the cause nearby, perhaps for a septic spot on the scalp. When the glands in the groin are enlarged, he looks for infection somewhere on the leg, because these glands are responsible for the whole leg area. You may have noticed these particular glands, which look like little lumps, while changing your baby's diaper, but it is unlikely that they worried you or that you checked up regularly to see if they changed size. You should disregard the glands in his neck in the same way.

The neck glands, in common with lymphoid tissue throughout the body, increase in size during childhood, so that in a child with a thin neck they may be noticeable even when uninfected (see p. 454). This is nothing to worry about. It does not mean that the child has infectious mononucleosis (glandular fever) (p. 531) or that the glands are chronically infected. Neither of these conditions is common and both make the child ill in other ways.

Should You Consult Your Doctor?

What about the occasions when the glands swell temporarily? Does this mean the doctor should see your child? Neck glands get bigger when dealing with germs that have penetrated the first line of defense, the tonsils and adenoids. However, in some children the neck glands seem to be the only site affected. Perhaps the child has had a sore throat, which he did not mention and which cleared up, leaving his neck glands still swollen. Glands remain enlarged for a considerable time after an infection and go back to normal without treatment; so if your child seems well, and has no other symptoms, you can ignore the swollen glands.

Sometimes there does not appear to be any infection to account for swollen glands. The doctor looks in your child's throat, down his ears, and feels his scalp, but finds no sign of trouble. If your child is well, nothing needs to be done, but your doctor will probably want to examine him again in a few weeks.

Sinuses and Sinusitis

The sinuses are air spaces in certain bones in the head. They lighten the bone, which would be considerably heavier if it were solid. They are apt to become infected but the frequency of this has been grossly overrated. "Sinusitis" used to be a fashionable disease, and many children were unnecessarily subjected to the unpleasant procedure of having their sinuses washed out.

At birth, there is only one pair of sinuses large enough to become infected, the ethmoids, which lie on either side of the bridge of the nose, close to the eye. Ethmoiditis is serious but rare—it appears as an acute inflammation of the eye.

The next sinus to grow large enough to become inflamed is the mastoid, which lies behind the ear. Acute mastoiditis used to be a dangerous form of infection in young children, but thanks to antibiotics and a greater watchfulness on ear infections it is now much less common and can be successfully treated, usually without the need for an operation.

The maxillary sinuses are the most liable to become infected but this happens much less frequently than was once thought. These two sinuses lie in the upper jaw behind the cheeks. At birth, the space in the bone is only a minute slit, which does not get big enough to become infected until a child is about four years old. Some of the children with rhinitis (p. 453) above this age have got sinusitis, but it is usually unnecessary to decide this point, since proper total care of the child will automatically deal with this in most cases. I rarely X-ray the face to see if maxillary sinusitis is present, nor do I ask for a light to be put in the mouth (transillumination), which is another way of checking for sinusitis.

Acute sinusitis responds well to antibiotics, with nose drops to reduce the swelling of the lining membrane of the sinus and of the nose itself. Persistent rhinitis associated with sinusitis is usually better treated with respiratory therapy to improve normal nasal breathing (pp. 466–67).

Croup

This is the name given to a particular type of acute laryngitis (inflammation of the vocal cords). The main thing you will notice is that breathing is difficult and that every breath in is accompanied by a high-pitched croaking noise. The reason is that the inflamed vocal cords are swollen, so that the narrow space between them is reduced still farther and breathing is therefore obstructed. The cause of the inflammation is infection with one of a number of different viruses that particularly attack the breathing system.

Croup tends to recur. Sometimes several members of the family are prone to it. It is most likely to occur in children between the ages of two and four.

When to Call the Doctor

It is not serious if your child has a slightly hoarse voice during a cold provided he does not seem ill, but if he shows any sign of difficulty in breathing you must contact your doctor, even if it is late at night.

The attack usually occurs quite unexpectedly, although it may be associated with a cold. Difficulty in breathing is worse at night, possibly because nighttime and darkness are always more frightening if anything is wrong, particularly if breathing is a problem. Your child may be worse when he is lying flat. His crying becomes hoarse; there is also a rasping cough.

Signs of difficulty in breathing are rapid heaving movements of the chest, and a pulling in of the lower end of the breastbone (sternum) and the lower ribs at the sides. The diaphragm is attached to the back of the breastbone and lower ribs; when it has to work harder its pull can draw these bones inward in a child, because they are still soft.

How to Help Your Child

Fear makes his breathing even more labored, so stay with your child and do your best to reassure him. Try not to convey your alarm to him. He will probably prefer to sit up; propping him up on pillows may help.

Hot dry air seems to encourage croup to develop, so opening the window of a heated bedroom will help your child breathe more easily. The humidity in the room can be increased by use of a commercial vaporizer, made for safe use near children. Sitting in a bathroom steamed up from the hot tap may also make him feel more comfortable.

Your doctor will be able to advise you on the treatment and management of croup so that you will know how to help your child if he has another attack, and how to assess its seriousness.

Bronchitis

Bronchitis is inflammation of the mucous membrane lining the bronchi or air tubes that branch out into the lungs from the big windpipe (trachea) in the neck.

Children are sometimes thought to have bronchitis because they breathe noisily, when in fact there is some other reason for this. For example, the large quantity of saliva produced when teething may run down the throat, making a child cough, so that he is said to "cut his teeth with bronchitis." Acute bronchitis is not very common in healthy children, and occurs more often when a child has some other condition, which makes him more likely to get it. Measles and whooping cough often masquerade as "bronchitis" at the beginning. The commonest variety of bronchitis in young children is "wheezy bronchitis."

Wheezy Bronchitis

With this type of bronchitis, a child's breathing sounds wheezy because his bronchial tubes are inflamed, full of mucus, and in a state of spasm, which makes them narrow.

Is He Asthmatic?   The wheezing does not mean the child is asthmatic; it is merely the noise he makes breathing through narrowed air passages. This is why the term "asthmatic bronchitis" should not be used to describe wheezy bronchitis. The child with bronchial asthma (see p. 504) suddenly gets a wheezing attack, whereas the child who gets wheezy bronchitis wheezes after he has caught a cold or started a chest infection.

However, a clear-cut distinction between the two conditions is not possible. A history of asthma, eczema, or hay fever in the family of a baby who wheezes makes asthma the more likely diagnosis. Some doctors regard asthma as the correct name to apply if the child wheezes on more than one or two occasions, but use of this label does not mean the condition is more serious.

The Fat Baby   Some babies, particularly those who are overweight, wheeze without any obvious sign of infection. The reason for this is not clear, though possibly fat babies cough less effectively, and their bronchi remain congested with mucus. The mucus can block and irritate the bronchi, making them more liable to infection and inflammation. The congestion encourages infection and the infection causes more congestion.

Treatment   The aim of treatment is to clear the tubes and break the vicious circle. The doctor may prescribe an antispasmodic drug to deal with the spasm, but the main treatment is to help the child cough up the mucus. Cough medicines do not do this, but postural drainage does (see respiratory therapy, p. 466). I like mothers to be taught how to tip down their child's head and thump his chest so as to bring up the mucus. When you do this your child is unlikely to cough out the sputum like an adult; he will probably swallow it, but this is just as effective in clearing his lungs, even if it sometimes causes vomiting. Antibiotics are seldom needed for children with wheezy bronchitis.

Pneumonia

The two commonest types of pneumonia in children, lobar pneumonia and bronchopneumonia, can be effectively treated with antibiotics, making them very similar from the nursing point of view, although bronchopneumonia is the more serious.

Lobar pneumonia tends to come on suddenly and unexpectedly, attacking the healthy, older child. Bronchopneumonia usually affects the child under five who already has another infection, such as a cold, middle ear infection, or gastroenteritis; it can also be a complication of measles or whooping cough.

Symptoms Lobar pneumonia begins suddenly with a high temperature, but in bronchopneumonia there is sometimes no rise in temperature—in fact, it may be subnormal. Although temperature alone can be a bad guide to the seriousness of an illness, it does indicate whether the child needs cooling or warming (see tepid sponging, p. 401).

Other symptoms of both types of pneumonia are: rapid breathing, a troublesome cough, vomiting, and diarrhea. The child may become drowsy. Occasionally, convulsions occur if the temperature is high. There is seldom any sputum with the cough, since if it is brought up from the lung a child will swallow it rather than cough it out. For this reason, a doctor requiring a specimen of sputum to discover the germ causing the infection may order "gastric washings." The child's stomach is washed out by a nurse or therapist before breakfast in the morning in order to test any sputum he has swallowed during the night.

Stiff Neck or "Meningismus" Sometimes a child with pneumonia develops a stiff neck. This may resemble meningitis to such an extent that the doctor has to undertake a lumbar puncture (see p. 614) in order to exclude the possibility. The reason children with pneumonia get this stiff neck is not understood; it is known as "meningismus" and may also occur with an acute infection in the middle ear, acute tonsillitis, acute appendicitis, and an acute infection of the kidney.

Difficulty in Diagnosis In an acutely ill adult, there is seldom any difficulty in distinguishing between acute tonsillitis, pneumonia, meningitis, and appendicitis. But you will now see why this is often difficult in children, especially because a child with pneumonia seldom complains of pain in the chest, whereas a child with tonsillitis may not complain of pain in the throat but feel it in the ear or stomach or both. Acute appendicitis may cause rapid breathing, just to add to the confusion that a children's doctor has to sort out.

The doctor must therefore be called if a child has any of these symptoms, or if he just seems ill. He must also be called back to any sick child who gets worse—this could be due to a number of causes, one of which is the start of bronchopneumonia, which has an under-handed way of attacking the child who is already ill.

Pneumonia can often be diagnosed from the end of the child's bed, because the doctor recognizes the typical rapid breathing, proba-bly accompanied by grunts, and the dilating nostrils.

Treatment The illness needs skillful nursing, although antibiotics make it unnecessary for all children to be sent to the hospital. Most children will be more comfortable if propped up, though a few prefer to lie flat. The child is unlikely to want solid food, but since his calorie intake must be kept up, he needs nourishing drinks containing sugar and vitamin supplements (see the sick child at home, p. 395). The doctor may prescribe respiratory therapy (see below).

Despite modern drugs, pneumonia can be lethal in small babies, striking so quickly that treatment is ineffective (see crib deaths, p. 650).

Respiratory Therapy

Today respiratory therapy is used more and more to treat children with respiratory complaints such as wheezy bronchitis and bronchial asthma; it is also used in pneumonia. You and your child will be taught exercises, which you then carry out regularly every day at home until your doctor decides there is no further need for them.

I like asthmatic children to attend a respiratory therapy clinic regularly, at increasing intervals as they improve, but children with less serious disorders, such as wheezy bronchitis, can often be taught the techniques and then discharged from the clinic.

How Respiratory Therapy Helps Breathing and postural exer-cises enable a child to breathe correctly through his nose. This means that he uses his air passages more effectively and helps to keep them clear. The exercises also help a child to relax, so that he can cope more easily with stress. The fact that he has learned a way of breathing rhythmically sometimes helps him to forestall a threatened attack of asthma. By using respiratory therapy, you and your child can help positively to control the tendency to asthma and to keep down the number of attacks. The exercises should become part of your child's life and should not be regarded as a separate chore to be done at a particular time of the day. You should encourage him to breathe in the way he has been taught while waiting at a bus stop, for instance, and at other suitable moments.

Postural Drainage and Percussion A respiratory therapist can teach you this technique. It is a mechanical method of draining a child's chest of the accumulation of mucus that is making him wheeze, and is useful for both bronchial asthma and wheezy bronchitis. Use the method whenever your child has an attack, and often enough between the attacks to keep you both in practice. Some children cannot tolerate respiratory therapy at the height of the asthmatic attack, in which case you should wait till he has started to improve. Others can be helped immediately.

Lay your child on his front across your lap with his head tipped downward; then tap his back and sides with your cupped hands in a drumming rhythm. The technique cannot be taught by book but a respiratory therapist will soon show you how to do it. You can use the method with small babies, and, provided you do it properly, children do not usually object.

Postural drainage and percussion is particularly useful in treating children, because their very small air tubes fill up with mucus much more rapidly than an adult's. Children are also less efficient than adults at coughing up secretions, and may not cough at all even when it is necessary. Cough medicines are ineffective and do not bring up mucus. The fact that the child is likely to swallow whatever he brings up as a result of the postural drainage and percussion does not matter; indeed, he may swallow so much that he vomits (see bronchitis, pp. 463–64). This is a nuisance, and unpleasant for you, but nevertheless vomiting is a very efficient way of draining the chest; it compresses the lungs, thereby squeezing the mucus out of the bronchial tubes.

34

Sight and Eye Problems

Nearly all babies have blue-gray eyes at birth, although a few, mostly those with dark skins, have brown eyes from the start. You won't know your baby's permanent eye color for certain until he is at least six months old.

A newborn baby seldom produces tears when he cries, but will probably start to do so when about a week old. Some babies cry without tears until they are two or three months old. Preterm babies produce tears later than full-term babies.

Vision is not developed fully until a baby is three to six months old. As his eyes develop he becomes able to focus and to see details. A new baby can probably distinguish only vague shapes, darkness and light. However, he can fix his vision on his mother for short periods during the first hour of life (p. 219). By about the age of one month he is beginning to have binocular vision, that is, he uses both eyes together. Until he can do this, it is natural for him to look slightly cross-eyed at times; the reason for this is that when the eyes are at rest it is natural for them to diverge—a child needs to be seeing properly and to have normal eye muscle power if his eyes are to move together. A baby does not develop this until about four months of age.

Squint ("Lazy Eye" or Strabismus)

If a baby between three and six months old persistently looks cross-eyed, the cause is usually an imbalance of the eye muscles. He should be seen promptly by his family doctor, who will probably need to refer him to an eye specialist. Treatment may be unnecessary or it may not start until he is older, but it is essential for the situation to be checked early. If the squint is causing double vision, the baby's brain will suppress one of the two images it sees. If vision is not corrected, the eye goes blind from lack of use. Because a squint can be so dangerous I dislike the expression "lazy eye," which is commonly used to describe it. This lulls parents into doing nothing when they should be consulting their doctor (see early detection, p. 574).

Treatment

The specialist may decide that the baby's good eye should be blanked off with a pad. For an older child, glasses with one lens blacked out may be prescribed. These maneuvers force the child to use his weaker eye, which becomes more efficient through being exercised.

When your child is old enough to co-operate, he may be given exercises to help the eye muscles to work effectively. Sometimes an operation to lengthen or to shorten one of the eye muscles is needed; occasionally, it takes more than one operation to correct the squint. Since your child will be young when the operation is carried out, it would be ideal for you to stay in the hospital with him (see the sick child in the hospital, pp. 410–11).

Other Types of Squinting

A squint can also start because a child has a defect of vision, either short or long sight or astigmatism (see below). These are termed "errors of refraction." In order to see things nearby, he has to turn in one eye; a child may even cover one eye with his hand while trying to focus on something. Again, it is important to seek your doctor's advice early. Glasses to correct the visual error will help the child to use both eyes together.

Squints caused by errors of refraction appear more often when a child is three or four years old. Sometimes a child of this age develops a squint after an illness such as measles. A child who does so has usually been long-sighted from birth and has compensated for this by forcing his eyes to converge. The illness causes him to lose this ability and a squint results. Glasses can restore the previous state of affairs.

Sometimes a baby has an alternating squint, that is, he uses first one eye and then the other. Because he exercises both eyes, there is less likelihood that the vision of one eye will fail through disuse. The tendency may right itself, but eye exercises may be needed to stop this kind of squint from developing into the more dangerous squint that affects one eye only.

Apparent Squint

A baby with normal eyes may look as though he is squinting because he has wide epicanthic folds; these are vertical folds of skin that overlie the inner corner of the eye. The tendency to have these folds often runs in families and they cause no harm. The baby's eyes merely look far apart, giving a false impression of a squint when he focuses. Let your doctor decide if this is why he appears to squint.

Screening Tests

Early detection of squints is so important that every baby should have a screening test for squint at the age of six months. But if you notice your baby crossing his eyes frequently after he is three months old, don't wait, but consult your doctor about it. It is particularly important to do so if squints run in your family, because there is a strong familiar tendency to the condition.

Defective Sight

Another reason for early and regular tests of a child's vision is to pick up and correct defective vision as soon as possible. Routine visual screening tests should start at two and a half years and be repeated at yearly intervals. Have extra tests if you suspect your child is not seeing perfectly; he may screw his eyes up or complain he cannot see the blackboard. Children have been accused of cheating at school because they have been seen looking at their neighbor's exercise book when the real reason for this was that they could not see the blackboard.

Wearing Glasses

The commonest reason a child needs glasses is short-sightedness, with or without astigmatism. Astigmatism means that the surface of the lens of the eye is not quite symmetrical with the retina, so the child sees things slightly crooked.

If your child does have to wear glasses, you will be given hints on how to get him to wear them happily.

Color Blindness

This is far commoner in boys than in girls; about 8 percent of boys are color blind to some degree, compared with only 0.4 percent of girls. If a child's ability to distinguish colors normally is only mildly affected, his handicap may go unnoticed. However, it may cause problems at school; for example, by affecting his ability to use color-coded apparatus. The mildly color-blind child might be considered backward or stubborn if his handicap continued to be unidentified.

A major degree of color blindness is usually obvious by the age of five, since you will have noticed that your child persistently muddles or misnames certain colors, especially red and green. When he goes to school, alert his teacher to the problem so that allowances can be made for it.

Although color blindness cannot be cured, a child will learn to adjust to it. Certain jobs will be closed to him as an adult—but there is no need to rub it in that he will never be a locomotive engineer.

Styes

A stye, which looks like a small boil on the eyelid, is an infection in the hair follicle of an eyelash. Some children never get styes, others get an occasional stye, while a few children get them repeatedly, in crops.

Home Treatment

A stye can usually be treated at home. One thing you can do is to apply heat to it, thereby increasing the blood supply to the area; this helps the infection to clear more quickly. Wrap gauze or soft cloth around a tongue depressor or a wooden spoon, soak it in warm salty water and hold it against the stye for a few moments. Another home treatment is to remove the lash at the center of the stye with tweezers. The hair comes out quite easily, enabling the pus to drain away, thus relieving the inflammation and discomfort as well as hastening healing.

Consulting the Doctor

If your child suffers from one stye after another, take him to your doctor. Sometimes repeated styes are due to seborrhea—in fact, you may be able to see flakes of seborrhea among the eyelashes. When this is treated, the styes stop. However, I am afraid we often do not know the cause of recurrent styes.

Styes may spread from one part of the eyelid to another because the child rubs his eyes, transferring the infection from the infected follicle to others. You must stop this. Make sure he uses only his own face cloth and towel, keeping them separate from the rest of the family's; otherwise someone else may get a stye.

Bloodshot Eyes (Conjunctivitis)

The conjunctiva is the membrane lining the inside of the eyelids and the exposed front portion of the globe of the eye. When the conjunctiva becomes inflamed (conjunctivitis) the eye looks bloodshot. If one of your child's eyes becomes suddenly bloodshot, you should try to see whether a foreign body such as a speck of dust has got in, and do your best to get it out (see below).

Alternatively, conjunctivitis may be due to an infection; this sometimes accompanies a cold and it may affect one or both eyes. It also commonly accompanies measles (p. 523). "Pink eye" is the name given to a type of infectious conjunctivitis that may occur in epidemics, especially in schools.

The first essential in the treatment of conjunctivitis is to check if something has got into the eye and remove it. Your doctor will prescribe antibiotic eye drops or ointment as necessary.

Something in the Eye

Small Foreign Bodies

When a foreign body gets on the eyeball or under the eyelid, the eye's normal reaction is to water and so flood out the intruder. Provided your child has not rubbed his eye so that the speck of dirt, eyelash, or other cause of trouble has entrenched itself more firmly, the increased watering will float it out. Teach your child to blink rather than to rub his eye when something goes in; if he must rub, it is better to rub the other eye, since this will encourage watering without pushing the speck farther in.

If watering does not work, you can try using an eyecup; the extra liquid may float it out. If not, you must find and remove the foreign body, but do not try to remove something from the eyeball until it has had a chance to move to the outer edge of the eye of its own accord.

Pull down the lower lid, and if this exposes the foreign body you can remove it by using the edge of a handkerchief. Be careful not to press the speck against the eye; lift it off gently. If you still cannot see the speck, lift the upper lid, holding on to the upper lashes; this encourages anything under the lid to float out. If you can turn back the lid, you will be able to remove a speck sticking to the underside. But if you find this too difficult, or if the foreign body is lodged right in the middle of the eye, over the pupil, take your child to your doctor or go to the hospital emergency department to have it removed. Don't leave a foreign body on the pupil itself, and don't try to get it off yourself.

Even after the object has been taken out, your child may complain that there is still something in his eye. This is because his eyeball has been slightly scratched. Put two or three drops of artificial tears into the eye to soothe it, cover the eye with a pad, and encourage him to rest for an hour. If his eye still hurts after this, take him to the doctor.

Injury to the Eye

You should of course take your child straight to the hospital if something has penetrated his eye causing a deep injury. Cover the eye with a clean pad before starting off. Discourage or supervise games such as archery or games involving running around with sticks.

If acid or corrosive liquid splashes into the eye, it is essential to dilute it at once, using ordinary water, since this is quickest. Irrigate the eye by pouring water over it—never mind about the mess. Telephone your doctor for advice.

Sticky Eye

A sticky eye in the first forty-eight hours of life is common; it is nearly always due to debris, such as amniotic fluid and blood, getting into the eye during birth. Although a bacterial swab should be taken to make sure, this is usually found to be negative, and all that is needed is for the eye to be bathed regularly with a salt solution so as to clear away the stickiness. In the hospital, a bottle of saline, as supplied for intravenous drips, may be used to provide a jet of fluid to wash the eye clean. At home, wet cotton balls may be used; these should be wiped outward from the inside corner of the eye to reduce the risk of carrying any debris across from one eye to the other. Discard after one wipe. For the same reason, the baby should be put on his side with the affected eye next to the mattress. If he was the other way around, with the bad eye on top, debris from the eye could flow across the bridge of the nose into the good eye.

After the first two days of life, a sticky eye is more liable to be due to infection by a staphylococcus, which can quickly spread to the other babies in the hospital nursery. More vigorous treatment is needed; as well as irrigation, an antibiotic ointment will be applied to the eye. Whatever the cause of the sticky eye, it can always be treated successfully and it never harms the eyes.

Persistent Watering

An eye that keeps on watering or a repeatedly sticky eye may be due to blockage of the tear duct, which leads the tears from the eye to the nose. This blockage occurs more often in babies with a flat bridge to the nose and wide epicanthic folds, an extra fold of skin over the inner part of the eye.

The majority of blocked lacrimal ducts open without treatment before the age of six months. Each episode of sticky eye is therefore dealt with along the lines outlined above, but nothing special is done about the duct. If the condition persists after the age of six months, the duct will be opened up by the ophthalmic surgeon under a general anesthetic, using a fine probe.

Black Eye

What is called "a black eye" does not affect or harm the eye itself, but is a bruise of the tissue surrounding it. There is swelling for a few days, but the discoloration may go on for a short while after the swelling has disappeared. No treatment is needed.

Occasionally, what looks like a black eye results from a fracture of the base of the skull. This type of black eye occurs more often on both sides, causing a bruise just below each eye. If you are in doubt about the cause of a black eye, consult your doctor.

35

Mouth Troubles

Thrush is the commonest cause of an inflamed mouth in babies under a year old (see disorders affecting young babies, pp. 434–35). From the age of one to three years, cold sores are the most common cause.

Cold Sores (Herpes Simplex)

These are due to infection with a virus called "herpes simplex." They are sore areas at the edge of the mouth and nostrils, sometimes with a crust on top. Babies do not seem to get them; the first attack usually occurs after the age of one year and before a child reaches school age.

The First Attack

The first attack is severe; shallow white ulcers suddenly appear anywhere inside the mouth. They may be on the tongue, gums, roof of the mouth, or on the inside of the cheeks. They are very painful; your child is likely to refuse solids and may even refuse to drink.

The attack lasts about ten days and will disappear of its own accord. At present we have no medicine to destroy viruses in the way that antibiotics destroy bacteria. Presumably this difference is due to the smaller size of viruses, which, unlike bacteria, are not visible with the ordinary microscope. Mouthwashes and gentian violet are sometimes prescribed, but they increase the pain without doing any obvious good and I have given up prescribing them.

Sores Around the Mouth

It is only the first attack of the herpes virus that causes the painful ulcers inside the mouth. After this a child is likely to get sores at the edge of his mouth or nose. This happens whenever his resistance is lowered, especially when he gets a cold or is under stress. For this reason the sores are commonly known as "cold sores," though the cold is not the primary cause.

Since anyone who gets cold sores is a carrier of the herpes simplex virus, he is likely to infect others, and nothing can be done to stop him. If a child gets cold sores, one usually finds that one of his parents or some other close relative gets them too. Some children who develop cold sores have had no previous known attack of ulcers in the mouth.

Cold sores disappear after about a week. An antibiotic ointment may reduce secondary infection and, being greasy, it may decrease the discomfort of the sore, which cracks when it is dry.

Adults who are liable to cold sores should not kiss children on the eyes, in case they cause a herpes infection of the cornea, which could damage the eyesight.

Repeated Single Mouth Ulcers

These are common, though their cause is unknown. They are not due to the herpes virus, but they may be connected with dental trouble, so it is wise to visit the dentist. Some children get mouth ulcers, frequently, while others never suffer from them.

Is It a Gum Boil?

A mouth ulcer may be inside the cheek or on the gum. Get your child to show you where it is. There will be a red area with a small yellowish-white ulcer in the middle. It is not the same as a "gum boil," which is an abscess under the tooth showing as a swelling on the gum margin. A gum boil needs prompt advice from the dentist; if it is not treated, it can lead to loss of a tooth.

A mouth ulcer goes away of its own accord after about ten days, but it is very unpleasant because it is so painful. It is best treated by cortisone ointment from your doctor. This is squirted onto it through a fine nozzle. Ordinary petroleum jelly or any greasy ointment will help by coating the ulcer so that it is protected from rubbing against the teeth.

"Dirty Tongue" and "Bad Breath"

Furring of the tongue, as seen in adults, does not occur in babies, because the taste buds on which the fur settles are not yet fully developed. Milk produces a white coating on the tongue, which can be scraped off. This is very different from the thick white coating caused by thrush, which cannot be scraped off and is usually present on the inside of the cheeks as well (see p. 435).

Do not make the mistake of checking your child's tongue to see if it is "dirty" or smelling his breath to check if it is "bad." The mothers who come to me complaining that their children have bad breath are the anxious ones whose children are healthy. It is true that some disturbances, such as tonsillitis or appendicitis, can cause bad breath; but children suffering from something like this are brought because they have abdominal pain, or sickness, or because they are unwell—not because their breath smells bad.

Constipation is not a cause of furred tongue or bad breath. My advice is to keep your nose and eyes out of your child's mouth unless he complains of pain there. Far too much attention has been paid to the state of the tongue and breath.

For more about mouth troubles, see cleft lip and cleft palate, pp. 423–24, and teeth, pp. 247f.

36

Stomach Troubles

Vomiting

Vomiting means the forcible expulsion of the contents of the stomach. Many things are incorrectly referred to as vomiting, especially regurgitation, which is nothing more than an effortless milk dribble and is usually just a pleasurable habit (p. 436). Vomiting always means something, but you cannot always tell what. Small children frequently vomit at the start of an infection such as a cold, tonsillitis, or an ear infection. Violent projectile vomiting in a baby may be due to pyloric stenosis (p. 438).

Sometimes a child is sick without warning but seems quite well immediately afterward. Provided he does not continue to be sick, you can ignore the incident and let him eat and drink whatever he wants. Some children are sick easily, and eating too much at a birthday party is sure to be followed by vomiting in the middle of the night; other children seem able to digest anything without trouble. Repeated bouts of sickness may be caused by emotional problems (see bilious attacks, pp. 539–40). Some children can be sick "on purpose," using it as a weapon in battles with parents (see feeding problems, p. 201). Travel sickness can start around the middle of the first year (p. 367).

Consulting Your Doctor

Ask your doctor's advice if your child is violently sick and does not begin to feel better shortly afterward, if he is violently sick several times in succession, or if sickness is associated with diarrhea or some other symptom such as fever. Food poisoning (pp. 483–84), appendicitis (p. 483), meningitis (pp. 613–14), and other infections are among the illnesses in which there may be vomiting (see also pp. 436–38).

If vomiting is serious, your child's general health will be affected within a matter of hours. If it goes on for days, or longer, without any obvious effect on his health, you can be sure that it is not due to a physical cause.

Diarrhea

Diarrhea means that the stools are looser, in other words, more fluid, than normal. In addition, they usually occur more frequently. The presence of diarrhea means that something is making the intestinal waves (peristalsis) work faster than normal—this could be a poison, an infection, or an emotional disturbance such as worrying about an exam. This intestinal hurry means that there is less time for the fluid to be absorbed from the stools, so that they are loose because of the excessive water they contain.

Intestinal hurry also means a change in color, especially in babies. At an early stage of digestion the bile is green, making the contents of the intestines green. Green bile is converted later to the usual brown color. Green stools indicate that there has not been sufficient time for the complete conversion of green bile to brown; in itself, this does not matter at all.

Is It Serious?

Whether diarrhea should be taken seriously depends on whether your child is ill with it, and particularly on whether he has lost his appetite or not. As long as he is eating and drinking normally you can disregard the fact that he has loose stools. Don't make the mistake of judging your child's health by the appearance of his stools; it may be perfectly normal for him to have bowel movements that are looser than the average. Even if he has lost his appetite for solids, provided he is still drinking normally and not vomiting, you need not be too concerned. It is when there is vomiting as well that urgent help is needed, because the combination of diarrhea and vomiting soon leads to dehydration, especially in babies (see below). Fretfulness in such a baby is far more likely to be due to thirst than to hunger.

For diarrhea without vomiting all you need do is to see that your child has enough to drink; if he does not want solid food there is no need to press him. He can have milk if he wants it, but if he prefers ordinary water or fruit juice, with or without a little sugar to sweeten it, that is perfectly all right. If he prefers a fizzy drink you will need to check whether this increases the diarrhea; if it does, he must have ordinary water instead.

Dehydration

Serious loss of fluid from vomiting or diarrhea leads to dehydration, or drying out of the body. The eyes look glazed and sunken, and the mouth becomes dry. The skin does not become dry for some time. It is dangerous because it means that the body chemistry is seriously deranged, and the correct fluid, based on chemical tests of the blood and urine, must be given without delay.

Medicines

Medicines make very little difference to the diarrhea itself. Many of them contain chalk (kaolin), which absorbs some of the water, making the motion more solid; however, it still contains the same amount of liquid, and the body is no better off. Some medicines contain opium or codeine or other substances, which aim to slow down the intestinal waves (peristalsis) so that they do not drive the food through the intestine so fast. This type of medicine is more effective and can also help the stomach ache. Antibiotics are only effective if the diarrhea is due to bacteria, as in dysentery, but this is relatively uncommon and can only be discovered by laboratory tests. Much more often the diarrhea is caused by viruses, and these are unaffected by antibiotic treatment.

Calling the Doctor

If the diarrhea is serious, or if it is accompanied by vomiting or by blood in the stool, you must call the doctor. Be sure to save the stools for him to see, as they will help him in coming to a diagnosis. He will need to find out whether the diarrhea is due to an infection in the bowel itself, such as food poisoning or dysentery, or whether there is infection elsewhere in the body, such as acute tonsillitis, acute inflammation in the middle ear, or a urinary infection. Only then can he prescribe the correct treatment. If your child cannot keep anything down by mouth, there is a danger of dehydration and he will need to be fed by a tube inserted into one of his veins (intravenous feeding). This requires immediate admission to the hospital.

Abdominal Pain in Babies

Your baby can only tell you his stomach hurts by crying. Consequently, when he cries furiously and draws up his legs you will very probably suspect colic or gas. But babies draw up their legs as a natural accompaniment to crying, whatever the cause. Gas is more likely to be the result of prolonged crying than its cause (see three-month colic, pp. 123f.).

How then are you to decide whether your crying baby, whom you suspect has a stomach ache, has something serious for which you should call the doctor? The clue lies in whether you think he is ill and whether there are other signs present. If he looks well and stops crying when you hold and comfort him, there is no need to call the doctor. Taking his feedings normally is another good sign; a baby who is crying and refuses his feedings may have an infection and must be seen by a doctor. If he goes pale during his bouts of crying, and especially if he also vomits, your baby should be seen by a doctor without delay, in case he has something seriously wrong such as an intussusception (see below).

If he has diarrhea it is likely that his crying is due to an illness. Although it may not be necessary to call your doctor after the first loose stool, he should certainly be contacted if the diarrhea continues, because babies can so quickly become dehydrated.

Acute Intussusception

This is not a common condition but it is a very serious one. It mainly affects babies between the ages of three and twelve months. It comes on suddenly, usually in a previously well baby, but sometimes when a baby already has a cold or a chest infection. A portion of the intestine telescopes into the bit immediately in front, causing the bowel to become obstructed. Pain occurs in bouts every few minutes as the intestine forces itself forward into the piece ahead. It is so severe that with each bout the baby screams and becomes very pale. When the bout is over his color returns and he will probably go to sleep, from exhaustion, until the next bout occurs. He usually vomits but may or may not be feverish.

Blood may appear in the stools, making them look like red-currant jelly. This happens later than the typical bouts of colic, so don't wait for it before going to the doctor. An intussusception must be diagnosed early so that the operation to pull the intestine back into position is as easy as possible. If it is left too late, the affected piece of intestine can become gangrenous from lack of blood, and the surgeon has to remove it—a serious procedure.

Other Causes of Acute Pain

If your baby is unwell and screaming with pain, the other most likely causes are infection of the middle ear (otitis media, p. 459), and acute urinary infection due to a germ in the kidney (see urinary infections, pp. 443–44).

Abdominal Pain in Children

A child may say he has a stomach ache when he really means he does not feel well. Sometimes he uses the words when he is about to be sick; alternatively, he may have a pain elsewhere but calls it "a stomach ache." Young children are often unable to describe accurately where a pain is, and the doctor can find out only from his examination.

Abdominal pain may be part of an infection elsewhere in the body. For example, acute tonsillitis is frequently accompanied by a stomach ache, possibly as a result of swollen abdominal glands (see tonsillitis, pp. 454–56). So if your doctor finds tonsillitis, he will often be able to explain the stomach ache.

Recurrent abdominal pains usually have an emotional cause (see recurrent pains, p. 536). Children who have been made anxious about eating and having normal movements sometimes complain of a stomach ache as part of their general tension about these subjects (p. 540). Mothers and sometimes doctors may ascribe an older girl's abdominal pains to impending menstrual periods. There is no evidence for this, and I believe the concept of "hidden periods" to be erroneous. It is just one more attempt to give a mechanical label to pain of emotional origin (p. 541).

Although a stomach ache may turn out to be nothing serious, you should always take your child's complaint seriously. Whether the cause of the pain is emotional, as in recurrent pains and feeding problems, or physical, as in the illnesses described below, the pain is real, not imaginary, and needs to be investigated.

Never treat abdominal pain yourself with laxatives. These may cause pain themselves and often make matters worse rather than better (see p. 486).

When to Call the Doctor

If you know your child suffers from recurrent abdominal pain (pp. 539–40), you can probably decide on each occasion whether the stomach ache is following its usual pattern. Remember that a child who has recurrent pains of emotional origin is not immune from pain caused by physical illness.

If your child is clearly in agony or seems very ill, call the doctor at once, even if it is midnight. Don't wait to see if the pain will go away. The degree of pain is an unreliable guide to its seriousness, and you cannot assume that a slight stomach ache is harmless. You have to judge this sort by your previous knowledge of your child and by whether there are accompanying symptoms such as vomiting, diarrhea, or fever. The combination of one or more of these with abdominal pain occurs in several illnesses, for example, in food poisoning, gastroenteritis, acute tonsillitis, and appendicitis.

It takes a doctor to decide which is the cause, so if your child has any combination of these symptoms it is safer to ask his advice. If the rest of the family is already suffering from food poisoning and your child wakes in the night with the same symptoms, it is reasonable to assume that he has the same thing and therefore to wait until morning before calling the doctor.

When your child's condition really worries you, telephone your doctor whatever the hour.

Acute Appendicitis

It is especially difficult to diagnose appendicitis in a child, which is why some operations for appendicitis turn out to have been unnecessary. When this happens, the surgeon usually removes the normal appendix anyway, because it is a vestigial and potentially troublesome organ. If the surgeon recommends an operation, it is always wise to accept his advice, since no harm is done by having a look inside, whereas a great deal of harm can result from waiting too long to operate.

Causes   Appendicitis means inflammation of the appendix. This is a small, obsolete, blind tube, 2 to 3 inches (5 to 8 cm) long, leading off the large, lower part of the intestine. Inflammation results from infection, which occurs more often in the appendix because it is a blind tube and therefore can only empty itself back into the intestine. Theoretically, any solid object, such as an apple seed, could get stuck in the appendix, but in practice this is such a rare cause of appendicitis that you need not be concerned about what your child eats from the point of view of preventing it. (See also threadworms, p. 490.)

Symptoms   Appendicitis happens suddenly. There is no such thing as a "grumbling appendix." The appendix either roars because it is inflamed or is silent because it is well. A pain that goes away by itself is not due to appendicitis. The inflamed appendix may burst within twenty-four hours, causing infection to spread dangerously throughout the abdomen (peritonitis); it is for this reason that appendicitis must be diagnosed quickly.

Children's symptoms often differ from those of adults. The pain stays around the navel instead of moving to the right side of the abdomen. In adults there is usually constipation, but in children there is often diarrhea. Vomiting is usual and there may or may not be a fever. The doctor confirms the diagnosis by examining the child's abdomen. This requires technical knowledge; don't try to diagnose appendicitis yourself. The more unwell the child, the more quickly you should get the doctor.

Food Poisoning

This comes on suddenly, with abdominal pain, diarrhea, and vomiting; sometimes there is a fever as well. Usually, more than one member of the family is involved. It more often strikes away from home, when you are especially likely to eat unfamiliar food that has not been hygienically prepared.

Food poisoning can be just a nuisance but it can also make a child very ill if he loses so much fluid through vomiting and diarrhea that he becomes dehydrated (p. 479). If this happens he will probably require intravenous feeding (p. 480), which means admission to the hospital.

Gastroenteritis

Again, the symptoms are vomiting, diarrhea, abdominal pain, and possibly fever. The cause is an infection in the bowels. There is a danger of dehydration if the child can keep nothing down and has severe diarrhea.

Gastroenteritis is a medical diagnosis, which can be made only by proving that the diarrhea and vomiting are due to an infection in the bowel by a special germ, such as those causing dysentery. Do not use the term "gastroenteritis" to explain your child's diarrhea and vomiting until your doctor has discovered this germ by a laboratory test. Diarrhea and sickness can be due to other serious conditions, such as appendicitis, which may be overlooked if the label "gastroenteritis" has already been applied.

Since dehydration is the danger from diarrhea, it is safe, provided the child is not vomiting, to give water contianing sugar and salt. The correct proportions are one flat teaspoonful of sugar and one flat saltspoonful of salt (½ teaspoon) to one pint of water. Special double-ended spoons are now being made for use in developing countries. However, if your child is obviously ill, even if not vomiting, please call your doctor without delay.

Celiac Disease

This is a relatively rare condition causing the stools to be bulky, pale, and offensive. It is due to an inborn inability to digest gluten, the protein present in cereal. It therefore appears as soon as the baby is started on cereal, which to him is poisonous. Treatment consists in giving a gluten-free diet for life.

Constipation

Constipation means infrequent bowel movements and uncomfortably hard stools. No doubt you know this, but you may have an inaccurate idea of the meaning of "infrequent" and probably of the term "hard," so that you may think your child is constipated when he is not. This would not matter if it did not lead some parents to dose their children with laxatives and make them excessively concerned about their bowels. Both policies can lead to genuine constipation by interfering with the natural action of the bowels.

Normal Patterns

The most important thing to know about bowels is that left to themselves bowels move whenever they need to, since the emptying reflex acts as soon as the rectum is full. The child then wants to have a bowel movement, and provided he visits the bathroom promptly he will have no problem.

The reflex has a different rhythm in different people; this is where trouble can arise if the point is misunderstood. An individual's bowels may move once or more each day, or every other day, or even only once every three or four days. Any of these patterns is normal, but if your child's pattern happens to be infrequent you may think he is constipated.

Avoid believing that it is your duty to make your child's bowels move every day. If you do, you will find yourself changing his diet, giving him more vegetables and making him drink more than he wants. You may also make the mistake of giving laxatives as well. At the same time you will find yourself waiting anxiously each day to see if he goes and then examining his stool. The extra vegetables do no harm unless they make him dislike meals, but the extra worry is bad for both of you, and before you know where you are you will be cooking food for stools!

Children should not be concerned about their bowel movements. There is no need even to ask whether or not your child has been to the bathroom or what his stool was like. Stools vary in firmness; only a degree of hardness that causes discomfort or pain matters.

Constipation Due to Illness

Constipation does not cause a child to be ill, but illness can cause constipation. It may be due to loss of appetite, which means that there is less food in the bowel. Alternatively, a child may be drinking less fluid, or perhaps fluid is being lost through vomiting or excessive sweating due to fever. Sometimes, because he is ill, a child suppresses the reflex calling him to have a bowel movement so that the next day the stool is slightly larger and firmer; this does not matter in the least. Any illness, by altering a child's normal routine of exercise and diet, may temporarily alter his bowel rhythm.

Laxatives

If a child is given a laxative to "help" him along, the pattern is much more likely to remain upset, since the laxative clears out the lower bowel. It takes longer for it to fill again and for the emptying reflex to act spontaneously. If he is then given another dose because you think this second delay means he is still constipated, there is yet another interruption to the re-establishment of his normal rhythm.

Is there ever a reason for giving a child a laxative? Over the years I have prescribed them less and less and now do not use them at all. I believe that normal rhythm returns more quickly if the body is left to readjust itself unhampered by the clumsy use of medicines. The only possible reason for a laxative would be to make the stool softer so as to reduce pain; milk of magnesia could be used for this (see anal fissure, below). But I would emphasize that there is absolutely no reason to give a medicine merely to have a bowel movement—the body will do this much more effectively by itself, when ready to do so.

It should now be clear to you that you must not give your child a laxative or, worse still, a purgative—a stronger medicine—when he is ill. Not only is it unnecessary, but also it can be harmful. If a child with abdominal pain is given a dose and the cause of the pain is acute appendicitis, the laxative may cause the appendix to rupture (see appendicitis, above).

Is Regularity Important?

Is there any advantage in having regular and predictable bowel movements, for example, at the popular time of after breakfast each day? This is certainly a convenient time to get it over and done with; your child then avoids having to ask permission to leave the classroom. A child who ignores the need to have a bowel movement because he is too embarrassed or too busy at the right time is not in danger of becoming constipated, since the reflex to move his bowels is far stronger than his will to resist it. Left to himself, he will either go at the next opportunity or be forced by nature to leave the classroom. Some children who are shy about going at school establish a pattern of rushing straight to the bathroom when they get home.

There is no harm in gently encouraging the after-breakfast habit from the time when your child is starting to use the toilet, if his bowels seem to move at around this time of day. There is a gastrocolic reflex whereby eating increases the strength of the digestive waves (peristalsis), which in turn sets off the emptying reflex, causing a bowel movement. After the long overnight interval without food, breakfast is particularly likely to have this effect.

Avoiding Anxiety

It is sensible to take advantage of this reflex, if it can be done easily. But it is certainly not worth doing if it makes your child anxious, so that he strains, although he feels no urge to move his bowels at the time. A child who is perfectly happy and unconcerned about his bowel movements may then start worrying about them, visiting the bathroom several times a day and trying to go when he does not really want to. This may stop him from registering the real signal to move his bowels.

Therefore, do not make the issue a matter of life and death. A child can understand that it would merely be convenient to go every day before leaving for school, particularly if it is difficult to get to the bathroom later, but he should not be given the impression that it is important in any other way.

What to Do

If your child does become temporarily constipated, does it matter, and what should you do about it? First, it does not matter in that being constipated does not make a child ill, or even produce symptoms like a coated tongue or bad breath (pp. 476–77). There are illnesses in which constipation is a symptom, but these make the child ill in other ways as well.

If you follow this advice you will seldom find yourself wondering whether you should give your child a laxative because, I hope, you will not even know whether he is having a bowel movement every day. If he complains of pain and has to strain, which will be very unlikely if you have adopted the matter-of-fact approach recommended, you can suggest he eat more fruit and drink more fruit juice.

I must emphasize that chronic constipation is almost always the result of excessive concern about bowels, and that it is therefore a man-made problem. Vets tell me that dog owners who are excessively concerned about their pets' bowels can create a situation where the dog continues to have his bowel movements in the living room or some other inappropriate place. The concern shown by his mistress can be conveyed to the dog, so that he develops the habit of eating his stools in order to destroy the evidence!

Anal Fissure

Hard stools can tear the lining membrane just inside the anus, producing an anal fissure. This increases the pain when the bowels are being opened and results in a vicious circle of further constipation. I still do not give any laxatives or local treatment for this, preferring to put all my emphasis on the need to remove all parental concern from the bowels; this I find to be effective. I appreciate, however, that some doctors may wish to give milk of magnesia to soften the stools, and they may give you an ointment containing a local anesthetic to apply to the anal fissure just before the child has a bowel movement in order to reduce the pain.

Chronic constipation may also lead to soiling (see below).

Soiling (Fecal Incontinence)

Frequent soiling is only very occasionally due to late development in acquiring bowel control; such a child may also wet his bed (see toilet training, pp. 243–44).

Accidents

A child who is already toilet trained and usually reliable may soil his pants by accident. The incident should be forgotten. Dirtying the pants deliberately could be a sign of jealousy or insecurity, like wetting again after the birth of a new baby. It is more likely to happen when toilet training has been intense and if your child knows you are anxious about his bowel movements, which he may therefore use to express his own emotions. He will stop soiling when he feels happier and when your attitude toward his bowels is less intense. Your family doctor can help here (see jealousy, pp. 148f., constipation, pp. 484–85).

Chronic Constipation

By far the commonest reason for soiling, in a child past the toilet-training stage, is chronic constipation. It sounds strange that constipation could cause soiling with loose stool, but this results from leakage of semifluid stool which accumulates behind the hard-stool blockage in the rectum. The muscles of the anus become loose and insensitive, so that the child has no control over the leakage. Obviously, it is pointless to be angry with him (see constipation, pp. 484–85).

Chronic constipation leading to soiling usually starts because for some reason a child has repeatedly "held on to" his stool instead of "letting go." This is the result of excessive family concern about bowels, leading to vigorous attempts to toilet train a child. He is likely to have a very normal reaction—negativism—which makes him fight his parents' wishes and hold on to his stool instead of letting it go. Such a child may have a bowel movement as soon as he gets off the toilet, since his defenses are now lowered. This may be into the diaper that has unwisely been applied—since he is no longer a baby—or onto the floor.

Emotional Problems

A child who soils cannot help being worried, because of the physical discomfort and because of the disgust and contempt of his schoolmates, who probably let him know that he stinks. So while soiling could be an indication of deeper emotional conflicts, it is more often the other way around and is the reason for the child's problems.

When the causes of his constipation have been identified and tackled, the soiling stops and so do the worries—although it may take a little time for the child to recover his self-confidence. After the doctor has explained the physical mechanism behind the trouble, the child feels reassured that it was not his fault. The doctor also has to correct the attitude of the child's parents toward bowels, which probably dates back to the attitude of their own parents when they themselves were children. Giving enemas and laxatives for this problem is now practiced less and less by doctors.

Rectal Prolapse

Sometimes the rectum—the last part of the intestine—projects through the back passage. This is usually the result of excessive family concern about bowel movements, leading to the child's straining to achieve what he has come to believe is so vital to please his parents or for his health. A child sitting on a training seat with his knees doubled up can, by straining, achieve such a powerful downward force through his pelvis that he causes a portion of his rectum to prolapse through the anus.

It is alarming, and was vividly described to me by one mother, who said, "His bottom's fallen out!"

Treatment Fortunately, the condition is not serious and the rectum will always go back. It is important not to panic and frighten your child. Just lying on his bed may do the trick; it sometimes help if you raise the foot of the bed on blocks or a pile of books. If you want to push it back, put a piece of toilet paper on your index finger and insert this into the channel in the center of the prolapsed rectum. Having pushed it back, remove your finger, leaving the paper inside to be passed with the next stool. If you push it back without paper, the intestine sticks to your finger and comes out again when you withdraw it.

To reduce the force of straining while passing a stool, get your child to use the toilet rather than a training seat, so that his knees are less doubled up. Provide him with a smaller seat, if necessary. It is a good idea to fix a footrest at a slightly lower level than it really needs to be, to reduce still more the extent to which he is doubled up.

37

Worms

There are several varieties of worm that enter the human body and live there as parasites. Some are visible to the naked eye and some can be seen only under the microscope. Some are common only in tropical countries, whereas others are common all over the world. Children from every type of home—immaculate or "dirty"—can catch worms, so if you discover that your child has them, don't feel ashamed, or try to keep it a deadly secret. Get them treated and forget them.

Threadworms

Symptoms

These are the most common type. They look like little white threads that move and can be seen in the stools or around the anus. The only symptom they produce is irritation around the anus, which is caused by the female worm when she comes out of the rectum to lay her eggs; bed-wetting can result from this irritation.

The appendix is the part of the intestine most often chosen by the threadworm. It is not surprising, therefore, if the surgeon finds that an appendix he has removed contains some threadworms. However, it is rare for threadworms to be the cause of acute appendicitis.

The Worm's Life Cycle

The eggs are fertilized while the worm is still in the intestine; the female prefers to lay her eggs outside the intestine but in warmth, so she comes out at night, when the child is particularly warm in bed. He scratches and may be restless. If he then puts his hands to his mouth, he will reinfest himself by swallowing some of the eggs, thereby starting the whole life cycle of the threadworm again. Alternatively, the eggs may stay under his nails until he holds hands with another child, and in this way the infection can be passed from one child to another.

Emotional Problems

Although threadworms do not cause loss of weight, loss of energy, abdominal pain, convulsions, or many of the symptoms once attributed to them, it is worth treating them, since there is a simple cure available. Also, it is difficult to rid yourself altogether of the feeling that worms are "shameful." Threadworms are insignificant little things in themselves but they can cause emotional problems out of all proportion to their importance, and therefore they should be treated. The child with threadworms sometimes feels "dirty" and may even get stomach aches caused by shame, not by the worms. Tell him that threadworms are more like threads than worms, and he may dislike the idea of them less.

Treatment

A single dose of a special medicine may be sufficient to eliminate the worms. But you must all take the medicine, not just the child who has them; otherwise worms can go around and around the family.

Additional measures should also be carried out to prevent reinfestation: cut your child's nails as short as possible, so that they are less likely to trap the eggs beneath them. Get him to wear gloves and tight pants at night to stop him from scratching and transferring the eggs to his mouth.

Roundworms

These are much less common than threadworms. They are more of a problem in tropical than in developed countries. They live in the small intestine, and look like earthworms, but are whitish; they are about 6 inches (15 cm) long, and are sometimes vomited out.

The eggs are passed in the child's stools and so may contaminate his hands; if he then puts his hands in his mouth and swallows the eggs, the cycle is started again. The eggs hatch into larvae in the small intestine and then migrate to the lungs via the blood. Afterward they return to the intestine, where they mature. The larvae are not dangerous and do no permanent damage to the lungs; in the majority of cases they cause no symptoms.

A single dose of a drug works as with threadworms.

Toxocara

This is the roundworm that infests dogs and cats, so that they pass stools containing the eggs. A child can be infected from his own pet but more often from contamination of his hands with infested stools while playing in the park or sand. The eggs are transferred when he puts his hands in his mouth and they hatch into larvae in the child's intestine. These penetrate the intestinal wall and pass to any of the organs of the body to cause disease by local irritation. This can lead to blindness and epilepsy.

The larvae can be killed by medicine but this does not affect the established areas of irritation. It is essential to create a greater public awareness of the condition so as to prevent the disease by regular deworming of puppies and the segregation of dogs from places where young children play.

Hookworms

These worms are a serious cause of ill-health and anemia in the tropics but are rare elsewhere. A few hookworms in a healthy person cause little trouble.

The eggs are passed in the stools and develop into larvae in the soil, from where they can tunnel into the skin of bare feet. This is one of the reasons why visitors to the topics should not walk about barefoot (see living in the tropics, p. 377).

Tapeworms

Becoming host to a tapeworm is usually the result of eating undercooked pork. This can occur in any country, so pork should always be cooked thoroughly.

Although a tapeworm may cause stomach or bowel trouble, in most cases nothing abnormal is noticed until flat, white segments are seen moving in the stool. The tail, which is the larger end, comes out first. Hundreds of segments may be noticed, but if the head is still inside the child's body, the tapeworm goes on growing. The doctor must see examples of the segments in order to diagnose the trouble and start treatment. The only sure way of knowing that treatment has been successful is to find the head of the worm in the stool. This is a laborious process, because it is very small.

38

Skin Disorders

Skin Types

You cannot alter the type of skin with which your child is born. You cannot make a greasy skin less greasy, a dry skin less dry, or a "sensitive" skin tougher from the inside by changing his diet or from the outside by applying creams or ointments. All you can do, once you know how an individual's skin reacts to washing and weather, for example, is to treat it appropriately.

The complexion of young babies is nowhere near as perfect as is commonly supposed; in fact, babies often have spotty faces in the early weeks of life, a condition that cures itself (see skin troubles, pp. 428–29, and infantile eczema, pp. 507f.). Young children, particularly toddlers, often have a rough patch of skin on the cheek; this also cures itself.

Greasy Skin

This is seldom a problem in babies and children, but it may give rise to acne during adolescence (see acne, pp. 496–97).

Dry Skin

You will soon notice if your baby's skin tends to be dry. Taking him out in a cold wind may chap his face, especially where he has dribbled, and make his hands rough and chapped. Vigorous scrubbing with a washcloth, soap, and water will make his face peel, so soap and water should be used sparingly and baby lotion or oil used for cleaning his face. The skin on his bottom may be equally sensitive and need similar treatment (see diaper rash, p. 431).

Sunburn

Skin can be burned by the sun's rays just as by other forms of heat. The skin of fair or red-haired people burns particularly easily and is less efficient than darker skin at building up a protective tan, so children with this coloring need special care to prevent sunburn.

Prevention

Sunburn only starts hurting several hours after the actual burning has taken place. Because a child does not complain while the damage is being done, you have to anticipate trouble. On the first days of hot and steady sunshine, do not let your child strip down for hours on end. Half an hour is long enough to sunbathe for the first day or two, and even this may be too long for a fair-skinned child on vacation at the beach; the sun's rays are reflected off the water, which means they are extra powerful by the sea. So put a shirt over your child's bathing suit when he is playing on the beach and in the water. His legs need protection too. Running around in a partially shaded yard is less of a hazard.

Creams and Lotions

The application of protective lotions and creams before and during sunbathing does help, but do not rely on them for complete protection against sunburn. They cannot prevent a child from getting over-heated even if they protect his skin, and heatstroke can make him ill (pp. 376–77).

Symptoms and Remedies

You will find it hard to convince your young child of the need for him to keep covered up in the heat, but it is better to insist than to have him suffer later. Explain that he will have to stay out of the sun altogether for a day or two if he does get sunburned, and that sun-burn is painful. It may hurt so much that even the pressure of the sheet makes a child restless at night. Blisters may form. Calamine lotion is soothing and acetaminophen may relieve the pain. It takes a few days for the burn to pass through its various stages of fading and peeling.

Folliculitis and Boils

Every hair grows upward to the surface of the skin from its root; it passes along a channel called a hair follicle. Each hair follicle has its own sebaceous gland, which produces a greasy substance called sebum to lubricate the skin and hair.

Inflammation at the point where the hair breaks through the skin is called "folliculitis"; this produces a white pimple or pustule. A rash of these pimples on the chest can be caused by overenthusiastic appli-cation of a "vapor rub" during a cold. These preparations do not help the cold and, since they may cause folliculitis, are best avoided.

Boils are caused by infection deeper down the hair follicle, near the root of the hair. The infection is usually the result of a germ (staphylococcus) entering the follicle. This happens more easily where the skin is rubbed, for example, at the back of the neck from a collar, or on the buttocks. Boils can complicate an existing skin complaint such as acne.

Recognizing a Boil

How do you know when a spot is a boil and not a pimple? A boil hurts. Starting as a small, red lump, it feels tender and goes on hurting until it comes to a point and bursts to discharge yellow matter (pus). This usually happens within two or three days.

Never squeeze a boil to try to bring it to a head, since this may make it worse, spread the infection to nearby hair follicles, and start more boils. Hot applications also encourage boils to spread.

Crops of Boils

The ease with which germs spread from one boil to cause others is one reason they often appear in crops. A child who is below par for some reason, such as a recent illness, is more likely to get a crop of boils, since his resistance to infection is lowered. Everyone's skin is constantly covered with germs, which usually cause no trouble; some people never get boils, although their skin is no cleaner than the skin of other people who do suffer from them.

Treatment

The boil will heal itself, and treatment probably makes very little difference to the time this takes. But treatment can reduce pain and prevent spread. If adhesive plaster is stretched across a developing boil it helps to reduce pain by splinting the skin and so reducing some of its movement. Nonstick dressings impregnated with antibiotics are now available. The antibiotic probably does not hasten recovery from the boil but it may help to reduce the spread of infection to nearby skin. Another way of reducing the risk of spread is to clean the surrounding skin with alcohol.

Consulting Your Doctor

You should consult your doctor if a boil is in an awkward place, such as the armpit or ear (see otitis externa, p. 458), or if it fails to come to a head. Red streaks running from the area of the boil and tender glands nearby mean that the infection is spreading to a serious degree.

Acne

This trouble occurs at puberty and is commoner in boys than girls. The tendency to acne often runs in families. The spots, which can be very disfiguring, occur mainly on the face but also on the back of the neck, the shoulders, and the chest.

Acne affects appearance, not physical health, but it can be severe enough to cause mental anguish by making a young person feel ugly at the very age when it is becoming more important for him, or her, to feel attractive. Parents and doctors must, therefore, take a child's worries seriously and do more than advise patience.

Cause

The cause of acne is the excessive greasiness of the skin that occurs at puberty. Under the influence of hormones (chemical substances) circulating during puberty, the sebaceous glands in the skin become especially active and produce extra amounts of the normal grease (sebum) that lubricates the skin. So much is produced that the mouths of the skin pores through which the sebum has to pass to get out become blocked. This blockage produces the "blackheads" that are characteristic of acne. These are very liable to become inflamed, causing pimples and boils, which can leave scars. It is now known that this inflammation is due not to infection but is the result of chemical changes in the sebum. Dandruff exaggerates the problem, and many sufferers from acne also have dandruff.

Remedies

Acne stops soon after puberty is completed and the associated chemical changes have settled down. Treatment to reduce the greasiness of the skin and to clear the blocked sebaceous glands does a great deal to keep the condition down until a natural cure occurs with the end of adolescence.

The face should be washed with soap in very hot water as often as possible; washing should be vigorous, and it is a good idea even to use a scrubbing brush. This helps to get rid of the blackheads. Squeezing blackheads is usually discouraged on the grounds that it increases the risk of infection. However, some skin specialists now feel that the risk of secondary infection has been exaggerated and that, since the inflammation is acne is chemical, it is safe for blackheads to be removed by hand after a thorough wash of hands and face. After the washing, a drying lotion, such as calamine and 3 percent sulphur, which you can get from the pharmacist without a prescription, should be applied. This is rubbed in when the face has dried in order to encourage peeling of the skin and cleaning of the blocked pore. The lotion can be used during the daytime because once it has been rubbed in it is not obvious. The slight color from the lotion may camouflage the spots without making a boy look made up.

This routine makes a child less likely to pick his skin, leading to further spots and scarring. It also shows him that his problem is being taken seriously.

Ultraviolet light also helps to dry the skin and encourage peeling. Children with acne should therefore spend as much time as possible out in the sun. Their hair should be cut in such a way that it does not stop the sun from reaching the face. Bangs may hide spots on the forehead but they also screen off the sunlight, so that the spots remain. Ultraviolet light can also be obtained from a special lamp, but the length of exposure must be strictly controlled. The eyes should be covered while the lamp is being used.

The hair must be shampooed often enough to keep down the dandruff, and no greasy hair oils should be used. Greasy cosmetics should also be avoided, but some cosmetics must be allowed if needed to give your daughter confidence to go out and lead a normal social life. Chocolate has often been blamed for aggravating acne, but diet probably makes very little difference.

If acne is severe your doctor may also give antibiotic treatment for a long period. The antibiotics used do not act in their usual way, by destroying germs, but alter the chemical composition of the sebum. Whatever line of treatment your doctor recommends, the aim is also reassurance. Sometimes the spots are not half as noticeable as your child imagines—he may not believe you, but tell him this if you suspect he is becoming morbidly self-conscious about his appearance. Also emphasize to him that acne does not last forever, pointing out that if he helps to prevent his skin from being permanently scarred there will be no lasting evidence of his adolescent complexion.

Benzoyl peroxide is probably the most effective local treatment for acne and is sometimes prescribed in combination with tretinoin. Local treatment must be applied to the back and chest, as well as to the face, if they are involved. It must be emphasized that treatment is lengthy, lasting for a minimum of six months.

Impetigo

This is caused by an infection. It may affect previously healthy skin or it can be a complication of another skin condition such as eczema, scabies, papular urticaria, or cold sores. It is contagious whichever way it starts, so if your child has impetigo, wash him and his things separately.

Impetigo usually appears on exposed parts of the body such as
the face, scalp, and hands. It starts as little red spots, which get
watery heads and then develop large brownish-yellow crusts. It
spreads quickly over the skin, so take your child to the doctor
promptly.

An antibiotic ointment may be enough to clear up impetigo, but
if it is very widespread, your doctor may also prescribe an antibiotic
drug to be taken by mouth.

Chilblains

These are painful, itching, red or purplish swellings, which appear on
the extremities of the body—fingers, toes, and the tips of the ears or
nose. Scratching causes breaks in the skin, so the chilblains may
become infected.

Exactly why some people tend to get chilblains and others never
do is uncertain. The cause is related to poor circulation and cold
weather, so if your child gets chilblains see that his arms and legs, and
particularly his hands and feet, are kept warm when it is cold, that
his boots are not tight, and that he dries thoroughly after washing.

There is no dramatic cure for chilblains but your doctor can
prescribe an ointment to reduce the itching.

Chilblains are quite different from the swollen red hands that
babies may get on cold days, when they take off their gloves in their
carriages. This results from slowing of the circulation due to cold, and
although it looks alarming, the hands return quickly to normal in the
home. Unlike chilblains, they don't seem to cause the child any discomfort.

Warts (Verrucae)

Warts are harmless growths on the skin due to a virus; the infection
may spread, causing a crop of warts. Some types are caught easily by
other children; this applies particularly to warts on the feet (plantar
warts, or verrucas, as they are popularly called). A child with a plantar wart should not walk about barefoot until it has cleared up. The
wearing of protective footwear (Plastsoks) prevents the transfer of
infection, thereby making it possible for a child to swim in public pools
or at beaches.

Any part of the body may be affected but the hands and feet are
the most common places. Most warts disappear eventually without
treatment, which probably accounts for stories of miraculous

"cures"; these probably happened to coincide with the wart's spontaneous disappearance.

Warts on the palms of the hands and soles of the feet tend to be flat, and because those on the soles are pressed inward by the pressure of walking, they become painful. Because of this, and because warts are catching, take your child to the doctor for advice. Treatment may be by the gradual method of applying ointment regularly, by soaking the plantar wart in formalin—difficult to manage with a small restless child, or by scraping or cutting out the wart.

Ringworm

Ringworm is caused by a fungus infection, of which there are a number of different types. It affects the skin, hair, or nails and is often found in the creases of the body—between the toes, for instance (athlete's foot, below). It can spread from the feet to other parts of the body. Although there are varieties of ringworm that can be caught from animals, the infection is most often passed from one person to another.

Ringworm of the Body

When it affects the body the fungus produces circular rashes, which spread in ever-enlarging circles while healing in the center. The edge is the active growing area of the rash and the skin here is raised into small bumps.

Ringworm of the body is fairly easy to treat but it is very important to deal with other hidden sites as well, especially athlete's foot (see below). Your doctor will probably prescribe Whitfield's ointment or Micopazole.

Ringworm of the Scalp (Tinea Capitis)

A child with ringworm of the scalp has one or more bald patches. These are round or oval with clearly defined edges. The ring grows from the outside, the center healing first. The skin is covered with dry, gray scales and the bald patch is studded with broken stumps of dull hair. Take a child with these symptoms to the doctor promptly, since ringworm is catching. He will probably use a Wood's lamp to show up the ringworm. Brushes, combs, and towels belonging to the child must be washed separately and should not be used by other members of the family.

A new antibiotic has dramatically changed the treatment of this type of ringworm. It works by preventing further growth of the fungus. When the infected part is shed as the new hair grows, the ringworm disappears. This process usually takes about three weeks and the hair recovers completely. During this time a child may be kept from school unless wearing special headgear. It is a reasonable compromise to let him mix with other members of the family, provided the precautions described above are taken.

In the past, because ringworm of the scalp was common and treatment very unsatisfactory, the disease caused much public alarm. Children with the disease had to be isolated for long periods. Now that a satisfactory treatment is readily available and the condition is relatively rare, these old fears should be dismissed.

Athlete's Foot (Ringworm of the Feet)

This form of ringworm is a "civilized" disorder in that wearing socks and shoes makes it easier for the fungus responsible to gain a hold. This is why visitors to the tropics whose feet are squeezed into sweaty shoes suffer far more frequently from athlete's foot than the native inhabitants; walking barefoot allows air to circulate between the toes and discourages the fungal infection.

However, in countries where people tend to walk barefoot indoors only, in bathrooms and swimming pools, bare feet encourage the spread of athlete's foot. It is highly contagious and once an outbreak starts in a school or family it is very hard to eradicate it. Your child may catch it at school, bring it home, and give it to the rest of you, unless you are very careful to prevent this happening at the first sign of infection. Keep his towels separate and try to stop him from walking barefoot in the house.

How do you recognize athlete's foot? The skin between the toes (often the little toe and its neighbor) is soft, white, and sodden. Your child may pick this dead-looking skin off because of itching and this reveals sore red skin underneath. See that his feet are washed and dried thoroughly every day and that he applies an antiringworm ointment between his toes. A dusting powder should be used in his shoes and socks. The pharmacist can recommend suitable preparations.

Continue this treatment for at least a week after all signs of athlete's foot have gone. Bare feet help hasten the cure but also spread infection, so open sandals or open clogs are a good compromise.

Bald Patch (Alopecia Areata)

Occasionally, a child over the age of five suddenly develops a bald patch or even loses all his hair. It is difficult to discover why, though sometimes an acute emotional shock is the cause.

This condition differs from ringworm, in which the bald patches are gray and scaly (see ringworm, above). In alopecia areata, the skin in the bald area is quite clear and smooth; you can see stumps of hair like exclamation marks around the edges of the patch. As long as the stumps remain, the area is still getting bigger.

There is now an effective treatment by injections of cortisone, which usually results in the hair growing again within a few weeks. Without treatment, the hair usually grows again of its own accord, but it takes time and increases the worry felt by you and your child. Your doctor will need to help you to identify and deal with any emotional factors that might be involved. The condition is not catching.

Louse Infestation (Pediculosis)

Two varieties affect children: the head louse and the body louse, both of which cause such intense irritation that infection with impetigo may result. The head louse sticks its eggs, called nits, to hairs. The eggs are grayish-white and are just visible to the naked eye.

The body louse lives in clothing and only comes onto the body to feed. It leaves small puncture marks where blood has been extracted, which are soon scratched and become infected. These occur anywhere on the body except the face, hands, and feet.

Gamma benzene hexachloride is commonly used for treatment, either as a shampoo for the head or as a cream or dusting powder for the body. Be sure to avoid getting the shampoo into the eyes and do not wash the hair for twenty-four hours after application. The dead eggs remain attached but can be removed with a specially fine comb.

39

The Allergic Child

Allergies

What Is an Allergy?

A child who suffers from asthma, eczema, hay fever, allergic rhinitis (hay fever is one variety of this), or urticaria (hives) probably has an allergy. This means that his body overreacts to something eaten, inhaled, or touched. The cause of this reaction, the "allergen," is a substance, usually a protein, though not necessarily in the form of food, that ordinarily produces no symptoms.

Who Suffers?

Why some individuals are born with or acquire sensitivity to certain substances that are usually harmless is a question still occupying much medical research. However, it is known that the tendency to allergy is shared by a high proportion of the population and that it often runs in families. If you and your husband both have allergies, your children are more likely to inherit the tendency than if only one of you suffers from it.

Allergy may come out in different forms in the same family: a parent with asthma may have a child who gets hay fever, or a parent with eczema may have a child who gets asthma. It is also quite common for an individual's allergy to change in severity or in form during the course of his life: eczema in a young infant may be replaced by asthma when the child is older. If the two occur together there is a remarkable tendency for one to improve as the other gets worse—if a child's asthma is bad his eczema will probably be better.

Being subject to allergy does not mean a child is going to suffer from symptoms all his life, since they are likely to improve as he gets older. Many people have only isolated attacks of symptoms; these may be trivial, so that the allergy makes no difference to life and can safely be ignored. Moreover, although doctors cannot cure allergy, there is a great deal they can do to reduce the symptoms.

What Can Be Done?

A doctor has three approaches in trying to help a child who suffers from an allergic disease. First, he can try to discover to which substance (allergen) the child is sensitive and then advise parents how to eliminate it from his environment. Secondly, he can give medicines that may prevent the attacks altogether, or at any rate make them less severe. These include the antiallergic drugs (antihistamines) and cortisone. Other drugs are used to widen the narrowed air tubes (bronchi) during an attack of asthma. The newest is a powder, which is inhaled. It is used in the prevention of asthma and, more recently, of hay fever. The third method is desensitization.

Skin Tests and Desensitization The child can be desensitized to the substance to which he is sensitive, if it is first identified by special skin tests. The doctor is likely to undertake skin testing only if the history of the child's illness suggests that he may be able to identify the cause of the allergy. For example, is there a family history of allergic diseases? Does the disease have a seasonal incidence, like hay fever, which occurs in the pollen season? Does the attack of asthma come on at night, making allergy to the house dust mite (pp. 505–6) a likely possibility? Unsatisfactory results prevent the use of skin tests before the age of four years.

Minute quantities of possible allergens, each contained in a drop of water, are pricked into the child's skin. If he is allergic to the test substance, a small itching wheal appears at the site.

Desensitization stops the child from overreacting to the substance every time he meets it. It is done by giving him a course of injections containing the allergen so that his body gradually learns to accept it without trouble. Desensitization is more effective if the child turns out to be sensitive to only one or two allergens. Unfortunately, it does not last for life and has to be repeated after one or more years, depending on symptoms.

Allergy is such a complicated business that simple desensitization does not always work. One person may be allergic to several substances, which reduces its effect, while other factors besides sensitivity to a protein may be involved. For example, emotional stress may play a part—starting a new school year may bring on asthma as well as sleeping on a feather bed; standing in a cold wind at the bus stop, wearing a wool shirt, worry, or eating strawberries could all be responsible at different times for one child's eczema or asthma.

Tracking Down the Allergen It is always worth trying to find the cause of a child's allergy but the extent of the search depends on the seriousness of his symptoms. It is sometimes possible to identify allergens and remove them from the diet or environment. If eating eggs is found to cause severe eczema or stroking the cat brings on an attack of asthma, dispense with eggs and cats. But tracking down an allergen may involve tests and changes in the child's routine that would worry him more than minor symptoms, such as mild eczema or asthma, or occasional hives.

An extensive search is worthwhile if the complaint is making the child's life miserable. The form the search takes will depend on which allergic disease he has. The cause of hives is likely to be something the child has eaten, so the doctor will advise cutting out certain foods, one by one, to see if any improvement follows. Alternatively, he might prescribe a very safe bland diet containing milk products only and then add one new food at a time to see if it brings on an attack of hives.

The allergic cause of asthma and of allergic rhinitis (the itching runny nose) is likely to be some substance in the air a child breathes to which he is sensitive. This could be dealt with by trying the effect of removing possible irritating substances such as hair and feathers from the bedding. Today there is a greater emphasis on skin tests, particularly since the importance of the house dust mite as a cause of asthma has been realized. Not only is it possible to reduce the size of the population of house dust mites in your home, but recently it has become possible to desensitize a child against them.

Learning to live with an allergy and the treatment of the various allergic disorders are dealt with more fully under the appropriate headings.

Bronchial Asthma

Symptoms

In bronchial asthma, severe spasm of the muscle of the bronchi occurs and breathing is difficult, particularly breathing out. The child is likely to be very frightened during an attack, thereby increasing his difficulty. Therefore it is important for you to be as calm and reassuring as possible.

In some children, especially the young ones, it may be difficult to distinguish wheezing from what is called "wheezy bronchitis" (pp. 463–64), and wheezing from asthma. This difficulty is not serious, since the treatment is similar for both—respiratory therapy (pp. 466–67) to clear the mucus from the narrowed bronchi and medicines to relieve the spasm. Your doctor will decide about antibiotics and other forms of treatment.

Asthma usually improves as the child gets older—though the allergic tendency may be passed on. For this reason, a family history of allergic disease helps to distinguish bronchial asthma. The attack of bronchial asthma often comes on out of the blue; it may be preceded by a clear discharge from the nose due to sensitivity, similar to hay fever; this is different from the thick discharge of the ordinary cold, which has probably affected other members of the family as well.

Causes

In the asthmatic child, the mucous membrane lining the bronchi is oversensitive, reacting by spasm and by the secretion of excessive amounts of mucus to various influences, which may be allergic, emotional, or due to infection; often there is a combination of factors, particularly allergy and emotion. The lining of the nose may also be sensitive, causing an attack to start with allergic rhinitis; this produces nasal irritation and sneezing, just like hay fever, which is one variety of allergic rhinitis (see p. 453).

The doctor will determine the likelihood of an allergic cause on the basis of his clinical history of the child's illness. From this he will decide whether to do skin tests, and in the light of the results of these, whether to desensitize the child (see above). With asthmatic children it is a wise precaution to avoid all bedding containing feathers, down, or hair, because these are common allergens and they also encourage the house dust mite.

The House Dust Mite The importance of the house dust mite as a possible cause of asthma has already been mentioned (above). The house dust mite is everywhere, but it can be seen only by using a microscope and it has only recently been discovered. It lives on the scales of dead skin that human beings are shedding all the time. Individuals who are sensitive to the house dust mite are allergic to protein contained in its body, so that they react to it even when it is dead; they may even react to its droppings alone.

Being so ubiquitous the house dust mite is very difficult to eliminate entirely from a home, but a great deal can be done to improve matters, particularly by the frequent use of a vacuum cleaner in the deepest crevices of upholstery on chairs. A plastic mattress cover should be used, making cleaning easier. Damp dusting of the furniture should be carried out often. Blankets should be well shaken and sheets changed frequently. Beds should be made when the child is out of the room and preferably out of the house.

Recently I saw a child who got asthma only when he was home from school on Saturdays. An emotional cause seemed likely, but the real answer was that this was the only day he was at home when his blankets were thoroughly shaken. Once the bed-making routine was altered, his asthma was much improved.

The discovery of the house dust mite has made an enormous difference to our understanding of, and our ability to help, those children who get asthma mainly at night. The absence of the mite from newly built houses explains why children with asthma sometimes get better when they move to a new home. Unfortunately, it is never long before the house dust mites arrive. Mites flourish more in damp homes—so there is now a scientific explanation for the statement that a child's asthma is worse when he lives in a damp home.

Emotional Factors These may act on their own or in combination with allergic factors. The emotional stress may be excitement of a pleasant or of an unpleasant kind. When emotional factors play a part, control of the asthma depends on making sure that the reasons for the stress are minimized. Children sometimes do better away from home, not because the air suits them in another part of the country, but because they are away from the cause of their stress. There is no point in moving to a new home in an attempt to find air that suits the child, except that asthmatics usually improve in the dust-free air of mountainous areas. Moving to a new home could make a child's asthma worse by increasing the family stresses—his father's new job might be less rewarding both in interest and financially. When I worked in Plymouth, England, I saw several children whose asthma was no better despite the move to what was hoped to be the better climate of Devon.

Treatment

The treatment for individual attacks consists of antispasmodic drugs, like Salbutamol or Ventolin, which relieve the symptoms of bronchial spasm. Cortisone may be used just to stop an acute attack or given over a long period to prevent attacks. The inhalation of special powder called sodium cromolyn, using an inhaler, is also used as a long-term method of treatment to prevent attacks. If infection is a factor, appropriate drugs will be given. Tonsils or adenoids are removed only for the same reasons as in other children and not just because the child has asthma.

Respiratory therapy is an important basic treatment for all children with asthma. The aim is to reduce the frequency and duration of attacks as well as to prevent permanent chest deformity, particularly pigeon chest, which can result from repeated attacks.

The whole approach to the child with asthma and his family should be that asthma is a nuisance but not an illness. By accepting it merely as a nuisance, so that it upsets his normal life less severely, the child will hasten the natural improvement that occurs as he gets older, particularly if he is also receiving respiratory therapy (p. 466).

Infantile Eczema

This problem does not usually arise before a baby is two or three months old. It is commoner in boys and there is often a family history of a relative who suffers from some kind of allergy—eczema, asthma, or hay fever. Like asthma, eczema is made worse by anything that upsets the child emotionally.

Symptoms

The trouble usually starts as an irritating red patch on the cheeks and forehead, which in severe cases becomes moist from acute inflammation, particularly when scratched. The rash may spread to cover most of the body, especially the creases. There is often dandruff on the head, and it is this that leads to inflamed cracks behind the ears. Severe eczema causes enormous discomfort; the unfortunate baby's continual need to scratch opens the skin to infection and makes it ooze. His poor mother has to try to stop him from scratching; she has a miserable and frustrated baby who looks pretty awful as well.

Because it is an allergic condition, there is no "cure" for eczema, but a great deal can be done to prevent it and to keep it down. Some children with eczema later develop asthma, and when the two occur in the same child there is a tendency for one to improve when the other gets worse. The reason for this is unknown.

Causes and Remedies

Infantile eczema is commoner in babies fed on cow's milk than those fed on breast milk. Total breast feeding for six months has been shown to reduce the chance of later eczema in those babies at risk. If sensitivity to cow's milk seems to be a possible cause, particularly if the rash began with a change from breast to cow's milk, the baby can be fed with milk containing soya bean instead of cow's milk protein.

Extensive tests to determine the cause of the sensitivity are seldom helpful, but any food that seems to make the skin worse must be avoided. Soap and water seem to irritate the affected skin, so it is preferable to clean it with cotton balls soaked in olive or mineral oil instead. Scratchy, rough, or fluffy materials like wool should not be worn next to the skin.

For severe eczema your doctor will probably prescribe cortisone ointment to keep down the inflammation. Cortisone has revolutionized the treatment of eczema. If the skin is weeping you may be given cortisone as a lotion to dab on, since an ointment would not get through to such severely inflamed skin. If the eczema is mild the doctor may try a tar ointment first.

Your doctor may give you an emulsifying ointment to make a lather in the bath and so reduce the harmful effect of ordinary water. As an alternative, two tablespoonfuls of sodium bicarbonate can be added to the bath.

Preventing Scratching

As well as dealing directly with the skin problem, you have to learn how to deal with your child, how to prevent him from scratching without driving you both insane. The best way is by distracting his attention from the itching, giving him so much else to do that he forgets about it. Organizing nonstop amusement is extremely hard work, because it means you may never be able to leave him playing by himself, even when he wants to be alone, but have to take him around the house and be ready to stop him from scratching at the first sign. This is a tedious addition to the strains of living with a toddler; the only comfort is that your child would probably insist on accompanying you everywhere at this age even without eczema.

With the help of the remedies your doctor provides to control the condition, and with luck, the itching phases should not last too long. A sedative may be prescribed to reduce the irritation in the early stages of eczema. Meanwhile, keep your child's fingernails short. If you find it impossible to distract him from scratching, it may be simpler to use cardboard splints. These are bandaged to his arms so that he cannot scratch but can still use his hands to play. A baby with very severe eczema involving a large part of his body may be admitted to the hospital for treatment—and to give his mother a rest.

Consolations

Most children grow out of the tendency to severe eczema in the first two or three years of life. In some it disappears altogether and in others the only traces remaining are patches in the creases in front of the elbows and behind the knees.

Eczema is not catching and leaves no scars—this at least is some consolation. Sometimes the skin may be left rougher than normal.

Vaccination

A child with eczema must not be vaccinated until his skin is completely healed, nor must he come into contact with anyone who has just been vaccinated. The reason for this is that the virus used for vaccination can spread on unhealthy skin.

Urticaria (Hives)

This condition looks like the rash produced by nettle stings: lots of small white wheals surrounded by reddened skin, or perhaps fewer but larger wheals. Occasionally, in a severe attack, the wheals are so big that they join up, forming a large raised pale area.

Urticaria itches furiously but does not usually last long; the wheals disappear in a few hours. However, other wheals may appear, with the result that a child has urticaria over a period of days or weeks. A person may get only one or two attacks in a lifetime, so if your child suddenly comes out in irritating bumps that soon disappear and do not reappear regularly, you need do no more than help relieve the itching.

Remedies

Dab on calamine lotion (an older child can be given the bottle and cotton balls to use whenever he wants to) and add two tablespoons of sodium bicarbonate to your child's bath water. In severe cases, where itching is persistent, the doctor may prescribe antiallergic drugs (antihistamines), though unfortunately these help only a few of the sufferers.

Causes

If the urticaria keeps coming back it is necessary to hunt for the cause of the sensitivity. Possible causes of urticaria include allergy to various foods, such as strawberries or shellfish; allergy to drugs, such as aspirin or penicillin; and reaction to insect bites. Emotional tension can also produce urticaria. Several factors may be at work together but the cause is often not discovered. Fortunately urticaria, although intensely annoying, is not a dangerous complaint.

Angioneurotic Edema

This is a less common disorder related to urticaria. A large area of skin suddenly swells up to form a large white wheal. The eyelid, lip, or some other part of the face, or the penis, are commonly affected. The cause can seldom be found, but the swelling goes down in a few hours. It is only dangerous if the larynx is affected and breathing becomes obstructed. This is very rare, and your child's difficulty in breathing would make you rush to the doctor anyway.

Papular Urticaria

Papular urticaria is common among children of all ages, but especially between six months and three years. It consists of red blotches and white wheals which differ from ordinary urticaria in that there is a round spot in the center topped with a blister of clear fluid. They may appear anywhere on the body but mainly on the trunk, arms and legs. Itching causes scratching and this may lead to impetigo (pp. 497–98). The blotches or wheals go away in a few hours but the spots may last longer.

Apart from looking different from ordinary urticaria, papular urticaria has a different cause. In most cases it is due to sensitivity to fleas from cat, dog, or bird rather than the human variety. The child may not actually be bitten by the fleas; mere contact with them, even if they are dead, is sufficient to produce the reaction. The child is sensitive to the protein in the body of the flea.

Papular urticaria occurs most often in summer, when cats suffer most from fleas. Dust the animal with antiflea powder and put a flea collar on the dog or cat. Put calamine lotion on the child's bumps; give him a bottle of his own so that he can dab it on whenever he wants to—this may discourage him from scratching. If impetigo does result, it must be treated (see impetigo, pp. 497–98). Your doctor may decide that antihistamine drugs are worth a trial.

40

The Diabetic Child

Diabetes Mellitus ("Sugar Diabetes")

Not many children get diabetes. However, the disease almost always strikes suddenly in childhood, sometimes so suddenly that a mother can tell the doctor the exact hour when her child showed the first symptoms.

Symptoms

The main symptoms are intense thirst and a greatly increased output of pale urine (some children start bed-wetting again). Some of the children develop abdominal pain and vomiting; the illness can therefore be mistaken for a stomach upset until the doctor tests the urine and finds that it contains sugar, indicating diabetes. In some children, the first sign is drowsiness, leading to loss of consciousness.

There is no need to worry that a healthy child who always drinks a lot and passes larger quantities of urine than his friends is developing diabetes. Some people drink more than others, or there may be a perfectly good explanation, like hot weather or a salty meal, to account for a child's sudden thirst. Output of urine may also vary from day to day—for example, a child visits the bathroom every few minutes when he is nervous about the start of a new school year.

The onset of diabetes in a child can cause difficult behavior. Such a child needs to have his change in behavior (and possibly its punishments) explained to him, so that he is not muddled into believing he has developed diabetes as a punishment for his bad behavior. A similar problem can occur if a child is admitted to the hospital feeling relatively well and is discovered to have diabetes. This may lead him to believe he has "caught" diabetes in the hospital.

Causes

Diabetes is caused by failure of part of the pancreas, a gland in the abdomen. The pancreas has two main tasks: one is to produce a juice, which it pours into the intestine to aid digestion; the other is to manufacture insulin, which passes straight into the blood. Insulin is the hormone or chemical messenger that deals with the sugar in the blood. Part of the sugar eaten is burned up as fuel to provide energy;

the rest is stored in the liver as glycogen, to be turned back into sugar when needed.

Lack of insulin, as in diabetes, causes a build-up of sugar in the blood because the sugar that is not required for energy cannot be stored in the liver. It passes out of the body in the urine, where it can be found on testing. Simple blood and urine tests are therefore used to diagnose diabetes. If left untreated, diabetes affects the body's ability to deal with the other two main constituents of food—fat and protein.

Treatment: Insulin Injections

All children with diabetes require insulin. Some adults can be treated by means of a strict diet and medicines by mouth, but because children are growing, the amount of food they eat should not be restricted in this way. The insulin has to be given by injection, since if it is taken by mouth it is destroyed in the stomach. It has to be given daily at regular times, which will vary according to the child and to the type of insulin that suits him best. Mothers are taught how to do urine tests and injections, but children can be shown how to do these for themselves when still very young. This enables them to be independent, a vital aspect of the management of diabetes.

Some restrictions on the diet may be necessary, according to the individual child's needs, but the tendency today is to allow as much freedom as possible, so that the child feels less unlike other children. By helping your child to understand the reasons for the restrictions on his diet, thus encouraging him to feel responsible for obeying them, you can avoid the need for hovering over him to see he sticks to the rules, which is bound to make him feel antagonistic. Parents have to be aware that one of the greatest difficulties for their child is that he is having to control himself in order to control his diabetes at a time when he finds being controlled particularly difficult.

The Child's Future

Diabetes cannot be cured, but the child can lead a completely normal life. People with diabetes have reached the top in all fields—politics, literature, music, even sports. The regular insulin injections and the need to look out for warning signs that more sugar or more insulin is required will become a familiar routine, although it is a mistake to underestimate the upset it can cause your child at first. Understandably, children resent feeling different and being unable to gorge themselves on candy like other children. You have to avoid becoming depressed and too concerned about your child, at the same time remaining alert enough to control the condition and keep him healthy. The problem is to reduce the psychological effect on the child of living with a permanent disorder without encouraging physical hazards: to help him take his condition for granted instead of allowing it to dominate his life. Explain the situation in advance to people who do not know him so that he is given some help in resisting the temptation of sweet foods at parties, for instance. When he is older he will prefer to deal with his problems himself.

41

Problems Affecting the Heart

Murmurs and "Holes in the Heart"

Innocent Murmurs

When your doctor listens to your child's heart he is checking whether the sounds he hears are of the normal number and character. A murmur is an extra sound, often like a musical note. Although it may indicate something wrong in the structure of the heart, it is often heard in normal hearts—especially in young children. In a nursery full of newborn babies, about half of them would be found to have heart murmurs if these were listened for very carefully; most disappear. An older child is sometimes found to have a murmur during a routine school physical examination or when he is being examined for a cough or cold.

The majority of murmurs heard during routine testing are found to be "innocent"—in other words, there is nothing wrong with the structure of the heart despite the presence of murmur. All it means is that the blood can be heard going around inside the heart.

Investigating a Murmur An "innocent" murmur varies in strength with the position of the child. A murmur that is due to something structurally wrong, such as a "hole in the heart," does not vary with position. When the doctor first hears the murmur he will therefore move your child from lying down to sitting up in order to decide whether it is innocent or not. He will usually be able to reassure parents that all is well as soon as he has finished his examination. Sometimes, however, a school doctor decides to refer a child for further tests. Do not be too worried if this happens; if there were something wrong with your child's heart due to congenital disease, it would most likely have been discovered much earlier in his life.

When there is doubt as to whether a murmur is innocent or is caused by a hole in one of the walls inside the heart, an X-ray of the heart can help. An electrical test—using the electrocardiogram—is also likely to be carried out to decide whether the electrical waves produced by the heart are normal.

Holes in the Heart

Holes in the heart are present at birth: they do not develop later. It makes it easier to understand if you think of the heart as a four-room house with two upstairs rooms—the auricles—and two downstairs rooms—the ventricles. The hole may lie in the wall between the two auricles (the upstairs rooms) or in the wall between the two ventricles (the downstairs rooms). If any doubt remains as to where the hole is, further tests can be made.

Helping the Child

Children with a congenital abnormality of the heart do not need to be told to rest. They are much better off if they are left to find their own level of activity; the majority of children will be able to do everything. A severe heart lesion will stop a child taking part in sports, but he should still be told he can do what he feels able to do. In days gone by, when doctors prescribed the amount of exercise that could be undertaken, the child often became so concerned about his heart that his fears turned him into a "cardiac invalid." It is easier to make a person, including a young child, anxious about his heart than about any other organ.

The heart is a complicated organ; it is not surprising, therefore, that sometimes it is structurally imperfect. However, even when it has an abnormal structure, its muscle is still normal. A hole in one of the inside walls will make the heart less efficient but only when efficiency is measured in extreme degrees—for example, the child might take a second or two longer to run a hundred yards than he would without the hole. It makes little difference to most aspects of living.

Treatment

Only recently have we realized that quite a number of holes in the heart close of their own accord. Nowadays, surgery is used less often, because the doctor will want to see if spontaneous closure occurs.

Parents sometimes wish doctors would get on and do something; but if a doctor does not operate at once on a child with a congenital heart defect, it means he is waiting for the best time to begin treatment from the point of view of the child and of the defect. For example, whenever possible, investigations that involve putting tubes (catheters) into the heart are left until a baby is older. Provided the heart is not under stress, it is safer to let him grow up a bit; the tests can then be carried out with less risk and greater efficiency. So if there seems to be a delay in the start of treatment, parents can be sure this is in their child's best interests.

"Blue Babies"

This condition results from severe forms of congenital heart malformation. The baby is blue because there is mixing of blood from the two sides of his heart. Blood becomes blue as it circulates around the body and has its oxygen removed. It becomes red again when it is pumped through the lungs to receive a fresh supply of oxygen before going around the body once more. A hole in the heart can cause some of the blue blood to be sent around the body without going to the lungs first for a new supply of oxygen; this makes the baby blue.

With modern surgery the outlook for blue babies is vastly improved. Today the condition is usually noticed early, even though not all such babies are "blue" at birth. A murmur may be heard on routine examination or the baby may become short of breath while feeding. This is quite different from the way a normal baby takes rests during a feeding without being short of breath (pp. 66, 73).

Penicillin Cover for Dental Extractions

Whatever the cause of an abnormality of the heart, whether it is congenital or due to rheumatic heart disease (below), there is a risk that removal of the teeth can force germs into the bloodstream which might light on the abnormal part of the heart, causing inflammation. To reduce this risk it is now the practice for a child with such an abnormality to be given penicillin immediately before the teeth are extracted. This procedure is also carried out before any operation entailing a similar risk, for example, the removal of tonsils or adenoids.

Rheumatic Fever

Rheumatic fever is a hypersensitivity reaction to infection with the streptococcus, the site of the infection usually being the throat. If the original throat infection is treated, the likelihood of rheumatic fever is reduced.

Today "strep throat" is treated with antibiotics, and as a result few children get rheumatic fever. Those who do must be given penicillin for long enough to prevent further streptococcal infections, since rheumatic fever can affect the heart (see rheumatic heart disease, p. 517). The doctor has to make sure he does not miss rheumatic fever, thereby failing to give the penicillin preventive treatment. Penicillin is usually given until the child is safely through adolescence; it has no side effects and the streptococcus is incapable of developing resistance to it (p. 393).

Penicillin is one reason why rheumatic heart disease is now relatively uncommon in Western countries. Rheumatic fever is still a major problem in developing countries. Medical students used to be taught that rheumatic fever was essentially a disease of damp, temperate climates such as the United Kingdom. This is just one more fact that has had to be erased from the old medical textbooks: rheumatic fever is now mainly a disease of the tropics, being related to poverty and overcrowding and not to dampness.

Symptoms

Rheumatic fever produces painful inflamed joints. It confines its activity to the large joints—shoulders, elbows, wrists, hips, knees and ankles—and very characteristically "flits" from one joint to another, causing symptoms in the affected joint for two to three days before moving on. The child is ill and feverish—so rheumatic fever should not be confused with "growing pains" (p. 542). Moreover, whereas the pain of rheumatic fever is felt in the joints, growing pains are felt in the muscle, particularly the calf or thigh.

The child with rheumatic fever will already have been ill with a sore throat, scarlet fever, or tonsillitis some ten to twelve days earlier. You will have consulted your doctor for the original complaint, but consult him again if your child does not make an uninterrupted recovery, and particularly if he gets painful joints.

Rheumatic Heart Disease

Today the number of children with rheumatic heart disease in which the heart valves are damaged is minute, thanks to better living conditions and to penicillin. Streptococcal throat infection, the usual precursor of rheumatic fever, is nipped in the bud by treatment with penicillin (see above). Even if a child does develop rheumatic fever, the chances of its going on to affect the heart are less, since recurrent attacks that increase the risk of damage to the heart can be prevented by giving penicillin.

42

Blood Disorders

Blood contains red cells that carry oxygen, white cells that deal with infection, and platelets that help in clotting. These three ingredients are contained in a liquid called plasma.

You cannot judge the health of your child's blood by the appearance of his skin; whether or not a child has pink cheeks depends on how close his small blood vessels are to the surface. Family coloring varies—a family of pale faces is not less healthy than a family of apple cheeks.

Anemia

This means there is a lack of hemoglobin, the substance in the red cells that transports the oxygen from the air in the lungs to every part of the body.

To discover whether or not a child is anemic the doctor looks at the lining of the eye (the conjunctiva) by pulling down the lower eyelid. He also looks at the inside of the lips and at the palms of the hands. The color of the mucous membranes (the conjunctiva and the inside of the lips) gives a true picture, since they do not vary between individuals as does skin color; the reason is that you are looking much more directly at the blood itself in these membranes than in the skin. If the doctor is in doubt he will have the child's blood tested for its level of hemoglobin.

Causes: Lack of Iron in the Diet

Hemoglobin contains iron. The commonest cause of anemia is a lack of iron, usually because there is not enough in the diet. In the fetus, iron is stored mainly in the last months of pregnancy; a normal baby gets enough iron from this source to last the first six months of life. However, a preterm baby lacks his full store of iron because he did not stay long enough in the uterus to receive it all; therefore he has to be given iron supplements to prevent the development of anemia. These are usually started when he is one month old and are continued until he is on a mixed diet containing enough iron for his daily needs (see low birth weight, p. 139).

A mother would have to be very anemic during pregnancy for her baby to be born anemic at the end of the full term; he acts rather like a parasite, taking what he needs from her. Good prenatal care ensures that any iron deficiency in a mother is corrected before it can affect her baby.

Repeated Infections

Another cause of anemia is severe or repeated infections. A vicious circle may begin—the infection leads to anemia, and an anemic child is more likely to get another infection. Infection affects the absorption, storage, and use of iron by the body, so it hits in every direction. However, do not assume automatically that because your child is a little pale after an illness he is anemic. As I have already said, you cannot tell by looking. Your doctor will arrange a hemoglobin test if he thinks it likely that your child has become anemic from his illness.

Treatment

An iron deficiency anemia is easily treated by iron medicine, which is given as tablets or in liquid form.

Rarer Causes

Occasional causes of anemia are severe loss of blood from an accident or blood destruction from certain diseases.

Leukemia

Leukemia is cancer of the white blood cells. Pallor is one symptom, but the pallor of leukemia is very severe and the disease produces other symptoms as well, so paleness by itself need not make you frightened about the possibility of leukemia. Leukemia produces easy bleeding from gums and other mucous surfaces, and there is excessive bruising for no good reason. Small children knock and bruise themselves frequently during play but the bruising of leukemia is far more extensive than this ordinary bruising. A pale child with the occasional bruise has not got leukemia.

Modern treatment can always prolong a child's life, and cures occur. Fortunately, it is a rare disease, although you might think it was common because of the publicity. If you are frightened that your child may have leukemia, mention it to your doctor. He is used to this fear and it is no problem for him to arrange a blood test that can set your mind completely at rest.

X-rays and Leukemia

Many parents will have heard that X-raying a mother during pregnancy increases the risk of leukemia in her child. Because this information is widespread, it must be emphasized that the risk of leukemia, even in children who were X-rayed in the uterus, is still very small. However, because of the risk, doctors do not order unnecessary X-rays during pregnancy. When an X-ray is taken—for example, to check for twins or to find out which way around the baby is lying— the risk to both mother and child is very much smaller than the risk they would run if the information obtained from the X-ray were not available (see p. 9).

43

Measles and the Infectious Fevers

The common infectious fevers are measles, mumps, whooping cough, scarlet fever, chickenpox, and German measles. They are naturally thought of as childhood complaints because, being so infectious, they are usually caught during childhood, particularly once a child starts mixing with other children.

Up to the age of about six months, babies have some immunity to the infectious fevers their mothers have had, since antibodies in the mother's blood can cross the placenta into the baby's circulation. These antibodies gradually disappear from the baby's blood during the first six months of life. This "passive" immunization (see p. 260), as it is termed, does not apply to whooping cough, since the antibodies to this disease are too large to cross the placental barrier. "Active" immunization is the term used for the immunization program discussed on pages 259 to 264. Protection is not yet available against all the other infectious fevers.

All these infections are spread directly from one child to the next, usually in minute particles carried in the air from the breath of the infected child. Second attacks are unusual, so that the probable explanation for a so-called second attack is that one of the attacks was incorrectly diagnosed.

Quarantine and Isolation

Quarantine is the length of time a child who has been in contact with one of these infections has to be isolated from people who have not had it, in order not to infect them. A contact is most infectious toward the end of the incubation period and in the early stages of the disease. The incubation period is the interval between catching the illness and developing its outward signs.

The strict quarantine regulations that used to cause so much loss of schooling are now known to have had little effect on the spread of infection. Most schools, therefore, no longer insist on children staying away from school throughout the incubation period but only when they begin to show signs of the illness. However, schools and institutions differ about their rules for quarantine, so you should ask the school for details.

Taking Reasonable Precautions

Warn parents of children who are visiting you about an infection in your home. Small babies should be protected from catching it and children who are already ill should not be exposed to another illness. Of course the children should have been immunized.

Coping with Infectious Fevers

If you suspect your child is developing one of these fevers, do not take him to the doctor's office and risk spreading the infection; telephone your doctor so that he can decide what to do. There may be no special treatment for the fever but the doctor can confirm your diagnosis and advise you how to look after your child.

Most often, your child can be left to set the pace as far as staying in bed and appetite are concerned (see the sick child at home, pp. 395f.). Consult your doctor again if your child does not make a steady recovery or if you are worried about anything, a rise in temperature, for instance. You must get him checked by the doctor if he remains persistently unwell or has a symptom such as a continuing cough.

Disinfecting toys and eating utensils is unnecessary and ineffective (see the sick child at home, p. 395). You need not keep him away from the rest of the family, unless you have a particular reason for trying to prevent the infection from running around the family—but you are probably too late in any case (see above). If you cannot care for your child at home because he is too ill or because there is no one who can be there all day, he will have to be sent to the hospital.

Measles

Measles is highly infectious; you should take it seriously because some of the complications are severe. Measles tends to come in epidemics, which affect so many susceptible children that two years used to elapse before the next wave because most children had already had it, but immunization has altered this.

Children are particularly liable to catch measles between the ages of one and six years; this is because passive immunity from their mothers wears off during the first year, and because it is a very infectious fever, they will probably catch it the first time they meet it. Vaccination to prevent measles should be carried out as soon as passive immunity has been lost (see p. 263). Vaccination is getting rid of the epidemics that used to occur. In developing countries, where vaccination is not yet available, measles will remain a hazard for many years. The illness is more serious in children under three.

Gamma Globulin

If you have a young child who has not been vaccinated and who has been exposed to measles, your doctor should be given the opportunity to decide whether he should be given gamma globulin, the blood ingredient that contains antibodies. This is prepared from the blood of people who have had the illness, and it can prevent an attack or lessen its severity. Gamma globulin is expensive and in short supply; it is generally only considered for the very young or for children whose resistance to infection is lowered—because they are already suffering from another illness, for instance.

Symptoms

Measles is spread by droplet infection from the nose and throat. The incubation period is from ten to fifteen days. The disease is probably catching from the first day the symptoms appear, which is usually three or four days before the main illness. The first signs are that your child seems to have a bad cold, with a running nose, cough, and red eyes. He may be feverish, he may vomit, and he may have diarrhea. He may seem better for a day or two, but then feels ill again. A few children are mildly ill throughout the incubation period. Your doctor may confirm suspected measles by looking in his mouth to see if there are small white spots, called Koplik's spots, on the inside of his cheeks.

The Rash

This usually comes out on the third to fifth day, but is sometimes much later. It begins behind the ears, spreads to the face and then to the rest of the body. You will see small, dark red spots which soon become irregular blotches. At this stage, your child should start to feel better. While the rash is developing he may feel very miserable, with high fever and possibly delirium.

Caring for Your Child

The rash does not itch and needs no treatment. If your child's eyes are crusted, wash them with boiled water and cotton balls; your doctor will decide if special treatment is necessary (in the case of severe conjunctivitis). There is no need to darken the room unless your child is troubled by the light.

Let him rinse out his mouth, since it may become dry and uncomfortable and his tongue may feel sore. He will probably not be hungry at the height of the illness, so leave the question of food to him; the only essential is that he has enough to drink. Similarly, let him decide whether he wishes to stay in bed or to get up (see the sick child at home, p. 396).

Complications

Complications should be suspected if your child does not get steadily better once the rash fades. If he seems worse for any reason, for example, if his temperature goes up, call your doctor, since he can treat complications. Measles affects the air passages, and a secondary infection such as bronchitis may occur, especially if the child is under two. Infection from the sore throat associated with measles may spread and cause earache.

Of all the infectious childhood fevers, measles is the most likely to be followed by inflammation of the brain (encephalitis), though this is still very rare. Complications are more severe and more frequent in developing countries because the general standard of health of native children is lower as a result of malnutrition, anemia, and malaria. The European or American child in the tropics has no more severe an attack than he would have had at home.

If your child fails to pick up after the illness or has a persistent cough, your doctor may order an X-ray to check that chest complications have not remained; in particular, he will want to check that the lungs are fully expanded. The lungs consist of thousands of balloons; the phlegm that collects during any lung infection may block the channel to some of the balloons so that they become deflated, because no air is going in and the air already there is absorbed into the blood. This is known as a "collapse," and the collapsed portion of the lung can be a continual source of trouble if it is not immediately made to expand. Respiratory therapy is used for this.

Back to Normal

The official period of isolation is ten days from the beginning of the rash, so your child will not usually be allowed back to school before this. However, once the symptoms have gone it is unlikely that he is infectious and he can start leading a normal life when he wants to; use your intuition to decide what seems reasonable.

German Measles (Rubella)

This has no connection with ordinary measles; it is less infectious and much milder. It spreads by droplet infection and tends to affect older children. It is uncertain how long the child remains infectious, but isolation for seven days after the rash has appeared is recommended to prevent the infection from spreading.

Symptoms

The incubation period is fourteen to twenty-one days. Your child may feel slightly unwell for a day or two before the rash appears. Your doctor will look for enlarged glands, particularly at the back of the neck; this is the characteristic feature of the illness. The glands sometimes remain swollen for several weeks afterward.

The Rash

The rash is often the first sign; it starts behind the ears and on the forehead, then spreads over the body. It lasts only one or two days, sometimes fading before the doctor arrives. The flat pink spots may merge so that the body merely looks flushed. Fever is mild, or there may be none, and complications are rare.

Why an Accurate Diagnosis Is Important

German measles causes such slight upset to a child that it would not really be important at all were it not for the damage it can cause to the developing fetus if an expectant mother catches it in the first four months of pregnancy. Because of this, always let your doctor know if you suspect German measles, which can easily be confused with a mild attack of measles or scarlet fever (see p. 10).

Accurate diagnosis is essential, so that your child can be kept away from any expectant mothers in the early months of pregnancy. Any mother who has already been in contact with your child should discuss the problem with her doctor; an injection of gamma globulin may give some protection to the baby (see p. 523).

The other reason for an accurate diagnosis is that a woman needs to know if she has already had the disease, in case she is later exposed to it when pregnant. One attack of German measles usually gives protection for life. Vaccination is now available (p. 263).

Roseola Infantum

This mainly affects children under three. It is easy to confuse with German measles, but it has one striking characteristic: it starts with a raised temperature, which lasts for about three days, and as this falls to normal the rash appears. This is made up of small pink spots. There are no complications apart from the risk of convulsions from high fever (p. 614). No special treatment is needed. The disease often goes unrecognized because it is so mild.

Chickenpox

Chickenpox is one of the most contagious but also one of the mildest of the infectious fevers; it mainly affects children under ten. It spreads by droplet infection. The spots are not infectious, since they do not contain a virus. A patient is infectious for seven days.

The virus causing chickenpox is the same one that causes shingles (herpes zoster). Because of this, an adult with shingles can give chickenpox to a child.

Symptoms

The incubation period is usually two weeks. The child may be slightly unwell for a day or two before the spots appear, but frequently spots are the first sign. They come out in crops for three or four days, so that soon they are present in all stages of development. At first they resemble dark red pimples, but in a few hours blisters form, looking like drops of water on the skin. These are fragile, and are easily rubbed off by clothing; they dry into scabs, which drop off after about ten days, leaving shallow pink scars. These soon fade and disappear.

Some children have so few spots that the illness passes unnoticed, whereas others are covered with spots, in the mouth, nose, and ears, as well as on the scalp and body. The arms and legs are least affected. If there are a lot of spots, the child is likely to have severe irritation and to want to scratch, but scratching the spots infects them more deeply and makes them more liable to leave a permanent scar.

Treatment

These infected spots are the only common complication; therefore the aim of treatment is to relieve itching. Dabbing the spots with calamine lotion dries them up and reduces the irritation. A bath containing potassium permanganate has the same effect, although the bathtub and the child will be temporarily stained brown. A cupful of bicarbonate of soda or cornstarch dissolved in the bath is also soothing. Keep your child's nails short to reduce the damage from scratching.

Whooping Cough (Pertussis)

This is possibly the most deadly of the infectious fevers. It is especially serious in babies under a year old. Since babies get no immunity to whooping cough from their mothers, they should be immunized as early as possible (see pp. 260–62). Keep your young baby away from anyone with whooping cough. Prompt diagnosis of the illness is essential.

Symptoms

The usual incubation period is seven to ten days and the child remains infectious for twenty-eight days from the start of symptoms. A cough is usually the first symptom, often accompanied by a clear watery discharge from the nose. At first there is nothing distinctive about the cough, but after a few days it becomes paroxysmal, that is, it occurs in runs, so that the child coughs several times on the same breath. The characteristic of whooping cough is that the cough catches the child by surprise, before he has time to take in a breath, as happens normally when you cough. This makes him very distressed from lack of air in the lungs. The "whoop" is a trick whereby air is replaced as rapidly as possible; the noise is made as the air rushes through the larynx, which has not yet had time to open fully. Young children, particularly babies, seldom acquire the knack of whooping and are therefore more distressed by the disease than older children. This lack of a whoop makes diagnosis more difficult, but your doctor knows that a paroxysmal cough in children, particularly if it is associated with vomiting, is most often due to whooping cough. Let him know if your baby has been in contact with whooping cough, since this will help him to make the diagnosis.

Children who have been immunized can catch the disease, but it will be milder. It is probably the commonest cause of a long-lasting cough in young children who have been immunized. Unfortunately, the germ is hard to discover, so that the cause is hard to prove; but such children are just as infectious as children who have not been immunized.

Complications

Middle ear infections and bronchopneumonia are the most common complications. If your child goes on coughing for more than a month, take him to your doctor; he will probably decide to X-ray the chest to check that the lungs are fully expanded (see measles, pp. 522f.). Some children go on coughing for weeks, often continuing to whoop out of habit; they may also whoop with their next cough. This probably accounts for reported "second attacks" of whooping cough.

Treatment

Antibiotics are effective against the germ that causes whooping cough, but only if given early in the disease. Nothing has yet been discovered that effectively suppresses the cough; cough mixtures make no difference. Respiratory therapy helps, so your doctor may show you how to tap your child's chest while he is lying head down; this helps to shift the phlegm, making it easier for him to cough it up (see respiratory therapy, p. 466). If your child is frightened during a bout of coughing, hold him securely and calmly.

Vomiting can make feeding a serious problem. Your child is more likely to keep food down if you offer it immediately after he has been sick. Frequent small meals rather than a few large ones reduce the risk of vomiting. Don't be afraid to take your child outside in fine weather—it will do him good.

Mumps

This is usually a mild illness in children and it is uncommon in children under five. It is not highly infectious, so it sometimes attacks adults who, though in contact with it during childhood, did not catch it. It is caused by a virus and it affects mainly the salivary glands, especially the parotid gland, which lies in front of the ear; other glands can also be involved.

Symptoms

The incubation period is about three weeks. Your child may feel unwell for one or two days beforehand, but a swollen and tender parotid gland is usually the first sign. One side often swells up a day or two before the other and sometimes one side only is affected. Since the parotid gland produces saliva, the lack of saliva resulting from the disease makes the mouth dry. Ask your doctor to confirm the diagnosis, since the swelling can be due to other causes.

Complications

There are various possible complications, the most common being inflammation of the testicles at or after puberty. Although sterility rarely results, men and adolescent boys should try to avoid contact with mumps if they have not already had it.

Occasionally, mumps meningitis develops some ten days after the onset of the illness. The symptoms are high fever, delirium, stiff neck, and sore throat. Fortunately, complete recovery is the rule. One sequel, which is easily overlooked, is deafness. If you wonder whether your child is hearing normally after an attack of mumps don't ignore your suspicions; ask your doctor to check his hearing. Such deafness is usually total and permanent but nearly always affects one ear only.

Second attacks of mumps are rare. Even if only one side of the face swells, the antibodies in the bloodstream give total immunity.

Treatment

There is no special treatment for the disease. The inflammation makes opening the mouth difficult and painful, so give your child nourishing drinks, such as milk containing a beaten egg, to ensure he has enough calories.

Lack of saliva is not only uncomfortable but can lead to infection in the mouth; for this reason keep your child's mouth clean by rinsing, by giving him frequent drinks, and by cleaning his teeth after food. If he is in a lot of pain give him acetaminophen. Warm gauze or a large scarf around the neck is comforting.

The swelling may be small or large and varies in the time it takes to subside. There may be slight fever, but often a child remains fairly well except that his mouth feels uncomfortable. Adults feel more ill with mumps.

The official period of isolation is seven days from the disappearance of the swelling.

Scarlet Fever

Scarlet fever is caused by a strain of streptococcus that can produce a rash as well as a sore throat. From the practical point of view, scarlet fever is just a streptococcal sore throat with a rash. Treatment and complications are the same as for a child suffering from the sore throat only (see p. 455).

Symptoms

The incubation period is two to five days. The illness may start suddenly with loss of appetite, vomiting, and fever. Some children complain of stomach ache, possibly due to glands in the abdomen being swollen. Pain in the throat is uncommon and may not be noticed. At this stage, the child appears to be getting tonsillitis.

The Rash

On about the second day a rash appears, starting around the neck and on the chest and spreading over the whole body. It is composed of tiny red spots on a flushed skin. The area of skin around the mouth remains pale and without spots; this area of pallor is so striking that it is one of the particular signs looked for by doctors to help make the diagnosis. After about a week the skin flakes off over each spot. This makes the whole skin look scaly.

Treatment and Complications

It is usual for the doctor to give antibiotics or sulphonamides to cut short the illness or at any rate make it milder. It is important that the infection is treated, however mild it seems, because in a few children a streptococcal infection leads to the serious complications of acute nephritis (inflammation of the kidneys, p. 446) or rheumatic fever (pp. 516–17), as well as the more common sequel of middle ear infection (p. 459).

Poliomyelitis (Polio)

This is highly infectious, but as a result of immunization it is no longer a problem in Western countries. Anyone traveling to the tropics should be immunized, because the disease is still very common there; I wish this was a legal requirement.

Infection is spread by droplets from an infected person, and also through the stools. The incubation period is up to three weeks.

Symptoms

The great majority of children have a mild illness only, resembling a cold or influenza, which is likely to go undiagnosed unless there is polio in the community. Ten percent of cases may be serious, with meningitis or paralysis. Anyone who has been in contact with polio must therefore be isolated for three weeks.

Diphtheria

Diphtheria is a serious disease, which used to cause many deaths. Immunization has practically eliminated it from Western countries, since the immunized child is fully protected against it. The disease develops a week after exposure, the first symptoms being fever, a sore throat, and hoarseness. It is essential to remember how many children used to die from diphtheria: be sure to get your children immunized and keep this up to date.

Smallpox

This is the most catching of the infectious fevers. It used to occur all over the world but has now been eliminated. Smallpox is caused by a virus that spreads by droplet infection and lives in the scabs, which remain infectious until they disappear. It can be a serious illness, leaving permanent scarring, especially on the face.

Vaccination gives immediate protection, in the unlikely event of anyone being exposed to the disease (see p. 264).

Infectious Mononucleosis (Glandular Fever)

This disease is caused by a virus. It is less common in children, and it is diagnosed more often than it really exists. Glands become enlarged for many reasons and there is no need to be concerned about them unless your child is ill. Moreover, glands of a normal size may look swollen in children because they show up more in a thin neck (see swollen glands, pp. 460–61).

The incubation period is about ten days but this is uncertain because it is only slightly infectious. It usually begins suddenly with a sore throat, which may have ulcers. The glands are very large and the child is feverish. The diagnosis is confirmed by blood tests. There is no special treatment but the severe throat infection may be treated with antibiotics.

Infectious mononucleosis leaves a patient feeling unwell for many weeks. This is particularly the case with adults, but do not be surprised if your child takes some time to get back to his normal self.

Influenza

To a doctor, influenza is an unsatisfactory diagnosis, because diseases like this, which are caused by a virus infection, are so difficult to prove. Only if an epidemic is raging can the diagnosis be at all certain.

Children, fortunately, usually get less severe attacks than adults. The illness commonly starts with a cold and perhaps a sore throat. The child is feverish and feels aches and pains anywhere in the body but especially in the abdomen and sometimes in the legs and arms. Nosebleeding is quite common and the eyes may be inflamed. The whole illness should be over in three to four days. Antibiotics cannot speed recovery, since they do not kill viruses, but your doctor may prescribe them if he suspects that there is a secondary infection with some bacteria.

44

Bone and Joint Disorders

Bowlegs

It is normal for young children to have bowlegs. The condition is most obvious in the first two years of life. It will disappear by itself, so nothing needs to be done about it. The only disease causing bowlegs is rickets, which is rare in Western countries today (see below).

The only point to remember is that thick layers of diaper, bulky enough to cause a small child to walk in a more bowlegged fashion than he would otherwise, may exert sufficient pressure to alter the shape of his legs. In other words, wearing a very bulky diaper all day for several months while learning to walk not only makes a baby look more bowlegged but may actually increase his natural tendency to be bowlegged. Nowadays, few babies need be condemned to such discomfort, since diapers are shaped or can be pinned to minimize bulk between the legs.

Knock-Knees

This also is part of normal development, though in a slightly older age group—three to seven years. A large proportion of children with knock-knees are too fat; being overweight increases the natural tendency to be knock-kneed. Once your child gets thinner, his knock-knees will disappear.

To test whether your child is knock-kneed, put your fingers between his ankles when he is lying on his back with his knees pointing directly at the ceiling. Normally, it is possible to fit two fingers, side by side, between the ankles; more than this indicates knock-knees.

In the past, all sorts of treatment were given for knock-knees— exercises, splints, manipulations and ultraviolet light. None did any good, but they were often credited with success because a natural cure occurs in 95 percent of children by the age of seven years.

Flatfoot

All babies' feet are flat, because of a pad of fat on the inner side of the sole, which later disappears. Babies have fat feet, not flat feet.

Flatfoot in older children is a grossly overrated problem. Feet vary; different types run in families, and it can be more of a problem to have too much arch than "too little." The important thing is not what the foot looks like (ballerinas have flat feet) but what it is like in action. To judge a child's arch, the doctor watches what happens when he is on tiptoe. Try it for yourself and you will see how your child's apparently flat feet are pulled up into a graceful arch. Some toddlers turn their feet out when first learning to walk; this exaggerates the appearance of flatfoot.

There is seldom any benefit from remedial exercises since they have little influence on the shape of a child's feet.

"Pigeon Toes" or Toeing In

Many normal toddlers turn their toes inward when first starting to walk; it seems they can balance better this way. If you are really concerned that, compared with others of his age, your child seems to toe in excessively, consult your doctor. However, the tendency today is away from alterations to shoes or any kind of appliance, because time has proved to be a better corrective. An older child may be encouraged to walk more "correctly" with exercises taught by a physical therapist.

In all problems affecting feet, check that socks as well as shoes fit correctly. Tight socks can cause crowding or clawing of the toes. Some nylon stretch socks may not stretch enough; cotton or wool-mixture socks are best for children.

Bent Toes

"Curly Toes" in Babies

A few babies are born with "curly toes." It is usually the fourth or fifth toe that is bent inward and the condition often runs in the family. Attempts to put it right with adhesive tape are a waste of time, since the toe always reverts to its earlier position when the strapping is removed. However, curly toes seldom cause trouble provided good care is taken to buy wide-fitting shoes which give them plenty of room. Occasionally, the toe may curl under the foot so far that surgical correction is required, but only when the child is older.

Acquired Bent Toes

The bent toes with which many adults are afflicted were not there at birth; they can be the result of wearing badly fitting or too small shoes during childhood, when the bones of the feet are still soft and can literally be bent out of shape. Presentable feet are one practical benefit you can ensure for your children. Take trouble in choosing shoes, buying new ones before the old ones pinch (this applies to socks too).

Posture

You cannot do much to alter your child's posture. Some children always sit up straight, others seldom do, except momentarily, when nagged. Unfortunately, no amount of nagging works for long, and if your child grows up round-shouldered you are not to blame.

The occasional reminder to "sit up straight" is worthwhile, especially if you suspect your child is slumping because of self-consciousness about his height or appearance (see pp. 212–13, 556–57); but also tackle suspected self-consciousness with general reassurance. Continual nagging may make a child feel more defiant or more intimidated, so that he slumps even when he would like to sit up straight. Probably the only time you notice your own posture is at the very moment you open your mouth to tell off your round-shouldered child. You will both sit up—for a moment.

Rickets

This disease does not occur in babies who are totally breast fed, but vitamin D supplements are necessary for those on cow's milk preparations. This is routinely added to cow's milk in the United States. Rickets is now rare, thanks to vitamin D supplements (pp. 181–83), but the risk is always there. A recent outbreak in Glasgow, Scotland, has brought this home. The risk is greatest in the first two years of life because growth is at its fastest and the bones therefore require more vitamin D. The child may feel pain in his limbs.

Rickets makes children irritable and causes softening and bending of the bones. If the disease occurs when a child is crawling, softening of the arm bones causes widening of the wrists. If he is walking, his legs become bowed.

Rickets delays the closure of the anterior fontanel (p. 39). The possibility of rickets therefore has to be considered if the fontanel is still wide open at twelve months. It used to be said that the fontanel should close by eighteen months, but today it is often nearly closed by about twelve months. I suspect the difference is due to the fact that rickets was common in the last century.

Limp

Pain is the commonest reason for a limp. This occurs more often in boys aged between two and twelve years. Since they are usually more active than girls, they are more liable to subject themselves to the mild injury to the hip that causes the limp. The child is not ill, and a few days' rest in bed is all that is needed for the hip to return to normal. If the child is ill, infective arthritis is the more likely cause.

Inequality of the legs will also cause a child to limp. This is more often due to shortening of one limb and can result from earlier poliomyelitis, congenital shortening of a leg bone, cerebral palsy, or injury to the growing end of the bone. Overgrowth of one leg occasionally occurs and is usually due to an abnormality of the blood vessels, leading to an increased blood supply. Apparent inequality of the legs can result from spinal curvature, causing tilting of the pelvis. Whatever the cause of the inequality the child compensates by walking on his toes on the short side and he may also need to tilt down his pelvis on that side.

Instability of the hip joint from congenital dislocation of the hip is a much less common cause of limping nowadays, thanks to early diagnosis (p. 426). A hysterical limp is very rare in children and only diagnosed after the most meticulous examination has excluded all forms of disease.

45

Recurrent Pains

The Interaction of Mind and Body

Illness and Emotion

Every physical illness has some effect on the emotions, causing a degree of emotional "overlay." Mind and body are so closely connected that it is usually as inaccurate to say of an illness "It is all in the body" as it is to claim that "It is all in the mind." Being ill can make you feel miserable and vice versa. Emotional tension and anxiety can have physical repercussions; an example we all experience is a tightly clamped stomach and loss of appetite after receiving bad news. Anger can make us look red as well as see red, and tension can make us run for the bathroom. Having "butterflies in the stomach" when we are anxious about something is all part of the same thing.

It is now many years since a Canadian surgeon made the first studies of the effect of emotion on the stomach. In his laboratory he employed a man who had been shot in the stomach, leaving him with a connection (fistula) between stomach and skin. The result was that some of the lining of the stomach was visible. By making the man angry the scientist could watch his stomach increase its normal waves of movement (peristalsis); its lining thickened and the color changed from its normal pink to red and even mauve. We now know that acute stomach ulcers can result from emotional distress and that these may bleed.

Being aware that our stomachs and intestines react to our feelings with congestion of the lining and increased movement helps our understanding of our bodies. No wonder unfortunate students often get diarrhea on the morning of an exam!

Temperamental Differences in Tolerating Pain and Illness

How a child reacts to pain and illness is therefore affected by his state of mind as well as by the physical discomforts produced by the illness itself. It is not a question of his "strength of character." Some individuals are lucky enough to possess an equable temperament and so find it comparatively easy to tolerate pain; they may also possess a high threshold of pain, meaning that they register less distress from a given amount of pain than other people with a lower threshold. A child who cries readily when hurt is not necessarily a crybaby or a coward compared with his brother who does not cry; he may be more sensitive to pain than his brother—it hurts him more. Perhaps the brother is also better at keeping a stiff upper lip, but this too may be a gift of temperament rather than evidence of superior will power. Extroverts complain more of pain than introverts.

An individual's normal threshold of pain and tolerance of discomfort can be altered by circumstances. If you already feel low, a slight cold makes you feel miserable. But if your spirits are buoyant, it is easy to ignore a blocked-up nose and a tickling throat. It is also possible that we withstand infection better when happy, and succumb to it more readily when "under the weather" emotionally. The children of anxious parents seem to get more colds than the children of parents who worry less about them.

People vary in "emotional lability," that is, in the rapidity and frequency with which their moods change and the degree to which they are affected by events. An emotionally labile person's mood swings would show on a graph as a series of sharp ups and downs, contrasting with the much steadier curve of a nonlabile person. Both extremes have their pros and cons.

Understanding the Ill Child

It is more constructive for parents, and doctors, to appreciate the advantages and difficulties of an individual child's temperament than to wish he were different. Understanding, or trying to understand, your child's temperament helps you to decide if and when he is ill, whether he needs a doctor on a particular occasion, when to give open sympathy and when he needs a brisk show of indifference (see growing pains, p. 542). It will also help you to recognize anything that is worrying him and contributing to an illness.

The Child with Recurrent Symptoms

The link between temperament and bodily symptoms is particularly clear in the recurrent aches and pains that are comparatively common in children—abdominal pains, headaches, and arm and leg pains. Recurrent fever can also come into this category. They tend to strike a child in a regular pattern.

The fact that your child suffers from recurring symptoms of emotional origin does not necessarily mean he is emotionally disturbed, although you should look for and deal with any causes of anxiety in his life. However, it does mean that he reacts to his share of stress in a certain way, producing physical symptoms. It is often found that other members of a family react in a similar way, suffering from recurring "nervous" symptoms such as headaches or indigestion.

Finding the Reason

The doctor needs to find out if recurring physical symptoms reflect recurring emotional patterns in a child's life in order to make a correct diagnosis as well as to be able to advise you and help your child. He has to make sure there is no underlying physical (organic) cause for the symptoms, and, once he is satisfied, you should take his word for it that there is no point in continuing the search for a "physical" cause. Endless investigations upset a child and can aggravate his troubles by making him worry more about his health. The doctor has also to help you to recognize when your child is not suffering from his usual pattern; for example, a child who suffers from recurrent vomiting can also vomit because of food poisoning.

Helping Your Child

Apart from following the doctor's advice, what is the best way for parents to handle a child who suffers recurrent attacks of symptoms, particularly if these come on whenever he is faced with a certain situation? For example, if your child complains of a stomach ache and is sick at the prospect of a birthday party, is it better to let him stay at home and avoid the pain and sickness, or should you insist that he go? However well you know the pattern, and even if your child agrees with you that there is nothing to be afraid of, it is impossible for him to prevent the symptoms. Saying "Pull yourself together" is as useless as it would be to say it to an adult suffering from an attack of migraine or a bout of depression.

It is not a simple problem, since if you "give in" and let your child stay at home each time, the physical consequences may be avoided but his anxiety remains—in fact, facing the dreaded event and finding it is not as bad in reality as in imagination may help a child accumulate self-confidence, whereas continually shirking it may increase his apprehension. On the other hand, knowing that his parents are completely inflexible, always insisting he go to the party however awful he feels, can make a child feel desperate, and increase his tension and his symptoms. If he knows that they sympathize and are flexible in their attitude he is more likely to relax and may build up enough confidence to decide to go for himself.

A long-term policy of gradual exposure to the frightening situation, plus playing down any aspects that appear to add to your child's anxiety, may be effective. For example, it may be obvious that it is the frantic preparations beforehand—dressing up in special clothes and making sure that everything is perfect—that sets off the stomach ache, rather than the outing itself. Many parents have discovered that a child who is sick and miserable before a party is usually quite happy going out in everyday clothes. So the best course would be to let him off the more formal occasions for a while and encourage him to go to the less formal ones with the minimum of fuss beforehand—avoiding special party clothes, for one thing.

Is His Pain "Real"?

A point to remember is that the amount of fear and pain a child feels in a particular situation bears little relation to the fearsomeness of the event—he may cope with really frightening events, such as being involved in a road accident, perfectly calmly. Fears do not have to be rational to be real, nor do pains have to be "physical" to be felt. Emotional pain can hurt more than physical pain. You cannot eliminate all the frightening situations from his life, and if he is "highly strung" or "sensitive," like the rest of the family perhaps, you cannot expect to change him altogether.

However, it is comforting that severe recurrent attacks of vomiting and abdominal pain tend to diminish and disappear as a child grows up, although they are sometimes replaced by other symptoms of emotional origin, such as migraine or a tendency to "indigestion."

Recurrent Abdominal Pain and Bilious Attacks

Abdominal pain can be a serious symptom; I have explained on page 482 when you should telephone the doctor promptly and when it is safe to "wait and see." Here we are discussing the abdominal pains, with or without other symptoms, that recur at intervals, turn out to have no physical basis, but are nevertheless real and painful for your child and worrying for you.

Just as the arm and leg pains common in childhood were once called "growing pains" (see below), because this name seemed to explain them, so recurrent abdominal pains were often blamed in the United Kingdom on a "grumbling appendix." However, nowadays we know that an appendix does not grumble; it either roars or keeps quiet (see appendicitis, p. 483).

Recurrent abdominal pain seems to come in two forms. The more serious and more acute attack is associated with vomiting and sometimes with fever. This type is referred to as "the periodic syndrome" or "cyclical vomiting." It was formerly known as "acidosis" or a "bilious attack" (see below). The other type is less acute and more frequent, consisting of abdominal pain, sometimes associated with nausea. Both represent a reaction to stress (see above).

Stomach Aches with Emotional Causes

Children tend to get pains in the abdomen for emotional reasons more than adults, perhaps because adults encourage children to focus their attention on their "insides." Eating is a duty rather than a pleasure in some families, and a stomach ache or vomiting can be a reaction to carrying out this pleasureless duty. "Bowel training" can turn the natural and pleasurable act of excretion into a matter of life and death, or so it must seem to a young child forced to sit on the toilet, particularly if his mother worries about the results. He may start to worry too; this may make him aware of the workings of his stomach and intestines. He becomes conscious of processes that are normally below the threshold of consciousness, and he may feel this as pain.

Explaining the Pain

It helps both child and parents to worry less if the doctor explains to the child why he has a pain, although there is nothing physically wrong with him. Using a simple diagram, I like to show the child how digestion depends on bowel waves so that the food is made to move along the intestine. Normally, we do not feel these waves, but they can be felt by a sensitive person in the same way as the heart, which normally works silently and unnoticed, can be felt beating from excitement or fear, as well as from physical exertion—this is the common cause of "palpitations." A lowered threshold of awareness causes the waves to be felt by the individual. This is more likely to occur when he is tense, and tenseness itself increases the force of the waves passing along the intestine. The result is a feeling of abdominal pain.

Once the child understands the reason for his pain and realizes there is nothing wrong with his inside, he will find it less frightening and pay less attention to it. The attacks will then occur less frequently, finally stopping altogether.

Causes

These recurrent abdominal pains come on at any time of the day or night. In some children they may be brought on by a particular stress, such as going back to school. In others, there may be no particular precipitating cause although the pain still recurs at more or less regular intervals. The doctor tries to work out why the child worries and helps his parents to reduce any avoidable anxieties in his life.

The clue may lie in the child's character. It is often found that the type of child most likely to be brought to the doctor with a "grumbling appendix" is the well-behaved, responsible child, always chosen as class leader and always trusted to do nothing even mildly outrageous. His family probably has high standards and high expectations for him, and has inculcated early a sense of correct behavior. But, reliable as this child is by nature and by training, the whole business of living up to his own and his parents' standards is more of a strain than any of them realize. He is too conscientious to admit it and relax, so the strain comes out in his most vulnerable spot, his abdomen.

Helping the Child

A doctor cannot change the parents' or the child's temperaments, but he can advise the family and the school to lighten any extra pressures on the child. The aim should be to help him to understand that his symptoms are the result of the exacting standards demanded by his perfectionist nature. The child needs encouragement to relax, perhaps to read comics instead of a book sometimes or go out and play; and he needs help in losing his anxiety to be top of the class every year.

The "Periodic Syndrome"

This is the name given to sudden attacks of abdominal pain which make the child physically ill; often there is vomiting and sometimes there is fever. The attacks come on suddenly and go away equally suddenly, usually within two days. Children who suffer from these attacks sometimes also get travel sickness. The attacks used to be known by a variety of names—among them "acidosis," "bilious attacks," "abdominal migraine"—but these were misleading. "Cyclical vomiting" is another unsatisfactory description, since vomiting is not necessarily part of every attack. The worst title is "irritable bowel or colon syndrome," since there is no evidence that the bowel is abnormally irritated and it suggests to parents that there is an organic basis to the disorder.

Causes

Although a child who suffers from these acute attacks is obviously ill and is therefore less likely to be accused of "imagining things" than a child whose recurrent abdominal pains produce no signs of illness, the origin of both types of pain is emotional. The child does not vomit because he periodically eats too much of the wrong things, so there is no point in altering his diet; the causes lie in the less easily defined regions of his emotions, described on page 536.

Treatment

Having satisfied himself that there is nothing physically wrong, the doctor does his best to reduce the family's anxiety. The explanation that an operation is not needed also helps.

The main aim of treatment is to determine the factors leading to the attack in order to reduce its strength. During the attack the child must be given enough to drink to replace the fluid lost by vomiting. Drinks should contain glucose, and he can be left to choose his favorite ones. Little and often is less likely to be vomited than a large amount at one time. Soda crackers are the most likely solid to stay down (see the sick child at home, p. 397). A pill for motion sickness is worth trying.

Recurrent Headaches

These are seldom caused by eyestrain and certainly not by "bad teeth," although the doctor will check for physical causes and prescribe any treatment needed. They usually turn out to be in the same category as recurrent abdominal and arm and leg pains—an emotional rather than a physical reaction.

It is older children who get this kind of pain. The headache is usually in the front of the head and occurs at any time of the day. There is no vomiting, although the child may feel sick. Treatment is similar to that for recurrent abdominal pain (see above).

Limb Pains ("Growing Pains")

Growing up may be painful, but growth, in the physical sense, is not. So why are the vague arm and leg pains of which children sometimes complain still called "growing pains"? The answer is that people like explanations for any kind of pain: the child is undoubtedly growing, so the process of growth itself is wrongly blamed. It is all part of the same approach that labels an older girl's recurrent stomach aches as being due to the impending onset of periods (p. 482).

Symptoms

The child who points at a limb, usually his thigh or calf, and says it hurts is not lying. But that does not mean there is anything wrong with the leg. Children submit their bodies to all kinds of outrageous assaults in the course of a day's play. They never stop and think "Am

I getting tired?" or "If I do that again, I'll be sorry later." Most of the time they get away with it, but sometimes the body protests;. a muscle starts aching and forces the child to stop playing.

Alternatively, the pain may come on at night and wake your child up. He tells you about it, and if you are wise you will simply give the aching place a rub; then he usually goes back to sleep. If it happens during the day he may sit quietly for a while and then rush out to play again. At this point, you may wonder if it is all right to let him go on playing. Suppose there is something wrong with his leg? How can you know?

Is He Ill?

You can assume your child is suffering from nothing more than insignificant muscle ache if he decides he wants to play again; if playing caused the pain he would soon stop. Don't be afraid that you might overlook the start of rheumatic fever—this produces pains in the joints, not in the muscles between the joints, and it does not pass off in a few minutes. As well as this, a child with rheumatic fever is obviously ill and feverish (see rheumatic fever, pp. 516–17). Children can usually point to the site of this pain with accuracy, so you should not have difficulty in deciding whether the pain has come from a joint or a muscle. Joint pains are, in fact, much less common than muscle pains.

Is It a Fracture?

Occasionally, a fracture is not obvious at first, particularly in young children, who may get a greenstick fracture, that is, a bend rather than a break. But the pain from a fracture stays in the same place and not only persists but gets worse if the child does not rest (see fracture, pp. 640–41). It always follows a fall or other accident, whereas "growing pains" do not follow a particular incident.

Does He Need Sympathy?

If your child sometimes complains of aches and pains in his arms or legs, it is unlikely that this is anything more than the result of vigorous play. It is safe to let him go on playing as soon as he wants to. Alternatively, he may want sympathy and the ache may be a good reason for coming to you for a kiss and a little undivided attention. The last thing he wants to hear is that he has not got a pain at all—if he says it hurts, it does hurt. There is the usual need to maintain the right balance and give him the right amount of sympathy without making him feel worse by overdoing the "Oh-you-poor-darling" treatment.

Recurrent Fever

A child who is well but whose temperature fluctuates above or below "normal" is sometimes brought to the doctor by his worried mother. For some reason she has been taking his temperature regularly, perhaps continuing a habit started during an illness, when the doctor asked her to check it. Although the child is now better, the fact that the thermometer registers a figure other than 98.6°F (37°C) convinces her that something is wrong. Is it?

Normal Fluctuations

"Normal" temperature can be anywhere between about 97° and 99.5°F (36.1° and 37.5°C) when taken by mouth and one degree higher when taken by rectum (see taking temperature, pp. 399–401). Everyone's temperature goes up and down in the course of a day—exertion, surroundings, and time of day all affect it. For example, crying makes a baby hotter, so that his temperature would be slightly higher if taken after a bout of crying. But normally, you do not compare your baby's temperature before and after he cries any more than you would check the temperature of an older child several times a day.

Temperature and Emotion

In most cases, the child is suffering from nothing worse than these normal variations in temperature. The doctor simply explains what is happening and gets his mother to promise to put the thermometer away! However, since emotion can affect temperature, making one feel hot not only under the collar but everywhere else too, a normal degree of variation can be increased if a child also becomes worried, either because of his mother's obsession with his temperature or because of other anxieties. He may then suffer from recurrent bouts of fever that are sufficiently uncomfortable to make him look and feel unwell. This is his way of reacting to anxiety, just as another child may react with recurrent abdominal pain or vomiting (p. 540). He is what is known as "thermolabile" —his temperature, more than the average person's, is liable to fluctuate in response to physical or emotional changes. This tendency is harmless in itself and the child does not need to be put to bed.

Consulting the Doctor

However, any child with a fever who is also unwell needs to see the doctor so that the reason for his symptoms can be diagnosed. Even when a child suffers from recurrent bouts of fever, parents and doctors have to take care not to overlook the possibility of there being another reason for his fever. It helps if they know and understand the usual pattern of his bouts.

46

Problems Affecting Behavior

Problems affecting behavior are universal though the area of behavior affected varies from child to child. What is regarded as a "problem" in one family may be regarded as normal behavior in another, for example, nail-biting or thumb-sucking.

The serious problems occur more often if a child is insecure. Thus they are found more frequently in children who come from broken homes or have a background of marital disharmony. Children who are overdisciplined may react by behaving badly or by producing symptoms of insecurity, such as bed-wetting. A similar reaction may occur in children who have to abide by a different set of rules for each parent. Rules for children should be common to both parents, and the fewer made the less likely a child is to break them and so to come into conflict with his parents (p. 268).

Conflict often results from parental rigidity: normal behavior is regarded as "naughty," and there is a failure on the parent's part to foresee an avoidable head-on collision with his child. Too much discipline is more likely to produce problems than too little. A child needs and likes to have a framework of "rules," but these should be as few as possible and should not be so cut and dried that there is no place for compromise between parent and child over any situation that develops between them (see discipline, p. 285). Whatever else you do, avoid being a perfectionist in your attitude to your child's behavior. Perfectionism is lethal; it is much better to err the other way.

Not all behavior problems result from insecurity. Many are due to a lack of knowledge about the normal development of children. Most parents know that it is normal for a baby to suck his thumb but few realize that this is an important step in his learning (see pp. 68 and 229–30). If you make the mistake of trying to stop your baby from sucking his thumb, you will prolong a stage of development out of which he should pass naturally, without difficulty. Normal development in this area of behavior can become arrested for a time and your child may continue to suck his thumb for years instead of for months as a result.

Another example of a problem resulting from mismanagement due to ignorance is persistent masturbation (pp. 339–40). Stealing may be a cry for help and understanding (p. 562). Temper tantrums are common at the toddler stage (see pp. 279–80).

It is clear, therefore, that "bad" behavior can be normal in a young child and should be tolerated. The same behavior in an older child may no longer be normal and it then constitutes a behavior problem.

Thumb-sucking

Why Sucking Is Necessary

Babies love sucking. It is a necessary pleasure, since it enables them to feed. Because it is so pleasurable, there is plenty of incentive to indulge in sucking for its own sake, so a baby soon learns how to put his thumb or fingers into his mouth (see development, p. 229). Occasionally, a baby sucks for pleasure even before birth, sucking his thumb while still in the uterus.

By sucking his thumb a baby explores his mouth, a necessary part of learning. A spastic child whose paralysis prevents this stage will be helped by the physical therapist and his mother to get his thumb into his mouth so that he does not miss out on this enjoyable and important learning process (see cerebral palsy, pp. 607-9).

Sometimes, making sucking noises or sucking his thumb is a sign that a baby is anticipating a feeding, but at other times he may do it as a pastime, about the only one he has at first. If you think he is hungry, feed him; otherwise, let him suck. There is no problem; it is not a sign of insecurity. It will not harm the position of his teeth; this is influenced only by prolonged thumb-sucking. Provided it has stopped by the age of six years, when the second set of teeth starts to appear, there can be no permanent effect.

The Older Baby

Once your baby starts to put objects in his mouth, he sucks them as part of his general curiosity about them. But he will also continue to suck his thumb. Since this stage comes at about the middle of the first year, when he is eating more by spoon and less by sucking, you may wonder whether he is missing the breast or bottle and whether you could prevent thumb-sucking by slowing down weaning. Some babies do seem to suck their thumbs less if allowed longer at the bottle or breast; this is an easy matter to ensure if a baby is breast fed, but sucking an empty bottle will simply fill him with air. For example, a baby may show that he is bored with the bottle and is quite ready to drink from a cup, but will still suck his thumb before going to sleep and at intervals during the day, especially when he is a bit bored or needs to relax.

What Should You Do?

Since the habit is harmless and cannot affect the second teeth unless your child still sucks his thumb persistently after the age of six, there is no need for you to do anything about it: no need to distract his attention, to keep taking the thumb out of his mouth—he will only keep putting it back—or to worry that he will suck his thumb forevermore. He will grow out of the habit as his interests develop and his mouth ceases to be his pleasure center. Most babies give it up during the second year. Some continue to thumbsuck, while others transfer their allegiance to an old piece of cloth or blanket which they suck or cuddle, perhaps while sucking their thumb as well.

The "Security Blanket"

Children who continue to suck their fingers or carry around their beloved rag after the age of a year are not necessarily insecure, although they may suck only when they need comfort or reassurance —just before going to sleep, for example. It is partly a habit, a trick to get them through the bad patches of their day or night, and partly simply still a pleasure in itself.

You may be ashamed of the "security blanket," which is likely to be grubby because your baby objects to its being washed; you have to wash it secretly, but he may then object because he misses the characteristic smell it acquires through sharing his life. This seems to be part of its charm, so that when your child has a cold he may complain that he can't get to sleep because he can't smell his rag. He may give it a name of its own, and will refuse all substitutes. Tell baby-sitters about the rag or they may remove it and then wonder why the child cannot sleep. Going away from home on vacation or to the hospital is a big change for a small child to cope with, and he will need his security blanket more than ever then, so do not leave it behind.

A child may go on needing his rag or sucking his thumb for years, and even when he has started school and is trying hard to be a "big boy" you may find him sucking his thumb in bed or while watching television. If you ask him why he does it, he will probably answer, "Because I like it!" If you fuss, he may do it more because he resents your interfering with his harmless habit. Nagging a child to stop thumb-sucking is no more effective than nagging a husband to stop smoking. The child will give up sucking his thumb eventually—the husband, unfortunately, may go on smoking forever. A child sometimes gives it up after another child has called him a baby, whereas parental urgings go unheeded.

When to Worry

It is not the age of your child that should make you concerned about his continuing habit of sucking: the only time to worry is when a child would rather suck his thumb continually than play (not the same as breaking off to rest and suck for a minute or two); when he spends his time looking vacant or worried and sucking while other children play; and when persistent sucking after the age of six starts to affect the alignment of his second teeth. The dentist may be able to convince your child better than you can about the effect on his teeth.

If a child needs the comfort of sucking for a large part of his waking hours, the problem is not the sucking but why he needs so much comfort. It is unlikely that the thumb in his mouth is the only sign of insecurity—and it is the insecurity that needs treatment, not the thumb-sucking.

A frequent feature of insecurity is the child's fear of losing his mother from his sight, so that he accompanies her everywhere, particularly when she tries to disappear into the bathroom. These children are usually in the toddler age group and I refer to them as "loo children," who must of course be allowed to accompany mother into the bathroom. Looked at from a child's point of view, this is the most frightening room in the house as far as losing mother is concerned, since it is the one place where she shuts the door to keep him out. Moreover, she possibly even locks it to make sure she disappears completely.

Nail-biting

Babies do not bite their nails, but many school-age children pass through a phase of nail-biting. It may start with copying another child or when the nails are long and tempting; the child finds the habit enjoyable and soothing and goes on doing it. Sometimes a child bites his nails whenever he is worried or feels shy, stopping when the difficult moment is over. An exciting television program or boredom may have the same effect.

It is wise to ignore nail-biting, since drawing attention to it does not stop the child and may make a passing habit more permanent. However, if your child continually bites his nails to the quick and the habit shows no sign of abating, you could try pointing out that it looks ugly. A useful trick with a girl is to help her feel proud of her nails by allowing her to use nail polish. Buy her a bottle of colorless nail polish to keep for herself and tell her schoolteacher that this is "medical" nail polish so as to ensure her co-operation. Your daughter will want to show off to her friends that she is allowed nail polish but she will not do so until she has let her nails grow. Giving her a manicure set and showing her how to use it also helps. Punishment or painting the nails with bitter substances only makes a child defiant and he soon gets it off.

Nail-biting is so common that to label all children who do it as "insecure" would be to condemn a good half of the child population, but compulsive nail-biting by a worried-looking child is a symptom of anxiety. The child will stop only when his anxiety has abated, and the hangover of the habit may well linger for some time afterward.

Dirt-eating (Pica)

All small children occasionally put something dirty into their mouths. Usually they spit it out, although since a baby has no preconceived ideas about what is edible and what is not, he may swallow it. Unless he is playing with something poisonous, which should be removed long before it gets near his mouth, it is best not to react too dramatically when your baby puts a lump of earth or something similar in his mouth; this may only encourage him to do it again to provoke another reaction from you.

A few children go beyond this normal tendency to try anything once and have what amounts to a perverted appetite for such things as earth, wood, paper, coal, and even feces. This disorder is called "pica," and is most common between the ages of two and four. It rarely makes the child ill, with one exception—lead poisoning. This will occur if the objects chewed are covered with lead paint, the greatest danger being a crib or a window sill that has been repainted (see equipment, p. 30).

Sometimes a child with pica is anemic; possibly his habit is a symptom of iron deficiency (see anemia, p. 518). But other children show no dietary deficiency and are healthy. Worms are not a cause of pica, although the child may get worms more easily as a result of eating dirt. Children who are emotionally disturbed or mentally retarded show a greater tendency to eat dirt, but normal children may also develop this perverted appetite.

Apart from treating anemia or any other health problem, it is necessary to curb the tendency because the child runs a higher than average risk of poisoning himself. Give him plenty of opportunity to play with things he can safely put in his mouth and remove all the dangerous objects. This is the kind of child who will take a swig of disinfectant which other children would find unpleasant after the first sniff, so parents have to be doubly careful to prevent accidental poisoning.

Tics (Habit Spasms)

A tic is one of those irritating nervous habits, usually involving the head or shoulders. Typical examples are twitching the nostrils, blinking, sniffing, shrugging the shoulders, rubbing the same place on the cheek and wrinkling the forehead. Most tics start as gestures with a useful purpose; for example, a child may have to toss his head back to get a lock of hair out of his eyes, but he continues to toss after he has had a haircut. Another child may rub his nose when someone is talking to him because he feels shy and it distracts his attention from the feeling—rather like the unnecessary gestures made by a nervous person appearing on television for the first time.

Annoying though a tic may be, it is wise not to demand that the child stop—although if your child has a tic you are bound to be irritated into the occasional reproof. He cannot stop the habit to order, but he can control the impulse for a time if he tries. This is how a tic is differentiated from chorea (St. Vitus's dance), a much rarer condition, which produces writhing movements that cannot be controlled to order.

The tic is not the child's fault and will disappear in time, but it may be followed by another, equally irritating, habit. Tics do no harm, but it is worth finding out if any particular worries are making your child tense. Drawing his attention to the movement and telling him to stop only makes things worse, because in the long run the more he tries to stop the more the movements increase.

Head-banging, Rocking, and Other Repetitive Habits

From the beginning of his life, a baby is comforted by rhythmic rocking—in your arms and in his cradle, and by the motion of travel in his carriage, by car and by train. Around the age of nine months, some babies start to provide this comfort for themselves. The most popular habits are banging the head against something hard, probably rocking the body back and forth at the same time; rolling the head from side to side; and bouncing back against a chair. Other repetitive habits include ear and hair pulling, lip and tongue sucking, and, more rarely, tooth-grinding.

What to Do

The problem is a serious one if your baby is having to provide his own comfort. Something has gone wrong in the mother/child relationship, and for some reason the baby's natural curiosity and his feeling of security have been lost. He has to rock for comfort and even "enjoys" banging his head. This suggests that he may have a lot of pent-up anger within him, which he is trying to express by turning it on himself.

Because this problem is serious, you should discuss it with your doctor or visiting nurse. Don't be put off with remarks to the effect that it is just a passing phase and your baby will "grow out of it." You must learn why his development has been diverted into these repetitive habits, which are so wasteful of his time because they restrict his natural opportunities for learning.

While you are discovering the cause, spend all the time with him that you possibly can. Try to catch his attention by some interesting game. If that does not succeed, then satisfy his need for extra comfort by cuddling instead of leaving him to get it for himself by rocking.

Fortunately, a child seldom causes himself physical damage by these habits, but it is wise to pad the head end of your baby's crib. Crib legs can be screwed to the floor, using right-angled metal struts, if the rocking movements start the crib moving. If your child is old enough, transfer him to a bed that is too heavy to be moved around. Don't leave him in his crib or bed until he is absolutely ready to fall asleep as soon as you go.

Breath-holding Attacks

These frightening attacks occur mainly in toddlers. The children who get them are usually bright individuals who react with exceptional force when frustrated, whether by people or by things; they may even be so angry that they blame the floor when they fall over. Breath-holding attacks are really an extreme form of temper tantrum (see pp. 279–80).

Is He Doing It on Purpose?

An attack rarely, if ever, occurs when a child is alone, since he requires an audience for his performance. In addition, one of his parents usually has to be in the audience. But this does not mean that the breath-holding is a deliberate attempt to get attention; this reaction to frustration, although requiring an audience, is subconscious, indicating the strength of feeling and the lack of personal control normal at this age. Each attack is a direct reaction to something the child has found particularly annoying.

Is He Ill?

Occasionally, these attacks are associated with anemia; your doctor will check for this and treat it if necessary (see p. 518).

Signs

In most cases the attack starts with the child taking a deep breath, as if he were preparing to let out an ear-splitting cry, but instead he holds his breath, and no sound comes out. Less often, he cries for a short period before holding his breath. He resembles an outraged adult who has opened his mouth to speak but is too flabbergasted to find words to express himself. His face usually goes dark red and then blue, though sometimes he goes pale for a short time at the beginning of an attack.

Is It Dangerous?

The attack itself is harmless, but there is a danger that if the child holds his breath for long enough he will have a convulsion from sheer lack of oxygen. It is for this reason that attacks should be cut short and, as far as possible, prevented altogether.

What to Do

By the time a mother consults the doctor about this problem she has often tried slapping her child or throwing cold water over him to startle him out of the attack, but has usually found these measures ineffective. A useful and often successful maneuver is to hook the index finger over the back of the child's tongue and draw it forward; this forces him to take a breath as a reflex. Once he has taken a breath the attack stops. You must do it as soon as he starts holding his breath and before he clenches his teeth. Some mothers have found that blowing into their child's mouth stimulates a breath.

Once a way to stop the attacks has been found you naturally become less anxious about them, so that you can handle your child normally and without "kid gloves." The attacks will also become less frequent when dealt with promptly.

Prevention must be tried as well as cure, but it is impossible to stop a child meeting frustrations, and to give in to him continually leads to a spoiled child and a distorted relationship between you. By tactfully leading him out of provocative situations and using the finger or blowing techniques to cut short attacks, you will usually be able to keep matters under control. The attacks will disappear by school age.

Bed-wetting (Enuresis)

If your child shows no sign of becoming dry at night by the age of about four, or has started wetting his bed again after being dry, it is wise to see your doctor (see pp. 244, 511). He will first check that everything is physically normal; then he will try to find out what is causing the delay and will give you advice on training methods.

Helping Your Child: Day Clock Training

Your doctor may suggest helping to stretch the bladder by a method called "day clock training." You use an alarm clock to remind your child to go to the bathroom at set intervals during the day—perhaps every two hours to start with, gradually increasing the interval until six hours is reached. This method often works and it gives both you and your child something positive to do about the problem. The child realizes that he is not to blame and that it is just a question of waiting till his bladder is large enough to last the night.

Games

Other children are helped by games of various kinds, aimed at giving them a sense of achievement when they manage a dry night, without making them feel guilty when they do not. It is no good promising a large present like a bicycle in the distant future when total dryness is achieved. This makes the child feel hopeless and gives him nothing immediate to look forward to.

Girls particularly seem to enjoy having a special calendar on which they ring the dry nights in red. Call it "Dr. X's calendar" and let your daughter bring it along to show the doctor on each visit. Another method is to put a penny (or more!) beside a bank, away from the child's bed, telling him that if he is dry in the morning, the money is his and he can put it in the bank. Children never seem to cheat at this game.

It is important to avoid the impression that the reward is for being good, which implies that your child is naughty if he fails. The whole thing should be treated lightly. Congratulate him on his successes; reassure him that he will soon succeed if the method does not work at first. To avoid any jealousy with other children in the family who have already achieved being dry, it is wise that they receive the same financial reward as the patient. The system then works to everyone's advantage and encouragement.

Drugs and Buzzers

Some doctors prescribe drugs for bed-wetting, but on the whole these seem to be less effective than working out with the child ways and means of helping him over his temporary delay in gaining control. An electric buzzer that goes off when the child starts to wet the bed is sometimes successful, particularly with older children. It works by conditioning the child so that after a short time he wakes up just before he wets the bed, when the buzzer would have gone off. Unfortunately, some children who wet the bed are such deep sleepers that the buzzer wakes everyone in the house except the patient!

Other Methods

Sometimes a child appears to wet the bed out of habit. Although able to last for long intervals during the day, he wets almost as soon as he is put to bed, even if he uses the toilet immediately beforehand. The child may or may not seem concerned—you may be quite relaxed about it but he may worry. Various policies may have been tried to break this habit, including rewards, threats, and taking to the toilet more frequently. Sometimes a sudden dramatic gesture works, such as new pajamas, new bedding, or leaving off the rubber sheet; but there should always be some sign that the time is ripe before you try this, otherwise the child may be deeply disappointed and discouraged by another failure.

Minimizing Worry and Work

Although bed-wetting problems disappear, given time, it is hard for you to stay calm and confident about this and natural for you to want to hurry up the process. The situation is all the more frustrating because you are usually dealing with a child who would like to cooperate but cannot.

The main thing to remember about bed-wetting is that your child will become dry in the end and that it will happen more quickly if you can avoid putting the pressure on him by trying to force him to be dry. Taking the pressure off yourself helps. Minimize the work involved by getting the most efficient laundering equipment you can afford. Remove some of the mental burden by reminding yourself that bed-wetters are not necessarily anxious or neurotic children. Worry over wetting his bed may make a child anxious, but he may not have been anxious beforehand. A child may wet his bed for emotional reasons, but there may be a perfectly "respectable" reason such as the size of his bladder, a family trait, or unavoidable stresses in his life (p. 244).

Bed-wetting as a Stress Signal

As well as the problem of the child who goes on wetting the bed later than most children, there is that of the child who becomes dry but then starts wetting again as the result of stress: illness, a new school, or the birth of a new baby are common reasons. This child may want a bottle like the new baby or start sucking his thumb again; or his jealousy or insecurity may show itself in bed-wetting. The obvious treatment for this type of bed-wetting is to reduce the cause of the stress, by making sure the child does not feel ousted by the baby and by allowing him to be a bit babyish himself. It is important to prevent him from worrying about wetting the bed, because anxiety may cause him to continue to do this after he has become accustomed to the baby. It is easy for a vicious circle of bed-wetting and anxiety to start.

Stress may also be responsible for bed-wetting in a child who has never achieved dry nights. He would have become dry, but at the point when he was ready he became ill or something distressing happened that interrupted his progress and interfered with learning the new skill—just as other skills are delayed if learning is interrupted at the vital moment.

Disfiguring Blemishes

Feeling "Different"

These may cause problems that affect behavior and for this reason are included here. A child who is disfigured is bound to feel different from other children and needs help to overcome his embarrassment. Without help he will probably try to avoid going out and mixing with others. In dealing with physical and mental conditions that cause genuine handicap I have emphasized that the effect on the child is not decided by the handicap alone but also by his reactions to it and by those of the people involved with him (see the handicapped child, pp. 578f.). A major physical handicap does not necessarily stop a child from being happy and living a full life, whereas a minor blemish sometimes causes enough unhappiness to make a child feel handicapped. As a result, his behavior is affected. Shyness, aggressiveness, or some other exaggeration of normal behavior may be the result of worrying about his appearance.

Children hate to feel different. They can become extremely self-conscious about any physical feature, for example, a prominent birthmark or protruding ears, which singles them out from the rest of their group, or becomes the focus of teasing. Everything depends on how the child himself feels about the blemish and how he deals with teasing if it starts.

Helping the Child Avoid Teasing

A small child may not notice a blemish and there is no need to draw his attention to it deliberately. However, if he does notice it and ask about it, or if you suspect he is worrying about it or think it would help him to deal with any teasing when he begins school, you can talk to him about it in a matter-of-fact way. Explain that lots of people have some feature that makes them look a little different but it is not always visible like his, so they are not teased about it. Tell him that everyone is different in some way, and that although he may hate feeling different now, grownups usually dislike feeling exactly like everyone else and enjoy finding ways in which to be different. People can't change what they look like and he can't help having his blemish, any more than the boy who teases him can help having red hair or a long nose. The teasers will soon get used to his appearance and become bored with teasing him about it, especially if he shows them that he is not worried either by the defect or by the teasing.

Of course, this attitude can be "caught" from the family without being explained in so many words. If the child is treated normally, so that he feels his defect is insignificant and his good points are appreciated, he will probably convey his lack of concern to other children, who will then be less likely to tease him; he will brush off any remarks so easily that they never become a serious problem. However, it is worth remembering that the child may become more self-conscious as he nears puberty, or that some incident can embarrass him temporarily so that he needs to talk about it.

Getting Help

It is always worth asking your doctor if there are any ways of dealing with the defect directly. Some physical features responsible for excessive self-consciousness in adolescence can be treated by plastic surgery. A bad birthmark can be camouflaged by special make-up (see birthmarks, pp. 419–20). Squints (p. 468) and protruding teeth (p. 257) should be corrected by prompt treatment.

Compulsions

These are a kind of magical insurance policy, taken out for luck, or, rather, to avoid bad luck. The child feels he must touch every other railing, take three steps between every sidewalk crack, chew his food a certain number of times, or repeat a sequence of actions all over again; unless he does, something awful may happen. This is no more foolish than an adult touching wood or not walking under ladders, but tends to come up rather more often in the course of each day. The child knows perfectly well that he is being "silly," but he would rather feel silly than suffer the anxiety of not carrying out the ritual.

Most adults can remember going through a similar stage, and some of us still have the occasional compulsion, like rechecking unnecessarily that the stove or oven or a light is switched off. But although you should not ridicule a child for his particular compulsion, it can still be irritating, particularly if it happens to involve you; being kissed fourteen times on the nose every night at bedtime instead of once on the cheek is very tedious.

Compulsions are common in the eight-to-ten age group. The child is becoming the keeper of his own conscience, and the gap between what he wants to be like and some of his unworthy, perhaps downright aggressive or sexual, feelings can seem so unbridgeable that he needs a little help; performing a ritual is a reliable way of making himself feel safe, temporarily.

Compulsive habits are eventually discarded, although your child may go through a series of different ones or have several going at once. There is no need to be concerned unless his life is becoming dominated by them.

When to Worry

A child who is obsessed with a compulsion, for example, with cleanliness, so that he has to wash himself over and over again, is obviously coping with something more than twinges of an awakening conscience and needs help. A child whose compulsive habit affects his health, by forcing him to eat or not to eat certain foods or quantities of food, is also in need of help. In short, a compulsion is a symptom of abnormal anxiety when it consumes a child's emotional energy and time; then it is no longer "silly" but a serious obsession. You should seek your doctor's help for such a problem.

Lying

The Preschool Child

"Lying" is an inappropriate word to apply to the tall stories and imaginative exaggerations, the doubtful explanations and hopeful fibs of the preschool child whose imagination is vivid, but whose sense of right and wrong, truth and falsehood, is cloudy. You will not help him to find out when it is important to distinguish the one from the other and how to behave honestly by calling him a liar or by demanding the whole truth at all times. But you can help by giving him the confidence to admit failure or weakness without fear, and by being honest with him yourself (see pp. 561–62). There is no need to take any other action.

Fantasies   Tall stories and fantasies are signs of a fertile imagination—listen and you will be entertained; you may also hear something that your child is trying to say indirectly, perhaps about his special fears and worries. Join in and add your own twist to the story occasionally, showing by your expression and tone of voice that you, and he, know that this is really only fun.

Don't accuse him of lying and refuse to listen when he tells you about the latest exploit of his imaginary friends (see friends, p. 303) or the fantastic happenings at play group that morning. You would not preface your reading of a bedtime story with the words "Of course, this is all lies," and you both know this is really a story too. Let him know you appreciate his talent for story making, and if he protests that this is not a story but all true, don't press the point.

If you feel your child is relying too much on his fantasy world, help him by showing more interest in his real life. He may feel that his own doings and achievements are uninteresting to you, perhaps because you are preoccupied with another child, so he tries to boost himself by inventing a more impressive version. By making plain your interest in him and in his less spectacular everyday life, you diminish his need to impress you with fantasy.

Fibs   A small child's untruthful explanations of how he acquired another child's toy or of how a vase got broken, for example, are usually laughably transparent. Rather than tell you the truth, which he fears would make you angry and also lead to loss of the coveted toy, he invents an explanation. This is understandable and should be taken lightly (see stealing, p. 562).

These fibs show that your child is beginning to grasp the difference between acceptable and unacceptable behavior; he knows that helping himself to other people's belongings, or knocking them over and breaking them, is vaguely wrong. But he is not yet clear why. Small children measure the seriousness of their own crimes by the anger they provoke: if you shout with rage and punish him when he breaks something, he will assume that this is very wicked and next time may "lie," saying another child did it. If you explain after your original outburst of anger that you are upset at losing your vase and that you are not really furious with him, he is less likely to be afraid to tell the truth if it happens again. Punishing a child frequently for his mistakes encourages him to lie to protect himself from further punishment. The less afraid he is of you, the less likely he is to lie to you.

The School Child

Fantasy   Fantasy in an older child usually takes the form of exaggerations of real events. After the age of about seven, the need to exercise his imagination by weaving elaborate fantasies becomes less as his ability to express himself in other ways grows. But he still needs to hold his own, particularly at school, and may boast and invent stories in order to do so.

He cannot help feeling small and unimportant in the crowd and it is natural for him to try to keep up with the little Joneses by exaggerating or inventing achievements or a more impressive background for himself. Your child may describe the family dinghy as a yacht to his friends; he is really saying that he thinks his family deserves a yacht rather than a dinghy.

Children give up trying to hoodwink their friends when they discover how difficult it is to keep up the pretense. There is no need to intervene and order your child to stick always to the facts; when he tries to impress you with an obviously glamorized version of the truth, you can show you are not taken in without calling him a liar.

A child who continually relies on obvious exaggerations and fantasies to gain attention needs to have his sense of personal worth bolstered by open appreciation of his actual achievements and qualities. He must not feel that his parents' love for him depends on success at school or elsewhere; in other words, he must feel that you love him for himself, not for his achievements. It may be necessary to discuss the problem with his teachers to discover whether he is finding school life a strain, and to work out how to take the pressure off him. He can then afford to be honest and will no longer need to impress you.

Fibs   Many fibs are nothing more than verbal compliance with some boring routine that is expected of the child, such as brushing his teeth. He gives the required answer without stopping to think about the truth. If found out, he is probably surprised that his mother ever expected him to obey. Adults manipulate truth just as much as children. If you want to check whether he brushes his teeth, you may need to be there.

What about apparently straightforward examples of lying, such as false accusations of "He did it," when it is plain that the accuser is to blame? Sometimes the situation is more complex than it seems; the child who kicks his companion may have been provoked beyond endurance until he finally retaliates, so in a sense both children are to blame for the outcome. It is simplest to avoid accusing one child of guilt unless there is no doubt about it, and to ask everyone to behave better, reminding them that they are all in the wrong sometimes (see playing with friends, pp. 301–4).

It is more serious when a guilty child accuses another of stealing or of being to blame for some mishap for which he is responsible. Extracting an outright confession from an unwilling child is usually impossible; he feels cornered and humiliated and his pride will not let him admit his fault. If you are absolutely sure of your position, there is no point in dragging a confession out of your child; it is better to let him know you know and take action accordingly. If it is impossible to discover the truth and find out if a child is lying, the chances are that he is guilty; he is learning his lesson through the unpleasantness caused and by his own sense of guilt.

Compulsive Lying Compulsive lying, that is, telling continual, senseless lies, without reason and without any benefit to the liar, is a cry for help and a demand for love, in the same way as are certain types of stealing (p. 562). The child wants to be found out because he cannot explain the problem in direct language. The compulsive liar's parents need expert advice, so that the reasons for his symptom can be diagnosed and help given.

Being Honest with Your Children

Children soon discover that adults are not totally honest. They hear their parents give different explanations of the same thing to different people, pretending to like what they don't like, making excuses that any child knows are untrue, breaking promises, and generally falling far short of the standards they wish their children to reach.

If you are less than perfect, like everyone else, it is best to admit this to your children rather than to attempt to keep up a permanent façade of perfection, which is bound to crumble sooner or later. By admitting to your child that you sometimes say you are too busy to play with him when really you do not want to at that moment, or that you said you liked the neighbor's new coat when you really hated it to avoid hurting her feelings, you help him to accept that you have difficulty, as he does, in being absolutely truthful; you also help him to understand that absolute honesty is not always desirable, since people's feelings are important too. Sometimes a choice must be made between speaking the unvarnished truth and sparing someone's feelings. You would be alarmed if your child always blurted out the truth, telling Mrs. X what you really thought of her new wallpaper. We expect our children to learn a sense of discretion, to know when to tell "white lies," keeping them to the minimum, and when to say too little rather than too much. It is unreasonable to expect them not to make some mistakes, not to slip in some unnecessary "lies" while they are in the process of learning.

However, it is essential for your children to be able to trust you to tell them the truth about important things. The rule should be "the more important the subject, the more important it is to tell the whole truth." Children need honest answers to their questions about sex (pp. 330f.), death (pp. 342f.), adoption (pp. 352f.), illness (pp. 388–89), and anything else involving their emotional well-being.

The main lesson to teach your children is the value of honesty in its deepest sense. Personal relationships that are based on falsehood are doomed to disaster.

Stealing

"Borrowing" Toys

Stealing means different things at different ages. It is not the right word to apply when your toddler has helped himself to another child's toy, but all the same you should point out to him that the toy belongs to someone else and must be given back. He has to learn to live in a society in which the rights of ownership are undeniable and therefore must be able to curb his magpie instincts.

Nearly every small child disturbs his mother at some time during his first five or six years by appearing with a strange toy; he looks proud, innocent (or perhaps guilty), and probably tries a little fibbing to bear out his claim to ownership. He may feel he should not have taken it, but at this age desire and impulse are stronger than conscience. It is best to treat the whole thing lightly. Let him know you are not taken in, even if he does not admit taking the toy, and insist he give it back; but don't call him a "thief" or treat him like one. He is far more likely to begin justifying the name if he is made to feel unduly guilty or resentful.

Repeated Stealing

A child over the age of about seven years who steals regularly is feeling guilty or apprehensive. He steals his mother's money but he is really trying to steal her affection, love, or forgiveness—something he feels short of. This interpretation of stealing can come as a shock to devoted parents. The child may be unable to acknowledge their love for some emotional reason—jealousy of a brother or sister, fear that he is not doing well enough at school, fear of his own destructive thoughts or of masturbation. He cannot talk about his problem, which he may be unable to recognize, so he asks for your help in an oblique way, by stealing.

In this kind of situation, where stealing is a symptom of emotional disturbance, the child often steals only from the person he loves and cares about most—his mother. Therefore the problem should be seen as a misguided effort to reach the most important person in his life. It is misguided because it has the opposite effect to that intended: the child loses approval instead of gaining it.

Occasional Stealing

If your child steals from your purse on one occasion, should you conclude that he is suffering from some inner hurt and rush him off to the doctor? If he seemed normal before, he is still normal and the explanation is probably simpler. Is he short of pocket money compared with his friends, or is he desperate to save up for a bicycle that he cannot yet have, or does he just want an ice-cream cone like every other child on the block?

Although an immediate pressing need for money is no justification, it is an explanation for a particular episode; it is best to try to discover and remedy the cause, and then to forget the incident. If a child continually finds pressing reasons and excuses for stealing, then he is covering up his real motives, which again are likely to arise from a feeling of insecurity needing investigation.

Helping the Child

Professional help is not always necessary even when stealing seems to be the symptom of inner worry. Parents can often work things out for themselves once they recognize the real problem. Many an adult can recall a period in his childhood when he stole and remembers that he knew, underneath, that it was really because he was jealous of a small brother; had he been younger, he might have wet his pants instead. For his parents to have made a fuss and treated him like a criminal could have turned a short interlude into a longer one, and fixed him in a role whose only function was to provide temporary relief from tension. Some adults remember stealing for fun during childhood and deny they had any sense of right or wrong at the time, although they now have normal standards of honesty.

Professional Help

If neither home nor school can uncover and relieve your child's reason for persistent stealing, then professional guidance is needed. Your family doctor can put you in touch with the local pediatrician or psychiatrist, whichever he feels to be the more appropriate.

The "Ugly Duckling"

I am frequently asked to see a child who is quite different from the others in the family. He is very difficult to handle because he is aggressive and unhappy, and he does badly at school and is frequently disruptive in class. In addition, he is likely to lie and to steal. It is usual to find that his mother feels differently toward him, compared with her other children, and that he does not like to be cuddled. Sometimes the child is described as being hyperactive and very often I am told that he was always crying as a baby.

By careful and sympathetic questioning it is usually possible to discover that something went wrong in the very early days, perhaps even before he was born. His mother may have become pregnant before she was ready; very often she was handled unsympathetically by medical and nursing staff when she was in labor and immediately afterward. Sadly, it is very often the "system," meaning the hospital staff, that has created the situation.

Some of the mothers have been separated from their newborn babies when they were needing to fall in love with them. Sometimes the hospital had such rigid rules that feeding times were ordained by the staff and not by the babies. Often the babies were kept in a nursery away from their mothers, all night. Many such mothers describe how they were scolded for picking up their crying babies between feedings.

When they came home from the hospital, things continued to be bad. The baby kept crying and mother was increasingly depressed while father could not understand what was happening. The doctor or visiting nurse may not have helped by using the word "colic" (p. 123) to describe the reason for the baby's behavior and assuring the mother that he would grow out of it when he was three months old. All this only increased her depression and her feeling that she was a "bad" mother, who could not love and care for her baby properly. The baby continued to respond by crying.

The next pregnancy and labor were quite different because the mother had confidence and knew she should pick up her crying baby. Consequently that baby was placid and easy to handle and to love, while the baby responded to his mother's affection. The first baby—the "ugly duckling"—was aware of the difference and in his longing to be loved and as a result of his insecurity he behaved in the way I have described.

47

Speech Problems

There is a wide variation in the speed and efficiency with which normal children learn to talk, although all go through the same stages on the way (see learning to talk, pp. 234f.). However, because speech is such clear evidence of intelligence and because it is such a pleasure for you to begin talking to your baby, apparent delays and difficulties are apt to make you particularly anxious and impatient.

The Late Talker

Anxiety is usually unnecessary. The most common reason why a baby is comparatively late in talking is a physiological one: he has not yet reached the age at which Nature intends him to start talking. There is an inbuilt time clock for speech, just as there is for walking and all other areas of your child's development.

However, lack of stimulus, that is, lack of being talked to, can affect the speed and the quality of a child's development of language by reducing his opportunity to learn and to practice. Your baby learns to speak while he is on your knee; he needs to hear you talking to him in normal clear language. By listening to you and by seeing your pleasure in the sounds he produces he is encouraged to go on producing more sounds himself.

By the time he has reached the toddler stage your child's speech should have developed a considerable way. But it is still important that he should be hearing you clearly. Normal household noises may be so loud that he does not hear you when you are speaking to him, especially if you are at the sink and he is playing in a corner.

Practice is essential. If you and your husband talk volubly to each other but not to your child, his speech development may be unnecessarily slow. Your task is to try to achieve the right balance: encourage him to develop speech, but do not be overanxious, since this could have the opposite effect. If you try to force him to talk, he may react by holding on to his words instead of producing them for you. This is exactly comparable to the reaction of the child whose mother is excessively concerned about moving his bowels—he holds on to his stool (p. 243).

Trying to make your child talk can result in his developing a grunt language of his own. Instead of producing the sounds you want he produces his own and gets you to learn to understand them. He probably points as well as grunts when he wants something, and you know what he wants. The trouble is that no one else does, so that he becomes frustrated with other people and probably also with you because you cannot understand all his grunts.

The right way to handle this situation is similar to the way you should handle feeding and bowel problems—don't get too intense and too involved in it. Where it is practical to answer your child's grunts by normal words and normal actions, do so. But on no account try to force him to speak correctly: this will only strengthen his reaction against saying what you want him to. Normal speech will develop when he finds that others, particularly children, do not understand his grunts. He will then adopt their lingua franca.

"Tongue-tie" is not a cause of indistinct or late talking (see tongue-tie, p. 41). Nor is "laziness"—there is no such thing as a lazy child. Children have an inbuilt zest for life and for learning; if they switch this off, thus giving the outward appearance of being lazy, it is as a reaction to stress. Very often the stress results from excessive concern on the part of parents about a child's performance in one area of development. We have already seen how a child can switch off speech development if you pressurize him to try to make him talk.

Problems such as stuttering, lisping, mispronouncing, and reversing words are often temporary and normal stages (p. 568). However, sometimes a speech problem is due to a genuine disorder, affecting the ability to learn or to use words normally. If in doubt, take your child to see your doctor.

Mental Retardation

The most common cause of real delayed speech is mental retardation, but this is much less common than the "normal" delayed speech of the child, already described, who happens to talk later than average. In contrast to the normal "late talker," who shows plenty of intelligence and increasing understanding of what you say to him, the mentally retarded child finds speech difficult to comprehend as well as to use —he can hear but he cannot listen (see learning to talk, pp. 234f.). In addition, he shows signs of slow development in several other areas and lacks the normal baby's curiosity and eagerness. Late talking will not be the only reason for concern.

Early diagnosis of mental retardation is important from many points of view, one of which is to assist speech development. All mentally retarded children should have skilled tests of hearing to ensure that his additional cause of delayed speech is not present.

Extra patience is needed to help the mentally retarded child make maximum progress in his speech. Progress is slowed by expecting either too much or too little. The advice of experts is needed to show how the child can best be helped (see mental retardation, pp. 590–91, and the autistic child, pp. 601–5).

The Deaf Child

A deaf baby begins making sounds at around the same time as a baby with normal hearing, which shows that the creation of sounds is not just imitation but begins as "verbal play." But he receives less encouragement to practice and to develop his range of noises. He can enjoy the physical sensations, such as the vibrations involved in using his vocal cords and his mouth, but he cannot hear and appreciate his own efforts; there is no playback. Nor does he have the stimulus of hearing all the sounds around him, which are both a reply and a source of inspiration to the baby with normal hearing. Consequently, the early sounds made by a deaf child have none of the tonal fluctuations of a normal infant.

Since deafness is usually only partial, so that he may respond to some sounds, he will also react to others because of visual clues—he sees your mouth move when you talk to him, and your lips smile. This increases the danger of his handicap remaining undetected and emphasizes the need for routine testing for deafness (p. 574). Particular care has to be taken when testing a bright deaf child, who can easily be missed because he is so clever. He is able to compensate for his deafness—almost as though he has eyes in the back of his head!

Vocalizing

Before the age of six months, it may be hard to tell from his vocalizing whether or not a baby is hearing properly, since he makes somewhat similar sounds to a baby with normal hearing except that they lack the tonal fluctuations already mentioned. However, a deaf baby tends to stop making sounds spontaneously, for the fun of it, only doing so when distressed or when actively encouraged. After about six months, it becomes clear to a professional or to an experienced parent that babbling, with its inflections, increased range of expression, and variety of sounds, is not appearing in the baby's repertoire.

It is essential to discover and treat deafness at the earliest possible moment, because vocalizing and babbling, and learning to listen, are the baby's preparation for speech. Missing these early experiences makes the task of learning to speak much harder. "Deaf and dumb" used frequently to go together simply because deafness had been overlooked and as a a result no attempt made to counteract its effects. The longer a child remains unable to hear adequately, the greater the delay in his learning to discriminate between sounds. This ability diminishes with age, which is why adults learning a foreign language find it more difficult to achieve the correct accent than do children.

Hearing Aids

A baby can wear a hearing aid as early as six months, preferably on both ears, since two ears hear better than one. Once the baby can hear better, he can begin to learn to listen. A normal baby has been learning this from the beginning of life, so he has a start of several months in the process of learning to speak (see pp. 234f.). Consequently, the deaf child needs about a year from the time his hearing aid is fitted before he can start using the words he can now hear. If you are the parent of a deaf child you will need guidance in helping him make up the leeway. The ear specialist will put you in touch with a special teacher or clinic.

Stuttering (Stammering)

"Normal" Hesitations

The tendency to trip over words, to repeat syllables, or to hesitate over speech is common between the ages of two and a half and six. This is the period when a child has a lot to say, is in a hurry to say it, and is trying to use longer and more complicated words and sentences. However, if his thoughts are more fluent than his speech, he gets into difficulties and it sounds as if a stutter is beginning.

This is not a real stutter, only a temporary holdup in fluency. The child usually seems not to notice his "stutter." It may be worse when he is anxious or jealous, but it is not of emotional origin.

Unless the child becomes worried because attention is drawn to his speech, the tendency nearly always disappears of its own accord within a few weeks or months. The worst thing to do is to look anxious and watch him while he is trying to get his words out, or to make him say them again "correctly"—in other words, to make him self-conscious about speech. Thinking twice before he speaks will not improve matters, but may turn a temporary difficulty into a persistent one, by causing the muscles involved in speaking to tense up. It is probable that nearly all persistent stuttering comes about because adults have overreacted to this normal stage in speech development, making the child overreact as well.

The Second Stage: Persistent Stuttering

Stuttering occurs, therefore, in two stages. The first or temporary stage, described above, occurs while he is learning to speak. The child is often unaware of what he is doing. In the second or persistent stage, the child has become aware of what he is doing, and attempts to correct the sounds by a deliberate effort. In doing so he makes writhing movements of his face and tongue and sometimes his whole body becomes contorted.

A Family Tendency

The reason some parents worry when a child begins to stutter, whereas others do not, may be that someone else in the family stutters. But while it seems that there is a family tendency to develop a stutter, and that it is commoner in boys than girls, this may be partly because the family has become "stutter conscious" and shows concern as soon as a child gives any sign of hesitancy in his speech, thereby increasing the likelihood of a persistent stutter developing.

Obviously, the right thing to do if your child stutters is not to take any notice. Never tell him to speak more slowly or to repeat words he has said indistinctly. In this way a temporary stutter will cure itself instead of becoming permanent.

Speech Therapy

If a child has developed a persistent stutter and has become so conscious of the problem that he is making movements of his face and tongue in an attempt to correct it, the help of a speech therapist is required.

Treatment of persistent stuttering aims at increasing the child's confidence by convincing him that he has all the normal mechanisms needed for normal speech. A metronome and earphones may be used to help him to build up the rhythm necessary for steady speech. The outlook is good: over half of the children who receive treatment are completely cured, and all can be improved.

Lisping

"Normal" Lisping

When someone wants to imitate a baby talking, he lisps. Lisping is normal when a baby is learning to talk and has yet to master all the sounds needed for clear speech. Some children go on lisping after the baby stage, out of habit or because they are copying another child. A temporary lisp is common when a child loses his front teeth and the second teeth have not yet appeared. Ignore all these types of lisp.

Lisping for a Serious Reason

Lisping and mispronunciation may be due to partial deafness and it also happens in children with a cleft palate. But these disorders should have been diagnosed long before persistent lisping causes concern (see pp. 423f.).

Occasionally, a lisp is due to faulty action of the tongue, and the child may need speech therapy. It is important to start treatment before he begins school, because unintelligible speech will handicap his progress and is likely to lead to teasing from other children.

Developmental Aphasia

This is the name for a complicated group of disorders, not yet fully understood by doctors, that make a child late in talking, although he is mentally normal. The lack of speech results from an inability to understand the spoken word (word deafness) or the written word (word blindness or dyslexia, see below). Children who suffer from this disability are able to see and hear in the ordinary sense. However, in present-day society, finding words difficult to understand in speech or in print is an enormous handicap. It is likely to cause a child to be labeled "slow" unless it is recognized at an early stage, and it is also likely to create serious emotional problems.

Whether these conditions are much commoner than is generally realized or whether they are really very rare is difficult to say because they often go unrecognized.

Dyslexia

Learning to Read   The dyslexic child can see perfectly well but the printed word is to him a confusing jumble of symbols, and he is unable to read. This is true, to a certain extent, of any child learning to read, especially if the tension involved in having to produce results and feeling foolish because he cannot stops him seeing "straight" and makes his mind go blank.

Is He Dyslexic?   If the child is normal, the help of a patient and sympathetic teacher makes him more confident, and he begins to be able to sort out the jumble of letters in front of him and to learn to read.

For the dyslexic child, the confusion is more persistent. Similar letters, like "b" and "d," are frequently muddled or reversed, both in reading and in writing, and his spelling may be completely illogical, so that there is no apparent connection between what he hears and what he writes down. In contrast, the ordinary poor speller shows some attempt to match sound and print. The dyslexic child may be the brightest child in the class when expressing himself in speech. This carries the danger that he will be labeled "lazy" or accused of "not trying" unless his teachers and parents recognize that he needs extra help.

The diagnosis of dyslexia requires special skills, particularly because large classes, poor teaching, and emotional problems can have a similar effect on a child's reading ability.

Helping the Child A great deal of harm is done if dyslexia is not recognized, and the child will certainly not reach his full potential. He is also likely to develop emotional problems because of the frustration he feels. The dyslexic child needs individual attention and sympathy, and his teacher needs to spend extra time and patience on teaching him to read and write, but he is usually best off remaining in the same class as his contemporaries. This can be achieved by means of individual lessons from a skilled "remedial teacher," in addition to ordinary lessons with an understanding class teacher. A dyslexic child, like a normal child, must be helped to understand that writing is speech on paper and not just a group of symbols which he has to learn to decipher like a code.

All this, basically, resembles the attention needed by any child with reading difficulties. Therefore, whether or not dyslexia exists as a distinct condition and whether or not it is mistakenly diagnosed in some children need not worry parents; any child who finds reading difficult can only benefit from the extra trouble taken to help him. If your child is eight or older and is worrying you, himself, and his teachers by his lack of progress in reading, find out what extra help he is receiving. Make sure he is not being overlooked or dismissed as "lazy." If his problems persist, press for proper testing to identify and treat the possible reasons for them.

Dyslexia is not related to a child's intelligence or economic group. It occurs in mentally retarded children, but also in intelligent children.

48

Problems Affecting All Handicapped Children

The handicapped child is one who suffers from a long-term disability, which affects his body, mind, or emotions sufficiently to hinder his normal growth, development, or capacity to learn. Inevitably, this puts him at a disadvantage compared with the average child, but a great deal can be done to reduce this disadvantage. The severity of the handicap does not necessarily decide the effect it has on the child, since his personality and the way he is helped to deal with it are often of greater importance. For this reason, if you are the parent of a handicapped child you are not faced with an unchangeable situation because your child has a particular handicap. Although each type of handicap does bring its own problems, the outlook for the individual child can always be improved by an appropriate and understanding management from his family and doctor.

The commoner handicaps are discussed separately below, but since all handicapped children and their families share a similar problem, you may find it useful to think about the subject as a whole.

Types of Handicap

Handicaps fall into three categories: physical handicaps, affecting a child's movement, appearance, or general health; mental handicaps, affecting his intelligence and learning ability; and emotional handicaps, distorting the development of personality and sometimes preventing the full use of a normal intellect.

In practice, these three categories often overlap. For example, physical handicap can lead to emotional maladjustment if a child is disturbed by his defect, or to educational backwardness if his schooling is constantly interrupted. Some children have several handicaps, which may interact—deafness affects the development of speech, for instance. Children with cerebral palsy may also be mentally retarded —this increases their difficulty in making the best use of their paralyzed arms and legs. It is one of the doctor's main tasks to look for "hidden" defects when treating the main handicap.

Physical Handicaps

The most common cause of physical handicap today is cerebral palsy (see pp. 606f.). However, spinal palsy from spina bifida has become commoner as more of these children have been helped to survive (see spina bifida, p. 425).

Medical advances are reducing some kinds of handicap, but others are replacing them because conditions like spina bifida and hydrocephalus can now be partially alleviated by treatment. The lives of some preterm babies who would formerly have died can now be saved, but some of these will be handicapped. The increased survival rate of preterm babies has not added to the total number of handicapped children, since improved medical techniques have reduced the incidence of brain damage in those who now survive. There has been an enormous swing in the climate of thought toward much greater help for handicapped children.

Some physical handicaps, such as cleft palate and cleft lip, can be repaired surgically so that they are not permanent, and the severity of almost all physical handicaps can be reduced by early diagnosis and correct management. This applies particularly to defects in eyesight and hearing. Since these faculties are closely linked with intellectual development, the child's general development will be delayed if the defects are not treated early. It is vital to recognize deafness early so that its effect on speech can be prevented (see pp. 565–66). Speech disorder is another serious and potentially frustrating handicap, whether due primarily to physical or to mental causes (see pp. 568f.). Inability to communicate normally is a serious cause of secondary emotional problems.

Mental and Emotional Handicaps

It is difficult to discover the relative frequency of these two types of handicap since mental retardation (see pp. 584f.) is so much more obvious. Certainly, emotional disorders are far commoner than realized and they may have a severe handicapping effect. A child with normal intelligence can be prevented from using it to the full if emotional problems interfere with his ability to concentrate and to learn. Maladjustment affects social and general development in a more surreptitious way than mental retardation, since it may be some time before the trouble is suspected and identified, and the child and his family given psychiatric help (see problems affecting behavior, p. 546).

Some children suffer from special difficulties resulting in educational problems, such as word blindness (see dyslexia, pp. 570–71). This kind of handicap is far less devastating if the reason for the child's backwardness is found early. In the past, such children were often thought to be "lazy" or mentally deficient.

Helping the Handicapped Child

Early Detection

Early detection of a handicap is an advantage from every point of view, preventing months or even years of uncertainty in the family and ensuring that treatment and correct management of the child start as soon as possible. Prompt treatment can stop the development of secondary handicaps as well as minimizing the effects of an existing one. A blind eye resulting from an untreated squint is an example of a preventable handicap. A squint causes double vision, that is, the child sees two objects when only one exists. After a few weeks the brain learns to suppress the image from one eye, and if this state of affairs is allowed to continue, that eye becomes permanently blind (see squint, p. 468). Conditions such as cerebral palsy and deafness can now be diagnosed much earlier than before, which improves the chance of preventing deformity in children with cerebral palsy and speech disorders in children who are deaf.

Regular checks should be carried out on all babies in the early months to make sure development is progressing normally and to enable the doctor to deal with any problems as they arise. To help doctors detect handicaps quickly, a special watch should be kept on any baby who runs a higher than average risk of handicap. Babies who should be given these extra checkups include those with a history of complications before, during, or just after birth; babies born to families with inherited disorders, such as congenital deafness; and babies who have had certain illnesses, such as jaundice.

Illegitimate babies need special care and handling, because of the emotional problems surrounding an illegitimate birth and the difficulties facing an unmarried mother bringing up a baby by herself. It has been shown that the intellectual performance of babies born illegitimate but adopted into a normal family is appreciably higher than that of babies brought up by an unmarried mother.

The babies at high risk are carefully followed in the hope of identifying every one with a predictable chance of developing a handicap. However, since it is impossible to predict every potential handicap, some babies who are not judged to be at risk will be handicapped, while many who do receive extra checks will not develop any handicap. The knowledge that your baby is being watched should not leave you on tenterhooks, waiting for a defect to show itself, provided the reasons for the extra attention are explained to you. For the great majority of parents, each checkup renews confidence that their child is making normal progress. If a problem is detected, it is a relief to know that your child is getting the earliest and most effective help because his handicap was found promptly.

The Doctor's Role

Several doctors and therapists may be involved in diagnosing and treating your child's handicap but one person, usually a doctor, co-ordinates their skills, providing a continuing source of advice and help for the family. He will be experienced in dealing with handicaps, is alert for any additional defects, and sees your child regularly to re-check his needs as he develops. He will make sure that all the appropriate services are helping you.

If your child is handicapped, the doctor needs your help to know about your home background and how the care of this child is affecting the rest of your family. He is aware that one child with a handicap may lead to trouble for the whole family unless problems are forestalled or detected as soon as they arise. For example, the doctor may see you are becoming so preoccupied with bringing up the handicapped child that your other children feel neglected and are beginning to be difficult as a result. This may be noticed by the doctor first because you are too involved in the situation to see it as a whole. You and your husband may disagree with each other over some aspect of managing your handicapped child—the doctor's advice, often combined with help from a social worker, can prevent this from souring your whole marital relationship.

The doctor will also tell you if the handicap is one that can be inherited, in which case you need to be told the degree of risk for future babies. You may be referred to a specialist for this genetic counseling (p. 417).

Relationships between Family and Doctor

These get off to a good start if the first diagnosis and news of the handicap are broken to you sympathetically and skillfully. If you are convinced the doctor has examined your child fully, has a consistent interest in him, and is always ready to review the situation, you will feel able to accept his advice, however unpalatable, and then relax in the certainty that you are doing your best for your child. Parents must feel that everything possible is being done, by the team and by themselves, if they are to avoid the frustrating and wasted energy of hunting for a new cure or better treatment. (See also cerebral palsy, p. 608.)

If it has taken you a long time to convince a doctor that there is something wrong with your baby, it will probably also take you a long time to regain confidence in his advice. Some handicaps only become obvious as a child develops; an experienced mother is often the first to notice that something is wrong. You should therefore always tell your doctor if you are concerned about your baby's development. Doctors have been trained to take parents' worries seriously, and an

important part of their role is giving reassurance when these worries
are unfounded and the baby is normal.

Parents' Reactions

It may be the doctor who has to convince the parents that a child is
handicapped, and it can take several meetings for the knowledge to
sink in and become bearable. Even parents who can grasp the news
at once are liable to have second thoughts, and agonized guilts and
doubts about its implications. You need to know that reactions of this
kind are normal and to be reminded that no parent has continually
admirable feelings even about a perfectly normal baby. The prospect
of providing continual love and care for any child is sometimes daunting; when a child is going to need extra attention, patience, and devotion, perhaps indefinitely, and is less able to give the rewards of
ordinary childhood in return, the prospect is naturally overwhelming
at times.

It is probably more difficult to have a natural loving feeling for
the handicapped child if he is the first in the family. Parents with other
children have achieved a normal, natural way of treating their children that is carried on with the handicapped one. Whereas, if the
handicapped child comes first and especially if he remains the only
child, too much attention may be focused on every detail of the handicap, so that the atmosphere in the family is tense. Every problem
seems special, though often many of the difficulties met are little
different from those in families with normal children.

Accepting Your Baby

If you have looked after your baby for some time before he is found
to be handicapped, you have already accepted him as a person and
made him one of the family. It is more difficult for parents of a baby
born with an obvious defect, such as spina bifida or Down's syndrome,
to think of him as an individual and to stop their feelings from being
dominated by his handicap. They may feel excessively protective, or
repelled by the abnormality—both are natural reactions. If the baby
is cared for by others, they do not get to know him and love him in
the normal way. Even when a baby is so badly deformed that he is
unlikely to survive, it is better for the parents to see the baby, since
imagination is worse than reality. By sensitive handling and the
skilled use of drapes an experienced doctor can show and explain the
deformity, thereby helping to make the baby a very different person
from the "monster" the parents might have imagined they had produced.

Once the problem is in the open, you can be helped to overcome
any unreasonable feelings of guilt and inadequacy. The cause of the

handicap, if known, can be explained to you, and suitable genetic advice given about the prospects of future children being handicapped. Once you accept the fact that your child is handicapped and are given help and support, you can turn your energies toward doing your best for him. There may be crises in the future, perhaps when you are very tired or the child's handicap presents a particular problem, so it is vital for you to have a doctor to whom you know you can turn for help and advice at any time.

Fundamental to knowing how to help the parents of a handicapped child is to be aware that they need time and understanding to mourn the loss of the perfect child for which they had hoped. Until this aspect has been worked through by counseling, the parents cannot begin to help their child in a rational manner.

Child Development Centers

Today, more and more hospitals are providing special centers where teams of experts can study every aspect of a child's development over a period of days or weeks in order to assess his total needs. This ensures that no defect is missed in the child with multiple handicaps. At such a center your child does not have to be fitted into an ordinary and perhaps hurried outpatient session, although he is likely to be seen at an outpatient department first and then referred for an appointment at the center.

Your child may attend the center every day for a week or more and, if necessary, return to it periodically. He will usually reach the center through the pediatrician to whom his family doctor or school doctor has referred him. The family doctor and the school doctor will be told the results of the assessment and will help work out how your child can be helped.

Teachers, speech therapists, psychologists, physical therapists, and occupational therapists (p. 609) work together in such a center. They also cooperate closely with their counterparts in the community, either working in schools and clinics or visiting your child at home.

Music Therapy

This is a relatively new discipline for helping handicapped children. The music therapist, who must be a skilled musician, is totally different from a music teacher, because she is taking her tune from the child rather than teaching him to play.

Children have to learn to listen before they can speak (p. 234). Listening requires concentration, but this is less well developed in those who are mentally retarded. Consequently, when a child is enjoying making music he is being helped to concentrate more.

Conversation with words requires more advanced learning than musical conversation, hence a handicapped child can be helped to converse musically before reaching the stage of words. Moreover, by using special objects (instruments) to make music, the child learns that he has the ability to make things happen and to get others to copy him or to converse musically with him.

The music therapist assesses the handicapped child's musical responses and awareness, the accent being on shared practical music-making in order to activate the child's responses. The child expresses himself through sound, the therapist accompanies, aiming to support and develop the child's music. By this means a musical picture of the child is built up so that child and therapist can begin to communicate on a nonverbal level. Having once communicated in this way he can start to move on to words.

Bringing Up a Handicapped Child at Home

The Need to Belong

All children need to be part of a family; with a handicapped child the need is even greater. In fact, he will usually be more dependent than ordinary children of the same age. The love and interest of his relatives make it easier for him to feel at ease with people outside the family circle; he is more likely than other children to be reserved and timid, although underneath he may feel exceptionally aggressive if his life is restricted by his handicap. If his mobility and independence are limited, preventing the normal widening of interests and loyalties as he grows older, it is all the more vital for him to feel he belongs in the family group.

The family itself often benefits too, despite the difficulties; caring for a handicapped child gives a new perspective on life and can strengthen family unity. The progress of a handicapped child, however limited, can be even more rewarding to watch than that of an ordinary child. It is natural for parents to question whether they are doing everything possible for their child.

In the case of some handicapped children the question of permanent residential care away from home may arise. Since this problem is largely confined to mentally retarded children it is discussed in Chapter 49 (pp. 584f.).

The Child's Attitude to His Handicap

In general, children accept handicaps more readily than adults, but they are helped in this if grownups also take a matter-of-fact, though sympathetic, attitude toward their handicap. The child should feel you are sorry about his handicap but not sorry for him. Nobody really wants to be pitied, but it is easy to become dependent on pity; making allowances for his handicap can degenerate into a permanent excuse for expecting too little of a child.

Encouraging Independence

If parents do too much for their child, it may become a habit for all of them. The child never finds out what he is capable of, and since in the long run his happiness is related to using his potential abilities, he needs every encouragement toward becoming as independent and self-reliant as possible. It is tempting, in bringing up any child, to keep him dependent in various ways for longer than is necessary. This is part of a natural wish to retain his love and to keep a share in his life as his interests become less and less centered on his home and family. The child with a severe physical or mental handicap is less well equipped than a normal child for the gradual breakaway from the family. He may have to stay at home a good deal and may not start school at the usual age of five, an event that provides ordinary children with the opportunity to widen their horizons and automatically helps ordinary parents to avoid too much dependence between parent and child.

As parents of a handicapped child you may have to remind yourselves deliberately that widening interests and loyalties are an inevitable and desirable stage in normal development. Just as you helped your handicapped baby to crawl or pick up a toy when he reached that stage of physical development, you must be ready to guide him through the normal stages of social development when he is ready. It is better to let him be independent, for example, in going out alone if he can, even if this is more trouble and worry than keeping him at home. Let him find out what he can and cannot do by trial and error rather than by deciding beforehand that his handicap prevents it. It is better to let a child do things for himself slowly and inefficiently, than to do everything for him. Visitors and relatives sometimes think a mother is being hard on her handicapped child because she lets him struggle with some problem she could easily solve for him in a second, but she has his long-term interests at heart as well as his immediate difficulty.

Behaving Normally

The handicapped child must be expected and encouraged to behave as well as any other child in the family, within the limits of his handicap. He will be more popular with his brothers and sisters and other children if he plays with them on equal terms and does his share of clearing up and helping in the house. The child with flippers instead of arms can be shown how to hold open a door with his back to let someone through, proving to himself and to them that he can help as well as be helped.

A child who knows his difficulties are appreciated, but feels he is just another member of the family, does not need constant sympathy; his handicap shades into the background of his life instead of dominating the foreground. His problems should be treated for themselves, and should not automatically be regarded as an inevitable part of his handicap.

Jealousy

Jealousy of a new baby is normal in young children; since the handicapped child is likely to be more dependent on his mother than most children of his age, the birth of another baby may be even more disrupting for him. However, his jealousy needs just the same treatment as any other child's—extra but not exaggerated love and attention.

He may also suffer from his brothers' and sisters' jealousy of him, because he takes up more of his mother's time. However, children often understand that the handicapped child needs this extra attention and may be no more jealous of him than of any other brother or sister.

Aggression

Behavior problems can be indirectly encouraged by the handicap but are not an inevitable part of it. Any small boy who could not roll about or play boisterous games to work off his aggressive feelings and use up his energy would be liable to show his aggression and energy in other ways, such as temper tantrums. The handicap is responsible for the temper tantrums to the extent that it prevents normal play, but it has not made the handicapped child more violent and aggressive by nature.

Apathy

Similarly, apathy and lack of interest are not part of a handicapping condition, but it is easier to become bored if you cannot move about and do things for yourself. A child can play alone for hours if he is able to follow up one game with another, fetching toys, moving from house to yard, and needing little help to develop his own ideas. If he had to ask for help every time he thought of another possibility, he might soon become discouraged and find it simpler to rely on other people's ideas for amusing himself. The handicapped child has to keep his curiosity and interest alive despite the restrictions of his handicap and his dependence on others. He has to work harder at it, but his original supply of natural curiosity and exploratory instinct can be preserved with the help of his family and his teacher.

Adventure Playgrounds

The development of adventure playgrounds for handicapped children has been a great step forward, and there are now many of these special playgrounds in the United Kingdom. Many handicapped children who have been denied the experience of adventurous play, because their parents were frightened they would hurt themselves, have blossomed when given the opportunity of playing in groups in an adventure playground. Those caring for the children know how to protect them without overprotecting them, and how to avoid rushing to their aid the moment any difficulty arises. In this way it has been found that handicapped children can play adventurous games as safely as those who are not handicapped. Consequently they need no longer be denied such important learning experiences.

Ask your child's doctor, nurse, or teacher for details of any adventure playground where your child might play.

Educating the Handicapped Child

How well you cope with bringing up your child is greatly influenced by the quality and amount of help you receive from the medical and social services, and on the educational facilities available. You may find you can manage to fit caring for your child into the family routine as long as it does not take up twenty-four hours a day.

Nursery School

The best solution, while your child is small, is for him to attend a nursery school for part of the day, provided he is ready to leave you. Ideally, this nursery school should be one catering for normal as well as handicapped children. Some communities provide such nurseries, while in other places play groups have been organized by parents. The children are stimulated by meeting others and playing together, which encourages their social and general development as well as giving their families a break.

Mutual Help

In many cases, parents have banded together to start groups to draw attention to their children's particular needs, and to give each other support. Joining a group helps parents to avoid the tendency to become socially isolated because of their handicapped child, and enables them to make new friends. Visiting nurses and social workers will know about such groups. If there are no nursery schools or play groups locally, it is important to try to make arrangements so that he can mix with other children.

Remember that the child who depends on his home to provide all his stimulus needs extra encouragement in exploring his surroundings if his movement is restricted by physical handicap. You have to anticipate some of his needs, bringing things to him if he cannot get to them, but letting him manage things for himself whenever possible.

Attending "Ordinary" School

Your child should become as much a part of the local community as possible. When the time comes, and if his handicap allows it, he will benefit from attending an ordinary school nearby. This makes the journey easier and enables him to make friends who live near and can come to play at your home.

The possibility of going to a local school depends partly on his handicap and partly on the attitude of the school toward taking a child with his particular handicap. For example, some schools will accept a child with cerebral palsy and others prefer to avoid the problem. Some schools have a special class for handicapped children (see pp. 599–600).

Special Schools

In the United Kingdom, if the handicap makes it impractical to educate your child at an ordinary school, he can still live at home if there is a special school near enough for him to attend as a day pupil. Special schools cater either for one type of handicap only, for example, cerebral palsy, or may take a cross section of handicapped children (see pp. 599–600). Children are regularly reassessed during their school careers so that any child whose handicap allows can be transferred to an ordinary school.

Parents are often worried that once their child has been placed in a special school he will remain there for the rest of his school life.

In fact, because it costs more to keep a child at a special school and because the number of places is limited, there is a constant aim to transfer him to an ordinary school if he is fit to attend. The extra expense of the special school results from the higher staff-pupil ratio and the fact that the staff are paid at higher rates because of their special training. Additionally, there is the expense of school transport and other special facilities.

If your doctor recommends special schooling, accept his advice and be confident that this is best for your child. You may worry that he will be held back if educated with children who are intellectually "worse" than he is although they share the same handicap; but with small classes, specially trained teachers, and regular reassessment, this is not the case.

The tendency today is to place the child according to his educational capacity, not according to his handicap, and new and sophisticated ways of measuring learning ability and difficulties are being used. Many handicapped children enjoy mixing with others who have handicaps; they feel less conspicuous and are relieved to know that they are not unique.

Leaving School

It is natural to worry about what will happen when your child leaves school. Many handicapped adults can earn their own living and lead normal lives. Others are found jobs in ordinary firms that take a certain proportion of disabled people; some severely handicapped adults work in sheltered workshops or centers for handicapped people. These workshops and centers often undertake work on a contract basis for local firms, so that the disabled are no longer expected to work only at special crafts like basket-making.

Another worry for the parents of a handicapped child who will never be fully independent is what will happen to him when they die. It is best to speak with a lawyer and, if possible, establish a trust fund for the child to provide care after the death of the parents.

It is impossible to predict any child's future; what parents and doctors can do is to provide each child with the opportunity to develop to his fullest capacity, whether he is handicapped or not.

49

The Mentally Retarded Child

A better term for mental retardation would be "mental handicap," because this is just one of several ways in which a child can be handicapped. A physically handicapped child is not regarded as a "subnormal" human being but as an otherwise normal person whose body has suffered a physical defect; similarly, a mentally handicapped child has suffered a defect affecting the development of intellect. He will make progress, but at a slower pace than the average.

Degrees of Mental Retardation

One of the measurements used in assessing the degree of mental handicap or retardation and in planning the child's education is his intelligence quotient (IQ) (pp. 593–94).

In the United States the classification of mental retardation is: borderline, 68–83; mild, 52–67; moderate, 36–51; severe, 20–35; profound, 0–19.

Causes of Mental Retardation

Mental retardation can afflict any family. The object in looking for the cause is to find out how the individual child and his family can best be helped.

The first question many parents ask on learning that their child is handicapped is "Why should this have happened to us?" The answer is frequently unknown, though in some cases inherited or environmental causes can be traced. Whose fault is it? Usually it is no one's fault. What could have been done to prevent it? Usually nothing.

Preventing Mental Retardation

The few cases where retardation can be prevented or reversed must be detected early, and where necessary parents should be given genetic advice about the chances of future children being similarly affected (see genetic counseling, p. 417). As more and more is discovered about the causes of mental retardation, the chances of future prevention and treatment increase.

Environmental Factors

In the majority of cases no cause can be found for mental retardation. This applies particularly to the large number of mentally retarded children coming from the lower economic levels. The reason for this is not clear but one factor is the overcrowded and understimulating environment. The home provides little opportunity for intellectual development and parents are often not interested in education and their children's progress at school. Children whose parents went to college are more likely to get to college themselves than those whose parents did not; a major reason for this is that their homes encourage an atmosphere of learning.

All children, whether normal or mentally retarded, are held back by lack of learning opportunities; some children who are educationally subnormal might have been normal had they not been pulled down by a poor environment. Emotional disturbances and physical illness can also prevent a child from reaching his full potential.

Known Causes

The same causes operate as for cerebral palsy: the child's brain may have been damaged before, or more particularly during, birth, or it may have been malformed during the stage of development in the womb. In the mentally retarded child, the damage is in the part of the cerebral cortex that is responsible for intellect. As this is close to the part that controls movement, some mentally retarded children also have cerebral palsy (see cerebral palsy, p. 606).

Brain cells, once killed or damaged, cannot be replaced or repaired; consequently, there is no chance of curing this type of mental retardation once the damage has occurred. Brain damage is not the label for a particular type of mental retardation but is an explanation of what has happened to the brain in a number of different circumstances. The only way of preventing such damages is for all mothers to receive full obstetric care in the prenatal period and during labor, and for all babies to have expert medical care available the moment they are born. This is why most doctors recommend that babies should be born in a fully equipped and staffed hospital.

Biochemical Causes

A few types of mental retardation have a biochemical origin. They are caused by inborn errors of metabolism. This is a small but very important group, since if the error is detected promptly and treatment begun, mental retardation can be prevented. An increasing number of these conditions are being discovered.

Phenylketonuria (PKU)   The most familiar is phenylketonuria (PKU), for which all newborn babies are tested. The modern test is carried out on a drop of the baby's blood obtained by pricking the heel, usually on the sixth day of life, so that he has received milk for at least four days. This test has superseded the urine test previously used, which was not always accurate. If the condition is diagnosed, the baby is put on a special diet, and provided this is done from very early in life, he can develop normally. It used to be thought that the diet would need to be continued for life; recent research suggests it may be possible to stop the diet at the end of childhood, when the brain has finished developing, without any harm coming to the child.

This condition is inherited: although the parents of children with PKU are not affected by the disease, each of them is the innocent carrier of one recessive gene for the disorder. Some of their children will be born with not one but two of these recessive genes, and it is these children who will inherit the disease (see congenital malformation, p. 418).

Thyroid Deficiency   Another kind of preventable mental retardation is that due to lack of sufficient thyroid hormone. A child may be born without a thyroid gland; or his gland may be incapable of producing enough hormone. In many countries it is now routine to screen for thyroid deficiency using the blood obtained for the PKU test.

Children born without any thyroid gland become mentally retarded if untreated; they are known as cretins. The condition does not usually show at birth. Very soon the baby becomes sluggish in his behavior and in his bowel movements; he gradually becomes more and more inactive and constipated. His cry becomes hoarse, because his vocal cords thicken, like those of adolescent boys. His features coarsen, and if the condition is untreated, his arms and legs become stunted and he remains short, because thyroid hormone is one of the hormones needed for normal growth. Parents of such babies often do not notice that anything is wrong for some time—they may think their baby is "good" because he is inactive and gives so little trouble. This is one of the conditions that doctors and nurses are trained to detect at an early stage in babies attending a well-baby clinic. If you are worried that your baby might have this condition, do not hesitate to ask your doctor.

Children born with a thyroid gland that produces insufficient thyroid hormone remain normal for longer. Their needs can usually be met for the first months of life, but between one and four years, when increasing growth causes increasing thyroid requirements, they too begin to suffer from lack of thyroid. The signs of this are a slowing up of growth, decreasing activity, and constipation. With treatment, the outlook for their mental development is better than that of children with no thyroid gland; since they had sufficient thyroid hormone during their first year, normal brain development could occur.

Malnutrition and Brain Development

Malnutrition affects brain development only if it occurs during the last weeks of pregnancy and the first three years of life. During this period the brain is growing at its fastest and is therefore particularly vulnerable (pp. 12, 213–14). This is why feeding programs in famine areas should give priority treatment to pregnant mothers and to children under three years of age. Older children and adults need to be given only enough to sustain life until there are sufficient food supplies for the whole population. For these reasons, war and famine can be regarded as preventable causes of mental retardation.

In the United States the WIC Program (Women, Infants and Children) provides supplementary feedings for high-risk mothers and babies. The program also includes pregnant mothers and breast-feeding babies.

Lack of Intellectual Stimulation

Although older children will not become mentally handicapped from lack of food, their intellectual performance can be affected by lack of the stimulation necessary for intellectual development (see pp. 216, 314–15). Play is food for the brain and for the development of personality; lack of it in the early years of life may have a permanent effect. Emotional disturbance may also affect a child's intellectual performance, so that he appears to be mentally retarded (see p. 592).

Postnatal Causes of Mental Retardation

Mental retardation very occasionally results from brain infections after birth, such as meningitis and encephalitis (pp. 613f.). Brain injury can lead to mental retardation, so that it could arise as the result of an accident. Certain kinds of poisoning can also be a cause, for example, lead poisoning, which results from chewing toys or furniture painted with lead paint (see pp. 30, 625).

Congenital Abnormality of the Brain

In some children, mental retardation is caused by a congenital abnormality of the brain. The commonest of these abnormalities are mongolism (Down's syndrome), microcephaly, and hydrocephalus.

Mongolism ("Down's Syndrome")

This is one of the commonest and most clear-cut types of mental retardation. All Down's children are mentally retarded. They also look similar because they share certain physical features, particularly the slanting oriental eyes that account for the name "mongol." The term "Down's syndrome"—after the doctor who first described the condition—is now preferred. Some parents have mistakenly believed that the children are "down," so the reason for the term needs to be explained.

In addition to being slanting, the Down's child's eyes are small. His nose has a shallow bridge, making him snuffly and particularly susceptible to colds and chest infections. Down's children are always floppy as babies; they are also more likely to be born with an abnormal heart than normal children. However, the idea that they all die young is incorrect. It used to be true, before the advent of antibiotics.

A doctor can usually tell at once if a newborn baby is a Down's child, though parents seldom notice that anything is wrong. Once the doctor is certain, he has to decide when to tell the parents. It is now felt wise to break the news on the day of birth. This avoids the bitter reactions felt by parents who have already sent off the news to friends that they have a normal baby. Moreover, many parents will immediately sense that something is wrong from the behavior of the doctors and nurses.

Bringing Up a Down's Child   Down's syndrome is incurable, but that does not mean there is nothing to be done for the children and their parents. A Down's child, like any other child, will do best if he grows up in a normal home atmosphere. To achieve this the family will need an enormous amount of medical, social, and educational help from the community (see pp. 575f.). It must be emphasized that for the first year or so the behavior of the Down's baby is little different from that of any other baby; it is only that some of his physical features are different. He will return his mother's love by his reactions, like any other baby.

Although Down's children are both physically and mentally backward, they are often friendly and cheerful, as well as active. Their placid nature probably results from the way they are handled by people, particularly by their parents. Because of their distinctive physical appearance their condition is recognized early and they have the good fortune not to be pressured to "do better," as are so many mentally retarded children whose handicap is not detected until they are much older (see pp. 597f.).

The degree of mental retardation varies; some Down's children learn to speak quite well. All of them learn to walk and do so nearly as soon as normal children.

Causes There are several types of Down's syndrome, all due to abnormalities of the chromosomes and all producing similar features. Chromosomes are contained in the nucleus of every cell in the body; they carry the genes that determine inherited characteristics. In the normal person each cell has forty-six chromosomes, but in Down's syndrome there is an extra one. Every cell is affected, so the whole body is involved; this is why the Down's child has typical physical features.

The majority of Down's babies are "regular," with a type of abnormality that affects the baby only; his parents' chromosomes are normal (see below). The chances of producing a Down's child of this type increase with the mother's age.

In the rarer types of Down's syndrome, one or both of the parents may show chromosomal abnormalities, although they are physically and mentally normal. In this inherited form of Down's syndrome, the parents must be advised of their increased chance of having more Down's children.

It is now usual for chromosome tests to be carried out whenever a Down's baby is born. Usually the chromosome test is carried out on the baby's blood first to determine if he has "regular" Down's syndrome; if so, the parents' chromosomes need not be studied, since the handicap has not been transmitted by them.

Similar chromosome tests on the amniotic fluid can now determine whether the unborn baby has Down's syndrome. Such tests are applied to mothers at particular risk, mainly the older pregnant woman (see p. 417). A positive result may lead such parents to decide to have the pregnancy terminated.

Microcephaly (Small Head)

This child is born with a small head, which grows very slowly, although his face is a normal size. The head is small because the brain is undersized as a result of faulty development before birth. The small brain continues to grow too slowly to stimulate normal growth of the skull bones—the size of the baby's head is not due to a small skull preventing brain growth. There is a separate and rare condition in which the skull bones join up too early.

A different reason for a small head is damage to a normal brain by, for example, lack of oxygen during delivery. If this is serious enough to cause major damage to the brain cells, which can never recover, the brain remains undersized and the head small from lack of normal brain growth. However, although many mentally retarded children have small heads, you cannot judge a child's intelligence by the size of his head. Obviously, the way the brain functions is more important than its size.

Hydrocephalus (Water on the Brain)

In this condition, the child's head is proportionately larger than his face. The skull is stretched by too much cerebro-spinal fluid accumulating inside the brain. This fluid flows through the inside and bathes the outside of the brain. Under normal circumstances, the amount of fluid remains constant, but if something goes wrong with its circulation, an accumulation of extra fluid occurs. This presses on the brain, gradually making it thinner and thinner; at the same time it pushes the skull bones outward, so that the head continues to grow rapidly after birth. The fontanel (soft spot), being stretched, feels harder than normal, and does not pulsate up and down like the normal fontanel. Thus the doctor is able to distinguish the baby with hydrocephalus from the baby whose head is large because this happens to be the family shape.

Hydrocephalus may start before or after birth. It is often associated with spina bifida (p. 425). Surgical treatment can prevent mental retardation by relieving the pressure of fluid on the brain before the brain cells are damaged.

Diagnosing Mental Retardation

Whatever the degree of mental retardation it is always important for it to be picked up early. This applies not only to the few types of retardation that can be treated but also to those for which there is no direct treatment. In this way parents can be spared years of doubt and can be taught how to help their child in a positive manner if he proves to be mentally retarded. By saving him the frustration and emotional disturbance that will result if too much is expected of him, parents can help him to perform to his maximum ability.

Although it may take some time to make the final diagnosis, most doctors now feel that parents should be kept frankly and fully informed. This is not only your right, but it also enables you to understand your child's problem and to treat him sympathetically from the earliest possible moment. If you and your doctor understand each other, you will be able to accept his advice more easily. You will be able to work as partners in the interests of your child.

If it turns out that your child is fundamentally normal, although he is developing slowly in some fields, you will be reassured that he is not mentally retarded. On the other hand, if mental retardation is diagnosed, you have to be helped to realize that there is no point in searching for a cure. The best way to help such a child is to encourage him to develop at his own pace and to co-operate in a program devised to fit his educational, psychological, social, and medical needs; this will be prepared by everyone involved in his care. The rate of progress of children with Down's syndrome has been remarkably improved by the provision of such a stimulating program of activity.

Reasons for Slow Progress

Some types of mental retardation are evident at birth because the baby also has certain physical characteristics, as in Down's syndrome. In other types, the baby seems normal at birth, and as every young baby's range of behavior is small, nothing is suspected until he fails to make normal progress in several fields. The doctor or visiting nurse may be concerned by the baby's lack of progress or his mother may be the first to notice it.

Some mothers tend naturally to think there may be other reasons, such as physical illness, for their baby's slowness, but it is more common for parents to worry excessively about a rate of progress that is in fact normal. Parents tend to underestimate the wide variations in normal development, expecting one baby to advance as quickly as another. You may worry particularly if your child is slow to reach one of the major milestones such as sitting up, but these physical stages on which so much parental anxiety and pride are focused are a poor guide to intelligence. A baby who is slower than average in reaching one or two of these milestones, but is otherwise normal, is not mentally retarded (see Is my baby developing normally?, p. 218).

Checking Your Baby's Development

If you are worried, you should not expect to diagnose the cause of your baby's slow progress yourself, any more than you would expect to diagnose the cause of an obscure physical illness. A detailed knowledge of normal development is necessary for the individual child's rate of progress to be assessed and compared with the usual rate for his age. When you have mentioned your concern to your doctor or visiting nurse, and if the doctor decides the child does need to be checked further, assessment by a specialist will be arranged. This can be either in a special center, which the child can visit on a day basis (see child development centers, p. 577), or in a children's unit at a hospital.

Although a mentally retarded baby will probably be late in reaching physical milestones like sitting and walking, the specialist will be more concerned with his general alertness, his natural curiosity and interest in his surroundings, and his response to other people. Particularly important is his understanding of language and the amount he communicates and speaks. The specialist will ask when your baby first smiled and started reacting to sounds and sights and looking at you, when he began lifting his head off the mattress, and how well he uses his fingers.

As well as tracing the baby's physical and social development with your help, and observing the baby's behavior himself, the doctor checks the prenatal and postnatal history and family background, in case these throw light on the baby's rate of progress. For example, prematurity or serious illness must be taken into account when considering a baby's achievements at a given age (see the low birth weight baby, pp. 133f.).

Screening Tests

Even if your baby appears perfectly healthy, he is given a thorough examination and any screening tests the doctor thinks necessary. This is to make sure there is no underlying physical cause, such as phenylketonuria (p. 586), thyroid deficiency, or deafness. A number of conditions that can give a false impression of mental slowness must always be excluded, including defective eyesight and hearing. The deaf baby's speech will be delayed, and since communicating with others is such an important part of his development, it obviously affects his growing intelligence in many ways and can make him seem mentally slow.

Cerebral palsy can make a child appear mentally retarded by interfering with control of the muscles used in speaking and by preventing the child from playing normally, as well as by delaying accomplishments like sitting up. It is very difficult to assess a child's intelligence if the channels through which he would normally express it are blocked.

Emotional Causes

Emotional factors can also make a child backward. For example, a baby brought up in an institution without individual care lacks the encouragement to learn that the ordinary baby gains through playing and communicating with a devoted mother or mother figure. Such a baby becomes apathetic; if nobody responds to your smiles and burblings there is little stimulus to practice and repeat them. It takes longer to reach and then to consolidate the various stages of development, and although individual attention and love help a child to catch up later, some children never manage to overcome the initial handicap. This applies particularly in a field like learning to speak, which depends on two-way communication. Thus a child with a normal level of intelligence can become permanently handicapped, emotionally disturbed, and educationally backward (see stimulating development, p. 216).

Diagnosing Educational Subnormality

It is comparatively easy to pick out severe mental retardation in babyhood because it shows in extreme slowness in a wide range of activities. It is more difficult to detect the mildly mentally retarded child early on, since he may hold his own as a baby and young child. Physical stages may be reached within the average time and he learns to speak.

It is the use the child makes of language that begins to single him out from other children. He probably asks fewer questions and shows less curiosity about the world than most children. But since normal children vary so much in this respect, his handicap may not become noticeable until he starts school and makes little progress. His teacher may be the first to feel that something is wrong and that he shows more than the normal variation in readiness to learn. Always discuss with your child's teacher any worries you have about his lack of progress.

Learning Difficulties

Many children are just not ready to read and write when they begin school at five; this is recognized as normal in several countries where formal schooling does not start until children are six or seven years old. An earlier start in the United States and in the United Kingdom is in many ways an opportunity to learn to mix and play with others, preparing the child for more conventional education after the age of seven.

A teacher takes this into account when seeking an explanation for learning difficulties, and also bears in mind that they may be due to a lack of stimulus in a child's preschool years or to worries connected with his home life. She has to be alert for the child who is not hearing or seeing properly, although deafness should be discovered long before starting school. She also bears in mind the possibility of special difficulties, such as dyslexia (pp. 570f.).

Teachers should always inform the school physician or school nurse of any child who is educationally slow. Procedures for assessing the child's needs vary from area to area, but it is best if teacher, doctor, and psychologist all take part in the investigation. Parents, of course, should be involved from the start. Part of the investigation will be an IQ test.

IQ Test

A child's IQ (Intelligence Quotient) is measured by an IQ test (see also p. 584). These tests are standardized on the basis of what the ordinary child can achieve at various stages. If a child succeeds at the test set for a given age, he is said to have the corresponding mental age. Thus a ten-year-old who can only manage the tests set for a five-year-old has a mental age of five and his IQ is half the normal level. With a mental age of five, his IQ, expressed as a percentage of his actual age, would be 50. The child whose performance exactly matches the standard set for his age has an IQ of 100.

Measuring intelligence is far more complex than measuring something like height, which starts from zero and can be measured with the same instrument at any age. Intelligence has no fixed starting point or upper limit and it changes in character as the child grows; the same techniques cannot be used for measuring intelligence at the age of two as at the age of ten, or even at five or six. In addition, the five-year-old retarded child with a mental age of three is not the equal of a normal three-year-old in other respects. Even if their IQs are equal, the retarded child is likely to lack the normal three-year-old's curiosity and drive, and to lag behind him in the use of language.

Testing the Retarded Child   It is particularly difficult to test a mentally retarded child because in many instances he cannot co-operate; he may have behavior problems and poor speech as well as low intelligence. He sometimes has other handicaps such as deafness which stop him from expressing himself. A standardized test may be useless for a severely handicapped child, but it has a place in discovering the capabilities and learning difficulties of many mentally retarded children.

Parents sometimes worry that the tests are not suitable for their child or that they are used just to exclude the child from a normal school. However, increasingly sophisticated tests are being devised to measure these children's learning characteristics and to give teachers more information about the individual child's educational needs.

You should not worry that your child will be labeled or assessed on his IQ test alone. The test can be compared with taking a temperature in physical illness—it reveals something about a child's condition at a particular time but will be only one factor in the diagnosis. It is useful in planning a child's education and management but it is only one of many types of assessment.

Doctors, teachers, psychologists, and others whose work with children requires knowledge of their intellectual capacity do not think in terms of an exact figure. The figure obtained as a result of an intelligence test is a measure of the child's achievement on a particular day and under a particular set of circumstances. If he was upset in any way at the time of the test the figure would be lower than his true potential. The test is administered by a psychologist, and all psychologists recognize this point and will always arrange to retest at a later date if they are not satisfied that the test is a correct assessment.

The test, therefore, is not an exam, giving a definitive result, but is one way of measuring a child's intellect. As the child gets older the tests become more difficult. The remarkable fact is that under optimum conditions, the figure for the individual child remains remarkably constant over the years.

Rate of progress in other fields is also important, for example, general behavior, ability to mix with other children, and emotional stability. Children with identical IQs may need different schooling because of different character traits. The determined child may succeed in keeping up with an ordinary class, whereas an equally intelligent child may lack his persistence, and need a slower pace of teaching.

Changing Attitudes to Mental Retardation

In the past, many mentally retarded children were "put away" in institutions because it was assumed that they needed only physical care and protection from life in society. Euthanasia would be considered intolerable by most people: being put away in a large hospital for the mentally subnormal, perhaps without visitors, has been described as "social euthanasia."

Today it is realized that the mentally retarded child has educational, emotional, and social needs that are just as important as his physical needs and as the needs of a child with normal intelligence. If these needs can be met, a larger proportion of mentally retarded people will be able to hold their own in the outside world.

Behavior Problems

We know now that much of the disturbed behavior that was thought to be an inescapable part of mental retardation is really the result of emotional deprivation and the frustration of stifled individuality. It is not an exaggeration to suggest that most normal children would become mentally retarded and disturbed if brought up in the circumstances once thought appropriate for mentally retarded children. The child was often admitted to an institution at an age when every child needs the security of a mother figure, sometimes as an infant and frequently before he was five years old.

Mentally retarded children are usually more, not less, emotionally dependent than other children. Considering the disturbance caused to the ordinary small child by separation from his mother, it is not surprising that a mentally retarded child, removed from his mother's care and brought up in the rigid atmosphere of an old-fashioned institution, should grow up to be a very disturbed adult.

Just imagine what it would be like if all your life you were subjected to rules and regulations as to when you got up and when you went to bed, when you ate and when you went to the bathroom. And that all these activities took place as part of a montonous program with a group of other mentally retarded individuals.

Advantages of Home Life

Mentally retarded children brought up in their own homes are found to have better speech, and to be able to mix with others and look after themselves to a greater extent by the time they reach adolescence. If they do have to enter an institution eventually, they make the adjustment more easily than younger children, and will always keep the advantage of a good start.

It is obviously in the interests of the individual child that he should be brought up to become self-sufficient socially, if possible, but it is also in the interests of society as a whole. The greater the proportion of mentally retarded children living at home, with all possible support for their families from doctors, teachers, social workers, and the community, the greater the chance of providing satisfactory residential care for the few children whose families really need it.

Alternatives to "Institution Life"

For those children requiring residential care, the ideal is a small hostel situated in a town as near as possible to the child's own home. The children in such a hostel will be organized in family groups, each group having its own house mother: a total contrast to the vast institutions run on hospital lines. The aim is to get away from rigid routines that force all the children in a large group to do the same things at the same time, with little respect for their personal needs.

In the past, all the children in the ward of a mental subnormality hospital might have had to use the toilet at the same time, every child sitting there until the slowest one had finished. Even children who were quite capable of using the bathroom normally had to take part in this routine, so that many relapsed and grew up incontinent. The children might spend almost all their time in one room, the ward, even having their meals there and never having a normal person eating at the same table. They would have no experience of ordinary domestic life to draw upon in their play: cooking, washing, and ironing would all be done away from the ward.

Life in an institution can never be the same as life in a family, but it is hoped that in future more effort will be made to provide these normal experiences for mentally retarded children who have to live away from home. Staff members will eat with the children, who will be encouraged to be as independent as possible, and will be helped to keep their individuality.

Managing the Mentally Retarded Child at Home

Much that applies to managing handicapped children of all types is also true of mentally retarded children (see the handicapped child, pp. 578f.). As a general rule, you should treat your child in a way that matches his emotional and intellectual level and his actual achievements, rather than his chronological age. You do this instinctively with a normal child, adapting to his changing needs and realizing that he does not "act his age" the whole time—sometimes he behaves as if he were older and sometimes as if younger than he really is. You encourage him toward the next stage without expecting too much of him at any time.

Maladjustment

Mentally retarded children have emotions and feelings that can be hurt just like a normal child's; being made to feel clumsy and stupid can therefore add to their problems. It is now realized that a high proportion of these children are emotionally maladjusted as well as mentally retarded. If maladjustment can be avoided or reduced, the child becomes easier to live with and some of the family's problems disappear as well. Mentally retarded children suffer from the same emotional difficulties as other children, and therefore require the same treatment; they may also need the help of a child psychiatrist.

Helping Him to Be Happy

You can help your child to be well adjusted by remembering that he may have emotional difficulties as well as mental retardation. The less severely mentally retarded child may suffer particularly, since he is intelligent enough to compare his accomplishments with those of his contemporaries, but all mentally retarded children easily become maladjusted. Even a severely retarded child may feel different and inadequate and, therefore, uneasy and afraid.

When a twelve-year-old plays and behaves in a way more appropriate for a five-year-old, it seems disturbing and odd at first sight; but it is normal for that particular child. If you accept your child's level of activities as being natural for him, they will soon seem natural to other people; the child himself will probably sense this, and become more relaxed and happy as a result. This is the probable reason why Down's children are usually placid and well adjusted. Because people recognize their condition and know they are mentally retarded, they are not expected to do better than their disability permits, as can happen with normal-looking children who are mentally retarded. The parents of Down's children do not have to explain their children's backwardness, as do the parents of mentally retarded children who look normal.

The mentally retarded child, like any other, will be at his best if he senses approval and acceptance rather than dislike or despair. Fear blocks learning and stifles individuality, whether a child is mentally above or below average. Therefore it is important for parents, and everyone involved with the mentally retarded child, to accept his emotional need for respect at his own level.

If you have a mentally retarded child the major step is for you to be helped to accept this fact (see pp. 576–77). Once you have done so you will be much better able to accept the help that can be offered, instead of chasing around from doctor to doctor in the hope of finding one who, wrongly, will say your child is normal, thereby postponing this help for your child.

Even when parents have been able to accept that their child is mentally retarded they are likely to ask the doctor if he will catch up and become normal. This is impossible unless he has a form of mental retardation that can be treated, such as lack of thyroid. If a mentally retarded child is to catch up he would have to develop intellectually at a faster rate than normal for a time—in others words, at the rate of a genius. Clearly this is impossible. Parents of a six-year-old mentally retarded child may have been told that his intellect is at a three-year-old level. This may lead them erroneously to conclude that at ten years of age he will be like a five-year-old.

It is parents who have been unable to accept their baby in the first instance who face the greatest problems. This is largely confined to parents of Down's babies, since they are the only ones whose condition is likely to be detected at birth. Such parents need enormous understanding and professional help to become aware that not only does their baby need them but they need their baby. Later guilt feelings are an inevitable part of rejection. In the early months, the needs of a Down's baby do not differ from those of a normal baby.

Leading a Normal Life

As the problem of mental retardation is brought into the open and becomes part of everyday life, instead of something that is hidden and forgotten, bringing up a mentally retarded child at home will become easier, although it will always be hard work because the child remains more dependent than an ordinary child and will continue to have special problems. For example, he may be difficult to feed because he chews inefficiently, which in turn affects his teeth and gums. (For this reason, a mentally retarded child tends to suffer from tooth decay, and special attention must be paid to his dental health.)

Bringing the problem into the open should help parents to stop feeling ashamed and guilty about their child so that they can treat him in a more normal manner. Some families feel so isolated and so different that the child leads almost as restricted a life in his own home as he would in an institution, never being taken out or mixing with other children. The advantage of living at home is partly lost, and the difficulty of keeping the child there greatly increased, by these illogical but understandable feelings of embarrassment.

Many voluntary societies have done much to help parents with their problems. It is encouraging that an increasing number of play groups are willing to take handicapped children (see the handicapped child, p. 581).

Education (see p. 581)

The Borderline to Mild Child

The slow-learning child whose behavior is normal and who mixes well with other children may be able to remain within the ordinary school system. This is particularly true of children whose backwardness is due to or is aggravated by social problems, such as a broken family background.

The child may be able to keep up in a normal but slow-moving class, and it is ideal if schools have a special small class for such children. These can be excellent: there is a specially trained teacher and each child has more individual attention than would be possible in an ordinary class. However, sometimes the range of abilities, ages, and handicaps contained in one class can be too wide for the teacher to deal with satisfactorily; and often the class is the first to suffer in teacher shortages or other school crises.

In some schools, the children feel themselves to be a class of rejects and the presence of other schoolchildren only makes them feel their difference from the rest of the community. In this case, or if the child has behavior problems as well as limited learning ability, he may be better off in a special school for slow-learning children. As with the education of other types of handicapped schoolchildren, the decision too often depends on what is available locally, rather than on the child's individual needs. Unfortunately, it may sometimes be necessary for parents to move to an area with better educational facilities.

The Severe to Profound Child

Now that the teaching of mentally retarded children is subject to guidelines from the Department of Special Education, the mentally retarded and their teachers are no longer cut off from the mainstream of education. This amounts to an official recognition that mentally retarded children, however severely affected, have the ability to learn and so to benefit from education. Their education will have the same general aim as that of other children: the development of their full potential.

Since the mentally retarded child develops at a much slower pace than an ordinary child, his education needs to continue beyond the normal school-leaving age; he may therefore be kept at a school for the mentally retarded into his mid-teens or later.

It must be emphasized that no school placement is permanent but is always subject to review. Children whose mental retardation resulted from environmental causes may so improve with the special teaching provided that they can be transferred to a normal school.

Social Learning

Much of what the child is taught, particularly in the early years, must necessarily be aimed at helping him to mix with others and to look after his own everyday needs as far as possible. With skillful teachers and a well-planned curriculum, this social learning can be integrated with other forms of learning and other skills. For example, playing shopping at school can lead to visits to real stores, traveling on public transportation, and handling real money. The aim of teaching the child something about numbers is not to give him a knowledge of arithmetic in the ordinary sense, but to enable him to go shopping, to use the telephone, and to undertake similar everyday activities.

Not all severely mentally retarded children are able to become independent to this extent, but all benefit from the encouragement of skilled teachers, and all deserve more than "passive" minding. As more and more such children live at home and attend schools daily, they will have a wider range of experience to draw upon. This in itself will help them to acquire an independence, a knowledge of normal life that could never develop in the restricted life of an institution for the mentally subnormal.

Behavior Modification

These techniques of treatment are being increasingly applied to the problems of mentally retarded children. Many of their associated behavior problems can be reduced under the guidance of a psychologist working through the parents. The aim of this method of treatment is to praise and reward "good" behavior and to disregard bad behavior.

Many parents have unwittingly been encouraging the very behavior they wished to eradicate. For example, a mother may complain that her child keeps shouting. On closer investigation it becomes clear that unless he shouts she takes no notice of him. It is almost as though she has been teaching him to shout. Now she is taught to disregard him when he shouts but, and most important, she must reward him when he is not shouting by playing with him and by encouraging him in every way possible.

What to Do if Your Child Has to Leave Home

If family and personal reasons make it impossible for you to keep your mentally retarded child at home, perhaps because your other children are suffering as a result, there is still much that you can do. First, you will want to ensure that the home or facility to which your child is admitted is satisfactory.

Secondly, make sure that every member of your family is aware that although your child is no longer living under your roof he is still very much part of the family. Visit him as often as possible, preferably with some of your other children as well as your husband. Take him out for trips and, if possible, have him home for some weekends. Write to him and send or bring him presents, just as you would for any other of your children.

Do not feel guilty if you find yourself no longer able to look after your child at home. The fact that he has been able to start his life in his own home will be an advantage he will never lose. You may be helped by not thinking of his stay away as necessarily permanent—events may make it practical for him to return home later on. Your main area of help for him now is to ensure that he still feels a member of the family.

The Autistic Child

Autism is an uncommon mental disorder that affects relatively few children, although the term is becoming well known. It is due to mental illness rather than physical damage to the brain. The cause is unknown; in fact, it is unlikely that there is only one cause, since the condition is not clear-cut (see below).

Characteristics of Autism

The most obvious feature is that the child appears to live in a world of his own. He seems aloof and indifferent to people, and may walk over them as though they were pieces of furniture. He is the exact opposite of the cuddly child; he does not seem to like or to respond to affection.

If a baby is born with the condition, as some such children are, it will be noticeable only when he reaches the stage at which a normal baby begins to enjoy responding to his mother, showing pleasure when she comes near and generally reacting as if he likes company and attention. The autistic baby may never seem to notice his mother's presence, and may never want to be held or cuddled. Having learned to walk, usually at the normal time, he does not use his new skill to make contact with other people and is unable to play normally with other children. He may hardly ever look at anyone directly. However, some autistic children later show that they have noticed a good deal more than was apparent at the time.

Speech Understandably, in a child who seems or is unable to communicate, learning to talk is always affected. A child may never start to speak, or may start and then stop; he may invent his own language or use words in a meaningless repetitive way rather than for communication.

Sense of Identity The child's attitude to himself is also odd. He lacks a sense of his own identity, so that he sometimes treats a part of his body as if it had nothing to do with him personally. His attitude to things as well as to people is abnormal. He cannot understand that objects have particular uses, and uses them merely for his own repetitive games. He reacts inappropriately to sights and sounds and to sensations like heat and cold.

Need for Routine While lacking a normal sense of fear, he may fear something quite ordinary or be acutely anxious for no apparent reason. This is why he needs and demands a monotonous sameness in his routine and surroundings. His mother may have a difficult time getting him to accept any step forward in childhood, such as the change from milk to solid food. Once he has accepted a change, he is likely to cling to it and resist the next change. Parents will need all their ingenuity to help him accept ordinary, everyday situations.

Intelligence The child is not mentally retarded in the usual sense, since for short periods he may behave normally. But his behavior makes it impossible for him to use properly whatever intelligence he possesses. His intelligence may be average or even high; an autistic child may possess an exceptional gift, for example for drawing or mathematics.

Some autistic children are also mentally retarded, with low intelligence, while others suffer from additional handicaps such as deafness. Many of the children look normal, which makes their odd behavior difficult for outsiders to understand; their parents, therefore, have the task of coping with a normal-looking child who behaves badly in public, without the sympathy that is often shown to the parents of an obviously handicapped child like one with Down's syndrome.

The Contrast with Normal Children   Nearly all the characteristics of the autistic child are shown by a normal child to some extent at different stages of his development. For example, every baby lacks a sense of identity at first; he is unaware of himself as an individual or of his mother as a separate person. He does not know that his toes are part of his own body and not just delightful playthings. Gradually, he becomes aware that he is an individual, and that his toes belong to him and are not just a kind of toy.

In the same way, all young children use words inaccurately when they are learning to speak. The baby babbling in his cot enjoys the sounds for their own sake but is delighted if his mother responds; her interest is his stimulus to communicate and his babbling eventually develops into true speech. He repeats things after his parents, but as part of learning to use language for his own purpose, not in the limited way of the autistic child.

Ordinary children play repetitive games; the normal baby learns by practicing the same movement over and over again. But ordinary children play in other ways as well. They begin to understand that a wooden spoon has uses in the kitchen as well as being a good toy.

Some normal babies dislike sitting still on their mothers' laps or being cuddled for more than a moment, but they show their friendliness in other ways and they are restless because they are interested in other things: the autistic baby seems indifferent to or even afraid of contact. Any child may become aloof temporarily when preoccupied with his own thoughts. For example, when ill in the hospital he may refuse to communicate or to look his mother in the eye. Children can be solitary and moody without being autistic.

In a normal child, these characteristics are temporary or usual at a particular stage of development. His general behavior shows that he is aware of himself, of other people, and of what is happening around him. The autistic child shows the same characteristics in an extreme and persistent form, and although they may alter as he grows older, he does not outgrow his inability to adapt to life in a normal way.

Causes

What cuts off the world from the autistic child? Some experts suspect that something prevents him from understanding in an ordinary way what he sees, hears, and feels. Because he does not receive impressions normally, he cannot interpret them and act upon them consistently—he never builds up a coherent picture of the world. The picture he receives may be so distorted and frightening that he tries to shut out new impressions and experiences, demanding routine and sameness in his surroundings to help him cope with them. His poor speech and his lack of incentive to communicate, for whatever reason, make it almost impossible for him to understand the consequences of events or actions. Therefore, it is difficult for him to trust others, to generalize, or to adapt himself as a normal child learns to do.

There are several theories about the cause of autism. It is no longer generally believed that any one cause is responsible; probably several causes interact in any one child. Although it seems that some previously normal children become autistic following an unhappy experience such as separation from their parents, it is unlikely that parental mismanagement is often an ingredient. The autistic child is often a member of a stable family with normal brothers and sisters, with nothing in his background to account for his condition. The child is not abnormal because his parents were cold and unfeeling to him when he was a baby.

Education

While the causes remain uncertain, the main hope of improving the child's condition remains with education, although the techniques used to reach the autistic child resemble therapy rather than formal teaching. Before he can learn anything else, the child must grasp that he exists as an individual with whom other individuals wish to make contact. This means he needs individual attention for a long period before he can make any progress in a group. The teacher has first to establish contact with him, by finding a chink in his armor of apparent indifference: having found it she must keep it open and make it wider.

Different teachers have different methods of helping autistic children. The aim is to help a child to behave more normally so that his behavior does not repel other people or prevent him from learning whatever his intelligence would otherwise allow. Some teachers emphasize learning acceptable behavior first, while others feel that this will follow more easily if the main emphasis is placed first on learning to communicate. Speech therapy is important, because once the child is using speech with more meaning, he tends to progress in other ways as well and to develop more normally from this point onward.

Communication

The teacher will need to learn the child's own language first in order to be able to communicate with him. Many teachers make use of the fact that autistic children seem to learn more easily through the senses of touch and smell than of sight and hearing. It is sometimes found that a child has noticed far more than he showed at the time, and will tell the teacher about something he had seemed unaware of, once he can communicate with her. Even when he can communicate through speech, it is a hard task helping an autistic child to make connections, to see the point of learning and doing new things.

50

Disorders Involving the Brain

The "Spastic" Child (Cerebral Palsy)

There are various types of cerebral palsy. In lay terms the word "spastic" is used to describe all forms of the condition, but in medical terms it is the description of only one form, though this is the largest group.

Cerebral palsy affects a child's movement and posture; it results from damage to the part of the brain that controls the movement and the tension of the muscles. Damage to the movement mechanism causes muscles to be paralyzed; damage to the tension mechanism causes muscles to be too stiff (spastic) or too floppy.

Causes

The damage occurs most often during birth, usually from an interruption of the oxygen supply to the brain; occasionally there is actual tearing of the brain itself. However, sometimes the brain is damaged before birth. Two varieties of damage can occur while the baby is still in the uterus: in the early weeks of pregnancy, when the brain is being formed, an infection, such as German measles in the mother, can attack the developing brain so that it is never properly formed; if in the later weeks of pregnancy, when the brain is growing at its fastest, it does not receive enough food, it fails to grow to its proper size. This lack of food can be due to severe maternal starvation, but it is usually the result of disease of the placenta, which means that not enough food is passed from the mother to her baby.

Babies whose birth weight is lower than average are more likely to suffer brain damage, so that there is a higher incidence of cerebral palsy among preterm babies. Occasionally the condition is due to a congenital malformation of the brain.

Although the condition is always present when the child is born, it may not become obvious for a few weeks or months, when the child should normally be gaining more control of his muscles (see below).

Handicaps Associated with Cerebral Palsy

The damage that causes cerebral palsy can also affect nearby parts of the brain that are responsible for other abilities. For this reason, the child with cerebral palsy is likely to have other handicaps besides those affecting movement and posture.

Intelligence The area of the brain responsible for intellect is near the area controlling movement and is therefore liable to be involved if the damage is extensive. This means that children with the most severe cerebral palsy usually run the greatest risk of mental retardation. However, it has to be remembered that lack of control of facial muscles alters a child's expression, making him look less bright than he really is. In addition, the emotional problems that result from coping with physical handicaps can mask or hinder the full development of intelligence, so that the child's intelligence cannot be gauged by appearance alone.

Sensation The area of the brain that interprets incoming sensations lies just in front of the part affected in cerebral palsy. If this area is damaged, the child's capacity to understand the position of his body in space is limited. Normally, we know where our arms and legs are without having to look at them. We take this for granted, like the ability to tell which side of the body is which, and where our body ends and space begins, but these abilities may be entirely absent in a child with cerebral palsy. He may also have lost the ability to feel sensations on his skin, so that he cannot tell the difference between a prick with the point or the head of a pin, or between hot and cold. In a young child tests for normal sensation are more difficult to carry out than tests of movement, so it may be some time before this aspect of his handicap can be assessed.

Hearing Damage to the brain can also affect the area controlling hearing, causing deafness. Every child with cerebral palsy must have a hearing test; early diagnosis of deafness is essential for its correct management, so that it handicaps the child as little as possible. (See deafness, pp. 567f.)

Eyesight Eye muscles can be among the muscles affected, resulting in a squint. Eyesight itself is seldom affected since it is controlled by the back of the brain, which is far away from the part controlling movement.

The Child with Spastic Cerebral Palsy

The spastic child, using the term in its medical sense (p. 606), suffers from increased muscle tension, although some spastic children start as abnormally "floppy" babies (see below). This increased tension affects different parts of the body according to the type and degree of spasticity, so leading to different types of deformity. The disease may be hardly noticeable or so severe that the child is practically helpless. Movements are slow and the consequent lack of exercise makes it easy for the child to become overweight.

Lack of muscle control leads to many other handicaps: the baby may have trouble sucking, swallowing, and chewing. Speech may be delayed and distorted, because it is controlled by muscles that may also be affected. The child may dribble because he cannot easily swallow his saliva, and this makes him look mentally backward, even if he is not.

The Child with Athetoid Cerebral Palsy

Diminished muscle tension causes "floppiness." The spastic baby is sometimes floppy at first, later becoming stiff; floppiness is also the early stage of athetosis, a form of cerebral palsy in which writhing movements are the main feature. These writhing movements are not present at birth and usually appear during the second year of life. The child is unable to stop them himself but they do stop during sleep, and sometimes when he is awake if he becomes completely relaxed.

The intelligence of a child with athetosis is often normal, because the area of the brain involved in this kind of cerebral palsy is farther away from the area responsible for the thinking processes than in the child with spastic cerebral palsy. The athetoid child is seldom fat, because of his great activity; he is often cheerful and has a great sense of humor.

The commonest cause of athetosis is severe jaundice in the first week of life, this being one reason exchange transfusions are necessary (see p. 441). Jaundice also damages the inner part of the ear, so that athetoid children are often deaf.

Diagnosis of Cerebral Palsy

It is still sometimes said that the early diagnosis of cerebral palsy is both difficult and unimportant because nothing can be done to help a young baby affected by it. This is incorrect; early diagnosis is not difficult for those trained in the normal development of babies, while correct handling, at the earliest possible stage, is essential for the parents as well as for the child.

The condition can be suspected as early as a week after birth. The mother may be the first to feel suspicious, because her baby does not "feel right" when she holds him. He may have difficulty in feeding and move his arms and legs very little. Lack of kicking is serious. Such suspicions must always be investigated by a doctor with specialized knowledge of normal development. The risk of failure to make an early diagnosis is reduced if all babies are checked for normal development as a matter of routine (see pp. 574–75).

Early diagnosis and correct management give the child the best chance of developing to his fullest capacity, with minimum emotional disturbance. Encouraging his attempts at early movement, with the emphasis on achieving balance rather than restraining with splints, reduces the chance of deformity, which can result from using the arms and legs incorrectly.

Parents' Reactions

If you are the parent of a child with cerebral palsy, you will be happier knowing the truth and knowing that your child is being helped; as long as you remain in ignorance you will be frustrated by suspicions that all is not well, while nothing is being done. One important advantage of early diagnosis is that it saves parents the emotional strain of uncertainty about the reason for their baby's problems.

There may be a time lag before you can fully accept the significance of the diagnosis, but if you are told sympathetically and kept informed, you can divert the energy you might otherwise have wasted in hopeless searches for a cure, or for a more hopeful explanation, into helping your child. Once your energies are being used constructively, the situation is likely to become more bearable for the whole family, and the child himself is less likely to develop behavior problems as a result of misunderstanding the cause of his difficulties.

Treatment

Unfortunately, no drug has been found that improves muscle power in children with cerebral palsy, and surgery is seldom advisable while the child is still growing.

The emphasis today is on continued support of parents by doctors, physical therapists, occupational therapists, speech therapists, teachers, psychologists, and social workers, combining together as a team to help the child and his family.

How You Can Help Your Child

As the mother of a child with cerebral palsy, you have the day-to-day responsibility of bringing him up. You have to learn to handle him with patience and skill but without overprotecting him. You must have help to understand his emotional as well as his physical needs; these are as closely linked in the handicapped child as in the normal child.

Development

Your child should be encouraged to follow the normal stages of development as completely as possible. For example, although he may not be able to get his fingers to his mouth by himself, he needs to enjoy sucking and to explore his mouth as much as any other baby; knowing how important this is, you can move his paralyzed fingers into his mouth for him (see p. 547).

He has to be guided through the various stages of childhood in the normal sequence, however slowly and awkwardly. If he is your first baby, you will need advice about this; if you already have other children, you may need reminding that a handicapped child has similar needs but must have more deliberate help from you. In fact, you must know more about normal development than the mother of an ordinary child (see development, pp. 214f.). You will then recognize that your child cannot be expected to stand before he has achieved a degree of head control and has mastered sitting and crawling sufficiently. In the past, many mistakes were made by failure to apply knowledge of normal development to the handicapped child (see the handicapped child, pp. 578f., 596f.).

Physical Therapy

Physical therapists have evolved new ways of helping children with cerebral palsy and can teach you the principles of treatment. Since muscles work in groups, the affected limb is not treated in isolation and forced to move correctly by the use of splints or other appliances; instead, the aim is to help the child to achieve good balance and to overcome abnormal muscle tension by special methods of treatment and handling. It is not just a matter of doing exercises once or twice a day but of learning how to handle him in all his activities throughout the day so as to encourage movement and minimize the risk of deformities developing. The child is encouraged to do things for himself, even if he does them clumsily. The accent is on efficient movement rather than appearance. A baby-bouncer (p. 296), while excellent for a normal child, is not appropriate for a child with cerebral palsy, since it could increase the amount of spasticity.

Occupational Therapy

The occupational therapist works closely with the physical therapist, and in the field of handicapped children both are termed developmental therapists. The occupational therapist concentrates on functional ability and the skills required for daily living. Consequently, the physical therapist is principally concerned with improving the large movements of the whole body, whereas the occupational therapist works on fine movements to improve manipulation of the hands and reduce clumsiness. Both therapists often combine together in their treatment of a child with cerebral palsy.

Adapting to Normal Life

Your child can become more independent if he is provided with suitably adapted clothing, dishes, and eating implements, and if such necessities as going to the bathroom are made as simple as possible for him. Don't be afraid to keep asking whether any new aids have been developed to help handicapped children. National and local societies provide information and support for parents of spastic children, and co-ordination of medical and social help is improving.

In the United Kingdom, toy libraries are now available in many units caring for handicapped children so that suitable toys can be selected and taken out on loan. Similarly, special appliances and other aids to easier living can be loaned.

Education

Whenever possible, the child should attend an ordinary school, although severely affected children may be better off at a special school where their particular needs are understood and physical therapy is part of the program. The severely paralyzed child with a good intellect has the greatest problem, since his ways of expressing himself, for example, through his hands in writing, or through speech, may be very restricted.

Clumsiness

The Normal Clumsy Child

Children, like adults, vary in efficiency and skill of movement. Some are naturally graceful, athletic, and good with their hands, while at the other end of the scale is the child who moves awkwardly, is hopeless at games, butter-fingered, and responsible for more than his share of breakages around the house. Many children are bad at tying up shoelaces because they have better things to do with their time; some of them are just slow to learn this particular skill.

Parents of a clumsy child have to steer a middle course, avoiding constant nagging or constant interference by doing everything for their child, while not completely ignoring the problem. Some children who are extremely good at using their hands when doing something they enjoy, like drawing or playing a musical instrument, are hopeless at things that bore them, like dressing themselves. As a child approaches school age, he needs to be able to look after himself, so a policy of encouragement and learning by trial and error is needed. Seeing children of his own age doing up their own buttons may provide a greater incentive than years of suggestions from you. Practice also is important; some children cannot put their coats on without help because their mothers have always done it for them.

Skill with fingers needs encouragement and practice at the right stage of development, like many other skills. The child who has had nothing suitable to play with and manipulate may not develop his manual dexterity to the full (see living in the tropics, pp. 378–79). However, babies vary in what they will do to help themselves and will often improvise, even if they have only the minimum of playthings.

Abnormal Clumsiness

Some children are abnormally unco-ordinated in their movements. These particularly clumsy children suffer from a slight degree of brain damage, which makes it difficult for them to control their movements. Although this is not a common cause of clumsiness, it is important to recognize it so that parents can be helped to understand why their child is so awkward. The family is then less likely to feel irritated and impatient with him. He can be encouraged in the things he does well, instead of continually being nagged over his inability to tie up shoelaces or to write neatly. Every step should be taken to make dressing easier; for example, he could wear slip-on shoes instead of tie shoes. When parents know why a child is clumsy and make allowances for it, the child is less likely to become frustrated and disturbed by trying to improve when he cannot. Some of these children also have squints (see p. 468).

As well as a slight lack of muscle control, the child may have difficulty in interpreting the information received through his senses; for example, he may be unable to tell which is the left or right side of his body, or to assess accurately the distance between objects. He cannot interpret these sensory messages properly and therefore cannot react to them correctly. This type of slight brain damage may be responsible for making a child abnormally liable to be involved in accidents (see accidents, pp. 620f.).

There is no clear cutoff point between normal and abnormal clumsiness, but if you are concerned because your child is especially clumsy you should consult your doctor.

Meningitis

This is inflammation of the meninges, the lining that surrounds the whole of the brain and spinal cord. It is due to infection by bacteria or viruses. The meninges can also be directly infected from outside as the result of a head injury that penetrates the skull. Whatever the cause of the meningitis, the general symptoms are similar, although the disease presents a different picture at different ages.

Meningitis in Babies

Diagnosis can be particularly difficult in babies, since at this age the symptoms of meningitis resemble those of other infections. The baby may simply be irritable and unwell, refusing his feedings, and vomiting. He may also have convulsions. Unlike adults and older children, babies seldom develop stiffness of the neck or dislike of light (photophobia). You will notice the doctor feeling the anterior fontanel (soft spot) on your baby's head; meningitis causes this to be tenser than normal, and sometimes it bulges up to form a bump on the head.

If there are only general signs of infection, and the doctor can find nothing to account for the baby's condition, he will investigate the two hidden sites of infection in children: the urine for urinary infection and the cerebrospinal fluid for meningitis. The latter is tested by a procedure known as a lumbar puncture (see below).

Meningitis in Children

The classical features of meningitis in adults—neck stiffness, headache, and dislike of light—are not necessarily early signs of meningitis in young children, although you may worry about these symptoms because they are associated with meningitis. A stiff neck can have many causes (see stiff neck, p. 465). It is not a common symptom of meningitis in children before the age of two years. Meningitis can cause headache in children, but this does not mean you should be worried about meningitis whenever your child develops a headache (see p. 542).

One of the most important signs of meningitis is a sudden and drastic change of mood. A child who becomes unaccountably irritable, behaving in a completely uncharacteristic way, and who also has other symptoms such as headache, vomiting, fever, and a stiff neck, needs the doctor. Since meningitis sometimes develops as a complication of another infection, any such change for the worse in a child who is already ill should be reported to your doctor.

Meningitis must be treated early, and in all cases a lumbar puncture will be done to confirm the diagnosis. This is repeated to show when recovery is complete. With modern antibiotic treatment the outlook for children with meningitis is good provided there is no delay in starting treatment.

Lumbar Puncture

Owing to difficulties in diagnosis, this test is needed far more frequently for children than for adults. The child lies down on his side, curled up, and is gently held so that his backbone is exposed. After giving him a local anesthetic, the doctor inserts a needle between two of the bones of the spine to draw off a sample of the cerebrospinal fluid, which bathes the spinal cord. The fluid is then tested chemically and examined under the microscope for evidence of meningitis.

Deafness as a Sequel

A child who has meningitis should have his hearing tested afterward, since partial deafness can result and must be dealt with promptly.

Encephalitis

Encephalitis is inflammation of the brain. It is usually the result of infection by one of a number of viruses that favor the brain as their site of attack.

Brain inflammation is also an occasional complication of infectious fevers such as measles, whooping cough, and German measles; very rarely, it is triggered off by vaccination for measles or whooping cough, but the risk involved in vaccination is far smaller than the risk of the actual disease.

Vaccination against whooping cough is not given to children who have had convulsions, since they have an increased risk of encephalitis (see immunization, p. 264).

The symptoms resemble those of meningitis (see p. 613). A lumbar puncture is needed to confirm the diagnosis (see above). There is no special treatment for most cases of encephalitis, but the outlook varies according to the virus causing the disease.

Febrile Convulsions

Causes

These are the commonest variety of convulsions or fits—the words mean the same thing—in young children, and are caused by a sudden high temperature. A young child's brain is less stable than an adult's and is therefore more easily irritated by fever. This irritation stimulates the nerves leading to the muscles, the muscles contract, and a convulsion results.

Many young children start even slight infections, such as colds, with a rapid rise in temperature. This tendency to react to infections with a high fever and to fever with a convulsion is most frequent between the ages of one and three, hardly ever occurring after the age of five.

Teething should never be regarded as the cause of a fever or of a convulsion; the fact that a child is teething at the time proves nothing except that he is at the age when cutting teeth is normal (see pp. 248–49). Similarly, constipation is not a cause of convulsions.

The tendency to febrile convulsions runs in families. As the child gets older he will lose the tendency, probably at the same age as other children in his family who have been similarly affected.

Symptoms

Convulsions are very frightening to parents. The child becomes unconscious, twitching uncontrollably; his whole body may shake. His eyes roll up; he breathes heavily and may froth slightly at the mouth. He clenches his teeth, though he seldom bites his tongue, so that more damage is done by prizing open the jaws to force an instrument between the teeth to protect the tongue than by leaving him alone. The child may wet himself during the convulsions, and, less often, he may also soil himself.

A convulsion is always followed by sleep—this is one way in which a doctor distinguishes it from fainting. The child comes to and then falls asleep, or he may slip straight into sleep after the convulsion. An unconscious child breathes in a noisy way, similar to snoring, and looks strange; if the child is just asleep he will look as he does normally; so you would be able to tell the difference.

What to Do

You must stay with your child throughout the convulsion; it often lasts only a few seconds and never more than a few minutes. Although you may long for support and advice, don't panic and leave your child while you rush to a neighbor or to telephone the doctor. Lay him on a bed or on the floor and kneel beside him. A convulsion is never fatal, but the danger in leaving a child alone is that he may be sick and inhale the vomit into his lungs, which can cause death. For this reason he should be placed in the prone position, that is, on his stomach, with his head to one side so that the vomit comes out of his mouth instead of going down into his lungs. The other reason for not leaving the child alone is the terror he would feel if he found himself alone when he came to.

Don't try to restrain the child's jerking arms and legs but do prevent him from striking them against hard furniture, and move him away from danger, such as a fire or heater. On no account should you shake or thump him in an attempt to bring him around. When he comes to or when he falls asleep, contact the doctor immediately. While waiting for him to arrive, start to cool the child (see below). It is safe to move him once the convulsion is over.

Prevention

The main way to prevent febrile convulsions is to prevent high fevers. When a child gets hot he needs to be cooled. Remove his blankets and sweaters and open the windows. The old idea that a child who is feverish should be kept warm is quite wrong, though some mothers whose children are actually convulsing from excessive heat wrap them up to keep them warm! If your child's temperature rises above 39.4°C (103°F) he should be tepid-sponged (see p. 401) until it comes down to 38.8°C (102°F). One children's aspirin or acetaminophen tablet may also help.

Doctors debate whether children who tend to get febrile convulsions are helped by long courses of anticonvulsant medicine, such as phenobarbital. Recent evidence makes this seem unlikely; therefore your doctor is unlikely to prescribe more than a week's course at the time of the feverish illness. I do not recommend asking a mother to give an anticonvulsant medicine such as phenobarbital as soon as her child becomes feverish. I prefer all the emphasis to be on preventing the temperature from getting high when he is ill. I find that a mother left with phenobarbital to give when there is a rise in temperature is perpetually giving her child a dose or worrying whether she should. Some mothers are needlessly frightened that a temper tantrum can cause a rise in temperature and lead to a febrile convulsion. In consequence they handle their child unnaturally in order to prevent him from ever getting angry.

Other Causes of Convulsions

If a doctor is uncertain about the cause of a convulsion, he will arrange for an electroencephalogram (see below). A lumbar puncture (p. 614) is sometimes ordered to exclude the possibility of meningitis or other brain disorder. A young baby who suffered brain damage at birth may have convulsions as a result. Febrile convulsions are by far the commonest type in young children. The next most common is epilepsy.

Epilepsy (Seizures)

The doctor diagnoses this conditon by eliminating other possible causes in a child who has had a convulsion. In most cases the child with epilepsy will already have had a number of convulsions before the term "epilepsy" is used.

Electroencephalogram (EEG)

To help him in his diagnosis the doctor is likely to arrange for an electrical test in order to record the brain waves—an electroenceph-alogram. Normal brains produce normal waves, which differ from those of people with epilepsy. Although the machine and its wires look alarming, the test causes no pain and the child remains awake. The ends of the wires are simply stuck to the scalp with special glue for the duration of the test, which takes one to two hours. The child does not have to stay in the hospital

"Petit Mal"

There are two main types of epilepsy, and a child may suffer from one type only or from both. In the milder type, "petit mal," the child suddenly loses consciousness for a moment, looking vacant and pale; sometimes his head droops. The episode lasts little more than a second or two, and the child then comes to and goes on with whatever he was doing before as if nothing has happened. He will pick up his conversation exactly where it was when the attack occurred. This may happen several times a day; the child usually has the same type of attack on each occasion. He does not fall down, nor does he pass urine.

Many children tend to look vague and "far away" without suffering from epilepsy. There is no difficulty in distinguishing between ordinary daydreaming and petit mal. The child who is daydreaming can easily be brought back into his surroundings, whereas the child with petit mal is, for the moment of the attack, cut off from his surroundings.

"Grand Mal"

This term is used for a major fit, which looks like a febrile convulsion (see above). The child loses consciousness, shakes, clenches his teeth, and may froth at the mouth. The difference is that the patient with epilepsy starts having fits at a later stage than the child with febrile convulsions—in fact, he is often an adult.

Although the convulsion in someone with epilepsy may be

brought on by a fever, it more often occurs "out of the blue." The muscular effort involved in a convulsion can cause a rise in temperature, and this can cause confusion as to whether or not the attack was caused by the fever. The doctor will therefore question you closely on the timing of the fever in relation to the start of the convulsion. If he is still in doubt, he will probably order an electroencephalogram (see above).

Helping the Child to Adjust to Epilepsy

A tendency to epilepsy does not in itself affect a child's personality. It is now realized that many of the behavioral and emotional problems suffered by people with epilepsy and previously ascribed to the disease were the result of other people's reactions to the condition and the way patients were treated. They used to be ostracized by society, especially if they were put together in an "epileptic" colony. Children with epilepsy should never be referred to as "epileptics."

Parents sometimes blame themselves, wrongly suspecting that the epilepsy is due to something they could have controlled, perhaps during pregnancy. They often feel guilty, yet ashamed of the fits; this leads to efforts to protect the child, and their own feelings, by restricting his activities and by discouraging him from mixing with other children. The original problem of coming to terms with the convulsions is sometimes overshadowed by the child's attempts to shield his parents and other people; he may even try to conceal his fits from them. However, provided a child is handled sympathetically, as an ordinary person, his emotional and intellectual development can be quite normal.

Treatment with Drugs

The tendency to major epileptic fits can be controlled by drugs. If the epileptic pattern of the brain waves can be subdued for long periods, the tendency to produce fits may disappear altogether. Treatment with drugs, which usually has little effect on alertness, makes it possible for the child to go to an ordinary school and to play games. This is very important in helping the child. Obviously some forms of activity would be dangerous, such as cycling, but swimming is safe if one adult takes total charge of the child while he is in the water. It is advisable to leave the door open while the child is in the bathtub, in case he has a fit while bathing. Your management of the individual fit is the same as that described for a febrile convulsion (p. 614).

Attacks of petit mal can also be prevented, though without such certainty as grand mal. However, since these attacks are much less dramatic and less disturbing to children who see them, the child has little difficulty in leading a normal life. He is best helped if you encourage him to accept the inconvenience, disregarding the attacks as far as possible.

In the past, the fear engendered by a convulsion did untold harm to the individual. Today the attitude of society is a great deal more enlightened.

Fainting

This problem particularly affects the older schoolchild. Fainting results from insufficient blood reaching the brain, and there can be several reasons for this. School assembly provides the ideal circumstances for fainting: the room is hot, stuffy, and overcrowded, causing blood to be diverted to the skin for cooling purposes. The child has to stand for long periods, thereby reducing the blood supply to the brain; he has probably had a hurried breakfast after jumping out of bed and then rushed to school, so that extra blood is still being used for digestion; in addition, he may have been worried about being late.

Preventing Anxiety

When one child faints, other children present are likely to become frightened that they will do the same thing. One way of tackling the problem is to ask the school principal to allow the children to sit down during assembly, even if on the floor, since attacks occur only when standing up. You can help the child who is worried about fainting by telling him he will get a warning—he may first feel dizzy and possibly sick.

What to Do

When a child feels faint he should immediately sit down and put his head between his knees; the feeling will then pass off. If a child has fainted, loosen his collar and let him have plenty of fresh air, preferably by taking him out of doors. A glass of water to drink helps. He does not need to be made to lie down or keep quiet for the rest of the day.

Why Do Some People Faint?

Some people never faint, others faint frequently. People with a tendency to faint probably suffer from an occasional inefficiency of the blood supply to the brain. The cause is unknown and no permanent harm results. The idea that fainting is due to anemia is mistaken.

51

Accidents

Reducing the Risk

In developed countries, now that illness kills fewer children, accidents have taken over as the largest cause of death and disabling injury in childhood. Every parent dreads the possibility of an accident to his child. The fear is hard to dismiss permanently, because however safe you make your home, and however skillfully you guide your child toward a sense of self-preservation, this is something over which you can never have complete control.

Emotional Consequences

When a child is involved in an accident, parents rarely feel entirely blameless, even if they are. They blame themselves, or each other, or another child. So an accident in the family causes emotional stress as well as physical injury.

The child has had a mental shock and needs to talk about the accident. His parents may begin treating him like a younger child until they get over their fright. This may go on far too long. A child who was trusted to cross the street alone until he was knocked over may be escorted everywhere for years longer than is necessary; a baby who banged his head in a fall may be restrained from climbing on even the lowest chair.

Avoiding Overprotection

It is particularly difficult to steer a reasonable course between over-protecting your child and allowing him an appropriate degree of freedom after an accident. It is hard not to hover over him when he is climbing the smallest tree because he once fell and hurt himself. But hovering over him is likely to do more harm than another fall, since an overprotected child either becomes too timid to enjoy himself with other children in the normal way or becomes defiant and takes more risks than he otherwise would. Moreover, he gets no practice in working out for himself the dangers of particular situations.

Self-preservation

Even the most daring small boy has some sense of self-preservation —he does not actually want to kill himself. If he is taught to use his penknife safely or to boil water, he will be safer than if these are forbidden areas and everything is done for him "just in case." However, a child may lack the experience to assess danger accurately, and what experience he possesses tends to evaporate when he is trying to impress his friends. He jumps off a high wall, even though he suspects it is too high for him, because he wants to keep up with a bigger boy.

An accident may happen when several children, scrambling about in excitement, forget their normal caution. It is wise to intervene in a potentially dangerous situation of this kind, but difficult to find the happy mean between unnecessary interference and too much looking the other way. You will get to recognize the situations in which your children become overexcited and danger-prone; you will know when to remove the penknife or stop the sword fight.

The Parents' Role

You can assume that your child will gain an increasing fund of sense and assurance concerning his own self-protection, provided he has had the opportunity to try things for himself, to test his surroundings, and to take some responsibility for mastering them. It is only while he is very young that you have to do all the testing and take all the responsibility. Even the baby in his crib can have an accident, though the dangers multiply dramatically when the baby is no longer immobile but an explorer, at first lacking the knowledge and experience to keep himself out of trouble. A preschool child is in the greatest danger in his own home and yard, the schoolchild when he is outside his home. After the first birthday, boys have more accidents than girls, because they involve themselves in situations of greater risk.

Making Your Home Accidentproof

As a parent, your job is to make your home as accidentproof as possible and to help your child to be safe both inside and outside it. Ask your local health center, visiting nurse, or your insurance company, which probably has a pamphlet, for advice. It would be ideal if an "accident prevention officer" were available to help parents by looking over homes and suggesting improvements in safety, because this is an area where the first mistake can be fatal.

However safe your home and however good you are at helping your child to become safety conscious, you cannot supervise every moment of his life. A critical outsider easily forgets that even if a parent does seem to be to blame for an accident, it is quite an achievement to steer a small child through each twenty-four hours and avoid the thousand and one other potential accidents along the way. Parents practically develop antennas to protect their children from danger under normal circumstances—which is why an accident is more likely to happen during house moving, after illness or bereavement, and when a baby-sitter, less used to the child and the house, is in charge, or in someone else's home, where the setting is unfamiliar and potentially dangerous objects may be within reach.

Accident-prone Families

Sometimes the antennas fail; parents become less capable of preventing accidents, perhaps through stress and worry; a child in the family has an accident, sometimes more than one accident, which he would not have had if his mother had felt her normal self. The house itself may be as safe as any other, and the remedy lies not in improving its safety, but in helping the parents to feel themselves again.

You may have noticed that if you are preoccupied with personal worries, you are less quick to see your baby lurching toward the pan of boiling water, and more apt to leave the handle of the pan sticking out over the edge of the stove where he can reach it. If you are lucky, you merely have a fright—if you are unlucky, the child is scalded. So it is wise to make a double effort to be careful at a time of domestic stress.

Family stress and emotional problems in the child are an important cause of repeated accidents in a family, but this is not to say that every run of accidents can be put down to emotional problems. Physical living conditions can increase the liability to accidents. Overcrowding, unsafe equipment, such as kerosene heaters kept because parents cannot afford to replace them, and the general difficulty of caring for children adequately in bad housing conditions, all contribute. Children may be turned out to play in traffic-laden streets because there is no room to play at home. Children living in apartments may be so unused to playing freely that they easily run into trouble when confronted with greater space and opportunity.

The Dangers of Affluence

Paradoxically, the most lavishly equipped and spacious home can contain more dangers than a poor home. A kitchen full of electrical gadgets and a yard with a swimming pool are hazards avoided by the children of a family that has to share a kitchen and water supply. Every kind of household has different problems in making its environment as safe as possible for the children, but there are general rules that apply to any household, and points that apply particularly to children at different ages.

Preventing Accidents

Special Dangers in the First Two Years

Safety in the Home   The impending arrival of a baby should make you take another look around your home and its equipment. It may seem ages before your baby will be old enough to get himself into trouble, but try to visualize him as an inquisitive toddler when buying new equipment. For example, new saucepans should preferably have small handles on both sides rather than one long handle; a new washing machine or stove should, ideally, have its knobs sited high up out of a small child's reach. All heaters and screens should be childproof, not just those bought for the nursery. Trailing electrical cords are dangerous and worn electrical cords must be replaced. Any new plugs should be shuttered and preferably placed out of reach; gas taps should be the kind that cannot be turned on easily.

It goes without saying that all the baby's own equipment and his room should be safe (see p. 23 and pp. 29f.). Have his upstairs window barred before he horrifies you by climbing on the sill and leaning out. The bars should be placed vertically to prevent climbing and should be too close for his head to get stuck between them.

Anticipating Trouble   Accidents involving babies frequently happen because a baby catches his parents unawares with a new skill. He may roll off the bed and bang his head because you did not realize he could roll. He may knock a cup of coffee out of your hand and over you both because he has decided waving his arms is more fun than sitting swaddled on your lap. He falls while climbing out of his crib before you realize he can. In other words, you must always be one step ahead of him.

Suffocation   A small baby who cannot crawl may not get himself into trouble but he cannot get himself out of it either. You have to protect him from the attentions of pets and other children. Put a net over the baby carriage in the yard if there are cats in the neighborhood. If you have a pet cat which makes a habit of climbing into the cradle, it is safer to use a net indoors also, or to shut the cat out of the baby's room. Once he can shuffle and turn his head, a baby will change position if the cat does come uncomfortably near his face. This applies to smothering in bedclothes too—a normal baby moves if his breathing is obstructed; the dangers of suffocation have been exaggerated in the past (see crib deaths, p. 650). But avoid using a pillow for the first twelve months—it is unnecessary anyway.

Plastic bags are a common cause of suffocation in young children. A bag put over the head instantly blocks the nose and mouth, and can kill almost at once. If you must keep these bags in the house, treat them like a deadly poison; keep them locked away or tie a knot in the top of each bag before storing.

Protecting Your Baby from Other Children   However safe your baby's carriage, crib, and highchair, another child, in particular a jealous small brother or sister, can make them dangerous, perhaps "accidentally on purpose." The steadiest carriage can be tipped over or set in motion by a determined child who cannot assess the amount of harm he is doing and who is expressing general resentment, rather than intent to murder. You will be more furious with him for tipping up the carriage than for doing something less dangerous, such as kissing the baby a little too hard, but the child may be feeling far more murderous when giving the kiss.

Prevention is best; when in doubt, don't leave the older child alone with the baby when you are at the other end of the house. Remove temporarily any sharp or hefty toys that could be used as missiles aimed at the crib. But if a small child does hurt or nearly hurt the baby, try not to make him feel too guilty. He has not yet learned to control his strongest feelings (see jealousy, pp. 148f.).

Choking   Mealtimes can be dangerous. Choking is one of the most common accidents in babyhood, and your baby should never be left eating alone even when he can hold his own toast or roll. If he does choke he needs you there to help at once. Never leave him feeding himself from a propped bottle; the milk may go down the wrong way, making him choke or vomit and possibly causing ear trouble by entering the Eustachian tubes (see p. 93).

When your baby begins mixed feeding, avoid small hard pieces of food. If he does begin to choke, especially if he also goes blue in the face, and you cannot get the piece of food out with your finger, turn him upside down and slap him on the back until he coughs it out. There is always fear with this action lest the object is forced further inward. Consequently, a new method has been developed called the Heimlich Maneuver. Stand behind the child, who is upright, putting both your arms around his *upper* abdomen *just below the ribs*. Make a fist with your clasped hands and jerk them back toward his spine. This empties the lungs of air so that the inhaled object is forced out.

Never give a young child peanuts, since they contain arachis oil that causes severe irritation and inflammation in the lungs if the nut is inhaled accidentally; therefore, the damage can persist even after the nut has been removed. Once your baby can pick things up, any small objects that may choke him should be kept out of his reach.

Safety at the Table   Another mealtime hazard is the pulled tablecloth, which brings everything on the table cascading over the baby. If this includes a scalding pot or sharp knives, the results can be catastrophic. Give up tablecloths and get into the habit of putting hot liquids and sharp knives out of his reach. Always strap your baby into his chair, even if he is only there a minute or two, because this is quite long enough for him to lean out and tip over. Avoid thin plastic bibs, which can suffocate your baby if he pulls them over his face.

Bathtime Bathtime is also full of potential dangers. A baby can drown in only an inch or two (a couple of centimeters) of water and should never be left alone in the bath. Let the doorbell and the telephone to ring or take your baby out of the bath to answer them. Always put cold water into the bath before hot to avoid the risk of scalding, and never leave a small child alone with the baby when he is in the bath—he may turn on the hot tap (see bathing the baby, pp. 97f.). If you take these safety precautions from the beginning, they become second nature very quickly.

Safe Toys What about safe toys for babies? It is comparatively easy to vet the safety of toys bought for your baby. Safety regulations control the manufacture of home-produced toys, but some imported toys escape the net. Points to look out for are small parts, such as the eyes of a soft toy, which your baby can detach and swallow; and avoid toys with sharp edges. Secondhand toys are sometimes repainted with poisonous lead-containing paint, which your baby may suck off.

Almost any toy can be dangerous if wrongly used, which is why a baby is more likely to be hurt by another child's toys than by those bought for him. When there is more than one child in the family it is impossible to ban every toy that could be dangerous to the baby. It is wise to discourage bead-threading within the baby's reach but difficult to justify forbidding beads altogether because there is a baby in the house who might choke on one. The humble marble could be outlawed on these grounds. A ball left on the stairs could kill. A toy car, safely made with smooth edges and lead-free paint, is unsafe when used as a weapon; so is a building brick; and a baby can choke on the small parts of a construction set.

The only answer is to ban obviously dangerous toys, like guns with pellets, bows with sharp arrows, and toys with cutting edges and sharp points. Keep the older child and baby separated by a playpen if necessary.

Protecting the Exploring Baby

Once your baby can move around, additional dangers loom up on every side. Even if you have thought ahead in terms of safety, there will be some unforeseen accident spots, which, with luck, you will spot before the baby does. Unsteady furniture, slippery floors, ornaments on coffee tables, grandfather clocks, and many other challenges to his investigating instinct must be dealt with before he damages them and possibly himself.

Keep him out of rooms that cannot be made safe. It is better to give a child the freedom of a small part of the house that is safe, than to allow him everywhere while you worry or tag along anxiously in case he hurts himself.

Learning the Meaning of "No" The mobile baby is also beginning to understand language, or at least the tone of your voice and the expression on your face; you start to use the word "no" with some hope of success. The less often you have to say "no" to prevent accidents, the more chance there is of his regarding it as a word with meaning, which he obeys promptly when it really matters, thus preventing an accident.

Distracting His Attention

Your baby will get to know what "no" means sooner if at first you reinforce it with action, stopping him from doing whatever he was about to do. It is best of all to stop him before he gets to the point of imminent danger, distracting him from his obvious intention to climb up the rickety bookcase before he puts his foot on the first shelf, not after he is halfway up (see discipline at different ages, pp. 275f.).

However well your baby understands and obeys the word "no," there are some areas in which it is not safe to rely on his obedience; you have to ensure that disobedience is not punished by injury, disfigurement, or death. One of these areas is burns and scalds.

Preventing Burns and Scalds

All new equipment should be bought with your children's safety in mind. If you have to make do with equipment that is potentially dangerous for a small child, you must make it safe.

Fires An open fire should have a screen which is hooked to the wall so that your child cannot move it. The screen must be fine so that he cannot poke a stick through it. A bar-type electric fire should also be protected with this kind of guard; the token guard provided with the fire is usually totally inadequate. A convector heater is safer, since it has no exposed elements; although your child may push things down the slots and put the heater out of action, it will not injure him. Kerosene stoves are a bad idea when there are small children in the home. Since they are seldom fixed in place, they can be tipped over accidentally, putting the whole family at risk. New oil stoves are safer than old ones, since safety regulations ensure that if they are used correctly, the risk of fire is minimized. A mirror over the fireplace and ornaments on the mantelpiece tempt a child to climb on a chair to reach them. Make the fireplace as uninteresting as possible.

Electrical Fittings   Children poke things into the holes of outlets unless they are closed. Even if the points are safe in your house, those in other people's homes may not be, and your child may receive a shock if he fiddles. For this reason, teach children never to play with plugs and electrical fittings, and never to touch electric switches with damp hands, since this increases the risk of a shock. Putting a plug in a socket and switching on looks like fun—it is just the kind of thing you encourage him to do with his educational interlocking toys, after all—but plugging in the television set is something he must leave strictly alone until he is old enough to do it properly.

Methods of prevention vary with the individual child. If your child is fascinated by plugs, and you cannot have them moved out of his reach, place a heavy piece of furniture in front of the outlets. The same could be done in the case of gas taps, which are easy for a child to turn on.

Inflammable Clothing   Never leave matches around, although it is a good idea to teach a child how to strike and use matches carefully. Nonflammable materials are used in the manufacture of children's sleepwear. Young children should wear pajamas, and never night-dresses, which get caught more easily in the fire or in a heater.

Safety in the Kitchen   It is in the kitchen that your child is in greatest danger of scalding and burns. He may spend much of his time in your company, and it would be hard to imagine a more danger-ous environment for a small child. A playpen in the corner of the kitchen is one answer if your child will stay in it; alternatively, he may be content to sit strapped in a highchair or a carriage for a short time or to play in a baby-bouncer (see play, p. 296). However, he may refuse to stay put, insisting on trailing around after you. You may become amazingly adept at not tripping and at maneuvering yourself safely around the kitchen and the child, but it is not an ideal situation.

Check your baby's whereabouts before transporting a hot pan, always remember to turn the pan handles away from the edge of the stove so he cannot pull hot liquid over himself, and never leave a pot of boiling water within his reach. But however careful you are, cook-ing with a small child around is full of hazards, and it is far safer to have a play area visible from but physically apart from the working area of the kitchen.

Preventing Poisoning

While you are slaving over the hot stove, trying to prevent your child from burning or scalding himself, he may be busy opening a cabinet door and sampling its contents.

Household Cleaners   Before your child gets at these for the first time, move your cleaning, disinfecting, and general household articles to a cabinet he cannot open. Limiting the number and variety of containers full of potential poisons also reduces the dangers. For instance, bleach can double as a bathroom cleaner, making a special cleaner unnecessary. Keep it out of reach, not on the bathroom floor. Never transfer anything that could be poisonous into another container. Children have died drinking "lemonade" from a bottle that turned out to contain kerosene, bleach, lye, or antifreeze.

Some small children are more than usually liable to taste or drink anything they can lay hands on. If your child is like this it is safest to lock up even your cosmetics. But any baby may experiment once, and once can be sufficient to kill him.

Pills and Medicines   Pills are the greatest danger because they often resemble candy and are left about in accessible places like bedside tables and handbags. In addition, some parents unwisely pretend that drugs are candies when trying to get their child to take his medicine. Never do this: always make it clear that medicine is medicine, to be taken in the correct dosage, even if this makes the job of giving it harder.

Don't take your tablets in front of your young child—he may copy you. Empty the family medicine cabinet of all obsolete drugs, half-full bottles, and pillboxes and make sure it is locked and inaccessible to children. Many drugs lose their effectiveness if stored, and your doctor would rather see you for a repeat prescription than for a case of poisoning.

Some of the commonest drugs are the most lethal to children. Iron tablets, which so many mothers have to take, can kill a child quickly. Antidepressants, sleeping pills, tranquilizers, and aspirin can kill. Even if the child escapes death, poisoning is a traumatic experience for him and for you (p. 636). All tablets should be supplied in child-resistant containers, whose caps are difficult for children to remove. But no one has made a perfect childproof container, one that children cannot open at times. Consequently, your aim must be that your child never can reach such containers.

Berries and Plants   Train a child never to taste berries in the yard or field without asking what they are. Laburnum and laurel are deadly, but it is far safer to train your child to regard any berry as potentially dangerous. Obviously you will not allow dangerous plants in the home.

Cigarettes Don't leave your cigarettes around either. Eating just one cigarette can poison a small child. In fact, try to cultivate tidiness about anything you do not want your child to eat or drink. For what to do if a child takes poison, see pages 637–38.

Preventing Falls

Small children frequently stumble when learning to walk, run, climb stairs, etc. Usually they do not hurt themselves, but it is best to eliminate any unnecessary obstacles such as loose rugs and move furniture your baby habitually bumps into. Awkward changes of level, such as a step from one room to another, cannot be eliminated, so teach him to negotiate them. He will probably get down on all fours to do so until he can walk down steadily.

Stair Gates Stairs must be barred with a gate once your baby is mobile, until he can climb efficiently. The gate must fit well and be strong enough to withstand his tugging. Once he can climb over it, it is safer to remove it. Encourage him to learn to cope with stairs by himself. Teach him to walk downstairs backward—he will be able to get up and down on all fours before he learns to walk properly. Keep the gate in place at the top of the stairs as long as there is a risk of his falling downstairs or of being accidentally pushed by another child.

Climbing Some children love climbing on furniture, and unless you dissuade them or are willing to accompany them everywhere, they will go on doing so. Good climbers rarely fall off if left to themselves, but they may if there are several children helping to put them off balance. Accidents on climbing frames are rare unless this happens (see climbing frames, pp. 630–31).

    With a climber in the family, it is important to check that the furniture he uses is steady; move it against a wall or remove it if it is not. If a child does fall, it is the effect the fall has upon him rather than the exact number of feet he has fallen that is significant (pp. 638–39).

Upstairs Windows These should always have guards placed so that the child cannot get his head stuck between the bars. To prevent their use as a climbing frame, the bars should be placed vertically. An alternative to bars is a screw that permits limited opening only.

Miscellaneous Perils

Locking Himself In Children easily lock themselves in when playing with locks and bolts. It is important to have bolts, especially in rooms like the bathroom, sited high above the reach of a small child. And remember that your child may slam the front door while he is still inside and you are already outside. If you have no key and have locked up efficiently, you may have to call the fire or police department to get in again—meanwhile, he may be getting into all kinds of danger and will probably be frightened too.

Wandering Outside   Your child may discover he can open the front door or yard gate and decide to go exploring without you, which could be disastrous if you live on a busy street. Use locks and padlocks and check the fence until he can be trusted not to wander out.

Slamming Doors   Teach children not to slam shut or kick open doors and never do so yourself when there is the possibility of small fingers getting caught and injured. Drawers and windows with broken glass can also injure hands and fingers, so have repairs done quickly.

Dangers in the Yard   It is of little use making your house safe if your yard or garage remain dangerous. Your child must not be able to get out of the yard without your knowledge (see above), and while he is in it he must be as safe as possible; you will then be able to allow him the freedom to play alone outside. A pond or swimming pool must be completely fenced off or, if this is impractical, drained. Otherwise, the risk and worry of a pool are simply not worth it while you have children of preschool age who can drown in the shallowest water. I am appalled by the number of children who drown in their own yards.

Lock a shed that contains dangerous tools such as garden shears and lawn mowers, and poisons such as fertilizers and weed-killers.

The Garage   The same applies to the garage; the car should be locked too, to prevent the possibility of your child climbing in, perhaps releasing the hand brake, or slamming the door on his hand. Always check that your child is not hidden by the back of the car when you are reversing; using the mirror is not enough—he is too short for you to see him if he is near the car. It is safer to reverse the car into the garage so that you can drive it out forward. Garages often contain tools and poisons, and these must be stored in a safe place. Remind your husband about this and also insist that he put away garden tools that could hurt your child; even the rake left lying on the lawn can cause serious injury.

Swings and Climbing Frames   Swings, climbing frames, and slides can lead to accidents, particularly if several children are playing on them at once. It is safest to site these on grass to make any falls that do occur less painful. Teach children never to push the swing at another child and always to look before starting to swing, in case someone is in the way. Most children are amazingly agile at an early age and rarely hurt themselves on this type of equipment.

Discarded Refrigerators   It is difficult to know what advice to give about avoiding the risk of your child's shutting himself into a discarded refrigerator. They are potentially lethal traps for children, and the disposal of them is a national problem. Hence some states have wisely introduced laws requiring the doors to be removed before discarding.

Preventing Road Accidents

Why Children Are at Special Risk   One of the most important and most difficult aspects of accident prevention is the teaching of road safety. Help your child to develop road sense from the moment he can walk; this is an opportune time because you are still holding on to him whenever traffic is around. You can never guarantee that he will arrive home safely once he starts going out by himself, but you can help to make him safety conscious. Nevertheless, however well you do your part, the mere fact that a child is a child makes this an almost impossible job to achieve.

First, there is his small size; this makes him difficult to see from a driver's seat and it makes it harder for him to see around and over vehicles. Then there is every child's natural preference for running rather than walking, particularly after being cooped up in school all day. Accidents involving children are often caused by a child running into a car, not a car running into a child.

A child does not do one thing at a time, like an adult, and does not stop playing just because he is going from one place to another. He tends to become absorbed in play and does not notice that he is in danger of falling off the curb into the path of oncoming traffic. You can teach him never to play ball in the street but you cannot expect him to switch off the games in his head.

Child harnesses are used less nowadays on the grounds that they are restrictive. However, a young child who is always being shouted at to take care when out for a walk or going shopping may have greater freedom on reins and will not need to be shouted at.

Road Safety Drill

Surveys have shown that many children who appear to know their road safety drill regard it as a ritual. A child may be able to recite his drill parrot fashion but be unable to apply those parts of the code requiring judgment of the speed and distance of approaching vehicles.

A young child tends to regard the drill as a kind of automatic protection, like touching wood, with the result that he may start crossing the road after doing it although there is something coming. He has not seen the vehicle at all, because his drill is only a mechanical head-turning involving no real observation. He may think the approaching car will stop because he has done his part; he thinks of the driver as an all-powerful adult in full control of the situation anyway.

When teaching your child safety drill, make sure he realizes that he is still responsible for himself. Learning a set drill, then regarding it as a magic protection, is worse than useless. Tell your child he must always take a good look, listen, and look again.

Is He Old Enough?   Long experience teaches adults to judge vehicle speed and general danger on the roads, so that when we have checked we know whether or not it is safe to cross. A child has a sense of self-preservation but no experience; road sense develops only gradually, at different ages in different children. It fluctuates: a child who is safe today may be quite unsafe tomorrow, when he is preoccupied, distracted by the company of other children, or meets a new situation —for example, when he sees a friend waving to him on the other side of the road. You have told him never to rush across should this happen, but he may not remember or connect your instruction with this situation.

It seems that a child is least likely to be involved in an accident when using a familiar route at a familiar time, going to school, for example. He is most at risk when dashing out to do a quick errand at an unusual time. But a child is not safe just because the street is familiar or quiet; children are more frequently knocked down just around the corner from their homes, often in a quiet back street where traffic is light and the child is off his guard.

So when can you relax and allow your child to navigate the streets alone? You can never be absolutely certain he is safe, if only because you cannot insure against the foolishness of other road users. The age at which you let a child start crossing the road alone will depend on your nerves, his good sense, and local conditions. If there is only one road to cross on the way to school, and it is patrolled by a crossing guard who takes the children across, you may feel you can trust your child to go to school by himself as soon as he wants to. It would still be wise to check at intervals that he is crossing the road at the right place, with the crossing guard, not with another child who crosses somewhere else. Ask if your child is behaving sensibly and whether he always waits on the sidewalk if the crossing guard is busy helping another child across. If you are doubtful, accompany your child to school for a few days to remind him of the importance of keeping to the rules.

Your child may be ready to take himself to and from school long before you can trust him to cross the town to visit a friend. Children between the ages of five and nine are the group most often involved in road accidents, probably because they are beginning to seem capable in some situations, and are therefore trusted beyond their true capabilities. If your child pleads that his best friend is allowed to go home from outings alone but you feel that he is not ready for this, do not give in until you consider that he is. Practice does help, but this is one area where mistakes can be fatal.

Bicycling The age at which you let your child bicycle alone also depends on your nerves, his capabilities, and local traffic. It is sensible to take advantage of cycling proficiency schemes and to insist that he pass a test before allowing him to bicycle on busy streets. Details of such schemes may be available from town halls or from schools. Make sure his bicycle is in good condition.

Encouraging Road Sense Children absorb a certain amount of road safety training at school and through posters and television, but it remains primarily the responsibility of parents. Your own good example, reinforced with deliberate reminders, is the best long-term policy. Resist the temptation to weave through traffic, holding your child's hand and muttering, "Never do this without me."

Crossing the Road Teach your child how to use different types of pedestrian crossings. If he must cross a road where there is no pedestrian crossing, subway, or bridge, teach him how to do it safely; warn him never to rush out from behind a parked car, and not to run across, because he might trip and be unable to get up in time. It is difficult for drivers to judge the speed of a running pedestrian. Help your child to understand traffic lights and road signs, and give him some idea of how to judge a driver's intentions—turning left or right, for example.

When driving with your child, point out the driver's problems. He will be better able to appreciate the danger of stepping suddenly into the road if he realizes that a car cannot stop instantly. Let him sit in the driver's seat while the car is stationary so that he can see for himself that there are blind spots where the driver cannot see a child near the car. This helps to impress on him the danger of playing near parked cars, which might reverse and knock him down, because he is out of sight.

If you drive past an ice-cream truck, seize the opportunity to mention the rashness of running into the road licking ice cream and forgetting about the traffic. This may sink in and may make him a more considerate driver in the future as well as a safer pedestrian now.

One of the great dangers is pushing a baby carriage in front of you as you cross a street, because you cannot see the situation properly. I have known a child in a carriage to be killed while being pushed beyond a stationary car on a pedestrian crossing.

Special Precautions A child who is unwell, excited, or anxious, or who has been crying and is still upset, is in double peril on the roads. Never let your child rush out of the house alone "in a state" or feeling rotten, even if he has long passed the stage of being accompanied. There is no harm in reminding the most trustworthy child to be careful on a foggy morning. Make sure your child can still see and hear properly when he is dressed for a cold day. Dress him in light-colored clothes, with a luminous armband or a luminous bag to carry if he has to go out in the dark.

Country Roads This is particularly important on ill-lit country roads, where cars may be few but speedy. The country child has his own traffic hazards to contend with—unexpected vehicles can be more dangerous than a steady stream. He will have to learn how to cope in town traffic sometime, so take the opportunity to teach him when you go into town together.

Safety in the Car

Children must be protected while inside a car as well as outside. Never let a child sit in the front passenger seat; this is particularly dangerous for a small child. An adult seat belt is no protection for a child. A sudden stop, even at a very low speed, can kill a child in this seat if he is thrown forward and hits his head on the windshield. There is also the danger of his fiddling with the controls or touching the driver.

Children should be provided with their own safety belts properly fitted in the back seat; if they are under four or five, they need special safety seats attached to the back seat. Hook-on chairs with trays which are not specially intended for car travel are useless in a collision, since the child can be thrown out of them. This is one area where it really pays to buy the best—that is the safest—equipment, even if it costs more.

Traveling Baby A baby can travel in his carry-bed, but it must be placed safely. It can slip off the back seat and fall between back and front seats unless it is well wedged in. The back of a station wagon may provide a good space for a carry-bed, but your baby will be in danger if something runs into you from behind. Use a harness once your baby can sit up in his crib. If he must sit on someone's lap, let this be in the back of the car.

Safety Catches Four-door cars must have safety catches on the back doors to stop children from opening them from the inside. Keep the safety catches on always, even if it means having to unlock adults from outside—this is better than forgetting and having a child fall out.

Children are better and, therefore, safer passengers if they are taught from the beginning that it is dangerous to distract the driver. They behave better if they are not bored, so it is worth taking trouble to keep them amused (see journeys, p. 365).

Dealing with Accidents

Burns and Scalds

The seriousness of a burn or scald is determined by the area of skin affected; the larger the area, the greater the loss of fluid from the skin and the greater the danger of infection entering via the damaged skin. Death is likely if more than half of the skin area is burned.

Trivial Burns   Only small burns and scalds, those under about an inch in diameter (2.5 cm), should be regarded as trivial and treated at home without being seen by a doctor. A safe home treatment for trivial burns and scalds is prompt immersion in cold water or holding the burn under the cold tap for a few minutes. The cold water reduces the pain and is also a quick way of cleaning the skin. Cooling is of no value five minutes after the burn. Do not touch the burn itself, and if there are no blisters, no dressing is required.

If there are blisters, a dressing is required, but do not prick them, because they protect the sensitive area underneath. The water inside the blister is absorbed in a few days. A medicated adhesive dressing is the simplest to use. Give acetaminophen to relieve pain. Leave the dressing on for several days, making sure that it does not get wet, since the burn should be kept dry to aid healing.

Serious Burns   A larger burn should also be immediately cooled in water, then covered with a clean dressing such as the inner surface of an ironed handkerchief (do not use a fluffy towel). Bandage the dressing in place and take the child to the hospital emergency department.

If a child's clothes are on fire, the first priority is to stop further burning: lay the child on the floor and put out the flames by wrapping him in a rug or blanket or rolling him on the floor. Burned clothes should not be removed. Cover him with a clean sheet before arranging to get him to the hospital. Clothes that have been soaked in scalding water must be removed before you wrap the child in a sheet, because heat is retained in the layers of clothing.

Calming Your Child Your child will be terrified and probably screaming. It is difficult but important to try to keep yourself looking calm and comforting while dealing with the situation. Burning is more likely to leave a child disturbed than other types of accident, so the way you handle him is vital. An extra minute or two spent in comforting your child is more important than getting him to the hospital that much quicker.

Taking Him to the Hospital Take the child to the hospital by car or ambulance, whichever is more rapidly arranged, having first wrapped him in a clean sheet, with a blanket over this if it is a cold day. Do not put on a dressing, since this will have to be removed before the doctor can start treatment.

In the hospital, the burned area is likely to be left exposed to the air to aid healing. This may be more frightening for both you and your child. You are bound to feel particularly guilty if your child gets burned, and most doctors and nurses understand this.

Burns from Chemicals Acids and alkalis burn the skin and must be washed off immediately with plenty of cold water. If your child has been playing with any liquid that "stings," such as the acid from an old car battery, make sure it is all washed away before you deal with the burned skin. (See also injury to the eye, p. 473.)

The same rules apply as for other types of burn—a small area can be treated at home by cooling with water and covering with a dressing, but a large burn must be seen by a doctor.

Electricity Burn An electric shock can leave a burn that may look small at first but may also be deep and slow to heal. After a couple of days you will see that the burn is much more serious than it looked, and that treatment from a doctor is needed.

Poisoning

The Consequences A child is rushed to the hospital after being found with an open bottle of pills, kerosene, or other poisonous substance. Whether or not it turns out to be a false alarm, the whole experience leaves a terrifying mark on the memory of both the child and his parents, because of the frightening sequence of events that inevitably follows.

If you find your toddler playing with an open bottle of aspirin and you are not sure how many tablets are missing, you will be terrified. Your probable reaction will be to grab the bottle from him, stick your finger down his throat to make him sick, and rush to the telephone to call the doctor. Any one of these actions is enough to alarm and bewilder a small child, but what follows is even worse. The doctor will probably advise you to take him to the hospital as quickly as possible.

The hospital doctor is faced with the same dilemma as you—could the child have swallowed a potentially lethal number of tablets? He cannot take a chance, so he has to empty the child's stomach. This is done by giving him a dose of Ipecac Syrup large enough to make him violently sick, or by passing a large tube down his throat and esophagus in order to wash out the stomach. Both maneuvers are unpleasant and frightening, particularly for a child too young to have them explained.

The child should now be out of danger, but he must still be kept in the hospital overnight for observation, in case his condition deteriorates. So on top of everything else he has the experience of separation from his parents when he is already very frightened.

It is impossible to deal with suspected poisoning in a psychologically harmless way. Obviously, prevention is the only satisfactory answer: the child must never get hold of the bottle in the first place (see preventing poisoning, p. 628).

What to Do if You Suspect Poisoning However, if the worst happens, the first move is to take away the bottle and any tablets still in your child's mouth and check the contents of the bottle; if possible, calculate how many are missing. If the child can talk or if another child can tell you how many tablets have been eaten, you have to decide whether their information is accurate. Unless you are certain it is, you must play safe, assume the worst, and act accordingly; you have to proceed as if the child had taken a dangerous amount of a poisonous substance. Call Poison Control if you know what the child took.

Antidotes Since there are few poisons with a specific antidote to render them harmless, it is a waste of time to try to find the right antidote for a particular poison. The most useful thing to do is to make the child sick, provided the substance he has taken is not a caustic or household kerosene, which could damage his lungs during vomiting. A list of poisons for which you should not induce vomiting is given below.

In some cases it is safe to give a drink of milk instead: this is soothing and also dilutes the poison (see the list below).

If it is safe to make the child sick, do so as soon as you have taken away the remaining poison and cleared out his mouth, and while you are waiting for an ambulance to arrive. If you have a car and the hospital is nearby, it is still better to try to make him sick before you start off.

Making Him Vomit To induce vomiting, give your child Ipecac Syrup, if he has not eaten recently; it is easier to be sick when the stomach is fairly full. Then put him over your knee as if you were about to spank him or lay him flat on a bed, with a basin to catch the vomit. This position avoids the risk of his breathing it in. Wiggle your finger about near the back of his throat until he vomits. Alternatively, you can use a spoon handle, but be careful not to damage his throat.

If you have no Ipecac Syrup, give him an emetic drink to make him sick. The easiest to make quickly is a tablespoon of salt or a teaspoon of mustard in warm water. Give it to him twice to make him vomit twice. But do not spend long over either of these measures. Time is important; the doctor will be able to empty the stomach one way or another (see above), and the aim should be to get the child to him as rapidly as possible.

Contraindications to Vomiting   Bringing up the poison is sometimes dangerous: it can burn the lining of the esophagus even more and damage the lungs if it is inhaled. For the following substances, vomiting should not be induced, although a drink of milk or water should be given:

Petroleum Products
Examples: gasoline, kerosene, liquid furniture and car polishes, benzene, lighter fuel, turpentine, dry-cleaning fluids.
Strong Acids
Examples: sulphuric, nitric, carbolic, hydrochloric, creosote.
Strong Alkalis
Examples: bleach, ammonia, washing soda, caustic soda.
Miscellaneous
Oil-based paints, insect sprays.

Identifying the Poison   Take the poisonous tablets or liquid with you to the hospital, even if you know their name; this will help the doctor. Nowadays, the pharmacist must write the name of drugs on the bottle, for easy identification. If you have no idea what your child has taken but know or suspect he has been poisoned, either from his appearance or because another child says so, take a sample of his vomit to the hospital.

What should you do if you are quite sure that the child has taken just one or two pills or a sip of something that might be poisonous? If he seems perfectly well and cheerful and you are certain he has only taken a small amount, there is probably no need to worry; but telephone your doctor if you need advice.

Head Injuries

Falls on the Head   When your child falls and bumps his head, the most important question is not how far he has fallen, but what effect the fall has had on him.

Any fall may make a child pale and frightened for a minute or two; a baby may cry from fear rather than pain, then fall asleep because he has exhausted himself crying. These are normal reactions, and provided the child seems himself again after getting over the initial shock, or if he goes to sleep and seems to be sleeping normally, you can assume all is well. He needs comfort, and may want to rest, but it is not necessary to consult your doctor unless you are uneasy. Remove anything your child had in his mouth when he fell, in case it chokes him, and stay with him until you are sure he is all right. A baby should be laid prone with his head to one side to avoid the danger of inhaling vomit if he is sick.

Danger Signs What are the danger signs after a fall? You should telephone the doctor if your child vomits, if there is a visible head wound, any bleeding from nose, mouth, or ears, or if he remains pale and in an unusual mood after the accident. Loss of consciousness, even for a moment, in the twenty-four hours after a fall should be reported. A child who goes to sleep after a fall should be checked to see if he is breathing in his normal way and looking normal. Noisy breathing, snoring in a child who does not usually snore, labored breathing, or continued pallor are signs to notice. If you cannot tell whether your child is asleep or unconscious, try to wake him up; if it is impossible or more difficult to wake him than usual, call the doctor.

Don't feel you must be absolutely certain something is wrong before asking your doctor for advice. You are right to do so even if you only feel vaguely uneasy.

Admission to the Hospital A parent cannot assess possible damage from a fall: even doctors find this difficult—which is why children are often taken into the hospital for observation. With the vast majority of children admitted for observation, this turns out to be nothing more than a precaution.

Fractured Skull If your child is sent to the hospital he will probably be X-rayed in case there is a fracture of the skull. No additional treatment is required for such a fracture unless the bone has been pushed inward, thereby causing pressure on the brain. A "depressed fracture" is raised surgically, but all other fractures are left to heal themselves.

The fact that the skull has been fractured does not of itself make the child's condition worse. This would depend on the amount of injury to the brain, which is sometimes less if the skull is fractured, since the skull has taken some of the force of the blow. The fracture, therefore, does not determine when the child is allowed up, and nowadays children with head injuries are usually allowed to get up as soon as they feel like it.

Swelling A bang on the head, particularly on the forehead, may be followed by a large swelling of alarming appearance. The swelling is caused by bleeding under the scalp but outside the skull. This bleeding always stops, the child never "bleeds to death," and it is never a sign of "brain damage." It is just another bruise, which may feel a bit tender but goes away without treatment in a few days.

Cuts on the Scalp Cuts on the scalp bleed profusely. Your child may rush in covered with blood, but when you find the cut beneath his matted hair, it may turn out to be less than half an inch (a centimeter) long. Since it is difficult to keep a bandage or plaster on the cut to hold the sides together while healing takes place, it may be necessary for a stitch to be inserted, even for a small cut. When in doubt, ask your doctor or take your child to the hospital. If the wound is large and continues to bleed, press your thumb or finger on it to control the bleeding until it can be stitched.

Broken Bones

Greenstick Fracture The bones of a young child bend rather than break, since they are softer than the bones of an older child or adult. This is known as a "greenstick" fracture: the bone cracks on one side only, rather like a bent green twig which refuses to break cleanly. Since it is not actually broken in two, the two parts of the bone do not get into a bad position, and there is no need to set them straight; Nature sees to this, provided the limb is kept still by some form of splint.

Is a Bone Broken? A doctor often needs X-ray evidence to confirm whether a bone is broken or not, so how can you tell whether an injured limb is fractured, sprained, or just bruised? A bruise hurts less as time goes by, but a fracture hurts more. A child with a hurt leg who goes on refusing to walk on it may have broken his leg. A child with a fractured collarbone finds it painful to lift his arm above his head and makes it plain that it hurts when you try to remove his shirt. He may refuse to lie down in bed, since it is less painful to sit up. (See also p. 543.)

The Emergency Department Once you suspect a fracture, take your child to the emergency department of a hospital. X-rays may be necessary to show whether he has a fracture or a sprain. Don't worry if you have taken some time to realize that the injury is more serious than a bruise.

"Compound" Fracture Occasionally, a child suffers a more serious type of fracture, a "compound" fracture, which means that the injury has penetrated the skin so that the broken bone is in direct contact with the outside air and therefore at great risk of infection. The child must be taken to the emergency department immediately, but the injured leg or arm should first be immobilized. A broken leg can be bandaged to the other leg; a broken arm should be loosely tied to the child's body or put in a sling made from a scarf or large handkerchief. When taking off a coat or shirt, remove the sleeve from the uninjured arm first. Do not try to apply wooden splints and do not give the child aspirin, or anything to eat or drink, because he may need an anesthetic.

Treatment in the Hospital   In the hospital, the fractured bones will be set if they are out of position. It may then be possible to put the limb straight into plaster to keep the broken bones in the right place. Alternatively, it may be necessary to pull the broken bones apart (traction) for a few days, either to get them into the right position or to keep them in the correct position before plastering.

Your Child's Reactions   Traction is often an alarming experience for a young child. He suddenly finds himself in a hospital bed to which he is tied by weights. It is not easy to explain the reasons for this to him. Even having an arm or leg put into a plaster cast can be an alarming experience, because on waking the child may think he has lost the part of his leg or arm that is covered by the plaster of Paris. You will need to reassure him that he is still in one piece and that the missing part of his leg or arm is still safely there, hidden by the plaster.

Treating Cuts and Grazes

Nine times out of ten, you will not see a bloody knee until some time after the event. The wound has bled and a scab is already forming. A cut or graze that was too trivial to worry your child when it happened is usually not serious enough for you to worry about. Apart from washing away dirt and dried blood from around the wound, it is best to leave it alone. Bleeding will have removed most of the dirt from the wound itself, and if you wash it or apply antiseptic, you dampen the scab and make infection more likely, not less. Particles of dirt remaining in the graze or cut generally come out when the scab comes off. You may dig dirt further in if you try to wash it out.

When to See the Doctor   You are most likely to worry about dirt in a cut or graze on your child's face because of the possibility of scarring; it is best to cover the spot with a dressing and take him to the emergency department of the nearest hospital for a doctor's opinion. Long, deep, and gaping wounds anywhere need cleaning by a doctor; he will decide if stitches are necessary.

Antiseptic Ointments It is impossible to clean a wound completely. Antiseptic ointments cannot kill every organism, and if they are too strong they hinder rather than help healing. Do not put ointment on a wound or scab as a "precaution" against infection; the scab itself is the best barrier to infection and the ointment makes it soggy and less effective. A child's natural resistance to infection can nearly always deal with any harmful organisms remaining in the wound (see infection, below).

Dressings Since the scab is a wound's best protection, dressings are only necessary to help control bleeding and to keep out dirt while a scab is forming. With a small child, it is sensible to put a bandage over a wound to stop him picking at the scab; he is also unlikely to remember the tender place when playing, and it may get knocked and hurt again before it has had a chance to heal, especially if it is on a vulnerable place like a knee. Putting on a bandage is a ritual that many children enjoy and demand: it is harmless and useful if it stops the child from crying and worrying about the hurt place.

However, the dressing or bandage does keep the wound moist and to a certain extent slows up healing, so do not leave it on too long.

Protection against Tetanus Cuts and grazes are an inevitable part of childhood and not something every good mother should try to prevent. The most useful insurance against possible ill effects is to keep your child's tetanus immunization up to date (pp. 261–62). Tetanus is rare in the United States because most children are immunized against it. Provided your child has been previously immunized against tetanus the doctor can give a booster dose which gives total protection. Those who have not been immunized may have to be given antitetanus serum (ATS), which can cause dangerous reactions because it contains horse serum. The doctor may decide that giving penicillin is sufficient protection, provided he can keep your child under observation.

Tetanus is caused by germs that live in animal manure but remain dormant in soil long after the last horse has left the paddock. Therefore the risk cannot be ignored if a child who has not been immunized cuts himself outdoors. Profuse bleeding removes some dirt and harmful organisms from a cut, but a deep puncture wound, such as that caused by a nail in the sole of a child's foot, seldom bleeds much, is impossible to clean adequately, and probably looks much smaller than it is. This is the kind of wound that carries the greatest risk of tetanus; you should check that your child's immunization is up to date, if in doubt.

Signs of Infection A small white or yellow patch means that a wound is slightly infected, but this usually clears up of its own accord.

Signs that infection should be taken seriously are: continuing pain in the area of the wound, reddened skin surrounding it and perhaps showing beyond the edges of the dressing, or red streaks running up the limb from the wound. The last sign is an emergency, but any of these symptoms need a doctor's advice and further treatment.

Controlling Bleeding A small cut, particularly on the scalp or face, can produce a large amount of blood, so that when you wash it away and manage to find the wound you are relieved and surprised. In fact, it is difficult to judge the amount of blood lost—a few spoonfuls may look like pints.

This type of bleeding is usually stopped by applying a dressing; a handkerchief or scarf will do if it is the nearest thing to hand. If the dressing alone is insufficient to control the bleeding, press with your fingers as well until it stops.

A wound that goes on bleeding as soon as pressure is eased may need stitching. Don't try to clean it; cover it with a dressing and take your child to the doctor.

Bleeding from an Artery Blood spurting dramatically from a wound means that an artery is damaged. It is essential to control the bleeding. Waste no time trying to remember the correct pressure point; don't apply a tourniquet—this is no longer recommended because of its dangers. Press hard at the point from which the blood seems to come. If this fails, try the spot just above.

Once you have discovered where to press to stop the spurting blood, apply a firm dressing and take your child directly to the emergency department, calling an ambulance if necessary. Should the bleeding begin again as soon as you remove your fingers, give up the idea of putting on a dressing and keep applying pressure with your fingers all the way to the hospital.

Nosebleeds

Nosebleeding is usually due to a blow, but it sometimes happens because a child has put something up his nose. Always ask about this if it seems a possibility, though the child may not admit what he has done. A bloodstained discharge that smells is usually the result of something being pushed up into the nose.

Frequent Nosebleeds Some children tend to have frequent nosebleeds, which can be severe. The usual cause is that the small blood vessels lining both sides of the partition wall (septum) between the nostrils are more numerous and even nearer to the surface than usual. When the nose becomes dry, the surface covering the blood vessels flakes off, leaving them exposed, so that bleeding occurs.

Your doctor can tell you whether this is the cause. The simplest way of avoiding this kind of nosebleed is to apply petroleum jelly to the partition inside the nose, night and morning; as long as the surface is prevented from drying, the blood vessels remain protected and they do not bleed.

Sudden Nosebleeds   A sudden nosebleed, such as one caused by a punch, eventually stops, like other bleeding, but the blood may look copious and alarm you and your child. Reassure him that it is not as serious as it looks. The best thing to do is to make him sit up with his head bent forward so that the blood drips out and is not swallowed. He should breathe through his mouth and sit still in order to assist the natural process of clotting.

If bleeding continues after five minutes, try gently squeezing the nostrils together for a further few minutes. If it persists for more than twenty minutes, ask your doctor's advice. Keys down the back and cold compresses on the back of the neck do not do much good.

Animal Bites

Dog Bites   In the United States there is the risk of rabies after a dog bite. The main risk is tetanus, so take your child to the doctor, unless you are certain his immunization is up to date (see tetanus immunization, pp. 261–62).

Snake Bites   Try to identify the snake, whether it is poisonous or nonpoisonous. If poisonous, apply a tourniquet above the bite. Comfort your child, treat him for shock, if necessary (see below), and take him straight to the nearest hospital emergency department; do not let him walk there.

Insect Stings   In this country most stings cause only minor irritation; relieving this is all that is necessary. Cooling the skin with a cold compress helps, and calamine lotion is soothing. If your child is well, you need not worry about identifying the insect that stung him.

Very occasionally, a wasp or bee sting causes an allergic reaction, so that the surrounding area becomes severely inflamed, the child is in pain, and, in rare cases, may even suffer from shock (see below). A sting in the mouth can cause so much swelling that it interferes with breathing; in this case the child should be taken straight to the hospital. It is wise to consult your doctor whenever your child is stung in the mouth.

If you can see the sting in the skin, scrape it out gently with a clean fingernail, but do this only if it is easy.

Any person developing an allergic reaction to a bee or wasp sting should be desensitized after recovery. A second sting in a sensitive individual can be fatal.

Shock

A shocked child is in a state of physical collapse, usually as the result of an accident such as a bad burn, poisoning, broken bones, or loss of blood. Allergic reactions, to bee stings, for example, can also cause shock (see above), and so can an acute illness or a severe emotional disturbance. The important thing from your point of view is to know how to recognize and deal with shock, rather than to understand the mechanism and causes.

Signs The shocked child may show some or all of many symptoms. He becomes pale or grayish and breaks out in a cold sweat. His breathing is quick but shallow; he may seem unable to get enough air. The pulse is rapid, though occasionally it is much slower than normal. He may be listless, restless, or frightened, or he may lose consciousness. He may be thirsty, giddy, and feel or be sick. In fact, he looks and acts "shocked."

Treating Shock If shock is the result of an injury, for example, if the child is bleeding or burned, the injuries must obviously be dealt with as well as the shock. There is no point in "treating for shock" while a child is bleeding to death.

Severe shock is an emergency and must be treated at once. Lay your child flat on his back. Reassure him, and loosen any tight clothing. Do not make the mistake of warming him with hot-water bottles; his skin is cold because in shock the amount of blood going to the skin is reduced to make extra available for more vital organs. Warming the skin dilates the blood vessels, thereby counteracting this safety measure; it also causes sweating, which makes the shocked person colder. It therefore does nothing to stimulate the circulation and may make the state of shock worse. A light blanket is sufficient. Since you cannot be sure whether your child will need an anesthetic, give no drinks— a hot cup of tea is not good treatment for shock.

A child usually recovers quickly from a slight degree of shock, such as may result from a minor injury. Severe shock is an emergency, and the child must be taken to the hospital as quickly as possible so that the shock and the injury can be treated together.

Mouth-to-Mouth Resuscitation by Artificial Respiration

Everyone should know how to give mouth-to-mouth resuscitation. When someone has stopped breathing there is no time to look up directions, let alone take him to the hospital. The brain and heart can survive a few minutes only after their oxygen supply is cut off be-

(a) Lay the child on his back.

(b) Sweep a finger around the mouth to clear any obstruction.

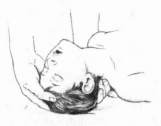

(c) Tilt his head back to ensure a clear airway.

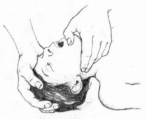

(d) Still supporting the head with one hand, press the chin farther forward with your other hand. This lifts the tongue clear of the throat.

(e) Close nostrils.

(f) Breathe gently into his mouth. With a baby or small child, seal your lips over both nose and mouth.

(g) External cardiac massage.

Fig. 15. Mouth-to-mouth resuscitation.

cause breathing has stopped. A child involved in an accident such as drowning, electric shock, or suffocation and who has stopped breathing, can sometimes be revived if artificial respiration is started quickly enough and continued long enough. Mouth-to-mouth resuscitation is the simplest and most effective method for parents to learn and use. First-aid classes are ideal; learning the basic rules from a book is second best but may enable you to save life in an emergency.

The Basic Rules

Never start artificial respiration if the child is still breathing for himself, however faintly. If he is not breathing, do not waste time searching for his pulse; even if you cannot feel his pulse, you may still be able to revive him. A child whose heart has stopped beating needs cardiac massage as well (see p. 648).

If you are alone with the child, start mouth-to-mouth resuscitation at once and work out how to get help while you are giving it. Carry on until ordinary breathing begins; the child can then be left for up to a minute while you telephone. If it is impossible to telephone within this time, drag the child gradually, between blowing, toward a telephone or to where you can shout for help.

The Technique

It is possible to give mouth-to-mouth resuscitation with the child in any position except face down, but it is best if he is lying on his back (Fig. 15a). You must be able to reach him with the minimum of discomfort, as this is exhausting work and sometimes has to go on for hours.

Start Immediately Remove any obvious obstruction from the child's mouth but do not waste time looking for hidden obstructions or in trying to empty the lungs of water in the case of drowning (Fig. 15b). The urgent thing is to start getting air into the lungs, and every second counts.

Push the Chin Forward It is important to ensure that the tongue does not sag backward over the back of the throat and block the windpipe; if this happens, air blown into the child's mouth goes into his stomach instead of his lungs. The way to prevent it is to push his chin forward; this automatically brings his tongue forward and arches his neck, opening the entrance to the windpipe and closing the entrance to the esophagus (Figs. 15c and d).

Close the Nostrils The nostrils must be closed to stop the air from escaping through the nose instead of reaching the lungs. Unless the child's face is small enough for you to get your mouth over both mouth and nose, pinch his nostrils shut, using either hand (Fig. 15e).

These preliminaries sound lengthy but should take only a very few seconds, provided you know what to do in advance.

Start Blowing   Take a deep breath and put your mouth right over the child's open mouth, making sure you seal it completely (Fig. 15f). Blow gently, watching whether the chest expands. If the abdomen rises, air is not reaching the lungs. The child's head may be in the wrong position, so pull his jaw farther forward and arch his neck more before blowing again (Fig. 15d). Pressing your hand on the abdomen also reduces the chance of air entering the stomach instead of the lungs.

Twelve to Fifteen Blows per Minute   After each blow into the child's mouth, take the chance of breathing normally yourself and relaxing as far as possible. When his chest contracts and you can no longer hear air being exhaled, blow again. Give the first half-dozen blows in quick succession, then continue blowing rhythmically every six seconds.

Continue Till the Child Recovers   The child may start to breathe of his own accord almost immediately, but sometimes artificial respiration has to continue for several minutes or even hours before he revives. This is exceedingly tiring for the person giving it but essential while a chance of survival remains. It is worth going on as long as the child's color is pinkish. Give artificial respiration in relays if someone competent is available to take over.

Continue to Watch Him   When the child starts breathing for himself, keep him lying down until the doctor comes or he reaches the hospital. Warm him with a blanket if possible, and keep an eye on him in case he stops breathing again, making further mouth-to-mouth resuscitation necessary.

External Cardiac Massage

When there is no sign of a heartbeat the child must be given external massage to the heart at the same time as mouth-to-mouth resuscitation. It is very difficult for one person to perform both maneuvers simultaneously.

The child must be flat on his back on a hard surface, either the floor or the ground. The "heel" of the hand (the rounded part of the palm below the thumb) is pressed rhythmically and firmly against the bottom of the breast bone so as to force it against the heart (Fig. 15g). The rate for this is about twice the rate for mouth-to-mouth resuscitation, that is every two to three seconds.

The First-Aid Kit

This should be readily accessible to you but not to your children. It is best kept near the place where accidents are most likely to happen, that is, in the kitchen or downstairs bathroom, rather than upstairs. Keep another kit in the car; this is useful for cut knees on picnics as well as for a possible car accident.

You can buy first-aid kits, but these tend to contain more than is really necessary and leave out important items like scissors. Assembling your own kit is cheaper, and you can choose exactly what you want. Only a few items are essential but they should be replaced promptly as they run out, and it should be a family rule that anything borrowed is put back at once.

Suggested Contents

Assorted dressings: these are available with medication, so that ointments, antiseptics, etc., are unnecessary.

Gauze dressings: packets of ready-cut dressings are simpler to use than a long roll.

Roll of adhesive tape to strap gauze dressings in place.

Bandages 1 inch and 2 inches (2.5 and 5 centimeters) wide.

A sling. This is not essential, because a bandage or a scarf can double as a sling.

Elastic bandage.

Tweezers to remove splinters.

Scissors to cut bandages and adhesive tape.

Absorbent cotton and paper tissues for cleaning wounds.

Safety pins to fix bandages.

Adhesive tape as an alternative to safety pins for fixing dressings and bandages. Used also over cuts to keep out dirt and to encourage healing without stitches by holding the edges of the cut together.

Soothing eye drops to use if something gets into the eye (p. 472).

52

When a Child Dies

Crib Deaths ("Sudden Infant Death Syndrome")

A tiny baby looks so fragile that it is easy to feel his life "hangs by a thread." Your feeling that your baby's very life depends on you is a biological necessity. A helpless new baby is safer if parents have too much concern for him rather than too little. But this natural sense of responsibility can be so exaggerated that it leads parents to check regularly that their baby is still breathing. A mother may become so tense that she no longer knows how her baby really is, or what he really wants. If this happens, her concern is no longer useful.

There are several reasons why some parents, particularly mothers, become obsessed by the fear that their baby may die suddenly. One is the headline "Baby found dead in crib" which appears now and then in local newspapers. It is a good idea to get the subject into perspective.

The number of babies who die suddenly and without warning symptoms is small; it may seem larger than it really is because, in developed countries, other causes of infant deaths have dropped in comparison with the number of "crib deaths." Whenever a baby dies like this, it is reported and discussed, reinforcing the fears of other parents of young babies. So it is useless to pretend it never happens —it is better to know the odds and whether there is anything constructive you can do about it.

Wider understanding will help the few families who do meet this tragedy, because in the past many have had to live with uncertainty and rumors about the "real" cause of their baby's death as well as with the tragedy itself. Years afterward, a mother may still feel obscurely to blame, wondering what more she could have done and what she might have done differently. The fear of the same thing happening again could ruin her enjoyment of her next baby. Parents may silently or openly blame each other, or their doctor, or an unfortunate baby-sitter who was in charge at the time.

There is no evidence to suggest that crib deaths are caused by some inherited family weakness. They occur in a particular age group, not particular families. One such tragedy is not a reason for putting off having another child.

Possible Causes

Suffocation   Guilt and misunderstanding are still the penalty of our hazy ideas of the cause of crib deaths, and only now is some light beginning to dawn on this difficult subject. For example, suffocation used to be made the scapegoat for many sudden infant deaths. Parents felt they were at fault for providing the "wrong" kind of bedding or, worse still, for letting the baby sleep in their bed. At worst, the suspicion of deliberate suffocation arose. Yet at the age when crib deaths are most common—two to six months—a normal baby can lift his head and change his position if he cannot breathe easily. The normal baby will not suffocate in his crib overnight: his reaction to a blocked airway is to wriggle about until he can breathe properly again. Bedclothes are soft and allow enough air through for breathing, even if they do cover the face, although it is wise not to use pillows until the baby is twelve months old and not to leave a plastic lining in a carry-bed uncovered.

In addition, there is the fact that the number of crib deaths has not fallen, although nearly all babies in developed countries sleep in separate beds and with "safe" modern bedding. We now know that many deaths were ascribed to suffocation because no other cause could be found and because of an exaggerated fear that a parent might lie on the baby and stop him breathing ("overlying"). In fact, in many developing countries it is still the rule for babies to sleep safely and warmly alongside their mothers, waking up at times to feed at the breast.

Chest Infection   One reason for sudden deaths in babies is chest infection. Occasionally, an overwhelming infection strikes and kills a small baby so quickly that there is no time to observe and treat it. In such a case neither the parents nor the doctors are to blame. The identification of the cause of death in such a tragedy at least spares the parents the horror of doubt and uncertainty. It is clear that in the past many crib deaths were put down to "asphyxia" because the acute respiratory failure that resulted from the infection was mistakenly thought to be the sole cause of death. However, just as suffocation has been blamed for too many crib deaths, so possibly has chest infection, giving parents an exaggerated fear of the likelihood of pneumonia or some other sudden chest disease carrying off their baby.

Allergy   Other theories have received publicity and startled parents, for example, the idea that some babies are sensitive to the protein in cow's milk and might therefore die suddenly because of a build-up of antibodies in the blood. Animal experiments have shown that guinea pigs sensitized to milk protein die if a minute amount of milk enters their air passages during sleep. If the same were true of babies it would be safer not to bottle feed, but there is no proof that this is the case, although it is true that crib deaths occur less often in babies who are breast fed.

All that is certain about crib deaths, at present, is that they are more frequent in the winter, and that the number of such deaths in a community seems to parallel the number of babies admitted to the hospital with chest complaints. Babies living in poor conditions are at greater risk, which may be because infection spreads more easily in overcrowded homes.

What Can You Do?

Although as yet no virus or bacterium has been isolated as the cause of crib deaths—and indeed there may be many causes—it is a sensible general precaution to protect your baby from outside infections when possible, particularly if he is born in the autumn and is still very small in the winter months (see the common cold, p. 450). This is really all you can do—apart from not being too concerned about this possibility. It is obviously unreasonable for the parents of a healthy baby to hover over his crib while he sleeps for fear of such a tragedy, though the occasional visit is very understandable. It possibly helps to get the problem in perspective if you know that crib deaths occur occasionally in the hospital in babies who were thought to be completely well.

It has been suggested that some crib deaths are due to overheating from excessive bedclothes. The guiding principle is to cover the baby with the same amount of bedding as you would want for yourself—no more.

The Dying Child

Telling the Parents

It is of course essential that this should take place in an office, out of sight of the child. I mention this because one mother was told in the nursing supervisor's office, which had glass walls looking out onto the unit. The mother could see her daughter watching her and knew she must not show her feelings in her face as the truth was being broken to her husband and herself.

The first reaction of parents is likely to be a feeling of total inadequacy and failure, because the doctors and nurses take over their child. They may feel they must be particularly good because their child is being held as a hostage. Many people are unaware that children can get cancer, apart from leukemia.

After learning the true facts of their child's illness, and this will take several talks to sink in, it is important for parents not to alter the way they handle their child. It would be understandable if they now felt the child must be given everything possible and no longer be told off for bad behavior. But if the code of discipline were to be altered suddenly, the child would be left bewildered, quite apart from being made aware that some new and very strange happening had taken place.

It is so easy for medical and nursing staff to fail to understand the needs and fears of parents faced with the impending death of their child. One mother told her family doctor that her daughter's death at home had been peaceful and he said he knew it would be. To this the mother reacted explosively, asking him why then had he not told her beforehand, because her greatest fear was that her daughter would suffer pain at the time of death.

Telling the Truth

When a sick child is certain to die, it is not automatically best to keep this a secret. A child is protective toward his parents and wants to save them distress, so although he may desperately need to talk about his fear of dying, he never gets near this point in conversation with them. Parents usually feel the only thing to do is to keep up a façade of hope, deflecting any remarks that indicate the child's suspicions.

Medical staff, if they have no special training in dealing with this situation, will also give the child false reassurance; they are likely to change the subject or pretend not to hear when a child asks them directly or indirectly if he is going to die. In some hospitals, beds are changed around in the unit after a child's death in the hope that the other children will not notice the absence—but, of course, they do. Healthy children think about death, so it is hardly possible for sick children in the hospital to ignore it (see a child's attitude toward death, pp. 342–43).

I am not saying that parents in this dreadful dilemma should always tell their child the full truth. A child who shows no suspicion of the possibility of dying and who appears happily ignorant should be left in ignorance. When there is a chance of recovery, however remote, the child should not be burdened with calculating the odds. His will to live depends to a considerable extent on positive hope of life. Only parents and trained staff who have watched the child react to his illness can attempt to judge his state of mind and decide how to help him.

Talking to the Child

What I am saying is that sometimes, more often than is suspected, a child spends his last days more happily when he realizes that he is dying than when he is left in a state of uncertainty, unshared worry, and doubt. He can actually help his parents and himself by talking about his impending death and sharing the feelings they have all been experiencing alone. He has shared everything with his parents in the past, when they have tried to work out what he has wanted to tell them and what he has needed; yet it is assumed that he does not need to share the greatest worry of all. This could cause him to feel that death must be even more frightening than he had imagined since no one will talk to him about this, his greatest fear.

Of course, sympathetic understanding between parents and child does not invariably need words to make it real. Often, a child will ask his nurse if he is going to die. He thus saves his parents the distress of answering his question, finding it easier to ask someone less emotionally involved with him. When hospital staff and parents are in tune, their pooled knowledge of the child's feelings enables them to help to make his remaining time peaceful, even happy.

Parents will vary in their capacity to cope with this situation. Those who have always talked openly to their child about life, death, sex, in fact about anything he has wanted to know, will find it less difficult than parents who have evaded the child's questions on awkward subjects.

It is to be hoped that every parent who needs it has the benefit of advice from an experienced and wise doctor, nurse, social worker, or chaplain.

Fear of the Moment of Death

People who have been involved with sick children have found that a child's major worry is fear of the moment of death; of dying, rather than of death itself. Nowadays, a child's idea of death is largely made up of what he has seen on the TV screen; to him death is a bloody business involving violence and agony. Red is the predominant color used in children's drawings illustrating death. He needs to be told that this is not the usual manner of death, and that more often death is peaceful rather than painful. As for what happens after death, he can be reassured that the individual's influence and memory live on, however ignorant we are about the rest (see p. 345).

It is really a question of using understanding, love, and energy in a positive fashion instead of allowing it to overflow into helplessness. Parents can be helped so that none of their time with their child is wasted in misunderstanding each other's true needs. Nothing can diminish grief, but knowing that they have done the best for their child reduces the element of agonized self-recrimination parents are likely to feel following the death of their child.

Help After the Child's Death

Parents continue to need help from the family doctor, social worker, clergyman, or others in the community after their child's death. This is the most lonely time of all, when the embarrassment of friends and neighbors keeps them away because they do not know how to help—to add to their problems the family members find that they have been put in quarantine. Without help, many parents go back to the hospital, walking around and around the building. Many people need help in order to allow themselves to mourn and to be able to express their grief in the family circle so that the loss is discussed.

It is part of the doctor's job to seek help for bereaved parents from members of the community, perhaps to help to find a compassionate friend who is prepared to listen while the parents do the one thing they need most—to talk about their dead child. This help must be extended to the bereaved brothers and sisters, whose depth of sorrow may not be realized by their parents because of their own immense personal grief. A surviving child has been known to commit suicide after the sudden loss of a brother or sister, because no one appreciated the seriousness of his own emotional tragedy.

Stillborn Babies

Much more needs to be done to help the parents of stillborn babies than has been the case in the past. In many maternity units the baby is hustled away without being seen by the parents and sometimes without their even being told the sex.

From talking with many parents and from numerous letters I have received I am certain that they are helped by seeing and holding their dead baby, even if the baby is handicapped (pp. 576–77). Parents see a very different child from that seen by the hospital staff. A baby who has died some hours or days before delivery develops "maceration" of the skin. The staff often considers that parents should be prevented from seeing such a baby in order to protect them from distress, but I remember a mother remarking "What a beautiful baby" as she held her "macerated fetus." It is very difficult to mourn someone you have never seen, and yet mourning is essential to recovery from bereavement. Mothers who have never seen the baby feel that their pregnancy has ended in a void; for this reason a photograph can give comfort. Taking part in the funeral is also most important, as for any other bereavement.

If the baby is known to have died before labor the parents should be told. In most instances a mother will already be aware, because movements have ceased. It is most important that the baby's father should be present at delivery to give comfort.

After the delivery the question arises as to whether the mother should be cared for in a unit with mothers and babies or in a room of her own. On the whole she will be able to talk over her feelings more easily if she has access to the main unit, even if she has her own single room. The mother should be asked if the other mothers in the unit can be told of her loss so that they do not find out or suspect the truth on their own and are then too embarrassed to be able to express their feelings of grief for her. The father should be given a bed (folding bed, if necessary) in the mother's room so that she is not left by herself at night. Mothers should be told that they are likely to lactate.

Some degree of depression is bound to be felt by all parents of stillborn babies, especially the mothers, who are likely to blame themselves. Some will feel that they have only been able to create death. Ongoing counseling must therefore be provided for as long as necessary in every case. One of the worst suggestions is tha the parents should have another baby as soon as possible to "replace" the dead one. Nothing can replace the baby who, though dead, has a permanent place in the family. Mourning and grief must be worked through before another pregnancy is considered. A stillborn baby removes the basic trust we all have in life. The very word is evocative—having been born silent, a stillbirth often continues to be shrouded in the silence of all involved and is powerful in its silence.

Miscarriages (Spontaneous Abortion)

A similar approach is needed for a mother who has experienced a miscarriage. For many years I have questioned mothers who have had a miscarriage about what the experience was like. Their answers are remarkably uniform: first, the amount of pain, which many describe as worse than a normal delivery, and second, the sense of emptiness and subsequent depression.

I suspect the pain is partly physical, from delivering a baby through a hard undilated cervix, which is resisting dilation, and partly emotional, from the loss being experienced at the same time.

One is perpetually shocked by the reported remarks of doctors and nurses and their lack of sensitivity, as though a miscarriage were an everyday occurrence. If only all staff members would ask mothers what it felt like to experience a miscarriage, their attitude would be very different. It is salutary to realize that few mothers who have suffered a miscarriage are visited by their family doctors or provided with any ongoing care to sustain them in their bereavement, particularly to realize that a mother is likely to feel guilty, that it was her fault, while a father commonly wants to forget it all and expects his wife to do the same. It is of course correct to tell parents that about half the fetuses aborted have chromosome abnormalities, but this does not influence the feeling of loss, nor does it help if the doctor goes on to say they were "lucky" to have had the miscarriage.

Bereavement

So far I have discussed bereavement from death but it is important to realize that bereavement occurs in other ways. The parents of a handicapped child have been bereaved of the perfect child they expected (pp. 576–77). The mother who gives her child for adoption has been bereaved. Adoptive parents who cannot have a baby of their own have first to come to terms with the bereavement of never being able to be natural parents. Occasionally, through the death of a child, parents also have to come to terms with the fact that they will always be bereaved of becoming grandparents.

INDEX

Abscess (breast), 72–73
Accidents, 620–49
  preventing, 620–35
  treating, 635–49
Achondroplasia, 418
Acidosis, 539, 541–42
Acne, 496–97
Adenoids: and rhinitis, 452–53. *See also*
  Tonsils and adenoids
Adolescents
  drug abuse and, 41–42
  growth of, 210–11
  modesty in, 341
  obesity in, 207
  sex education and, 335–40, 354
Adoption, 347–54
Advice
  from grandparents, 172–75
  from professionals, 173–74
"Afterpains," 61
Alcohol: in pregnancy, 14
Allergies, 502–10
Alopecia areata, 500–501
Ambidexterity, 230, 233
Ammonia dermatitis, 431–32
Amniocentesis, 417
Anal fissure, 487–88
Anemia, 518–19
Anencephaly, 417
Anger: in children and parents, 286–87,
  289–91, 414–15. *See also* Child
  abuse
Angioneurotic edema, 509
Animal bites, 313
Antibiotics, 392–93
Antiseptic ointment, 642
Aphasia: developmental, 570–71
Appendicitis, 465, 483
Appetite
  and growth, 189, 200, 208
  loss of, 198, 248, 390, 433–35
  small, 199–200
Artificial respiration, 645–48
Aseptic sterilizing, 92
Asthma, 466–67, 504–6
"Asthmatic bronchitis," 464

Astigmatism, 470
Athlete's foot, 377, 500
ATS (antitetanus serum), 260, 261
Attachment, 219
Autism, 601–5

Baby. *See* Newborn
Baby-bouncers, 227, 296
Baby carriages, 25, 28–31, 112–14
Baby equipment
  carriages, 28–31
  clothing, 31–35
  room furnishings, 22–25
  secondhand, 30
Babysitters, 155, 157–61, 175–76
"Baby talk," 3
Baby teeth. *See* Milk teeth
"Bad breath," 476–77
Bald patch, 500–501
Baths: and newborns, 97–103
Battered children, 177–79, 289–90.
  See also Child abuse
BCG vaccination, 264, 373
Bedding: for newborn, 26
Bedtime, 130, 269–70
Bed-wetting, 445, 554–56
Behavior
  modification, 267, 600–601
  problems, 546–64
Bent toes, 533–34
Bereavement. *See* Death
Bilingualism, 237
Bilious attack, 539, 541–42
Birth, 19–20. *See also* Home birth;
  Hospital
Birthmarks, 40, 419–21
Bites, 644
Blackheads, 496–97
Blankets
  for newborn, 26–27
  security, 120, 548–49
Bleeding
  controlling, 643–44
  from newborn's vagina, 39
Blemishes: disfiguring, 556–57. *See also*
  Acne; Birthmarks